THE COMPLETE GUIDE TO
TWENTIETH CENTURY ANTIQUES

THIS IS A SEVENOAKS BOOK

Design copyright © 2005 Carlton Publishing Group
Text copyright © 2005 Martin Miller

This edition published in 2007 by
Sevenoaks
An imprint of the Carlton Publishing Group
20 Mortimer Street
London
W1T 3JW

A CIP catalogue for this book is available from the
British Library.

ISBN 978 1 86200 532 7

Printed and bound in Dubai

COMPLETE GUIDE TO
TWENTIETH CENTURY ANTIQUES

20th

MARTIN MILLER

SEVENOAKS

CONTENTS

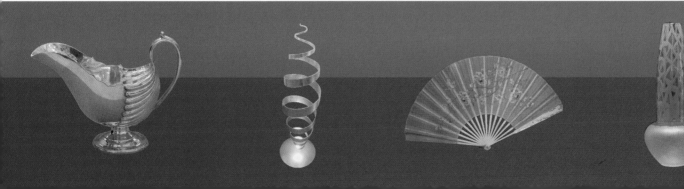

ACKNOWLEDGEMENTS

GENERAL EDITOR
Martin Miller

EDITORS
Marianne Blake
Peter Blake
Simon Blake
Richard Bundy
Abigail Zoe Martin
Caroline Proctor
Michael Spilling
Charlotte Stock
Clair Whiteman

PHOTOGRAPHERS
Neil Fox
Anders Gramer
Ryan Green
Carmen Klammer
Anna Malni
Abigail Zoe Martin
Julia Morley
Chris Smailes
James Bean Van Etten
Lee Walsh

DESIGN
Michelle Pickering

HOW TO USE THIS BOOK

I started publishing antiques guides in 1969 – and they have always been very successful – but one criticism has been, 'I loved the book, but what a pity that so many of the items were already sold'. And it was true. The books were designed more as compilations of information from auction sales that had already taken place than as immediate guides; as reference books rather than handbooks.

The difference between *The Complete Guide to Twentieth Century Antiques* and other antiques guides is that here we have used retailers, rather than auction houses, as our source of guide prices. A reputable and experienced dealer's assessment of the price of an antique is at least as reliable – and usually a great deal more reasoned – than a price achieved at auction. Even though prices may vary slightly from one dealer to another, it gives a useful guide to the sort of prices you should be paying. You can also get an idea of what else is available in your particular area of interest, or spending range.

The Complete Guide to Twentieth Century Antiques is designed for maximum visual interest and appeal. The guide price shown against an entry is per individual item, unless the heading and description refer to more than one item, a set, or pair. The Contents and Index will tell you in which area to find specific items, but the collector, enthusiast or interior designer will profit most from reading through a section, or several sections, and gathering information and inspiration as they go.

Good luck and enjoy your journey into the world of antiques.

Martin Miller

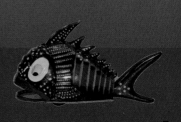

INTRODUCTION

The Complete Guide to Twentieth Century Antiques is a timely and comprehensive guide to the fastest-growing area in the antiques trade. With modern interiors – even in older houses – becoming more popular, many people don't want to clutter up their living space with heavy antique furniture or objets d'art, preferring instead to collect clean, minimalist pieces from the middle of the twentieth century – ceramics from the 1920s, art deco glass, furniture from the 1960s or lighting from the 1910s.

Collectables and other desirable objects that don't fall under the 'over 100 years old' rule, by which antiques are commonly defined, is what everyone is talking about. Even buying and wearing vintage clothing and jewellery is becoming an increasingly fashionable trend and with the explosion of the 'e-Bay generation' making it easier for everyone to source such items, a guide like this has never been more timely. The Complete Guide to Twentieth Century Antiques covers all the essential categories of interest including books, cameras, toys, clocks, glass, ephemera, telephones, handbags, jewellery, art, ceramics and posters.

Unlike many publications, I have selected antiques,

collectables and works of art that have recently been for sale in antique shops or markets in Great Britain. All the illustrations have been photographed and selected by our team to bring the reader a comprehensive cross section of twentieth century items that are available in the market place. One of the difficulties for the newcomer to antiques is in valuing an item. Once you have satisfied yourself that the items you are looking to acquire are indeed what you want and what they purport to be, then the problem is determining their worth. *The Complete Guide to Twentieth Century Antiques* offers a guide to the retail value of over 4,000 items. So whether it's a 1950s radio, Eames chair, Susie Cooper plate, marcasite jewelry or art deco table lamp, you will have a better idea of what you can expect to pay.

The world of antiques is probably one of the most fascinating, challenging and can also be one of the most confusing and impenetrable. Whether you are a beginner or a serious collector *The Complete Guide to Twentieth Century Antiques* is an invaluable part of your arsenal.

ADVERTISING
& PACKAGING

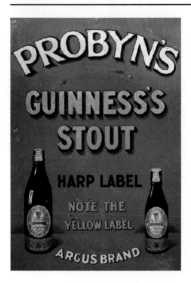

Probyn's Sign ▲

- *circa 1930*

An enamel sign for Probyn's Guinness's Stout – the Harp label. From the Argus Brand showing a picture of two stout bottles.

- *65cm x 40cm*
- **Guide price £400/$756**

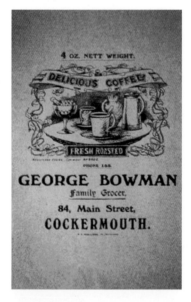

Coffee Packet ▲

- *1920s*

A packet of "delicious coffee", "fresh roasted" by George Bowman of 84 Main Street, Cockermouth. 4oz nett weight.

- *24cm x 19cm*
- **Guide price £5/$9**

McVities & Price's
Digestive Biscuits ▼

- *1930*

Small red tin with a cream lid and a boy seated on a red tin of McVitie & Price's Digestive Biscuits.

- *diameter 8cm*
- **Guide price £12/$23**

Redbreast Tobacco Tin ▼

- *1930*

Ogden's Redbreast Flake tobacco tin, made in Liverpool, decorated with a robin shown perched on a branch.

- *width 14cm*
- **Guide price £12/$23**

Sandwich Tin ▼

- *1930*

Yellow French sandwich tin with a red handle and trim, showing Mickey Mouse offering Pluto some sweets on the lid.

- *8cm x 18cm*
- **Guide price £150/$284**

Thorne's Creme Toffee ▲

- *1924*

Royal blue tin with gold scrolling and the words, "Thorne's Extra Super Creme Toffee and British Empire Exhibition Souvenir".

- *height 5.5.cm*
- **Guide price £30/$57**

Bisto Tin ▲

- *1960*

Tin of Bisto with a girl wearing a green hat and a boy with a red hat, both sniffing the aroma from a gravy boat.

- *height 19cm*
- **Guide price £14/$27**

Ty-Phoo Tea ▼

- *circa 1950–60*

Ty-Phoo tea in a grey box surrounded by a foliate wreath with the words 'Delicious, Economical, Refreshing'.

- *height 12.5cm*
- **Guide price £7/$13**

Book Mark ◀

- circa 1910

A book mark advertising giveaways for Wright's Coal Tar Soap. The Nursery Soap, inscribed with the words "The Seal of Health and Purity".

- length 15.4cm
- **Guide price £12/$23**

Castle Polish ▲

- 1930

Red tin of Castle Ballroom floor polish with a picture of a castle.

- height 11cm
- **Guide price £13/$25**

Cherry Blossom Shoe Stand ▼

- circa 1930

A tin and wood shoe stand advertising Cherry Blossom shoe polish in dark tan, with printed transfer on its sides.

- height 30cm
- **Guide price £150/$284**

Aero Chocolate ▲

- circa 1930

Unused bar of Aero chocolate in a brown wrapper with cream writing by Rowntrees.

- width 11cm
- **Guide price £20/$38**

Pearce Duff's Custard Powder ▼

- 1950

Tin of Pearce Duff's custard powder with a picture of a bowl of custard and pineapple, plums and pears on each side.

- height 11.5cm
- **Guide price £13/$25**

Huntley and Palmers Biscuit Tin ▼

- 1927

A British toy tank containing Huntley & Palmers biscuits.

- height 9.5cm
- **Guide price £800/$1,512**

Gray Dunn's Biscuits ▲

- 1915

Yellow ochre bus with red roof and wheels with figures looking out of the window and a bus conductor. With the letters "Gray Dunn's Biscuits" in red and "Lands End to John O' Groats".

- height 9.5cm
- **Guide price £1,500/$2,835**

Ashtray ▼

- 1955

Ashtray with "Don't forget your Anadin tablets" written in white writing on a red background and decorated with a two-tone green Anadin packet.

- 15cm square
- **Guide price £12/$23**

Senior Service Tobacco ▲

- *1940*

Red plaque with the written inscription "Senior Service Satisfy – Tobacco at its best".
- *height 28cm*
- **Guide price £15/$28**

Everyman's Hair Cream ▲

- *1950*

Everyman's brilliantine hair cream in a glass bottle with a pink rose beneath the words, 'Kenrosa made in England'.
- *height 13cm*
- **Guide price £12/$23**

Player's Ashtray ▲

- *1930*

Pottery Player's ashtray showing an interior scene with a man seated smoking a pipe, a lady in a green dress, a hound, and the words "Player's Tobacco Country Life and Cigarettes".
- *width 11.5cm*
- **Guide price £25/$48**

Golden Leaf Tobacco Tin ▼

- *circa 1912*

Golden leaf navy cut tobacco tin, manufactured by Louis Dobbelmann, Rotterdam. Showing an angel blowing a horn and flying on wings in the center of the tin, surrounded by flowers and the Dutch flag.
- *width 8cm*
- **Guide price £60/$114**

Brasso ▼

- *1960*

Tin of Brasso with 'Brasso' written in white letters on a red ground with a blue and white striped sun design in the background.
- *height 13cm*
- **Guide price £7/$14**

Dried Eggs U.S.A. ▼

- *circa 1940*

Gold tin inscribed with the words 'Pure dried whole eggs U.S.A. 5 ounces net weight equal to 12 eggs' in black writing.
- *height 11cm*
- **Guide price £16/$32**

Ty-Phoo Tea ▲

- *circa 1950–60*

Ty-Phoo Tea in a red box with white writing and the words 'Ty-Phoo Tea' in white, surrounded with a foliate wreath and 'Authorised 1/9 price'.
- *height 12.5cm*
- **Guide price £7/$14**

BP Anti-Frost ▼

- *1962*

Green oil can with BP in yellow writing on a green shield with the words 'Anti-Frost' in red on a white background.
- *height 14cm*
- **Guide price £20/$38**

Chillexine for the Udder ▼

- *circa 1930*

Bell & Sons in white writing with 'Limited Chillexine' in yellow writing on a brown background and 'For the Udder' in white writing with a picture of a cow's udder.
- *height 20.5cm*
- **Guide price £26/$50**

Lyons Pure Ground Coffee ▲

- *1930*

Green tin of Lyons pure ground coffee.
- *height 10.5cm*
- **Guide price £17/$34**

Evening in Paris Hair Cream ▲

- *1940*

Evening in Paris hair cream by Bourjois, in a dark blue glass bottle with dark blue writing on a pale blue background.
- *height 15cm*
- **Guide price £13/$25**

Persil Soap Powder ◄

- *1950*

Persil in a green box with a red circle the words 'Persil washes whiter Yes it does!' in white.
- *height 18cm*
- **Guide price £15/$28**

My Fair Lady Talc ▼

- *1960*

Cusson's My Fair Lady talc, showing a photograph of a blonde-haired lady.
- *height 14cm*
- **Guide price £14/$27**

Saturday Night Lotion ▼

- *1930*

Saturday Night Lotion in a clear glass bottle decorated with a man in a top hat and a lady in evening dress.
- *height 14cm*
- **Guide price £15/$28**

Chipso Soap Flakes ▲

- *circa 1930*

White cardboard box for Chipso soap flakes with a blue and yellow design and inscribed with the words, 'Fine for fine things'.
- *height 15cm*
- **Guide price £10/$19**

Cue Hair Dressing ▲

- *1955*

Glass bottle of Cue Hair dressing, a Colgate Product.
- *height 14cm*
- **Guide price £10/$19**

Orlox Beef Suet ▲

- *circa 1930*

Cardboard box of Orlox Beef Suet with the picture of a red bull. In excellent condition.
- *height 9cm*
- **Guide price £5/$9**

Kay-Tee ▼

- *1958*

Plastic bottle of Kay-Tee golden washing up liquid by Kearley and Tong Ltd, London.
- *height 20cm*
- **Guide price £9/$17**

Tide Washing Powder ▼

- *1950*

Yellow packet of Tide with orange circles and the words 'Tide' and 'Gives clothes a whiteness bonus' in dark blue.
- *height 17cm*
- **Guide price £19/$36**

Lyons Tea ▲

- *1925*

Set of four Lyon's tea tins, each one inscribed with a different slogan, 'Degrees Better', 'Lyons has stood the test of time', 'Mirror for reflection, Lyon's tea for perfection', 'All the year round drink Lyon's tea'.

- *height 14cm*
- **Guide price £200/$378**

Gramophone Needle Tins ▲

- *1910-1940*

Six tins: The National Band, Pathé, Salon-Tanz Nadeln. Sem Aero-needles.

- *4cm square*
- **Guide price £30–£100/ $57–$189 each**

A1 Salt ▲

- *1940*

Metal sign with two ladies, one cutting salt and the other opening a packet of 'A1 crushed lump salt.'

- *height 25cm*
- **Guide price £20/$38**

Player's Glass Ashtray ▼

- *1950*

Glass ashtray depicting a man in naval uniform surrounded by a white life ring and inscribed with 'Player's Navy cut' in black writing.

- *width 15cm*
- **Guide price £20/$38**

My Guinness Tray ▲

- *1955*

Metal tray with a pelican balancing a mug of Guinness inscribed with the slogan, 'My Goodness My Guinness'.

- *diameter 27cm*
- **Guide price £55/$104**

Ipso Washing Powder ▲

- *circa 1930*

Red cardboard box with the inscription 'The Wonder Worker IPSO washes by itself' displayed on a sheet and basket.

- *height 13cm*
- **Guide price £10/$19**

Oxo Cube ▼

- *1950*

Dark blue painted red metal box with 'Oxo cube' in yellow writing and the slogan 'Invaluable for cooking'.

- *35cm square*
- **Guide price £40/$76**

Ideal Home Cleanser ▼

- *1930*

Unopened cardboard packet of soap with a metal lid and a picture of a house and garden. Inscribed in dark blue and bordered in white with the words 'Ideal Home Cleanser' and below in yellow 'contains Pure Palm & Olive Oil Soap.'

- *height 25cm*
- **Guide price £44/$83**

Colman's Mustard ◀

- *1935*

Small red, yellow and black tin of Colman's mustard, with a red bull's head in the centre.

- *height 5cm*
- **Guide price £8/$15**

Reeves Colour Box ◄

- *circa 1940*

Light and dark blue cardboard box with the inscription 'Reeves Students Colour Box', decorated with a seated dalmatian.
- *width 20cm*
- **Guide price £20/$38**

Jester Towel Soap ▲

- *1930*

Orange and red box of Jester towel soap with a picture of a jester and the words 'for economy and cleanliness' printed on the side.
- *length 15.5.cm*
- **Guide price £15/$28**

Oxydol ▼

- *1950*

Yellow box of Oxydol with dark blue circles and the words 'Oxydol' in white with a white star.
- *height 13.5cm*
- **Guide price £11/$21**

Glass Jug ▲

- *1950*

Glass water jug inscribed in blue with the words 'Senior Service Satisfy'.
- *height 21cm*
- **Guide price £15/$28**

Collecting Box ▲

- *1914*

Alexandra Day collecting box.
- *height 13cm*
- **Guide price £16/$30**

Rinso Box ▲

- *1950*

Green box of Rinso showing a clothing line with two dresses and sheets blowing in the wind.
- *height 14.5cm*
- **Guide price £12/$23**

Guinness Mug ▼

- *1955*

Large plastic mug of Guinness inscribed on black with white writing 'Guinness is good for you'.
- *height 32cm*
- **Guide price £120/$227**

Cure-C-Cure ▼

- *1960*

Yellow tin of tube repair outfit with a red car and the words 'Cure-C-Cure by Romac', made in England.
- *length 13cm*
- **Guide price £12/$23**

Oxo Cubes ▲

- *circa 1930*

Metal tin with red and black geometric design with the inscription 'Oxo Cubes' in cream writing on the top of the lid.
- *width 10cm*
- **Guide price £12/$23**

Robin Starch ▲

- *1930*

Box of Robin Starch, which can also be used as a dry shampoo. Decorated with green and white stripes and a robin on a branch with a yellow sunburst background. Inscribed 'Robin The new starch', on the lid and 'Nursery & Dusting powder'.
- *height 9cm*
- **Guide price £14/$27**

Johnnie Walker Figure ▲

- *1940*

Striding jovial figure of a gentleman in a gold top hat with a brown bow, red jacket with tails, cream breeches, black boots with gold trim and tassels, carrying a black cane and standing on a dark green base with 'Johnnie Walker' in gold writing.

- *height 37cm*
- **Guide price £120/$227**

Nestlé's Chocolate Bar ▲

- *1930*

Unopened Nestlé's honey and almond milk chocolate bar.

- *width 10cm*
- **Guide price £20/$38**

Peter's Ideal Chocolate ▼

- *1950*

Peter's ideal milk chocolate shop dummy in a brown wrapper with gold writing.

- *width 11cm*
- **Guide price £15/$28**

Lifebuoy Soap ▶

- *1938*

Lifebuoy soap in a red box showing a lifeguard throwing a life-ring with a cartoon bubble above with the words 'More than a good soap - a good habit!' written on it.

- *height 15.5cm*
- **Guide price £18/$34**

Volga Caviar ▲

- *1930*

Turquoise tin of Caviar Volga Malossol from Russia.

- *diameter 10.5cm*
- **Guide price £28/$53**

William Lawson's Figure ▲

- *1930*

Figure of a boxer in fighting pose, with brown hair and moustache, blue eyes, red breeches and a gold sash, and black boots, standing on a yellow ochre and black base with the inscription 'William Lawson's Rare Scotch Whisky'.

- *height 36cm*
- **Guide price £160/$303**

Black & White Scotch Whisky Jug ▼

- *1960*

Burleigh Ware white pottery jug, made in Great Britain, with two small terrier dogs, one black and one white, and the words 'Black & White Scotch Whisky Buchanan's', decorated on the side with the Royal Crest.

- *height 12cm*
- **Guide price £30/$57**

Slazenger Advert ▼

- *1960*

Cardboard advertisement for cricket bats by Slazenger with photographs of cricketers in action including Garfield Sobers, Colin Cowdrey and Mike Smith.

- *height 35cm*
- **Guide price £30/$57**

Huntley & Palmers Tin ▲

- *1930*

Yellow tin for Huntley & Palmers biscuits showing a young lady smiling with dark hair and eyes, wearing a blue scarf.

- *width 13.5cm*
- **Guide price £24/$47**

Cocktail Biscuit Tin ▲

- *circa 1950*

Circular biscuit tin with a pink and white striped sunshade above a garden chair and table with cocktail shaker and glasses and a tin of cocktail biscuits.

- *diameter 18cm*
- **Guide price £15/$28**

Walter Palm Toffee Tin ▼

- *1950*

'Walter's Palm Toffee' tin with a lady in a red and white striped bikini with matching sunshade, towel and holding a bottle of orange juice on the beach.
- *24cm square*
- **Guide price £25/$48**

Camay Soap ▼

- *1950*

Unused Camay soap with a turquoise and yellow wrapper showing a cartouche of a lady and inscribed in black 'Camay the soap of beautiful women'.
- *length 8cm*
- **Guide price £6/$12**

Macleans Toothpaste ▼

- *1960*

Macleans toothpaste in a white box with a dark blue line, by Beecham of Ireland Limited, Dublin.
- *width 19cm*
- **Guide price £8/$16**

Pottery Figure ▲

- *1950*

A painted pottery figure of a shoemaker holding a shoe, advertising Phillips Soles and Heels.
- *height 30cm*
- **Guide price £200/$378**

Rennies Indigestion Tablets ▲

- *1960*

Yellow box of Rennies Indigestion tablets containing 24 boxes, inscribed with the words, 'Just the right size for pocket or handbag'.
- *width 9cm*
- **Guide price £16/$31**

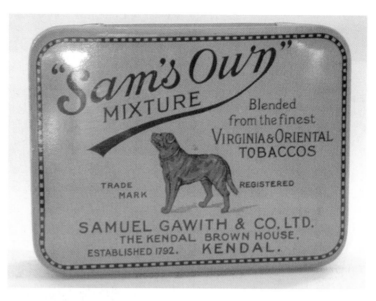

Sam's Own Tobacco ▲

- *1930*

Yellow ochre tin with a brown Labrador and black writing stating 'Sam's Own mixture blended from the finest Virginia and Oriental Tobaccos' by Samuel Gawith and Co. Ltd., Kendal, 1792.
- *width 11cm*
- **Guide price £19/$36**

Palmolive Soap ▲

- *1930*

Unused Palmolive soap in green paper wrapping with a black band and the word 'Palmolive' in yellow.
- *length 8cm*
- **Guide price £5/$9**

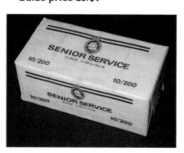

Carton of Cigarettes ▲

- *1960s*

A carton of Senior Service cigarettes. In original white paper wrapping with navy blue lettering, unopened.
- *13cm x 5cm*
- **Guide price £40/$76**

India and China Tea Sign ▼

- *1920*

White enamel sign for Indian and China tea in red writing, with heads of an Indian and a Chinese man.
- *width 71cm*
- **Guide price £55/$104**

Duncan Chocolates ▼

- *1930*

Cardboard box for Duncan Edinburgh chocolates, showing a young girl wearing a yellow ruff holding a bunch of flowers, wearing a blue hat with yellow pom-poms.
- *height 5cm*
- **Guide price £15/$28**

Gin Fizz Stocking Box

- circa 1956

Cardboard box for stockings with a picture of a lady sitting cross legged on a stool at a bar holding a glass, and inscribed with, 'Gin Fizz Crestmont created in Italy' in red lettering on a white background.

- 18cm square
- **Guide price £18/$34**

Packet of Condoms

- 1950s

An assortment of 1950s condoms.

- 16cm x 5cm/packet
- **Guide price £10/$19**

Bottle of Broseden

- 1930s

A bottle of "Broseden" made in Germany. A drink used to calm the troops during lonely times.

- height 9cm
- **Guide price £5/$9**

Dresden Figurine

- 1910

A Dresden porcelain group of figures advertising Yardley perfumes and soaps.

- height 17cm
- **Guide price £350/$662**

Ink Bottle

- 1930s

A bottle of blue black Swan ink.

- height 8cm
- **Guide price £6/$12**

Manufacturer's Sign

- 1930s

A sign cut from hardwood of the figure of John Bull, advertising John Bull Tyres.

- height 65cm
- **Guide price £120/$227**

Boat Biscuit Tin

- circa 1935

A French biscuit box in the shape of the ill-fated liner, Normandie.

- length 62cm
- **Guide price £350/$662**

Nib Boxes

- 1920s

An assortment of unopened pen nib boxes.

- width 7cm
- **Guide price £7/$14**

Toffee Tin ▲

- *20th century*
A Macintosh's toffee tin bearing a portrait of King George VI and Elizabeth Bowes-Lyon, and produced to commemorate the Royal wedding.
- *diameter 14cm*
- **Guide price £20/$38**

Art Deco Tin ▼

- *1920*
Art Deco tin showing a smiling lady in a white dress, holding a letter and seated on a large cushion. Beside her is a Pekinese wearing a pink bow,, a vase and a large pink lampshade on a red circular table.
- *width 23cm*
- **Guide price £20/$38**

Bournvita Mug ▼

- *1950s*
A white Bournvita mug in the shape of a face with a blue nightcap and a red pom-pom. With large handle.
- *height 14cm*
- **Guide price £40/$76**

Shop Sign ▼

- *1940s*
A wrought iron shop sign, with scrolled decoration surrounding a clover leaf emblem with the hand-painted letters "Sunshine Bakery". In original condition.
- *102cm x 65cm*
- **Guide price £220/$416**

Battery Advertisement ▼

- *circa 1960*
An Oldham Batteries metal advertising sign, incorporating the 'I told 'em – Oldham' slogan.
- *height 37cm*
- **Guide price £28/$53**

Biscuit Tin ▲

- *circa 1910*
A biscuit tin in the shape of a book, made by Hoffman Suisse.
- *height 36cm*
- **Guide price £90/$171**

Talcum Powder ▲

- *circa 1950*
A 'Jolly Baby' talcum powder container, with voluptuous cover.
- *height 15cm*
- **Guide price £40/$76**

Polish Box ▼

- *circa 1930*
A metal polish box with a secondary use as a string dispenser.
- *height 15cm*
- **Guide price £35/$67**

Sanitary Products ▲

- *1950s*
An assortment of female sanitary towel and tampon boxes.
- *8cm x 4cm/packet*
- **Guide price £5/$9**

Royal Busts ▲

- *1902*
Busts of Edward VII and Queen Alexandra made by Britains.
- *height 5cm*
- **Guide price £55/$104**

Babycham Glass ◄

- *circa 1960*
Babycham promotional champagne glass.
- *height 12cm*
- **Guide price £14/$27**

Trumps Markers ▼

- *1930s*
Two trumps markers for use in card games.
- **Guide price £20/$38**

Tape Measure ▼

- *circa 1950*
A promotional tape measure with the inscription, "With compliments of A.H. Manning". Includes original box.
- *10cm x 9cm*
- **Guide price £14/$28**

Queen of Hearts Box ▼

- *circa 1920*
A sweet box from *Alice in Wonderland* in the shape of Tenniel's Queen of Hearts.
- *height 20cm*
- **Guide price £75/$142**

Horlicks Mug ▼

- *circa 1940*
A white porcelain Horlicks mug with blue lettering with solid handle.
- *height 11cm*
- **Guide price £18/$34**

V.D. Matches ▼

- *circa 1940*
An assortment of V.D. matches from World War II.
- *5cm x 3cm*
- **Guide price £5/$9**

Toffee Tin ▲

- *1930*
A "Felix the Cat" toffee tin. With Felix the cat on one side and a cartoon of Felix on the other side.
- *16cm x 16cm x 10cm*
- **Guide price £500/$945**

Cigarette Tin ▲

- *1910*
A green cigarette tin with the painting of a lady in red wearing a straw hat, with the lettering "Muratt's young ladies cigarettes" written on the tin.
- *14cm x 9cm*
- **Guide price £120/$227**

Michelin Ashtray ▲

- *1940s*
A premium give-away Bakelite ashtray with a seated figure in the form of the Michelin Man.
- *height 18cm*
- **Guide price £150/$284**

Horlicks Mixer ▼

- *circa 1950*

A Horlicks promotional glass jug with a metal mixer.

- *height 15cm*
- **Guide price £10/$19**

Michelin Man ▶

- *1966*

A bakelite Michelin Man used for advertising in petrol stations and shops.

- *height 150cm*
- **Guide price £85/$161**

Commemorative Tin ▼

- *1951*

A "Festival of Britain" commemorative tin.

- *6cm x 14cm*
- **Guide price £200/$378**

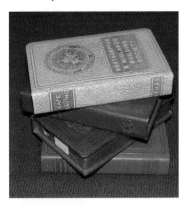

Lollipop Man ▲

- *1960s*

A porcelain figure of a Robertson's Golly Lollipop Man.

- *height 12cm*
- **Guide price £12/$23**

Savings Bank Tin ▼

- *1930s*

A savings bank tin issued by various banks of the 1930s.

- **Guide price £150/$284**

Match Holder ▼

- *1910*

An Apploinaris match holder and striker.

- *height 8cm*
- **Guide price £30/$57**

Guinness Toucan ▼

- *1955*

A toucan with a glass of Guinness on a stand advertising the beer with the slogan – "My goodness – my Guinness".

- *height 7cm*
- **Guide price £250/$473**

Dog Food Sign ▲

- *1950*

A Spratt's wooden sign advertising dog food with the picture of a Highland terrier in the form of the word "Spratts".

- *50cm x 80cm*
- **Guide price £100/$189**

Money Tin ▲

- *1934*

A Crawfords biscuit cum money tin fairy house by Lucie Attwell.

- *height 21cm*
- **Guide price £300/$567**

Guinness Tray ▲

- *circa 1950*

Circular tray advertising Guinness.

- **Guide price £50/$95**

AERONAUTICA

Four Cannon Shells ▲

- *circa 1942*

Four fighter-plane cannon shells, converted into a desk pen holder and mounted on oak and brass. The result of a dogfight between British and German fighter planes.

- *15cm x 15cm*
- **Guide price £45/$85**

Aircraft Propellor ▲

- *circa 1920*

A four-bladed wooden coarse-pitched, wind-generator propellor, in mahogany with lamination and holes in the centre intact.

- *length 61cm*
- **Guide price £165/$312**

Concorde Postal Cover ▲

- *circa 1978*

Commemorating the first flight from London to New York, with colour print showing an early Concorde in blue sky.

- *19cm x 11.5cm*
- **Guide price £15/$28**

Qantas Empire Airways ▼

- *circa 1930*

A Qantas flying-boat map of the Sydney to Singapore route. Good condition.

- *length 24.5cm, width 12cm*
- **Guide price £50/$95**

Route Map ▼

- *circa 1930*

Imperial Airways route map from Southampton to Alexandria.

- *22cm x 14cm*
- **Guide price £50/$95**

Model Airplane ▶

- *circa 1940*

A brass twin-engined aircraft on a beechwood base.

- *height 10cm*
- **Guide price £70/$133**

Brooklands Flying Club ▲

- *circa 1920*

A Brooklands trophy, in pressed steel with an alloy finish.

- *height 11.5cm*
- **Guide price £1,500/$2,835**

Pan-Am Ticket ▲

- *1949*

Pan-American Clipper ticket, sponsored by the Bulova watch company, in half green and half white with black and white print.

- *diameter 11cm*
- **Guide price £20/$38**

Aerial ABC Gazetteer ▼

- *August 1929*

Light brown in colour with black and white print. In mint condition.

- *22cm x 14.5cm*
- **Guide price £40/$76**

Comet Model Plane ▼

- *circa 1940*

A balsa-wood model kit of the B-4 Superfortress. Made by the Comet model factory, Chicago, Illinois. In mint condition.

- **Guide price £10/$19**

Princess Flying Boat ▼

• *circa 1950*
Photograph of the *Princess*, the biggest flying boat ever made.
• *119.5cm x 15cm*
• **Guide price £25/$48**

Aero Club Badge ▼

• *circa 1920*
Brooklands club badge in pressed steel with coloured enamels. The club was established in the 1920s.
• *height 10cm*
• **Guide price £600/$1,134**

Qantas Ticket ▼

• *circa 1941*
Flying-boat hotel ticket, from Australia to Singapore, with Qantas Empire Airways.
• *16.5cm x 11cm*
• **Guide price £15/$28**

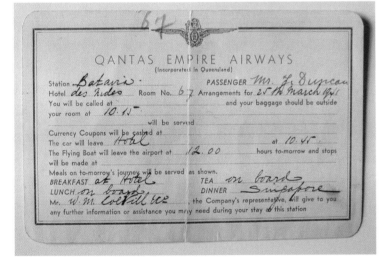

Model Messerschmitt ▼

• *circa 1940*
Hand-made model of a Messerschmitt ME110 fighter plane on perspex and beaten steel base, with Nazi insignia modelled into base of stem.
• *wingspan 31.5cm*
• **Guide price £350/$662**

Souvenir Programme ▼

• *1930*
Illustrated souvenir programme from the British Hospitals' Air Pageant, 1930. In good condition.
• *21.5cm x 14cm*
• **Guide price £40/$76**

BOAC Sales Leaflet ▲

• *circa 1970*
Advertising standard merchandise of the era. With colour pictures.
• *length 20cm*
• **Guide price £10/$19**

Airship Safety Award ▲

• *circa 1959*
An American 'Aviation Safety Award' with brass engraving set in a plaque of beechwood.
• *16cm x 13cm*
• **Guide price £25–£30/$48–$57**

Aircraft Timetable ▲

• *1926*
An Imperial Airways Ltd summer timetable, second edition, in good condition.
• *15cm x 11cm*
• **Guide price £40/$76**

Fighter Plane Model ▼

• *circa 1980*
Model of a battle-camouflaged Tornado fighter plane. On a steel frame with rubber feet.
• *height 10cm*
• **Guide price £30/$57**

Spanish Airline Leaflet ▼

• *circa 1922*
In good condition, but with a folding crease down the centre.
• *15.5cm x 12cm*
• **Guide price £25/$48**

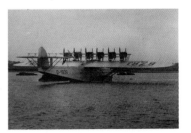

German Flying Boat ▼

• *circa 1929*
A black and white photograph of the six-engined German Dorrier Dox flying boat, off Calshot Spit, in Southampton Water.
• *21.5cm x 15cm*
• **Guide price £15–£20/$28–$38**

ARCHITECTURAL & GARDEN FURNITURE

Prague Lantern
- *20th century*

A hexagonal lantern from Prague, with heraldic and floral swag decoration, surmounted by a finial with pierced designs.
- *height 100cm*
- **Guide price £425/$803**

Stone Flower Pot
- *1970*

Stone flower pot with a fluted body with carved designs in relief.
- *height 24cm*
- **Guide price £24/$47**

Garden Folding Stool
- *1950*

Folding picnic stool with a candy striped linen seat supported by four teak legs.
- *height 41cm*
- **Guide price £78/$150**

French Chair
- *circa 1950*

One of a set of four French wrought iron garden chairs with pierced geometric designs to back splat and seat.
- *height 87cm*
- **Guide price £680/$1,286**

Garden Trolley
- *circa 1920*

A wrought iron garden trolley with a pierced floral design and original white enamel paint.
- *71cm x 48cm*
- **Guide price £225/$426**

Roll Top Bench
- *20th century*

A two-seater roll top iron bench, with ladder back and seat, and scrolled arms and legs.
- *width 1.2m*
- **Guide price £425/$803**

Galvanised Flower Bucket
- *1960*

French flower vendor's galvanised display bucket with carrying handles.
- *height 48cm*
- **Guide price £22/$41**

Cast Iron Bull
- *circa 1950*

Impressive cast iron bull with left leg raised in an aggressive manner, mounted on a stylised rocky base.
- *1.55m x 2.5m*
- **Guide price £16,580/$31,336**

One of a Pair of Urns ▲

- *1910*

Pair of cast iron urns with egg and dart moulded rim above a lobed body, raised on a fluted, splayed foot on a square base.

- *58.5cm diameter*
- **Guide price £460/$870**

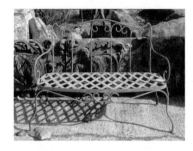

Garden Bench ▲

- *20th century*

Iron lattice garden bench with scrolled back and arms, above a lattice seat, supported by shaped legs on pad feet.

- *width 130cm*
- **Guide price £395/$748**

Enamel Bucket ▲

- *1920*

French enamelled water bucket with a red rim, pale green body, hand-painted strawberries and original handle.

- *height 29cm*
- **Guide price £78/$150**

Zinc Urns ▼

- *1920*

One of a pair of French urns made from zinc with unusual angular designs and a marbled finish.

- *height 31cm*
- **Guide price £680/$1,286**

Brass Urns ▼

- *circa 1910*

One of a pair of brass urns from the modern movement, with unusual angular double handles, the whole on a pedestal foot resting on a square base.

- *height 48cm*
- **Guide price £880/$1,664**

Green Stucco Pot ▲

- *1950*

Stoneware urn of ovoid form with green glazed lip and neck with rusticated finish to the body.

- *height 44cm*
- **Guide price £240/$454**

Salt Glazed Urn ▲

- *1910*

French salt glazed pottery urn with pinched lip and banding, the body centred with a flower motif in relief on a pedestal base.

- *height 41cm*
- **Guide price £120/$227**

Wrought Iron Chairs ▲

- *circa 1950*

Set of four French wrought iron patio chairs with a heart-shaped back, scrolled arms and original white enamel paint.

- *height 87cm*
- **Guide price £680/$1,286 for set**

Shanks Canopy Bath ▼

- *circa 1910*

Shanks, cast iron canopy bath, with original nickel fittings including numerous water-jets and large shower rose.

- *height 32cm*
- **Guide price £9,800/$18,522**

Balloon Back Chairs ◄

- *circa 1920*

Two wrought iron balloon back chairs being part of a set of six with a circular wrought iron table, original paint.

- *height 83cm*
- **Guide price £2,500/$4,725**

Stone Torso ▼

- *circa 1920*

A French stone statue of the torso and thighs of a woman, with attention to form.
- *height 1.5m*
- **Guide price £3,600/$6,804**

Lounge Bath ▲

- *circa 1910*

Lounge bath with ball and claw feet with original nickel plated fittings including built in waist and plunger units.
- *width 86cm*
- **Guide price £1,950/$3,686**

Garden Lantern ▼

- *1920*

An oval wirework Chinoiserie garden lantern, lined with decorative parchment on a circular wooden base.
- *height 60cm*
- **Guide price £210/$397**

Copper Container ▲

- *1915*

A very unusual large copper container which was originally used as a dying vat for military uniforms and is now converted into a bath.
- **Guide price £15,000/$28,350**

Christening Font ▲

- *circa 1930*

An unusual 20th century carved stone christening font in the Gothic style with octagonal oak lid from a church in Farnham Surrey.
- *height 130cm*
- **Guide price £1,950/$3,686**

Watering Can ▲

- *1920*

Zinc watering can with an elongated spout.
- *height 26cm*
- **Guide price £34/$66**

Pink Pottery Bucket ▼

- *1910*

French ceramic pail with salmon pink glaze and white interior with a raffia covered handle.
- *height 24cm*
- **Guide price £18/$34**

London Ceramic Trap ▲

- *circa 1910*

London porcelain trap with bracket and seat, with rose and leaf decoration, to the inside and outside of the unit.
- *height 46cm*
- **Guide price £1,125/$2,126**

Park Bench ▼

- *1940s*

English garden seat with scrolled arm rests in original condition.
- *184cm x 88cm x 69cm*
- **Guide price £299/$567**

Art Deco Fireplace ▼

- *circa 1920*
Art Deco tiled fireplace with mottled effect and a reeded design running vertically either side of the hearth.
- *94cm x 138cm*
- **Guide price £350/$662**

Pottery Urns ▼

- *circa 1940*
One of a pair of pottery urns with lobed designs around the body and egg and dart motif to the splayed lip, standing on a pedestal base.
- *height 43cm*
- **Guide price £480/$908**

Wicker Chair ◄

- *circa 1920*
French provincial wicker conservatory chair painted pistachio green with a deep horseshoe back, apron front and splayed legs.
- *height 67cm*
- **Guide price £240/$454**

Wood-Burning Stove ▲

- *1910*
Cast-iron wood-burning stove with decorated top, made by G. Portway & Son of Halsted in Essex, model No. 6 Tortoise.
- *height 105cm*
- **Guide price £1,475/$2,788**

Musgraves Conservatory Radiator ▲

- *circa 1910*
One of a pair of cast iron Musgraves conservatory radiators consisting of twelve columns.
- *height 75cm*
- **Guide price £850/$1,607**

Wall Fountain ▲

- *20th century*
A large, marble, 'Roman', carved lion wall fountain, with water aperture to the mouth.
- *height 57cm*
- **Guide price £3,200/$6,048**

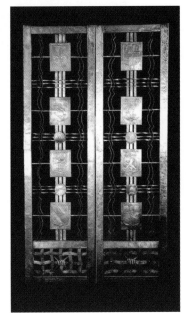

French Plaques ▲

- *circa 1930*
A pair of French, Art Deco doors with armorial plaques.
- *height 2.15m*
- **Guide price £1,850/$3,497**

Jardinières ▼

- *circa 1910*
An early 20th-century Art Nouveau period pair of galvanized steel hanging wall planters, with 'Theatre des Fleurs' engraving.
- *height 51cm*
- **Guide price £380/$719**

Watering Can ▼

- *circa 1940*
Galvanized watering can of classic design with large-bore spout and pivotal carrying handle.
- *height 45cm*
- **Guide price £12/$23**

Garden Recliner ▼

- *circa 1930*
A garden or conservatory recliner made from steamed and shaped bamboo with full-length cushion and original spoked wheels.
- *length 2.2m*
- **Guide price £350/$662**

ARMS & ARMOUR

Buffalo Bill Revolver ◀
- *circa 1970*
Percussion Revolver, 31 calibre, as used on frontier mining camps from the "Buffalo Bill" Historical Society Museum, Wyoming. Non-firing replica, with pellets and brass powder containers set in a presentation box.
- *width 30cm*
- **Guide price £750/$1,418**

Schutzenschnur Silver Luftwaffe ▼
- *1940*
Pilot officer's silver braid of the Luftwaffe with an eagle and national insignia.
- *length 14cm*
- **Guide price £100/$189**

Japanese N.C.O. Sword ▼
- *circa 1939*
Japanese N.C.O. Katena sword with polished folded steel blade and original paintwork to handle. No. 79275, with matching scabbard number.
- *length 59cm*
- **Guide price £290/$549**

Kriegsmarine Colani Jacket ▲
- *1940*
A rare Kriegsmarine Colani Jacket-Haupt Feldwebel, Coxwain rank, complete with breast eagle, shoulder boards and all original buttons.
- *medium*
- **Guide price £315/$595**

General's Aiguilettes ▲
- *1940*
Third Reich General's aiguilettes, in good condition with only minor damage to parts of the gilt wiring.
- *length 42cm*
- **Guide price £185/$350**

Officer's Peaked Cap ◀
- *1940*
Officer's peaked cap of the Kriegsmarine Administration Service, with silver wire eagle cockage and braid, in excellent condition. Items of this branch of the Kriegsmarine are rarely seen!
- *size 8*
- **Guide price £795/$1,504**

SS Kepi Cap ▲
- *1940*
Early SS Kepi with Skull and leather strap.
- *size 8*
- **Guide price £975/$1,843**

Luftschutz Dagger ▲

- *1939*

Luftschutz dagger, lst pattern rankers issue, complete with single strap hanger, with the maker's mark 'Kroneck Ernst Erich Witte Solingen' on blade and 'RZM M5/71 OLC' on the hanger clip.

- *length 40cm*
- **Guide price £825/$1,559**

Luftwaffe Belt ▲

- *1940*

Luftwaffe other ranks late pattern standard leather belt, with some wear, but complete.

- *5cm x 3cm*
- **Guide price £45/$85**

Artillery Parade Tunic ▲

- *1936*

Waffenrock Gebirgsjaeger artillery parade tunic, complete with ribbon bar of 5 and breast eagle shoulder boards.

- *medium*
- **Guide price £325/$614**

SS Steel Helmet ▼

- *1940*

SS M-44 Steel helmet, a rare early double decal version complete with inner lining and chin strap, stamped "54" on lining and a maker's stamp on inside of helmet, with most of original finish still present.

- *size 8*
- **Guide price £1,195/$2,259**

Helmet Plate ▼

- *1914*

Baden Reservists gilt metal helmet plate, modelled as a griffin centered with shield and cross swords.

- *width 14cm*
- **Guide price £65/$123**

Prismatic Compass ▼

- *circa 1917*

British officers, First World War, military prismatic compass with original fitted leather case, dated.

- *diameter 5.5cm*
- **Guide price £200/$378**

Pith Helmet ▲

- *circa 1915*

Turn of the century linen pith helmet for the overseas campaign in India, in fine original condition.

- *size 7*
- **Guide price £120/$227**

Scottish Full Dirk ▲

- *circa 1905*

Scottish military full dress dirk blade etched with battle honours for the Highland Light Infantry, coloured stones, regimental crest.

- *length 46cm*
- **Guide price £1,800/$3,402**

Airforce Honour Dagger ▲

- *1937*

Airforce honour dagger lst pattern known as Bordoich, complete with hanging chains.

- *length 39cm*
- **Guide price £295/$558**

Luftwaffe Flying Helmet ▼

- *1940*

Luftwaffe flying helmet. Summer issue version, with canvas hood, straps, leads and sockets still present. Stamped inside earpiece. Ln 26602.

- *height 19cm*
- **Guide price £245/$463**

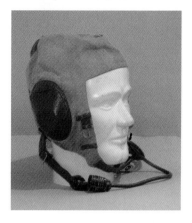

Infantry Tunic ▼

- *1941*

Africa Corps infantry tunic with four pockets complete with all insignia and buttons. In excellent condition.

- *large*
- **Guide price £375/$709**

German Peaked Cap ▼

- *1940*

German W.W.II, peaked cap of the Luftwaffe Artillery. Blue with red piping, in good condition, badges and cockade. Makers mark 'Deutsche Wert Arbeit' inside.

- *size 8*
- **Guide price £285/$539**

Royal Engineers Busby ▲

- *circa 1910*

Royal engineers officer's bear fur busby with the gilt flaming bomb incorporating the Regiment's insignia and patent leather chinstrap.

- *height 14cm*
- **Guide price £375/$709**

Korean War Pilot's Helmet ▼

- *1950*

A fighter pilot's helmet, Soviet-made for a MiG fighter, used by a North Korean pilot in the Korean War.

- **Guide price £150/$284**

Trooper's Sabre ▼

- *circa 1908*

British trooper's sabre, pattern dated and inscribed WWI paint.

- *length 1.1m*
- **Guide price £275/$520**

German Sailor's Jacket ◄

- *1939*

A German naval rating's summer tunic from the beginning of World War II, with insignia.

- **Guide price £100/$189**

Luftwaffe Nachrichten Signals Tunic ▲

- *1940*

Luftwaffe Nachrichten (Signals) NCO tunic with four pockets, NCO shoulder boards with silver braid, one pip, tan piping and number 11, with piping and silver braid collar.

- *large*
- **Guide price £395/$748**

Royal Engineers Officer's Tunic ▲

- *1914*

An officer's full dress tunic of the Royal Engineers, in scarlet, dating from the beginning of World War I.

- **Guide price £185/$350**

SA Dagger ▲

- *circa 1932*

SA honour dagger Rohm Widmung with partly erased inscription. The Ernst Rohm has been neatly erased from the blade but the rests remains. Some light wear on the scabbard, otherwise dagger in very good condition.

- *length 39cm*
- **Guide price £695/$1,314**

Gerbirgsjaeger NCO's Peaked Cap ▼

- *1940*

Gerbirgsjaeger N C O's peaked cap. Maker's diamond on the inside. Uniform Krungshaus Karl Petrasch Klagenfurt. All outside emblems attached, complete and in good condition.

- *size 8*
- **Guide price £495/$936**

Lifeguard Boots ▼

- *1950s*

A pair of post-World War II dress boots of a trooper from the Royal Regiment of Lifeguards.

- *height 43cm*
- **Guide price £150/$284**

Great War Picture Frame ◄

- *1917*

A World War I picture frame made from the tip of a wooden aeroplane propellor blade and mounted on a mahogany stand, showing the photograph of a uniformed nurse from the period.

- **Guide price £45/$85**

World War II RAF Ashtray ▼

- *World War II*

An aluminum ashtray made from the piston of a Rolls Royce Merlin engine. Includes RAF emblem and Churchill dedication.

- *diameter 31cm*
- **Guide price £25/$48**

Welsh Guards Bearskin ▼

- *1980*

An NCO's bearskin from the Welsh Guards regiment, showing plumed insignia and brass retaining strap. This headgear is current issue.

- *height 64cm*
- **Guide price £585/$1,106**

Luftwaffe Dagger ▼

- *1937*

German Lufwaffe dagger, 2nd type, with yellow bakelite grip and original maker's mark 'Eickhorn Solingen', hanger straps and epee portopee.

- *length 37cm*
- **Guide price £325/$614**

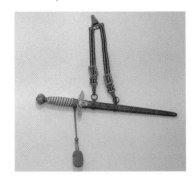

Great War Commemorative Frame ▲

- *circa 1918*

A World War I commemorative picture frame in bronze, modelled as a relief map of France and Belgium, with a circular glass portal displaying the photograph of a soldier.

- *height 16cm*
- **Guide price £85/$161**

Tin of Boer War Chocolate ▲

- *1900*

A hinged metal tin from the Boer War, originally containing chocolate and showing the royal crest, the profile of Queen Victoria, the inscription "South Africa 1900" and a signed message in the Queen's handwriting wishing the recipient, "A happy new year".

- *19cm x 11cm*
- **Guide price £145/$274**

Boer War Two Pound Shell Case ▲

- *1900*

A Boer War two-pound "Pom Pom" artillery shell case, in brass with projectile head in place but powder and percussion cap removed.

- *length 20cm*
- **Guide price £15/$28**

British SAS Uniform ▼

- *1990*

A British SAS sergeant's uniform and medals for the Falklands and Gulf War period (medals are replacements).

- **Guide price £250/$473**

Commemorative Scroll ▼

- *World War II*

A World War II illuminated memorial scroll for Driver L.S.D. Butcher who was killed in action during the North African campaign.

- *38cm x 20cm*
- **Guide price £25/$48**

World War I Binoculars ▼

- *1917*

A pair of military binoculars dated 1917, with leather carrying case inscribed with the name of a soldier serving with the Highland Light Infantry.

- *length 18cm*
- **Guide price £115/$217**

World War II Flying Helmet ▲

- *1944*

A World War II RAF "C" type flying helmet with intrinsic radio earpieces and MK VIII goggles with webbing strap and H-type oxygen mask for high altitude.

- **Guide price £185/$350**

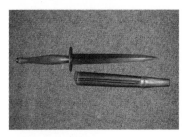

World War II Commando Knife ▲

- *1944*

A World War II British Commando fighting knife in steel and brass, complete with scabbard.

- *length 30cm*
- **Guide price £85/$161**

Girl's Hitler Youth Uniform ▲

- *circa 1940*

A blouson from a girl's uniform of the Hitler Youth, dating from the beginning of World War II and emblazoned with the insignia of the National Socialist party.

- *length 34cm*
- **Guide price £150/$284**

World War I German Helmet Badge ▼

- *1914*

The helmet badge of a Prussian soldier from the beginning of World War I, with the crowned eagle of the emperor and the inscription, "Mitt Gott fur Koenig und Vaterland".

- *height 9cm*
- **Guide price £50/$95**

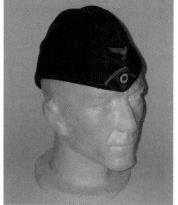

German Naval Artillery Forage Cap ▲

- *1942*

A German Naval Coastal Artillery soldier's forage cap in field grey wool, from World War II. With badge and insignia.

- **Guide price £140/$265**

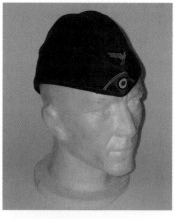

World War II RAF Cap ▲

- *1940*

A Royal Air Force warrant officer's uniform cap dating from the beginning of World War II.

- **Guide price £85/$161**

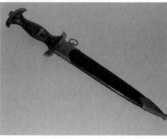

German Dagger ▲

- *1937*

A pre-war Third Reich Brownshirt's dress dagger, made by Friedrich Geigis. Complete with scabbard and nickel fittings; showing insignia.

- *length 30cm*
- **Guide price £225/$426**

British Army Sword ▼

- *1920*

A post-World War I officer's dress sword belonging to an officer of the Royal Army Service Corps. The sword in steel with brass hilt and the scabbard in highly polished tan leather.

- *length 92cm*
- **Guide price £185/$350**

Cigarette Gift Tin ▶

- *1914*

An example of a gift tin sent by Queen Mary to the troops fighting in France for the first Christmas of World War I. Complete with photographs, monogrammed cigarettes and all the original contents.

- *18cm x 11cm*
- **Guide price £125/$237**

Copper Powder Flask ▼

- *20th century*

Powder flask with copper body and brass mounts.

- *length 17cm*
- **Guide price £180/$341**

World War I German Helmet ▼

- *1916*

A World War I camouflaged German army helmet of 1916 design, with original camouflage paint and chinstrap fittings.

- **Guide price £200/$378**

Dress Busby ▲

- *1916*

A dress Busby with white plume and brass fittings and chin strap, showing insignia of the Royal Engineers and dating from World War I.

- *height 33cm*
- **Guide price £275**

Paper Rack ▲

- *1940*

A paper rack from World War II, hand-crafted and scrolled in wrought iron and mounted on a splay-footed stand constructed of pieces of collected shrapnel.

- *height 46cm*
- **Guide price £100/$189**

World War I German Sweetheart Brooch ▲

- *1917*
A World War I German Eindekker sweetheart's brooch in the shape of a monoplane, with a German cross insignia attached by a chain. In original box with inscription in gold print.
- *length 3.8cm*
- **Guide price £1,917/$3,624**

Silver Regimental Spoon ▲

- *World War I*
A silver regimental teaspoon showing the ornate crest of the London Rifle Brigade, topped with a crown.
- *length 9cm*
- **Guide price £25/$48**

German Pilot's Log Books ▲

- *1936–1939*
Completed pilot's log books covering the years 1936 to 1939. Details the flights taken by a German pilot.
- **Guide price £175/$331**

Grenadier Guards Cap ▲

- *circa 1940*
A World War II period Grenadier Guards peaked dress cap, with regimental cap badge insignia.
- **Guide price £40/$76**

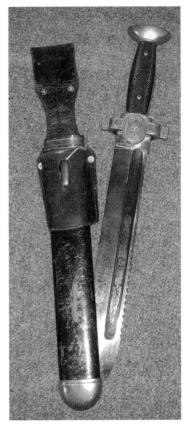

World War II German Red Cross Dagger ▲

- *World War II*
A World War II German red cross man's "heuer" dress dagger, with serrated edge and blood gutter.
- *length 30cm*
- **Guide price £375/$709**

Old Bill Mascot ▼

- *1920*
A bronze car mascot mounted on a wooden base of Bruce Bairnsfather's "Old Bill" character.
- **Guide price £200/$378**

World War I "Brodie" Helmet ▲

- *1917*
A British army second type "Brodie" steel helmet, from the latter part of World War I, complete with adjustable leather strap.
- **Guide price £75/$142**

World War II German Army Helmet ◄

- *1940*
A World War II German army 1935 pattern helmet with single army decal. With evocative bullet hole sustained in battle.
- **Guide price £175/$331**

Miniature Cavalry Helmet ▲

- *1920*
A one third-sized cavalry helmet of the 2nd County of London Yeomanry, with purple horse-hair plume. Possibly made as an officer's desk ornament.
- **Guide price £450/$851**

World War I Dagger ▼

- *World War I*
A World War I German fighting knife by "Ern". Has a studded wooden handle and is complete with a leather and steel sheath.
- *length 70cm*
- **Guide price £70/$133**

AUTOMOBILIA

Eagle Insignia Car Mascot ▼

- circa 1960

Square black and white Car Recovery Service Club badge with eagle insignia.

- height 14cm
- **Guide price £8/$16**

A.A. Badge ▼

- circa 1960

Automobile Association metal badge with yellow ochre background.

- 11cm x 10cm
- **Guide price £22/$41**

Horn-Playing Satyr Car Mascot ▷

- 1960s

A rude devil cocking-a-snook car mascot for rear mounting. Chromed brass by Desmo.

- length 12cm
- **Guide price £150/$284**

Brighton & Hove Motor Club Badge ▲

- 2001

Brighton & Hove Motor Club badge of the present day, cut brass, chrome and plastic-based enamel colours.

- diameter 6cm
- **Guide price £20/$38**

R.A.C. Key ▲

- circa 1960

Metal key, property of the Royal Automobile Club, London, SW1.

- height 7cm
- **Guide price £7/$14**

B.A.R.C. Badge ▷

- 1930s

Brooklands Automobile Racing Club membership badge issued during the inter-war period up until the closure of the circuit in 1939. Die struck brass, chrome plated and vitreous coloured enamels. Produced by Spencer. London. Usually with members issue No. stamped on the reverse.

- height 14cm
- **Guide price £400/$756**

Bentley Mascot ▲

- 1950s

Bentley flying winged B radiator mounted mascot, designed by Charles Sykes. This example is post World War II and is shown to be leaning forward. Cast brass, chronuim plated.

- height 7cm
- **Guide price £250/$473**

Jaguar Mascot ▼

- 1950s

Small Jaguar leaping cat bonnet mascot, in die cast brass chrome plated for MK.10. Jaguar still used today on modern Jaguars.

- length 11cm
- **Guide price £20/$38**

Chrome Lady Car Mascot ▼

- circa 1960

Chrome flying lady mascot for car.

- height 14cm
- **Guide price £120/$227**

S.A.M.T.C. Lion Badge ◀

- *circa 1960*
S.A.M.T.C. white badge with enamelled crown and badge with rampant lion.
- *14cm x 12cm*
- **Guide price £65/$123**

Lines Bros. Car ▶

- *1930s*
Morris-type open roadster, pressed steel with folding windscreen, period running boards and opening driver's door.
- *40cm x 90cm*
- **Guide price £1,750/$3,308**

Bentley Winged B Badge ▼

- *1960–80*
Bentley winged B radiator shell badge, pressed steel, chrome-plated with enamel central black B label.
- *height 14.5cm*
- **Guide price £100/$189**

A.A. Key ▲

- *circa 1970*
Metal A.A. key.
- *height 7cm*
- **Guide price £4/$8**

Brighton & Hove Motor Club Badge ▼

- *circa 1920s*
Brighton and Hove Motor Club membership badge of the inter-war period. Die stuck brass, chrome plated with vitreous enamel.
- *diameter 6cm*
- **Guide price £200/$378**

J.C.C. Badge ▼

- *1960–70*
The Junior Car Club existed to cater for light cars and motorcycles including Morgan type three wheelers. Membership badge in die struck brass, nickel or chrome-plated with vitreous enamel colours.
- *height 14cm*
- **Guide price £200/$378**

B.A.R.C. Badge ▼

- *1950s–70s*
British Automobile Racing Club member's badge in die struck brass chrome plated with coloured vitreous enamels.
- *height 10cm*
- **Guide price £75/$142**

Word Wildlife Fun Panda Car Mascot ◀

- *circa 1960*
World Wildlife Fund badge with a panda on a bottle green background being held by a pair of hands.
- *height 14cm*
- **Guide price £25/$48**

Bugatti Racing Car ▲

• *1990s*
Bugatti type 35 Grand Prix racing car replica produced by Elantec-Eureka. Aluminium body, working gearshift and handbrake levers and authentic dashboard.
• *50cm x 125cm*
• **Guide price £2,750/$5,198**

Brookland's Junior Racing Drivers' Club Badge ▲

• *1930s*
Brookland's Junior Car Club badge for the Junior Racing Drivers' Club. Multi-coloured vitreous enamels on chromed shield.
• *height 12cm*
• **Guide price £1,500/$2,835**

Bentley Flying B Mascot ▼

• *1920*
Bentley flying winged B radiator mounted mascot designed by Charles Sykes.
• *height 17cm*
• **Guide price £300/$567**

R.A.C. Silver Jubilee Badge ▼

• *1977*
R.A.C. Queen's Silver Jubilee 1977 specially produced limited edition commemorative badge sold with certificate. Die struck brass chrome plated with plastic based enamel colours.
• *diameter 10cm*
• **Guide price £200/$378**

Brooklands Society Badge ▼

• *circa 1990s*
B.S (Brooklands Society) membership badge in cut brass, chromium plated with plastic based coloured enamels.
• *height 14.5cm*
• **Guide price £25/$48**

Mercedes Radiator Grille ▲

• *circa 1950*
Mercedes Benz radiator shell with grille and star mascot, pressed steel chromium plated.
• *width 65cm*
• **Guide price £100/$189**

R.A.C. Badge ▲

• *circa 1930s*
Royal Automobile Club associate badge affiliated to the Junior Car Club (J.C.C.) Inter-war period. Chromed brass and vitreous enamel collars.
• *height 13cm*
• **Guide price £150/$284**

Austin Pathfinder Pedal Car ▲

• *circa 1949*
Pressed steel monocoque body with vinyl upholstered seat. Has dummy engine under removable bonnet and perspex windscreen.
• *40cm x 1.1m*
• **Guide price £2,500/$4,725**

Brooklands Society Badge ▼

• *circa 1960s–1980s*
B.S (Brooklands Society) membership badge in die struck brass, chrome plated with vitreous coloured enamels.
• *height 14.5cm*
• **Guide price £100/$189**

Pressed Steel Pedal Car ▼

• *1960s*
A Ford style saloon, made by Tri-Ang Toys Ltd, marketed as a "Lightning".
• *30cm x 90cm*
• **Guide price £125/$137**

Bentley B Mascot ▲

• *1940s*

Bentley flying winged B radiator mounted mascot, designed by Charles Sykes. This example is shown to be leaning backward. Cast brass, chronium-plated.

• *wing span 17cm*

• **Guide price £300/$567**

Bentley Drivers Club Badge ▲

• *1950s*

Bentley Drivers Club wheel spinner style club membership badge in chrome and painted enamel.

• *diameter 8cm*

• **Guide price £45/$85**

Brookland's Automobile Racing Club Badge ▲

• *1921*

Brookland's Automobile Racing Club Badge in original box, membership number stamped on reverse, brass and red enamel.

• *10cm x 4cm*

• **Guide price £250/$473**

Morgan Club Badge ▼

• *2001*

Morgan Sports Car Club present day membership badge, known as 'Sex Mog.' Cut brass with plastic based enamel colours.

• *diameter 7cm*

• **Guide price £25/$48**

British Motor Racing Badge ▼

• *circa 1940s*

British Motor Racing Marshall's badge produced in die struck brass, chrome plated with vitreous enamel colours.

• *12cm x 9cm*

• **Guide price £150/$284**

Rolls-Royce Mascot ▶

• *circa 1920s*

Rolls-Royce flying lady known as 'The Spirit of Ecstasy' designed by Charles Sykes and patented in 1911. This very tall example is from the pre World War 1 period. In cast brass, nickel plated sometimes silver plated.

• *height 17cm*

• **Guide price £1,250/$2,363**

J. R. D. C. Badge ▲

• *circa 1920s*

Junior Racing Driver Club, die struck thin brass shield shape badge.

• *height 10cm*

• **Guide price £200/$378**

Morgan Pedal Car ▼

• *1980*

A Morgan 4/4 Roadster with a fibreglass body and chrome detailing, and has working headlights and horn.

• *122cm x 50cm*

• **Guide price £950/$1,796**

Bentley Mascot

- *1920s*

Bentley flying winged B radiator mounted mascot designed by Charles Sykes. This example is from the 1920s roadster sports model and is a large brass-casting used for a short period.

- *wing span 22cm*
- **Guide price £400/$756**

Steering Wheel Ashtray

- *circa 1950s*

Ashtray in the form of a steering wheel in moulded porcelain produced by Beswick, England for Les Leston (Motoring Suppliers).

- *diameter 19cm*
- **Guide price £55/$104**

B. A. R. C. Badge

- *circa 1930s*

Brookland Automobile Racing Club committee members' badge (a standard issue badge with the legend 'Committee' on a yellow label beneath the wings, only a very few were issued) 1,500.

- *height 14cm*
- **Guide price £2,000/$3,780**

Jaguar Mascot

- *circa 1925–30*

Jaguar leaping cat car mascot by Desmo, after a design by Frederick Gordon Crosby, cast brass, chrome plated and mounted on a radiator cap. An after sales accessory mascot popular during the inter-war period.

- *length 20cm*
- **Guide price £300/$567**

Brooklands Society Badge

- *1960s–70s*

Brooklands Society membership badge in pressed steel with plastic covered circuit emblem within a shield.

- *8cm square*
- **Guide price £65/$123**

B. A. R. C. Badge

- *1920–30s*

Brookland Automobile Racing Club. Special speed award for attaining a timed lap speed of 120 mph or more on the outer circuit. The red vitreous enamel label riveted beneath the wings.

- *height 14cm*
- **Guide price £5,500/$10,395**

Morgan Badge

- *circa 1945–1995*

50th Anniversary Morgan three wheeler club badge die struck brass chrome plated with coloured plastic based enamels.

- *height 9cm*
- **Guide price £45/$85**

J.C.C. Ashtray

- *circa 1920s*

Ashtray of the J.C.C. Junior Car Club produced in epns, with the club badge positioned in the centre.

- *diameter 14cm*
- **Guide price £75/$142**

B. R. D. C. Badge

- *circa 1950*

British Racing Drivers Club die struck brass and nickel plated with coloured vitreous enamels.

- *height 11cm*
- **Guide price £350/$662**

Brighton & Hove Badge

- *1950s–70s*

Brighton & Hove Motor Club membership badge. Die struck brass, chrome plated with vitreous enamel colours.

- *diameter 6cm*
- **Guide price £40/$76**

Dolphin Brighton & Hove Mascot

- *circa 1920–30*

Brighton and Hove Car Club mascot for radiator mounting in the form of a dolphin like sea monster. Cast brass nickel plated. This car club is the oldest club in the UK.

- *height 14cm*
- **Guide price £200/$378**

R.A.C. Award Plaque ▲

• *1939*

Award plaque for 'Eighth Annual Rally of the R.A.C. London to Brighton' 1939, in pressed hollow cast brass. Mounted on a wood plinth.

• *17cm x 11cm*
• **Guide price £100/$189**

B.A.R.C. Badge ▼

• *From 1907*

Brookland Automobile Racing Club member's and guests brooches. Every year on joining a member would be issued with a pin brooch tag in gilt brass with vitreous coloured enamel centre with two smaller versions on coloured string for the guests. These were sent in an official box with the matching year date shown. The dates issued were from the opening of the circuit in 1910.

• *height 14cm*
• **Guide price £200/$378 (for boxed sets)**

Morgan Badge ◄

• *circa 1970*

The Morgan three wheeler club. A die struck aluminium badge with the design on the front of a Morgan Aero Super Sports three wheeler trike.

• *9cm x 8cm*
• **Guide price £30/$57**

Bentley Flying 'B' Mascot ▲

• *circa 1950*

Bentley flying winged B radiator mascot in die cast brass chrome plated for S type Bentley.

• *height 6cm*
• **Guide price £150/$284**

Brookland's Entry Pass Badges ▲

• *1912*

Brass and enamel Brookland's annual entry pass badges for members (large central badge) and guests pair of brooches in original box of issue.

• *10cm x 4cm*
• **Guide price £250/$473**

Measuring Cans ◄

• *circa 1930*

A two-gallon and a five-gallon metering vessel with copper bodies and heavy-duty brass banding. The cans show funnel tops and brass spouts, positioned to prevent over-filling.

• **Guide price £195/$370 (5 gal); £180/$341 (2 gal)**

Club Badge ▲

• *1950s–70s*

British racing and Sports Car Club badge in die struck brass, chrome plated with coloured vitreous enamels.

• *height 10cm*
• **Guide price £75/$142**

Japanese Cadillac ▲

• *1950*

A tin-plate Japanese 50s Marysan Cadillac, cream and green with working lights. Forward and reverse, very rare, in original box.

• *length 30cm*
• **Guide price £250/$473**

B. R. D. C. Badge ▲

- *circa 1920s*

British Racing Drivers Club badge. Die struck gilded brass with coloured vitreous enamels, produced with holes on either side of the wings for radiator grille fixing.

- *height 11cm*
- **Guide price £400/$756**

M. S. C. C. Badge ▲

- *circa 1970–80*

M.S.C.C. Morgan Sports Car Club shield shape membership badge of the 4/4 owner's (special anniversary issue dates thereon) Die struck with vitreous coloured enamels.

- *height 14cm*
- **Guide price £75/$142**

Morgan's Commemorative Badge ▶

- *1962*

Morgan's finest hour 23–24 June 1962 commemorative badge in die struck brass chrome plate with plastic based coloured enamels.

- *height 8cm*
- **Guide price £40/$76**

Jaguar Badge ▲

- *circa 1950*

Jaguar Drivers Club members badge in the form of a steering wheel. In die struck brass chrome plated with central cats head in brass and red vitreous enamel legend on scroll beneath. Made by Pinches, London with member's name engraved on reverse.

- *diameter 8cm*
- **Guide price £75/$142**

Jaguar Bonnet Mascot ▼

- *circa 1920s*

Jaguar leaping at bonnet mascot in die cast brass chrome plated with lozenge shaped base, designed by Frederick Gordon Crosby.

- *length 19cm*
- **Guide price £200/$378**

Bentley B Mascot ▼

- *circa 1931*

Bentley flying winged B of the single wing early experimental type design of 1931 die cast, nickel plated brass.

- *height 6cm*
- **Guide price £400/$756**

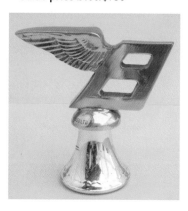

Morgan Badge ▼

- *circa 1990*

A 'Morgan in Coburg' pressed steel badge, with Art Deco polychrome design, with front of red Morgan in foreground.

- **Guide price £30/$57**

Moscovich Pedal Car ▶

- *early 1980s–mid 1990s*

A Moscovich pressed-steel pedal car with working lights and horn.

- *109cm x 44cm*
- **Guide price £350/$662**

Brooklands Club Award ▼

- *circa 1930s*

Brookland Automobile Racing Club Special speed award for attaining a timed lap speed of 130mph or more on the outer circuit. The red vitreous enamel label riveted beneath the wings. Only about a dozen or so of the 130mph badges were awarded and they are recorded in the W B Boddy book 'History of Brookland Motor Course' showing the date of issue and the speed attained and in which car.

- *height 14cm*
- **Guide price £5,500/$10,395**

Club Badge ▼

- *circa 1985*

Brighton Morgan Sports Car Club. Perspex front on steel, chrome-plated badge.

- **Guide price £35/$66**

Bugatti Pedal Car ▼

- *late 1920s*
A Bugatti Eureka made in France. Two-seater replica of the type 35 Grand Prix Sports with very fine chrome and leather detailing.
- *165cm x 56cm*
- **Guide price £3,500/$6,615**

Autocourse ▼

- *1980-81*
Autocourse annual for 1980–81, published by Seymour Press Limited.
- **Guide price £125/$137**

Bugatti Book ▼

- *circa 1997*
Memoirs of a Bugatti Hunter by Antoine Raffaëlli.
- *height 42cm*
- **Guide price £33/$63**

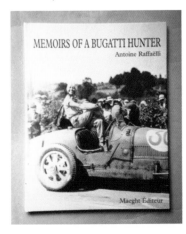

Bentley Pedal Car ▲

- *mid 1960s*
A Tri-Ang Bentley continental convertible. Plastic body with chrome detailing.
- *122cm x 46cm*
- **Guide price £950/$1,796**

Klemantaski Books ▲

- *circa 1998*
The memoirs of Louis Klemantaski with photographic portfolio. Edition limited to 300, signed by the author.
- **Guide price £400/$756**

Chrysler Pedal Car ▼

- *late 1920s*
An American-made Chrysler "Airflow" with an all-pressed steel body and chrome detailing. Built by Steelcraft.
- *120cm x 55cm*
- **Guide price £3,000/$5,670**

Pedal Car ▼

- *1980–90*
A Tri-Ang Sharna Rolls Royce Corniche convertible. Pedal-powered car in plastic.
- *122cm x 53cm*
- **Guide price £500/$945**

Pedal Fire Truck ▲

- *early 1920s*
An American-made fire truck with fine detailing. Wooden ladder with mascot on bonnet.
- *105cm x 52cm*
- **Guide price £3,500/$6,615**

Jaguar Pedal Car ▲

- *1950s–mid 1960s*
A Jaguar XK-120 open Roadster. Fibreglass body with chrome detailing, pedal powered car.
- *length 150cm, width 53cm*
- **Guide price £950/$1,796**

Ford Pedal Car ▲

- *Early 1960s*
A Tri-Ang Ford Zephyr-style police car with working siren and chrome detailing.
- *84cm x 36cm*
- **Guide price £300/$567**

BOOKS & MAPS

Map of Menorca
- *1974*

By John Armstrong, the governor of Menorca. Published by Laurie and Whittle. Showing an inset of Mahon and two inset views of the harbour. This harbour was an important position for controlling the Mediterranean Sea.
- *55 x 45cm*
- **Guide price £450/$851**

The Noh Plays of Japan
- *1922*

The Noh Plays of Japan by Arthur Waley. New York: Alfred A. Knopf. First American edition. Translations of the most celebrated Noh plays. Eight plates of masks. Original linen-backed boards.
- **Guide price £125/$137**

A Treatise on Money
- *1930*

A Treatise on Money by John Maynard. New York: Harcourt, Brace & Co. First edition: the American issue of the London sheets. Two volumes. Demy 8vo.
- **Guide price £350/$662**

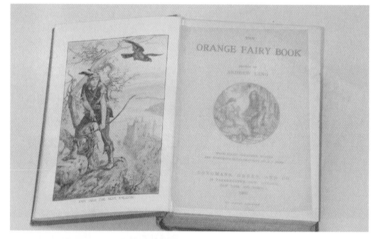

Peter Rabbit
- *1902*

The Tale of Peter Rabbit by Beatrix Potter. First edition, and first issue of the flat spine.
- *14cm x 10cm*
- **Guide price £50,000/$94,500**

A Christmas Carol
- *1915*

A Christmas Carol by Charles Dickens, illustrated by Arthur Rackam and published by William Henemann, London.
- *19cm x 12cm*
- **Guide price £1,450/$2,741**

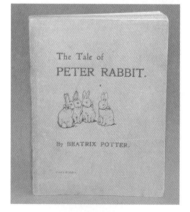

Shakespeare's Plays
- *1925–32*

The Tragedies, Comedies and Histories of Shakespeare. London. Oxford University Press. A prettily bound set of the three separately published volumes of the Oxford India-paper edition. Edited by W. J. Craig with a full glossary.
- **Guide price £250/$473**

Voltaire
- *1930*

A unique copy of *Historie de Jenni*, with hand-coloured illustrations throughout by Lauro with original cover and gilding.
- *19cm x 24cm*
- **Guide price £1,800/$3,402**

The Saint
- *1961*

The Saint to the Rescue by Leslie Charters, published by Hodder and Stoughton London and printed by G. Bertram.
- *19cm x 13cm*
- **Guide price £220/$417**

Orange Fairy Book
- *1906*

First edition of the *Orange Fairy Book* by Andrew Lang. Published in 1906.
- **Guide price £300/$567**

Casino Royale
- *1953*

Casino Royale, author Ian Fleming published by Jonathon Cape, Bedford Square, London. First edition, second issue.
- *19cm x 13cm*
- **Guide price £2,950/$5,576**

Peer Gynt

- *1920*

Peer Gynt, first Rackham edition, published by George G. Harrap & Co. Ltd., illustrated by Arthur Rackham.

- *27cm x 20cm*
- **Guide price £245/$463**

Arabian Horse

- *1914*

The Arabian Horse His Country and People by Major General W. Tweedies. C.S.I. with fine coloured illustrations published by William Blakwood and sons, Edinburgh and London bound in green leather.

- *31cm x 25cm*
- **Guide price £1,800/$3,402**

Thunderball

- *1961*

Thunderball by Ian Fleming. First published by Glidrose Publications.

- *19cm x 13cm*
- **Guide price £550/$1,040**

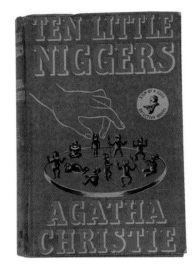

Ten Little Niggers

- *1939*

Ten Little Niggers by Agatha Christie. First edition, published for the Crime Club by Collins, Pall Mall, London.

- *19cm x 13cm*
- **Guide price £6,500/$12,285**

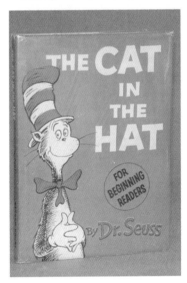

The Cat in the Hat

- *1957*

First edition of *The Cat in the Hat* by Dr. Seuss. Original pictorial paper covered boards complete with dust wrapper. Illustrated throughout by the author.

- *29cm x 21cm*
- **Guide price £8,500/$16,065**

Harry Potter Set

- *1997–2000*

An extremely scarce set of first editions of the *Harry Potter* series by J.K. Rowling, which includes: *The Philosopher's Stone*, *The Chamber of Secrets*, *The Prisoner of Azkaban* and *The Goblet of Fire*. Published by Bloomsbury, London. All signed.

- *20cm x 13cm*
- **Guide price £27,500/$51,975**

Charles Dickens

- *1906*

The Works, Letters, and Life of Charles Dickens with plates by illustrators Cruickshank Leech & co., London. The National Edition in 40 vol. Chapman and Hall Ltd., 1906-8 with a signed manuscript and letter addressed to Dr. Hudson in superb contemporary binding by Birsall Morocco with raised bands, gilt titles to spines top edged gilt. The Dr. Hudson to whom Dickens' letter is addressed is presumably Fredrick Hudson, surgeon of Manchester. With regard to the arrangement for the performance of *The Frozen Deep*, the play he wrote with Wilkie Collins.

- *18cm x 13cm*
- **Guide price £8,500/$16,065**

Three Guineas

- *1938*

First edition of *Three Guineas* by Virginia Woolf. Published by The Hogarth Press, London. Pale yellow cloth, gilt titles to spine, complete with dust wrapper. Illustrated with photographic plates.

- *18cm x 12cm*
- **Guide price £500/$945**

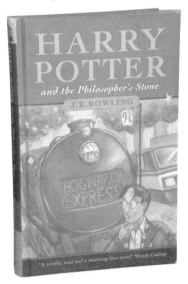

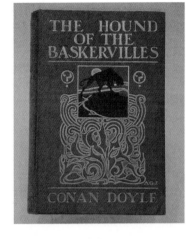

The Hound of the Baskervilles

- *1902*

The Hound of the Baskervilles, a Sherlock Holmes adventure by A. Conan Doyle, published George Newnes London.

- *19cm x 14cm*
- **Guide price £2,500/$4,725**

Sea Kings of Crete

- *1910*

The Sea Kings of Crete by James Baikie. Publishers: Adam & Charles Black, London. First edition. Plates. Maps. Original decorative cloth, top edge gilt.

- **Guide price £75/$142**

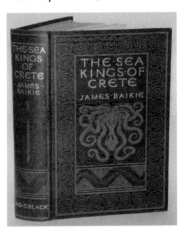

Fishing Stories

▼

- *1913*

First edition of *A Book of Fishing Stories* by F .G.Aflaco. Published by JM Dent and Sons Ltd., Aldine House, Covent Garden and E.P. Dutton & Co., New York

- *30cm x 23cm*
- **Guide price £375/$709**

Hunting with Eskimos

▼

- *1911*

Hunting with the Eskimos by Harry Whitney, a unique record of a sportsman's year among the northernmost tribe. Illustrated with photographs, published by The Century Co., New York.

- *19cm x 15cm*
- **Guide price £75/$142**

The Hound of Death and Other Stories

◄

- *1933*

The Hound of Death and Other Stories by Agatha Christie. First edition. Published by Odhams Press Limited, London.

- *18.5cm x 13cm*
- **Guide price £350/$662**

Constant Gardener

▲

- *2001*

The Constant Gardener signed first edition by John Le Carré. Published by Hodder and Stoughton, London.

- *25cm x 18cm*
- **Guide price £85/$161**

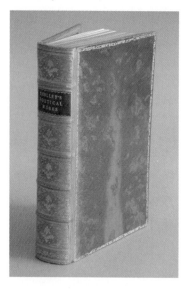

The Poetical Works of Percy Bysshe Shelley

▲

- *1908*

The Poetical Works of Percy Bysshe Shelley. Macmillan and Co., Limited London. Bound by Riviere in full tree calf, and gilt lettered green morocco label and gilt decoration to spine with marbled end papers, all edges gilded.

- *18cm x 12cm*
- **Guide price £475/$898**

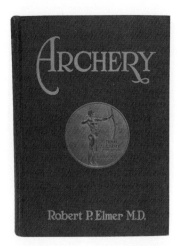

Archery

▲

- *1926*

Archery by Robert P. Elmer former champion archer of the United States. Published by The Penn Publishing Co., Philadelphia.

- *18cm x 14cm*
- **Guide price £95/$180**

Rubaiyat

▲

- *1922*

First edition of the *Rubaiyat of Omar Khayyam.* English verse by Edward Fitzgerald with illustrations by Fish. Published by John Lane, London. Plates by Geo. Givvons & Co., Leicester.

- *29cm x 23cm*
- **Guide price £60/$114**

The Tempest

▼

- *1926*

Deluxe edition of Shakespeare's *The Tempest,* illustrated by Arthur Rackham. Published by William Heinemann Ltd. London. Limited to 520 copies of which this is No. 128. Signed by Rackham.

- *32cm x 26cm*
- **Guide price £3,250/$6,143**

Fragonard

▼

- *1906*

Fragonard, a limited edition of 500 copies with good quality sepia illustrations by Pierre de Nothac Groupil & Co. Editors Manz Joyant & Co. Bound with original red leather.

- *33cm x 28cm*
- **Guide price £550/$1,040**

Winnie the Pooh

◄

- *1926*

Limited to 1/350 *Winnie the Pooh* by A.A. Milne, with wonderful onlaid binding, and decorations by Ernest H. Shephard. Methuen & Co. London, numbered copies, signed by Milne and Shephard.

- *23cm x 17cm*
- **Guide price £8,500/$16,065**

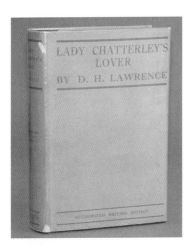

Lady Chatterley's Lover ▲

- *1932*

First authorised UK edition of *Lady Chatterley's Lover* by D.H. Lawrence. Publisher's brown cloth with gilt title to spine. Complete with dust wrapper. Published by Martin Secker, London.

- *19cm x 12.4cm*
- **Guide price £450/$851**

Brighton Rock ▼

- *1938*

First edition of *Brighton Rock* by Graham Greene, published by William Heinemann Ltd London, bound by the Chelsea Bindery.

- *18.5cm x 13cm*
- **Guide price £950/$1,796**

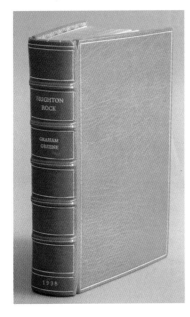

Kew Gardens ▶

- *1919*

Kew Gardens by Virginia Woolf with woodcuts by Vanessa Bell. There were only 150 copies made and Virginia Woolf set the type.

- *23cm x 14cm*
- **Guide price £18,000/$34,020**

Mr. Punch on the Links ▼

- *1929*

Mr. Punch on the Links by E.V. Knox consisting of 8 volumes with 32 illustrations, numerous golf anecdotes, and green cloth cover. Published in New York, Rue D Hendle Co. Inc.

- *23cm x 17cm*
- **Guide price £245/$463**

Brazilian Wilderness ▲

- *1914*

Through the Brazilian Wilderness by Theodore Roosevelt, published by Charles Scribner's and Sons, 332 illustrations and map of the entire South American journey and River of Doubt.

- *28cm x 10cm*
- **Guide price £495/$936**

The Hound of the Baskervillles ▼

- *1902*

First edition of *The Hound of the Baskervilles* by Arthur Conan Doyle. Published by George Newnes Limited, London. Bound in recent full burgundy morocco, gilt lettering and decoration to spine.

- *19cm x 12cm*
- **Guide price £1,200/$2,268**

The Kingdom of the Pearl ▼

- *1920*

The Kingdom of the Pearl by Leonard Rosenthal, illustrated by Edmund Dulac. Limited edition of 675 copies of which this is No. 67. Published by Nisbet & Co. London, with ten captioned tissue-pasted colour illustrations.

- *30cm x 24cm*
- **Guide price £600/$1,134**

Ulysses ◀

- *1922*

First edition of *Ulysses* by James Joyce. Limited to 1000 copies on Dutch handmade paper. This is one of 750 printed on handmade paper and numbered 501 (of 251–1,000). Published by Shakespeare and Company, 12, Rue de L'Odeon, Paris.

- *height 26cm*
- **Guide price £23,500/$44,415**

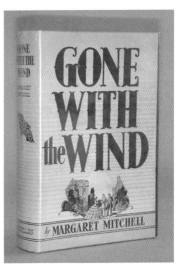

Gone with the Wind ▲

- *1936*

Gone with the Wind by Margaret Mitchell. First edition. Macmillan Company, New York. Original publisher's grey cloth, complete with dust wrapper.

- *height 22cm*
- **Guide price £3,950/$7,466**

The Lion, the Witch and the Wardrobe

- *1950*

The Lion, the Witch and the Wardrobe by C.S. Lewis. First edition. Illustrations and colour frontispiece by Pauline Baynes. The first and best known of the Narnia chronicles. Post 8vo. Bound in an elegant recent green quarter-morocco, banded and gilt. Published by Geoffrey Bles.
- **Guide price £850/$1,607**

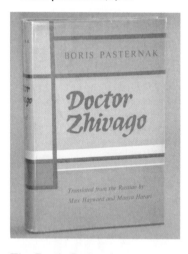

The Earth-Owl and Other Moon-People

- *1963*

By Ted Hughes. Faber & Faber, London. First edition. Illustrated by R.A. Beard. Very good copy.
- *16 x 23cm*
- **Guide price £95/$180**

George and the Dragon

- *1951*

Manifeste Mystique a pen and ink drawing within a book of *George and the Dragon*, together with original etching from a drawing of the famous Christ of St. John on the Cross, signed and dated by Salvador Dali.
- *40cm x 27cm*
- **Guide price £15,000/$28,350**

Doctor Zhivago

- *1958*

First edition of *Doctor Zhivago* by Boris Pasternak translated from the Russian by Max Hayward and Manya Harari. Collins and Harvill Press, London. Original publisher's red cloth, felt lettered spine, complete with dust wrapper.
- *21cm x 14cm*
- **Guide price £150/$284**

Alone

- *1938*

Alone by Richard E. Byrd. Published by Putnam, London. First British edition. Admiral Byrd's harrowing account of his Antarctic sojourn. Decorations by Richard E. Harrison. Demy 8vo.
- **Guide price £60/$114**

Spaniard in the Works

- *1965*

A Spaniard in the Works, First edition by the singer songwriter John Lennon, published by Jonathan Cape, London.
- *14cm x 10cm*
- **Guide price £140/$265**

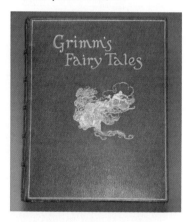

Hans Andersen's Fairy Tales

- *1913*

Signed limited edition of *Hans Andersen's Fairy Tales*. Constable and Company Ltd, London. Limited to 100 copies, this one being numbered 59 and signed on the limitation page by W. Heath Robinson. White illustrations.
- *height 29.5cm*
- **Guide price £3,950/$7,466**

The Hobbit

- *1951*

First edition of *The Hobbit or There and Back Again* by J.R.R. Tolkien illustrated by Aland Lee, published by Harper Collins.
- *26cm x 20cm*
- **Guide price £150/$284**

The Fairy Tales of the Brothers Grimm

- *1909*

A beautiful copy of *The Fairy Tales of the Brothers Grimm*, limited edition: number 41 of 750, signed on the limitation page by Arthur Rackham. Originally bound by Bayntun Riviere of Bath and more recently in full burgundy morocco, with gilt titles.
- *height 29.5cm*
- **Guide price £4,950/$9,356**

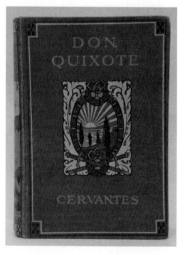

Don Quixote

- *1920*

Don Quixote de le Mancha by Cervantes with 206 illustrations by Sir John Gilbert R.A. in original hand back cover. Published by G. Routledge & Sons Ltd., New York, E. P. Dutton & Co.
- *21cm x 18cm*
- **Guide price £45/$85**

Vile Bodies ▼

- *1930*

Vile Bodies by Evelyn Waugh. First edition of Waugh's scarce second novel, with his own striking title-page design in red and black. Crown 8vo. Bound in a smart recent full morocco, banded and gilt.

- **Guide price £450/$851**

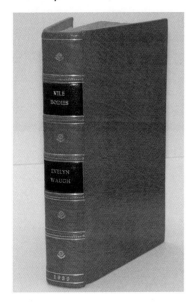

The Wind in the Willows ▼

- *1908*

First edition of *The Wind in the Willows*, by Kenneth Grahame. With a frontispiece by Graham Robertson. Methuen & Co. Ltd. London. Publisher's blue cloth with gilt titles and illustrations.

- *height 20cm*
- **Guide price £4,500/$8,505**

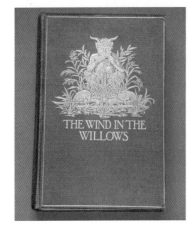

Arabian Nights ▶

- *1937*

The Arabian Nights by Parish Maxfield. Edited by Kate Douglas Wiggin and Nora A. Smith published in New York by Charles Scribner and Sons. Illustrated by Maxfield Parish with 9 colour illustrations.

- *24cm x 17cm*
- **Guide price £75/$142**

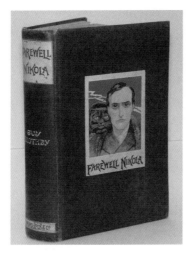

Farewell Nikola ▲

- *1901*

Farewell Nikola by Guy Boothby. First edition. The final adventures of one of the world's first fictional super-villains. Plates by Harold Piffard. Crown 8vo. Original bevelled cloth with pictorial onlay; white enamel on spine. Publishers: Ward, Lock & Co, London.

- **Guide price £75/$142**

Winnie the Pooh ▼

- *1924-8*

Set of books by A.A. Milne including: 'When We Were Very Young', 'Winnie the Pooh', 'Now We Are Six', and 'The House at Pooh Corner'.

- *22cm x 15cm*
- **Guide price £12,000/$22,680**

Tarantula ◀

- *1966*

First edition of *Tarantula* by the singer and songwriter Bob Dylan.

- *18cm x 12cm*
- **Guide price £75/$142**

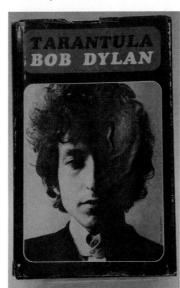

Old French Fairy Tales ▲

- *1920*

Old French Fairy Tales by Comtesse de Segar illustrated by Virginia Frances Sterrett, published in Philadelphia by Penn Publishing Co.

- *30cm x 26cm*
- **Guide price £650/$1,229**

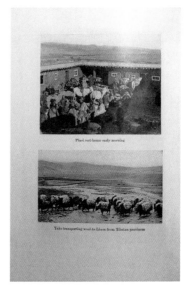

To Lhasa in Disguise ▲

- *1924*

By William Montgomery McGovern. The Century Co., New York & London. An Account of a Secret Expedition through Mysterious Tibet. First American edition. 8vo, profusely illustrated with attractive photographic plates throughout. Previous bookseller's label pasted on rear endpaper. Original blue decorated cloth. Gilt lettering to upper cover and spine. Original pictorial dustjacket. An excellent copy.

- **Guide price £200/$378**

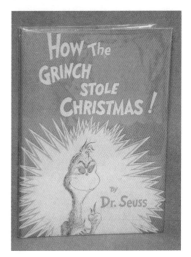

How the Grinch Stole Christmas ▲

- *1957*

First edition of *How the Grinch Stole Christmas* by Dr. Seuss. Published by Random House, New York. Original pictorial paper covered boards. Housed in a red cloth solander box with a green gilt lettered label. Illustrated by the author. Inscribed in the first blank page, 'for Pamela Benepe! Dr. Seuss'.

- *29cm x 20cm*
- **Guide price £6,500/$12,285**

Poems by Christina Rossetti ▲

- *circa 1920*

Poems by Christina Rossetti with illustrations by Florence Harrison published by Blackie and Son.
- *26cm x 21cm*
- **Guide price £475/$898**

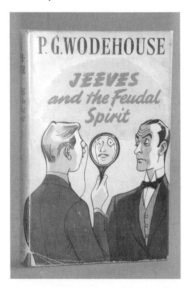

Gulliver's Travels ▼

- *1909*

By Jonathan Swift. 'Journey Into Several Remote Nations of the World'. Illustrated by Arthur Rackham. Published by J.M. Dent & Co., London. Fine quality.
- **Guide price £150–£180/$284–$341**

Jeeves and the Feudal Spirit ◄

- *1954*

First edition of *Jeeves and the Feudal Spirit* by P. G. Wodehouse. Herbert Jenkins Limited, London. Fine publisher's red cloth with black titles on spine. Complete with a dust wrapper.
- *19cm x 13cm*
- **Guide price £250/$473**

Bill the Minder ▼

- *1912*

Bill the Minder by W. Heath Robinson. Limited edition of 380 copies, of which this is no.167. Signed on the limitation page by Arthur Rackham. Bound by the Chelsea Bindery, others untrimmed. With sixteen colour plates and many monochrome illustrations by W. Heath Robinson.
- *height 29.5cm*
- **Guide price £2,750/$5,198**

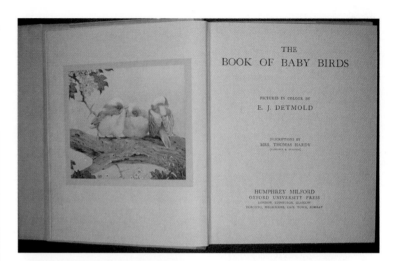

The Long Good-Bye ▲

- *1953*

The Long Good-Bye by Raymond Chandler. First edition. Hamish Hamilton, London, 1953. Original publisher's brown cloth, complete with dust wrapper.
- *18.5cm x 12cm*
- **Guide price £950/$1,796**

The Book of Baby Birds ▲

- *1919*

A full-colour illustrated book of baby birds by E.J. Detmold, accompanied by poetry.
- *height 35cm*
- **Guide price £300/$567**

Madeira, Canary Islands, Azores, Western Morocco ▼

- *1939*

By Karl Baedeker. Karl Baedeker, Leipzig, 1939. First edition. Extremely rare. 23 maps and plans, original pictorial wrappers, slight wear to the covers; overall a very good copy.
- **Guide price £1,000/$1,890**

Matilda ◄

- *1988*

First edition of *Matilda* by Roald Dahl. Jonathan Cape, London. Illustrated by Quentin Blake. Publisher's red cloth, with gilt title on spine.
- *23.5cm x 15cm*
- **Guide price £85/$161**

Brave New World ▲

- *1932*

First edition of *Brave New World*, signed by the author Aldous Huxley.
- *20cm x 13cm*
- **Guide price £15,000/$28,350**

Wind in the Willows ▲

- *1940*

Wind in the Willows by Kenneth Grahame, with an introduction by A.A Milne and 16 colour illustrations by Rackham. Limited edition of 2020 copies of which this is number 420. New York: The Limited Editions Club.
- *height 28cm*
- **Guide price £2,000/$3,780**

The Great River ▲

- *1911*

The Great River by Frederick Oakes Sylvester. The book contains poetry and illustrations throughout and has an embossed and gilded leather binder.
- *15cm x 21cm*
- **Guide price £350/$662**

Mobile Etude ▼

- *1962*

Mobile Etude pour une Representation des Etats Unis by Michel Butor. Published in Paris by Gallimard. One of 25 numbered copies with contemporary black leather backed dark grey boards and an intricate mosaic onlay of coloured paper cubes. Preserved in original grey board cover with perspex back, t.e.g., matching grey board slipcase. This work is dedicated to Jackson Pollock.
- *23.6cm x 18.7cm*
- **Guide price £5,000/$9,450**

The Salmon Rivers and Lochs of Scotland ▼

- *1909*

The Salmon Rivers and Lochs of Scotland by W.L. Calderwood with original binder and in good condition. A limited edition book, only 250 produced.
- *height 23cm*
- **Guide price £550/$1,040**

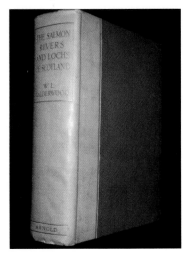

Mirage ▶

- *1906*

A book of various Arab stories compiled by Sliman Ben Ibrahim Bamer. It contains hand-painted illustrations throughout by E. Dinet. Decorative French binding by Rene Kieffer.
- *23cm x 17cm*
- **Guide price £1,400/$2,646**

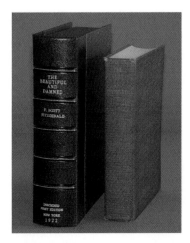

The Beautiful and Damned ▲

- *1922*

Presentation copy of *The Beautiful and Damned* inscribed twice by F. Scott Fitzgerald. The first inscription reads:- 'Sincerely F Scott Fitzgerald' and the second reads: 'Believe it or not this was in this book when it came to me from the Tyron bookshop. I must have autographed it for some book-seller and it fell into a stock of remainders. Such is fame.' Charles Scribner and Sons.
- *height 19cm*
- **Guide price £22,500/$42,525**

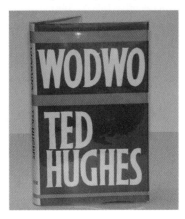

Wodwo ▲

- *1967*

Wodwo by Ted Hughes. London, Faber & Faber. First edition: in the first issue binding, lettered in gilt rather than silver. Poems, stories and a radio play. Demy 8vo. In the Berthold Wolpe dust-jacket.
- **Guide price £125/$137**

The Tempest ▼

- *1926*

The Tempest by William Shakespeare, illustrated by Arthur Rackham. London, William Heinemann. In contemporary full deep-blue morocco du cap, the lower board and decorated doublure are decorated in an elaborate grolieresque retrospective design consisting of onlaid, interlaced strapwork in three colours, red, saffron and tan, all edged in gilt. The book itself is one of 520 copies, reserved for America and signed in ink by Arthur Rackham.
- *29.5cm x 23cm*
- **Guide price £2,500/$4,725**

Bambi ▼

- *1928*

Bambi: A Life in the Wood by Felix Salten. Published in London by Jonathan Cape. First edition in English. Translated from the original German by Whittaker Chamber, with an introduction by John Galsworthy. Crown 8vo. Bound in a smart recent half green morocco, banded and gilt retaining the original pictorial endpapers.
- **Guide price £350/$662**

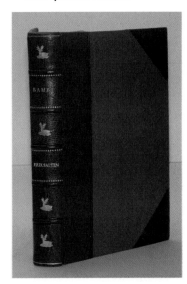

The Compleat Angler ▲

- *1931*

The Compleat Angler by Izaak Walton with fine, hand-coloured illustrations of rural themes by Arthur Rackham. Limited edition.

- *27cm x 20cm*
- **Guide price £750/$1,418**

A Morbid Taste for Bones ▲

- *1977*

By Ellis Peters. Macmillan, London. A mediaeval whodunnit. A fine copy.

- **Guide price £900/$1,701**

Night and Day ▼

- *1919*

First edition of *Night and Day* by Virginia Woolf, published by Duckworth & Co., Covent Garden London.

- *19.6cm x 12cm*
- **Guide price £23,500/$44,415**

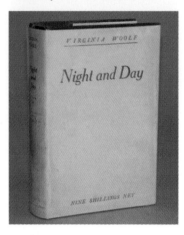

British Birds ▼

- *1915*

A book of the birds of Britain by Thorburn comprising four volumes, which contain 80 finely illustrated hand-coloured plates. Published by Longmans, Green & Co.

- *32cm x 27cm*
- **Guide price £680/$1,286**

Fairy Tales ▶

- *1924*

By Hans Andersen. Illustrated by Kay Nielsen. Hodder & Stoughton, London. First edition. 4to. Book has original green moiré cloth. Pictorial gilt with slightly faded spine. A very good copy.

- **Guide price £650/$1,229**

Bouquets et Frondaisana ◀

- *1920*

By Segay Eugene. Original cloth backed portfolio. Paris. Twenty sticky pochoir plates, comprising 60 designs based on flowers and foliage.

- *45x32cm*
- **Guide price £250/$473**

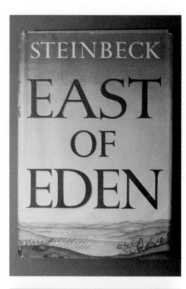

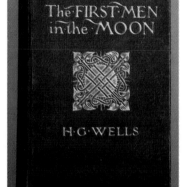

The First Men in the Moon ▲

- *1901*

Early 19th-century novel by H.G. Wells. Illustrated with 12 monochrome plates. Publisher's blue cloth. A very good copy with bright boards. First edition.

- **Guide price £150–£180/ $284–$341**

East of Eden ◀

- *1952*

By John Steinbeck. The Viking Press, New York. First edition in dustjacket.

- **Guide price £120–£150/ $227–$284**

A Midsummer Night's Dream ▲

- *1914*

By William Shakespeare. Illustrations by W. Heath Robinson. Constable & Co Ltd.

- **Guide price £200–£250/$378–$473**

The Sporting Adventures of Mr Popple ▲

- *1907*

By G.H. Jalland. Bodley Head, London. Landscape folio. Illustrated title page. Ten full-page captioned colour plates. Each with facing illustrated textleaf in sepia. Original linen-backed colour pictorial boards. A very good copy.

- **Guide price £250/$473**

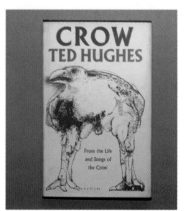

Crow ▲

- *1970*

A poem by Ted Hughes from *The Life and Songs of the Crow*. Published by Faber & Faber, London. First edition.

- *22cm x 15cm*
- **Guide price £125/$137**

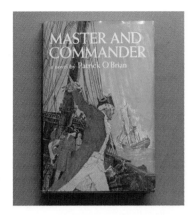

Master and Commander ▲

- *1969*

By Patrick O'Brian. J.B. Lippencott Co., New York and Philadelphia. First edition, precedes the later edition published by Collins in 1970. In very good condition.
- *15cm x 22.5cm*
- **Guide price £650/$1,229**

Viala Paul V. Vermod ▲

- *1910*

Traité Gérard de Viticulture: Amplography. Six volume folio, Paris: Marsonet Cie. Five hundred chromolithograph plates of grapes. Publisher's maroon cloth. Blind-stamped art nouveau.
- *35 x 26cm*
- **Guide price £7,500/$14,175**

Musical Instruments ▼

- *1921*

A book by A.J. Hipkins, consisting of 48 plates covering historic, rare and unique musical instruments, bound and gilded.
- **Guide price £280/$530**

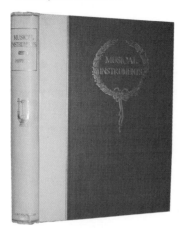

The Frequent Gun and a Little Fishing ▼

- *1950*

By Patrick R. Chalmers. Published by Phil Allan & Co., London
- *22.5 x 15cm*
- **Guide price £80/$152**

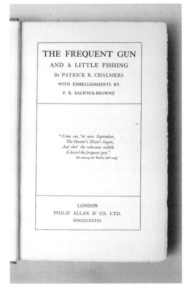

The World is Not Enough ▶

- *1999*

By Raymond Benson. Hodder & Stoughton. As new. First edition. Signed. Very small print run.
- **Guide price £80–£100/$152–$189**

Animal Portraiture ◀

- *1930*

By B.A. Ludekken. Contains fifty studies. Reproduced original paintings in full colour. Frederick Warne & Co., New York.
- *37 x 29cm*
- **Guide price £350/$662**

Tales of Mystery and Imagination ▲

- *1919*

By Edgar Allan Poe. First edition. 4to. Original blindstamped limp suede. Rebacked preserving original covers.
- **Guide price £150/$284**

The Spy Who Loved Me ▲

- *1962*

By Ian Fleming. Near fine first edition of James Bond caper, in dustwrapper.
- **Guide price £200–£250/$378–$473**

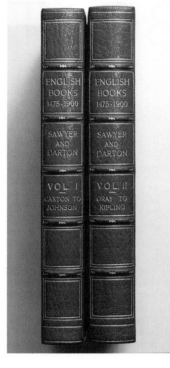

English Books 1475–1900 ▲

- *1927*

By Charles J. Sawyer and F.B. Darton Harvey. A signpost for collectors. London. First edition. 2,000 copies. Two volumes.
- *15 x 23cm*
- **Guide price £200/$378**

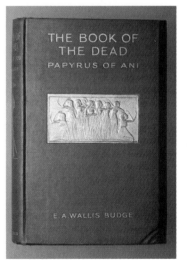

The Book of the Dead ▲

- *1913*

'The Papyrus of Ani' by Sir Ernest Alfred Wallis Budge. Phillip Lee Warner, London and G.P. Putnam Sons, New York. A reproduction in facsimile. Two volumes, 8vo. 37 folding colour plates and numerous illustrations in the text. Signature on endpapers, original gilt blindstamped red cloth, gilt lettering to spines. A fine and scarce copy.
- **Guide price £450/$851**

BOTTLES

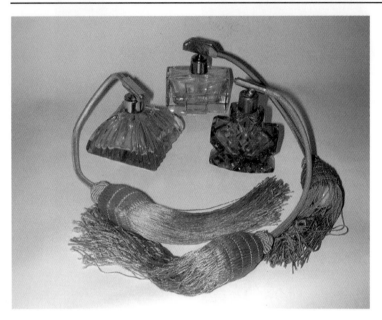

English Scent Bottles ▲

- *1920*

Three English Art Deco scent bottles, in red, pink and blue glass, each carrying a long silk tassel.

- *height 9cm*
- **Guide price £125/$237**

Black Tassle Bottle ▼

- *circa 1920*

Moulded Art Deco glass bottle with black circular design and black tassle.

- *height 14cm*
- **Guide price £120/$227**

Ruby Bottle ▼

- *1911*

Ruby red perfume bottle with a foliate design engraved in the silver stopper.

- *height 7cm*
- **Guide price £98/$185**

Faceted Bottle ▶

- *1930*

Glass perfume bottle faceted design with a silver-plated rim and a pink silk action pump spray with tassle.

- *height 15.5cm*
- **Guide price £158/$299**

Wedgwood Bottle ▼

- *circa 1930*

Wedgwood blue bottle with silver plate stopper.

- *height 4cm*
- **Guide price £85/$161**

Art Deco Bottle ▲

- *circa 1930*

European Art Deco glass bottle with fine floral and foliate engraved stopper.

- *height 22cm*
- **Guide price £250/$473**

Shalimar Scent Bottle ▲

- *1960*

Shalimar clear glass perfume bottle with scrolling and bee design, one of a limited edition of a 100 manufactured.

- *height 20cm*
- **Guide price £150/$284**

Pump Action Perfume Bottle ▼

- *circa 1920*

Red glass perfume bottle with silver screw top lid with a pump action spray and a hand painted butterfly on one side.

- *height 13cm*
- **Guide price £250/$473**

Gold Tassle Bottle ◀

- *circa 1920*

Art Deco clear glass perfume bottle with yellow spots, and royal blue leaf design around the base and gilt stopper and gold tassle.

- *height 15cm*
- **Guide price £250/$473**

Art Deco Scent Bottles ▼

- *1920*

A pair of English Art Deco perfume bottles in clear glass with black geometric designs.

- *height 18cm*
- **Guide price £268/$507**

Red Glass Scent Bottle ▼

- *1920*

Art Deco perfume bottle in deep red glass, with a tassle and opaque glass stopper.

- *height 14cm*
- **Guide price £168/$507**

Cut Glass Perfume Bottle ▲

- *circa 1910*

A glass perfume bottle with lattice design around the middle and a silver stopper.

- *height 11.5cm*
- **Guide price £150/$284**

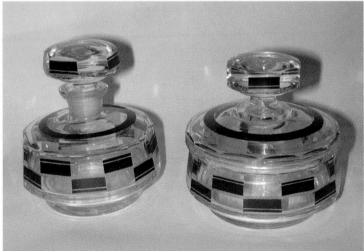

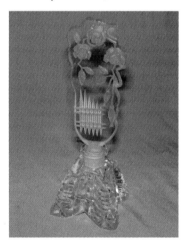

Cut-Glass Scent Bottle ▲

- *1920*

A cut-glass Art Deco scent bottle with stopper. Decorated with engraved flowers.

- *height 12cm*
- **Guide price £125/$237**

Joy de Jean Patou Scent Bottle ▲

- *circa 1950*

Large black plastic bottle, large red stopper, Joy de Jean Patou.

- *height 15cm*
- **Guide price £95/$180**

Prince Matchabelli Bottle ▲

- *circa 1930*

Prince Matchabelli perfume bottle in the shape of a ceramic crown with gilt cross stopper, in original box.

- *height 4cm*
- **Guide price £125/$237**

Heart-Shaped Porcelain Bottle ▲

- *circa 1906*

A heart-shaped porcelain scent bottle, with a silver stopper. Decorated with a pair of eighteenth century figures.

- *diameter 4cm*
- **Guide price £178/$337**

Eau de Cologne ▼

- *1950*

Scrolling glass bottle with burgundy flame stopper.

- *height 16cm*
- **Guide price £120/$227**

Cylindrical Bottle ▲

- *circa 1920*

Cylindrical shape perfume bottle with a silver stopper with inset with green stone.

- *height 8cm*
- **Guide price £110/$208**

Lancôme Bottle ▼

- *1960*

Lancôme perfume bottle with a foliate design on the stopper complete with original box.

- *10cm x 4cm*
- **Guide price £85/$161**

Art Deco Scent Bottle ▼

- *1920*

An Art Deco perfume bottle in turquoise and silver, with stopper. Decorated with geometric design and inscribed "R.M.S. Homeric".

- *height 6cm*
- **Guide price £68/$129**

Glass Perfume Bottle ◄

- *circa 1920*

Cut glass perfume bottle with a generous silver stopper encrusted with flowers and decorated with a foliate design.

- *height 14.5cm*
- **Guide price £445/$842**

English Scent Bottle ▼

• *1920*
English salmon pink Art Deco perfume bottle, styled in the shape of a sailing boat with sail.
• *height 14cm*
• **Guide price £150/$284**

Schiaparelli Perfume ▼

• *1960*
Clear glass bottle in the form of a female model. In a moulded glass case.
• *10cm x 6cm*
• **Guide price £250/$473**

Chanel Tester Kit ▶

• *circa 1950*
A perfume tester kit from Chanel, comprising five tester bottles some of which hold deleted perfumes.
• **Guide price £280/$530**

Art Deco Bottle ▲

• *circa 1920*
Art Deco glass perfume bottle with geometric design and a circular faceted lozenge shaped stopper.
• *height 14.5cm*
• **Guide price £135/$256**

Bourjois Kobako ▲

• *circa 1925*
A fashionable oriental-style perfume bottle, designed by Bourjois of Paris, with bakelite cover and carved stand.
• **Guide price £390/$737**

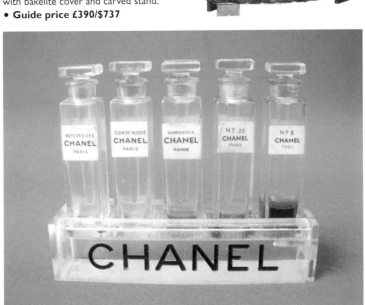

Circular Scent Bottle ▲

• *1902*
A circular scent bottle painted with two Japanese ladies in traditional dress embracing each other, set against a background of green foliage.
• *diameter 7cm*
• **Guide price £155/$293**

Glass Perfume Bottle ▼

• *circa 1903*
Cut glass perfume bottle with a silver rim and glass lozenge shaped stopper.
• *height 8cm*
• **Guide price £85/$161**

Art Deco Perfume Bottle ◀

• *circa 1920*
Art Deco perfume bottle with stopper set in a silver plated base with blue stone set in the centre.
• *14cm x 12cm*
• **Guide price £155/$293**

Square Scent Bottle ▲

• *1930*
Square glass Art Deco perfume bottle, with a clear glass stopper and large grey silk tassel. Decorated with a black floral design.
• *height 10cm*
• **Guide price £138/$261**

Cut Glass Bottle with Black Banding ▲

- *circa 1920*

Art Deco cut glass oval bottle with black enamel banding.

- *4cm x 11cm*
- **Guide price £185/$350**

Hour Glass Bottle ▲

- *circa 1920*

Hour glass shape perfume bottle with a silver stopper.

- *height 6.5cm*
- **Guide price £150/$284**

Art Deco Set ▼

- *1920*

An Art Deco dressing-table set, consisting of a perfume atomiser and a powder box with lid, both in smoked glass.

- **Guide price £170/$322**

Unknown Heart-Shaped Perfume Bottle ▼

- *circa 1940*

With etched glass and bakelite base with dipper.

- **Guide price £65/$123**

Grossmith 'Old Cottage' Lavender Water ▼

- *circa 1930*

A bottle of English lavender water of etched glass.

- **Guide price £95/$180**

Glass Bottle ▲

- *circa 1930s*

Glass perfume bottle with moulded base, and a lozenge shaped stopper.

- *height 20cm*
- **Guide price £145/$274**

Jacinthe De Coty ▲

- *circa 1920*

Bottle with metalic plaque and beaded decoration; the stopper has floral designs.

- **Guide price £150/$284**

Bourjois 'Mais Oui' ◄

- *circa 1938*

A bottle of Boujois 'Mais Oui', in perfect condition with original inner and outer box.

- **Guide price £175/$331**

Guerlain 'L'Heure Bleue' ▲

- *circa 1940*

Made by Baccarate perfume, with original box.

- **Guide price £125/$237**

Christian Dior 'Miss Dior' ▼

- *circa 1950*

A Christian Dior 'Miss Dior' perfume bottle, unused and in its original packaging.

- **Guide price £250/$473**

Nina Ricci 'Coeur-Joie' ▼

- *1946*

Lalique bottle with heart-shaped centre and floral decoration.

- **Guide price £210/$397**

Saville London 'June' ◄

- *circa 1930*

A novelty perfume bottle in the form of a sundial.

- **Guide price £125/$237**

Christian Dior 'Miss Dior' ▲

- *circa 1945*

A Christian Dior perfume bottle of obelisk shape.

- **Guide price £450/$851**

Prince Matchabello 'Beloved' ▲

- *circa 1950*

Enamel crown bottle. With inner and outer box.

- **Guide price £220/$416**

Decanter Bottle ▼

- *circa 1920*

A decanter bottle with handle in original wicker coat.

- *height 23cm*
- **Guide price £25/$48**

Lancôme Tresor ◄

- *circa 1950*

Original Tresor with cut glass bottle stand.

- **Guide price £195/$369**

Bourjois 'Evening in Paris' ▼

- *circa 1935*

A novelty perfume bottle in perspex wheelbarrow.

- **Guide price £250/$473**

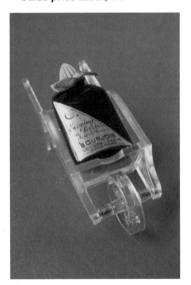

Jardin des Bagatelle ◄

- *circa 1980*

Window display bottle. With brass mounts.

- **Guide price £275/$520**

CAMERAS

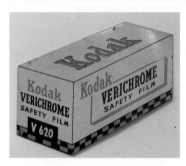

Kodak Advertisement ▲

- *circa 1950*
An advertisement in the shape of a yellow box of film with the words "Kodak Verichrome Safety Film" with black and red check border.
- *41cm x 43cm*
- **Guide price £99/$187**

Camera Sign ▲

- *circa 1950*
Yellow sign with red writing with the words "Appareils Pellicules" a sign for cameras and films.
- *26cm x 93cm*
- **Guide price £95/$180**

Rajar Bakelite Camera ▲

- *1929*
Rajar black bakelite No.6. Folding camera. With 120 roll film, with 6 x 9cm negative size.
- *height 17cm*
- **Guide price £49/$95**

Ikonta Camera ▼

- *circa 1950*
Ikonta model no.524/2. Novur Lens. F stop 4.5.
- *16cm x 10cm*
- **Guide price £149/$284**

Zeiss Strut Camera ▼

- *1928*
A 4.5 x 6cm Strut-type camera, with compur shutter.
- *10cm x 9cm*
- **Guide price £199/$378**

Ensign Cupid Camera ▶

- *1922*
Ensign Cupid simple metal-bodied camera. 4 x 6cm exposures on 120 film. The design is based on a 1921 prototype for a stereo camera, which was never produced. Mensicus achromatic F11 lens. Available in black, blue, grey and some other colours.
- *height 8cm*
- **Guide price £89/$171**

French Sign ▲

- *circa 1940*
Advertisement with a picture of a camera and the words "Film appareils Lumière – En Vente Ici".
- *85cm x 80cm*
- **Guide price £200/$378**

Mamiya ▲

- *1959*
Japanese Mamiya 16 camera.
- *width 11.5cm*
- **Guide price £49/$95**

Soligor Camera ▼

- *circa 1960*
Soligor 50mm lens, Japanese made auto lens.
- *height 7cm*
- **Guide price £74/$142**

Contina Zeiss Camera ▼

- *circa 1960*
Zeiss Contina camera with an F2.8 45mm Novica lens.
- *height 7cm*
- **Guide price £30/$57**

Tennent's Lager Can Camera ▲

- *1980*
Promotional Tennent's lager can camera.
- *length 12cm*
- **Guide price £39/$76**

Sign for Photos ▲

- *circa 1950*
Cream metal sign with the word "Photo" in red with red and yellow border.
- *40cm x 59cm*
- **Guide price £50**

Revere Stereo 33 ▶

- *1950*
Revere Stereo 33 made in the U.S.A. 35mm F3.5 Amaton. Complete with its original leather case.
- *width 19cm*
- **Guide price £249/$473**

Rolleiflex Camera ▲

- *circa 1955–65*
Rolleiflex camera with a Tessar 1.3.8. F7.5mm lens.
- *height 19cm*
- **Guide price £70/$133**

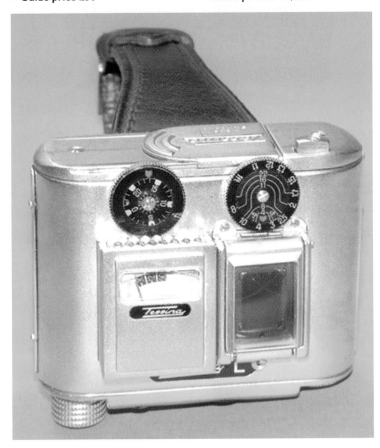

Robin Hood Camera ▼

- *1930*
Black marbelised bakelite Robin Hood camera with a picture of Robin Hood by Standard Cameras of Birmingham. Takes darkroom loaded single sheets of 45 x 107mm film. Originally came with film, paper and darkroom safelight. Sometimes seen in England, but rarely seen elsewhere.
- *height 5cm*
- **Guide price £69/$133**

Retina Kodak Camera ▼

- *circa 1960*
Retina-Xenar F2.8 45mm lens by Kodak.
- *height 8cm*
- **Guide price £70/$133**

Miniature Tessina ◀

- *1960*
Swiss-made miniature Tessina camera in the style of a watch, with meter and strap. It took exposure on 35mm film, which was divided up in special cartridges.
- *width 6.8cm*
- **Guide price £899/$1,701**

The New Special Sybil ▼

- *1914–35*
The new special Sybil. Ross Xpress F4.5 112mm. N & G special shutter.
- *height 16cm*
- **Guide price £149/$284**

Franke & Heidecke Rolly Camera ▼

- *1921–40*
Frank & Heidecke Braunschweig, Germany, Rolley Heidoscop three lens stereo camera including its own case. 7.5cm F4.5 Tessar Lens.
- *height 17cm*
- **Guide price £699/$1,323**

Balda Camera ▲

- *circa 1960*

Balda proximeter 2 and a quarter square camera with a range finder. 35mm lens including poxymetre.

- *height 9.5cm*
- **Guide price £90/$171**

Kodak Stereo Camera ▲

- *1954–59*

Kodak stereo 35mm camera with Kodak Anaston F3.5 35mm lens, Kodak flash 200, shutter 25-200 with stereo viewer. With original box.

- *width 17cm*
- **Guide price £249/$473**

Bolex Projector ▼

- *circa 1960*

An M.A. Bolex projector.

- *height 50cm*
- **Guide price £150/$284**

Mick A Matic ▼

- *1971*

Mick A Matic American camera in the shape of Mickey Mouse made by Child Guidance Product Inc.

- *height 20cm*
- **Guide price £49/$95**

Kodak Eastman ▲

- *circa 1920*

No.2 Hawkette brown tortoiseshell effect bakelite folding camera by Kodak.

- *height 18cm*
- **Guide price £69/$133**

Hasselblad 550c Camera ▼

- *circa 1970*

A Hasselblad. Model 500c, 18mm with 2.8 planner lens.

- *17cm x 10cm*
- **Guide price £700/$1,323**

Perkeo Camera ▼

- *circa 1954*

A Perkeo with rangefinder Color Skopar lens in Prontor SVS shutter. Voigtlander.

- *6cm x 12cm*
- **Guide price £199/$378**

Super Nettle Camera ▼

- *circa 1920*

Zeiss Super Nettel. 11. F2.8. Black leather covered press camera.

- *9cm x 14cm*
- **Guide price £499/$945**

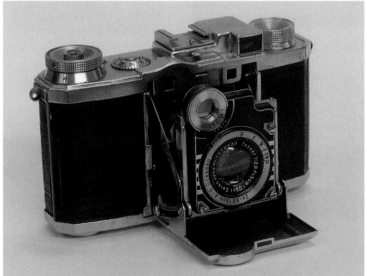

Lizars Challenge ▲

- *circa 1903*

Lizars Challenge made in Glasgow mahogany frame and brass fittings, Bush and Long Lens.

- *17cm x 21cm*
- **Guide price £249/$473**

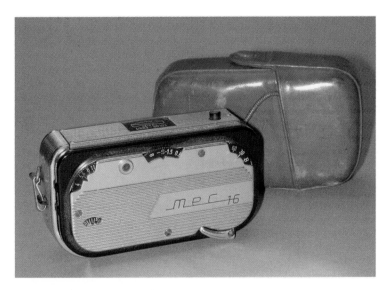

Miniature Mec 16 ▲

- *1950*

German miniature Mec 16 camera with an unusual pressed gold tin casing. With original leather case.

- *width 10cm*
- **Guide price £99/$189**

Newman Sinclair ▲

- *circa 1946*

A Newman Sinclair, London. Used generally in the Antartic. London 35mm spring-driven movie camera. Polished patterned Duralumin body. Ross Xpres F3.5 lens.

- *24cm x 25cm*
- **Guide price £2,000/$3,780**

Zenit B Camera ▼

- *circa 1960*

Zenit B camera with 300mm lens.

- *height 8cm*
- **Guide price £69/$133**

Speed Graphic ▼

- *circa 1948*

Miniature "Speed Graphic" camera. Optar Lens 101mm.

- *23cm x 16cm*
- **Guide price £299/$567**

Nikon Red Spot Camera ◄

- *1965*

Nikon F known as Red Spot. Lens 50mm F1.4.

- *height 14cm*
- **Guide price £349/$662**

Franke & Heideck Rolleiflex Camera ▼

- *mid 20th century*

A Rolleiflex 2.8F Lens Zeiss, made by Franke & Heideck.

- *13cm x 12cm*
- **Guide price £599/$1,134**

Ensign Auto-speed Camera ▼

- *1932*

Ensign auto-speed camera inscribed on the side, 100mm F4.5 lens, with focal plane shutter speed of 15–500 sec.

- *height 20cm*
- **Guide price £199/$378**

Bolex Camera ▼

- *circa 1960*

A Bolex P1 zoom cine camera.

- *height 38cm*
- **Guide price £149/$284**

Petie Vanity Camera and Compact ▲

- *circa 1956*

Petie camera housed in a make up compact. Front door opens to reveal mirror and powder. One top knob contains a lipstick, another provides storage for an extra roll of film. Beautiful Art deco marblelized finish in either red, green or blue made by Kreher and Bayer Offenbach, Germany. Kigu a British make of powder compacts. Highly collectable.

- *8cm x 10cm*
- **Guide price £499/$945**

Meopta Admira 8F Camera ▲

- *circa 1960*

Meopta Admira 8F- similar to the A8G but with BIM.

- *16cm x 16cm*
- **Guide price £30/$57**

Weston Master Light Meter ▲

- *circa 1940*

English Weston Master light meter.

- *9cm x 6cm*
- **Guide price £20/$38**

Kodak Camera ▼

- *circa 1960*

Kodak 35 camera with an F4.5 51mm lens.

- *height 6cm*
- **Guide price £50/$95**

Sputnik Camera ▲

- *1950*

Russian Sputnik camera and case with 75mm F4.5 Lomo lens.

- *height 8cm*
- **Guide price £149/$284**

Weston Lightometer ▲

- *1940*

Weston lightometer 703 Weston Electrical Instrument Corp Neward. N.J. U.S.A.

- *width 12cm*
- **Guide price £50/$95**

Rolleicord Camera ◄

- *circa 1955–65*

Rolleicord Triotar Camera 1.3.5 F 75cm.

- *height 19cm*
- **Guide price £70/$133**

Bolex Super 8 ▲

- *circa 1970*

Bolex Super 8 480 Macrozoom.

- *height 19cm*
- **Guide price £170/$322**

Bolex H16 ▼

- *circa 1950*

Swiss-made Paillard Bolex H16 Cine camera still used by students today for animation. Black leather body.

- *23cm x 24cm*
- **Guide price £299/$567**

Eastman Kodak Camera ▲

- *circa 1950*

Eastman Kodak camera. The shutter is made in Rochester, N.Y. with an F7.3 10mm lens.

- *height 16.5cm*
- **Guide price £70/$133**

No. 4 Ensign Camera ▲

- *circa 1950*

No.4 Ensign carbine camera made in England with a Trichro shutter F77 lens anaston.

- *height 15cm*
- **Guide price £40/$76**

Plate Camera ▲

- *circa 1950*

Plate camera by Aldiss-Butcher with an F4.5 lens with 6 inch focus.

- *height 18cm*
- **Guide price £70/$133**

Balda Jubilette Camera ▲

- *1938*

German Balda Jubilette camera commemorating the 30th anniversary of Balda Werk. Folding 35mm similar to the Baldina. F2.9 50mm lens. Baltar, Trioplan, or Corygon. Compur shutter.

- *height 13cm*
- **Guide price £69/$133**

Wrayflex ▼

- *1950*

English Wrayflex 1 with outfit lens. Only approximately 1600 ever made. With original leather camera and lens case. Lens 50mm F2. Unilite.

- *height 9cm*
- **Guide price £799/$1,512**

Wallace Heaton ▶

- *1925–35*

Wallace Heaton Zodel model folding camera with a 105mm F3.8. Zodellar lens and original leather case with handle.

- *height 14cm*
- **Guide price £149/$284**

Coronet 3 D Camera ▲

- *1953*

Coronet 3 D marbelised bakelite stereo camera. Takes 127 film. Single speed shutter. Twin F11 meniscus fixed focus lenses.

- *height 8cm*
- **Guide price £79/$152**

Sakura Petal Camera ▲

- *1948*

Sakura Petal camera with film and case included. This is the world's smallest mass-produced camera.

- *2.5cm x 1.2cm*
- **Guide price £250/$473**

Widelux Super Wide Angle Camera ▲

- *circa 1970s*

Widelux super wide angle viewfinder camera with an unusual rotating lens. The camera uses 120 film.

- *23cm x 28cm*
- **Guide price £1,399/$2,646**

Microtechnical Camera ▲

- *circa 1970s*

Microtechnical MK8 camera with a 150mm Symmar lens. Accompanied by a guide book.

- *18cm x 18cm*
- **Guide price £599/$1,134**

C8 Cine Camera ▼

- *1954*

Bolex Standard 8 cine camera with a clockwork windup and single interchangeable lens.

- *12.5cm x 6cm*
- **Guide price £50/$95**

Kodak Medallist II Rangefinder Camera ▼

- *1946–253*

Rare Kodak Medallist II rangefinder camera, fitted with an F3.5 100mm Ektar lens.

- *20cm x 13cm*
- **Guide price £349/$662**

Rectaflex Camera ▲

- *1950s*

Rare Rota Rectaflex camera with three French-made Angenieux rotatable lenses. The lenses have three focal lengths: 50mm, 35mm and 135mm.

- *15cm x 9cm*
- **Guide price £3,000/$5,670**

Thornton Pickard Camera ▲

- *circa 1909*

Triple extension, Thornton Pickard camera which uses ½ plate-sized negatives (glass plates used, not films). Made of wood with leather bellows.

- *21cm x 25.5cm*
- **Guide price £300/$567**

Voigtlander Camera ▲

- *1958–60*

Rare Voigtlander Prominent II camera with an Ultron 50mm F2 lens. The camera has a 35mm rangefinder with interchangeable lenses and a clear viewfinder.

- *14cm x 8.5cm*
- **Guide price £699/$1,323**

Voigtlander Bessamatic SLR Camera ▼

- *circa 1950s*

Voigtlander Bessamatic SLR camera, with a 36–82mm F2.8 zoom lens. This was the first commercially produced zoom lens for a 35mm camera.

- *16cm x 10cm*
- **Guide price £149/$284**

Rolleiflex TLR Camera ▼

- *1960s*

Rolleiflex 2.8F twin lens camera (TLR), which uses standard 120 roll film.

- *15cm x 10cm*
- **Guide price £649/$1,229**

Rollei 35 Camera ▲

- *1971*

Gold Rollei 35 camera, supplied with a brown leather case and a red felt-lined wooden box. Fitted with an F3.5 Tessar lens.

- *9.5cm x 6cm*
- **Guide price £899/$1,701**

Kodak "Girl Guide" Camera ▲

- *1933*

Blue Kodak "Girl Guide" camera with an F6.3 Anistigmat lens. Supplied with blue case.

- *13cm x 7cm*
- **Guide price £200/$378**

Canon IV Camera ▼

- *circa 1950s*

Canon IV range finder camera with detachable flash unit and a 50mm 1.9 Serenar lens. Supplied with a brown leather case. This model is based on a Leica design.

- *14cm x 7cm*
- **Guide price £499/$945**

Teleca Bino Camera ◄

- *1950*

Relatively rare, subminiature 16mm Teleca Bino camera, which is built into a pair of binoculars. Fitted with standard 10mm x 14mm lenses and supplied with a brown leather case.

- *10 x 9cm*
- **Guide price £299/$567**

Bolex 16mm Cine Camera ▶

- *circa 1960s*
Bolex 16mm cine camera, model number H16m, with a Swiss-made body and Som Berthiot 17–85mm zoom lens.
- *33cm x 21.5cm*
- **Guide price £500/$945**

Kodak Suprema Camera ▲

- *circa 1950s*
Kodak Suprema camera fitted with an 8cm Xenar lens. Uses 120 standard film.
- *15cm x 10cm*
- **Guide price £349/$662**

Kodak Retina II F, 35mm Camera ▲

- *1963*
Kodak Retina II F, 35mm camera with an F2.8, 45mm Xenar lens. The built-in flash bulb holder is an unusual feature for this style of camera.
- *13cm x 8.5cm*
- **Guide price £100/$189**

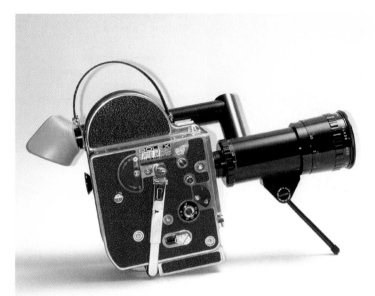

16mm Cine Camera ▼

- *1928*
Bell and Howell 16mm cine camera with a 20mm F3.5 lens with 100ft spool, and a clockwork motor. The model is covered with grey tooled leather and is quite rare, especially outside the United States.
- *20.5cm x 3.7cm*
- **Guide price £150/$284**

"Boy Scout" Camera ▼

- *1933*
Green Kodak "Boy Scout" camera, fitted with an F6.3 Anstigmat lens. The model is supplied with a brown leather case and uses 127 Kodak film.
- *12.5cm x 7cm*
- **Guide price £150/$284**

L35 Concava Camera ▶

- *circa 1960s*
Rare miniature Tessina L35 Concava camera, designed to fit on the wrist in the style of a watch, and comes with a leather strap. It has a 25mm Tessinon lens and is supplied with 35mm film in special cassettes.
- *6.5cm x 6.5cm*
- **Guide price £899/$1,701**

Rollei Camera ◀

- *1966–7*
Rollei 35 standard camera fitted with an F3.5 Tessar lens.
- *9.5cm x 6cm*
- **Guide price £299/$567**

Houghton Ticka Camera ▲

- *1905–14*
Houghton Ticka Spy camera. This is designed to look like a pocket watch with an engraved monogram on the cover. The camera is hidden underneath the winding mechanism.
- *6.5cm x 5cm*
- **Guide price £249/$473**

Midget Coronet Camera ▲

- *circa 1930s*
Art-Deco style, blue bakelite, Midget Coronet camera, fitted with a Taylor Hobson F10 lens. The colour is very rare.
- *2cm x 6cm*
- **Guide price £325/$614**

Ensign Silver Midget Camera ◄

- *1935*

Ensign Silver Midget Jubilee model camera, made by Houghton, model number 22. Fitted with an Ensarlens F6.3 lens and uses E10 film which is now discontinued.

- *9cm x 4cm*
- **Guide price £175/$331**

Blair Stereo Weno with Case ▼

- *1902*

Blair stereo Weno camera with case (as seen underneath), made in Rochester, New York. Supplied with a pair of Plastigmat lenses. Uses 116 Kodak film which has now been discontinued.

- *26.5cm x 11.5cm*
- **Guide price £299/$567**

Leica Range Finder Camera ▲

- *circa 1930s*

Leica Range Finder camera fitted with a Summar 5cm F2 lens. This camera remains in production.

- *13cm x 7cm*
- **Guide price £299/$567**

35mm SLR Camera ▲

- *circa 1965*

Leicaflex 35mm SLR with f/2 semi-micron lens.

- **Guide price £400/$756**

Filma Projector ▼

- *circa 1970*

Filma 240f 8mm sound projector. Standard 8 sound and silent. Portable and with outfit case.

- **Guide price £100/$189**

Reflex Camera ▼

- *circa 1960*

Rolleiflex 2.8f twin lens reflex camera with built in light meter and overhead viewfinder.

- **Guide price £600/$1,134**

Hollywood Splicer ▲

- *circa 1960*

Hollywood stainless-steel splicer. 8mm x 16mm, in original box.

- **Guide price £30/$57**

8mm Cine Camera ▲

- *1927*

Extremely compact 8mm Kodak cine camera. This was the first model to use standard 8 film.

- *15cm x 11.5cm*
- **Guide price £120/$227**

Rollei Camera ◄

- *circa 1975*

Rollei 35S gold 35mm camera. A specially finished precision compact camera. Limited edition of 1500, gold-plated.

- **Guide price £900/$1,701**

Minox Camera ▲

- *circa 1950s*

Minox A camera which was used in the World War II as a spy camera. It takes 8 x 11mm negatives, has a brushed aluminium body and a Complan 15mm, 3.5 lens.

- *1cm x 10cm*
- **Guide price £180/$341**

Leicaflex SLR Camera ▲
- *circa 1970*
Leicaflex 35mm SLR camera with f2.8/90 Elmarit lens.
- **Guide price £500/$945**

M.P.P. Plate Holder ▲
- *circa 1960*
M.P.P. plate holder for 5x4 plate camera used by large format cameras.
- **Guide price £10/$19**

Cartridge System Camera ▼
- *circa 1975*
A 110 cartridge system camera modelled as a caricature of a British Airways Aeroplane. In good condition.
- **Guide price £60/$114**

Flash-Bulb Holder ▼
- *circa 1949*
Leica Chico flash-bulb holder for Leica cameras.
- **Guide price £20/$38**

Mamiya 120 Camera ▼
- *circa 1970–1980*
Mamiya C33 first professional 120 camera with interchangeable lens. 6x6 image.
- **Guide price £170/$322**

Skeky Camera ▼
- *1947*
Subminiature Skeky camera with a tele-lens. The camera uses 16mm film and comes with a brown leather case.
- *2cm x 1cm*
- **Guide price £299/$567**

Purma Roll Camera ▲
- *circa 1932*
Purma 'Special' bakelite 127 roll camera with telescoping lens.
- **Guide price £30/$57**

Pentax Asahi ▼
- *circa 1970*
Pentax Asahi 'Sportmatik' 500 camera with a 55mm fixed lens f1.8. All metal body.
- **Guide price £100/$189**

Field Camera ▲
- *circa 1930*
Deardorff 10x8-inch camera made of mahogany with nickel-plated fittings. Schneider and Symmar 300mm lens.
- **Guide price £2,000/$3,780**

Kodak Field Camera ▲
- *circa 1950*
Kodak No.1 Autographic 120mm film field camera with folding case.
- **Guide price £70/$133**

Cine Camera ▲

• *circa 1960*
Bell & Howell 'Sportster Standard 8'
8mm cine camera.
• **Guide price £30/$57**

Editor with Viewer ▲

• *circa 1970*
8mm Crown editor with magnified and
backlit viewer. All-metal body and hand-
operated spools.
• **Guide price £30/$57**

Miniature Spy Camera ▶

• *circa 1958*
Minox B sub miniature spy camera,
which takes 8x11mm negatives. With
brushed aluminium body.
• **Guide price £180/$341**

Canon Ixus Camera ▲

• *circa 2000*
18 ct. gold limited edition with
certificate of authenticity and remote
control.
• **Guide price £400/$756**

Brownie Six-20 Camera ▲

• *circa 1960*
A model 'C' Brownie Six-20 camera.
Made in England by Kodak Ltd.
• **Guide price £30/$57**

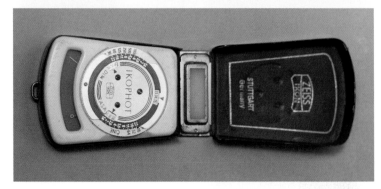

Rolleiflex Camera ▼

• *circa 1950*
German Rolleiflex camera with flip-top
view finder and Carl Zeiss twin lenses.
120 film.
• **Guide price £70/$133**

Asahi Pentax Camera ◀

• *1979*
Asahi Pentax Auto 110 camera, fitted
with a 24mm lens. The camera comes as
part of a kit which includes a flash unit,
filters and carrying bag.
• *9cm x 6cm*
• **Guide price £200/$378**

Light Exposure Meter ▲

• *circa 1960*
1 Kophot light exposure meter by Zeiss
in a folding burgundy leather case.
• **Guide price £30/$57**

16mm Cine Camera ▲

• *circa 1960*
AGFA 16mm cine camera and telephoto
lens with 100ft spool. All metal body.
• **Guide price £90/$171**

Pyramid Tripod ▼

- *circa 1960*
Camera base with wooden legs and adjustable tubular metal stands.
- **Guide price £15/$28**

Brownie Box Camera ▶

- *circa 1960*
Brownie Box camera, for 127 film, made in Canada by Kodak Eastman Co Ltd.
- **Guide price £30/$57**

Light Meter ▲

- *circa 1960*
A pocket-sized Weston Master V Selinium light meter with all-metal body construction. In good condition.
- **Guide price £40/$76**

Stereo Plate Camera ▲

- *circa 1926*
Rollei Heidoskop camera. It takes two parallel pictures to create a 3D image.
- **Guide price £700/$1,323**

Press Camera ▼

- *circa 1930*
A 9x12 VN press camera with sports finder, ground-glass screen.
- **Guide price £250/$473**

Light Meter ▶

- *circa 1950–1960*
Sixtus light meter with folding bakelite case. No batteries required.
- **Guide price £30/$57**

Slide Projector ◀

- *circa 1960*
Aldis 35mm slide projector with original box.
- **Guide price £30/$57**

35mm Range Finder ▲

- *circa 1957*
Minolta super A 35mm range finder interchangeable lens camera with standard lens.
- **Guide price £200/$378**

Pentax Roll Film Camera ▲

- *circa 1969*
Pentax 6x7 roll film camera. This has been a very popular professional camera for the last thirty-one years.
- **Guide price £900/$1,701**

Light Meter ▼

- *circa 1950–1960*
An electro BEWI light meter in metal case.
- **Guide price £30/$57**

Polaroid Camera ▼

- *circa 1960*
The first Polaroid instant film camera – the 900 Electric Eye Land Camera.
- **Guide price £90/$171**

Leica M3 35mm Camera ▼

- *circa 1954*
Leica M3 with 50mm f2 standard lens. One of the most highly regarded cameras ever made. Used by many photographers.
- **Guide price £1,000/$1,890**

CARPETS & RUGS

Luri Gabbeth Rug ▲

- *mid 20th century*

A Luri Gabbeth rug from the Zagros mountains of southern Persia. With bold design of red, blue, brown and cream, the borders with red squares and cream centres.

- *length 180cm*
- **Guide price £1,450/$2,741**

Bownat Marriage Rug ▲

- *circa 1920*

Bownat marriage rug, produced by a small tribe in Southern Iran. The rug shows courting birds and the name and date in Arabic of the couple to be married. These rugs are some of the most beautiful tribal weaving produced today.

- *210cm x 293cm*
- **Guide price £1,650/$3,119**

Luri Jijim Rug ▶

- *20th century*

Luri Jijim rug with brown, navy, blue and cream, woven striped design, and navy, blue and red binding on the edge.

- *length 283cm*
- **Guide price £990/$1,872**

Sarouk Rug ▲

- *circa 1940*

Typical Harati design with a large medallion in the centre, the ground colour is coral with blue, pink and cream. Sarouk is a small village of approximately 1,000 houses, west of Iran.

- *89cm x 118cm*
- **Guide price £1,100/$2,079**

Karabagh Cushion ▼

- *1920*

Karabagh kilim converted into a cushion cover.

- *35cm square*
- **Guide price £50/$95**

Bibibaff Quajquoli ▼

- *circa 1940*

An unusual and fine example of a Bibibaff Quajquoli.

- *80cm x 118cm*
- **Guide price £1,100/$2,079**

Kilim Stool ▲

- *1930*

Anatonian kilim upholstered stool.

- *30cm x 40cm*
- **Guide price £125/$237**

Striped Rug ▲

- *circa 1920–30*

Antique Gabbeh rug, by Luri tribe in Zagros mountains, southern Persia (code NZ00192).

- *122cm x 120cm*
- **Guide price £720/$1,361**

Western Anatonian Kilim Cushion ▲

- *1920*

Western Anatonian kilim converted into a cushion cover.

- *35cm square*
- **Guide price £45/$85**

Bakhtiari Rug ▲

- *circa 1940*

Bakhtiari rug with a glorious central medallion design in blue, green, coral and cream. The reverse of the carpet shows a very open weaving technique with wefts which may have a bluish hue.

- *127cm x 207cm*
- **Guide price £490/$927**

Tekke Rug ▼

- *circa 1920*

Acha-Tekke are woven by the famous tribesmen from the Tekke tribe who are noted for their fine work. A geometric design in reds, cream and black.

- *20cm x 200cm*
- **Guide price £1,400/$2,646**

Kashan Rug ▶

- *circa 1920*

Kashan pictorial rug with peacocks in red, blue and green design surrounding a central vase.

- *137cm x 207cm*
- **Guide price £4,500/$8,505**

Tent Trappings ▲

- *1940*

Tent trappings in red, purple, orange and cream with beaded tassles.

- *55cm x 13cm*
- **Guide price £65/$123**

Kashan Medallion Rug ▲

- *circa 1920*

Kashan rug with classical elongated medallion designs in coral and dark blue and corner decorations. Extremely good example of a curvilinear Persian floral rug.

- *137cm x 207cm*
- **Guide price £4,500/$8,505**

Sharshavan Cushion ▶

- *1920*

Cushion made from a Sharshavan rug, which was originally part of a cradle.

- *35cm square*
- **Guide price £65/$123**

Western Anatonian Kilim Cushion ▲

- *1920*

Western Anatonian kilim converted to a cushion cover.

- *35cm square*
- **Guide price £45/$85**

Anatonian Kilim Stool ▼

- *1930*

Western Anatonian kilim covering a stool.

- *width 65cm*
- **Guide price £240/$454**

Anatonian Kilim ▲

- *1920*
Western Anatonian kilim covering a beechwood chest.
- *50cm x 90cm*
- **Guide price £750/$1,418**

Persian Rug ▲

- *early 20th century*
Persian Quashquai Gabbeh rug incorporating a strong central design within a geometric border on a red ground (code NZ00174).
- *165cm x 104cm*
- **Guide price £760/$1,437**

Gabbeh Carpet ▼

- *20th century*
Luri Gabbeh carpet from the Zagros mountains, southern Persia.
- *148cm x 121cm*
- **Guide price £770/$1,456**

Persian Cushion ▼

- *circa 1960*
A Persian cushion with cover woven by the Shasavan into geometric, polychromatic designs with a hexagonal central panel.
- *40cm x 40cm*
- **Guide price £69/$131**

Tent Trappings ◄

- *1920*
Tent trappings in red, purple, orange and cream with red, yellow and brown tassles.
- *height 50cm*
- **Guide price £65/$123**

Bakhtiari Rug ▼

- *circa 1940*
Bakhtiari rugs woven by nomads and villagers of Luri, Kurdish and other ethnic origins from the Chahar Mahal region of Iran. Featuring a medallion design.
- *140cm x 228cm*
- **Guide price £2,300/$4,347**

Persian Kilim ▼

- *early 20th century*
A rare kilim from a dowry treasure found in Luristan. Little-used, with fine naive design in natural dyes.
- *length 198cm, width 128cm*
- **Guide price £1,200/$2,268**

Tibetan Cushion ►

- *circa 1995*
A modern Tibetan cushion with a traditional design of stylized lotus flower in part silk.
- *40cm x 40cm*
- **Guide price £90/$171**

Karabagh Cushion ▲

- *circa 1920*
Karabagh kilim converted into a cushion cover.
- *width 48cm*
- **Guide price £60/$114**

Belouch Rug ▲

- *circa 1920*
Belouch rug from western Afghanistan and eastern Iran, where lions from the nomadic and semi-nomadic Belouch Tribes represent courage. All Belouch rugs are made with woollen warps and wefts with lustrous wool pile, and the Belouch are noted for their "prayer rug" designs. Typical Botay design.
- *92cm x 184cm*
- **Guide price £420/$794**

Persian Rug ▲

- *early 20th century*

Luri Gabbeh rug from southwest Persia. Includes a strong geometric pattern in blue and red and an alternating zig-zag border.

- *200cm x 147cm*
- **Guide price £950/$1,796**

Indian Rug ▲

- *circa 1999*

An Indian Agra rug. An interpretation of the 16th-century Indian Agra designs. Using vegetable dyes.

- *length 190cm, width 124cm*
- **Guide price £750/$1,418**

Nepalese Cushion ▼

- *circa 1995*

A Tibetan design cushion from Nepal in part silk, with a key-pattern border and floral central decoration.

- *40cm x 40cm*
- **Guide price £90/$171**

Indian Rug ▼

- *circa 1996*

A vegetable-dyed Indian kilim rug with squared, polychrome pattern, with the red colouring derived from the madder plant.

- *length 269cm, width 188cm*
- **Guide price £950/$1,796**

Kilim Stool ◀

- *1920*

Western Anatonian kilim covering a stool.

- *60cm square*
- **Guide price £395/$747**

Turkish Cushion ◀

- *circa 1960*

A Turkish (Anatolia) kilim cushion, the cover of which originally came from a rug.

- *40cm x 40cm*
- **Guide price £39/$74**

Shahsavan Cushion ▲

- *circa 1940*

A Persian Shahsavan kilim cushion. Woven by the nomadic Shahsavan people.

- *40cm x 40cm*
- **Guide price £69/$131**

Quashquai Gabbeh Rug ▲

- *20th century*

A wool carpet of striking design created without the use of dye. From the Zagros mountains, South Persia.

- *175cm x 118cm*
- **Guide price £1,050/$1,985**

Indian Rug ▲

- *circa 1998*

A rug from Rajput with an old Mughal design, using all natural dyes and clay washing.

- *length 159cm, width 91cm*
- **Guide price £575/$1,087**

Persian Rug ◀

- *circa 1940*

A Persian bidjar kilim, the blue ground woven with geometric patterns, with a strong border.

- *length 212cm, width 120cm*
- **Guide price £770/$1,456**

CERAMICS

Ribbed Italian Jug ▼
- *1950*

Brown Italian jug of conical form with small neck and ear-shaped handle with a ribbed incised design.
- *height 19cm*
- **Guide price £45/$85**

Crown Ducal Cup and Saucer ▼
- *1930*

Crown Ducal yellow glaze cup and saucer with a gilded interior.
- *height 5cm*
- **Guide price £75/$142**

Goldscheider Figure ▶
- *circa 1930*

An Art Deco figure by Goldscheider, designed by Claire Herezy, of a young lady in a blue dress profusely decorated with flowers.
- *height 35cm*
- **Guide price £795/$1,503**

Royal Dux Centrepiece ▲
- *circa 1910*

An Art Nouveau Royal Dux centrepiece of two nude maidens intertwined among the waves.
- *20cm x 40cm*
- **Guide price £595/$1,125**

Retino ▲
- *circa 2000*

"Retino" by E. Sottsass, container of conical form, with a design of turquoise and gold banding above a gilded circular base.
- *height 16cm*
- **Guide price £250/$473**

Shelley Ceramic ▼
- *1920*

Shelley made cup and saucer with green and black geometric design Art Deco.
- *height 9cm*
- **Guide price £195/$370**

Highland Pottery Vase ▼
- *circa 1974*

Highland Stoneware Pottery baluster-shaped vase, hand painted with a coastal scene.
- *height 25cm*
- **Guide price £150/$284**

Butter Dish ▼
- *circa 1930*

Cream Poole Pottery butter dish designed by Truda Carter with yellow and red flowers.
- *height 9cm*
- **Guide price £72/$137**

Hammersley Floral Cup and Saucer ▲
- *circa 1930*

Pink floral Hammersley cup and saucer with floral decoration.
- *height 4cm*
- **Guide price £65/$123**

Festival of Britain ▲
- *1952*

Tulip-shaped vase designed by Alfred Read for the Festival of Britain with cream stripes and oblong design circling the vase.
- *height 20cm*
- **Guide price £230/$435**

Green Crown Devon Cup and Saucer ▲
- *circa 1930*

Crown Devon cup and saucer with a green pearlised interior.
- *height 6cm*
- **Guide price £95/$180**

Royal Worcester ▲

- *circa 1930*

Royal Worcester cup and saucer with a trailing foliate decoration with clusters of berries.

- *height 5.5cm*
- **Guide price £75/$142**

French Grey Vase ▲

- *1950*

Small French vase of conical form with a textured finish and a black geometric design with a large red dot.

- *height 16cm*
- **Guide price £55/$104**

Poole Pottery ▲

- *circa 1930*

A Truda Carter design vase from Poole Pottery by Rene Hayes.

- *height 18cm*
- **Guide price £330/$624**

Cruet Set ▼

- *circa 1950*

Festival of Britain cruet set designed by Alfred Read with a lattice pattern.

- *height 8cm*
- **Guide price £60/$114**

Poole Vase ▼

- *early 1950s*

Poole carafe designed by Alfred Read made of hand-thrown white earthenware with a pattern of purple stripes and the rim in red.

- *height 30cm*
- **Guide price £340/$643**

Calypso Pot ▼

- *circa 1980*

Black and turquoise lustreware Poole Calypso range pottery. Owned by Lord Queensbury.

- *height 25cm*
- **Guide price £600/$1,134**

Fruit Bowl ▲

- *1920*

Blue and white fruit bowl with a rural scene with cows in the foreground, within a bold floral border.

- *diameter 19cm*
- **Guide price £140/$265**

Rye Pottery ▲

- *circa 1950*

A Rye pottery jug with light grey glaze decorated with a trailing stylised foliate design.

- *height 20cm*
- **Guide price £125/$237**

Butterfly Handle Cup ▼

- *1930*

Unusual primrose yellow Ainsley cup with gilt rim on cup and saucer with unusual butterfly handle.

- *height 6cm*
- **Guide price £125/$237**

Read Bowl ▼

- *1950*

Alfred Read design bowl with grey glaze and a lattice design in red and white.

- *diameter 20cm*
- **Guide price £210/$397**

Foley Trio ▼

- *circa 1920*

Trio of cup saucer and plate with orange flowers and banding with an unusual geometric handle.

- *height 8cm*
- **Guide price £75/$142**

Biscuit Jar ▼

- *1930*

Poole pottery biscuit jar painted by Claire Heath with lid and wicker handle in original condition.
- *height 18cm*
- **Guide price £190/$360**

Royal Doulton Cup and Saucer ▼

- *circa 1930*

Cream Royal Doulton cup and saucer with sprays of violets and gilding to rim of cup and handle.
- *height 9cm*
- **Guide price £55/$104**

Royal Winton ▼

- *circa 1920*

Blue Royal Winton with sprays of apple blossom on a royal blue background.
- *height 6cm*
- **Guide price £95/$180**

Floral Vase ▲

- *1930*

Fine Poole Pottery vase painted by Ruth Paverley with stylized tulips and roses.
- *height 20cm*
- **Guide price £420/$794**

Honiton Pottery Water Jug ▲

- *circa 1930*

Bulbous-shaped water jug by Honiton pottery with a foliate and a floral design.
- *height 55cm*
- **Guide price £110/$208**

Art Deco Wall Mask ▼

- *circa 1930*

An Art Deco terracotta coloured wall mask of a woman with black hair and turquoise collar. Marked "Kunstkeramik Adolf Prischl Wien".
- *height 25cm*
- **Guide price £145/$274**

Burleigh Ware Cup and Saucer ▼

- *circa 1930*

Burleigh Ware cup and saucer with painted daffodils and leaves and rusticated leaf handle.
- *height 7cm*
- **Guide price £46/$87**

Clarice Cliff Pallet Plate ▼

- *circa 1900*

Clarice Cliff palette plate by Wilkinson with a lady in the wind, her scarf blowing, and a ship in turbulent seas.
- *diameter 24cm*
- **Guide price £400/$756**

Basket Pattern ▲

- *1956–7*

Basket pattern Poole pot designed by Anne Read.
- *height 19cm*
- **Guide price £220/$416**

Royal Paragon Trio ▲

- *circa 1930*

Royal Paragon cup, saucer and plate painted with yellow blue and pink flowers and three green circular green bands and stylised handle.
- *height 9cm*
- **Guide price £85/$161**

Katzhutte Figure ▲

- *circa 1930*

An Art Deco figure by Katzhutte of a woman in a pink floral dress.
- *height 26cm*
- **Guide price £445/$841**

Tissue and Cotton Jars ▲

- *circa 1950*

Italian jars by Fornasetti for cotton and tissues with mermaids, scallop shells and gilt banding.
- *height 23cm*
- **Guide price £250/$473**

Italian Fishbone Vase ▲

- *1970*

Grey Italian flask-shaped vase with a raised grey fishbone design on a burnt orange ground.
- *height 33cm*
- **Guide price £95/$180**

Doulton Art Nouveau Jug ▲

- *circa 1905*

Doulton jug with pink and green Art Nouveau design with brown edging.
- *height 19cm*
- **Guide price £225/$426**

Susie Cooper Trio ▲

- *1950*

"Green Dresden Spray" two tone green cup, saucer and matching plate trio with floral entwined sprays by Susie Cooper.
- *height 5cm*
- **Guide price £48/$91**

Cheese Dish ▲

- *circa 1940*

Cream-coloured cheese dish and cover with a floral design and moulded rim.
- *14cm x 20cm*
- **Guide price £30/$57**

Paragon Art Deco Cup and Saucer ◄

- *circa 1920*

Fine Paragon pink floral Art Deco cup and saucer.
- *height 10cm*
- **Guide price £45/$85**

Goldscheider Wall Mask ▼

- *circa 1930*

An Italian Art Deco wall mask, executed in the Goldscheider style, of a young woman with stylized turquoise ringlets.
- *height 27cm*
- **Guide price £375/$709**

Clarice Cliff Cup and Saucer ▼

- *1934*

Clarice Cliff cup and saucer with a 'tulip' pattern and wedge-shaped handle, the saucer with pink and blue banding.
- *height 8cm*
- **Guide price £350/$662**

Bell-shaped cup ▼

- *circa 1920*

Ainsley bell-shaped cup saucer and plate with a profusion of yellow and white flowers.
- *height 7cm*
- **Guide price £75/$142**

Beswick Wall Mask ►

- *circa 1930*

An English Art Deco wall mask by Beswick depicting a young lady in profile.
- *height 27cm*
- **Guide price £395/$748**

Totem ▲

- *circa 2000*

"Giogold" by E. Sottsass, a vase of cylindrical form with dark blue and gold banding above a blue circular base.
- *height 38cm*
- **Guide price £380/$719**

Paragon Trio ▲

- *circa 1920*

Paragon trio with octagonal plate with orange floral sprays, dramatic black and orange handle.
- *height 7.5cm*
- **Guide price £115/$217**

Queen Anne Shelley Cup and Saucer ▲

- ℗ circa 1927
White hand-painted Shelley cup with saucer with black trailing vine and yellow pink and blue stylised flowers.
- height 8cm
- **Guide price £85/$161**

Valaurido Plate by Capron ▲

- 1970
Plate by Roger Capron for Valaurido with a red and orange design within borders of matt grey.
- diameter 22cm
- **Guide price £85/$161**

Torso by Zaccagnini ▼

- circa 1940
Ceramic torso of a nude lady by Zaccagnini.
- height 61cm
- **Guide price £1,050/$1,985**

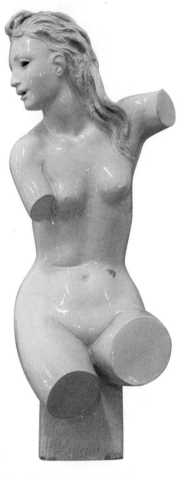

Coral Firs Cup and Saucer ▼

- circa 1930
A Clarice Cliff "Coral Firs" design from the Bizarre range with stylised terracotta trees.
- height 9cm
- **Guide price £335/$633**

Rosenthal Pottery ◄

- circa 1950
Peynet vase of conical form designed by Rosenthal Pottery entitled "The Marriage".
- height 29cm
- **Guide price £300/$567**

Crown Devon Trio ▲

- 1950
Crown Devon cup saucer and plate, with exotic birds their wings outstretched on a red glazed background.
- height 8cm
- **Guide price £165/$312**

Alan Caiger-Smith Goblet ▲

- circa 1963
Lustre glaze goblet by Alan Caiger-Smith, the bowl with swirled designs above a knopped stem, raised on a circular base.
- height 14cm
- **Guide price £100/$189**

Poole Pottery Vase ▼

- circa 1930
Poole pottery bulbous vase with stylised yellow lilac flowers and green foliage.
- height 13cm
- **Guide price £75/$142**

Clarice Cliff Trio ▼

- circa 1930
Clarice Cliff orange green and cream star decoration cup, saucer and plate.
- height 7cm
- **Guide price £395/$748**

Taurus ▼

- 1950
Blue stylised bull "Taurus" standing on all fours with head bowed and tail up by Gambone.
- height 25cm
- **Guide price £2,000/$3,780**

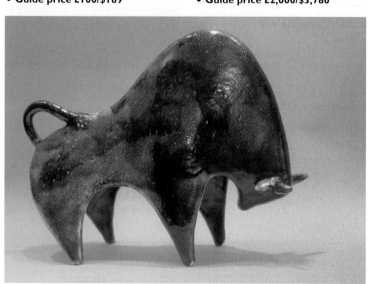

Katzhutte Art Deco Figure ▼

• *circa 1930*
A German Katzhutte Art Deco figure of a stylish woman dancing in a multi-coloured dress.
• *height 29cm*
• **Guide price £475/$898**

Poole Floral Vase ▼

• *circa 1930*
Poole pottery vase with stylised yellow and purple flowers and a purple, green and lilac design around the rim.
• *height 20cm*
• **Guide price £200/$378**

Melba Nasturtium Trio ▼

• *1931*
Unusual octagonal Melba trio with yellow and orange nasturtiums and floral handle.
• *height 8cm*
• **Guide price £55/$104**

Shelley Tea Plate ▼

• *1927*
Shelley tea plate with orange border, black trees and green woodland border.
• *diameter 16cm*
• **Guide price £20/$38**

Lorenzl Art Deco Figure ▼

• *circa 1930*
An Art Deco figured designed by Lorenzl of a stylish young woman posing in a grey lace effect dress.
• *height 30cm*
• **Guide price £595/$1,125**

Porcelain Busts ▲

• *20th century*
Pair of German porcelain busts of Royal children, after models by Johann Joachim Kaendler.
• *height 15.5cm*
• **Guide price £635/$1,200**

Ovoid Vase ▲

• *circa 1920*
Italian bottle-shaped vase with yellow, green and brown abstract design.
• *height 29cm*
• **Guide price £250/$473**

Pink Floral Trio ▲

• *circa 1930*
Royal Doulton trio with pink floral design and a blue and cream gilded background.
• *height 8cm*
• **Guide price £75/$142**

Peynet Design Vase ▼

• *circa 1950*
Rosenthal Germany pottery vase, showing spring with a couple on a bridge.
• *height 30cm*
• **Guide price £200/$378**

Shelley Vogue Trio ▼

• *1930*
Shelley Vogue trio with various shades of green with a triangular shape handle.
• *height 7cm*
• **Guide price £275/$520**

Pink Azalea Trio ▼

• *1950*
Pink Azalea cup, saucer and plate trio, by Susie Cooper.
• *height 8cm*
• **Guide price £55/$104**

Poole Vase

- circa 1930

Poole vase of ovoid form with yellow, blue and green design.

- height 26cm
- **Guide price £400/$756**

Spode Copeland Trio

- 1910

Spode Copeland trio with pale pink roses, gilding on a dark blue background.

- height 6.5cm
- **Guide price £65/$123**

Katzhutte Figure

- circa 1930

An Art Deco figure by Katzhutte, posing in a pink dress, with Katzhutte marks.

- height 26cm
- **Guide price £545/$1,030**

Carlton Ware Cup and Saucer

- circa 1900

Carlton Ware orange lustre cup and saucer with stylized birds and gilding.

- height 6cm
- **Guide price £165/$312**

Vase Tulip Pattern

- 1934

Vase of baluster form, hand-painted by Clarice Cliff with a "tulip" pattern and green and red banding on a blue ground.

- height 12cm
- **Guide price £650/$1,229**

Wedgwood Cup

- 1910

Wedgwood cup and saucer with separate silver gilt holder.

- height 7cm
- **Guide price £125/$237**

Grindly Floral Trio

- 1920

Hand-painted Grindley cup, saucer and plate with yellow floral decoration and a pale pink raised background.

- height 9cm
- **Guide price £55/$104**

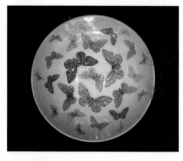

Butterfly Charger

- 2001

Charger with painted butterflies by Tania Pike for Dennis China Works.

- diameter 37cm
- **Guide price £445/$841**

Ocelot Vase

- 2000

Catherine Mellor vase with a design of a leopard in blue on a leopard spot ground.

- height 24cm
- **Guide price £411/$777**

Butter Container ▲

- *circa 1940*

Cream ceramic butter dish with a lattice and apple blossom design in relief.

- *12cm x 18cm*
- **Guide price £30/$57**

Janice Tchalenko Vase ▲

- *circa 1999*

Poole pottery vase of baluster form with a vibrant candy strip design by Janice Tchalenko.

- *height 37cm*
- **Guide price £200/$378**

Italian Ceramic Jug ▲

- *1950*

Matt brown Italian jug of ovoid form with stylised black and white enamel horses and strap handle.

- *height 22cm*
- **Guide price £75/$142**

Terracotta Wall Mask ▼

- *1930s*

An Art Deco terracotta wall mask, in the German/Austrian style, of a woman with black glazed hair, a mottle glazed face, and orange lips.

- *height 27cm*
- **Guide price £155/$293**

Wedding Band Cup and Saucer ▼

- *circa 1930*

Susie Cooper coffee cup with a wedding band pattern.

- *height 7cm*
- **Guide price £45/$85**

Shelley Cup and Saucer ▼

- *1930*

Hand-painted Shelley dainty shape cup and saucer with orange and yellow floral spray of flowers.

- *height 10cm*
- **Guide price £185/$350**

Cigarette Holder ▼

- *1950*

Circular cigarette holder with push-action lid to extinguish the cigarettes.

- *height 21cm*
- **Guide price £38/$72**

Dutch Jar ▼

- *circa 1923*

Dutch jar with cover by Corona Gouda, designed by W. P. Harispring.

- *height 11cm*
- **Guide price £280/$530**

Highland Stoneware Vase ▲

- *circa 2000*

Highland stoneware vase of baluster form with a narrow neck and splayed lip painted with trout underwater.

- *height 31cm*
- **Guide price £145/$274**

Gunnar Nylund Vase ▼

- *1950s*

A vase by Gunnar Nylund for Rorstrand, incised "R" and three crowns. Stoneware with a brown and black glaze.
- *height 17cm*
- **Guide price £110/$208**

Troika ▲

- *circa 1965*

Troika pottery vase with cream and turquoise geometric design from St. Ives.
- *36cm x 17cm*
- **Guide price £895/$1,692**

Carp Charger ▲

- *circa 2000*

Pottery charger with a design of two carp on a green background, by Dennis China Works.
- *diameter 36cm*
- **Guide price £540/$1,021**

Nuage by Clarice Cliff ◄

- *1935*

"Nuage" bowl by Clarice Cliff, with hand painted flowers and leaves with an orange centre on a green ground.
- *diameter 19cm*
- **Guide price £950/$1,796**

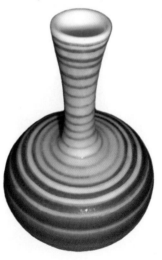

English Cup and Saucer ▼

- *circa 1920*

English cup, saucer and plate with a cartouche of a painted bird within gilt borders, surrounded by pink roses and cornflowers.
- *height 7.5cm*
- **Guide price £38/$72**

Bulb Vase ▼

- *1936*

Clarice Cliff bulb vase with metal rim from the "Citrus Delicier" collection.
- *diameter 20cm*
- **Guide price £350/$662**

Italian Ribbed Vase ▲

- *1950*

Italian elegant bottle-shaped vase with long neck, ribbed body and a matt black finish.
- *height 33cm*
- **Guide price £65/$123**

Rorstrand Miniature Vase ▲

- *1950s*

Miniature stoneware vase by Gunnar Nylund for Rorstrand with a matte white glaze with stripes of brown.
- *height 8cm*
- **Guide price £110/$208**

Floral Design Plate ▼

• *1970*

Circular plate with a floral design in red, black and yellow enamels by Geramim S. Rocco, Torrita de Sirvo.

• *diameter 38cm*

• **Guide price £145/$274**

Spode Copeland Cup and Saucer ▲

• *circa 1930*

Spode Copeland cup and saucer with floral sprays.

• *height 4cm*

• **Guide price £69/$131**

Hand Painted Wall Plaque ▼

• *1930s*

A quality china wall plaque hand painted in pastel colours and unsigned, but most likely a Beswick piece.

• *27.9cm x 20.3cm*

• **Guide price £280/$530**

Cornish Moon Troika ▲

• *circa 1960*

Pottery blue vase of conical form by Troika St. Ives with cream circles on a textured brown and green ground.

• *height 26cm*

• **Guide price £285/$539**

Leather Texture Bowl ▼

• *1960s*

Oval stoneware bowl by Rorstrand with dark brown leather-textured glaze, with incised parallel lines.

• *19cm x 16cm*

• **Guide price £80/$152**

Keramik Wall Mask ▲

• *1930s*

A terracotta Gmundner Keramik wall mask made in Austria and printed with flowerpot mark.

• *height 20cm*

• **Guide price £165/$312**

Fantasque by Clarice Cliff ▲

• *1936*

Plate by Clarice Cliff from the Fantasque collection centered with a hand-painted design of a country setting within black and orange borders.

• *diameter 18cm*

• **Guide price £450/$851**

Poole Butterfly Pattern Vase ▲

• *1956–7*

Poole vase designed by Alfred Read and decorated by Gwen Haskins. Hand-thrown white earthenware decorated with purple and red butterflies.

• *height 21cm*

• **Guide price £200/$378**

Shelley Bon-Bon Dish ◄

• *1927*

Bon-bon dish with a serpentine rim, orange centre and four black trees.

• *diameter 11cm*

• **Guide price £65/$123**

Tea Cup and Saucer

- *1936*

Clarice Cliff 'Spring' cup and saucer hand painted with crocuses with gilt banding and pale green borders.

- *height 7cm*
- **Guide price £110/$208**

Martin Brothers Pot

- *circa 1960*

Medium size grey pot of bulbous proportions with variegated sized yellow spots, with separate raised moulding, by Martin Brothers.

- *height 17cm*
- **Guide price £1,906/$3,603**

Denby Vase

- *circa 1960s*

Bourne Denby vase of conical form with white vertical stripes within a border of variegated dots.

- *height 30cm*
- **Guide price £45/$85**

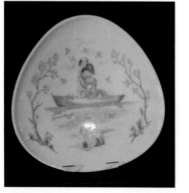

Alan Caiger-Smith Jug

- *circa 1978*

Large white pottery water jug with green and blue design by Alan Caiger-Smith.

- *height 38cm*
- **Guide price £400/$756**

Rosenthal Pottery

- *circa 1950*

Peynet design plate of ovoid form, depicting a hand-painted design of a couple in a boat with birds circling.

- *diameter 20cm*
- **Guide price £100/$189**

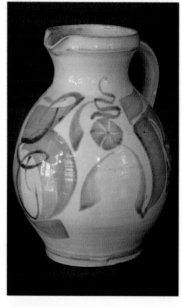

Spring Vase

- *1936*

'Spring' vase of ovoid form with a hand-painted design of crocuses by Clarice Cliff.

- *height 15cm*
- **Guide price £465/$879**

Susie Cooper Jug

- *1929*

'Cubist' collection cream jug by Susie Cooper for Gray's Pottery.

- *height 13cm*
- **Guide price £350/$662**

Vase by John Criswick

- *1960*

John Criswick vase of inverted conical form, dated and signed on the base "10.11.1960".

- *height 44cm*
- **Guide price £380/$719**

Ceramic Jar

- *circa 1940s*

Pale green ceramic biscuit jar and cover, with a raised Chinoiserie cherry blossom design and basket-style handle.

- *13cm x 10cm*
- **Guide price £65/$123**

Cake Server ▼

- *circa 1930*

Cream ceramic cake stand with orange and yellow flowers and folia, and a geometric metal handle.

- *13cm x 23cm*
- **Guide price £30/$57**

German Red Vase ▼

- *1950*

Red vase of inverted conical form with a raised black and white abstract design around the middle of the vase.

- *height 22cm*
- **Guide price £30/$57**

Whieldon Ware Vase ◄

- *circa 1930*

Whieldon Ware bulbous blue and orange floral design vase with gold leaves by F. Winkle & Co. Ltd, England. Orient design.

- *height 11cm*
- **Guide price £160/$303**

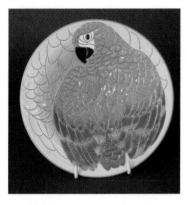

Parrot Plate ▲

- *2000*

Parrot designed by Sally Tuffin and painted by Tania Pike for Dennis China Works.

- *diameter 16cm*
- **Guide price £70/$133**

Zebra Vase ▲

- *1999*

Dennis China Works vase with a zebra design on a zebra pattern background, designed by Sally Tuffin and painted by Heidi Warr.

- *height 23cm*
- **Guide price £298/$563**

Crown Devon Jug ▶

- *circa 1930*

Crown Devon yellow, black, orange and aubergine geometric design jug by Fieldings of England.

- *height 14cm*
- **Guide price £240/$454**

Plate and Bowl ▲

- *1930–40*

A Susie Cooper twin-handled bowl with plate with a graduated green glaze with floral design.

- *diameter 16cm*
- **Guide price £45/$85**

Shelley Jug ▲

- *1930*

Porcelain Shelley milk jug with swallow and pastoral scene with a yellow handle.

- *height 10cm*
- **Guide price £55/$104**

Gray's Pottery Jug ▼

- *1929*

Water jug with an abstract pattern and gilding designed by Susie Cooper for Gray's pottery.

- *height 35cm*
- **Guide price £300/$567**

Clarice Cliff Jam Pot ▼

• *1934*
Bon-jour shape pot by Clarice Cliff with a 'tulip' pattern painted on the lid, with stylised acorn finial and a blue and green glazed body.
• *height 9cm*
• **Guide price £750/$1,418**

Clarice Cliff Mustard Pot ▲

• *1934*
Clarice Cliff mustard pot with a 'tulip' pattern.
• *height 5cm*
• **Guide price £160/$303**

Troika ▶

• *circa 1965*
Troika pottery vase of abstract design with a rusticated finish from St. Ives.
• *36cm x 17cm*
• **Guide price £895/$1,692**

Ceramic Plate ▼

• *1973*
Large ceramic plate with six-eye design, on a grey base, by Salvatori Meli.
• *diameter 59cm*
• **Guide price £3,000/$5,670**

Royal Worcester ▲

• *circa 1930*
Royal Worcester turquoise bulb vase with dark blue butterflies and birds.
• *height 27cm*
• **Guide price £850/$1,607**

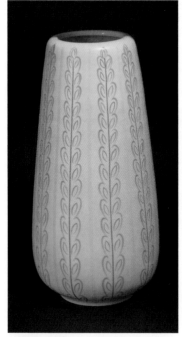

Figure of a Seated Lady ▲

• *1950*
A figure of a young girl in nineteenth century dress on a garden seat accompanied by a macaw. The whole on an oval moulded base with gilding.
• *19cm x 18cm*
• **Guide price £195/$370**

Alfred Read ▲

• *circa 1953-4*
Poole pottery vase No. YHP, designed by Alfred Read.
• *height 25cm*
• **Guide price £175/$331**

Eduardo Paolozzi Plate ▼

- circa 1950

Wedgwood bone china plate made in England by Eduardo Paolozzi with a red, black and gold geometric design.

- diameter 27cm
- **Guide price £150/$284**

Teapot by Clarice Cliff ▼

- 1936

'Blue Chintz' collection teapot with pink crocus by Clarice Cliff.

- height 15cm
- **Guide price £450/$851**

Susie Cooper Tea Set ▼

- 1929

Seventeen piece Susie Cooper tea set consisting of five cups and saucers, a milk jug and a sugar bowl, with a black, yellow, orange and grey geometric design.

- height of cup 9cm
- **Guide price £2,600/$4,914**

Ross's of Belfast ▲

- 1929

Small bowl by Susie Cooper inscribed with the advertisement for Ross's of Belfast and Lime Juice Cordial.

- diameter 14cm
- **Guide price £250/$473**

Cheese Dish ▼

- circa 1912

A Spode blue- and white- transfer cheese dish and cover.

- height 6cm
- **Guide price £90/$171**

Macintyre Vases ▼

- 1900–4

Pair of Macintyre vases in cornflower design by William Moorcroft.

- height 17cm
- **Guide price £1,650/$3,119**

Moon and Mountain ▲

- 1928

'Moon and Mountain' plate with a hand-painted abstract design by Susie Cooper.

- length 26cm
- **Guide price £325/$614**

Bee Vase ▲

- late 1990s

Dennis China Works ceramic vase of baluster form, decorated with a repeated honeycomb pattern with bees in the foreground.

- height 11.25cm
- **Guide price £300/$567**

Bauhaus Jug ▲

- circa 1930

Bauhaus pink and orange moulded jug by Leuchtenburg.

- height 19cm
- **Guide price £450/$851**

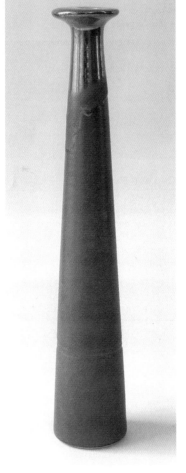

Enamel Vase ▲

- 1960

Enamel vase of conical form with a gilded neck and lip.

- height 20cm
- **Guide price £45/$85**

Susie Cooper Tea Trio ▲

- *1929*

Susie Cooper tea trio cup and saucer and plate with a yellow, green, black and yellow 'lightning' pattern.
- *height 9cm*
- **Guide price £450/$851**

Cup and Saucer ▲

- *1940–50*

Royal Copenhagen blue and white cup and saucer, decorated with interlaced banding and floral arrangements.
- *height 8cm*
- **Guide price £45/$85**

Arts Stable Jug ▼

- *circa 1930*

Arts stable jug with geometric design by Poole Pottery.
- *height 17cm*
- **Guide price £400/$756**

Royal Worcester Cup and Saucer ▼

- *1936*

An English Royal Worcester cup and saucer, with interlaced scroll decoration.
- *height 9cm*
- **Guide price £150/$284**

Figure in White Gown ◄

- *1983*

A Royal Doulton figurine of young girl in a flowing white gown with her hands clasped and her head tilted to one side.
- *height 20cm*
- **Guide price £120/$227**

Stephanie ▼

- *1975*

A Royal Doulton figurine entitled "Stephanie" showing a young girl dancing in period costume.
- *height 28cm*
- **Guide price £125/$237**

Art Deco Plates ▼

- *1930*

An Art Deco Shelley ceramic cake plate and side plate with swallow and foliate design.
- *width 25cm*
- **Guide price £55/$104**

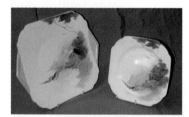

Gilded Vase ▼

- *1910*

Satsuma vase of baluster form, showing figures in a garden setting, and decorated with gilded and stylised floral patterns.
- *height 21cm*
- **Guide price £355/$671**

Poole Ware Jug ▼

- *1932*

Small Poole ware bulbous jug with a yellow, black and grey abstract design on a chalk white ground.
- *height 13cm*
- **Guide price £350/$662**

Minton Cup and Saucer ▲

- *1912–50*

A Minton cup and saucer made in New York by Cilman Collamore & Co., 5th Avenue and 30th Street, New York.

- **Guide price £85/$161**

Royal Doulton Bulldog ▲

- *20th century*

Porcelain Royal Doulton bulldog, shown recumbent, with a patch over one eye and draped in the Union Jack flag.

- *16cm x 23cm*
- **Guide price £395/$748**

Susie Cooper Milk Jug ▲

- *circa 1930s*

A Susie Cooper milk jug with graduated banding and stylised bird lip. Stamped "698 83".

- *height 20cm*
- **Guide price £63/$119**

Royal Copenhagen Ware ▲

- *1945*

Royal Copenhagen blue and white cup and saucer, with interlaced banding and foliate designs.

- *height 10cm*
- **Guide price £35/$66**

Sèvres Group ▼

- *1920*

'Les Pecheurs', a Sèvres group showing two ladies and two children. One of the ladies holds a fishing net beside a basket of fish, the whole on a rustic base.

- *height 27cm*
- **Guide price £1,500/$2,835**

English Abstract Dish ▶

- *circa 1950s*

An English ovoid dish with an abstract geometric pattern on a black ground with a white rim.

- *32cm x 23cm*
- **Guide price £75/$142**

Royal Doulton Figurine ▼

- *1950*

A Royal Doulton ceramic figure of a young girl in a red and white dress and bonnet, holding a posy.

- *height 13cm*
- **Guide price £95/$180**

Kaffe Fasset Vase ▼

- *late 20th century*

Scottish Highland stoneware baluster vase, hand painted with leaf and fruit designs by Kaffe Fasset.

- *height 36cm*
- **Guide price £600/$1,134**

Spode Figure ▲

- *1910*

A Spode figure of a lady in courtly dress with chinoiserie design, holding an extended fan to her side.

- *height 12cm*
- **Guide price £268/$506**

Dresden Dancing Figure ▲

- *1945*

Dresden figurine depicting a Flamenco dancer, standing on an oval moulded base with gilding.

- *height 12cm*
- **Guide price £65/$123**

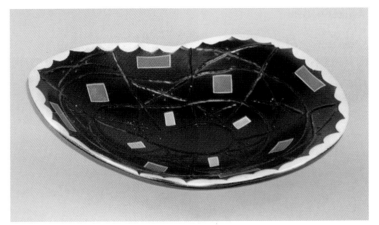

Dresden Figurines ▼

- *20th century*
Dresden group of porcelain figures, modelled as a monkey band.
- *height 17cm*
- **Guide price £255/$482**

Haddon Hall Set ▼

- *1940*
A polychrome Minton Haddon Hall cup and saucer, with profuse floral decoration.
- *height 11cm*
- **Guide price £45/$85**

Vegetable Dish ▼

- *1930–40*
A Susie Cooper vegetable dish with a graduated pale blue glaze with flower designs and banding.
- *18cm x 9cm*
- **Guide price £78/$150**

Soup Bowl ◄

- *1930–40*
A Susie Cooper soup bowl with a variegated pink glaze and a central pink rose.
- *diameter 23cm*
- **Guide price £85/$161**

Shelly Regent Bowl ▼

- *1930*
An English Art Deco Shelly Regent bowl of deep proportions with wide splayed lip and a swallow and foliate design.
- *height 9cm*
- **Guide price £55/$104**

Croismare Jug ▼

- *20th century*
Finely crafted gourd-shaped jug with abstract designs, made by Muller Croismare.
- *height 15cm*
- **Guide price £2,200/$4,158**

Royal Worcester Set ▼

- *1951*
A Royal Worcester cup and saucer with large, colourful fruit decoration. Includes gilding inside the cup, base and handle.
- *height 7cm*
- **Guide price £335/$633**

Lawrence McGowan Vase ▼

- *late 20th century*
Lawrence McGowan vase decorated with a foliate design, with scrolled handles.
- *height 28.75cm*
- **Guide price £140/$265**

Mortlake Cup and Saucer ▼

- *1945*
A Mortlake cup and saucer with gilded floral designs around cartouches with floral sprays.
- *height 11cm*
- **Guide price £38/$72**

Quenti Pot ▲

- *mid-20th century*
Very large impressively constructed Quenti pot, with diagrammatic decoration.
- *65cm x 45cm*
- **Guide price £1,800/$3,402**

Sauce Boat ▲

- *1930–40*
A Susie Cooper sauce boat with a crimson band around the body and grey matt finish above.
- *height 15cm*
- **Guide price £45/$85**

Royal Doulton Lady ▲

- *1982*
A Royal Doulton figurine of a young lady in a yellow dress with green waistband, holding a parasol over her shoulder and gazing upwards.
- *height 20cm*
- **Guide price £100/$189**

Poole Ceramic Plate ▲

- *20th century*
Poole pottery plate with a one-off abstract pattern, designed by Tony Morris.
- *diameter 40cm*
- **Guide price £450/$851**

Dennis Jar and Cover ◄

- *late 1990s*
Jar painted with a polar bear and cub in an arctic setting, with a polar bear finial, by Dennis China Works.
- *height 10cm*
- **Guide price £305/$576**

Minton Bowl and Base ▲

- *20th century*
A Minton bowl with base, fluted design and twin ribboned handles. The bowl and base have interlaced flower designs and a central panel of flowers.
- *9cm x 12cm*
- **Guide price £25/$48**

Picasso Bowl ▲

- *1952*
A Picasso bowl with a wide rim. The centre of the bowl is hand painted in a charcoal and grey wash, with a stylised picture of a raven with stones at its feet.
- *diameter 15cm*
- **Guide price £755/$1,427**

Pair of Spirit Barrels ▼

- *1910*
Pair of attractive salt glaze spirit barrels for brandy and whisky.
- *height 27cm*
- **Guide price £245/$463**

Ceramic Pots ▲

- *circa 1930*
Three assorted ceramic pots.
- *29cm x 18cm*
- **Guide price £155/$293**

Shelley Cup and Saucer ▼

- *1930*
A Shelley cup and saucer with floral pattern with the handle and base painted blue.
- *height 6cm*
- **Guide price £55/$104**

Highland Stoneware Bowl ▲

- *1990–9*
Highland stoneware bowl decorated with a repeated scene of gold fish within blue borders, with ear-shaped handles.
- *diameter 16.25cm*
- **Guide price £95/$180**

Art Deco Coffee Set ▼

- *1930*
An Art Deco Carlton Ware coffee set comprising six cups and saucers, a sugar bowl, milk jug and coffee pot. In emerald green glaze with gilt banding and gilded interiors.
- *height 27cm/pot*
- **Guide price £295/$558**

Royal Doulton Figure of Clarissa ◄

- *20th century*
A Royal Doulton figure of a young girl in flowing dress with a wicker basket containing flowers entitled "Clarissa".
- *height 14cm*
- **Guide price £110/$208**

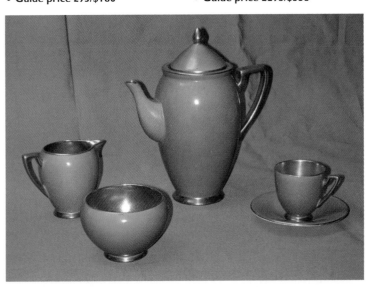

Toucan Vase ▲

• *late 20th century*

English vase decorated with a toucan on a black ground, by Dennis China Works.

• *height 30cm*
• **Guide price £470/$889**

Porcelain Teapot ▲

• *circa 1990s*

English porcelain teapot, with hand-painted ribbon decoration, by Graham Clarke.

• *height 27.5cm*
• **Guide price £75/$142**

Minton Cup and Saucer ▲

• *1950*

Cup and saucer with a Minton white and blue leaf pattern.

• **Guide price £25/$48**

Poole Pottery Pot ▼

• *1970*

Green Poole Pottery pot decorated with large lime green and darker green scrolls, by Caroge Holdan.

• *height 45cm*
• **Guide price £580/$1,097**

Royal Worcester Cabaret Set ▼

• *1918–19*

A Royal Worcester cabaret set with six cups, saucers and spoons in a presentation box. Signed by Stinton, with spoons by Henry James Hulbert.

• **Guide price £2,850/$5,387**

Poole Owl Plate ▼

• *late 1990s*

Poole pottery plate painted with an black owl, with a sunset in the background, by Tony Morris.

• *diameter 40cm*
• **Guide price £450/$851**

Aynsley Cup and Saucer ▲

• *circa 1926*

An Aynsley cup and saucer with scrolled handle and gilt banding on a cobalt blue ground.

• *height 9cm*
• **Guide price £60/$114**

Figure of Young Lady ▶

• *1977*

A Royal Doulton figure of a young lady standing posed in an evening dress, entitled "Harmony".

• *height 29cm*
• **Guide price £125/$237**

Royal Doulton Figure ▲

• *1954*

A Royal Doulton figurine of a sixteenth century young lady in courtly dress. Entitled "Catherine Clergon Sitzendore".

• *height 14cm*
• **Guide price £110/$208**

Susie Cooper Trio ▼

• *1930–40*

A Susie Cooper trio comprising a white teacup, blue saucer and plate with a moulded rim.

• *diameter 19cm/plate; 9cm/saucer*
• **Guide price £75/$142**

Bone China Cup and Saucer ▼

- *1945*

A bone china cup and saucer with gilt rim interspersed with pink rose detail.

- *height 10cm*
- **Guide price £45/$85**

Bisque Rabbit ▼

- *20th century*

Bisque porcelain model of a rabbit with ears erect and head turned to the side.

- *height 30cm*
- **Guide price £340/$643**

Dennis Iris Vase ▼

- *late 1990s*

English ceramic vase decorated with irises by Dennis China Works.

- *height 36cm*
- **Guide price £940/$1,777**

Dinanderie Plate ▲

- *20th century*

Red and black glazed Dinanderie dish signed by Linossier.

- *diameter 19cm*
- **Guide price £2,400/$4,536**

Water Jug ▲

- *1990–9*

Ceramic water jug decorated with a rooster by Maureen Minchin.

- *height 27.5cm*
- **Guide price £95/$180**

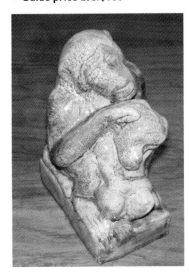

Ceramic Monkeys ▲

- *20th century*

Italian ceramic group of two monkeys preening each other, with a rusticated green and blue glaze.

- *height 19cm*
- **Guide price £550/$1,040**

Royal Doulton Service ▼

- *20th century*

Royal Doulton teaset of six cups and saucers, with sugar bowl, decorated with an orange pattern with gold borders.

- *height 8cm/cup*
- **Guide price £450/$851**

Sicart Ashtray ▲

- *circa 1970s*

Italian circular ceramic ashtray with metal insert by Sicart.

- *6cm x 21cm*
- **Guide price £185/$350**

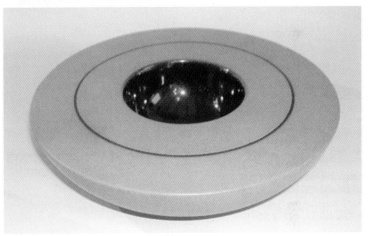

French Ceramic Lamp ▲

- *20th century*

French amber-coloured ceramic lamp which also can be a perfume burner, with a turned wooden cover and base.

- *height 28cm*
- **Guide price £200/$378**

Signed Dinanderie Saucer ▼

- *20th century*

A red and black glazed Dinanderie saucer signed by Linossier.

- *diameter 10cm*
- **Guide price £550/$1,040**

Salt and Pepper Shakers ▲

- *1960–70*
English Carlton Ware red salt and pepper shakers.
- *height 11.25cm*
- **Guide price £35/$66**

Porcelain Bowl ▲

- *1999*
British porcelain bowl with a hand painted scene of Felbrigg Hall, Norfolk, by Graham Clarke.
- *diameter 35cm*
- **Guide price £450/$851**

Carlton Ware Service ▼

- *1960–70*
Orange Carlton Ware ceramic table service consisting of salt and pepper shakers and sugar holder.
- *height 16.25cm*
- **Guide price £75/$142**

Italian Ceramic Vase ▼

- *circa 1950s*
Italian three-sided bottle-shaped vase with abstract cartouches on a green ground, by Cossa.
- *height 12cm*
- **Guide price £150/$284**

German Ceramic Vase ◄

- *1960*
A German ceramic vase decorated with a romantic scene, with a chinoiserie influence, from the Lover's collection by Raymond Peynet.
- *height 20cm*
- **Guide price £700/$1,323**

Ceramic Jar and Cover ►

- *20th century*
A cylinder-shaped ceramic jar and cover with an orange glaze, gilded handles and finial, made by Hutschenreuther.
- *height 22cm*
- **Guide price £200/$378**

Egg-Shaped Vase ▲

- *1960–70*
German ceramic vase of ovoid form decorated with an embracing couple on a bench, by Raymond Peynet.
- *height 21.25cm*
- **Guide price £300/$567**

Ceramic Painted Figure ▲

- *1925*
French ceramic painted figure modelled as a female reclining on a plain base, by Parvillee.
- *24cm x 60cm*
- **Guide price £1,800/$3,402**

Porcelain Plate ▼

- *late 1990s*
Porcelain plate hand painted with a Norfolk scene in a blue glaze, by Graham Clarke.
- *diameter 40cm*
- **Guide price £450/$851**

Cockran Bowl ▼

- *1990–9*
British ceramic deep bowl decorated with a blue octopus, by Roger Cockran.
- *15cm x 21.25cm*
- **Guide price £130/$246**

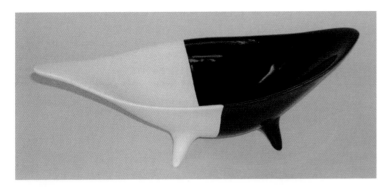

Italian Ceramic Dish ▲

- *1950s*

Italian black and white ceramic dish of ovoid form on three conical feet by Antonia Campi.

- *8cm x 29cm x 9cm*
- **Guide price £200/$378**

Highland Dish ▲

- *late 1990s*

Octagonal Highland stoneware dish, hand painted with a floral design of lillies on a lustre ground.

- *46.25cm x 40cm*
- **Guide price £189/$358**

Bosch Frères Vase ▼

- *1920*

Bosch Frères vase of oval form with splayed lip incorporating a geometric design in orange, black and cochineal glaze on a white ground.

- *height 26cm*
- **Guide price £280/$530**

Dinanderie Saucer ▼

- *20th century*

Fine French Dinanderie saucer, signed by Linossier.

- *diameter 13cm*
- **Guide price £950/$1,796**

Foxglove Bottle ▶

- *late 1990s*

Foxglove ceramic bottle-shaped vase painted with foxgloves on a blue ground, by Dennis China Works.

- *height 37.5cm*
- **Guide price £517/$977**

Enamel Ashtray ▲

- *1960*

Square enamel ashtray with two figures outlined in white on a purple base with a raised black rim.

- *16cm square*
- **Guide price £120/$227**

Asymmetric Vase ▲

- *1950s*

Italian ceramic vase of asymmetric form with a green and white design on a black ground.

- *height 30cm*
- **Guide price £40/$76**

Dinanderie Tray ▲

- *20th century*

A rectangular Dinanderie tray with a red glaze and gilded decoration, signed by Linossier.

- *21cm x 12cm*
- **Guide price £1,200/$2,268**

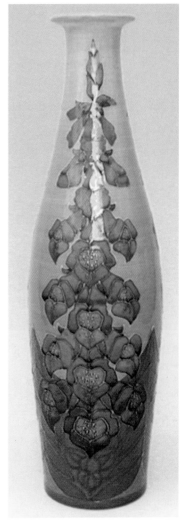

Ceramic Cat ▼

- *20th century*

Cat in red living glaze, a type of glaze pioneered by Poole Pottery.

- *height 28.75cm*
- **Guide price £28/$54**

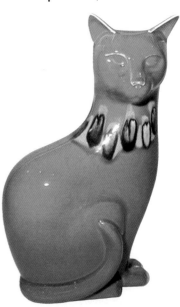

Balinese Dancer ▲

- *20th century*

A ceramic figure of a Balinese dancer by Royal Copenhagen.

- *height 14cm*
- **Guide price £120/$227**

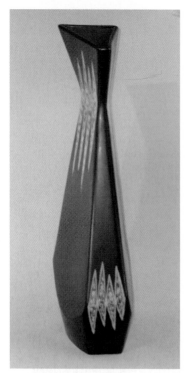

Danish Ceramic Vase ▲

- *1950s*

Danish ceramic vase of asymmetric form with a white elongated diamond-shaped pattern on a black ground, by Soholm Bornholm.

- *height 57cm*
- **Guide price £400/$756**

Cream-glazed Vase ▼

- *circa 1930*

French ceramic vase of ovoid proportions with a cream glaze and a rusticated finish.

- *height 20cm*
- **Guide price £150/$284**

Bonzo the Dog Plate ▼

- *1998*

Ceramic plate decorated with a repeated pattern of Bonzo the dog, by Richard Dennis Publications.

- *diameter 21.25cm*
- **Guide price £155/$293**

Holyrood Pottery Vase ▼

- *1917–27*

Holyrood pottery bulbous vase with crazing to base.

- *height 34cm*
- **Guide price £95/$180**

Cockran Plate ▲

- *late 1990s*

British ceramic plate showing a fish leaping out of the foaming sea, on a blue ground, by Roger Cockran.

- *diameter 26.25cm*
- **Guide price £125/$237**

Moorcroft Vase ▼

- *1913–7*

Early Moorcroft pomegranate vase by William Moorcroft.

- *height 19cm*
- **Guide price £575/$1,087**

Italian Ceramic Vase ▼

- *1950s*

Italian bottle-shaped ceramic vase by GTA, decorated with stylized faces.

- *height 48cm*
- **Guide price £250/$473**

Rhead Water Jug ◄

- *circa 1920*

Blue water jug with a floral trellis pattern by Frederick Rhead.

- *height 17.5cm*
- **Guide price £295/$558**

Glazed Candlesticks ▲

- *1917–34*

One of a pair of candlesticks by Minton Hollins Astraware, with a distinct variegated blue green glaze.

- *height 21cm*
- **Guide price £200/$378**

Bonzo Plate ▲

• 1998
Ceramic plate showing Bonzo the dog with the words "Pot Luck" on the rim, by Richard Dennis Publications.
• diameter 15cm
• **Guide price £12/$23**

French Vase ▲

• 20th century
French green vase, on a bronze tripod base by Daum Majorelle.
• height 15cm
• **Guide price £1,200/$2,268**

Bonzo the Dog Mugs ▶

• 1998
One of a pair of mugs decorated with Bonzo the dog, with a gold band around the rim by Richard Dennis Publications.
• height 8.75cm
• **Guide price £11/$21**

Enamelled Daum Vase ▲

• 1900
Daum vase of rectangular form, showing a winter scene with an enamelled silver birch and orange sunset.
• height 9cm
• **Guide price £1,500/$2,835**

Yellow Bonzo Mug ▲

• late 1990s
Yellow mug with a Bonzo the dog handle by Dennis China Works.
• height 12.5cm
• **Guide price £165/$312**

English Ceramic Bowl ▲

• 1990–9
English bowl of deep proportions painted with three hares in a woodland setting by Maureen Michin.
• diameter 42.5cm
• **Guide price £300/$567**

Art Deco Figure ▼

• 1926
Art Deco ceramic figure by Stanley Nicholson Babb showing a romantic figure.
• height 25cm
• **Guide price £600/$1,134**

McGowan Plate ▼

• late 20th century
Lawrence McGowan plate, with a central panel of a tree with robins and a poem on the rim.
• diameter 36.25cm
• **Guide price £250/$473**

Highland Stoneware Vase ▲

- *late 20th century*
Scottish Highland stoneware vase painted with a seascape. Limited edition of 250.
- *height 24cm*
- **Guide price £150/$284**

Burmantoft ▲

- *early 20th century*
An amber glazed Burmantoft of amphori form with two elongated handles.
- *height 20cm*
- **Guide price £235/$445**

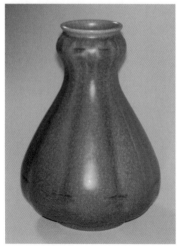

Dunmore Vase ▼

- *early 20th century*
Scottish Dunmore ovoid vase in a turquoise glaze with a splayed neck with moulded rim.
- *height 29cm*
- **Guide price £80/$152**

Moorland Vase ▼

- *1999*
A Moorland thistle vase. Cast and turned on a lathe with hand-painted metallic glaze. Signed and dated.
- *height 26cm*
- **Guide price £95/$180**

Royal Lancastrian Vase ◄

- *circa 1920*
Green Royal Lancastrian vase of organic form in matt green glaze.
- *height 18cm*
- **Guide price £195/$370**

Morris Ware Vases ▲

- *circa 1910*
Pair of Morris ware vases in thistle pattern by George Cartridge.
- *height 32cm*
- **Guide price £1,360/$2,571**

Flambé Pot ▲

- *1912*
Red and bronze flambé glazed pot of conical form, tapering to the foot with a small finial lid, by Howsons.
- *height 22cm*
- **Guide price £265/$501**

Mowart Vase ▼

- *1930*
Unusual vase of bulbous proportions with bubble inclusions within a deep red glaze, by Mowart.
- *height 22cm*
- **Guide price £595/$1,125**

Wedgwood Vase ▼

- *circa 1918–20*
Wedgwood fairyland lustre vase. Pilaster-shaped, showing patterns and decorations with fairies and scenes from folklore. Made by Daisy Makeig Jones.
- *height 31cm*
- **Guide price £4,500/$8,505**

Lustre Vase ◄

- *1910*
Pilkington Royal Lancaster lustre vase with floral decoration on a rich flambé ground by Annie Burton.
- *height 20cm*
- **Guide price £665/$1,257**

Dennis Bowl ▼

- *1998*

Dennis Chinaworks bowl of oriental shape with blue and pink glaze. Two dragonflies are imprinted on the inside of the dish. Bowl rests on a small base.
- *diameter 18cm*
- **Guide price £100/$189**

Wedgwood Trophy Plate ▲

- *circa 1960*

Wedgwood trophy plate dipped in black jasper with white cameos, decorated with musical instruments and trophies. Centre shows Pegasus surrounded by ribbons intertwined with grape vines and fruit.
- *diameter 22cm*
- **Guide price £750/$1,418**

Galileo Chini Vase ▼

- *circa 1910*

Very large, Galileo Chini lustre with decoration from Manfactura Di Fontebuoni.
- *height 55cm*
- **Guide price £7,000/$13,230**

Crown Derby Cup and Saucer Set ▲

- *circa 1931*

Early 20th-century Crown Derby cup and saucer set, decorated with an Imari pattern. Both pieces have gilding around the edges.
- *height 6cm*
- **Guide price £95/$180**

Gouda Deep Dish ▲

- *1928*

Early 20th-century Zuid-Holland factory Gouda deep dish on stand. Dish designed by Rembrandt Pottery.
- **Guide price £600/$1,134**

Two-Handled Vase ▲

- *April 1920*

Large two-handled baluster vase by Zuid-Holland factory. Gouda design 'Crocus'.
- *height 44cm*
- **Guide price £1,100/$2,079**

Baluster Vase ▲

- *1929*

Zuid-Holland factory. Gouda vase. Design 'Unique' by G.P. Van der Akker.
- *height 67.5cm*
- **Guide price £2,250/$4,253**

Wemyss Ware Piggy Bank ◄

- *circa 1930*

Early 20th-century Wemyss ware piggy bank painted with pink clover. Pink ears, nose, feet and tail. With slot below head for pennies.
- *height 28cm*
- **Guide price £2,500/$4,725**

Roger Low Vase ▲

- *20th century*

In association with Dartington pottery. High-fired deep red and purple glaze with iguana appliqué.
- *height 24cm*
- **Guide price £120/$227**

Art Nouveau Set ▲

• 1920

Art Nouveau-style jug and bowl set, comprising five pieces.

• **Guide price £195/$370**

Moorcroft Vase ▲

• 1995

Lisa Moorcroft urn-shaped vase or planter with a raised design of mushrooms in red on a tobacco backround.

• height 60cm
• **Guide price £175/$331**

Moorland Vase ▼

• 1999

Moorland conical vase with a repeated pyramid pattern in white, black and grey. Metallic banding running around neck.

• height 19cm
• **Guide price £40/$76**

Poole Vase ◄

• 1950

Poole vase with printed Poole mark. The vase is of a conical shape with a hand-painted basket pattern in purple and yellow.

• height 19cm
• **Guide price £400/$756**

Unusual Teapot ▲

• 1998

David Burnham Smith teapot is of unusual shape with a fish-like quality. Intricately painted with architectural scrolling pattern. It is signed and dated.

• height 10cm
• **Guide price £700/$1,323**

Bosch Frères Vase ▲

• 1925

Early 20th-century Keramis baluster vase by Charles Catteau.

• height 31cm
• **Guide price £500/$945**

Stamped Poole Vase ▼

• circa 1980s

A bulbous vase with short neck stamped with the Poole pottery mark. The detailing shows a bracelet pattern of bands running around the base, middle and neck. Banding also around base and rim.

• height 20cm
• **Guide price £500/$945**

Eggshell Porcelain Pot ▼

• 1902

Mocca pot with lid by H.G.A. Huyvenaar, from Rozenburg of the Hague, in the finest eggshell porcelain. Painted with purple floral decoration and in perfect condition.

• height 25cm
• **Guide price £10,000/$18,900**

Flambé Vase ◄

• 1905–15

Flambé vase of bottle shape form with a deep red glaze, made by Bernard Moore.

• height 15cm
• **Guide price £195/$370**

Porcelain Cup and Saucer ▲

- *1903*

Rozenburg of The Hague eggshell porcelain cup and saucer, with orchid and parrot design by Rudolph Sterken.

- *height 8cm*
- **Guide price £1,100/$2,079**

Large Gouda Vase ▲

- *1910*

Zuid-Holland factory. Gouda two-handled large vase.

- *height 43cm*
- **Guide price £2,050/$3,875**

Dennis Pot ▲

- *1999*

Dennis Chinaworks pot and cover decorated in a cobweb pattern in black and brown glaze with cobweb and leaf indentation. A spider is painted on the inside of the lid.

- *height 10cm*
- **Guide price £180/$341**

Dennis Plate ▼

- *1999*

A Dennis Chinaworks plate showing a cockerel with head turned and tail feathers on display. Brightly painted on a beige base, with a green glaze to the reverse.

- *diameter 36cm*
- **Guide price £423/$799**

Highland Dish ▼

- *1999*

A Highland Stoneware painted salmon dish. The dish has a representation of a Salmon in blue and purple glazes with a yellow underbelly.

- *height 42cm*
- **Guide price £53/$101**

Pantomime Vase ▼

- *1997*

Vase decorated with pantomime buttons and the ugly sisters. Showing three faces with different expressions, detailed painting inside and out with enamelling. By David Burnham Smith.

- *height 10cm*
- **Guide price £950/$1,796**

Ceramic Model of a Tower ▲

- *1998*

A tower, inspired by scenes from the Bayeux tapestry, by David Burnham Smith. Demonstrates highly dedicated and intricate technique in painting and craft. The painting is internal as well as external.

- *height 30cm*
- **Guide price £1,100/$2,079**

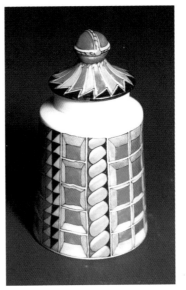

Burnham Smith Owl ▶

- *1999*

A David Burnham Smith owl, laboriously hand-painted in intricate detail with a matt glaze. Highly collectable. The owl is signed and dated D.B.S.

- *height 19cm*
- **Guide price £600/$1,134**

Gouda Wall Plate ▼

- *1928*

Zuid-Holland factory. Gouda wall plate. 'Corona' design by W.P. Hartsring.

- *height 31.5cm*
- **Guide price £380/$719**

Dartington Plate ▼

- *1999*

A Dartington plate ovate in shape with flower decorations and high-fired reduction glaze.

- *length 43cm*
- **Guide price £65/$123**

D. Burnham Smith Pot ◀

- *1998*

A small pot and cover decorated with an architectural repeated pattern on a blue ground. The lid is also similarly decorated and signed by David Burnham Smith.

- *height 11cm*
- **Guide price £150/$284**

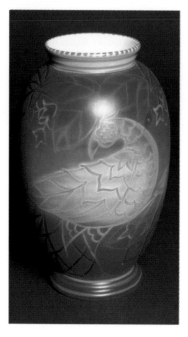

Poole Studio Vase ◄

- *1997*

Signed and dated. The design shows peacocks and floral decorations on a blue background with a painted green rim.

- *height 21cm*
- **Guide price £100/$189**

Royal Worcester Spaniel ▲

- *circa 1909*

Royal Worcester model of a brown and white spaniel recumbent on a tasselled gilt cushion. Mark to the base.

- *height 4cm*
- **Guide price £355/$671**

Baxter Plate ▼

- *1999*

Glen Baxter plate created for the Poole pottery showing cartoon printed on the face, wording around the edge of the rim and Glen Baxter's signature.

- *diameter 22cm*
- **Guide price £18/$34**

Ceramic Group ▼

- *20th century*

Fine ceramic group depicting Diana the huntress after the hunt, by Giovanni Grande for the Lenci Factory, Italy.

- *height 39cm*
- **Guide price £4,300/$8,127**

Worcester Pot Pourri ▲

- *1904*

Worcester pot pourri and cover.

- *height 25cm*
- **Guide price £800/$1,512**

Worcester Cup and Saucer Set ▼

- *20th century*

Early 20th-century Worcester cup and saucer, decorated with gilded swirls to the rim and solid gilding to centre and handle of cup, the whole on a blue ground.

- *height 5cm*
- **Guide price £45/$85**

Moorcroft Vase ▲

- *1994*

Lisa Moorcroft vase of oriental shape, with poppy flower and leaf design in red and green, on a green base.

- *height 14cm*
- **Guide price £105/$198**

Poole Studio Plate ▼

- *1999*

Showing a scene of a sunset with seagull, predominantly in black, orange and blue glaze. By Tony Morris, with Poole dolphin mark.

- *diameter 40cm*
- **Guide price £450/$851**

Swedish Sculpture ▲

- *1953*

Swedish abstract sculpture in avant garde style, of interwoven, architectural designs forming an asymmetrical whole and painted in black and white. The shape and the colour combine to create a complex play on light and form.

- *height 25cm*
- **Guide price £1,500/$2,835**

Deep Dish on Stand ▼

- *1928*

Made at the Rembrandt factory in Gouda and decorated at the Zuid-Holland factory. Tulip border with water lily in centre.

- *diameter 36cm*
- **Guide price £600/$1,134**

Lotus Pattern Poole Plate ▲

- *1999*

A contemporary and highly collectable Poole studio plate, printed with dolphin mark and signed "N. Massarella". Painted with a lotus pattern with orange glaze. Black glaze on the reverse.

- *diameter 40cm*
- **Guide price £300/$567**

Gouda Tile ▲

- *1923–1930*

Zuid-Holland factory. Gouda tile, with stork motif, designed by Jan Schonk.

- *11 x 19cm*
- **Guide price £350/$662**

Gagnier Vase ▼

- *circa 1998*

Double cone form with spherical centre around which are four nodules. Olivier Gagnier, Italy.

- *height 49cm*
- **Guide price £250/$473**

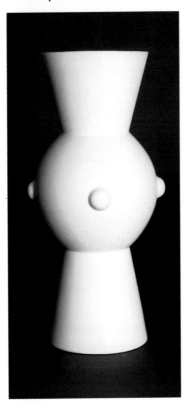

Blue-rimmed Bowl ▼

- *1999*

A bowl showing a hare positioned among woods and hills with the crescent moon and two stars. Corn and bean decoration and blue rim.

- *diameter 18cm*
- **Guide price £36/$68**

Royal Worcester Bird ◄

- *1936*

American bluebird of a limited edition perched on apple blossom branch. Shown to life size depicting a spring scene, the whole standing on a wooden plinth.

- *height 30cm*
- **Guide price £900/$1,701**

Gouda Night Light ▲

- *1915*

Zuid-Holland factory. Design 'A Jour'. Made for La Marquise de Sevigne Rouzand'.

- *height 17.5cm*
- **Guide price £300/$567**

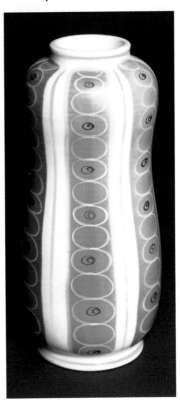

Poole Vase ▲

- *circa 1950s*

Organic shape with blue, grey and green abstract vertical banners, interlacing circles. Stamped with dolphin mark.

- *height 20cm*
- **Guide price £450/$851**

Bird on Pine Cone ▼

- *circa 1950*

Poole pottery. Bluetit on a pine cone. Heavily modelled naturalistic representation, with pine-cone design reflected in the plumage.

- *height 12cm*
- **Guide price £70/$133**

Albino Rabbit ▼

- *circa 1930*

Japanese model of a comical, albino rabbit, with pink highlights, painted red eyes, disproportionately small feet and large, caricatured ears.

- *height 22cm*
- **Guide price £780/$1,475**

Solitary Polar Bear ▼

- *1920s*

Royal Copenhagen solitary polar bear walking on all fours, all feet on the ground. Dated and signed.

- *height 10cm*
- **Guide price £280/$530**

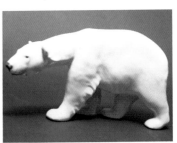

Paysage Vase ▲

- *circa 1930*

Zuid-Holland factory. Gouda 'Paysage' vase. Realistically painted farmer with horse ploughing, with sunset sky in background.

- *height 47cm*
- **Guide price £950/$1,796**

Elephant Bookends ▲

- *circa 1920s*

Pair of pink French elephant bookends in working pose, on octagonal plinths.

- *height 15cm*
- **Guide price £150/$284**

Jersey Cow ▼

- *circa 1950*

A Royal Worcester Jersey cow, standing on a wooden plinth. Part of a limited edition, all modelled on champion stock by Doris Lindner.

- *height 19cm*
- **Guide price £490/$927**

Picasso Plate ▼

- *1930s*

Ovate form, raised decoration of face. Hand-painted and glazed. Foundry stamped and numbered 22/100.

- *height 31cm*
- **Guide price £6,000/$11,340**

Glazed Inkwell ▼

- *1915*

Zuid-Holland factory. Gouda. Glazed inkwell with two lids. By A.M. Rijp.

- *length 22cm*
- **Guide price £250/$473**

Royal Bonn Vase ◄

- *1916*

'Old Dutch' design vase of bulbous form, with disproportionately narrow, baluster-shaped neck. By Frank Anton Mehlem.

- *height 21cm*
- **Guide price £350/$662**

Vienna Baluster Vase ▲

- *circa 1925*

Ernst Wahliss 'Pergamon' Vienna baluster vase. Abstract floral pattern with lustre finish.

- *height 32cm*
- **Guide price £300/$567**

Lion's Head Vase ▲

- *1999*

Dennis Chinaworks vase of bulbous form, showing three resplendant lion heads on an interlacing background of burnt orange and yellow glaze.

- *height 21cm*
- **Guide price £300/$567**

Eagle and Pine Tree Vase ▶

- *1924*

Unusually large Royal Copenhagen vase, signed and dated. Baluster form vase with eagle and pine tree decoration.

- *height 49cm*
- **Guide price £7,500/$14,175**

Dessert Plates ▲

- *1935*

Part of set of Royal Worcester plates in silver form with beaded gilt edge. Fruit Worcester design of apples, peaches and grapes painted by Smith.

- *diameter 24cm*
- **Guide price £200/$378 each**

Gouda Bowl ▲

- *1931*

Zuid-Holland factory. Gouda bowl. Design 'Floro'.

- *height 12cm*
- **Guide price £225/$426**

Poole Pottery Vase ▼
- *circa 1950*
A hand-painted and hand-decorated Poole pottery vase, decorated in blue and yellow with a vertical alternating pattern.
- *height 18cm*
- **Guide price £250/$473**

Spiral Poole Plate ▼
- *1999*
A Poole pottery plate showing a spiral pattern in red glaze with blue overglaze and black overglaze on the reverse. Signed by Janice Tchalenko.
- *diameter 40cm*
- **Guide price £375/$709**

Polar Bears ▲
- *circa 1920s*
Royal Copenhagen model of two adult polar bears fighting. The whole design is circular in form, giving it momentum. Signed.
- *height 15.5cm*
- **Guide price £475/$898**

Union Jack Poole Plate ▲
- *1999*
A Poole pottery plate showing the Union Jack pattern in red, white and blue glaze. Yellow glaze on the reverse with dolphin mark and date and signed by Nicky Massarella.
- *diameter 40cm*
- **Guide price £400/$756**

Painted Poole Vase ▼
- *circa 1950s*
Poole pottery vase showing the printed dolphin mark. Paint has been applied directly to the pot, unlike the ealier pre-war models which were terracotta with a tin glaze. Decoration shows an asymmetrical serpentine pattern with yellow and black detailing.
- *height 29cm*
- **Guide price £500/$945**

Gouda Baluster Vase ▼
- *1920*
From Regina factory, Zuid-Holland. A baluster vase in the 'D'Arla' design, with repeated design of stylised bird, swirls and floral decoration, with matt gilding, rich blues and black.
- *height 43cm*
- **Guide price £300/$567**

Two Bluetits ◄
- *1961*
A pair of Royal Worcester bluetits, male and female, made by Dorothy Doughty. Made to lifesize, showing a spring scene with pussy willow, each mounted on a wooden plinth.
- **Guide price £750/$1,418**

Monkey with Baby ▲
- *1920s*
Royal Copenhagen model of a monkey with baby. Signed and dated. Matt stone finish with grey and blue glaze.
- *height 17cm*
- **Guide price £750/$1,418**

Zuid-Holland Candlesticks ▲
- *1923*
Gouda pair of candlesticks in the 'Rio' design, with extra-large, moulded drip-pans and globular bases tapering upwards.
- *height 30cm*
- **Guide price £360/$681 (pair)**

Tea Service ▲
- *circa 1920s*
Belleek Irish porcelain tea service with shamrock pattern and a basketweave design with twig handle. Stamped with black mark. Made in Fermanagh.
- **Guide price £1,500/$2,835**

CLOCKS & WATCHES

Small Gold Hunter Coin Watch ▼

- *circa 1910*
A Swiss cylinder in a small gold full hunter case, the lids formed from the two halves of a French 20 franc coin dated 1908. When closed the watch resembles a stack of three gold coins.
- *diameter 2cm*
- **Guide price £975/$1,843**

Eight-Day French Clock ▲

- *circa 1930*
Unusual boulle mantel clock with French eight-day movement regulated by a cylinder escapement.
- *height 15cm*
- **Guide price £1,275/$2,410**

Blue Enamel Clock ▲

- *circa 1930*
Art Deco blue enamel guilloche clock.
- *height 11cm*
- **Guide price £675/$1,276**

Tiffany & Co. Watch ▼

- *1920s*
Ladies Tiffany & Co. Set in 9ct rose gold white enamelled dial with arabic numerals and a red number 12.
- *diameter 2cm*
- **Guide price £500/$945**

Gunmetal World Time Watch ▼

- *circa 1910*
A Swiss lever with world time dial in a gunmetal open face case. White enamel dial with gold decoration.
- *diameter 52mm*
- **Guide price £1,750/$3,308**

Art Deco Clock ▲

- *circa 1930*
Art Deco chinoiserie-decorated clock with mother-of-pearl dial with geometric blue enamelling.
- *height 10cm*
- **Guide price £1,475/$2,788**

Aviator's Chronograph ▲

- *circa 1968*
An aviator's "Navitimer" chronograph by Breitling, with subsidiary dials for sweep seconds, minute and hour recording. Outer rotating bezel allowing various aviation calculations. Case # 1307320 Ref # 806.
- **Guide price £1,800/$3,402**

Chinoiserie Clock ▲

- *circa 1930*
A brass dial with a blue chinoiserie figurative frame resting on a brass stand.
- *20cm x 20cm*
- **Guide price £420/$794**

Ladies Movado Watch ▼

- *1940s*
Ladies Movado Swiss-made 8ct rose gold wrist watch with a square face and two-tone dial with arabic numerals.
- *diameter 1.9cm*
- **Guide price £450/$851**

Art Deco Timepiece ▼

- *circa 1930*
Art Deco silver clock with enamel flying birds in the chinoiserie style.
- *11cm x 8cm*
- **Guide price £1,275/$2,410**

Boudoir Clock ▲

- *circa 1930*
A rare silver and enamel clock with watch inset.
- *6cm x 8cm*
- **Guide price £2,450/$4,631**

Rolex Watch ▶

- *circa 1920s*
Silver tonneau-shaped gents wrist watch. The white enamel dial signed Rolex, with luminous numerals and hands and subsidiary seconds. The 3pc case signed "Rolex 7 Worlds Records Gold Medal Geneva Suisse (RWC Ltd) #64948". The lever movement signed Rolex Swiss made. 15 rubies.
- **Guide price £2,550/$4,820**

Silver Swiss Half Hunter ▼

- *circa 1910*
A Swiss lever in a silver half hunter case. White enamel dial with subsidiary seconds, arabic numerals and blue steel hands.
- *diameter 5cm*
- **Guide price £495/$936**

Omega Watch ▼

- *1950s*
Swiss-made gents Omega 18ct gold mechanical movement watch with auxiliary sweep seconds and a gold dial with gold hands and gold digits.
- *diameter 3.1cm*
- **Guide price £650/$1,229**

Universal Geneve ▼

- *circa 1939*
An early 18ct gold Compax two-button chronograph with subsidiary seconds, minute and hour recording dials.
- **Guide price £3,900/$7,371**

Rolex Oyster Watch ▲

- *1920s*

Rolex Oyster precision auxiliary sweep seconds white dial. Two, four, eight, ten and 12 in arabic numerals, set in stainless steel.
- *diameter 1.6cm*
- **Guide price £650/$1,229**

Travelling Timepiece ▲

- *circa 1930*

Art Deco silver with enamel travelling clock stamped "Levi Nande".
- *2.5cm x 2cm*
- **Guide price £825/$1,559**

Bulova Wrist Watch ▼

- *1920s*

Ladies Bulova wrist watch set in 18ct gold with white dial. three, six, nine and 12 in arabic numerals with serrated lugs, on a black leather cocktail strap.
- *diameter 1.1cm*
- **Guide price £200/$378**

Ladies Swiss Watch ▼

- *1920s*

Ladies Swiss made 18ct gold with a white enamelled dial with Roman numerals.
- *diameter 2.7cm*
- **Guide price £400/$756**

Hexagonal Watch ◄

- *1920s*

Ladies silver hexagonal wrist watch with white enamel dial, auxiliary sweep seconds and a red number 12.
- *diameter 2cm*
- **Guide price £250/$473**

Gents Rolex Watch ▲

- *1960*

Gents Rolex Oyster perpetual explorer wristwatch on a Rolex Oyster expandable bracelet.
- *diameter 3cm*
- **Guide price £2,400/$4,536**

Green Enamel Clock ▲

- *circa 1931*

Silver and green Art Deco guilloche enamel clock.
- *10cm x 11cm*
- **Guide price £875/$1,654**

Bracelet Watch ▲

- *1920s*

Ladies Swiss-made wrist watch in 18ct rose gold with enamel dial with old cut diamonds on the bezel, on an expandable 18ct rose gold bracelet.
- *diameter 1.7cm.*
- **Guide price £500/$945**

Romer Wrist Watch ▼

- *1950s*

Ladies Swiss-made Romer wrist watch set in 9ct gold on a 9ct gold bracelet with safety chain. White dial with three, six, nine and 12 in arabic numerals.
- *diameter 1.2cm*
- **Guide price £250/$473**

Ladies Oyster Watch ▼

- *1930s*

Rolex Oyster precision ladies stainless steel wrist watch with a white dial and trianglular digits.
- *diameter 1.8cm*
- **Guide price £650/$1,229**

Omega Watch ▼

- circa 1938

An 18ct gold wrist chronograph with subsidiary seconds and 30 minute register dial. Inner pulsations scale and base 1000 scale. The case signed "Omega &" with Swiss control marks. CS #9174757. The movement signed "Omega Watch Company. 17 Jls #9388131.C333."

- **Guide price £6,500/$12,285**

Lemania Chronograph ▶

- 1953

An Air Ministry RAF issue, pilots high-grade one button chronograph with a steel case. The dial signed "Lemania &" with MOD Arrow, minute recording dial and sweep second dial. The case with fixed bar lugs and back with ordinance marks, "Arrow AM/6B/551 333/53".

- **Guide price £1,800/$3,402**

Omega Watch ▲

- 1950s

Gents Omega watch set in 9ct gold on a white dial with gold arabic numerals and auxiliary sweep seconds.

- diameter 2.9cm
- **Guide price £350/$662**

Silver and Blue Clock ◀

- circa 1930

Silver and blue enamel Art Deco strut clock with Swiss dial.

- height 11cm
- **Guide price £765/$1,446**

Omega Seamaster Wrist Watch ▲

- 1940s

Gents Omega Seamaster wrist watch set in stainless steel automatic movement, two-tone dial with gold digits.

- diameter 2.9cm
- **Guide price £300/$567**

Hunting Chronograph ▶

- 1907

Swiss-made Hunting Split Secondsi Chronograph with subsidiary minute recording and sweep second dials. Case ~ 130519. The white enamel dial signed "S. Smith & Son 9. The Strand London Maker to the Admiralty. # 142B 68. Non Magnetizable Swiss Made."

- **Guide price £2,950/$5,576**

Fly-Back Chronograph ▲

- circa 1970

A rare German air force issue aviator's "Fly-Back" chronograph by Heuer in steel. The black dial with subsidiary seconds and minute recording dial 1 and red "3H" in circle, case # 6445-12-146-3774 and stamped "BUNDWEHR".

- **Guide price £2,200/$4,158**

Omega Seamaster Watch ▲

- 1950s

Gentleman's Omega seamaster wrist watch set in stainless steel with a black dial with white roman numerals. Mechanical movement and a screw back case. Red second hand.

- diameter 2.9cm
- **Guide price £300/$567**

Vacheron Constantin Watch ▼

- 1960s

Gents Vacheron Constantin 18ct white gold wrist watch with oblong design black dial with white gold digits.

- diameter 1.9cm
- **Guide price £1,300/$2,457**

Benson Watch ▲

- *1940s*

J.W. Benson ladies wrist watch set in 9ct gold with fancy lugs amd white dial with arabic numerals.

- *diameter 1.7cm*
- **Guide price £250/$473**

Mappin & Webb Clock ▲

- *circa 1911*

A well-made mahogany eight day double fusée English bracket clock retailed by Mappin & Webb Ltd, Oxford Street, London W1. The finely figured mahogany case includes olive wood inlaid panel and boxwood stringing sitting on ball feet. With engraved silvered convex brass dial signed "Mappin & Webb", with blue steel counter poised moon hands.

- *37cm x 23cm*
- **Guide price £2,500/$4,725**

Gents Longines Wrist Watch ▼

- *1930s*

Gents Longines wrist watch with oblong design and set in 14ct. rose gold, with white dial set with gold arabic numerals and auxiliary sweep seconds.

- *diameter 1.8cm*
- **Guide price £950/$1,796**

Asprey Dial Clock ▼

- *circa 1920*

Rosewood with satinwood inlays and the dial signed by Asprey. French eight-day cylinder escapement.

- *height 45cm*
- **Guide price £1,700/$3,213**

Flightmaster Chronograph ◄

- *circa 1978*

A steel aviator's "Flightmaster" chronograph by Omega, with multifunction dial and internal rotating bezel. This watch comes with the original box and papers.

- **Guide price £1,800/$3,402**

Propelling Pencil ▼

- *circa 1920*

French propelling pencil with timepiece in engine turned body. With Swiss lever 15 jewelled movement. French control marks and struck. 925 monogram to case "MA".

- **Guide price £1,950/$3,686**

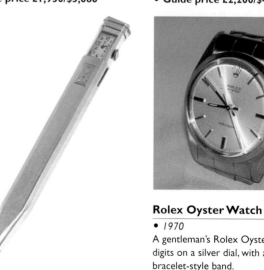

Globe Clock ▲

- *circa 1920*

Unusual globe converted to a clock with circular timepiece on a mahogany stand with attached movement, made in Leipzig.

- *61cm x 30cm*
- **Guide price £2,200/$4,158**

Rolex Oyster Watch ▲

- *1970*

A gentleman's Rolex Oyster watch with digits on a silver dial, with an Oyster bracelet-style band.

- *diameter 3cm*
- **Guide price £650/$1,229**

Air King Wrist Watch ▲
- *1960s*

Gentleman's Rolex Oyster perpetual Air King Model wrist watch in steel and gold. Automatic movement, white dial with gold digits, with a sunburst bezel.
- *diameter 3cm*
- **Guide price £1,400/$2,646**

Gold Rolex Watch ▼
- *1935*

A 9ct gold gents Rolex wrist watch. The dial signed "Rolex Swiss Made", with subsidiary seconds. The case signed "Rolex 25 World Records Geneva Suisse R.W.C. Ltd. # 19736 ref # 2356. Movement Sig Rolex Precision 17 Rubies Patented Superbalance Swiss Made."
- **Guide price £4,500/$8,505**

Oyster Speedking Watch ▼
- *1950s*

Boys size Rolex Oyster Speedking. Stainless steel mechanical movement with silver digits and expandable Rolex Oyster bracelet.
- *diameter 2.8cm*
- **Guide price £950/$1,796**

Cushion-shaped Watch ◄
- *1924*

Gents silver cushion-shaped wrist watch. The movement signed "Rolex 15 Jewels Swiss Made" Cal 507 Rebberg Depose. The case back signed "RWC Ltd." (Rolex Watch Company). The case frame # 655. The dial signed "Rolex Swiss Made". Lug size 22.5mm.
- *diameter 2.3cm*
- **Guide price £2,850/$5,387**

Rolex Wrist Watch ▲
- *1918*

Ladies Rolex wrist watch with white enamelled dial set in 9ct gold. Black arabic numerals.
- *diameter 2cm*
- **Guide price £580/$1,097**

Rolex Cushion Watch ▲
- *1920s*

Gentleman's Rolex cushion wrist watch set in 9ct gold. With white enamel dial, auxiliary sweep seconds and a red number 12. Rolex signature underneath the dial.
- *diameter 2.5cm*
- **Guide price £950/$1,796**

Folding Clock ▼
- *circa 1927*

English silver and enamel folding travelling clock. Birmingham.
- *height 4cm*
- **Guide price £675/$1,276**

Trench Guard Watch ▼
- *circa 1915*

A First World War large size officer's wrist watch with original mesh "Trench Guard". The white enamel dial with subsidiary seconds, signed "Omega." The case struck Omega Depose No. 9846 case # 5425073. The movement with Swan Neck Micro Reg. Signed Omega # 211504.
- *diameter 4.2cm*
- **Guide price £2,250/$4,253**

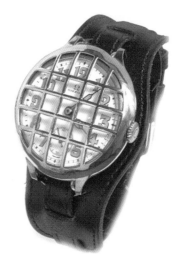

Pocket Watch ◄
- *circa 1920*

A high grade fully jewelled minute repeating open face pocket watch, with dial with subsidiary seconds. The case with Swiss control marks for 18ct gold and case # 62837. Repeating activated by a slide on the band.
- **Guide price £4,800/$9,072**

Longines Watch ▲
- *1940*

Ladies Longines wrist watch set in stainless steel with 3, 6, 9 arabic numerals. Screw back, for original waterproofing.
- *diameter 1.9cm*
- **Guide price £340/$643**

Mantel Clock ▲

- *1904*
A small red leather and silver fronted timepiece mantel clock. Silver hallmarked Birmingham 1904. Eight-day movement on platform escapement in very original condition, white enamel dial with Roman black numerals and black spade hands.
- *20cm x 10cm*
- **Guide price £850/$1,607**

Jaeger-LeCoultre Watch ▲

- *circa 1960*
Jaeger-LeCoultre Memovox (alarm) Stainless steel wrist watch with silver digits on a silver face and automatic movement.
- *diameter 4cm*
- **Guide price £1,500/$2,835**

Oyster Wrist Watch ▶

- *1950s*
Gents Rolex Oyster Royal watch set in stainless steel with a white mottled dial with 3,6,9 arabic numerals, Mercedes hands and mechanical movement.
- *diameter 2.6cm*
- **Guide price £800/$1,512**

Oyster Royal Watch ▲

- *circa 1947*
An Oyster "Royal" waterproof Rolex wrist watch, with centre seconds. The case signed "Rolex Geneve Suisse" with screw down Oyster button and case # 506021. Ref # 4444.
- **Guide price £1,550/$2,930**

Ladies Oyster Watch ▼

- *1920s*
Ladies Rolex Oyster wrist watch set in 14ct gold with mechanical movement, a sunburst dial, auxiliary sweep seconds and a white face with gold numbers.
- *diameter 2cm*
- **Guide price £1,500/$2,835**

Peerless Wrist Watch ◀

- *1934*
A gents wrist watch, the movement jewelled to the centre signed "Peerless" Swiss Made # 332257 with S & Co Logo. The case # 331618-2 & FB fo Francis Baumgartner Borgelle case designer Enamel dial subsidiary seconds.
- *diameter 3.3cm*
- **Guide price £2,750/$5,198**

Ladies Rolex Wrist Watch ▼

- *1940*
Ladies 18ct rose gold Rolex wrist watch with original expanding strap with the Rolex symbol on the buckle square face with scalloped lugs. Gold digits on a white face.
- *diameter 2cm*
- **Guide price £1,800/$3,402**

Russian Wall Clock ▲

- *1960*
An unusual geometrically designed Russian wall clock in painted red wood, with a white dial and a raised white circular hoop. Designed by Jantaz.
- *height 40cm*
- **Guide price £45/$85**

English Bakelite Clock ▲

- *1950*

An English brown, bakelite clock with circular dial, free standing on square base and feet. Manufactured by Smith Electric of England.

- *15cm x 12cm*
- **Guide price £45/$85**

Peerless Ladies Watch ▼

- *circa 1930s*

An hexagonal, Peerless ladies watch in platinum with a light silvered dial, black arabic numerals and hands, and an expandable gold bracelet. Swiss movement with an English case.

- *diameter 2cm*
- **Guide price £1,875/$3,544**

Navigational Stop Watch ▼

- *circa 1940*

A rare Hamilton navigational stop watch with a black dial including subseconds and a minute recorder. The chrome nickel case has U.S. ordinance marks: "FCCS No.88-W-590 MERS PART NO.37297 SERIAL NO.3560-42". The movement with micrometer adjustment, adjusts to temperature with three positions. Includes original US military issue box.

- **Guide price £1,200/$2,268**

Gilt Lacquer Clock ◄

- *circa 1970*

A gilt lacquer Atmos Jaeger-LeCoultre mantel timepiece with the original white fitted case. Silvered dial on a gilt pierced sunburst ground with a pendulum aperture, in a rectangular black lacquer case, together with the original fitted case.

- *35.5cm x 23cm x 15cm*
- **Guide price £950/$1,796**

Military Pocket Watch ▲

- *circa 1939*

A rare British military issue Rolex pocket watch. The dial signed "Rolex A9172", has sub seconds and luminous numerals and hands. The nickel case signed inside "Rolex", with ordinance marks "A9172 G.S.M.K.II" on the back of the outside case and "A9172" on the outside band.

- **Guide price £975/$1,843**

Rolex Prince Watch ▲

- *circa 1929*

Rare Prince chronometer gents watch. Dial features original, enamelled numerals and tracks.

- **Guide price £6,650/$12,569**

Rolex Pocket Watch ▼

- *circa 1930*

A Rolex sterling silver pocket watch with white enamel dial with subsidiary seconds. The 17-jewelled movement signed "Rolex". Swiss-made British import marks for the year 1930.

- **Guide price £2,250/$4,253**

Ladies Wrist Watch ◄

- *circa 1960*

An 18ct. gold Jaeger-LeCoultre ladies wrist watch with square face and white dial with roman numerals.

- *diameter 1.5cm*
- **Guide price £645/$1,219**

Omega Ladies Watch ▼

- *circa 1950*

An 18ct. covered gold Omega ladies watch with a gold-linked bracelet strap which, together with the lid, is encrusted with diamonds and Burma rubies.

- *diameter 3cm*
- **Guide price £2,750/$5,198**

Desk Compendium ▲

- *circa 1902*

A gilt bronze and green enamel French desk compendium in an original leather travelling case. Eight-day movement with original silvered English lever platform escapement. Presented to "VWL Parnett Botfield Esq" by the servants of the Hut on his coming of age, December 29, 1902.
- *15cm x 16.5cm x 6cm*
- **Guide price £2,300/$4,347**

Constellation Watch ▲

- *1960*

A stainless steel gents Omega constellation watch with digits on a silver face with a steel flip-lock bracelet.
- *diameter 3cm*
- **Guide price £425/$803**

Cartier Watch ▼

- *1968*

An 18ct. gold Cartier tank watch with a square face and a white dial with roman numerals. Sapphire winding button. French marked.
- *diameter 2cm*
- **Guide price £2,250/$4,253**

Cocktail Watch ▼

- *circa 1930s*

A ladies platinum cocktail watch with diamonds set around the face and arabic numerals on the dial, with a white expandable platinum bracelet.
- *diameter 3cm*
- **Guide price £1,150/$2,174**

Longines Cocktail Watch ◄

- *circa 1960s*

A delicate Longines ladies platinum and diamond manual wind cocktail watch, with a diamond encrusted strap. Swiss movement with an English case.
- *diameter 1.5cm*
- **Guide price £3,250/$6,143**

Propeller Clock ▲

- *circa 1917–18*

An Hispana Suiza working clock mounted on a mahogany propeller from a Sopworth Dolphin Scout airplane.
- *260cm x 26cm x 17cm*
- **Guide price £1,780/$3,365**

Ladies Dress Watch ▲

- *circa 1930s*

Delicate ladies dress watch in platinum with diamonds on a silk strap. Swiss movement with an English case.
- *1.5cm x 1cm*
- **Guide price £1,100/$2,079**

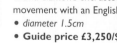

Pin Set Wrist Watch ▼

- *circa 1915*

A rare gents pin set wrist watch by H.Y. Moser & Cie in 14ct. pink gold with high-grade lever movement and engraved and enamelled dial. Features a very large tonneau-shaped case with hinged lugs. The case is signed "H.Y. Moser & Cie No. 635235", with Russian hallmarks.
- **Guide price £2,750/$5,198**

Art Deco Watch ▼

- *circa 1940*

A ladies curved 18ct. heavy gold bracelet cocktail watch with an Art Deco design. Swiss movement.
- *width 2cm*
- **Guide price £875/$1,654**

Vintage Ladies Watch ◄

- *circa 1925*

An hexagonal vintage ladies 9ct. gold watch with a 9ct. gold expandable bracelet. With arabic figures on a white porcelain face, and a second minute dial.
- *diameter 2.5cm*
- **Guide price £275/$520**

Swiss Chronograph ▶

- *circa 1950*

A high grade Swiss-made sterling silver, hunting case "Split Seconds" chronograph with subsidiary minute recording and sweep second dials. Case number 130519. The white enamel dial signed "S.Smith & Son, 9 The Strand, London, Maker to the Admiralty, No. 142B 68, Non Magnetizable Swiss Made".

- **Guide price £2,950/$5,576**

Omega Ladies Watch ▲

- *1970s*

An Omega ladies watch in 18ct. white gold with diamonds set around the bezel and a smooth 18ct. satin integral bracelet of average size. With roman numerals on an enamelled dial.

- *diameter 2.5cm*
- **Guide price £1,125/$2,126**

Gold Pocket Watch ▲

- *1920*

A gents gold pocket watch with top-wind button set by Thomas Russell.

- *diameter 4cm*
- **Guide price £250/$473**

Swiss Mantel Clock ▲

- *1960*

A Swiss Jaeger-LeCoultre Atmos timepiece with white chapter ring and gilt arabic numerals. Signed "Swiss made". This clock never needs winding.

- *22cm x 17cm x 14cm*
- **Guide price £1,200/$2,268**

Asprey Watch ▼

- *circa 1916*

Silver Asprey rectangular curved watch with white metal dial and Roman numerals.

- **Guide price £260/$492**

Hexagonal Rolex Watch ▼

- *1920*

A hexagonal 9ct. gold lady's Rolex watch with arabic figures on a gold dial.

- *diameter 2.5 cm*
- **Guide price £550/$1,040**

Chagrin Mantel Clock ▲

- *1920*

English-made chagrin leather cased clock, with a white face and white ivory stringing, the whole resting on ivory feet.

- *height 14cm*
- **Guide price £2,750/$5,198**

Lustre Ware Clock ▶

- *1905*

Ceramic lustre ware clock by Louis Fuler, an American who revolutionised dance in France.

- *height 27cm*
- **Guide price £350/$662**

Ladies Platinum and Diamond Watch ▼

- *circa 1930s*

A ladies platinum and diamond watch by Longines, with arabic numerals on a white face and a gold integral twin snake bracelet. Swiss movement with an English case.

- *diameter 1.5cm*
- **Guide price £895/$1,692**

Bulova Wrist Watch ▼

- *1930*

A gents rectangular, gold plated and curved, manual wind wrist watch by Bulova. White dial with gold arabic numerals and subsidiary seconds.

- *3.5cm x 2cm*
- **Guide price £295/$558**

Swiss Wrist Watch ▶

- *1950s*

A Swiss-made 18ct. gold wrist watch with roman numerals and gold batons on a silvered face with subsidiary seconds.

- *diameter 3.5cm*
- **Guide price £2,300/$4,347**

Hamilton Watch ▲

- *1930*

A rectangular gents gold-plated manual wind watch by Hamilton with gold roman numerals on a white enamel dial with subsidiary seconds.

- *3.5cm x 2.5cm*
- **Guide price £375/$709**

Oyster Submariner Diving Watch ▲

- *circa 1964*

Oyster Perpetual Submariner automatic diver's wrist watch, on a Rolex steel "flip-lock" bracelet.

- **Guide price £2,950/$5,576**

Military Issue Watch ▼

- *1940*

A military issue pocket watch by Waltman, with white arabic numerals on a black dial with subsidiary seconds.

- *3.5cm diameter*
- **Guide price £75/$142**

Signed Rolex Watch ▼

- *1940*

A 9ct. gold ladies Rolex watch, with a linked gold bracelet strap. Back plate signed "MA".

- *2.5cm square*
- **Guide price £275/$520**

Rolex Precision Watch ▲

- *1958*

A 9ct. gold Rolex Precision watch with an original Rolex strap.

- *diameter 3cm*
- **Guide price £1,100/$2,079**

Rolex Oyster Perpetual ▲

- *circa 1952*

18ct. gold Rolex Perpetual wrist watch with moon-phase calendar.

- **Guide price £35,000/$66,150**

Rolex Silver Pocket Watch ◀

- *circa 1920*

A silver Rolex pocket watch with a circular blue enamel insert to the outer casing of the watch.

- *diameter 4cm*
- **Guide price £700/$1,323**

Lord Elgin Wrist Watch ▲

- *1950*

A rectangular, gold-plated Lord Elgin gents wrist watch with subsidiary seconds by the Elgin National Watch Company.

- *width 3.5cm*
- **Guide price £275/$520**

Olympics Commemorative Watch ▲

- *1972*

A rare, limited edition commemorative wrist watch by Longines, which features a stamp from the Olympic games in Munich. With silvered baton numerals on a white dial.

- *diameter 3cm*
- **Guide price £295/$558**

Longines Wrist Watch ▲

- *1980*

A rectangular ladies 9ct. gold quartz Longines wrist watch with a diamond-set linked bracelet. White dial with arabic numerals.

- *2.5cm x 2cm*
- **Guide price £495/$936**

Breitling Navitimer Chronograph ◀

- *1960s*

A gents silver aviator's watch with the chronograph operated by two pushers on the case band. Made by Breitling Navitimer. The black dial has subsidiary seconds and minute recording dial.

- *diameter 4cm*
- **Guide price £950/$1,796**

Bulova Gentleman's Wrist Watch ▼

- *1940*

A rectangular, gold-plated, curved gentleman's wrist watch by Bulova. With gold baton and black arabic numerals on a white dial, with subsidiary seconds.

- *width 3.5cm*
- **Guide price £395/$748**

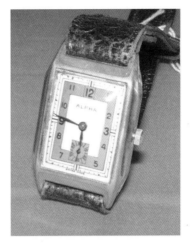

IWC Octagonal Watch ▶

- *circa 1923*

An octagonal IWC 18ct. wrist watch with arabic numerals on a silver face.

- *width 3cm*
- **Guide price £1,000/$1,890**

Vintage Ladies Watch ◀

- *circa 1930s*

Ladies 18ct. gold watch with leather strap. White porcelain dial with roman numerals and a red number 12, with black cathedral hands. Swiss lever movement and a black leather bracelet.

- *width 3cm*
- **Guide price £275/$520**

Ladies Gold Watch ▲

- *1915*

Rolex 9ct. gold watch with red numeral 12, enamel dial and expanding bracelet.

- **Guide price £700/$1,323**

Cine Alpha Wrist Watch ▲

- *1940*

A gold-plated gents Cine Alpha wrist watch, with black arabic numerals on an orange band within a white dial.

- *diameter 3.5cm*
- **Guide price £95/$180**

Platinum Watch ▼

- *circa 1930*

A platinum and diamond wrist watch with a sprung platinum bracelet. A light silvered face with five numerals in black and a red number 12 with an outer chapter ring

- *1.5cm x 1cm*
- **Guide price £1,275/$2,410**

Movado Wrist Watch ▲

- *1950s*

A gents 18ct. gold Movado wrist watch, with an interesting dial arrangement with silver batons and a crocodile strap.
- *diameter 4cm*
- **Guide price £650/$1,229**

Ladies Rose Gold Watch ▲

- *circa 1940s*

A square ladies precision Rolex watch in 18ct. rose gold with an original Rolex flexi-strap.
- *diameter 1.5cm*
- **Guide price £1,800/$3,402**

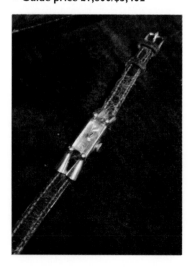

White Gold Watch ▼

- *circa 1950s*

Ladies Rolex watch in 18ct. white gold. Integral strap with a square white dial with silvered batons and black hands. Leaver movement, Rolex case and named movement.
- *1.5cm square*
- **Guide price £875/$1,654**

Duel-Dial Wrist Watch ▼

- *late 1940s*

A Rolex Prince 9ct. gold, dual-dial, curved-back wrist watch. Features flared sides and a crocodile strap.
- *length 3.5cm*
- **Guide price £2,900/$5,481**

Juvnenia Ladies Watch ◄

- *circa 1940s*

A rectangular 18ct. gold ladies watch by Juvnenia with an original crocodile strap.
- *1.5 x 2cm*
- **Guide price £1,200/$2,268**

Vacheron Constantin Watch ▲

- *circa 1960s*

A rectangular white gold 18ct. Vacheron Constantin manual movement watch, with silver digits on a black dial.
- *3.5cm x 2cm*
- **Guide price £1,500/$2,835**

Rolex Ladies Watch ▼

- *1920*

Rolex ladies sprung bracelet 9ct. gold watch with a Rolex-named movement and back plate. Features a white porcelain face with a red number 12, and a secondary minute dial.
- *diameter 3cm*
- **Guide price £750/$1,418**

Fob Watch ▼

- *1910*

Large gold fob watch by Vertex Revue, with black roman numerals on a white face with a subsidiary seconds dial.
- *diameter 5cm*
- **Guide price £223/$422**

Rolex Gents Dress Wrist Watch ▼

- *1933*

A rare Rolex 9ct. gold gents dress watch with rectangular cut corner case. Marked "Ref#1918 Case #9817", plus British import marks for the year 1933. The movement is signed "Rolex Hairspring 15 Rubies Swiss Made". The dial is signed "Rolex & Swiss Made" with a subsidiary dial showing seconds.

- **Guide price £3,350/$6,332**

Rolex Prince "Brancarde" ▼

- *circa 1930*

A Rolex Prince "Brancarde" wrist watch in sterling silver, case number "0559 Ref #971", movement number "#72147". This magnificent chronometer is in its original box with the original two-part chronometer rating certificate dated 1930, the original strap and Rolex sterling silver buckle.

- **Guide price £12,500/$23,625**

Victorian Ladies Dress Watch ▶

- *circa 1900s*

A Victorian 15ct. gold ladies dress watch with rubies and diamonds on a gate-type sprung bracelet with numerals in blue and red. With gold decoration on a white porcelain dial.

- *diameter 2.5cm*
- **Guide price £1,700/$3,213**

Ladies Rolex Watch ▲

- *circa 1957*

A 9ct. gold ladies Rolex watch with black arabic numerals on a white enamelled dial with subsidiary seconds.

- *diameter 2.7cm*
- **Guide price £525/$992**

Longines Watch ▲

- *1930*

A rectangular Longines, stainless steel mechanical watch, with luminous green arabic numbers on a white face.

- *2cm x 1.5cm*
- **Guide price £350/$662**

Rolex Earl Wrist Watch ▼

- *1930*

A gentleman's Rolex Earl manual-wind wrist watch, with a stainless steel case and a white dial with clear digits and subsidiary seconds.

- *diameter 3cm*
- **Guide price £375/$709**

Oyster Wrist Watch ▼

- *circa 1926*

A very early 9ct. pink gold Oyster waterproof wrist watch. The octagonal case signed "Rolex 20 Worlds Records", case number "#23681". The movement signed "Rolex Prima", 15 jewels timed to six positions for all climates. Swiss made. The white enamel dial signed "Rolex Oyster".

- **Guide price £4,900/$9,261**

German Aviator's Watch ▶

- *circa 1942*

A very rare aviator's wrist watch by A. Lange & Sohne Glashutte I Sa. model No. FI23883. German military ordinance marks to inside of case back: "Mvt #213092 Case #213092 Gerrat #127-560A-1 Werk #213092 Anforderz #FI23883".

- *diameter 5.5cm*
- **Guide price £3,500/$6,615**

Rolex Military Pocket Watch ▲

- *circa 1940s*

A Rolex military-style pocket watch, model number "GS MK II", with a black dial with gold Arabic numerals and subsidiary seconds.

- *diameter 4.2cm*
- **Guide price £650/$1,229**

IWC Automatic Watch ▲

- *circa 1950*

An automatic high-grade wrist watch in steel by the International Watch Co., with waterproof screw-on back.

- **Guide price £2,000/$3,780**

Rolex Pocket Watch ▼

- *circa 1920*

A gold-plated Rolex pocket watch with luminous arabic numerals and hands and subsidiary seconds.

- *diameter 4.2cm*
- **Guide price £600/$1,134**

Omega Seamaster Wrist Watch ▼

- *circa 1950*

An Omega Seamaster automatic waterproof wrist watch in steel with early automatic bumper movement.

- **Guide price £875/$1,654**

Sterling Silver Watch ▶

- *circa 1918*

A Longines sterling silver, early pin set one-button chronograph with minute recording dial and subsidiary second dial. The sweep centre seconds chronograph operating through the winding stem. The hinged lug case is marked "#2974806 Mvt#2974806". Eighteen jewels and five adjustment case dial and movement signed "Longines".

- **Guide price £2,950/$5,576**

Vacheron Constantin Wrist Watch ▲

- *1950*

An 18ct. gold wrist watch with gold baton numerals on a white dial by Vacheron Constantin.

- *diameter 4cm*
- **Guide price £1,900/$3,591**

Omega Flightmaster Wrist Watch ▲

- *circa 1970*

An Omega Flightmaster aviator's multifunctional wrist watch in steel. Supplied with the original box, instructions and guarantee.

- **Guide price £1,800/$3,402**

French Air Force Chronograph ▼

- *circa 1950*

A Breguet-type XX French Air Force Pilots "Fly-Back" chronograph in steel with rotating bezel marked "1–12". The dial with subsidiary seconds and minute recording dial. The waterproof screw-on back with case mark "20645".

- **Guide price £4,900/$9,261**

Aviator's Chronograph ▼

- *1968*

An aviator's Breitling "Navitimer" chronograph in steel with subsidiary dials for sweep seconds, minute and hour recording. Outer rotating bezel allowing various aviation calculations. Case marked "#1307320 Ref#806 806".

- **Guide price £1,800/$3,402**

Ladies Cocktail Watch ▶

- *circa 1940s*

A gas-tube bracelet ladies watch, inset with natural Burma rubies, with jointed finials on a circular silvered dial with black numerals. Mechanical movement.

- *width 1.2cm*
- **Guide price £2,100/$3,969**

Vintage Ladies Watch ▲

- *circa 1910*

An 18ct. gold ladies watch set with demantoid garnets and diamonds around the bezel. White porcelain face with black numerals and red number 12, decorated with gold pips with an 18ct. expandable bracelet.

- *diameter 2.2cm*
- **Guide price £1,275/$2,410**

French Art Deco ▲

- *1939*

Clock by JAZ. Typical of French Art Deco style. Maroon and black case with chromium embellishments. Embossed with stylized face.

- *height 18cm*
- **Guide price £300/$567**

Longines Water-Resistant Watch ▼

• *circa 1950*

A gents Longines water-resistant two-button chronograph with minute recording dial and subsidiary seconds dial. The caseback stamped 18ct. (Swiss control marks), with the words "Shock-absorber waterproof Antimagnetic" engraved. The high grade movement dial and case signed "Longines".

• **Guide price £2,450/$4,631**

Cartier Cocktail ▶

• *circa 1930*

Cartier ladies cocktail watch, in platinum with diamonds.

• **Guide price £1,000/$1,890**

Demi-Hunter Pocket Watch ▼

• *1905*

A 9ct. gold demi-hunter pocket watch by Wilson and Sharp of Edinburgh. With three-quarter plate movement.

• *diameter 4cm*

• **Guide price £495/$936**

Smiths Mystery Clock ▲

• *1930*

English, 240v mains-powered, in chrome, bakelite and glass. Hands move without apparent mechanism.

• *height 22cm*

• **Guide price £275/$520**

Waterproof Watch ▼

• *circa 1930*

Omega rare, double-case waterproof wrist watch.

• **Guide price £3,250/$6,143**

Pocket Watch ▼

• *circa 1910*

A 14ct. gold-filled pocket watch, with top-wind button set, by Thomas Russell.

• **Guide price £800/$1,512**

French Carriage Clock ▼

• *1922*

Brass corniche-cased repeating carriage clock retailed by Barraud & Lunds Ltd, London. French eight-day movement.

• *height 18cm*

• **Guide price £1,450/$2,741**

English Gravity Clock ▲

• *1910*

Made by Eleison, London. With mahogany pillared case and clock in serpentine marble case. The weight of the clock powers the movement.

• *height 30cm*

• **Guide price £1,200/$2,268**

German Brass Clock ▲

• *1900*

Diane mystery clock with spelter figure and swinging clock face by Junghans.

• *height 28cm*

• **Guide price £650/$1,229**

Omega Dynamic ▲

- circa 1968

Omega Dynamic automatic day and date watch.

- **Guide price £350/$662**

Vitascope Clock ▲

- 1944

'Vitascope' electric automation, 240v mains-powered. From Isle of Man, with bakelite case.

- height 32cm
- **Guide price £450/$851**

Masonic Watch ▲

- circa 1950

A gold-plated watch with masonic symbols as numerals.

- **Guide price £150/$284**

Marine Chronometer ▼

- 1900

English chronometer, by Victor Kulber, in rare coromandel, brass-strung case. 56 hours duration.

- height 20cm (closed)
- **Guide price £3,500/$6,615**

Gold Watch ▼

- circa 1960

Jaeger-LeCoultre 18ct. gold movement watch, designed by Kutchinsky, with nine diamonds and seven graded rubies on either side of the band.

- **Guide price £3,250/$6,143**

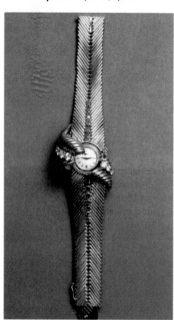

First World War Officer's Watch ▶

- circa 1913

Original, enamelled dial with roman numerals and traditional red twelve. Subsidiary second dial and minute recording. Fabulous example of one of the very earliest wrist watch chronographs. Good condition and extremely attractive.

- **Guide price £2,650/$5,009**

French Electric Clock ▲

- 1920

'Bulle', powered by 1.5 volt battery with heavy cut-glass crystal cover.

- height 34cm
- **Guide price £900/$1,701**

Art Deco Ladies Rolex ▲

- circa 1945

With hooded lugs. The case, dial and movement signed by Rolex.

- **Guide price £1,550/$2,930**

Double-Dialled Watch ▼

- circa 1910

A silver, keyless, lever double-dialled calendar watch with moon phases, time and subsidiaries on an enamel dial with roman numerals on the obverse, and world time indications for seven cities on the reverse dial. The watch, which is unsigned, was made in Switzerland.

- **Guide price £2,750/$5,198**

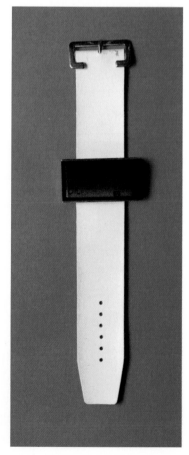

Pierre Cardin Watch ▼

- circa 1960

Pierre Cardin-designed watch with original white-leather strap and Jaeger manual-movement.

- **Guide price £220/$416**

Cartier Wrist Watch ▼

• *circa 1998*
Wrist watch with 18ct. gold body and bracelet. Roman numeral dial with date.
• **Guide price £4,500/$8,505**

English Electric Clock ▼

• *1910*
By Frank Holden, powered by 1.5 volt battery.
• *height 26cm*
• **Guide price £1,250/$2,363**

Art Deco Wrist Watch ▶

• *circa 1935*
Gentleman's high-quality wrist watch of Art Deco design. Case with hooded lugs and thick raised UB glass. The jewelled lever movement with original gilt dust cover.
• **Guide price £775/$1,465**

'Eureka' Clock ▲

• *1908-14*
Made in London, powered by 1.5 volt battery, serpentine brass case.
• *height 32cm*
• **Guide price £2,000/$3,780**

Aviator's 'Antimagnetic' ▲

• *circa 1953*
Rare, Swiss-made watch with military specification fixed-strap bars and screw-on waterproof back. Made of high-grade stainless steel.
• **Guide price £1,750/$3,308**

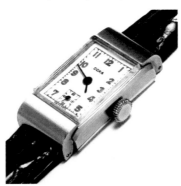

Openface Karrusel Watch ▼

• *circa 1930*
An 18ct. gold, keyless lever chronograph watch with register and vari-coloured tracking for the tachometer. Swiss, unsigned.
• *diameter 5cm*
• **Guide price £850/$1,607**

Rolex Watch ▼

• *circa 1923*
A medium-sized Rolex gents watch in sterling silver, with 'Sunray' dial, hinged lugs and subsidiary seconds.
• **Guide price £1,800/$3,402**

Cartier Pocket Watch ▼

• *circa 1930*
18ct. gold and onyx. With European Watch and Clock Co movement.
• **Guide price £9,200/$17,388**

Ladies Rolex ▲

• *circa 1924*
A 9ct. gold, ladies Rolex watch, with expanding bracelet holding 15 rubies.
• **Guide price £1,000/$1,890**

French LIP Watch ▲

• *circa 1950*
Military-style wrist watch with stainless-steel case and subsidiary seconds. Clear digits on face.
• **Guide price £140/$265**

'Reason' Electric Clock ▼

- *1910*

English, powered by 1.5 volt battery. Invented by Murday.

- *height 32cm*
- **Guide price £3,800/$7,182**

Bracelet Watch ▼

- *circa 1950*

An 18ct. gold and sapphire set bracelet watch with backwind movement.

- **Guide price £9,500/$17,955**

Rolex Officer's Wrist Watch ▼

- *circa 1916*

An early First World War officer's wrist watch. The silvered dial signed "Rolex & Swiss Made". The movement # 4636 and signed "Rolex Swiss 15 Jls." Case signed with "W & D" for Wilsdorf & Davis, the original founders of the Rolex empire. Case # 769936.

- **Guide price £2,500/$4,725**

German Novelty Clock ▲

- *1900*

By Junghans. In papier maché, original glass dome. The head and tail move as clock ticks.

- *height 30cm*
- **Guide price £1,250/$2,363**

Pilot's Wrist Watch ▲

- *circa 1951*

An RAF-issue, pilot's wrist watch with centre 'hacking' seconds hand and screw-back case with anti-magnetic inner case. Made by the International Watch Company with case, dial and movement signed and showing the Ministry of Defence arrow insignia. With factory guarantee.

- **Guide price £2,850/$5,387**

Golf Ball Watch ▲

- *circa 1920*

Swiss watch with silver case modelled as a golf ball. With subsidiary seconds.

- **Guide price £550/$1,040**

Gents Rolex Watch ▼

- *circa 1915*

9ct. gold precision watch, by Rolex, with subsidiary seconds and a white-metal dial.

- **Guide price £950/$1,796**

Ladies Cartier ▼

- *circa 1925*

Cocktail watch of 18ct. gold, platinum and diamonds set with matching deployant buckle.

- **Guide price £16,000/$30,240**

Gent's Triple Date Watch ◄

- *circa 1940*

Gents triple date calendar wrist watch with moonphase, in 10ct. gold. By Jaeger-LeCoultre.

- **Guide price £4,850/$9,167**

Ladies Rolex ▲

- *1914*

Ladies silver Rolex watch, of circular form, with original expanding bracelet and early example metal dial with roman numerals in black, 'XII' in red.

- **Guide price £675/$1,276**

'Naviquartz' Timepiece ▲

- *circa 1975*

Brass-bound mahogany timepiece with certificate, by Patek Philippe of Geneva.

- *length 16cm*
- **Guide price £3,500/$6,615**

Small Travelling Clock ▲

- *1903*

English silver-cased clock with hallmark and French eight-day movement. Original English lever platform escapement. Signed on the movement.
- *height 10cm*
- **Guide price £1,100/$2,079**

Eberhard Chronograph ▲

- *circa 1945*

Chronograph by Eberhard & Co, showing hour/minute registers.
- **Guide price £3,500/$6,615**

Gents Rolex Wrist Watch ▲

- *circa 1959*

9 ct. gold precision wristwatch. With black dial and sweep second hand. Coin edge to case.
- **Guide price £1,100/$2,079**

First World War Wrist Watch ▼

- *circa 1916*

A very rare officer's First World War 'Hunting' cased wrist watch, with waterproof screw-back. The movement is signed by Rolex and the case is marked 'Rolex' with 'W&D', standing for Wilsdorf and Davis, the original founders of the Rolex company. The case is numbered 773185 and the enamel face shows luminous numerals and subsidiary seconds.
- **Guide price £3,450/$6,521**

Chronograph Watch ▼

- *circa 1905*

An 18ct. gold hunter, keyless lever, minute-repeating chronograph watch with register, enamel dial and thief-proof swivel bow, by Dent, London.
- *height 5.3cm*
- **Guide price £11,500/$21,735**

Omega Chronograph ▼

- *circa 1932*

Rare, steel-cased Omega single button chronograph wrist watch with enamel dial in red and black and sweep second hand.
- **Guide price £7,000/$13,230**

Swiss-made Chronometer ▼

- *circa 1945*

A gents chronometer wrist watch with 3, 6, 9 and 12 in roman numerals. The centre seconds dial signed "Rolex Chronometer." Swiss made.
- **Guide price £3,650/$6,899**

Gent's Rolex Precision ◄

- *circa 1956*

A gentleman's high grade 9ct. gold wrist watch with subsidiary seconds and dial signed 'Rolex Precision', with British import marks for the year 1956. The dial has been sympathetically restored to the highest standard.
- **Guide price £3,350/$6,332**

Oyster Waterproof Watch ▲

- *circa 1937*

Fine example of an early Oyster waterproof gents 'Chronometer' wrist watch, the case with the original, screw-down 'Oyster' button.
- **Guide price £2,650/$5,009**

Art Deco Rolex ▲

- *circa 1937*

A gentleman's Art Deco period Rolex wrist watch in 9ct. gold, with stepped sides and high-grade movement timed to two positions. British import marks for the year 1937.
- **Guide price £3,650/$6,899**

'Eiffel Tower' ▲
- circa 1953

An 18ct. gold, rectangular dialled Patek Philippe wrist watch with enamel and gold face and subsidiary seconds.
- **Guide price £29,000/$54,810**

Ladies Rolex Watch ▼
- 1928

A 9ct. gold ladies Rolex watch with a white enamel dial and a matching 9ct. gold expanding bracelet.
- diameter 2cm
- **Guide price £650/$1,229**

Longines 'Lindbergh' ▼
- circa 1940

Steel and silver cased Longines 'Lindbergh' aviator's wrist watch. This design first used by the pilot, Charles Lindbergh, during his famous transatlantic crossing.
- **Guide price £9,000/$17,010**

Boudoir Balloon Clock ◀
- circa 1903

Silver and enamel, French and English hallmarked, Birmingham. Signed "L. Leroy & Cie of Paris."
- height 16cm
- **Guide price £1,600/$3,024**

'Moving Eye' Clock ▲
- 1930

Novelty dogs by Oswold, Germany. One eye is on the hour, the other on the minute.
- height 14cm
- **Guide price £350/$662**

German Air Force Issue Chronograph ▲
- circa 1970

A rare German Air Force issue aviator's 'fly-back' chronograph wrist watch, with the chronograph operated by two pushers on the case band. Made by Heuer, the chronograph has the benefit of a 'fly-back' facility, allowing the centre second hand to zero and immediately resume timing. The black dial has subsidiary seconds and minute recording dial and the steel-case body has a non-reflective, anti-glare finish and a rotating, dull matt-finish black bezel with minute increments.
- **Guide price £1,950/$3,686**

Gold Cartier Watch ▼
- circa 1920

An 18ct. gold and platinum Cartier tank watch with square face and enamelled dial with black, Arabic figures.
- **Guide price £22,000/$41,580**

Brass Carriage Clock ▼
- circa 1900

Small sized pediment-topped polished brass carriage clock timepiece. Eight-day movement with platform escapement.
- height 18cm
- **Guide price £1,900/$3,591**

French Carriage Timepiece ◀
- 1900

A French carriage timepiece combined with barometer, thermometer and compass with gilt brass, glass panels and carrying handle.
- height 16cm
- **Guide price £1,750/$3,308**

Hermetique Waterproof ▼

- *circa 1923*

Rare, hermatically sealed 'Waterproof' wrist watch, in double case with hinged lugs. Swiss make, by Hermetique, in 9ct. gold.

- **Guide price £2,750/$5,198**

Rolex 'Prince' ▼

- *circa 1929*

Rare 'Prince' Chronometer gent's watch. Dial with original, enamelled numerals and tracks.

- **Guide price £6,650/$12,569**

Dress Pocket Watch ▼

- *circa 1915*

An 18ct. gold, Swiss pocket watch with gold-washed dial and subsidiary seconds.

- **Guide price £395/$748**

French Pendulum ▼

- *1930*

Designed by ATO. First battery-operated French pendulum clock. Spider's web design to dial. Aztec Gothic numerals.

- *height 17cm*
- **Guide price £350/$662**

British Military Issue ◄

- *circa 1940*

A British military issue wrist watch, with black dial and subsidiary seconds dial and MOD arrow. By the International Watch Company.

- **Guide price £2,250/$4,253**

'Scott' Electric Clock ▲

- *1910*

English, powered by 1.5 volt battery. By Herbert Scott in oak, nickel plated and glass case.

- *height 40cm*
- **Guide price £2,000/$3,780**

Rolex Oyster ▲

- *circa 1970*

Date precision with silver face, stainless body. Bracelet-style band.

- **Guide price £725/$1,370**

Spaceman Watch ▲

- *circa 1970*

Swiss-made watch with stainless steel body and bracelet. Manual and water resistant.

- **Guide price £220/$416**

Keyless Lever Watch ▲

- *circa 1908*

An 18ct. gold open-face watch with split seconds chronograph and register. By Dent of London.

- *diameter 5.4cm*
- **Guide price £4,750/$8,978**

COINS & MEDALS

German Long Service Cross ▼

- *1936–45*
NSDAP Long Service Cross, German Third silver for 25 years. GVF.
- *diameter 5cm*
- **Guide price £225/$426**

Naval Service Medal ▼

- *1914–19*
Naval Distinguished Service medal with GVR bust, as awarded to: A8654. J. Crorkran. Sea. R.N.R. Mediterranean Service, 23 March, 1918. This award was mentioned in the *London Gazette* on 7.8.1918, and was approved for services in action with enemy submarines.
- *diameter 4cm*
- **Guide price £395/$748**

Third Luftwaffe ▲

- *1936-45*
German Third Luftwaffe Wireless Operator Air Gunners' Badge.
- *diameter 3cm*
- **Guide price £225/$426**

Inter-allied Victory Medal ▲

- *1914–19*
Inter-allied Victory medal for the Great War, this is the Italian version, with maker's mark: "Sacchimi – Milano".
- *diameter 4cm*
- **Guide price £14/$26**

Cyprus Coin ▲

- *circa 1928*
First Colonial Crown Cyprus coin, 45 Piastres.
- *diameter 3.5cm*
- **Guide price £120/$227**

Kitzbuhel Shooting Badge ▼

- *1943*
Attractively enameled Kitzbuhel shooting badge, maker's mark 'Ges Gesch' and the inscription "Meisterklasse Kitzbuhel".
- *diameter 4cm*
- **Guide price £165/$312**

Campaign Service Medal ▼

- *1970–82*
Campaign Service medal with one clasp; Northern Ireland, South Atlantic medal 1982, with rosette, UN Cyprus medal (UNFICYP), as awarded to: 24501637 Gunner J.C Howe Royal Artillery. Group mounted court style for wear.
- *diameter 12cm*
- **Guide price £345/$652**

German Red Cross ▼

- *1934*
German Red Cross, second class, white enameled cross with eagle in black and without swastika. The ribbon is in the style of a lady's bow.
- *diameter 4cm*
- **Guide price £125/$237**

British Victory Medal ▲

- *1914–19*
British Victory medal, as awarded to Lieutenant J.C Holmes RAF, and Ceylon Planters Rifle Corps medal. Inscribed on rim with: "Marathon Race, L.C.P.L.J.C. Holmes Kandy 1913". This man was killed in action on Sunday the first September 1918 in Egypt, aged 29. Having served in the Ceylon Planter's Rifle Corps, transferred on 17/11/1915 to the Yorkshire Regiment, was later commissioned as a second Lieutenant and joined the Royal Flying Corps and latterly the Royal Air Force.
- *diameter 12cm*
- **Guide price £325/$614**

Cape Colony Medal ▲

- *1902*
South African Cape Colony Medal – Coldstream Guards.
- *diameter 4cm*
- **Guide price £75/$142**

Gold Post Master Jewel ▲

• 1930
Nine carat gold Post Master jewel representing the guild of Freeman Lodge, decorated with the City of London's coat of arms.
• **Guide price £140/$265**

German Third Spanish Cross ▲

• 1939–45
Bronze German Spanish cross with swords, no maker's mark.
• *diameter 4cm*
• **Guide price £465/$879**

Burmese Rupee ▲

• 1920
Burmese rupee centred with a peacock. While of exceptionally high quality this example is one of the more common seen on the market.
• **Guide price £120/$227**

Air Force Cross ▼

• 1960–present
US Air Force cross.
• *diameter 5cm*
• **Guide price £43/$81**

Military Cross ▼

• 1910–36
The Military Cross, GV, with inscribed name on reverse N.P. Spooner.
• *diameter 4cm*
• **Guide price £35/$66**

Anna-Luisen Order ▼

• 1918
Medal commemorating the Anna-Luisen (Schwarzbury-Rudelstadt).
• *diameter 3cm*
• **Guide price £395/$748**

Founder Jewel ▲

• 1940
Hallmarked silver founder jewel with Masonic symbols painted on the enamel, set between two pillars
• **Guide price £40/$76**

Purple Heart Award ▲

• 1932–present
Purple heart medal of the Vietnam period. This is awarded for gallantry, the wounded or those killed in action in the service of the military forces of the United States of America.
• *diameter 4cm*
• **Guide price £24/$46**

German Iron Cross Bar ▲

• 1939
Second-class Bar badge of an eagle clutching a wreath.
• *diameter 4cm*
• **Guide price £160/$303**

Distinguished Service Medal ▼

• 1970–present
US Defence Distinguished Service medal.
• *diameter 5cm*
• **Guide price £43/$81**

WWI Death Plaque ▼

• 1917
World War I Death Plaque for Albert James Donovan 35th Battalion, Australian Infantry.
• *diameter 4cm*
• **Guide price £65/$123**

Military Cross ▼

• 1914–19
Military Cross, GVR, unofficially named on reverse: A. Melville Kennedy. 8th BN. Royal Scots Fusiliers June 1917.
• *diameter 4cm*
• **Guide price £395/$748**

SS Long Service ▲

- *1936–45*

German World War II SS Long Service
Medal for eight years. Bronze with
original blue moiré silk ribbon.
- *diameter 4cm*
- **Guide price £345/$652**

Royal Air Force Brooches ▲

- *circa 1918*

One of a pair of Royal Air Force
sweetheart brooches made from
15 carat gold, with original box.
- **Guide price £200/$378**

Royal Red Cross ▲

- *1913*

Royal Red Cross, second class
(Associate), ARRC, GVR initials
engraved on the reverse. In Garrad and
Co. titled case of issue, with wearing pin.
- *diameter 4cm*
- **Guide price £100/$189**

Victoria Cross ▼

- *2003*

A modern example of a Victoria Cross
in good condition.
- *diameter 4cm*
- **Guide price £30/$57**

Good Conduct Medal ▶

- *1909*

Volunteer Long Service Good Conduct
medal with Edward VII bust, awarded to:
1538 Sgt I. Harrison. 2nd V.B. Notts &
Derby R. With Daily Mail Empire Day
rifle competition. Silver award medal,
named to recipient and dated 1909.
- *diameter 4cm*
- **Guide price £65/$123**

War Merit Cross ▲

- *1939*

War Merit Cross, first class, with
maker's mark.
- *diameter 4cm*
- **Guide price £75/$142**

British War Medal ▼

- *1914–19*

1914–15 Star, British War medal, Victory
medal, and Royal Naval Volunteer
Reserve Long Service Good Conduct
medal, as awarded to: 1/945. R. Ryandell.
Sig. R.N.V.R. Bristol DIV.
- *diameter 4cm*
- **Guide price £135/$255**

War Service Cross ◀

- *1912*

War Service Cross of Imperial Austria
made from gold with enameling and
official mint maker's mark. Hallmarked
1912.
- *diameter 3cm*
- **Guide price £280/$530**

Hitler Youth Medal ▼

- *1939*

Hitler Youth Kreisseiger 1939 bronze and
enamel medal, maker's mark "H. Aurich,
Dresden".
- *diameter 4cm*
- **Guide price £195/$370**

Sports Badge ▼

- *circa 1937*

Weightlifting bronze athlete's sports
badge.
- *diameter 3cm*
- **Guide price £325/$614**

Army Roll of Honour Clasp ▼

- *1941–45*

Very rare Army Roll of Honour Clasp.
An actual presentation award piece, the
clasp is a superb fire-gilt tombak
swastika in very high relief with slight
wear.
- *diameter 3cm*
- **Guide price £850/$1,607**

Indian Army Long Service Medal

- *1910–36*
Indian Army Long Service and Good Conduct Medal for Indians. GVR Kaisar-i-hind bust.
- *diameter 4cm*
- **Guide price £30/$57**

Order of the War Cross

▼

- *1936–39*
Order of the War Cross "Cruz de guerra", second class, breast star in silver, awarded during the Spanish Civil War of 1936–39. In deluxe box of issue with the maker's name, "Insustrias Egana" Motrico.
- *diameter 4cm*
- **Guide price £200/$378**

Luftwaffe Retired Pilot's Badge

▲

- *1935–45*
Luftwaffe retired pilot's badge with maker's mark: C.E. Junker Berlin SW66.
- *diameter 4cm*
- **Guide price £925/$1,748**

Efficiency Decoration

▲

- *1936–52*
The Efficiency Decoration, GVI, with second award long service bar, territorial top bar, and Honourable Artillery Company ribbon.
- *diameter 3cm*
- **Guide price £40/$76**

Masonic Jewel

◄

- *1930*
St John's Lodge whole Masonic jewel. This hallmarked jewel bears a good quality enamel of St John the Martyr.
- **Guide price £70/$133**

Luftschutz Cross

▲

- *1938*
Luftschutz Cross, first class, in gold with original loop and ring suspender and pin-back ribbon. Rare, with less than 150 awarded.
- *diameter 4cm*
- **Guide price £675/$1,276**

Imperial Service Medal

▼

- *1901–10*
Early star-shaped EVII Imperial Service Medal, unnamed in case of issue.
- *diameter 4cm*
- **Guide price £75/$142**

Order of Medjidiek

▲

- *1916–17*
Order of Medjidiek together with Royal Society of Arts Silver Medal awarded to A. J. Todd, Professor of the Khedivial School of Law.
- *diameter 4cm*
- **Guide price £385/$728**

Masonic Collar Jewel ▲

- *1920*

Thirtieth degree Masonic collar jewel with hinged crown above a double-headed phoenix clutching a double-edged sword.

- **Guide price £60/$114**

Military Cross ▲

- *1918*

In original case of issue and inscribed on reverse '2nd Lieut. S.G. Williams 1st Battalion, Devonshire Regiment'.

- **Guide price £325/$614**

Third Reich Medals ▼

- *1935–45*

1939 Iron Cross 2nd Cl., Danzig Cross, 2nd Cl., the latter, one of only 254 awarded, maker's mark on reverse: B.V.A. Hulse-Berlin.

- *diameter 4cm*
- **Guide price £365/$690**

Iron Cross ▼

- *1914*

An Iron Cross 2nd Class, awarded to a German soldier at the beginning of World War I.

- **Guide price £20/$38**

Third Reich Army Long Service Cross ◄

- *1935–45*

Gold Third Reich Army Long Service Cross awarded for 40 years service, with gilt eagle standard and oak leaves on ribbon. A very fine specimen.

- *diameter 4cm*
- **Guide price £225/$426**

Lapland Shield ▲

- *1939–45*

Lapland shield made from zinc on a cloth backing.

- *diameter 3cm*
- **Guide price £295/$558**

WWI Military Medal ▲

- *1914–18*

A Great War Military medal for gallantry. Awarded to Private L. Goldthorpe, 10th Battalion, Worcester Regiment. Killed in action 13/07/17.

- **Guide price £225/$426**

Luftwaffe Combined Pilot/Observer's Badge ▼

- *1935–45*

Luftwaffe combined pilot/observer's badge. Two part gilt and silver, mid-war version, in super crisp condition. Makers marked: CEJ for Junckers.

- *diameter 4cm*
- **Guide price £650/$1,229**

German Pilot's Badge ▼

- *1940*

WWII German air force pilot's badge in silver by Bruder Schneider, Vienna.

- **Guide price £350/$662**

German Imperial Group ▼

- *1900–18*

Iron Cross 2nd Cl., 1914; Prussia, German Service Cross 1900–1918; Officer's Long Service Cross for 25 yrs; Friedrich Wilhelm 3rd Civil Service medal, 2nd Cl., 1847–1918, in silver; Army Lower Ranks Long Service medal for 15 yrs; Wilhelm 1st Centenary medal 1897; Braunschweig: Military Service Cross 2nd Cl., 1914–1918 and Service Cross 1st Cl., in gold. All mounted court style for wear.

- *diameter 18.5cm*
- **Guide price £475/$898**

Military Medal Trio

- *1918*

A trio of World War I medals, including the Victory medal, awarded to Private H. Codd of the East Yorkshire Regiment.
- **Guide price £35/$66**

Officer's Cap Badge ▲

- *1914*

Irish Guards Officer's silver and enamel Great War cap badge. Attributed to Captain M. Gore-Langton MC.
- **Guide price £195/$370**

Military Badge ▲

- *1940*

WWII German navy U-boat badge, an early plated brass example.
- **Guide price £225/$426**

WWI Medal Group ▼

- *WWI and later*

A WWI medal group of five medals, consisting of 1914–1915 Star Trio, 1935 Jubilee medal, RAF Long Service Good Conduct medal. Awarded to Corporal L. Thornton RAF.
- **Guide price £250/$473**

Air Force Medal ▶

- *1945*

A European Aircrew Star, awarded to a serving member of the Royal Air Force in World War II.
- **Guide price £105/$198**

Cap Badge ▲

- *1914–18*

Leicestershire Regiment Other Ranks cap badge.
- **Guide price £10/$19**

Memorial Plaque ▲

- *1914*

Great War memorial plaque dedicated to Ernest George Malyon of the 2nd/16th Battalion London Regiment and inscribed "He died for freedom and honour".
- *diameter 12cm*
- **Guide price £25/$48**

Leopold II Medal ▼

- *1915*

Order of Leopold II 2nd Class neck badge.
- **Guide price £175/$331**

Medal Group ▼

- *1914–45*

WWI and WWII group of eight medals to Masters at Arms P. McArthur "H.M.S. Tamar".
- **Guide price £225/$426**

Russian Medal ▲

• *1915*
Imperial Russian Cross of St. George IV class.
• **Guide price £45/$85**

Great War Medal ▲

• *1911–37*
A distinguished service order (George V) in Garrard & Co, in case of award.
• **Guide price £450/$851**

India General Service Medal ▲

• *1908*
1908 India General Service medal with clasp, "North West Frontier". Awarded to 65 Barghir Daroska of the 51st Camel Corps.
• **Guide price £60/$114**

Cap Badge ▼

• *1939–45*
Royal Armoured Corps WWII plastic cap badge.
• **Guide price £25/$48**

Miniature Medals ▼

• *1918*
A set of KCMG, CB(Gold) group of ten miniatures attributed to Major General Sir Andrew Mitchell Stuart. Royal Engineers.
• **Guide price £385/$728**

Cap Badge ▶

• *1914–18*
Royal Sussex Regiment silver and enamel officer's cap badge.
• **Guide price £100/$189**

DFC Medal ▼

• *1939–45*
Distinguished George VI Flying Cross, reverse dated 1943, in case of award.
• **Guide price £450/$851**

German Assault Badge ▲

• *1942*
World War II German army/SS General Assault badge, showing eagle, Nazi insignia and combat dagger in oak-leaf and acorn surround. Mid-war plated zinc example.
• **Guide price £40/$76**

Military Medal ▼

• *1962 onwards*
Campaign Service medal with three clasps awarded to Bombardier A.J. Williams of 2/9 Commando Royal Artillery.
• **Guide price £125/$237**

Soviet Military Medal ▼

- *1945*

World War II USSR Order of the Red Banner Military medal awarded for valour to members of the Soviet army.

- **Guide price £30/$57**

Commemorative Coin ▼

- *1935*

A gold coin commemorating the Silver Jubilee of King George V. The coin shows the King and Queen Mary with Windsor Castle on reverse.

- *diameter 3.1cm*
- **Guide price £250/$473**

Austrian Coin ▼

- *1936*

Gold Austrian 100-schilling coin with Madonna on obverse and Austrian shield on reverse.

- *diameter 3.2cm*
- **Guide price £450/$851**

Medal Group ▲

- *1914–18*

A medal group consisting of the NBE, The Military Cross, 1914 Star Trio, Defence medal, War medal and Special Constabulary medal. Awarded to Lieutenant Colonel T.L. Wall of the Fifth Lancers.

- **Guide price £1,550/$2,930**

Five-Pound Coin ▲

- *1902*

A very rare gold Edward VII five-pound coin.

- *diameter 3.5cm*
- **Guide price £700/$1,323**

Iron Cross ▲

- *1939*

A World War II German Iron Cross Second Class, awarded for bravery and / or leadership. Ring stamped with swastika and with red and white ribbon.

- **Guide price £38/$72**

Military Cigarette Case ▼

- *1943*

A Russian presentation silver cigarette case, celebrating victory over the Germans in World War II, with inscription.

- **Guide price £250/$473**

Gulf War Medal ▼

- *1991*

Gulf War medal with clasp, awarded to Steward I. McMillan of the Royal Fleet Auxiliary.

- **Guide price £135/$255**

RAF Flying Medal ▲

- *1939–45*

World War II RAF distinguished flying medal. For gallantry. Awarded to Sgt. G. Jones.

- **Guide price £950/$1,796**

General Service Medal ▲

- *1962*

A Northern Ireland service medal, awarded to L/CPL R. Scott, Scots Guards. With purple and green ribbon.

- **Guide price £42/$80**

COMMEMORATIVE WARE

Joseph Chamberlain Plate ▲
- *1904*
Ridgeway earthenware plate commemorating Joseph Chamberlain.
- *diameter 25cm*
- **Guide price £70/$133**

Mason's Jug ▲
- *1935*
Mason's ironstone jug commemorating King George and Queen Mary, a limited edition of 1,000. With King George and Queen Mary in profile within a wreath border.
- *height 19cm*
- **Guide price £275/$520**

Royal Albert Commemorative Mug ▶
- *1935*
Bone china Royal Albert commemorative mug of the Silver Jubilee of King George V and Queen Mary.
- *height 7cm*
- **Guide price £58/$110**

King Edward Coronation Earthenware Jug ▼
- *1902*
Royal Doulton earthenware jug from the Lambeth factory to commemorate the coronation of King Edward VII.
- *height 21cm*
- **Guide price £150/$284**

German Knight ▶
- *1918*
German bronzed spelter figure of a knight in armour on a stained wood plinth, with a dedication plate on the side to Major Niemann from his brother officers of the 39 Field Artillery Regiment, 22 March to 16 November, 1918.
- *height 45.5cm*
- **Guide price £325/$614**

Commemorative Plaque ▲
- *1914–15*
Bone china plaque commemorating the alliance between Germany and Austria, Kaiser Wilhelm II and Franz Joseph.
- *diameter 23.5cm*
- **Guide price £170/$322**

Coronation Mug ▲
- *1911*
Green and white coronation mug of George V. Manufactured by Booths.
- *height 7.5cm*
- **Guide price £70/$133**

Edward VII Earthenware Mug ▼

- *1910*

An earthenware mug to commemorate the demise of Edward VII.

- *height 10cm*
- **Guide price £110/$208**

Paragon Mug ▼

- *circa 1935*

Silver Jubilee bone china paragon mug of George V and Queen Mary.

- *height 8cm*
- **Guide price £75/$142**

Princess Mary Mug ▼

- *1929*

Earthenware mug to commemorate the visit of Princess Mary Viscountess Laschelles to Castleford.

- *height 8.6cm*
- **Guide price £175/$331**

Memorial Plaque ▲

- *1972*

An oval basalt plaque of the Duke of Windsor in memoriam.

- *8.3cm x 10.8cm*
- **Guide price £48/$91**

Prince William Bone China Mug ▲

- *2003*

Royal Collection English bone china mug to commemorate the 21st birthday of Prince William.

- *height 15cm*
- **Guide price £21/$40**

Crown Devon Jug ▼

- *1937*

Crown Devon jug musical "Super Jug" to commemorate the coronation of King George VI and Queen Elizabeth. Limited edition. With a lion handle.

- *height 30.5cm*
- **Guide price £2,250/$4,253**

King's Beaker ▼

- *1902*

Royal Doulton beaker commemorating the King Edward VII's coronation dinner, with a silver hallmarked rim, presented by His Majesty.

- *height 10cm*
- **Guide price £130/$246**

Doulton Mug ◀

- *1901*

Doulton bone china mug depicting Queen Victoria in memoriam with purple decoration around the rim, and decorated with a prayer book, inscribed below with the words, "She wrought her people lasting good".

- *height 7.6cm*
- **Guide price £475/$898**

Royal Doulton Beaker ▲

- *1902*

Royal Doulton earthenware King's coronation beaker celebrating the coronation of Edward VII in rare purple.

- *height 9.8cm*
- **Guide price £95/$180**

Booths Coronation Mug ▲

- *circa 1911*

Ceramic coronation mug to commemorate King George V and Queen Mary, by Booths.

- *height 9cm*
- **Guide price £60/$114**

Wall Plaque ▲

- *1938*

German black ash wall plaque with metal relief of artillery crew serving their gun, and metal label reading: "Res. battr. Opel 39.8.38. 11.10.38".

- *23cm x 32.5cm*
- **Guide price £115/$217**

Loving Cup ▲

- *1977*
Limited edition of 250 loving cup for the Silver Jubilee of Elizabeth II.
- *27cm x 37cm*
- **Guide price £1,250/$2,363**

Wedgwood Mug ▲

- *1939*
Wedgwood mug to commemorate the visit of King George and Queen Elizabeth to America with the inscription "Friendship makes Peace".
- *height 10cm*
- **Guide price £165/$312**

Royal Wintonia Mug ▲

- *1911*
Royal Wintonia earthenware mug for the Investiture of Edward Prince of Wales made for the City of Cardiff.
- *height 8cm*
- **Guide price £90/$171**

King George and Queen Mary Beaker ▶

- *circa 1911*
Enamel on tin beaker to commemorate the Coronation of King George V and Queen Mary and also the investiture of the Prince of Wales.
- *height 10cm*
- **Guide price £70/$133**

Hammersley Bone China Mug ▲

- *circa 1935*
Bone china mug to commemorate the Silver Jubilee of King George V and Queen Mary – transfer with enamel colours.
- *height 10cm*
- **Guide price £95/$180**

Princess of York Mug ▲

- *1937*
Royal Doulton bone china mug depicting a picture of Princess Elizabeth as a young girl.
- *height 9cm*
- **Guide price £400/$756**

Lions' Heads Beaker ▼

- *2002*
Limited edition beaker of 2,500 from the Royal Collection to commemorate the Golden Jubilee of Queen Elizabeth II.
- *height 22cm*
- **Guide price £50/$95**

Ovaltine Jubilee Mug ▼

- *1977*
Ovaltine Jubilee mug inscribed with the words, 'This was presented to you by Ovaltine and *Woman's Own* because you were born in the week February 6th-12th, 1977, The Silver Jubilee of Queen Elizabeth II'.
- *height 10.7cm*
- **Guide price £29/$56**

Prince William Porcelain Mug ▼

- *1982*
Porcelain mug by J. & J. May to commemorate the birth of Prince William depicting a pram with the royal crest.
- *height 9cm*
- **Guide price £65/123**

Copeland Mug ▼

- *1936–7*
Earthenware mug for the proposed Coronation of Edward VIII, made by Copeland for Thomas Goode of London.
- *height 9.8cm*
- **Guide price £95/$180**

Birthday Mug ▼

- *1991*
Bone china mug by Aynsley to commemorate the thirtieth birthday of Princess Diana.
- *height 9.5cm*
- **Guide price £70/$133**

Winston Churchill Figure ▲

- *circa 1943*

Ceramic figure of Winston Churchill, with the inscriptions "Our Gang Copyright The Boss" on the base of his right foot and "The Bovey Pottery England" on the base of his left foot.

- *height 12cm*
- **Guide price £150/$284**

Loving Cup ▲

- *1936–37*

Loving cup to commemorate the proposed coronation of Edward VIII.

- *height 25.3cm*
- **Guide price £135/$255**

Toby Jug ▲

- *circa 1939*

Small earthenware toby jug of Neville Chamberlain, the handle modelled as an umbrella. Manufactured by Lancaster.

- *height 7.7cm*
- **Guide price £65/$123**

Kitchener Figure ▼

- *circa 1915*

Staffordshire figure of Kitchener standing with his hand on his belt and a sword by his side on an oval base with the word 'Kitchener' on it.

- *height 35cm*
- **Guide price £220/$416**

The Queen's Vesta Box ▶

- *1939*

The Queen's regiment vesta box with "The Queen's" in relief.

- *width 5cm*
- **Guide price £35/$66**

Bone China Mug ▼

- *1937*

Bone china mug by Hammersley to commemorate the coronation of King George VI and Queen Elizabeth. Transfer with enamel colours.

- *height 7.8cm*
- **Guide price £75/$142**

Bronzed Imperial Eagles ▶

- *1914*

Two bronzed metal imperial eagles mounted on marble. Each with an iron cross 1914 2nd Cl., swinging from their beaks. Both fine unusual pieces, which would have been used in the officers mess as decoration.

- *height 14cm*
- **Guide price £295/$558**

Wedgwood Plaque ▲

- *1974*

Black basalt Wedgwood plaque to commemorate the centenary of the birth of Winston Churchill.

- *diameter 16.4cm*
- **Guide price £65/$123**

Child's Teapot and Jug ▼

- *1937*

Child's teapot and jug with transfers showing Princess Elizabeth and Princess Margaret as children.

- *height 8.8cm (teapot)*
- **Guide price £70/$133**

Porcelain Roundel ▼

- *1914*

German domed porcelain roundel, decorated with a coloured portrait of General Field Marshall Hindenburg shown in uniform.

- *diameter 7cm*
- **Guide price £70/$133**

Prime Minister ▼

- *circa 1941*

Pottery jug modelled as the Prime Minister of South Africa by J.C. Smutts.

- *height 13cm*
- **Guide price £98/$185**

Queen Elizabeth II Bust ▼

- *1953*

Bust of Queen Elizabeth II to commemorate her coronation in 1953, by Staffordshire Morloy.

- *height 18cm*
- **Guide price £80/$152**

Miners' Strike Plate ▶

- *1984*

Bone china plate to commemorate the great miners' strike of 1984–1985. Issued by the National Union of Mineworkers.

- *diameter 27cm*
- **Guide price £58/$110**

Caricature Mug ▼

- *1991*

A caricature mug of the former Prime Minister Margaret Thatcher and her husband.

- *height 9cm*
- **Guide price £33/$62**

Princess Diana Mug ▲

- *1996*

Bone china by Chown. Limited edition of 70 to commemorate her 35th birthday and was her last mug made before her death and is rare.

- *height 9cm*
- **Guide price £95/$180**

Wedgwood Mug ▲

- *2000*

Black basalt mug issued by Wedgwood in commemoration of the Millennium. Designed by Richard Guyatt in a limited edition of 500.

- *height 10cm*
- **Guide price £190/$360**

Coronation Mug ▼

- *1902*

Copeland mug for the coronation of King Edward VII and Queen Alexandra, showing the correct date of August 9, 1902. Most items give the date as June 26, 1902, which was postponed because of the king's appendicitis.

- *height 7.5cm*
- **Guide price £160/$303**

Curtseying Cup ▼

- *1977*

Carlton Ware porcelain cup in a curtseying pose, commemorating the silver jubilee of Queen Elizabeth II.

- *height 11cm*
- **Guide price £50/$95**

Engagement Mug ▲

- *1981*

China mug depicting Prince Charles's ear. Drawn by Marc Boxer, made at the engagement of Charles and Diana.

- **Guide price £5/$9**

Loving Cup ▲

- *1987*

Bone china loving cup by Royal Crown Derby. Commemorating the third term in office of Margaret Thatcher. Limited edition of 650.

- *height 7.75cm*
- **Guide price £160/$303**

Pottery Folly ▲

- *1969*

Caernarvon castle folly in Keystone pottery, issued to commemorate the investiture of Prince Charles in July 1969,

- *height 21cm*
- **Guide price £65/$123**

Ainsley Plate ▲

- *1953*

An elaborate commemorative plate by Ainsley in cobalt blue with gold border centred with a portrait of the Queen.

- *diameter 26.4cm*
- **Guide price £250/$473**

Silver Jubilee Ashtray ▼

- *1935*

King George V and Queen Mary silver jubilee ashtray in Burleigh ware.

- *diameter 22cm*
- **Guide price £55/$104**

Four Castles Plate ▲

- *1901*

Black transfer on earthenware plate to commemorate the death of Queen Victoria.

- *diameter 24.5cm*
- **Guide price £240/454**

Toby Jug ▼

- *1940*

A wartime Toby jug of Winston Churchill as first Sea Lord.

- *height 17cm*
- **Guide price £125/$237**

Royal Visit Teapot ▲

- *1939*

Teapot issued in commemoration of a royal visit to Canada made by George VI and Queen Elizabeth II in 1939.

- *height 13cm*
- **Guide price £85/$161**

Coronation Mug ▲

- *1911*

Bone china mug commemorating the coronation of George V.

- *height 8.5cm*
- **Guide price £58/$110**

Coronation Cup and Saucer ▲

- *1902*

Bone china cup and saucer commemorating the coronation of Edward VII. Made by Foley.

- *height 5.5cm*
- **Guide price £58/$110**

Jubilee Mug ▲

- *1935*

Ceramic mug celebrating the silver jubilee of King George V and Queen Mary.

- *height 7cm*
- **Guide price £24/$41**

Bone China Mug ◄

- *1936*

Bone china mug made for the proposed coronation of Edward VIII with abdication details on the reverse.

- *height 9cm*
- **Guide price £170/$322**

Minton Loving Cup ▲

- *1953*

Bone china loving cup by Minton. Coronation of Queen Elizabeth II, designed by John Wadsworth.

- *height 10.5cm*
- **Guide price £190/$360**

Coronation Mug ▲

- *1936*

Bone china mug made for the proposed coronation of Edward VIII.

- *height 9cm*
- **Guide price £40/$76**

Paragon Loving Cup ▲

- *1980*

Large Paragon bone china loving cup with gold lion handles, commemorating the Queen Mother's eightieth birthday. Limited edition of 750.

- *height 13.25cm*
- **Guide price £245/$463**

Porcelain Mug ▼

- *1996*

Porcelain mug depicting the divorce of Prince Charles and Princess Diana.

- *height 9.5cm*
- **Guide price £18/$34**

Coronation Vase ▼

- *1937*

Single-handled vase to commemorate the coronation of King George VI and Queen Elizabeth. Designed and signed by Charlotte Rhead.

- *height 18.5cm*
- **Guide price £325/$614**

Chocolate Tin ▼

- *circa 1953*

Royal blue enamelled tin with fleur-de-lys motif, commemorating the coronation of Queen Elizabeth II.

- *height 7cm*
- **Guide price £5/$9**

Slipware Charger ▶

- *circa 1977*

Charger by Mary Wondrausch to commemorate the silver jubilee of Queen Elizabeth II.

- *diameter 46cm*
- **Guide price £390/$738**

War Effort Teapot ▼

- *1939*

A teapot commemorating War against Hitlerism, liberty and freedom, given in exchange for aluminium utensils. Made by Crown Ducal.

- *height 14cm*
- **Guide price £140/$265**

Musical Teapot ▲

- *circa 1953*

Teapot in the form of a coach, commemorating the coronation of Queen Elizabeth II. Plays the national anthem.

- *height 13cm*
- **Guide price £240/$454**

Ink Well ▲

- *circa 1915*
Hand grenade casing used as an ink well to commemorate the World War I.
- *height 10.5cm*
- **Guide price £80/$152**

Whisky Decanter ▲

- *1911*
Spode decanter made for Andrew Usher & Co, distillers, Edinburgh, commemorating the coronation of George V.
- *height 25cm*
- **Guide price £160/$303**

Dutch Delft Plaque ▶

- *circa 1945*
To commemorate the liberation of Holland. Showing mother, child and aeroplane.
- *height 20cm*
- **Guide price £150/$284**

Jigsaw Puzzle ▼

- *circa 1934*
With original box showing the young Princess Elizabeth and Princess Margaret in front of Windsor Castle.
- *28 x 34cm*
- **Guide price £75/$142**

Commemorative Plate ▼

- *circa 1937*
For the proposed coronation of Edward VIII. Made by Paragon with the Royal coat of arms.
- *diameter 27cm*
- **Guide price £450/$851**

Officer on Horseback ▶

- *circa 1910*
German. Napoleonic period. Probably Dresden.
- *height 38cm*
- **Guide price £2,500/$4,725**

Winston S. Churchill Toby Jug ▼

- *circa 1941*
With anchor handle, by Fieldings, representing Churchill's second appointment as First Lord.
- *height 15cm*
- **Guide price £190/$360**

Pottery Mug ▼

- *circa 1969*
A mug from the Portmerion pottery to commemorate the first landing of men on the moon by Apollo 11.
- *height 10cm*
- **Guide price £70/$133**

Wedgwood Mug ▲

- *circa 1937*
A Wedgwood mug commemorating the coronation of King George VI, designed by Eric Ravilious.
- *height 11cm*
- **Guide price £475/$898**

Poole Pottery Vase ▲

- *1977*
Vase commemorating the silver jubilee of Queen Elizabeth II, showing the lion and unicorn.
- *height 25cm*
- **Guide price £125/$237**

Boer War Mug ▲

- *circa 1902*
Mug commemorating the end of the Boer War on the front, with the back celebrating the coronation of King Edward VII.
- *height 8cm*
- **Guide price £125/$237**

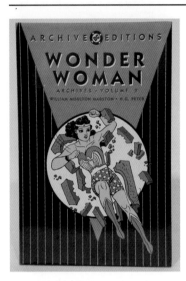

Wonder Woman ▲

- *2000*
Wonder Woman. An archive- volume No. 9. By William Mouton Marston & H.G. Peter.
- **Guide price £38/$72**

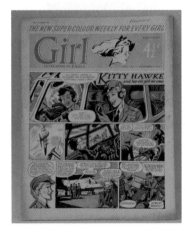

Hunt Emmerson ▼

- *2000*
A biblical cartoon with reference to Jesus and the story of the loaves and fishes.
- **Guide price £90/$171**

Exciting Comics ▼

- *1947*
Exciting Comics featuring, The Black Terror, Nemesis of Crime. No. 58, published by Better Comics. Art Cover by Xela.
- **Guide price £95/$180**

Girl ◄

- *1951*
Girl . No. 1. Published by Hulton Press.
- **Guide price £25/$48**

Iron Man and Captain America ▲

- *1965*
Tales of Suspense featuring Iron Man and Captain America. Published by Marvel.
- **Guide price £65/$123**

X-Men ▲

- *1966*
The X-Men – Holocaust. Published by Marvel Comics Group.
- **Guide price £18/$34**

Batman Year One ▲

- *1988*
Batman Year One by Frank Miller and David Mazzucchelli with Richmond Lewis. Published by D.C.
- **Guide price £9/$17**

Look and Learn ▶

- *1962*
Look and Learn No.2, published by Odhams.
- **Guide price £2/$4**

Mickey Mouse Weekly ▼

- *circa 1950*
Mickey Mouse Weekly published by Odhams.
- **Guide price £3/$6**

Blackhawk ▼

- *1956*
Blackhawk, The Delphian Menace. A Quality Comic Publication.
- **Guide price £35/$66**

The Amazing Spiderman ◄
- *1963*
The Amazing Spiderman, 'The Enforcer'
No.10, published by Marvel Comics.
- **Guide price £140/$265**

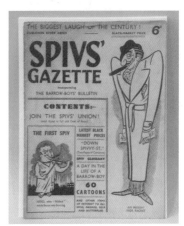

Film Fun ▲
- *1958*
Film Fun published by Amalgamated
Press.
- **Guide price £13/$25**

Courage ▶
- *circa 1950*
Courage. Vol.1. No.1. Published by Miller
& Son Ltd.
- **Guide price £4/$8**

Rupert Weekly ▶
- *1983*
Rupert Weekly published by Marvel
Comics.
- **Guide price £2/$4**

Teen Titans ◄
- *1967*
Teen Titans No.12 - published by D.C.
- **Guide price £7/$14**

2000 AD Year Book 1992 ▲
- *1992*
2000 AD Year Book 1992 published by
Fleetway.
- **Guide price £5/$9**

Fantastic Four ▲
- *1963*
Fantastic Four – the Living Bomb-burst.
Published by Marvel Blastaar.
- **Guide price £22/$42**

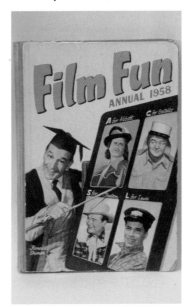

Spivs' Gazette ▲
- *circa 1950*
Spivs' Gazette published by Clare & Son
Ltd.
- **Guide price £3/$6**

The Comet ◄

• 1958

The Comet published by J.B. Allen No. 57.

• **Guide price £5/$9**

The Eagle ◄

• 1951

The Eagle, Vol.2 No.3. Published by Hulton Press.

• **Guide price £6/$12**

Countdown ◄

• 1971

Countdown Dr. Who. Published by Sun Printers.

• **Guide price £11/$21**

Sensation ◄

• 1949

Sensation Comics featuring Wonderwoman, 'The End of Paradise Island!' No.104.

• **Guide price £68/$129**

Film Fun Annual ▲

• 1938

Film Fun Annual. Published by Amalgamated Press.

• **Guide price £25/$48**

The Flash ▲

• 1961

The Flash featuring Superman C.C. National Comics featuring, 'Flash of two worlds!' No.123.

• **Guide price £120/$227**

Chris Riddell ▲

• circa 1977–8

Cartoon of John Bull by Chris Riddell.

• **Guide price £80/$152**

Strange Sports Stories ▶

• 1963

The Brave and the Bold presents Strange Sports Stories, July issue, No.48, published by D.C.

• **Guide price £10/$19**

The Fantastic Four ◄

• 1961

The Fantastic Four, featuring the Fantastic-Car, and Fantastic Four's skyscraper hide-out! Published by Marvel Comics.

• **Guide price £300/$567**

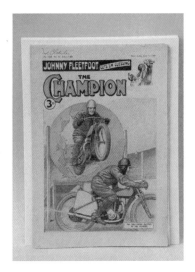

The Champion

* 1949

'Johnny Fleetfoot gets' em guessing'. The Champion. No.1428 Vol.55.

* **Guide price £4/$8**

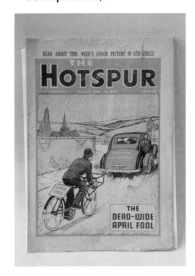

The Hotspur

* 1950

The Hotspur No.699.

* **Guide price £3/$6**

Batman's Detective Comics ▼

* 1977

Batman's Detective Comics published by D.C. No.471.

* **Guide price £8/$16**

Mystery in Space ▼

* 1962

Mystery in Space- featuring The Robot-Wraith of Rann! Published by D.C.

* **Guide price £17/$32**

Comic Cuts ◄

* 1955

Comic Cuts No.2983. Published by Amalgamated Press.

* **Guide price £4/£8**

Kabuki ▲

* 1999

Kabuki published by Wizard Entertainment.

* **Guide price £8/$16**

Essential Avengers ▼

* 2001

Essential Avengers Vol.1, published by Marvel Comics.

* **Guide price £12/$23**

Roobarb and Custard ◄

* 2000

Cartoon of Roobarb and Custard by Bob Godfrey.

* **Guide price £250/$473**

Here Comes Daredevil ►

* 1964

Daredevil the Man Without Fear! Published by Marvel.

* **Guide price £45/$85**

Tales of Suspense ▼

* 1963

Tales of Suspense approved by the Comics code - No. 37.

* **Guide price £50/$95**

Cheyenne ▼

* 1960

Cheyenne, Exciting Adventure. Published by Dell.

* **Guide price £10/$19**

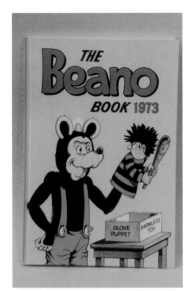

The Beano Book ◄

- *1973*

The Beano Book. Published by D.C. Thompson.

- **Guide price £20/$38**

X-Men ▼

- *1963*

The X-Men published by Marvel Comics Group.

- **Guide price £175/$331**

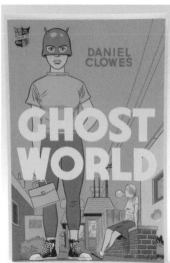

Star Spangled Comics ▲

- *1947*

Star Spangled Comics – Batman's famed partner-in-peril Robin – the boy wonder in Solo Action! No. 65.

- **Guide price £160/$303**

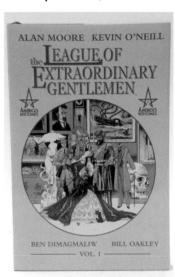

League of Extraordinary Gentlemen ▲

- *2000*

The League of Extraordinary Gentlemen published by America's Best Comics Vol.1.

- **Guide price £19/$36**

Ghost World ◄

- *2000*

Ghost World by Daniel Clowes– published by Jonathan Cape Random House Comic Books Inc.

- **Guide price £7/$14**

Love and Rockets ▼

- *1982*

Love and Rockets - No.1. Published by Fantagraphics Books Inc.

- **Guide price £12/$23**

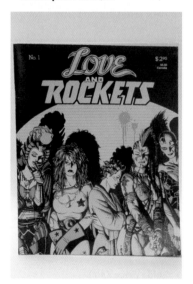

Drawn & Quarterly ◄

- *2000*

Drawn & Quarterly Vol.3.

- **Guide price £19/$36**

X-Men ▼

- *1963*

The X-Men published by Marvel Comics Group. No. 1.

- **Guide price £250/$473**

Wonder Woman ◄

- *1947*

Wonder Woman No.22. 'Wonder Woman and the Color Thief!' published by D.C. Comics.

- **Guide price £135/$255**

Torso ▲

- *2000*

Torso, a true crime graphic novel by Bendis/Andreyk.

- **Guide price £19/$36**

Superman ▶
- *1943*

Superman No. 20. Published by D.C.
- **Guide price £230/$435**

The Amazing Spider-Man ▲
- *1966*

The Amazing Spider-Man.
- **Guide price £30/$57**

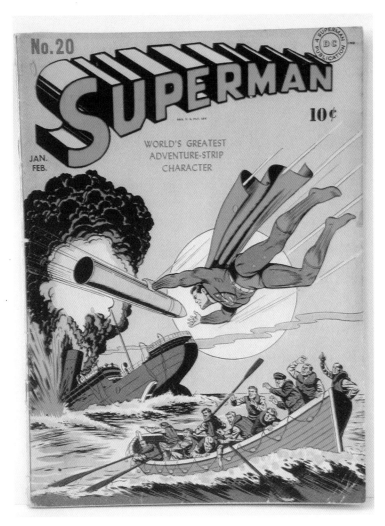

Aquaman ◀
- *1963*

Aquaman featuring Aqualad and The War of the Water Sprites! Published by D.C. No.10.
- **Guide price £8/$16**

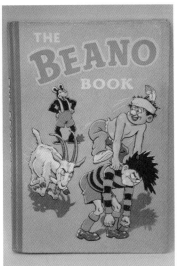

Beano ◀
- *1959*

The Beano Book. Published by D.C. Thompson.
- **Guide price £70/$133**

Soba ▶
- *1998*

Soba, Stories from Bosnia by Joe Sacco. No.1.
- **Guide price £3/$6**

Eagle Annual ◀
- *1951*

Eagle Annual No.1. Published by Hulton.
- **Guide price £15/$28**

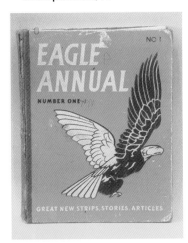

Rupert Adventure Book ▲
- *1955*

Rupert Adventure Book, published by Express Newspapers Ltd.
- **Guide price £10/£19**

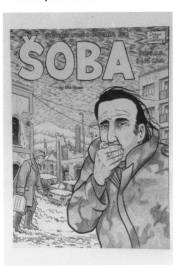

Mclachlan ▼
- *1998*

Cartoon of Eskimos by Mclachlan with the words, "Well, so much for solar panel heating".
- **Guide price £180/$341**

Diana ◀
- *1968*

'Diana' No.305, an English comic published by D.C.Thompson.
- **Guide price £1/$2**

Superman ▶

- *1994*

Superman Archive – Vol. 4, by Jerry Siegel and Joe Shuster.

- **Guide price £38/$72**

X-Men ◀

- *1986*

X-Men published by Marvel. 25th anniversary edition.

- **Guide price £6/$12**

The Essential Hulk ◀

- *1999*

The Essential Hulk Vol. I. Selections from Tales to Astonish.

- **Guide price £12/$23**

Legion of Super-Heroes ▲

- *1973*

Legion of Super-Heroes – The lad who wrecked the Legion. No. I.

- **Guide price £8/$16**

Green Lantern ◀

- *1959*

Showcase presents Green Lantern published by D.C. No. 23.

- **Guide price £280/$530**

All Winners ▲

- *1941*

All Winners starring The Human Torch, Captain America No. 3, Winter Issue Timely.

- **Guide price £650/$1,229**

Justice League of America ▼

- *1960*

Justice League of America – published by D.C. No. 23.

- **Guide price £50/$95**

100 Bullets ▼

- *1999*

100 Bullets – Vertigo by D.C. Publications.

- **Guide price £8/$16**

Cerebus ▲

- *1977*

Cerebus – the Aardvark Vol. I.

- **Guide price £450/$851**

Rupert ▲

- *1979*

Rupert the Daily Express Annual, published by Express Newspapers Ltd.

- **Guide price £10/$19**

V for Vendetta ▼

- *1990*

V for Vendetta by Vertigo/D.C. Comics.

- **Guide price £15/$28**

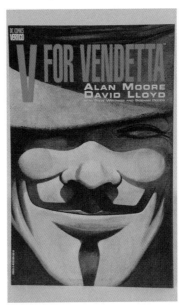

Steve Bell Cartoon ▶

- *1998*

Cartoon of Prince Charles and General Pinochet by Steve Bell.

- **Guide price £250/$473**

Special Edition Comics ▶

- *1940*

Special Edition Comics featuring Captain Marvel, No.1. A Fawcett Publication.

- **Guide price £400/$756**

Buffy ▲

- *2001*

Buffy the Vampire Slayer by Dark Horse Comics, featuring Angel.

- **Guide price £10/$19**

Green Arrow ▲

- *2001*

Green Arrow – Quiver, Part one.

- **Guide price £5/$9**

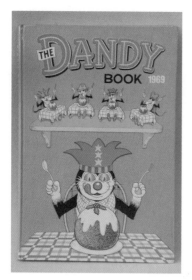

The Dandy

- *1969*

The Dandy Book published by D.C. Thompson.

- **Guide price £30/$57**

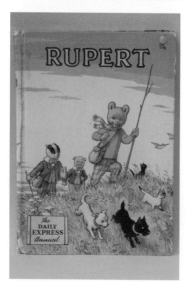

Batman Annual ▼

- *1964–5*

Batman Annual with Batman and Robin also John Jones from Mars and Congo Bill.

- **Guide price £20/$38**

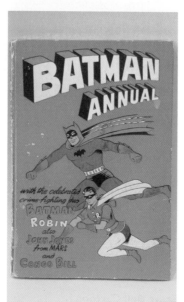

Hellboy the Conqueror Worm ◄

- *2001*

Hellboy the Conqueror Worm by Dark Horse. Maverick Publications.

- **Guide price £215/$406**

All Winners ▲

- *1941*

All Winners Comics starring Captain America. Fall Issue No. 2. Published by Timely.

- **Guide price £1,050/$1,985**

Rupert Annual ◄

- *1955*

Rupert the Bear Annual. No. 20.

- **Guide price £40/$76**

Planetary ▼

- *2001*

Planetary by Wildstorm Publications.

- **Guide price £175/$331**

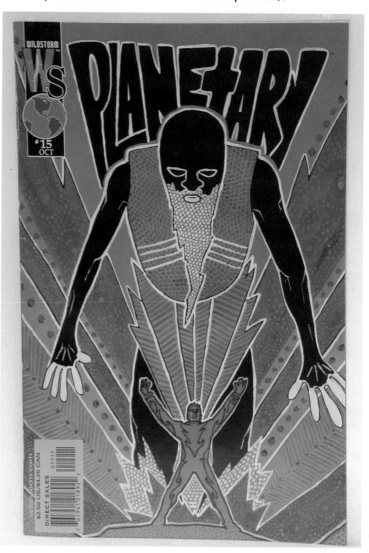

The House of Secrets ◄

- *1971*

The House of Secrets No. 92, published by D.C. Artist: Wrighton.

- **Guide price £60/$114**

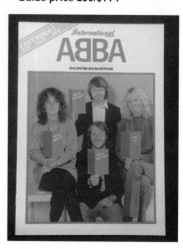

Abba International ▲

- *1981*

Issue No. 1 of Abba fan magazine.

- **Guide price £4/$8**

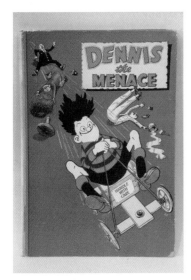

Dennis the Menace ▲

- *1958*

Dennis the Menace, published by D.C. Thompson.

- **Guide price £15/$28**

Scene ▲

- *1962*

Issue No. 14 of *Scene*, a theatre review magazine.

- **Guide price £4/$8**

Fantastic Four ◄

- *1966*

Issue No. 48 of *Fantastic Four*, a classic silver age comic in good condition.

- **Guide price £40/$76**

Second Coming ▼

- *1974*

Issue No. 3, Volume II of Second Coming with a special feature on Charles Bukowski.

- **Guide price £35/$66**

Bulletman ►

- *1941*

Bulletman featuring Bulletman and Bulletgirl 'Be an American', No.1 by Fawcett.

- **Guide price £475/$898**

Tales of Suspense ▼

- *1962*

Tales of Suspense – The Teenager who ruled the World!

- **Guide price £75/$142**

Do It Yourself ▲

- *1999*

Cartoon by Ian Baker entitled 'Do it Yourself'.

- **Guide price £75/$142**

The Alchemist ▼

- *1998*

Cartoon by Chris Riddel – The Alchemist I.

- **Guide price £300/$567**

Zig Zag ▼

- *1976*

Issue No. 65 of rock music magazine, *Zig Zag*, with feature on the Beach Boys.

- **Guide price £4/$8**

Ian Baker, The Bar ▼

- *1999*

Cartoon by Ian Baker entitled, "I wish you'd stop playing hard to get... rid of !".

- **Guide price £15/$28**

Buster ▲

- *1960*

Buster No.1, published by Fleetway.

- **Guide price £30/$57**

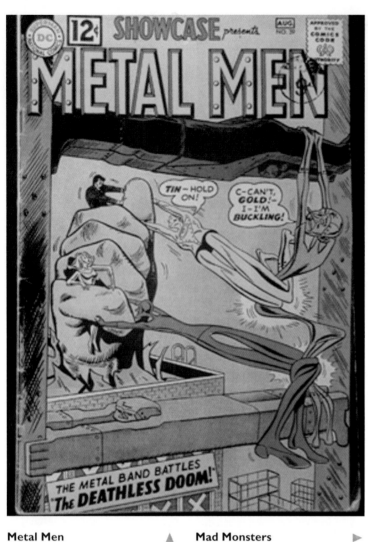

Metal Men ▲

- *1962*

Issue No. 39 of *Metal Men* comic, featuring a special appearance by "The Thanker". Published by DC Comics.

- **Guide price £20/$38**

i-D ▲

- *1989*

Issue No. 73 of fashion and lifestyle magazine, *i-D*.

- **Guide price £3/$6**

Mad Monsters ▶

- *1964*

Issue No. 7 of comic *Mad Monsters*.

- *height 30 cm*
- **Guide price £2/$4**

Rolling Stone ▲

- *1970*

October 1970 issue of US rock music magazine, *Rolling Stone*, featuring the life story of Janis Joplin.

- **Guide price £6/$12**

Animated Cerebus Folder ▲

- *1990s*

Book of art for cancelled film project.

- **Guide price £30/$57**

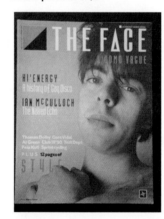

The Face ◀

- *1984*

Issue No. 52 of fashion and lifestyle magazine, *The Face*.

- **Guide price £1/$2**

Playboy ▼

- *1969*

August 1969 issue of adult magazine, *Playboy*, featuring Penny Spinster and the living theatre.

- **Guide price £12/$23**

Continental Film Review ▷

- *August 1968*
August 1968 issue of adult film magazine.
- **Guide price £3/$6**

The Beano ▲

- *1969*
Issue No. 1,405 of popular UK children's comic, *The Beano*.
- **Guide price £1/$2**

Zeta ▲

- *1960s*
Issue No. 5, Volume 2, of erotic photography magazine, *Zeta*.
- **Guide price £10/$19**

Bulletman ▲

- *1941*
Bulletman, a Fawcett Publication No. 3.
- **Guide price £160/$303**

Crawdaddy ▽

- *July 1973*
US music magazine, *Crawdaddy*, featuring Marvin Gaye.
- **Guide price £4/$8**

Video Watchdog ▲

- *1990*
First issue of cult underground magazine, Video Watchdog.
- **Guide price £4/$8**

Gent ▽

- *1961*
Men's magazine, *Gent*, featuring interviews with Mark Russell and Klaus Rock.
- **Guide price £8/$14**

Cry for Dawn ▽

- *1992*
Issue No. 9 of the *Cry for Dawn* comic book.
- **Guide price £8/$16**

Sun ▽

- *1947*
The Sun No.1. Published by J.B. Allen.
- **Guide price £20/$38**

Viz ▲
- *1981*
Issue No. 7 of adult humour comic, *Viz*.
- **Guide price £4/$8**

Sir! ▲
- *1962*
April 1962 issue of adult magazine, *Sir!*, featuring "Death of the Hoover" on the cover.
- **Guide price £4/$8**

Robotech ▲
- *1985*
The Macross Saga 7 issue, signed by the translator Frank Yonco with characteristic beard and glasses doodle. Published by Comico comics.
- **Guide price £8/$16**

Bomp! ▲
- *1976–77*
Music magazine, *Bomp!*, featuring Brian Wilson.
- **Guide price £5/$9**

Town ▲
- *1963*
September 1963 issue of fashion and lifestyle magazine, *Town*.
- **Guide price £10/$19**

Les Rendez-Vous de Sevenoaks ◀
- *1994*
Hardback edition of *Les Rendez-Vous de Sevenoaks*, featuring the first appearance of Richard Hughes.
- **Guide price £5/$9**

Shadow Hawk ▼
- *1992*
A first copy of the comic, with a glossy cover.
- *height 30cm*
- **Guide price £2/$4**

The Incredible Hulk ▼
- *1976*
Issue No. 202 of *The Incredible Hulk*, feautring the Origin of Cadavros. Published by Marvel Comics.
- **Guide price £2/$4**

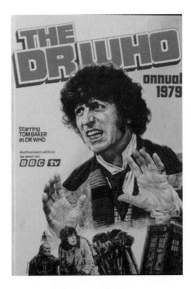

The Dr Who Annual ▲

• 1979

1979 annual based on the cult TV series *Dr Who*.

• **Guide price £5/$9**

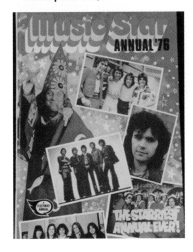

True Romances ▼

• *November 1938*

November 1938 issue of women's magazine, *True Romances*.

• **Guide price £4/$8**

Dr Who Discovers ▼

• 1979

Early Man issue from a spin-off non-fiction series, *Dr Who Discovers*. Booklet with colour poster.

• **Guide price £4/$8**

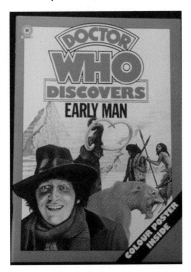

Music Star ◄

• 1976

1976 annual of teenage pop magazine, *Music Star*.

• **Guide price £4/$8**

Venus Moderne ▼

• 1950s

Issue No. 1 of digest-sized nude photography magazine, *Venus Moderne*.

• **Guide price £4/$8**

Men in Vogue ▶

• 1970

One of the few issues of this magazine to appear, featuring B.A.L Newman on the cover. Contains features on men's fashion.

• **Guide price £15/$28**

Sh-Boom ▲

• 1990

American rock magazine, *Sh-Boom*, featuring Rolling Stones' vocalist Mick Jagger on the front cover.

• **Guide price £2/$4**

Boyfriend ▼

• 1964

1964 annual of teenage pop magazine *Boyfriend* featuring Elvis Presley on the cover.

• **Guide price £10/$19**

The Lone Ranger ▼

- *1958*

The Lone Ranger comic book published by Gold Key.

- **Guide price £6/$12**

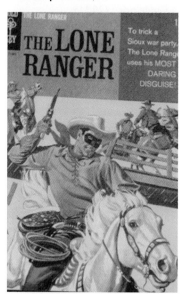

Young Physique ▼

- *1960s*

Issue No. 3 of the vintage muscle magazine, *The Young Physique*.

- **Guide price £4/$8**

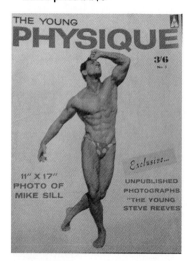

Titanic Series ▼

- *1999*

Set of 25 large-scale cards of the Titanic, produced by Rockwell Publishing at the time of James Cameron's film.

- **Guide price £10/$19**

Interview ▲

- *1977*

Newspaper format of Andy Warhol's magazine, *Interview*.

- **Guide price £18/$34**

The Atom ▼

- *1962*

First issue of *The Atom* comic, published by DC Comics.

- **Guide price £40/$76**

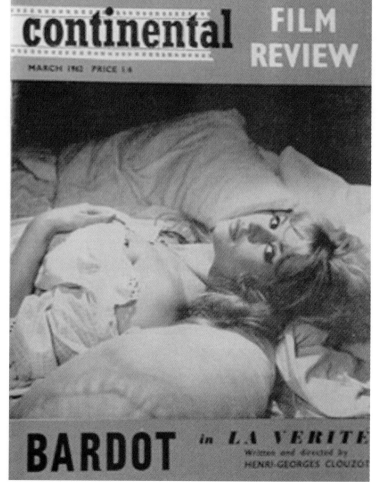

International Times ◄

- *1974*

Issue No. 2, Volume 2, of UK underground newspaper, *International Times*.

- **Guide price £2/$4**

Psychotronic ▲

- *1992*

Issue No. 13 of US film magazine, *Psychotronic*.

- **Guide price £4/$8**

Continental Film Review ▲

- *March 1962*

March 1962 issue of *Continental Film Review*, featuring Brigitte Bardot on the cover.

- **Guide price £4/$8**

Jamming ▲

- *1964*

Issue No. 12 of rock music magazine, *Jamming*.

- **Guide price £3/$4**

Fantastic Adventures ▼

• *1951*
March 1951 issue of US science-fantasy
magazine, *Fantastic Adventures*.
• **Guide price £5/$9**

Bat Masterson ▼

• *1960*
Issue No. 3 of *Bat Masterston*, a comic
published by Dell.
• **Guide price £5/$9**

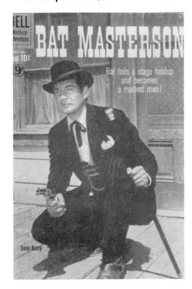

Ray Lowry Cartoon ▼

• *1992*
An original cartoon drawing by Ray
Lowry.
• **Guide price £65/$123**

Dr Who Annual ▲

• *1989*
Twenty-first anniversary annual of cult
TV series, *Dr Who*.
• **Guide price £3/$6**

Amazing Stories ▲

• *1954*
Issue No. 5, Volume I of sci-fi magazine
featuring a story by Philip K. Dick.
• **Guide price £5/$9**

Famous Crowns Series ▲

• *1938*
Set of 25 cards, by Godfrey Phillips Ltd.
Illustration shows an Italian crown.
• **Guide price £8/$16**

Thor ▼

• *January 1970*
The Mighty Thor, No. 172, original price
one shilling, from Marvel Comics.
• **Guide price £10/$19**

Searle Lithograph ▼

• *circa 1960*
A Ronald Searle lithograph from 'Those
Magnificent Men in Their Flying
Machines'.
• **Guide price £420/$794**

Strange Tales ▼

• *1967*
Strange Tales No.161– *Doctor Strange –
The Second Doom*. Published by Marvel
Comics.
• **Guide price £15/$28**

Star Trek

- *1970*

Star Trek No.7 March 1970. Published by Gold Key.

- **Guide price £50/$95**

The Incredible Hulk ◄

- *September 1968*

The Incredible Hulk, issue No. 107, by Marvel Comics.

- **Guide price £14/$26**

Superman Series ▼

- *1968*

Set of cards, issued as series 950 by Primrose Confectionery Co, with sweet cigarettes. Illustration shows 'Space Nightmare'.

- **Guide price £15/$28**

Amazing Spiderman ◄

- *February 1966*

Amazing Spiderman No. 333 – *The Final Chapter!* – published by Marvel Comics.

- **Guide price £50/$95**

Spawn ▲

- *May 1992*

Spawn magazine, issue No. 1, published by Image.

- **Guide price £13/$25**

Billiard Series ▲

- *circa 1905*

Set of 15 cards of *double entendre* billiard terms, from Salmon & Gluckstein.

- **Guide price £825/$1,559**

Soho International ▲

- *1971*

Volume 1, No. 1.

- **Guide price £10/$19**

Playboy ◄

- *May 1969*

May 1969 issue of Playboy magazine, in good condition.

- **Guide price £6/$12**

Romantic Story ▼

- *September 1958*

No. 40 – *Love's Tender Moments* – published by Charlton.

- **Guide price £18/$34**

Whitbread Inn Signs Series ▼

- *1974*

Set of 25 cards of Isle of Wight pubs. This one shows The Railway Inn, Ryde.

- **Guide price £80/$152**

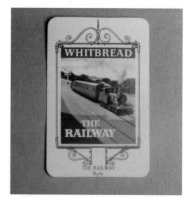

Political Cartoon ▼

- *1997*

A political cartoon – *Springs in Spring* – by John Springs.

- **Guide price £150/$284**

Kensitas Flower Series ▼

• *1933*
An unusual series of 60 cigarette collecting items with silk flowers enclosed in envelopes. By J Wix & Sons.
• **Guide price £168/$318**

Herbie ▼

• *January 1965*
Herbie issue No.13 – *Private Gold Man's New Coat* – published by ACG Comics.
• **Guide price £15/$28**

Monte Hale ▼

• *1952*
Monte Hale Western comic. Issue No. 76, price 10 cents.
• **Guide price £15/$28**

Blakes 7 ▲

• *October 1981*
Blake 7 magazine issue No. 1, published by Marvel UK.
• **Guide price £10/$19**

Stan Eales Cartoon ▲

• *1998*
A cartoon by Stan Eales of a man standing on the ledge of a burning building.
• **Guide price £250/$473**

Taddy's Clown Series ▲

• *1920*
One of 20 known sets of Taddy's 'Clowns' – the most prized of British cigarette cards, with completely blank backs.
• **Guide price £13,000/$24,570**

Strange Tales ▲

• *March 1964*
Strange Tales issue no. 118 – *The Human Torch* – published by Marvel Comics.
• **Guide price £17/$32**

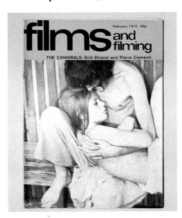

Star Spangled Comics ◄

• *May 1942*
Star Spangled Comics issue No. 8 by DC Comics.
• **Guide price £185/$350**

Watchmen ▼

• *1987*
The collected edition of a comic original in 12 issues, retelling the super-hero story.
• **Guide price £15/$28**

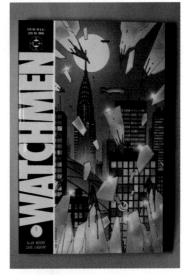

Esquire Magazine ▼

• *1959*
A publication of *Esquire* magazine for March 1959.
• **Guide price £8/$16**

Films and Filming ◄

• *February 1975*
Published by Hanson Books.
• **Guide price £5/$9**

London Standard Strip ▲

• *1997*
A London *Evening Standard* strip of 'Bristow' by Frank Dickens.
• **Guide price £60/$114**

Marvel Masterworks ◀

- *1997*
Spiderman Volume 1.
- **Guide price £25/$48**

X-Men ▲

- *January 1969*
X-Men magazine, issue No. 52 – *Armageddon Now!* – published by Marvel Comics.
- **Guide price £20/$38**

Famous Film Scene Series ▲

- *1935*
Set of 48 cigarette cards, by Gallaher Ltd. Shows Laurel & Hardy from "Babes in Toyland."
- **Guide price £36/$68**

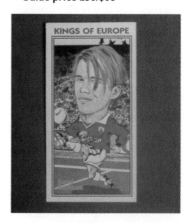

King of Europe Series ▲

- *1999*
Set of 15 cards by Philip Neill comemorating Manchester United FC's historic treble in 1999. Illustration shows a caricature of David Beckham.
- **Guide price £6/$12 (set)**

Buffy the Vampire Slayer ◀

- *1999*
Mail order only. Premium Darkhorse publication.
- **Guide price £10/$19**

Star Wars, Episode I Series ▶

- *1999*
Set of 20 cards collected through Kentucky Fried Chicken.
- **Guide price £6/$12**

Guardian Strip ▼

- *1997*
A strip cartoon for *The Guardian*, called 'If', by Steve Bell.
- **Guide price £135/$255**

Independent Cartoon ▼

- *1997*
A political cartoon from *The Independent*, by Chris Priestley.
- **Guide price £200/$378**

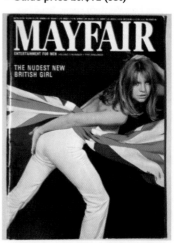

Mayfair Magazine ▲

- *1970*
Volume 3, No.1. British edition.
- **Guide price £20/$38**

Beatles Series ▲

• *circa 1998*
A set of 10 cards in a limited edition of
2,000. The illustration shows Paul
McCartney.
• **Guide price £5/$9**

Builders of the British Empire Series ▲

• *circa 1929*
Set of 50 cards by J A Pattreiouex.
Illustration shows General Gordon.
• **Guide price £135/$255**

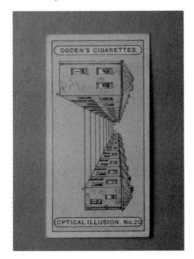

Witchblade ▼

• *November 1996*
Issue No. 10. Published by Top Cow and
signed by the artist.
• **Guide price £20/$38**

The Observer Cartoon ▼

• *1997*
Political cartoon by Chris Riddell, from
The Observer.
• **Guide price £225/$426**

Optical Illusions Series ◄

• *1923*
Set of 25 cigarette cards from Ogdens.
• **Guide price £65/$123**

A MARVEL COMICS LIMITED SERIES

WOLVERINE

Radio Times Cartoon ◄

• *1998*
A topical cartoon for *Radio Times* by
Kipper Williams.
• **Guide price £120/$227**

Wolverine ▲

• *September 1982*
Issue No. 1 by Marvel Comics.
• **Guide price £8/$16**

Curious Beaks Series ▲

• *1929*
Set of 50 cigarette cards from John
Player & Sons. Illustration shows
Australian Jacana.
• **Guide price £40/$76**

Fantastic Four ◄

• *March 1966*
Issue No. 48 – *The X-Men!* – published by
Marvel Comics.
• **Guide price £225/$426**

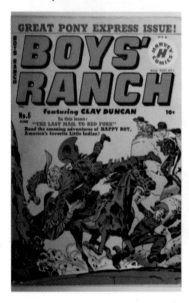

Studio International Art ▲

- *April 1964*

Issue of the art magazine.

- **Guide price £6/$12**

Vogue ▼

- *March 1967*

Volume 124, No. 4 of Condé Nast's *Vogue* magazine.

- **Guide price £15/$28**

Akira Comic ▼

- *1988*

Akira issue No. 2, by Epic publishers. Signed by the translator Frank Yonco.

- **Guide price £10/$19**

Boys' Ranch ◀

- *June 1951*

Boys' Ranch issue No. 5 – *Great Pony Express Issue* – published by Home Comics.

- **Guide price £45/$85**

Roses Series ▲

- *1912*

Set of 50 cigarette cards from Wills. Illustration shows a "Mrs Cocker" rose.

- **Guide price £50/$95**

The Dandy ▶

- *April 1973*

The Dandy, issue No. 1640, published by D.C. Thompson.

- **Guide price £1/$2**

Vogue ▲

- *November 1946*

A November 1946 copy of *Vogue* by Condé Nast.

- **Guide price £10/$19**

Hawkman ▲

- *July 1961*

Hawkman issue No. 36 – *The Brave and the Bold* – published by DC Comics.

- **Guide price £90/$171**

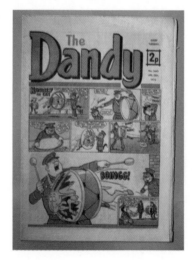

Famous Monsters No.46 ▼

- *1967*

Famous Monsters of Filmland.

- **Guide price £8/$16**

Notable MPs ▼

- *1929*

Series of 50 cigarette cards of politicians, from Carreras Ltd. Illustration shows caricature of David Lloyd George.

- **Guide price £45/$85**

Original Cartoon ▼

- *1998*

A cartoon titled 'Great Moments in Science' by Hunt Emerson.

- **Guide price £100/$189**

Film Fun ▲
- *1957*

Issue no. 1971. Published by The Amalgamated Press.
- **Guide price £2/$4**

The Topper ▲
- *April 1957*

Issue no. 220 by DC Thompson.
- **Guide price £2/$4**

Knockout ▲
- *1954*

Issue No. 806 of Knockout comic, by The Algamated Press.
- **Guide price £1/$2**

Custard Drawing ▼
- *1999*

A drawing of the character Custard, by Bob Godfrey, taken from the TV series 'Roobarb'.
- **Guide price £130/$246**

Playboy ▼
- *November 1968*

A 1968 issue of *Playboy* magazine with election cover.
- **Guide price £8/$16**

X-Men ▼
- *December 1977*

X-Men issue No. 108 – *Twilight of the Mutants* – published by Marvel Comics.
- **Guide price £12/$23**

Sunday Times Cartoon ▼
- *1997*

A cartoon for *The Sunday Times* by Nick Newman.
- **Guide price £120/$227**

Vogue ▶
- *July 1949*

A July 1949 edition of *Vogue* magazine by Condé Nast.
- **Guide price £10/$19**

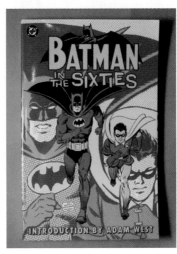

Batman in the Sixties ▲
- *1997*

Television series spin-off magazine, published by DC Comics.
- **Guide price £15/$28**

Aircraft of the Royal Air Force ▲
- *1938*

Set of 50 cigarette cards from Players. Illustration shows Hawker Hurricane.
- **Guide price £45/$85**

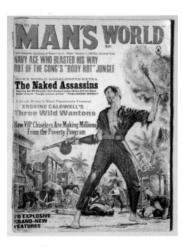

Man's World ▲
- *1967*

Man's World Volume 13. No.1.
- **Guide price £4/$8**

Vanity Fair Series ▼
- *circa 1902*

Set of 50 cigarette cards of *Vanity Fair* caricatures from Wills. Illustration shows George Wyndham, MP.
- **Guide price £225/$426**

Daily Telegraph Strip ▲
- *1998*

An original 'Alex' cartoon strip for *The Daily Telegraph*. By Peattie & Taylor.
- **Guide price £165/$312**

Konga ▲
- *1960*

An issue of Konga magazine, published by Charlton Comics.
- **Guide price £15/$28**

History of the VC ▼
- *1980*

Set of 24 cards, from Doncella cigars, commemorating winners of the Victoria Cross.
- **Guide price £18/$34**

Sandman Comic ▼
- *1989*

Issue No. 1 of Sandman Comic, from D.C. Comics.
- **Guide price £20/$38**

Original Cartoon ▶
- *1997*

A drawing by Ed MacLachlan for NET magazine.
- **Guide price £140/$265**

Modeling with Millie ▲
- *December 1964*

Modeling with Millie magazine, issue No. 36 – *The Greatest Love Story!* – published by Marvel.
- **Guide price £10/$19**

Dope Fiend Funnies ▼
- *1974*

Published by Cosmic Comics.
- **Guide price £8/$16**

Incredible Hulk ▲
- *1969*

Incredible Hulk, issue No. 112 – *The Brute Battles On!* – published by Marvel Comics.
- **Guide price £12/$23**

Land Rover Series ▼
- *2000*

Set of seven cards, showing seven seater. Illustration shows 86-inch seven-seater.
- **Guide price £3/$6**

The Invincible Iron Man ▼
- *June 1968*

Issue No. 2 of *The Invincible Iron Man* – *Enter the Demolisher!* – published by Marvel comics.
- **Guide price £24/$41**

'X Files' Series ▼
- *1996*

Set of 72 spin-off cards, from the X Files TV series, by Topps Chewing Gum, USA.
- **Guide price £12/$23**

Imperial Dog Collection Series ▲

- *1999*

Set of six cards by Imperial Publishing. Illustration shows an English bulldog.

- **Guide price £3/$6**

Private Eye Strip ▲

- *1997*

YOBS cartoon strip, from *Private Eye*, by Tony Husband.

- **Guide price £120/$227**

Waterloo Series ▲

- *circa 1914*

Set of 50 cigarette cards from Wills, never issued because of fear of offending French during First World War.

- **Guide price £4,750/$8,978**

Noted Cats Series ▼

- *1930*

Set of 24 cards by Cowans Confectionery, Canada. Shows a Persian male cat.

- **Guide price £132/$251**

Types of Horses ▼

- *1939*

Set of 25 large cigarette cards from John Player & Sons. Illustration shows a Cob horse.

- **Guide price £85/$161**

Film Directors ▼

- *1992*

A set of 20 famous film directors, issued by Cecil Court Collectors Centre.

- **Guide price £6/$12**

Racing Yachts Series ▼

- *1938*

Set of 25 cards, from paintings by Charles Pears. Illustration shows X.O.D. class.

- **Guide price £80/$152**

Highland Clan Series ▶

- *1907*

Set of 25 cigarette cards from Players. Illustration shows a representative of the Murray clan.

- **Guide price £80/$152**

Batman ▲

- *May 1942*

Very early Batman magazine – issue No. 10, by DC Comics.

- **Guide price £220/$416**

New Statesman Cover ▲

- *1999*

Cartoon by Chris Riddell, used on cover of *New Statesman*.

- **Guide price £250/$473**

Daily Telegraph Cartoon ▲

- *1998*

A cartoon for *The Daily Telegraph* by Matt.

- **Guide price £100/$189**

Daredevil ▲

- *June 1964*

Daredevil issue No. 2, published by Marvel Comics.

- **Guide price £135/$255**

Guardian Cartoon ▲

- *1999*

A cartoon for *The Guardian* newspaper, by Steve Bell.

- **Guide price £250/$473**

FURNITURE

Italian Bombe Bed ▼
- *early 20th century*
An unusual Italian "bombe" bed made in solid walnut with marquetry inlay incorporating tireless attention to detail.
- *1.63m x 1.83m x 2.24m*
- **Guide price £3,350/$6,332**

Black Lacquer Chairs ▼
- *early 20th century*
A pair of folding chairs, black lacquer over elm with cane seat and back. Made in Shanghai, where a more Westernised style was popular.
- *height 90cm*
- **Guide price £395/$748**

Shagreen Box ▼
- *circa 1920*
An English Art Deco geometric shagreen box with ivory stringing. -
- *5cm x 10cm x 12.5cm*
- **Guide price £450/$851**

Macassar Sideboard ▲
- *1929–30*
Art Deco period Heal's Macassar ebony veneered sideboard having top panels of green shagreen and sides and front veneered in boldly figured timber supported on ivory feet.
- *89cm x 152.5cm x 51cm*
- **Guide price £29,500/$55,755**

Ring Box ▲
- *1906*
A silver and tortoiseshell ring box with swag inlay 'H Matthews', Birmingham.
- *height 3.8cm*
- **Guide price £330/$624**

Open-fronted Walnut Cabinet ◄
- *circa 1930*
Open-fronted walnut corner display cabinet with shaped moulded pediment.
- *1.85m x 68.6cm*
- **Guide price £1,850/$3,497**

Burr Walnut Bureau Bookcase ▲
- *1920*
Bureau bookcase with upper doors enclosing shelves and drawers above a bureau and base.
- *2.34m x 56cm x 1.12m*
- **Guide price £4,750/$8,978**

Painted Walnut Cabinet ◄
- *circa 1930*
Fine quality walnut cabinet with painted panel set into the door of still life with roses.
- *73.6cm x 43.2cm x 1.143m*
- **Guide price £3,250/$6,143**

Balloon Back Chairs ▼

- *circa 1920*
One of six balloon back chairs with cane seats.
- *89cm x 38cm x 40.6cm*
- **Guide price £765/$1,446**

Edwardian Stationery Box ▶

- *1904*
Unusual Edwardian slope front stationery box with 1904 Birmingham hallmarked silver decoration, probably by John Angel.
- *26cm x 17cm x 24cm*
- **Guide price £995/$1,881**

Edwardian Child's Chair ▲

- *circa 1910*
Simple country-style chair with shaped armrests, turned legs and cross rails, with good patina.
- *75cm x 34cm x 38cm*
- **Guide price £185/$350**

Cherry Dining Chairs ▲

- *circa 1920*
One of six Provençal dining chairs in cherrywood with rush seats.
- *height 96.5cm*
- **Guide price £1,295/$2,448**

Mahjong Set ▼

- *1920*
Impressive and imposing Mahjong set of the highest quality in a solid oak case with extensive brass work decoration to the sides and top. With solid brass handle and sliding front panel revealing five similarly decorated drawers containing solid ivory tiles, game sticks and dice. Provenance: The Right Honourable The Viscount Leverhulme, K. G. of Thornton Manor.
- *29cm x 32cm*
- **Guide price £5,950/$11,246**

Chinese Rocking Chair ◀

- *early 20th century*
A rocking chair with turned legs and arm supports showing a very Western-influenced style. Blackwood with cane seat and back, with a simple floral motif carved into the back rail.
- *height 1.1m*
- **Guide price £490/$927**

Oak Canopy Bar ▶

- *early 20th century*
Oak canopy bar with carved panels and galleried and turned designs and etched mirrors. The moulded cornice with leaded glass decorative panels.
- *width 1.22m*
- **Guide price £4,500/$8,505**

Tortoiseshell Box ▲

- *1909*
A tortoiseshell and silver ring box with floral piqué.
- *height 3cm*
- **Guide price £235/$445**

Leather Desk Chair ▲

- *circa 1920*
Walnut desk chair with leather upholstery.
- *94cm x 48cm x 58.4cm*
- **Guide price £950/$1,796**

Black Lacquer Cabinet ▲

- *Early 20th century*
English lacquer cabinet in the Chippendale style incorporating fine peacock design, the whole surmounted by a galleried cornice.
- *1.80m x 43.2cm x 68.6cm*
- **Guide price £2,950/$5,576**

Walnut Chest of Drawers ▲

- *circa 1930*
Walnut chest of drawers on cabriole legs.
- *86.4cm x 50.8cm x 76.2cm*
- **Guide price £2,750/$5,198**

Mahogany Kneehole Desk ▶

- *circa 1910*
A mahogany desk of large size, standing on ogee bracket feet and retaining original handles.
- *width 1.37m*
- **Guide price £1,850/$3,497**

Domed Walnut Cabinet ▼

- *circa 1930*
Pretty walnut cabinet with domed bookcase, raised on cabriole legs.
- *60cm x 40.6cm x 58.4cm*
- **Guide price £2,250/$4,253**

Walnut Writing Table ▼

- *circa 1910*
Writing table with leather inlay, two side drawers on carved cabriole legs.
- *76.2cm x 53.4cm x 89cm*
- **Guide price £565/$1,068**

Walnut Display Cabinet ▲

- *circa 1920*
Walnut display cabinet with doors opening to reveal shelves, scrolled apron with central finial on turned legs with double stretcher.
- *1.55m x 28.1cm x 99cm*
- **Guide price £3,950/$7,466**

Waterfall Screen ▲

- *20th century*
A two-fold Japan paper screen painted in ink on a gold ground with a taki (waterfall), signed by Kunsai.
- *1.67m x 1.68m*
- **Guide price £9,800/$18,522**

Secretaire Bookcase ▼

- *mid-20th century*
Mahogany breakfront secretaire with brass fittings surmounted by glass-fronted bookshelves.
- *2.1m x 36cm x 1.7m*
- **Guide price £4,750/$8,978**

Walnut Sideboard ▼

- *circa 1930*
Pretty serpentine-fronted walnut cabinet and sideboard with moulded panel doors.
- *81.3cm x 40.6cm x 81.3cm*
- **Guide price £2,250/$4,253**

Yew Library Steps ▼

- *20th century*
Hand-made solid yew library steps with brass fittings.
- *88.9cm x 38.1cm*
- **Guide price £820/$1,550**

Bijin and Sakura Screen ▼

• *Taisho period 20th century*
A two-fold silk screen painted in ink and colour on a buff ground with two young bijin (beauties) beside a palanquin and beneath a flowering sakura (cherry tree). One is making a garland from the fallen blossoms she is collecting while the other looks on.
• *1.72m x 1.73m*
• **Guide price £8,000/$15,120**

Oak Office Desk ▲

• *20th century*
An all-in-one oak office desk, having seven drawers.
• *1.14m x 68.6cm*
• **£375**

Small Carved Table ◄

• *circa 1910*
A pretty two-tier table with scroll and lotus carved detail and carved foliate edge.
• *68.6cm x 33cm x 33cm*
• **Guide price £165/$312**

Shaped Front Chest of Drawers ▼

• *circa 1920*
Walnut shaped front chest of drawers of lovely faded colour.
• *50.8cm x 40.6cm x 69cm*
• **Guide price £3,950/$7,466**

Mahogany Corner Bar ▲

• *early 20th century*
Elaborately carved panelled and canopied corner bar, with medallion decoration and scrolled moulding below a moulded cornice.
• *width 1.52m*
• **Guide price £4,750/$8,978**

Walnut Cabriole Leg Desk ▲

• *Early 20th century*
Fine walnut leather-topped writing desk raised on cabriole legs, with curved front, the central drawer flanked by two deep drawers.
• *71cm x 61cm x 1.22m*
• **Guide price £1,950/$3,686**

William and Mary Long Stool ▲

• *circa 1920*
A William and Mary style upholstered long stool with early 18th century tapestry covering. On turned legs with pad feet, joined by shaped moulded stretchers with three turned finials.
• *17cm x 18cm x 60cm*
• **Guide price £4,600/$8,694**

Oak Canted Corner Bar ◄

• *Early 20th century*
Highly decorated oak canted corner bar; a hybrid of architectural elements, panelled with scrolled and turned columns and mirrored rear.
• *height 2.2m*
• **Guide price £5,250/$9,923**

Walnut Chest on Stand ▼

- circa 1920

Pretty walnut chest with seven drawers on cabriole legs.

- 1.27m x 43cm x 76.2cm
- **Guide price £2,450/$4,631**

Teak and Glass Coffee Table ▼

- 1950s

A teak and glass coffee table, the boomerang-shaped legs and cross stretchers supporting a circular glass top.

- 40.5cm x 73.5cm
- **Guide price £65/$123**

Walnut Side Table ▲

- circa 1920

Walnut drop-leaf side table with drawer on barley twist legs and curved cross stretcher.

- 68.6cm x 35.5cm x 96.5cm
- **Guide price £1,750/$3,308**

Walnut Sofa Table ▲

- circa 1930

Walnut sofa table with two side extensions, standing on a turned stretcher, drawers and feet with brass fittings.

- 71cm x 56cm x 73.7cm
- **Guide price £2,750/$5,198**

Edwardian Three-Tier Stand ▼

- circa 1905

An unusual wrought iron and copper Edwardian three-tier stand with scrolled decoration.

- 95cm x 25cm
- **Guide price £135/$255**

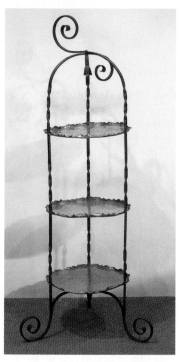

Art Deco Occasional Table ◀

- 1930s

Art Deco occasional circular table with a quartered veneered top in an attractive warm "golden" burr walnut and a quartered sectioned base in differing heights.

- 60cm x 58.5cm
- **Guide price £390/$738**

Hessian Ottoman ◀

- circa 1910

Ottoman covered in cross-stitch hessian with red and blue floral patterns.

- 61cm x 53.3cm x 98cm
- **Guide price £345/$652**

Swedish Desk ▲

- 1920–30

Gustavian-style Swedish free-standing desk.

- 76cm x 1.44m
- **Guide price £2,900/$5,481**

Red Leather Chairs ▼

- *circa 1960*

One of a pair of Italian chairs, one red and the other black leather, with teak legs and back rest.

- *height 98cm*
- **Guide price £800/$1,512**

Arts and Crafts Table ▶

- *circa 1910*

Arts and Crafts oak table of solid construction with straight supports and circular stretcher.

- *52cm x 69cm*
- **Guide price £280/$530**

Art Nouveau Bureau ▲

- *circa 1905*

Art Nouveau oak bureau with folding writing slope above a single drawer with organically designed copper metalwork.

- *1.2m x 90cm*
- **Guide price £565/$1,068**

SP4B Armchair ▲

- *circa 1931*

An SP4B armchair by Oliver Bernard for PEL, the seat fully upholstered in green rexine and supported on a canterlevered chrome frame.

- *height 71cm*
- **Guide price £195/$370**

Dieter Rams Armchairs ▼

- *1962*

Armchairs by Dieter Rams, for Vitsoe, made from green leather on a white fibreglass base.

- *69cm x 86cm*
- **Guide price £2,900/$5,481**

Supporto Office Chair ▼

- *circa 1979*

A Supporto office chair, by Fred Scott for Hille, with grey enamel finish and black cloth upholstery.

- *height 1.24m*
- **Guide price £275/$520**

"Reigate" Rocker ▲

- *1965*

William Plunkett rocker and footstool with coated steel frame, aluminium seat and arms, rubber webbing and cushions upholstered in original orange tweed fabric.

- *92cm x 56cm x 84cm*
- **Guide price £700/$1,323**

Arts and Crafts Chairs ▲

- *circa 1905*

One of three Arts and Crafts single chairs with moulded top rail and curved splat with fruitwood inlay standing on straight square legs.

- *88cm x 44cm*
- **Guide price £2,250/$4,253**

Hans Wegner Daybed ▲

- *1960s*

Danish daybed designed by Hans Wegner and upholstered in oatmeal tweed. Has a dark oak frame and the back lifts up to reveal storage and a canvas roll-out cover to protect sofa while sleeping.
- *1.95m x 86cm x 76cm*
- **Guide price £800/$1,512**

Plywood Coffee Table ▲

- *1930s*

A circular two-tiered coffee table made by 'Gerald Summers, Makers of Simple Furniture'. Made of birch plywood, formed and stained.
- *41cm x 68cm*
- **Guide price £550/$1,040**

Arts and Crafts Lamp Table ▼

- *circa 1905*

Arts and Crafts mahogany occasional table with three supports and carved and pierced decoration.
- *69cm x 43cm*
- **Guide price £220/$416**

Nursery Chest ◄

- *circa 1930*

Heal's oak nursery chest with double and single panelled doors, three short drawers and two long drawers.
- *1.5m x 1.15m*
- **Guide price £1,850/$3,497**

French Leather Chairs ▼

- *1977*

Pair of chairs by Michel Cadestin and George Laurent for the Library of the Centre Pompidou Beaubourg, made from wire with leather seat and back. Illus: Les Années 70, by Anne Bony.
- *height 74.5cm*
- **Guide price £1,200/$2,268**

Italian Lounge Chair ◄

- *1960s*

"Lady" lounge chair designed by Marco Zanuso, made by Arflex. Wood and fibreglass frame, on tubular brass legs with black ferrules, fully upholstered in yellow fabric.
- *78cm x 78cm x 78cm*
- **Guide price £650/$1,229**

Chrome Dining Chairs ▲

- *1975*

One of a set of four dining chairs with grey leather and chrome, by Prebenfabricus & Dorgen Kastholm for Alfred Kill.
- *height 70cm*
- **Guide price £2,200/$4,158**

Japanese Chest ◄

- *circa 1920s*

Special Japanese Isho Dansu (storage chest) for fabrics. The wood has not been sealed or lacquered first.
- *1.02m x 54cm*
- **Guide price £2,650/$5,009**

Ercol Occasional Table ▼

- *20th century*

An Ercol occasional table, the elm top supported on a beech frame.
- *49.5cm x 84cm*
- **Guide price £125/$237**

Wine Table ▼

- *1900–15*

Edwardian wine table with a circular top, satinwood banding and a central flower, the whole standing on a turned column with a tripod base.

- *47cm x 26cm*
- **Guide price £169/$320**

Arts and Crafts Carvers ◄

- *circa 1905*

One of a pair of oak Arts and Crafts carvers with scrolled arms and turned supports.

- *1.05m x 58cm*
- **Guide price £550/$1,040**

Stool by Verner Panton ▲

- *circa 1960*

Wire stool with original circular suede padded cove, by Danish Verner Panton.

- *height 43cm*
- **Guide price £745/$1,408**

Magistretti Coffee Table ▼

- *1964*

Low coffee table by Vico Magistretti in ebonised wood with end drawers, drop flap sides, a central storage well and brass top.

- *1.28m x 96cm*
- **Guide price £500/$945**

Mahogany Dining Chairs ▼

- *circa 1950s*

One of a set of six mahogany dining chairs with pierced backsplat, drop-in seat cushion and cabriole legs.

- *1m x 48cm*
- **Guide price £1,250/$2,363**

Walnut Bureau ◄

- *circa 1940*

A very good early twentieth century figured walnut bureau in the George II style.

- *1.04m x 84cm*
- **Guide price £1,895/$3,544**

Art Deco Cabinet ▲

- *circa 1930*

Art Deco figured mahogany walnut cocktail cabinet of circular design with pull-out mixing surface.

- *1.61m x 85cm*
- **Guide price £995/$1,881**

Teak Chairs ▼

- *circa 1960*

One of a set of four Danish teak chairs with black vinyl seats.

- *height 80cm*
- **Guide price £160/$303**

French Bedside Cabinet ◄

- *1930s*

Art Deco French bedside cabinet with heavily figured walnut veneers and almost organic shape.

- *58.5cm x 60cm x 32cm*
- **Guide price £255/$482**

Burr Walnut Table ▼

- *1930s*

Art Deco burr walnut table featuring a beautifully grained walnut veneered top, with a second tier underneath and four tapering ebonised legs.

- *59cm x 80cm x 52cm*
- **Guide price £225/$426**

Bird's Eye Circular Coffee Table ▲

- *1930s*

Art Deco pale blonde bird's eye maple circular coffee table. This rare table features grained maple veneers and a classic Deco circular base with walnut feather banded decoration.

- *56cm x 73cm*
- **Guide price £545/$1,030**

Leather Armchair ▼

- *1970s*

Danish leather armchair with formed beech frames and upholstered in grey leather with buttoned back and seat.

- *76cm x 57cm x 60cm*
- **Guide price £200/$378**

Modernist Chest of Drawers ▼

- *1930s*

Art Deco modernist style chest of drawers. The underwood is mahogany which has been grained in a blonde colour, surrounding the front edging is walnut feather banding. There are six graduated drawers.

- *96cm x 38cm x 50cm*
- **Guide price £585/$1,106**

U-Base Table ▲

- *1930s*

Original Art Deco U-base occasional table in a figured burr walnut with two walnut columns and glass top for protection.

- *62cm x 70cm x 70cm*
- **Guide price £475/$898**

Italian Leather Chair ▲

- *1930s*

Very rare large Italian Art Deco leather chair. In excellent condition with little sign of wear.

- *78cm x 1.16m x 92cm*
- **Guide price £285/$539**

Harlow Chairs ▼

- *1971*

Set of four "Harlow" chairs with red wool-padded seats and backs, standing on aluminium bases and stands, by Ettore Sottsass for Poltronova.

- *height 82cm*
- **Guide price £3,500/$6,615**

White Folding Bench ▲

- *circa 1920*

Continental pine folding bench, painted white, on metal legs and arms.

- *90cm x 1.25m*
- **Guide price £220/$416**

Cocktail Table ▼

• *1930s*
Art Deco walnut cocktail table featuring a central compartment in the top, accessed by sliding open two covers. Octagonal in shape, this piece also has two shelves and a ribbed pattern on the side panels.

• *62cm x 60cm*
• **Guide price £375/$709**

French Chinese-style Chairs ▲

• *circa 1920*
One of a pair of French oak chairs with a strong Chinese influence and a distressed paint effect, standing on straight square legs.

• *height 74cm*
• **Guide price £1,250/$2,363**

Art Nouveau Door ▼

• *circa 1920*
Mahogany door frame in Art Nouveau style with glass panels within organic styled mouldings, with brass door furniture.

• *220cm x 74cm*
• **Guide price £1,400/$2,646**

Red Stereophonic Chair ▲

• *circa 1960s*
Red moulded fibreglass egg chair on a circular metal base, with grey and white wool-padded upholstery and leather-padded seat cover and back rest, with fitted stereo and matching ottoman, designed by the Lee Co. of California for a commission.

• *1.29m x 86cm*
• **Guide price £4,200/$7,938**

Art Deco Three-Piece Suite ▲

• *circa 1930*
A very rare and unusual Art Deco upholstered leather three-piece suite.

• *86cm x 95cm*
• **Guide price £5,330/$10,073**

Savoy Trolley ◄

• *1930s*
English Art Deco circular "Savoy" hostess trolley with three walnut shelves, frame and castors.

• *78cm x 70cm x 43cm*
• **Guide price £345/$652**

Cocktail Cabinet ▲

• *1930s*
Art Deco cocktail cabinet in figured walnut, shaped like a half drum. The top part of the cocktail cabinet has an all-mirrored interior and internal light. The doors to the top and base storage areas roll open and shut.

• *1.38m x 1.14m x 35cm*
• **Guide price £1,100/$2,079**

Dressing Table ◄

• *circa 1950*
Modernist oak dressing table with two columns of graduated drawers and single drawer above knee hole.

• *1.65m x 1.22m*
• **Guide price £225/$426**

Edwardian Bedsteads ▲

• *1910*
A pair of Queen Anne style Edwardian moulded single bedsteads in burr walnut, standing on cabriole legs.

• *width 111cm*
• **Guide price £4,500/$8,505**

Walnut Buffet ▲

* 1930

Art Deco breakfront walnut buffet with solid supports and moulded decoration.

* 84cm x 1.06m
* **Guide price £650/$1,229**

Arts and Crafts Dining Chairs ▲

* circa 1910

One of a set of six light oak English Arts and Crafts single dining chairs and two carvers.

* 104cm x 38cm
* **Guide price £2,995/$5,661**

Adelphi Door ▼

* 1920

Pine Aldephi door, painted yellow with brass door furniture, circular foliate design on handle and the head of Pan on the door plate.

* 160cm x 89cm
* **Guide price £950/$1,796**

Shakespeare's House ▶

* circa 1920

Whimsical novelty jewel box in the form of a model of Shakespeare's house, inset with a clock and barometer on the side. Probably a tourist item.

* height 18cm
* **Guide price £2,950/$5,576**

Modernist Table ▲

* circa 1930

Modernist table for use as a library table or cocktail cabinet, made from oak with crossbanded decoration raised on moulded bracket feet.

* 51cm x 60cm
* **Guide price £185/$350**

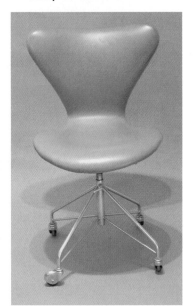

Flamed Mahogany Doors ▼

* circa 1910

One of a pair of fine quality six-panelled, flamed mahogany doors, with egg and dart moulding and fine interior pencil beading.

* 201cm x 94cm
* **Guide price £2,400/$4,536**

Leather Rotating Chair ◀

* 1970

Tan leather rotating and adjustable desk chair with padded seat and back, and metal legs on wheels.

* height 74cm
* **Guide price £495/$927**

Charles Perriand Chairs ▼

- *circa 1973*

Set of four chairs with brown leather upholstery, stitching and metal studs looped to moulded tubular chrome, designed by Charles Perriand.

- *height 84cm*
- **Guide price £950/$1,796**

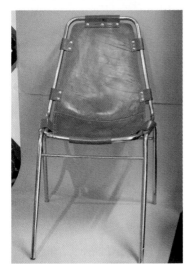

Eames Armchairs ◄

- *circa 1975*

One of a pair of Eames padded brown armchairs with aluminium arms and base.

- *height 1.01m*
- **Guide price £1,450/$2,741**

Franco Albini Chairs ▼

- *circa 1950*

One of a pair of Italian walnut chairs with green upholstered padded seats and back, by Franco Albini.

- *height 78cm*
- **Guide price £1,200/$2,268**

'Medea' Chairs ►

- *circa 1955*

One of a pair of moulded beechwood 'Medea' chairs by Vittoria Nobli, with an oblong hole in the seat and straight black metal legs.

- *height 82cm*
- **Guide price £450/$851**

Walnut Sofa ▲

- *circa 1920*

A fine walnut three-piece suite with caned back rest and side panels and turned decoration, raised on circular bun feet.

- *91cm x 182cm*
- **Guide price £3,900/$7,371**

Revolving Bookcase ►

- *circa 1905*

An Edwardian mahogany revolving bookcase with pierced side panels raised on four splayed legs.

- *80cm x 43cm*
- **Guide price £795/$1,503**

Walnut Coffee Table ◄

- *circa 1920s*

Walnut reproduction coffee table with scalloped decoration and cabriole legs with acanthus leaf carving.

- *52cm x 100cm*
- **Guide price £275/$520**

Jason Stacking Chairs ▼

- *1950*

A set of five "Jason" stacking chairs designed by Carl Jacobs for Kandya. Formed plywood seat section over a turned beech base.

- *74cm x 52cm x 38cm*
- **Guide price £700/$1,323 for set**

Kasthole Armchairs ▼

- *circa 1970*

One of a pair of leather and bent rosewood armchairs with metal and leather arms by Fabricius and Kastholme.

- *82cm x 72cm*
- **Guide price £1,950/$3,686**

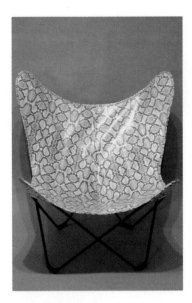

Butterfly Chairs ▲

- *circa 1950*

One of a pair of plastic mock snakeskin butterfly chairs on an early tubular frame, manufactured by Knoll.

- *height 1m*
- **Guide price £550/$1,040**

Brass Umbrella Stand ▼

- *circa 1910*

Art Nouveau brass brolly stand with hand-beaten finish and embossed tulip design.

- *height 63cm*
- **Guide price £375/$709**

Italian Red S-Chairs ◄

- *circa 1960*

One of a pair of Italian red padded soft man-made fabric S-bend chairs with tubular metal base.

- *height 80cm x 46cm*
- **Guide price £600/$1,134**

Car Radiator Chair ▲

- *circa 1970*

French-commissioned green fibreglass chair with square vinyl cushions, in the style of a car radiator and wings with headlights in working order.

- *82cm x 120cm x 75cm*
- **Guide price £2,200/$4,158**

Art Nouveau Chairs ▲

- *circa 1910*

One of a set of six Art Nouveau oak chairs consisting of two carvers and four single chairs, with slated back splat and curved top rail above square tapered legs.

- *140cm x 53cm*
- **Guide price £825/$1,559**

Art Deco Table ▲

- *circa 1940s*

An oak two-tier Art Deco side table with square tapered supports.
- *70cm x 53cm*
- **Guide price £225/$426**

Edwardian Chest of Drawers ▲

- *circa 1905*

Edwardian chest of two small and two long drawers, with metal foliate handles standing on straight legs.
- *82cm x 1.08m*
- **Guide price £240/$454**

Art Deco Chest ▲

- *circa 1930s*

A very good quality Art Deco chest in solid oak with wonderful early plastic handles.
- *83cm x 94cm*
- **Guide price £450/$851**

Bedside Cabinet ▼

- *circa 1920s*

Figured walnut bedside cabinet with pull-out writing slope and plain panelled door, raised on carved feet.
- *74cm x 38cm*
- **Guide price £325/$614**

Black Leather Armchair ▶

- *circa 1960*

Black leather armchair with padded seat and back, with metal and leather arms, standing on a rotating star-shaped metal base.
- *height 89cm*
- **Guide price £750/$1,418**

Chairs by Carl Jacobs ▲

- *circa 1950*

One of a set of six red chairs by Carl Jacobs for Kandya Ltd., with teak legs.
- *72cm x 51cm*
- **Guide price £485/$917**

Edwardian Occasional Table ▲

- *circa 1905*

A very good quality Edwardian satinwood and inlaid octagonal occasional table.
- *72cm x 54cm*
- **Guide price £495/$936**

Butterfly Stool ▼

- *circa 1950*

Butterfly stool designed by Son Yanagi for Tendo Mokko.
- *height 46cm*
- **Guide price £985/$1,862**

Edwardian Plant Stand ▼

- *circa 1910*

Oak plant stand with copper banded decoration, raised on three carved supports with tripod stretcher.
- *88cm x 28cm*
- **Guide price £145/$274**

Walnut and Chrome Table ▼

- *circa 1980*

Small circular walnut table with metal circular ashtray standing on a teak pedestal and circular base with metal turned legs.
- *height 58cm*
- **Guide price £365/$690**

Reclining Armchair ▲

- *1920s*

Oak reclining armchair with carved and turned decoration with slated side panels.

- *100cm x 65cm*
- **Guide price £395/$748**

Hardwood Dining Table ▼

- *circa 1920*

Oak dining table from a West Country cricket club, with pull-out leaves above square chamfered legs, raised on bun feet.

- *76cm x 91cm*
- **Guide price £975/$1,843**

Arne Jacobsen Egg Chair ▼

- *1958*

Padded wool turquoise 'Egg Chair' by Arne Jacobsen, together with footstool.

- *height 130cm*
- **Guide price £2,850/$5,387**

Walnut Side Table ◄

- *circa 1905*

Walnut Arts and Crafts table. The design and quality of this table suggests the work of C. R. Ashbee and the Guild of Handicraft.

- *52cm x 40cm*
- **Guide price £650/$1,229**

Oak Bookcase ►

- *circa 1910*

Glazed oak bookcase with arched pediment and double-glazed doors above two panel doors.

- *190cm x 80cm*
- **Guide price £890/$1,682**

Oak Sideboard by Richter ▼

- *circa 1930*

Oak sideboard with central stepped cupboard flanked by two short and two long drawers with bun handles, standing on square straight legs. Made in Bath, England and illustrated in Modern British Furniture.

- *height 112cm*
- **Guide price £1,490/$2,816**

Edwardian Bookcase ▲

- *circa 1905*

A good quality Edwardian bookcase with moulded decoration above three-tiered shelves.

- *118cm x 125cm*
- **Guide price £995/$1,881**

White Fibreglass Lounger ▲

- *circa 1960*

Moulded fibreglass lounger with oval headrest, square moulded body and raised moulded leg rests, by Olivia Morgue.

- *length 164cm*
- **Guide price £500/$945**

Teak Armchairs ▶

- *circa 1960*

Pair of teak and black leather armchairs by Hans Wegner for Carl Hanse.
- *height 70cm*
- **Guide price £2,800/$5,292**

Harry Bertoia Wire Chair ◀

- *circa 1950*

Wire chair and stool by Harry Bertoia, who was born in Italy and later worked with Charles and Ray Eames at Evans, and also with his ground-breaking wire chairs at Knoll International.
- *height 104cm*
- **Guide price £1,800/$3,402**

Circular Table ▶

- *circa 1950s*

Oak circular coffee table with turned supports and circular moulded stretcher, raised on bun feet.
- *51cm x 100cm*
- **Guide price £495/$936**

Eames Chair ▼

- *circa 1950*

Leather lounge chair designed in 1946 by Ray Eames and manufactured by Herman Miller. Sold as a set with a stool.
- *height 83cm*
- **Guide price £3,950/$7,466**

Universe Chair ▲

- *circa 1967*

'Universe' design black plastic stacking chair by Joe Columbo.
- *70cm x 43cm*
- **Guide price £220/$416**

Tortoiseshell Box ▼

- *1930*

Atractive petite Art Deco tortoiseshell box.
- *length 10cm*
- **Guide price £145/$274**

Edwardian Revolving Bookcase ▶

- *1901–10*

An Edwardian mahogany revolving bookcase of small proportions, on a stand with cabriole legs and shelf.
- *84cm x 40cm*
- **Guide price £1,450/$2,741**

Charles and Ray Eames Chair ◄

- *circa 1950*

Bent birchwood chair by Charles and Ray Eames, for Evans.

- *height 84cm*
- **Guide price £1,150/$2,174**

Nursing Chair ▲

- *1910*

An Edwardian rosewood inlaid nursing chair with lyre back, standing on square tapered legs with a splayed foot.

- *height 74cm*
- **Guide price £895/$1,692**

Mahogany Armchair ▲

- *circa 1950s*

Mahogany elbow chair with pierced back splat, curved arm rests and cabriole legs.

- *110cm x 62cm*
- **Guide price £250/$473**

Finnish Armchair and Footstool ▼

- *circa 1970*

Armchair and footstool in brown padded leather and aluminium by Ilmari Lappalainen, Finland.

- *height 77cm*
- **Guide price £1,600/$3,024**

Antelope Chairs ►

- *circa 1950*

One of a set of six 'Antelope' painted metal chairs, with 'Ernest Rays, London, England' on the base of the seat. Made for the Festival of Britain.

- *83cm x 55cm*
- **Guide price £1,050/$1,985**

European Pine Cupboard ◄
- *circa 1940*

European pine cupboard of two long drawers and panelled cupboards below, standing on a moulded base.
- *85cm x 113cm*
- **Guide price £420/$794**

French Secretaire ►
- *1920*

A bombe fall-front secretaire à l'abattant with three small drawers, profusely decorated with foliate design, standing on splayed legs.
- *132cm x 72cm x 40cm*
- **Guide price £1,150/$2,174**

Danish Sideboard ▼
- *1960*

Danish sideboard Jacaranda, by Korod Larsenfor Faarup Mobel Fabarik.
- *78cm x 230cm x 50cm*
- **Guide price £3,500/$6,615**

Folding Chair ▼
- *circa 1930*

Eastern European painted green metal folding chair.
- *90cm x 44cm*
- **Guide price £35/$66**

Biedermeier Bookcase ▼
- *circa 1910*

Swedish birchwood bookcase in the style of Biedermeier, with ebonised pillars and details, plus a moulded top.
- *201cm x 165cm x 40cm*
- **Guide price £9,800/$18,522**

Painted Fauteuils ►
- *early 20th century*

A pair of French painted fauteuils in the manner of Louis XVI.
- *87cm x 60cm x 58cm*
- **Guide price £350/$662**

Officer's Chair ►
- *1901–10*

Edwardian officer's revolving ladder back chair on brass castors.
- *88cm x x 53cm*
- **Guide price £665/$1,257**

Pine Secretaire ▲

- *20th century*
A painted pine miniature secretaire with broken pediment above the fall, with fitted interior, on shaped bracket feet.
- *height 80cm*
- **Guide price £675/$1,276**

Teak Bedroom Suite ▲

- *circa 1930s*
Teak Art Deco bedroom suite.
- *175cm x 95cm*
- **Guide price £1,650/$3,119**

Green Chairs by Carl Jacobs ▼

- *circa 1950*
One of a set of six lime-green chairs by Carl Jacobs for Kandya Ltd., with teak legs.
- *72cm x 51cm*
- **Guide price £485/$917**

Gripsholm Armchairs ▶

- *circa 1930*
Pair of Swedish Gripsholm armchairs with original paint on ball feet.
- *height 78cm*
- **Guide price £2,900/$5,481**

School Cupboard ◀

- *circa 1940*
European pine cupboard with panelled cupboards below and above, standing on a straight square base.
- *227cm x 167cm*
- **Guide price £1,100/$2,079**

Coromandel Lady's Necessaire ▼

- *1920–30*
A coromandel lady's necessaire with fitted interior containing original bottles and pull-out flaps, and a stretcher below. Standing on squared tapered legs on splayed feet.
- *72cm x 25cm*
- **Guide price £3,450/$6,521**

French Gothic Cabinet ◀

- *1910*
A French gothic carved oak cocktail cabinet in seventeenth century-style with extensive gothic tracery.
- *182cm x 112cm x 58cm*
- **Guide price £2,250/$4,253**

School Cupboard ▶

- *1900s*
English oak school cupboard with two interior shelves the moulded panel doors with bun handles.
- *140cm x 153cm*
- **Guide price £600/$1,134**

Victorian Fire Screen ▲

- *1900s*
A brass fire screen with enamelled floral designs within a brass frame.
- *61cm x 43cm*
- **Guide price £80/$152**

Biedermeier Cabinet ▼

- 1920
A Biedermeier light mahogany cabinet inlaid with figurative and floral designs.
- height 130cm
- **Guide price £3,850/$7,277**

Edwardian Desk ▼

- 1908
Edwardian rosewood writing desk with inlaid foliate designs on the drawers, standing on tapered legs with brass castors.
- 73cm x 107cm x 57cm
- **Guide price £3,800/$7,182**

German Table Mirror ▼

- circa 1910
German table mirror, mounted on ivory tusks on a wooden base with convex glass.
- 44cm x 20cm
- **Guide price £3,000/$5,670**

English Blanket Box ▲

- 1900s
An English well-figured pine chest in restored condition on turned bun feet.
- 51cm x 99cm x 59cm
- **Guide price £225/$426**

Walnut Wall Mirror ▼

- circa 1920s
George II-style walnut and parcel-gilt wall mirror with swan neck pediment and beaded edges.
- 112cm x 68cm
- **Guide price £1,250/$2,363**

Painted Mirror ▶

- 1910
A carved wood mirror with unusual paint effect with C-scroll border.
- 65cm x 55cm
- **Guide price £380/$719**

Reproduction Lowboy ◀

- circa 1930
Reproduction of a four-drawer. eighteenth century, walnut lowboy, with crossbanded marquetry and raised on cabriole legs with pad feet.
- height 75cm
- **Guide price £395/$748**

French Mahogany and Satinwood Cabinet ▲

- circa 1910
A French mahogany and satinwood cabinet with marble top over a moulded frieze drawer, the panelled doors with decorative inlay in satinwood with moulded front on cabriole legs and ormolu decoration.
- 162cm x 220cm x 42cm
- **Guide price £1,400/$2,646**

Toy Cupboard ▲

- 1900s
A pine cupboard with two panel doors below a moulded pediment with original brass fittings.
- 142cm x 137cm x 56cm
- **Guide price £420/$794**

Pine Dresser ▼

- 1900s
Pine dresser with original glazed doors with two interior shelves above two drawers and two cupboards, with brass fittings to the cupboards, complete with original brass key.
- 180cm x 103cm x 52cm
- **Guide price £600/$1,134**

Arts and Crafts Wardrobe ▲

- *circa 1910*
Art and Crafts oak wardrobe with central mirror and one long drawer, standing on bracket feet.
- *212cm x 112cm x 55cm*
- **Guide price £975/$1,843**

French Occasional Table ▼

- *circa 1950*
A French occasional table, with painted pierced metal apron on a tripod base.
- *70cm x 55cm*
- **Guide price £680/$1,285**

Glazed Pine Dresser ◄

- *1900s*
Pine dresser consisting of three glazed doors with shelving above a pine base, with two shallow drawers and panelled cupboard with brass fittings.
- *128cm x 98cm x 55cm*
- **Guide price £700/$1,323**

Pine Chest of Drawers ◄

- *1900s*
A pine chest having three tiers of drawers with scrolled decoration, brass fittings, standing on bun feet.
- *95cm x 58cm x 77cm*
- **Guide price £400/$756**

Chinese Cupboard ▲

- *1930*
A Chinese red-lacquered cupboard with butterfly and floral painted decoration.
- *190cm x 103cm*
- **Guide price £1,960/$3,705**

Orkney Chair ▼

- *circa 1905*
Child's stained oak Orkney chair with carved arms and legs. Original Liberty & Co London enamel label on underside of chair.
- *height 82.5cm*
- **Guide price £475/$898**

Swedish Dining Table ◄

- *circa 1920*
Swedish Biedermeier-style dining table made from birchwood, with masur birch banding on a square pedestal base.
- *136cm x 196cm*
- **Guide price £10,500/$19,845**

Leopard Chest ▲

- *circa 1990s*
A chest of drawers decorated with leopards in a jungle setting, by Formasetti, Italy.
- *82.5cm x 100cm*
- **Guide price £6,400/$12,096**

Edwardian Occasional Tables ▼

- *1910*

A nest of three Edwardian occasional tables with boxwood inlay and banding and tapered straight legs.

- *55cm x 50cm*
- **Guide price £495/$936**

Scandinavian Art Deco Hall Stand ▼

- *circa 1928*

Scandinavian Art Deco hall stand, with large oval central mirror and stainless steel and light elmwood side panels, with three central drawers with large stainless steel and plastic handles.

- *184cm x 139cm x 28cm*
- **Guide price £1,700/$3,213**

Occasional Table ▶

- *1910*

Small English occasional table with a large decorative cat on the surface, with one central drawer and slender legs on pad feet.

- *74cm x 87cm x 50cm*
- **Guide price £1,200/$2,268**

Pine Wardrobe ▲

- *1900s*

A pine wardrobe, with arched pediment above three panelled doors with three shallow drawers below.

- *211cm x 142cm x 62cm*
- **Guide price £800/$1,512**

French Mirror ▲

- *20th century*

French wrought-iron mirror designed by Raymond Subes.

- *120cm x 95cm*
- **Guide price £2,800/$5,292**

Cone Chair ▼

- *1958*

A Danish Verner Panton cone chair, with red wool upholstery and cushioned seat and backrest.

- *height 84.5cm*
- **Guide price £850/$1,607**

Three-Drawered Chest ▼

- *1900s*

A pine chest of drawers consisting of three deep drawers with porcelain bun handles with carved moulding to the side.

- *127cm x 102cm x 63cm*
- **Guide price £495/$936**

Carved Oak Mirror ▲

- *1940*

An Italian heavily carved oak mirror, carved with large golden apples and pears.

- *102cm x 159cm*
- **Guide price £2,800/$5,292**

Art Deco Bed ▲

- *1920*

A painted Art Deco bed with carved headboard and gilt foliate decoration, standing on turned bun feet.

- *1.5m x 1.8m*
- **Guide price £3,200/$6,048**

Italian Sofa ▼

- *circa 1950s*

Italian sofa with shaped back and buttoned upholstery, by Gio Ponti.

- *100cm x 192.5cm*
- **Guide price £5,500/$10,395**

Child's Chair ▲

- • *circa 1990s*
Swedish child's chair in shaped wood
with black and white cowhide
upholstery, by Caroline Schlyter.
- • *height 57.5cm*
- • **Guide price £980/$1,853**

Finnish Leather Armchairs ▲

- • *1970*
One of a pair of tan leather moulded
armchairs with a metal circular base, by
Wryo Kukkapuro, Finland.
- • *height 80cm*
- • **Guide price £1,500/$2,835**

Charles Eames Chair ▼

- • *1960*
Charles Eames swivel office chair with a
chrome tripod stand.
- • *height 91cm*
- • **Guide price £1,960/$3,705**

English Oak Stools ▼

- • *1910–15*
One of a pair of Art Nouveau oak
English stools on tapered square legs,
with metal ringed stretcher.
- • *height 82cm*
- • **Guide price £500/$945**

Italian Rosewood Table ▶

- • *1900*
Italian inlaid rosewood octagonal
occasional table, with circular satinwood
inlay standing on eight square tapering
legs.
- • *72cm x 60cm*
- • **Guide price £900/$1,701**

Mirrored Dressing Table ◀

- • *1920*
An Art Deco dressing table, the whole
being made of mirrors with elegant
sabred legs and a fixed mirror with glass
handle to drawer.
- • *70cm x 86cm x 45cm*
- • **Guide price £800/$1,512**

Egg Chair ▲

- • *1958*
Egg chair in black leather on a metal
base, by Arne Jacobsen, Denmark.
- • *105cm x 85cm*
- • **Guide price £4,000/$7,560**

Edwardian Wardrobe ◀

- • *circa 1901*
An Edwardian inlaid mahogany wardrobe
with central mirror and side panelling,
and long drawer below.
- • *180cm x 138cm*
- • **Guide price £975/$1,843**

Swivel Office Chair ▲

- • *1970*
Charles Eames, high-back office swivel
and tilt chair, with black wool upholstery
and aluminium stand on castors.
- • *height 82cm*
- • **Guide price £600/$1,134**

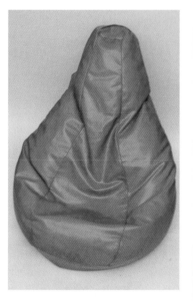

Sacco Beanbag ▲

- • *1960*
Red leather and vinyl beanbag of
teardrop shape, by Gatti-Paolini-Teodori
of Italy.
- • *height 82.5cm*
- • **Guide price £800/$1,512**

Mahogany Desk ▲

- *1925*

Fine mahogany partner's desk with embossed and gilded leather top. Two cupboards at front and rear, standing on bun feet.

- *79cm x 175cm x 84cm*
- **Guide price £12,500/$23,625**

French Cast-Iron Chairs ▲

- *1940*

One of a pair of French cast-iron chairs with intertwined lattice back and yellow leather seats, on cabriole legs.

- *height 95cm*
- **Guide price £1,400/$2,646**

Dressing Chest ▲

- *circa 1910*

An Arts and Crafts dressing chest with two large and three smaller drawers, original brass handles, and a swing mirror.

- *167cm x 107cm x 53cm*
- **Guide price £600/$1,134**

Spiral Umbrella Stands ◀

- *1960*

Italian Pluvium interlocking spiral umbrella stands in red and white plastic, designed by Giancarle Piretti for Castelli.

- *height 62.5cm*
- **Guide price £125/$237**

Italian Dining Table ▼

- *circa 1950s*

Italian interlocking sycamore dining table by Ico Parisi.

- *252.5cm x 77.5cm*
- **Guide price £8,500/$16,065**

Seagull Chairs ▲

- *circa 1990s*

A pair of seagull chairs by Arne Jacobsen of Denmark, for Fritz Hansen.

- *height 75cm*
- **Guide price £980/$1,853**

Set of Three Occasional Tables ◀

- *1900–15*

An Edwardian set of three mahogany card tables with satinwood banding.

- *85cm x 56cm*
- **Guide price £485/$917**

Rosewood Chair ▶

- *circa 1904*

Rare Art Nouveau rosewood chair raised on turned legs with pad feet. Designed by Walter Cave for Liberty & Co.

- *92.5cm x 62.5cm*
- **Guide price £3,500/$6,615**

Oak Sideboard ▲

• *circa 1910*
Medium oak Arts and Crafts sideboard, with mushroom bracket supports on upper shelf, above an arched recess between two panelled doors.
• *127.5cm x 147.5cm*
• **Guide price £2,250/$4,253**

Art Nouveau Music Cabinet ▶

• *circa 1910*
Mahogany Art Nouveau music cabinet with boxwood and ebony inlays, lined shelves and leaded glass door decorated with floral motifs. With carved top and side columns, by Liberty & Co.
• *height 120cm*
• **Guide price £4,500/$8,505**

Swedish Art Deco Desk ▼

• *circa 1920*
A rare example of a Swedish Art Deco desk. It is unique and is veneered in a particularly beautiful masur birch.
• *76cm x 120cm x 60cm*
• **Guide price £4,500/$8,505**

Limed Oak Desk with Art Deco Chairs ▼

• *20th century*
A limed oak partner's desk with drinks bar concealed behind curved panel doors, with two Art Deco chairs.
• *77cm x 140cm x 80cm*
• **Guide price £4,500/$8,505**

X-Chair ▲

• *1958*
An X-chair in wood and cane, by Huidt and Nielson, Denmark.
• *height 82cm*
• **Guide price £1,600/$3,024**

Hathaway Table ▲

• *circa 1905*
Extendable medium oak draw table with panelled top, X-shaped cross stretcher and tapered legs, by Liberty & Co.
• *height 137.5cm*
• **Guide price £2,350/$4,442**

Occasional Tables ▲

• *1950*
German wood occasional tables inlaid with gilt porcelain plaques, by Rosenthal.
• *42.5cm x 42.5cm x 60cm/largest*
• **Guide price £1,400/$2,646**

Bamboo Umbrella Stand ▲

• *1920*
A provincial bamboo painted umbrella and stick stand with original metal liner.
• *height 80cm*
• **Guide price £340/$643**

French Art Deco Brown Leather Chairs ▶

- *1925*
One of a pair of brown leather French Art Deco chairs with a curved padded back, scrolled arms and turned feet.
- height 120cm
- **Guide price £3,500/$6,615**

Parisian Café Table ▼

- *circa 1920*
A small Parisian wrought-iron café table, on a heavy moulded cast iron tripod base.
- height 70cm
- **Guide price £320/$605**

Swedish Art Deco Rosewood Table ▼

- *20th century*
Swedish Art Deco rosewood table, with a flat top, lyre-shaped support on a splayed base.
- 73cm x 150cm x 100cm
- **Guide price £3,200/$6,048**

Victorian Stick Stand ▼

- *1900*
Victorian stick stand with pierced back rail with a repeated heart motif, and ebony and boxwood inlay.
- 70cm x 85cm
- **Guide price £475/$898**

Brass Magazine Rack ▶

- *circa 1915*
An Edwardian brass magazine rack, with carrying handle.
- height 80cm
- **Guide price £245/$463**

Storm Oak Chairs ▲

- *1987–88*
One of a pair of oak chairs, part of a set which includes a sofa. The oak is a relic of the great storm in 1987.
- 106cm x 94cm
- **Guide price £2,750/$5,198**

Edwardian Gong ▼

- *circa 1913*
An oak and horn gong with baton and trophy plaque.
- height 34cm
- **Guide price £165/$312**

Invalid's Chair ▼

- *circa 1910*
An invalid's chair with original green upholstery.
- height 1.36m
- **Guide price £190/$360**

Globe Werniker ▲

- *circa 1915*
Six-stack, oak Globe Werniker bookcase with lifting glass panels.
- height 2m
- **Guide price £950/$1,796**

Make-up Table ▲

- *circa 1910*

An Edwardian ladies make-up table in rosewood, with inlay, two drawers and two side cabinets, the whole on tapered legs with castors.
- *height 88cm*
- **Guide price £750/$1,418**

Oak Bookcase ▲

- *circa 1910*

An oak bookcase originally from a post office, more lately from an author's library.
- *height 1.33m*
- **Guide price £1,450/$2,741**

Victorian Cabinet ▼

- *circa 1910*

Mahogany bookcase with fine glazed doors, raised on slender turned feet. By Maple & Co.
- *height 98cm*
- **Guide price £1,485/$2,807**

Dressing Table Set ▼

- *circa 1930*

Art Deco turquoise shell dressing table set in original silk-lined leather box. Set comprises two wooden hair brushes with handles, two clothes brushes and bottles and pots of cut glass in various shapes and sizes, with
a mirror and tray in the lid.
- **Guide price £1,450/$2,741**

Breakfront Bookcase ▶

- *circa 1930*

A fine neo-classical breakfront bookcase in elm.
- *height 2.3m*
- **Guide price £9,500/$17,995**

Corner Cabinet ◀

- *circa 1920*

A glazed cabinet with carved decoration, on three cabriole legs.
- *height 1.78m*
- **Guide price £2,950/$5,576**

Tortoiseshell and Silver Perfume Box ▼

- *circa 1918*

Original and complete. The box contains an inset of floral panel decorations. Made in England.
- *height 7.5cm*
- **Guide price £1,270/$2,401**

Travelling Dressing Case ▼

- *circa 1934*

An early 20th-century, fine-quality, Art Deco, crocodile-skin, gentleman's travelling dressing case. Made by Cartier of London. Hallmarked silver, inscribed 'Sir W. Rollo'.
- **Guide price £3,995/$7,551**

Sovereign Sorter ▲

- *early 20th century*

Originally used by shopkeepers to sort sovereigns and half sovereigns. Mahogany with brass fittings and escutcheon to the lower drawer.
- *height 27.5cm*
- **Guide price £650/$1,229**

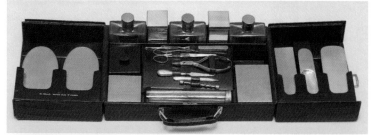

Music Stand ▲

- *circa 1920*

Regency-style painted, wrought-iron music canterbury with profuse floral pierced decoration and splayed legs.
- *height 68cm*
- **Guide price £1,275/$2,410**

Waste Paper Baskets ▲

- *circa 1910*

Silver plated. With pierced rim and frieze of rabbits below.
- *height 33cm*
- **Guide price £880/$1,663**

Birdcage ▼

- *circa 1940*

A 20th-century birdcage of rectangular shape with covered back and sides.
- *height 31cm*
- **Guide price £22/$£42**

Mahogany Desk ▲

- *circa 1920*

Early 20th-century mahogany desk in the George III manner. The top is inlaid with calf leather and decorated with gold tooling.
- *height 79cm*
- **Guide price £1,500/$2,835**

Two-fold Paper Screen ▲

- *20th century*

A Taisho period screen painted in ink and colour with hydrangea, peony and poppy.
- *height 1.8m, length 1.6m*
- **Guide price £8,600/$16,254**

Sabre-leg Stools ▶

- *circa 1950*

Pair of regency-style stools with turned supports in fruitwood.
- *height 95cm*
- **Guide price £1,000/$1,890**

Carlton House Desk ▼

- *circa 1910*

Fine Sheraton revival English mahogany Carlton House desk. Signed, with brass handles.
- *height 1m*
- **Guide price £9,500/$17,955**

Folding Bronze Doors ▼

- *circa 1930*

A very substantial and unusual pair of 1930s double folding bronze doors with twenty-eight raised and fielded panels. The doors show some patination.
- *height 2.64m*
- **Guide price £6,500/$12,285**

Writing Desk ▲

- *circa 1920*

Mahogany Hepplewhite writing desk with brass-bound and leather top on carved cabriole legs.
- *height 73cm*
- **Guide price £695/$1,314**

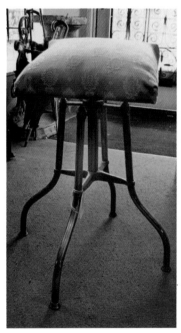

Brass Stool ▲

- *circa 1910*

Edwardian brass piano stool of adjustable height with red fabric.
- *height 90cm*
- **Guide price £175/$331**

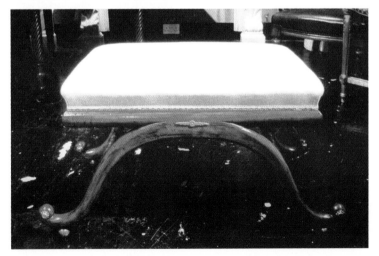

Walnut Canterbury ▼

• *circa 1910*
An Edwardian canterbury with frame surmounted by finials mounted with turned and reeded columns.
• *height 52cm*
• **Guide price £1,650/$3,119**

Arts and Crafts Buffet ▼

• *circa 1905*
English walnut buffet carved with strapwork decoration.
• *height 93cm*
• **Guide price £10,000/$18,900**

Corner Cabinets ▼

• *circa 1910*
One of a pair of Edwardian mahogany cabinets with glazed upper part and a cupboard base.
• *height 2.16m*
• **Guide price £750/$1,418**

Satinwood Table ▲

• *circa 1920*
Two-tier, Edwardian satinwood table on square, splayed legs.
• *height 70cm*
• **Guide price £2,100/$3,969**

Three-part Mirror ▲

• *circa 1910*
A Majorellel mirror, leather backed with glass behind door.
• *height 18cm*
• **Guide price £2,800/$5,292**

French Trolley ◄

• *circa 1930*
Nickel-plated trolley on castors with removable top.
• *height 84cm*
• **Guide price £600/$1,134**

Ladies Armchair ▼

• *circa 1910*
A Hepplewhite-style armchair in painted satin wood, with turned legs and stretchers.
• *height 87cm*
• **Guide price £1,000/$1,890**

Oak Door ▼

• *circa 1920*
Panelled oak door with carved and pierced roundel of birds and foliate designs.
• **Guide price £2,500/$4,725**

Pedestal Desk ▲

• *circa 1930*
A continental Art Deco pedestal desk made in birch with two panelled cupboards with four sliding shelves and three drawers with locks and keys.
• **Guide price £1,600/$3,024**

Biedermeier-style Chairs ▲

• *circa 1915*
A pair of Swedish masur birch chairs in cream ultra-suede.
• *height 93cm*
• **Guide price £4,900/$9,261**

Steel Medical Cabinet ▲

• *circa 1930*
Copper and brass fittings, two glass shelves glazed on the front and sides. With a hinged door.
• *height 45.5cm*
• **Guide price £140/$265**

Silk Screen ▲
- *early 20th century*
Two-fold silk screen painted in ink with birds flying above rose mallow on which are a praying mantis and a cricket.
- *height 1.8m, length 1.2m*
- **Guide price £6,800/$12,852**

Orange Chair ▲
- *circa 1970*
Thermoplastic, injection-moulded chair by Verner Panton from his 'series 2' range.
- *height 78cm*
- **Guide price £450/$851**

Art Deco Coffee Table ▲
- *circa 1925*
Swedish walnut table with inlays of heart, burr elm and fruitwood.
- *diameter 100cm*
- **Guide price £2,700/$5,103**

Marquetry Cabinet ▼
- *circa 1920*
An 18th century-style Dutch marquetry vitrine on a bombé chest base and standing on bracket feet.
- *height 2m*
- **Guide price £2,250/$4,253**

Coffee Table ▶
- *circa 1925*
Empire-style table in French mahogany, with gilt mounts and curved frame stretchers.
- *length 100cm*
- **Guide price £2,900/$5,481**

Four-fold Paper Screen ▼
- *20th century*
Silver and gold leaf on buff ground with imprint of three fuki.
- *height 1.7m, length 2.7m*
- **Guide price £8,500/$16,065**

Art Deco Armchairs ▼
- *circa 1925*
Pair of French armchairs with inlays of exotic woods, covered in artificial tiger skin print.
- *height 80cm*
- **Guide price £5,900/$11,151**

Pair of Side Tables ▶
- *circa 1910*
Pair of early 20th-century birchwood and masur birch side tables with top drawer and lower platform, the whole resting on four square tapering legs.
- *height 74cm*
- **Guide price £2,900/$5,481**

Factory Stool ▲
- *circa 1940*
Factory worker's stool. Originally painted mild steel. Adjustable elm seat on three legs. English made.
- *height 56cm*
- **Guide price £145/$274**

Silk Screen ▲

• *20th century*
Ink and colour on a buff ground with pine trees, bamboo fences, paths and lanterns.
• *height 90cm, length 1.76m*
• **Guide price £5,600/$10,584**

Art Deco Coffee Table ▼

• *circa 1925*
Masur birch and rosewood coffee table with inlays of satinwood and cross-banding in 'tiger' birch.
• *length 99cm*
• **Guide price £2,700/$5,103**

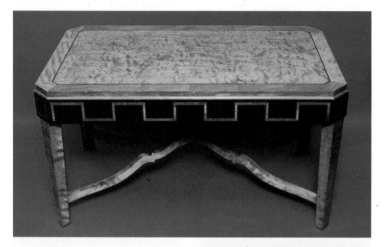

Pub Table ▼

• *circa 1920*
Mahogany and copper pub table, on square legs with turned feet and crossed stretchers.
• *height 71cm*
• **Guide price £225/$426**

Arrow Armchair ▼

• *20th century*
An armchair of neo-classical design with arrow-design back and a white bamboo frame.
• *height 80cm*
• **Guide price £995/$1,881**

Swedish Settee ▼

• *circa 1940*
A Swedish settee in brown leather with tapered legs.
• *width 1.95m*
• **Guide price £2,500/$4,725**

Three-Piece Suite ▼

• *circa 1930*
French Deco walnut three-seater sofa with two matching chairs.
• *width 1.8m*
• **Guide price £2,200/$4,158 the set**

Egyptian Design Chairs ▲

• *circa 1920*
Pair of English elbow chairs with hand-worked tapestry covers.
• *height 94cm*
• **Guide price £4,950/$9,356**

Swedish Sofa Table ▲

• *circa 1915*
Swedish sofa table in birchwood, with central, ebonised column, folding side flaps and a central drawer.
• *length (flaps up) 90cm*
• **Guide price £3,900/$7,371**

Display Cabinet ▲

• *circa 1905*
An unusually small, English Edwardian, mahogany, inlaid, bow-fronted cabinet, well proportioned with solid wood stretcher and tapered legs on spade feet.
• *height 1.66m*
• **Guide price £2,950/$5,576**

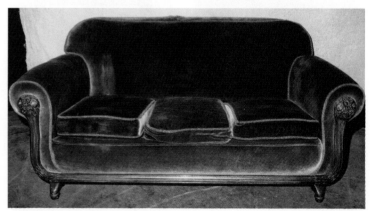

Art Nouveau Table ▼

- *circa 1918*
Art Nouveau table with organic inlay
designs on four pierced legs.
- *height 81cm*
- **Guide price £420/$794**

Extending Table ▲

- *circa 1920*
Swedish birchwood extending table with
ebonized feet.
- *length 2.63m (extended)*
- **Guide price £4,900/$9,261**

Ganesh ▲

- *circa 1990*
A Southern Indian ganesh with
polychrome decoration.
- *height 1.25cm*
- **Guide price £1,800/$3,402**

Plate Drainer ▶

- *circa 1910*
A pine draining board for drying dishes,
with carved ends.
- *width 64cm*
- **Guide price £150/$284**

Ash Sideboard ▼

- *circa 1915*
An English sideboard of substantial
construction.
- *height 1.02m*
- **Guide price £1,295/$2,448**

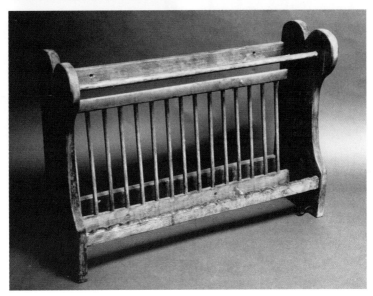

Bamboo Table ▲

- *early 20th century*
Bamboo and rattan table by Maples in
original condition.
- *height 66cm*
- **Guide price £240/$454**

Perspex Sculpture ▼

- *1961*
'Red Object' by Michael Kidner,
sculpture in perspex.
- *height 1.1m*
- **Guide price £1,750/$3,308**

Diner Stools ▲

- *circa 1940*
A set of four round American diner
stools with chromed steel base and red
leather-covered seats. Very typical of the
Art Deco, American café style.
- *height 51cm*
- **Guide price £350/$662**

Wicker Chair ▲

- *circa 1960*
An Eero Aarnio wicker chair of circular form.
- *height 65cm*
- **Guide price £675/$1,276**

End Table ▲

- *20th century*
A mahogany end table with carved swan heads. Made by Maitland-Smith.
- *height 68cm*
- **Guide price £1,750/$3,308**

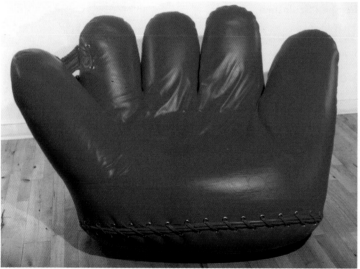

English Table ▼

- *circa 1930*
Tubular aluminium base, on three legs with cast bakelite top.
- *height 52cm*
- **Guide price £250/$473**

Arts and Crafts Chairs ▼

- *circa 1910*
Set of six oak chairs with rexine seats.
- *height 92cm*
- **Guide price £1,800/$3,402 the set**

The 'Joe' Sofa ▼

- *circa 1970*
Inspired by the American baseball legend, 'Joltin' Joe DiMaggio. Designed by J.de Pas, D. D'Urbino and P. Lomazzi and produced Poltronova, Italy. The design is that of a surreal, giant baseball glove.
- *width 1.05m*
- **Guide price £2,750/$5,198**

Auditorium Chair ▲

- *circa 1950*
Italian, by Carlo Mollino, for the Auditorium in Turin. Rust-coloured velvet upholstery with brass fittings and flip-up seat.
- *height 85cm*
- **Guide price £2,500/$4,725**

White Table ▲

- *circa 1965*
Small, Italian white 'Tulip' occasional table.
- *height 1.25m*
- **Guide price £300/$567**

Red Onyx Desk ▼

- *1973*
Moulded compartments with adjustable chrome metal lamp.
- *width 1.02m*
- **Guide price £1,350/$2,552**

'Safari' Seating Booth ▼

- *circa 1975*
Glass-fibre reinforced-polyester frame with leather upholstery, designed by Poltronoua for Archiroom Associati.
- **Guide price £18,000/$34,020**

Wall Cabinet ▼

- *circa 1920*
A French figured beechwood wall cabinet with ebonized mouldings, featuring two large panelled doors above two smaller ones.
- *height 84cm*
- **Guide price £1,550/$2,930**

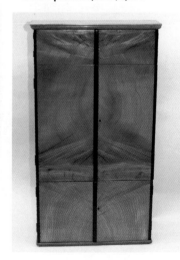

Danish Bench Seat ▶

- *circa 1950*
Special commission for a bank with button-cushion leather.
- *height 87cm*
- **Guide price £1,650/$3,119**

German Fan ▼

- *circa 1940*
German bakelite fan designed by Dieter Rams.
- *height 27cm*
- **Guide price £400/$756**

'Spring' Lamp ▼

- *circa 1970*
French chrome 'spring' lamp with coiled innovative design and spherical, light bulb holder.
- *height 36cm*
- **Guide price £145/$274**

French Fruitwood Chairs ▲

- *20th century*
Set of four provincial chairs in fruitwood, with asymetric backs and rush matted seats.
- *height 89cm*
- **Guide price £680/$1,286**

Ministry Locker ◀

- *circa 1950*
A steel Air Ministry locker with four doors, vents and label holders. In government grey.
- *height 1.65m*
- **Guide price £175/$331**

School Desk ▼

- *circa 1940*
English elm school desk with child-size chair. Good patination.
- *height 84cm*
- **Guide price £175/$331**

Aalto Armchair ▲

- *1932*
An Alvar Aalto cantilever armchair. Model no. 31
- *height 77cm*
- **Guide price £2,000/$3,780**

Corner Suite ◀

- *circa 1980*
An upholstered corner seating suite, covered in vermillion cloth, with all-moveable components.
- *height 1.2m*
- **Guide price £650/$1,229**

Club Chair ▼

- *20th century*

Leather and rattan club chair, made by Maitland-Smith, with metal, lion's paw feet.

- *height 80cm*
- **Guide price £1,850/$3,497**

Art Nouveau Sideboard ▼

- *early 20th century*

Oak sideboard with organic designs and copper handles.

- *height 1.87m*
- **Guide price £1,250/$2,363**

Oak Hall Seat ▲

- *circa 1910*

Unusual carved oak hall seat with side table and umbrella stand.

- *height 79cm*
- **Guide price £995/$1,881**

Bathroom Cabinet ▲

- *circa 1930*

An Art Deco tin bathroom cabinet with mirrored door and one shelf.

- *height 36cm*
- **Guide price £55/$104**

Set of Four Chairs ▼

- *circa 1965*

One of a set of four single chairs with detachable squab seats. Designed by Harry Bertoia.

- *height 31.5cm*
- **Guide price £865/$1,635 the set**

Cocktail Cabinet ▼

- *circa 1930*

A modernist, Art Deco British cocktail cabinet.

- *height 80cm*
- **Guide price £2,900/$5,481**

Wall Panels ▼

- *circa 1970*

Four decorative Verner Panton wall panels, in red perspex plastic, of bulbous design.

- *height 1.2m*
- **Guide price £480/$908**

Steel Desk ◄

- *circa 1950*

Twin pedestal with black rubber top, central locking mechanism and seven chrome handles.

- *height 76cm*
- **Guide price £475/$898**

'Up' Chair ▲

- *1969*

From the 'Up' series designed in 1969. Beige and red striped stretch fabric over moulded polyurethane foam.

- *height 65cm*
- **Guide price £4,500/$8,505**

Gout Stool ▲

- *circa 1920*

An adjustable stool for the gout-sufferer, made of oak and metal, on roller castors.

- *height 33cm*
- **Guide price £150/$284**

Red Chairs ▲

- *20th century*

Pair of red 'Champagne' chairs, in plastic, on central metal column and circular base.

- *height 77cm*
- **Guide price £2,500/$4,725**

Toleware Vase ▲

• *circa 1935*
A Toleware vase with tortoiseshell finish.
• *height 43cm*
• **Guide price £295/$558**

Coffee Table ▲

• *circa 1970*
A unique chrome and glass crossbar coffee table. Of rectangular form.
• *height 32cm*
• **Guide price £265/$501**

Figure-backed Chair ▼

• *circa 1980*
Fornasetti, Italian design. With a printed and lacquered figure in red dress above a black seat.
• *height 96cm*
• **Guide price £1,600/$3,024**

Indian Throne ▼

• *circa 1990*
An elaborately carved chair with carved canopy of mother-of-pearl and bone inlay. The carved chair back with floral inlays, flanked with carved lions. The whole resting on four carved elephants.
• *height 3m*
• **Guide price £10,000/$18,900**

'Airborn' Armchairs ◄

• *20th century*
A pair of 'Airborn' armchairs, in black leather. Exact period unknown, but of Art Deco style.
• *height 70cm*
• **Guide price £1,500/$2,835**

'Amphys' Red Sofa ▲

• *1968*
Designed by Pierre Paulin for Mobilier International.
• *length 2.14m*
• **Guide price £2,800/$5,292**

'Wave' Sofa ▼

• *circa 1968*
A sofa designed by the French designer Pierre Paulin and entitled 'The Wave'.
• *length 1.67m*
• **Guide price £2,750/$5,198**

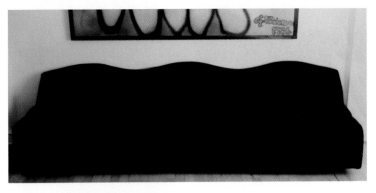

Lounge Chair ▼

• *circa 1950*
Aluminium and bent rosewood ply lounge chair, covered in natural leather.
• *height 1.05m*
• **Guide price £3,950/$7,466**

Art Deco Armchairs ◄

• *circa 1930*
A pair of English-made Art Deco armchairs, upholstered in leather with walnut sides.
• *height 84cm*
• **Guide price £1,200/$2,268**

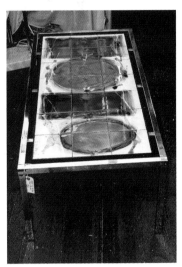

Coffee Table ▲

• *circa 1970*
Chrome and ceramic tile-topped coffee table by Belanti, Italy. Glazed in avant-garde style.
• *height 38cm*
• **Guide price £345/$652**

GLASS

Kosta Paperweight ▲

- *1955–63*
A Kosta paperweight, the teardrop shape consisting of internal cranberry pink glass surrounded by a controlled pattern of bubbles encased in clear glass.
- *height 8cm*
- **Guide price £75/$142**

Cameo Glass Vase ▼

- *circa 1905*
A large Art Nouveau cameo glass vase by Richard, the body carved and etched with a landscape.
- *height 33cm*
- **Guide price £875/$1,654**

Abstract Glass Structure ◄

- *circa 1990*
Orange and black abstract glass vase of cylindrical form with gold flaked inclusions, by Nichetti for Murano.
- *height 27cm*
- **Guide price £380/$719**

Glass Paperweight Abstract Sculpture ▶

- *circa 1960*
Italian orange, red, black and white abstract glass sculpture.
- *height 16cm*
- **Guide price £125/$237**

Lalique Bowl ▲

- *1920s*
An opalescent Lalique bowl in the Poisson pattern, marked "R. Lalique France".
- *diameter 24cm*
- **Guide price £550/$1,040**

Murano Paperweight ▶

- *circa 1960*
Murano paperweight of compressed globular form with an abstract pattern of blue, white, lime green, pink and gold.
- *diameter 23cm*
- **Guide price £325/$614**

Art Deco Decanter ▲

- *circa 1930*
Art Deco conical ruby cased decanter cut to clear with horizontal bands of broad flutes. Original clear conical stopper cut with broad flutes.
- *height 23cm*
- **Guide price £425/$803**

Orrefors Ariel Vase ▲

- *1972*

A strikingly beautiful Orrefors Ariel vase designed by Ingeborg Lundin. A thick slightly flaring vase with a continuous design, the inner in olive green glass, the whole cased in clear glass.

- *height 18cm*
- **Guide price £1,550/$2,930**

Blue Cactus Vase ▼

- *circa 1950*

Blue glass "Cactus" vase by Recardo Licata for Murano.

- *height 44cm*
- **Guide price £1,200/$2,268**

Cordonato d'Oro Vase ◀

- *1950s*

Cordonato d'Oro vase of red glass in a tapering ribbed shape above a bulbous body, with gold leaf.

- *height 26.5cm*
- **Guide price £300/$567**

Amber Bowl ▲

- *circa 1970*

Amber glass bowl on a clear stand by Cevedex.

- *height 23cm*
- **Guide price £500/$945**

Set of Conical Goblets ▲

- *circa 1930*

Two of a set of six Art Deco conical goblets decorated in intaglio with stylised zigzag pattern on conical uranium green feet.

- *height 20.3cm*
- **Guide price £495/$936**

Toso Glass Vase ▲

- *contemporary*

Heavy clear glass vase by Stefano Toso of Murano with swirls of orange and blue.

- *height 22cm*
- **Guide price £350/$662**

Lalique Box Lid ◀

- *1920s*

An opalescent Lalique box lid, marked "R. Lalique". This lid was used on a presentation set by Houbigant during 1928–30.

- *diameter 14cm*
- **Guide price £145/$274**

Mosaic Vase by Ferro ▼

- *1998*

Mosaic Murano glass vase by Ferro, for the Venice Biennale 1998.

- *height 29cm*
- **Guide price £1,200/$2,268**

Cameo Glass Vase ▼

- *circa 1920*

Le Verre Français cameo glass vase, acid-etched, with an orange and green design on a yellow ground, applied with the Millifiori cane mark.

- *height 30cm*
- **Guide price £795/$1,503**

Red and Yellow Murano Vase ▲

- *1950s*

Murano sommerso vase, red and yellow cased in clear glass, with original label.

- *height 11cm*
- **Guide price £65/$123**

Tiffany Centrepiece ▼

- *circa 1930*

L. Tiffany's gold iridescent centrepiece with organic designs.

- *diameter 25cm*
- **Guide price £4,000/$7,560**

Fish in Glass by Cenedese ▼

- *1950*

Glass object with a seascape design including a tropical fish with underwater plants, by Cenedese for Murano.

- *width 14cm*
- **Guide price £225/$426**

Art Deco Lemonade Set ▲

- *circa 1930*

Art Deco lemonade set consisting of a tall jug with an amber handle and six matching glasses with amber stems and feet, all engraved with vertical lines.

- *height 24cm*
- **Guide price £195/$370**

Large Murano Glass Vase ▼

- *contemporary*

A large glass vase designed by Stefano Toso of Murano with dominant colours of green, yellow and red.

- *height 38cm*
- **Guide price £450/$851**

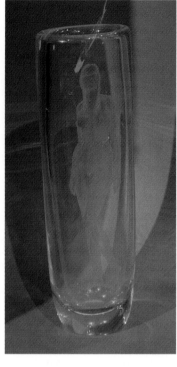

Hutton Vase ▲

- *circa 1920*

Clear glass vase by Orrefors and etched by John Hetton.

- *height 33cm*
- **Guide price £1,000/$1,890**

Italian Glass Fish ◄

- *1960*

Italian glass object fashioned as a stylised coiled fish.

- *height 24cm*
- **Guide price £285/$539**

Art Deco Candelabras ▼

- *circa 1935*

Pair of American Art Deco candelabra with ribbed arms and icicle drops suspended on rectangular bases cut underneath with diamonds.

- *height 19.7cm*
- **Guide price £695/$1,314**

Green Vase with Cactus ▼

- *circa 1950s*
Green Cactus vase by Recardo Licata for Murano.
- *height 44cm*
- **Guide price £1,200/$2,268**

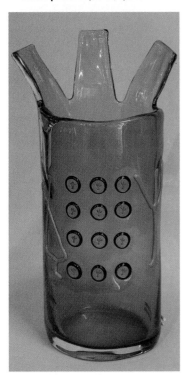

Martini Jug by Baxter ▼

- *circa 1962*
Whitefriars kingfisher-blue Martini jug with a clear handle. A Whitefriars Studio range by Peter Wheeler.
- *height 36cm*
- **Guide price £95/$180**

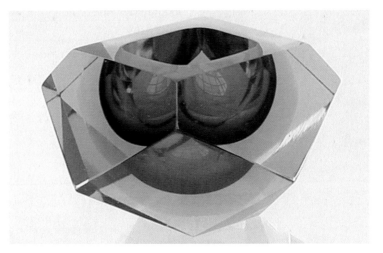

Green and Yellow Murano Vase ▲

- *1950s*
Murano sommerso vase, emerald green and lemon yellow cased in heavily facetted clear glass.
- *height 7.5cm*
- **Guide price £65/$123**

Glass Vase ▼

- *1973*
Glass vase with circular design by Olle Alerius. Orrefors Co. 1973, Expo A 248, signed and illustrated by Lilane.
- *height 20cm*
- **Guide price £2,200/$4,158**

Tangerine Vase ▶

- *1969*
Tangerine vase with concentric circular design and a textured finish by Baxter.
- *height 18cm x 17cm*
- **Guide price £140/$265**

Tall Italian Vase ◀

- *1982*
Italian tall glass vase with a moulded lip, cerulean blue variegated to paler blue with moulded banding within the glass.
- *height 63cm*
- **Guide price £1,000/$1,890**

Mosaic Murrina Vase ▼

- *1998*
Mosaic vase of baluster form, with blue and yellow organic design by Murrina.
- *height 29cm*
- **Guide price £1,500/$2,835**

Red Bubble Ashtray ▼

- *1958*
Ruby red lobed bubble ashtray with an organic moulded design by Harry Dyer.
- *diameter 13cm*
- **Guide price £25/$48**

Glass Vase by Laura Diaz ▶

- *1990–1*
Incalmo ink-blue glass vase, with a cane pattern neck and white glass wheel carved bulbous base by Laura Diaz, Ref: *il vetro a venezia* by Marino Baronier.
- *height 30cm*
- **Guide price £1,800/$3,402**

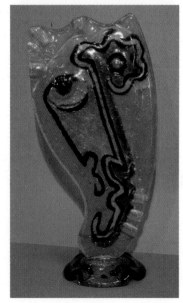

Swedish Translucent Vase ▲

- *1955–6*
Swedish translucent tall glass vase with white trailing lines and one red line made for Kosta.
- *height 38cm*
- **Guide price £2,200/$4,158**

Whitefriars Vase ◀

- *circa 1969*
Rare Whitefriars ovoid brown and orange vase. Studio Range by Peter Wheeler.
- *height 22.5cm*
- **Guide price £245/$463**

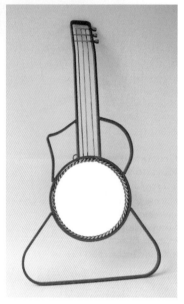

Guitar Mirror ▲

- *1950*
Guitar-shaped metal mirror.
- *length 83cm*
- **Guide price £120/$227**

Spanish Abstract ▲

- *circa 1960s*
Spanish hand-blown abstract glass object, with yellow, black and blue design. Signed Vinas.
- *height 27cm*
- **Guide price £850/$1,607**

Silvio Vigliaturo Sculpture ◀

- *1999*
Glass Ikomos series sculpture by Silvio Vigliaturo, signed and dated.
- *height 40cm*
- **Guide price £1,200/$2,268**

Vase by Baxter ▲

- *circa 1969*
Whitefriars kingfisher-blue vase by Baxter with an abstract design and textured finish.
- *height 29cm*
- **Guide price £235/$445**

Nichetti Vase ▼

- *circa 1990*
Hand-blown orange vase with a gold and grey abstract geometric design and a moulded rim, by Nichetti for Murano.
- *height 28cm*
- **Guide price £380/$719**

Archimede Seguso Vases ▼
- *circa 1950*
Italian Murano green and orange dimple vases of globular form, with a gold leaf border and a crumpled moulded design.
- *height 30cm*
- **Guide price £800/$1,512**

Gilded Glass Bowls ▼
- *early 20th century*
Three of a set of ten dimple-ribbed bowls and stands gilded with rural scenes.
- *diameter 15cm*
- **Guide price £300/$567**

Barovier and Toso ◄
- *circa 1970*
Italian Murano vase of globular form by Barovier and Toso with black, green and red geometric design.
- *height 35cm x 19cm*
- **Guide price £950/$1,796**

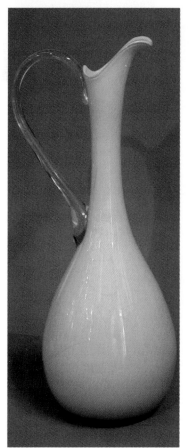

Mila Schon for Arte Vetro Murano ►
- *circa 1970*
Large Murano purple glass plate with circular vortex design, by Mila Schon for Arte Vetro. It has the option of being wall-mounted.
- *width 63cm*
- **Guide price £450/$851**

Pale Pink Jug ◄
- *1960*
Pale pink Murano jug with slender neck, pinched lip and clear strap handle.
- *height 49cm*
- **Guide price £85/$161**

Cenedese Ash Tray ▲
- *circa 1970*
Lime-green ash tray in the form of a halved lime, by Cenedese.
- *width 35cm*
- **Guide price £185/$350**

Mazzega Murano Glass ▲
- *circa 1960*
Italian circular clear and dark blue glass object, designed by Mazzega, with the option of being wall-mounted.
- *diameter 40cm*
- **Guide price £400/$756**

Mazzega Murano Glass ▼
- *circa 1960*
Italian glass object with a red and white glass dome within a circular clear glass halo, has the option of being wall-mounted, designed by Mazzega.
- *diameter 40cm*
- **Guide price £400/$756**

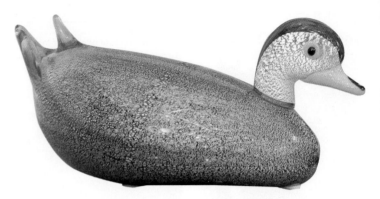

V. Ferro for Murano ▼

- *1998*

Yellow vase of bulbous proportions with black cobweb effect, raised on a splayed circular foot.

- *height 28cm*
- **Guide price £1,500/$2,835**

Murano Glass Duck ▲

- *1950*

Murano glass duck with silver and gold iridescence.

- *length 34cm*
- **Guide price £590/$1,116**

Spanish Abstract by Vinas ▲

- *circa 1990*

Spanish hand-blown lozenge-shaped glass with yellow, black and turquoise abstract circles and geometric design. Signed.

- *width 28cm*
- **Guide price £780/$1,475**

Scandinavian Green Glass Vase ▼

- *1950*

Scandinavian green glass vase of conical form with blue abstract inclusions.

- *height 29cm*
- **Guide price £180/$341**

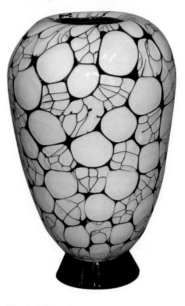

Venini Bottle ▶

- *circa 1950*

Italian emerald-green bottle with large stopper by Venini.

- *height 36cm*
- **Guide price £800/$1,512**

Green Vase ◀

- *1960*

Green Murano bottle-shaped vase with long slender neck and black and white banding around the rim.

- *height 49cm*
- **Guide price £65/$123**

Lalique Bird ▲

- *1920*

Lalique naturalistically formed glass finch.

- *length 13cm*
- **Guide price £280/$530**

Amber Glass ▼

- *circa 1940*

Amber glass jelly mould by William Wilson of globular design. No 9250.

- *17cm x 20cm*
- **Guide price £140/$265**

Antonio Da Ros ▼

- *circa 1960*

Clear Murano glass with dark blue teardrop and secondary droplet, by Antonio Da Ros, designed for Cenedese.
- *height 29cm*
- **Guide price £600/$1,134**

Orange Striped Vase by Venini ▼

- *1960*

Venini Murano glass vase with an orange and white striped design within the glass and a moulded, pinched rim.
- *height 34cm*
- **Guide price £650/$1,229**

Vase for Venini ▲

- *1965*

Blue vase for Venini designed by T. Zucheri.
- *height 31cm*
- **Guide price £1,200/$2,268**

Ruby Red Bubble Vase ▼

- *1965*

Ruby red bubble vase Whitefriars Studio range, by Harry Dyer.
- *height 18cm*
- **Guide price £130/$246**

Whitefriars Drunken Bricklayer ◄

- *circa 1969*

Large tangerine Drunken Bricklayer object by Baxter.
- *height 33.5cm*
- **Guide price £650/$1,229**

Venini Glass Bowl ◄

- *1962*

Glass bowl with bright red trailing design signed Venini Italia and designed by Ludovioc di Santilliana.
- *diameter 25cm*
- **Guide price £2,000/$3,780**

Studio Range Vase ▼

- *circa 1969*

Whitefriars old gold and amber striped vase of conical form, Studio range No. S6.L13 by Peter Wheeler.
- *height 29cm*
- **Guide price £130/$246**

Tangerine Oblong Vase ◄

- *1969*

Tangerine Whitefriars rectangular vase with twelve globular inclusions, resembling a mobile phone, by Baxter.
- *height 16.5cm*
- **Guide price £95/$180**

Vase with Poppy Design ▲

- *1920*

Glass vase by Lalique with raised poppy-head border and tapering stems with blue patina.
- *height 14cm*
- **Guide price £950/$1,796**

Scrolled Pattern Lalique ◄
- *1920*

Lalique glass vase with raised interlaced scrolled design.
- *height 14cm*
- **Guide price £1,400/$2,646**

Tangerine Log Vase ►
- *1969*

Tangerine Whitefriars log vase of cylindrical form with a bark textured finish, by Baxter.
- *height 23cm*
- **Guide price £140/$265**

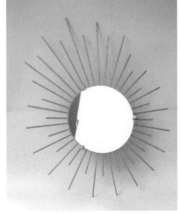

Toni Zuccheri for Venini ►
- *circa 1970*

Fine glass and bronze stork by Toni Zuccheri for Venini.
- *height 33cm*
- **Guide price £550/$1,040**

Sunburst Mirrors ▲
- *1950*

One of a pair of sunburst mirrors.
- *diameter 63cm*
- **Guide price £285/$539**

Modernist Lalique Vase ▼
- *1920*

Rare Modernist Lalique vase with raised geometric structural design.
- *height 15cm*
- **Guide price £1,400/$2,646**

Whitefriars Candle Holders ▲
- *1964*

A pair of Whitefriars Studio Range red glass candle holders of globular form by Harry Dyer.
- *height 24cm*
- **Guide price £125/$237**

Raison by Lalique ▲
- *1920*

Raison design vase by Lalique, with a raised floral design.
- *height 16cm*
- **Guide price £1,200/$2,268**

Cucumber Vase ►
- *1967*

Whitefriars red Cucumber vase, with a frosted textured finish, by Baxter.
- *height 30cm*
- **Guide price £185/$350**

Bubble Vase by Baxter ▲
- *circa 1957*
Whitefriars strawberry bubble glass vase by Baxter of organic form with a blue recess.
- *19.5cm x 16cm*
- **Guide price £115/$217**

Incalmo Glass Vase ▲
- *1990–91*
'Incalmo' glass vase with a vermilion red cane design neck, and a white glass globular shape base, by Laura Diaz de Santillana.
- *height 41cm*
- **Guide price £2,400/$4,536**

Lalique Vase ▶
- *1920*
Estoril pattern Lalique glass vase of conical design with concentric leaf pattern in relief.
- *height 13cm*
- **Guide price £1,000/$1,890**

Scent Bottle ▲
- *1901*
Small rose glass perfume bottle, diamond cut and faceted with clear stopper.
- *height 3.5cm*
- **Guide price £55/$104**

Murano Glass Ash Tray ▲
- *1950*
Fish-shaped Venetian Murano glass ash tray decorated with gold medallion splashes.
- *2cm x 8.5cm*
- **Guide price £45/$85**

Patterened Glass Bowl ▲
- *early 1970s*
Italian glass bowl with a blue and yellow swirling pattern within the glass.
- *9cm x 11.5cm*
- **Guide price £58/$110**

Venetian Vase ▼
- *circa 1950s*
Italian vase with air bubbles and aquatic scenes of fish and organic forms.
- *38cm x 18cm*
- **Guide price £1,250/$2,363**

Little Empress ◀
- *circa 1990s*
Little Empress, a twisted glass and steel sculpture by Danny Lane.
- *height 207cm*
- **Guide price £19,000/$35,910**

Fern by Lalique ▼
- *1920*
Lalique vase of ovoid form with narrow circular neck and a raised Fern pattern.
- *height 19cm*
- **Guide price £1,400/$2,646**

Italian Glass Sculpture ▲
- *1970*
Glass sculpture with red, yellow, green and turquoise freeform shapes within the glass, by Livio Seguso.
- *height 25cm*
- **Guide price £4,000/$7,560**

Art Deco Glass Bowl ▲
- *1920*
Art Deco French aubergine glass bowl, decorated with silver plated bands, signed Fains.
- *28cm x 30cm*
- **Guide price £350/$662**

Venetian Plate ▼
- *circa 1958*
A circular Venetian plate with white abstract design on a scarlet ground.
- *diameter 18cm*
- **Guide price £235/$445**

Danish Indigo Vase ▼
- *early 1970s*
Danish indigo blue glass vase of bottle shape form with splayed lip by Holmegaard.
- *14.5cm x 7cm*
- **Guide price £125/$237**

Venetian Glass Vase ◄
- *circa 1950s*
Venetian glass vase with applied white, green and black spun and dripped decoration.
- *50cm x 28cm*
- **Guide price £3,750/$7,088**

Murano Glass Ash Tray ▲
- *1950s*
Italian, Murano glass basket-shaped ash tray, with sea green and black design within the glass.
- *diameter 13cm*
- **Guide price £35/$66**

Jug and Glass Set ▼
- *circa 1950s*
Rare French glass water jug with two glasses from a set of eight, with gold banding and black geometric patterns.
- **Guide price £165/$312**

Circular Bowl ▼
- *1969*
Round glass bowl with orange design by Tagliapietra.
- *diameter 21cm*
- **Guide price £450/$851**

English Vase ◄
- *1960*
Indigo and turquoise blue English vase with pinched lip by Whitefriars.
- *24cm x 9cm*
- **Guide price £45/$85**

The Wave ▲
- *circa 1980s*
"The Wave", a clear glass sculpture by Colin Reid with internal colouring of blues, grey and rust.
- *42cm x 39cm*
- **Guide price £5,750/$10,868**

René Lalique Bowl ▲
- *1920*
René Lalique bowl, with four clam shells at the base.
- *diameter 18.2cm*
- **Guide price £600/$1,134**

Cenedese Vase ▼

- *circa 1980s*
Glass vase of ovoid form with red and blue spiral design and tears, by Cenedes.
- *height 28cm*
- **Guide price £850/$1,607**

French Vase ▼

- *1950*
A French pink and clear vase of ovoid form.
- *35cm x 25cm*
- **Guide price £65/$123**

Ice Relief Vase ▲

- *circa 1960s*
An amorphous glass vase with moulded ice relief by Mazzuccato.
- *height 41cm*
- **Guide price £400/$756**

Italian Murano Glasses ◄

- *circa 1960s*
A pair of Murano glasses of globular form on a circular base, by Barovier & Toso.
- *height 13.5cm*
- **Guide price £200/$378**

Gallé Vase with Bluebells ▲

- *1900*
Gallé vase, with bluebells and a variegated translucent blue and white background, signed.
- *height 32cm*
- **Guide price £2,800/$5,292**

French Crystal Vase ▲

- *circa 1950s*
French crystal vase styled as water with a fluted body and gobs of glass around the rim.
- *height 45cm*
- **Guide price £125/$237**

Signed Lalique Cat ▲

- *1970*
Lalique cat shown sitting with tail curled, with signature etched on the base.
- *height 21cm*
- **Guide price £750/$1,418**

Italian Glass Decanter ▼

- *20th century*
Italian red glass decanter with an exceptionally tall glass stopper, designed by Cenodese.
- *height 50cm*
- **Guide price £550/$1,040**

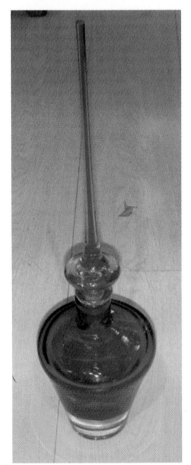

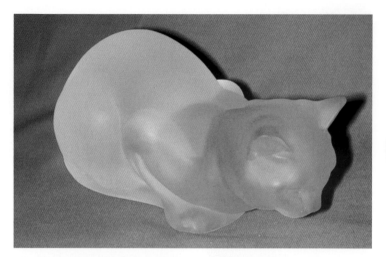

Crouching Lalique Cat ◀
- *1970*

Lalique cat in a crouching position.
- *length 23cm*
- **Guide price £750/$1,418**

Gallé Vase with Prunus Design ▼
- *1900*

Gallé vase with a prunus design on an amber ground with black rim and base.
- *height 30cm*
- **Guide price £2,400/$4,536**

Daum Vase ▲
- *1900*

Daum vase with pink poppies and green foliage with dragonflies.
- *height 12cm*
- **Guide price £2,400/$4,536**

Italian Teardrop Vase ▲
- *circa 1950s*

A glass vase of teardrop form with gold leaf set within the glass, by Seguso.
- *height 30cm*
- **Guide price £400/$756**

Veart Glass Vase ▲
- *1969*

An Italian glass vase with an avocado green wave pattern within the glass, by Veart.
- *height 25cm*
- **Guide price £450/$851**

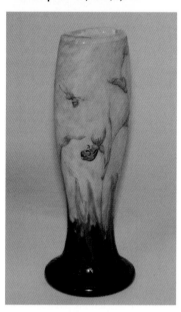

Maltese Medina Glass ▲
- *1978*

Maltese Medina glass with an abstract marine design on an aqua green ground.
- *height 7.5cm, width 5cm*
- **Guide price £65/$123**

Daum Art Nouveau Vase ▲
- *1900*

Daum Art Nouveau vase with translucent blue and white ground, decorated with flowers, butterflies and insects.
- *height 27cm*
- **Guide price £2,500/$4,725**

René Lalique Ash Tray ▶
- *1920*

Cendrier ash tray incorporating a celtic design on the border, signed "Gao' René Lalique".
- *diameter 9cm*
- **Guide price £450/$851**

Daum Vase ▲
- *1900*

A slightly waisted green Daum vase with a forest pattern, on a moulded foot.
- *height 16cm*
- **Guide price £2,600/$4,914**

Italian Oval Dish ▽

- *circa 1970s*
Italian emerald glass oval dish, by
Cenedese.
- *34cm x 15cm*
- **Guide price £250/$473**

Gallé Cameo Vase ▽

- *1900*
Gallé cameo glass vase with white and
orange floral design.
- *height 31cm*
- **Guide price £900/$1,701**

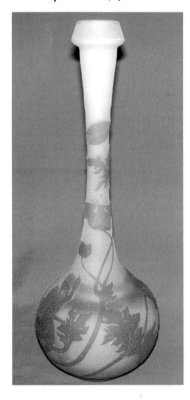

Cherry Blossom Vase ◀

- *1900*
Signed Galle vase of oval form with
trailing red cherry blossom.
- *height 21cm*
- **Guide price £2,400/$4,536**

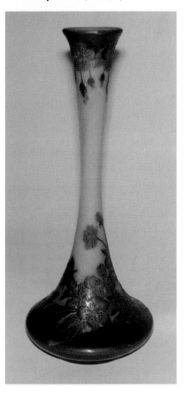

Tinted Cameo Vase ▲

- *1900*
French Gallé tinted cameo glass vase,
decorated with purple flowers around
the base and neck.
- *height 22cm*
- **Guide price £950/$1,796**

Cenedese Glass Vase ▽

- *circa 1980s*
Italian amorphous glass vase with orange
Murrina design by Cenedese.
- *height 38cm*
- **Guide price £950/$1,796**

Italian Ash Tray ▲

- *circa 1950s*
Italian amber coloured, shell-shaped,
glass ash tray with Venturina design by
Barovier.
- *21cm x 16cm*
- **Guide price £200/$378**

French Gallé Vase ▲

- *1900*
A red and yellow Gallé vase decorated
with pink apple blossom.
- *height 14cm*
- **Guide price £2,000/$3,780**

Venetian Glass Bowl ▲

- *circa 1960s*
Venetian glass bowl with a red spiral
design within the glass, with white
enamel on the reverse.
- *9cm x 16cm*
- **Guide price £58/$110**

Daum Enamelled Vase ▶

- *1900*
French Daum vase with splayed lip,
showing a summer scene with enamelled
trees.
- *height 21cm*
- **Guide price £3,500/$6,615**

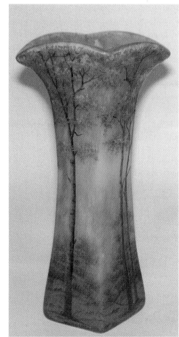

Purple Perfume Bottle ▲

- *circa 1960s*

Purple glass perfume bottle of bulbous form, with an oversized stopper by Cenedese, Italy.

- *height 45cm*
- **Guide price £650/$1,229**

Bottle-Shaped Vase ▲

- *1900*

Galle bottle-shaped vase with a long tapering neck, decorated with a pastoral scene with purple trees on a soft green background.

- *height 18cm*
- **Guide price £1,500/$2,835**

Chrysanthemum Bowl ▶

- *1910*

A green bowl with domed lid by Gallé, decorated with chrysanthemums.

- *height 14cm*
- **Guide price £2,400/$4,536**

Cenedese Glass Vase ▲

- *circa 1980s*

An amorphous Cenedese glass vase sculpture, with blue and amber designs within the glass.

- *height 31cm*
- **Guide price £850/$1,607**

Loetz Glass Bowl ▼

- *circa 1910*

A Loetz bowl of ovoid form, with pinched lip, in rose amber with gold-lustre finish.

- *height 13cm*
- **Guide price £1,900/$3,591**

Blue Cylindrical Vase ▼

- *circa 1960*

A blue, cylindrical Holmegaard vase, by Per Lütken, with intrinsic purple streak.

- *height 17cm*
- **Guide price £75/$142**

Italian Glass Vase ◀

- *circa 1950*

A glass vase by Archimede Seguso, decorated with a spiralling pattern in white, dark purple and mauve.

- *height 29cm*
- **Guide price £1,500/$2,835**

Art Nouveau Inkwell ▲

- *circa 1920*

A German glass inkwell, by Loetz, with brass top. Stamped with design registration mark.

- *height 6cm*
- **Guide price £265/$501**

Glass Sculpture ▶

- *1999*

Glass sculpture by Sir Terry Frost (b. 1915), entitled Millennium Disc and made from Murano glass with spiralled motif.

- **Guide price £3,800/$7,182**

Murano Shell Ash Tray ▲

- *circa 1960s*

Murano glass shell-shaped ash tray with gold leaf flakes within the glass.

- *14cm x 16cm*
- **Guide price £100/$189**

Small Gallé Vase ▲

- *1900*

A small Gallé vase with purple foliate design on a graduated blue and yellow ground.

- *height 15cm*
- **Guide price £1,900/$3,591**

Stained Glass Panel ▲

- *circa 1910*
Decorative panel showing tulip-shaped
floral image of nineteen, geometric
leaded sections.
- *height 58cm*
- **Guide price £45/$85**

Loetz Bowl ▲

- *circa 1905*
A Loetz bowl with blue Papillon oxide
finish. The bowl rests on three lemon
iridescent feet.
- *height 10.5cm*
- **Guide price £950/$1,796**

Green Glass ▼

- *circa 1939*
Green glass, by Barovier & Toso, in fluted
design with pinched double handles,
lustre finish and gold inclusions.
- *height 30cm*
- **Guide price £600/$1,134**

Loetz Vase ▼

- *circa 1910*
A Loetz vase with silver overlay with
organic patterns applied to the surface.
Iridescent oxides.
- *height 19cm*
- **Guide price £5,500/$10,395**

Rostrato Vase ▼

- *circa 1939*
A Rostrato vase, by Ferro, Barovier and
Toso, in Murano glass.
- *height 16cm*
- **Guide price £3,500/$6,615**

Pair of Glass Candlesticks ▼

- *circa 1950*
A pair of glass-pedestalled candlesticks
with metal liners.
- *height 21cm*
- **Guide price £480/$908**

Perfume Bottle ▲

- *circa 1955*
A Cenedese perfume bottle with an
oversized stopper and yellow and amber
centres.
- *height 44cm*
- **Guide price £800/$1,512**

Vistosi Glass Fist ◄

- *circa 1960*
Made from polychromatic glass, with red
soda predominant.
- *height 46cm*
- **Guide price £4,000/$7,560**

Barovier Glass Set ▲

- *circa 1950*
Ashtray, vesta and other receptacle, of
globular design with gold and bronze
inclusion, by Barovier, Italy.
- **Guide price £570/$1,078**

Two Red Gul Vases ▲

- *circa 1960*

Two Gul vases, designed by Otto Braver for Holmegaard, in red over white glaze.

- *height 26cm (left)*
- *height 30cm (right)*
- **Guide price £50/$95 (left)**
- **Guide price £70/$133 (right)**

Whitefriars Bowl ▲

- *circa 1960*

An English, Whitefriars bowl, of Geoffrey Baxter design.

- *height 18cm*
- **Guide price £125/$237**

Iceberg Vase ▼

- *circa 1950*

A Finnish vase by Tapio Wirkkala. Signed.

- *height 21cm*
- **Guide price £1,200/$2,268**

Three Whitefriars Vases ▼

- *circa 1960–70*

A selection of Geoffrey Baxter-designed, Whitefriars kingfisher blue vases in textured glass.

- **Guide price £33–£48/$62–$91**

Murano Glass Vase ▲

- *circa 1950*

A Murano Flavio Pozzi glass vase, showing eliptical design and colour graduation.

- *height 25cm*
- **Guide price £650/$1,229**

Cenedese Deep Bowl ◄

- *circa 1950*

A deep, Cenedese bowl with aquatic scenes of fish, jellyfish and organic forms.

- *height 25cm*
- **Guide price £850/$1,607**

Whitefriars Glass Bowl ▲

- *circa 1940*

An English glass bowl, by Whitefriars, of circular form with ribbon-trailed decoration.

- *height 24cm*
- **Guide price £180/$341**

Antonio Da Ros Dish ▲

- *circa 1958*

Cenedese dish of oval form with amber and cream design.

- *diameter 26cm*
- **Guide price £850/$1,607**

Murano Beakers ▼

- *circa 1960*

A pair of Aureliano Toso Murano glass beakers.

- *height 14cm*
- **Guide price £120/$227**

Timo Sarranera Vase ▼

- *circa 1950*

A vase, designed by Timo Sarranera for littala.

- *height 22cm*
- **Guide price £50/$95**

Poppy Vase ▼

- *circa 1920*

Argy-Rousseau pâté de verre vase, of coloured glass with repetitive poppy design.

- *height 7.5cm*
- **Guide price £4,200/$7,938**

Pinched Lip Decanter ▼
- *circa 1950*
An amber tinted circular-form decanter with pinched lip and splayed base. Signed by Venini.
- *height 23.5cm*
- **Guide price £180/$341**

Veart Glass ▼
- *circa 1970*
Italian object of teardrop form with inverted organic centre and amber tints.
- *height 72cm*
- **Guide price £550/$1,040**

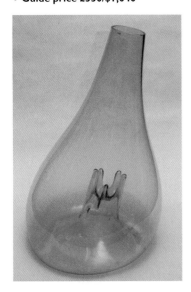

Biomorphic Bowl ◄
- *circa 1962*
A Holmegaard glass bowl by Per Lütken, with organic lines and a doubled, pinched lip.
- *height 35cm*
- **Guide price £90/$171**

Whitefriars Powell Vase ▲
- *circa 1930*
An English vase of baluster form in cloudy French blue colour.
- *height 25cm*
- **Guide price £345/$652**

Swedish Vase ▶
- *circa 1950*
A Skruf Talaha Swedish vase, with engraved base.
- *height 20cm*
- **Guide price £3,800/$7,182**

Cenedese Vase ▲
- *circa 1950*
Of ovoid form with small reservoir and red and blue spiral with tears.
- *height 26cm*
- **Guide price £1,350/$2,552**

Aubergine Vase ▼
- *circa 1972*
A textured, Whitefriars vase coloured aubergine, designed by Geoffrey Baxter.
- *height 14cm*
- **Guide price £48/$91**

Daum Lampstand and Shade ◄
- *circa 1900–10*
A toadstool-shaped lampstand and shade with purple overlay showing an evening scene with a lake setting and trees.
- *height 32cm*
- **Guide price £4,000/$7,560**

Monart Bowl ▶
- *circa 1930*
A Scottish, aqua-green bowl, by Monart, with single-folded rim.
- *height 8cm*
- **Guide price £90/$171**

Oriental-Style Vase ▼
- *circa 1980*
A blue and white vase, by Michael Bang for Holmegaard, from his Atlantis series.
- *height 16cm*
- **Guide price £72/$137**

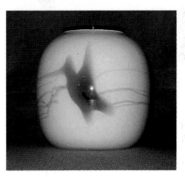

Teardrop Vases ▼
- *circa 1988*
Two, teardrop-shaped vases by Peter Layton, with blue swirled patterns within the predominantly white glass.
- *height 32cm (left)*
- *height 35cm (right)*
- **Guide price £250/$473 each**

HANDBAGS

Petit Point Handbag ▼

- *circa 1940*
A handbag with black petit point background decorated with flowers in a vase.
- *width 21cm*
- **Guide price £275/$520**

Bakelite Bag ◀

- *1950*
American silver grey bakelite bag with lucite top. With a flower and foliate design standing on ball feet.
- *height 15cm*
- **Guide price £265/$501**

Blue Beaded Bag ▲

- *circa 1940*
Blue beaded circular bag with an unusual gilt ball clasp and generous beaded looped handle.
- *diameter 16.5cm*
- **Guide price £295/$558**

Cocktail Mirror Bag ▼

- *circa 1950*
Ladies black cocktail oval silk bag with handle and small square mirrored sides.
- *8cm x 15cm*
- **Guide price £60/$114**

Two Owls Bag ▲

- *1930*
Brown leather bag with strap decorated with two owls with beaded glass eyes, surrounded by a foliate design.
- *width 21cm*
- **Guide price £145/$274**

Belgian Crewell Handbag ▲

- *1910*
Belgian crewell work of pink roses and purple flowers with a blue scrolling design on black silk and a floral gilt frame and jewelled clasp.
- *19cm x 20cm*
- **Guide price £160/£303**

Dogs Head Clasp Handbag ▼

- *circa 1920*
Silver lamé rose fabric with lilac silk lining and an unusual dog's head clasp with ruby eyes.
- *21cm x 20cm*
- **Guide price £106/$200**

Red Plastic Bag ▼

- *1930*
Red plastic bag with a gold and black geometrical design, with a gilt chain handle.
- *width 19cm*
- **Guide price £395/$748**

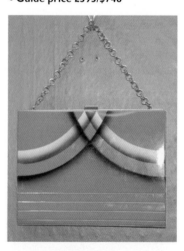

Pink Sequinned Bag ◀

- *1960*
English baby pink beaded and sequinned small evening bag.
- *width 22cm*
- **Guide price £160/$303**

Velvet Strawberries Purse ▼

- *circa 1960*

Plastic cream wicker bag with handle with pink and red velvet strawberries on the lid, pearls set in the green velvet leaves and pink velvet and gold trim.

- *18cm x 26cm*
- **Guide price £130/$246**

Leather Handbag ▼

- *1930*

Brown leather handbag with chrome and orange bakelite clasp.

- *width 21cm*
- **Guide price £295/$558**

Flowers and Butterflies Handbag ▼

- *circa 1960*

Woven wool bag with butterflies and floral design with carrying handles.

- *27cm x 25cm*
- **Guide price £75/$142**

Pink Beaded Bag ▼

- *circa 1930*

Very unusual soft pink beaded bag with circular beaded tassels.

- *height 25cm*
- **Guide price £115/$217**

Beaded Deco Purse ▼

- *circa 1920*

Black Art Deco silk ladies bag with a scrolling design of silver and black jet beads.

- *11cm x 17cm*
- **Guide price £65/$123**

Sequined Bag ▲

- *circa 1930*

Small ladies Art Deco sequined bag with fine cream beaded scrolling and ribbon design.

- *10cm x 14cm*
- **Guide price £55/$104**

Buffalo Skin Purse ▲

- *1903*

Art Deco buffalo skin purse with a silver chain and frame, hallmarked with unusual silver circular ring handle for use with a chatelaine.

- *9cm x 10cm*
- **Guide price £75/$142**

Plastic Strawberries Purse ▲

- *circa 1950*

Woven wicker bag with plastic strawberries and white flowers on the lid with red velvet trim.

- *height 20cm x 26cm*
- **Guide price £80/$152**

Clear Perspex Bag ▼

- *circa 1950*

Clear perspex American bag with foliate design on the lid.

- *height 11cm*
- **Guide price £248/$470**

Moiré Silk Evening Bag ▼

- *circa 1940*

Brown moiré silk evening back with a geometric gilt clasp by Josef.

- *height 17cm*
- **Guide price £265/$501**

Chinese Silk Purse ▼

- *1920*

Delicate rose Chinese silk and gold thread overlay handbag with enamel and green stone clasp.

- *26cm x 25cm*
- **Guide price £95/$180**

Wicker Bag ▲

• *1950*

Wicker bag made by Midas of Miami, decorated with birds, and green, orange and blue sequins.

• *width 37cm*
• **Guide price £135/$255**

Ken Lane Handbag ▲

• *1960*

Ken Lane brown handbag with a dramatic coral circular diamante handle.

• *height 15cm*
• **Guide price £295/$558**

Chrome Velvet Bag ▲

• *circa 1960*

Velvet ladies evening bag with chrome stripes and handle.

• *height 25cm*
• **Guide price £125/$237**

Beaded Bag ▼

• *circa 1920*

Gold metal beaded bag with pink lotus flowers and a green and pink geometric design, with a metal clasp and gold and silver looped fringing.

• *height 20cm*
• **Guide price £395/$748**

Silver Mesh Bag ▼

• *circa 1930*

Silver mesh bag with a delicate pink and orange floral design, a silver foliate design frame and chain handle.

• *height 18cm*
• **Guide price £225/$426**

Petit Point Bag ▶

• *circa 1940*

Petit point bag decorated with figures on horseback outside a castle, with an opaline beaded and enamel frame.

• *width 21cm*
• **Guide price £395/$748**

Brown Bakelite Bag ▲

• *1950*

America brown bakelite bag with lucite cover with faceted foliate design, made by Solar.

• *height 15cm*
• **Guide price £395/$748**

Evening Bag ▲

• *circa 1950*

Evening bag with paste diamante.

• *width 20cm*
• **Guide price £29/$56**

Bulaggi Bag ▼

• *circa 1950*

Bulaggi plastic bag with gold metal fittings and handle, with the inscription "Bulaggi" on the right-hand side.

• *width 17cm*
• **Guide price £85/$161**

Floral Handbag ▼

• *circa 1940*

Petit point floral design bag with black enamel frame with gilt scalloped edge and gilt chain.

• *width 19cm*
• **Guide price £295/$558**

Clochette Evening Bag ▼

• *circa 1920*

Clochette shaped beaded evening bag, with rows of blue and pink with a black metal filigree clasp and silver and black handle.

• *height 18cm*
• **Guide price £395/$748**

Wicker Bag ▼

• *1950*

Simulated wicker bag with a fabric head of palomino horse made by Atlas of Hollywood.

• *width 32cm*
• **Guide price £165/$312**

Plastic Tyrolean Bag ▼

• *1950*

New York made Tyrolean plastic bag with brass filigree foliate design, a red and black plaid pattern and a red leather handle.

• *width 20cm*
• **Guide price £195/$370**

French Beaded Bag ▲

• *circa 1950*

French beaded bag decorated with pink roses and a gold and white beaded frame inset with enamel roses.

• *width 22cm*
• **Guide price £695/$1,314**

Metal Beaded Bag ▲

• *circa 1920*

Metal beaded bag with a blue, pink and gold floral design and a gilt frame and chain.

• *height 22cm*
• **Guide price £695/$1,314**

Powder Compact Bag ▲

• *1930*

Black suede French bag inset with a powder compact. A Jeannes Bernard Paris creation.

• *height 11.5cm*
• **Guide price £245/$463**

Silk Evening Bag ▼

• *circa 1920*

Black silk evening bag decorated with flowers in blue, red and green with steel chips decoration.

• *height 18cm*
• **Guide price £295/$558**

Navy Chagrin Bag ▼

• *1930*

Navy chagrin bag with unusual metal fittings and chain handle.

• *width 19cm*
• **Guide price £495/$936**

Pink Suede Purse ▶

• *circa 1960*

Pink suede handbag with gilt oval clasp.

• *height 26cm*
• **Guide price £165/$312**

Amethyst Clasp Handbag ▲

• *circa 1910*

Art Nouveau ladies evening bag of finely woven material with delicate silver scrolling frame, silver chain handle and an amethyst clasp.

• *18cm x 19cm*
• **Guide price £165/$312**

Leather Pochette ▲

• *circa 1930*

Small leather pochette decorated with two cartouches; one with a sleeping cat with a peony, and the other with a red Chinese bridge over a river.

• *width 16cm*
• **Guide price £125/$237**

JEWELLERY

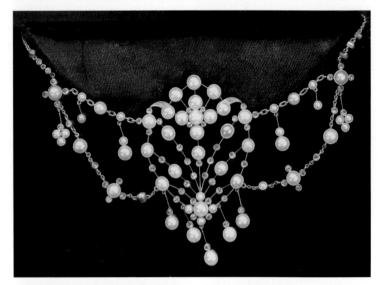

Pearl and Diamond Necklace ◄

- *circa 1905*

Edwardian pearl and diamond necklace with droplets and swag designs.

- *length 6cm*
- **Guide price £3,950/$7,466**

Diamond Earrings ▲

- *1920*

Pair of diamond earrings with oval, circular and rectangular diamonds within gold settings.

- *length 2.5cm*
- **Guide price £4,400/$8,316**

Art Deco Diamond Clasp ▲

- *1920*

Art Deco jade and diamond clasp together with a re-strung twisted cultured pearl necklace.

- *clasp 4cm*
- **Guide price £3,950/$7,466**

Salvador Dali Brooch ▼

- *1950*

Eighteen carat gold stylised leaf brooch in the form of a hand with red painted nails, signed "Dali" on the right-hand leaf.

- *length 6.5cm*
- **Guide price £3,750/$7,088**

Silver Gilt Brooch ▲

- *1940s*

American large silver gilt and cut-glass sapphire floral brooch.

- *7cm x 6cm*
- **Guide price £95/$180**

Flower Head Earrings ▲

- *circa 1910*

Sapphire and diamond earrings set in a flower head design of platinum and gold.

- *length 3cm*
- **Guide price £4,850/$9,167**

Diamond Leaf Earrings ◄

- *circa 1925*

Mille grain set in platinum diamond earrings in the form of a leaf.

- *length 2cm*
- **Guide price £3,475/$6,568**

Edwardian Jade Earrings ▼

- *1910*

Edwardian circular jade earrings set in plain gold with two bands of roping.

- *width 1.5cm*
- **Guide price £1,200/$2,268**

Austrian Violet Brooch ▲

• 1950

Austrian violet brooch with diamonds and jade leaves, set in silver.

• height 6.5cm
• **Guide price £1,650/$3,119**

Glass Italian Necklace ▼

• circa 1990

Hand blown glass necklace, made from blue, gold, red, green and clear glass squares.

• length 37cm
• **Guide price £135/$255**

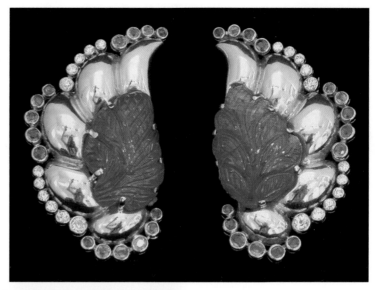

American Gold Bracelet ▲

• 1950

American heavy-textured gold link bracelet with geometric engraving on some of the links.

• 4cm/link size
• **Guide price £3,300/$6,237**

Boucheron Diamond Pin ◄

• 1920

Diamond-encrusted pin in the shape of a tie by Boucheron.

• length 4cm
• **Guide price £11,500/$21,735**

Snake Bracelet ▼

• 1930

Gilt bracelet styled as a coiled serpent with a spiralled chainlink, body and scale design to the head and tail.

• 8cm x 8cm
• **Guide price £85/$161**

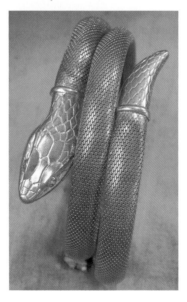

Pearl and Diamond Earrings ◄

• circa 1925

Pendulous natural pearl and diamond earrings set in 18ct gold and platinum.

• length 3.5cm
• **Guide price £3,785/$7,154**

Pair of Ruby Clasps ▲

• 1940

Pair of ruby and diamond clasps set in stylised gold leaf.

• length 5cm
• **Guide price £2,500/$4,725**

La Cloche Pendant Watch ▲

• circa 1930

A diamond and gemset pendant watch – the rectangular watch back set with brilliant-cut diamonds, suspended by a run of diamonds, and the top and base embellished with carved rubies, sapphires and emeralds.

• length 11.5cm
• **Guide price £42,250/$79,853**

Navajo Bracelet ▲

- circa 1950

Antique Navajo American turquoise and coral feather shadow box design with the artist's initials etched into the bracelet "ML Fowler".

- width 3cm
- **Guide price £500/$945**

Zuni Bow-guard ▲

- circa 1920

Pendant or pin and bow-guard, petit point design by Zuni Native American Indians.

- height 6cm
- **Guide price £299/$565**

Zuni Needlepoint ▶

- circa 1920

Unusual antique bracelet from Zuni, Arizona. Needlepoint with "Sleeping Beauty" turquoise.

- width 8cm
- **Guide price £850/$1,607**

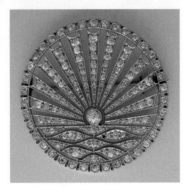

Art Deco Diamond Brooch ▲

- circa 1915

Diamond brooch with a circular plaque depicting a stylised rising sun over water, the lower section of undulating form with an old brilliant-cut diamond sun above.

- diameter 4.1cm
- **Guide price £12,500/$23,625**

Butterfly Belt ▲

- circa 1920

Silver Navajo butterfly belt with green turquoise conchos stamped "AJC" on the belt buckle, from Arizona.

- length 83cm
- **Guide price £1,390/$2,627**

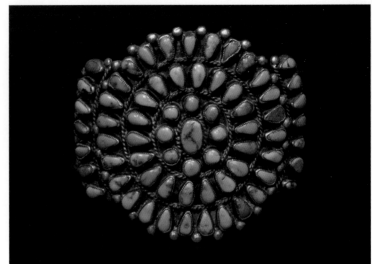

Necklace with Detachable Brooch Pendant ▼

- circa 1950

Dramatic white paste necklace with closed back silver setting, and detachable pendant with brooch fittings.

- length 43cm
- **Guide price £550/$1,040**

American Earrings ▼

- 1950

American turquoise glass earrings by Tiffany, modelled as flower petals within gold settings.

- 3.5cm x 3.5cm
- **Guide price £85/$161**

Silver and Turquoise Necklace ◀

- circa 1920

Unusual Navajo necklace with five silver and turquoise drops from Arizona.

- length 44cm
- **Guide price £395/$748**

Thunderbird Earrings ▲

- circa 1950

Zuni Thunderbird earrings with turquoise petit point design.

- height 7cm
- **Guide price £180/$340**

French Gold Necklace ▲

- 1960

Fine French gold necklace with a graduated design of icicles.

- length of largest drop 4cm
- **Guide price £2,400/$4,536**

Art Deco Feather Pin ▲
- *1920*

Art Deco peacock feather pin encrusted with diamonds on each side.
- *length 8cm*
- **Guide price £4,500/$8,505**

Zuni Cuff ▼
- *1950*

"Sleeping Beauty" Zuni cuff with 33 turquoise stones set in silver in a traditional design.
- *diameter 9cm*
- **Guide price £1,200/$2,268**

English Silver Brooch ▼
- *1940s*

English silver and enamel brooch modelled as a butterfly.
- *6.5cm x 3cm*
- **Guide price £125/$237**

Sterle Coral Earrings ▲
- *1960*

Coral earrings set in gold with gold balls.
- *height 8cm*
- **Guide price £6,600/$12,474**

French Art Deco Bracelet ▲
- *1920*

French Art Deco sapphire and diamond bracelet by Trabert and Hoeffer, Mauboussin.
- *length 19cm*
- **Guide price £44,500/$84,105**

Venetian Earrings ▼
- *1950s*

Venetian glass earrings modelled as sugared oranges and lemons.
- *2.5cm x 2.5cm*
- **Guide price £45/$85**

Silver Belt ▼
- *circa 1930*

Second-stage concho belt with turquoise stones.
- *length 97cm*
- **Guide price £2,500/$4,725**

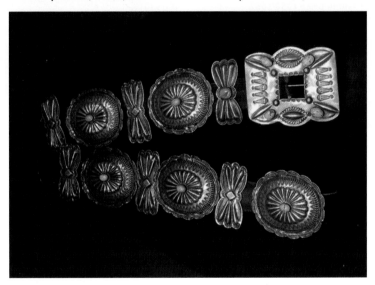

Glass Fruit Necklace ▲
- *20th century*

Venetian glass orange, lemon and strawberry necklace.
- *length 50cm*
- **Guide price £150/$284**

Zuni Turquoise Pin ▲
- *1920*

Zuni pin flower design with 30 turquoise stones, set on a silver base.
- *diameter 8cm*
- **Guide price £799/$1,510**

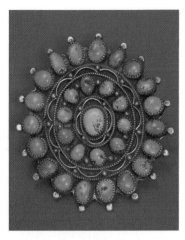

Men's Bracelet ▼
- *circa 1940*

Navajo men's seven stone bracelet with unusual silver setting with a feather one side.
- *diameter 7cm*
- **Guide price £799/$1,510**

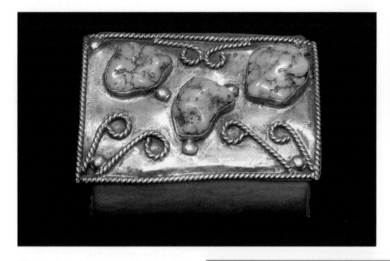

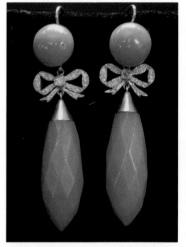

Austrian Bracelet ▼

- *1920*

Austrian Art Deco diamond bracelet set with a large central diamond surrounded by emeralds.

- *length 16cm*
- **Guide price £15,000/$28,350**

Deco Lapis Bracelet ▲

- *1950*

Art Deco bracelet with circular lapis lazuli discs with gold links and rectangular enamels with dragon designs.

- *length 19cm*
- **Guide price £4,500/$8,505**

Turquoise Bow-guard ▲

- *circa 1940*

Navajo silver and turquoise bow-guard on its original leather.

- *length 9cm*
- **Guide price £350/$662**

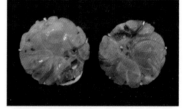

Zuni Ceremonial Ring ▼

- *1920*

Lady's Zuni traditional ceremonial ring set with 17 turquoise stones in a flower design.

- *diameter 5cm*
- **Guide price £269/$509**

Coral and Diamond Earrings ▲

- *circa 1910*

Carved coral ball and lozenge-shaped earrings set in platinum and 18ct gold with a diamond bow linking the upper and lower sections.

- *length 5.5cm*
- **Guide price £2,475/$4,678**

Butterfly Pendant ▲

- *circa 1950*

Navajo silver butterfly pendant with turquoise stone.

- *height 5cm*
- **Guide price £189/$358**

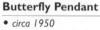

Jade Earrings ▲

- *1930*

Carved flower jade earrings set in 14ct gold.

- *width 2.5cm*
- **Guide price £1,150/$2,174**

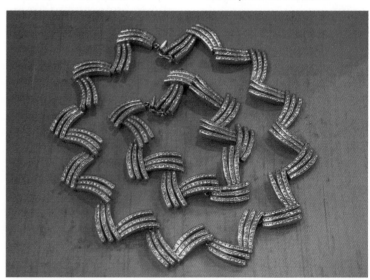

Zuni Silver Cuff Set ▲

- *circa 2000*

Zuni silver cuff set with jet and turquoise stones in a geometric pattern radiating from a stylised eagle, signed "Benji & Shirley Tzuni".

- *diameter 6cm*
- **Guide price £899/$1,699**

Necklace and Bracelet Set ▶

- *1930s*

Rare interlinked diamante necklace and bracelet set by DRGM, Germany.

- *necklace length 36cm; bracelet length 18cm*
- **Guide price £350/$662 for the set**

Gold Chainlink Bracelet ▲

- *circa 1940*

Gold 18ct double chainlink bracelet with light and dark gold linkages.

- *length 15cm*
- **Guide price £1,350/$2,552**

Navajo Green Bracelet ▲

- *1930*

Navajo silver bracelet with two rosettes each side of a large green stone.

- *length of stone 6cm*
- **Guide price £459/$868**

Black Pearl and Diamond Brooch ▲

- *circa 1935*

A brooch crafted of yellow and white gold and set with a highly iridescent Tahitian pearl of a rich metallic ebony colour. Surrounding the pearl are 46 round, pear and oval cut diamonds.

- *length 4.5cm*
- **Guide price £950/$1,796**

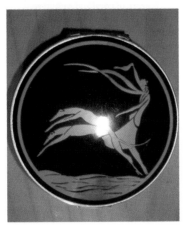

Stratton Powder Compact ▲

- *1920s*

English Stratton powder compact, with celluloid lid depicting stylised lady and two borzois on a gold-toned engine-turned back case.

- *diameter 7cm*
- **Guide price £130/$246**

Scottie Dog Brooch ◄

- *early 1930s*

Art Deco Scottie dog brooch made of celluloid on chrome.

- *height 5cm*
- **Guide price £38/$72**

Lanvin Pendant ▼

- *circa 1950*

Large circular black plastic pendant with red circular disc by Lanvin.

- *diameter 5cm*
- **Guide price £150/$284**

Deere Power Compact ▼

- *late 1920s*

American Deere book powder compact with geometric enamelled lid in black, white, gold, red and green with 'Deere' written on the spine of the book.

- *5cm x 7cm*
- **Guide price £120/$227**

Ruby and Emerald Pendant ▲

- *1950*

French ruby and emerald flower pendant with diamonds and pearls.

- *length 9.5cm*
- **Guide price £19,500/$36,855**

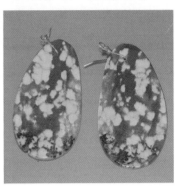

Santa Domingo Earrings ▲

- *1960*

Pair of oval Santa Domingo turquoise and black earrings from Arizona.

- *length 4cm*
- **Guide price £129/$244**

Zuni Bracelet ▼

- *circa 1930*

Zuni turquoise bracelet with petal design set on silver. There are arrow heads to each side and a hopi cactus and bird engraving.

- *length 14cm*
- **Guide price £370/$691**

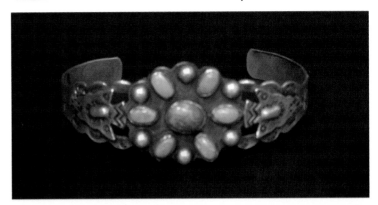

Metal Enamel Pin ▲

- *circa 1930*

English metal enamel pin by Dismal Desmond, with a seated black dog with a purple bow around its neck.

- *7.5cm x 2.5cm*
- **Guide price £75/$142**

Gold Floral Bracelet ▲

- *circa 1910*

French carved gold bracelet with flowers in oval panels.

- *length 18cm*
- **Guide price £925/$1,748**

Yacht Brooch ▲

- *early 1930s*

Art Deco German celluloid and chrome yacht brooch.

- *6.5cm x 6cm*
- **Guide price £58/$110**

Platinum Bracelet ▼

- *circa 1910*

A French platinum bracelet mounted with sapphires, diamonds and carved jade and moonstone.

- *length 16cm*
- **Guide price £6,800/$12,852**

French Tortoiseshell Compact ▼

- *late 1920s*

French celluloid tortoiseshell lady's head powder compact.

- *diameter 8.4cm*
- **Guide price £120/$227**

Gold Oval-cut Amethyst Ring ▼

- *circa 1920*

A ring crafted of 14ct yellow gold and set with a mixed oval-cut African amethyst, a vibrant violet in colour.

- *2.35cm x 1.9cm*
- **Guide price £360/$681**

Bear Claw Belt Buckle ▲

- *1950*

Bear claw set in silver foliate design with two flowers of coral and turquoise. Stamped 'E. King' and found on an Apache reservation.

- *diameter 7cm*
- **Guide price £699/$1,321**

Scottie Dog Brooch ▲

- *late 1920s*

Art Deco chrome and red enamel Scottie dog brooch.

- *6cm x 5cm*
- **Guide price £38/$72**

French Jade Brooch ◄

- *1940*

French jade carved dragon bar brooch set in gold with gold scrolling.

- *length 9cm*
- **Guide price £2,400/$4,536**

Swiss Balainot Bracelet ▲

- *1960*

Swiss gold bracelet by Balainot from the Sheet Range.

- *height 6cm*
- **Guide price £3,950/$7,466**

Vogue Brooch ▲

- *early 1920s*

Art Deco brooch of a flapper with a dog, given as a gift with a year's subscription to *Vogue* magazine. Metal with red detailing.

- *5cm x 7cm*
- **Guide price £58/$110**

Arrow Brooch ▲

- *early 1920s*

Art Deco sterling silver arrow brooch by Neja.

- *7cm x 2cm*
- **Guide price £125/$237**

Zuni Butterfly ▲

- 1960

Butterfly with a black and mother of pearl head and turquoise coral and mother of pearl body and wings, set in silver.

- width 6cm
- **Guide price £599/$1,132**

Navajo Ring ▲

- 2000

Navajo natural coral from the 1920s, designed with a turquoise stone in a heavy silver setting with scrolling, by Rowan Horse.

- length 4cm
- **Guide price £399/$754**

Turquoise Concho Belt ◄

- 1980

Turquoise Zuni 'concho' belt on black leather with nine large turquoise flowers, set in silver. Highly collectable due to the large size. Made by J. W. and M. S.

- diameter 8cm
- **Guide price £3,999/$7,558**

Navajo Bear Claw Necklace ▼

- 1970

Rare necklace with six bear claws set in silver with five large 'Sleeping Beauty' turquoise nuggets from the Arizona mine.

- length of claw 4cm
- **Guide price £1,899/$3,589**

Zuni Belt ▲

- 1930

Zuni delicate turquoise flower belt set in silver on brown leather.

- diameter 2.5cm
- **Guide price £1,200/$2,268**

Art Deco Diamond Necklace ▼

- circa 1925

Art Deco necklace with an alternating design of bar and circular cut diamonds, set in 8ct, platinum.

- length 47cm
- **Guide price £9,750/$18,428**

Indian Ring ▲

- 1980

Indian blue lapis ring with large amber stone set in gold.

- length 2cm
- **Guide price £8,880/$16,783**

Christian Dior Brooch ▲

- 1960

Circus horse brooch by Christian Dior.

- **Guide price £295/$558**

Zuni Pendant and Chain ▲

- 1920

Circular silver pendant set with 18 stones surrounded by silver scrolling, and a silver necklace.

- diameter 6cm
- **Guide price £699/$1,321**

Pink Enamel Compact ▼

- *1920s–30s*
American pink enamelled handbag compact, with silvered link chain, engine-turned back for rouge and powder, stamped with the maker's mark 'E.A.M.'
- *5cm x 6.5cm*
- **Guide price £130/$246**

Rectangular Tortoiseshell Compact ▼

- *1920s–30s*
Rectangular tortoiseshell enamel powder compact with trigger-action lid and stylised motif to the front.
- *6cm x 9cm*
- **Guide price £100/$189**

Red and Yellow Enamel Compact ▲

- *1920s–30s*
American red and yellow compact for powder, rouge and lipstick, with fine gilded interior detailing, engine-turned rear case and red and yellow enamelled lid suspended on silvered link chain.
- *5.5cm x 7.5cm*
- **Guide price £130/$246**

Compact with Yacht Decoration ▲

- *circa 1928*
English Gwenda powder compact in pink enamel with celluloid trigger-action lid depicting a yacht in foil finish.
- *4.5cm x 8cm*
- **Guide price £95/$180**

Federal Building Compact ▼

- *1934*
Green enamel powder compact with metal lid from the World's Fair, Chicago, 1934 depicting the Federal Building.
- *diameter 8cm*
- **Guide price £120/$227**

Suffragette Brooch/Pendant ▼

- *circa 1910*
Edwardian half pear, peridot and pink tourmaline pendant incorporating the colours white, green and pink of the Suffragette movement.
- *length 7cm*
- **Guide price £1,975/$3,733**

Corsage Brooch ▶

- *1940*
Flower corsage brooch styled as two exotic flower heads with leaves.
- *13cm x 6cm*
- **Guide price £65/$123**

Stylized Art Deco Brooch ◀

- *late 1920s*
French Art Deco celluloid brooch of a stylized man and woman leaning against each other.
- *4cm x 9cm*
- **Guide price £85/$161**

Lady Golfer Brooch ▲

- *early 1930s*
American Art Deco gold tone metal brooch of a stylised lady golfer.
- *height 6cm*
- **Guide price £25/$48**

Italian Glass Necklaces ▲

- *circa 1990*
Italian glass necklaces, made up of blue, turquoise, lilac, indigo and clear glass beads linked by gold metal beads.
- *length 37cm*
- **Guide price £85/$161 each**

Mixed Gem Stones Earrings ▲

- *circa 1910*
Pendulous set of earrings set in gold
with mixed gem stones of garnet,
sapphire, zircon, and citrine.
- *length 6.5cm*
- **Guide price £985/$1,861**

Bakelite Brooch ▲

- *1930s*
French bakelite black and white brooch,
with an incised feather design.
- *8cm x 4cm*
- **Guide price £65/$123**

English Jewellery Set ▶

- *circa 1940s*
English jewellery set with silver gilt top
hat pin with faux pearl and earrings.
- *8cm x 3cm*
- **Guide price £120/$227**

Combination Compact ▶

- *circa 1926*
Combination compact in green enamel
with marbled lid detail and yellow
diagonal band. Sections for powder,
cigarettes and money with additional
pull-out lipstick holder with attached
original tassle.
- *10cm x 5cm*
- **Guide price £130/$246**

Gold Tone Powder Compact ▲

- *circa mid-1920s*
Gold tone powder compact with
enamelled lid depicting lady and fan.
- *diameter 5cm*
- **Guide price £125/$237**

Lady Diver Brooch ▲

- *mid-1930s*
Art Deco red enamel and chrome lady
diver brooch, made in Czechoslovakia
and still on its original card.
- *6cm x 4cm*
- **Guide price £65/$123**

Organ Grinder and Monkey Brooch ▲

- *circa 1928*
American Art Deco brooch of an organ
grinder and monkey linked by a chain
with separate pin holders for each.
- *height 5.5cm*
- **Guide price £68/$129**

Lady and Mirror Compact Case ▲

- *early 1930s*
French chromed mirror powder
compact of lady looking at herself in a
mirror, with engine-turned back case
inscribed 'MUGUET DE MAI'.
- *4.8cm x 4.8cm*
- **Guide price £130/$246**

Aeroplane Brooch ▼

- *mid-1930s*
Celluloid black and white Art Deco
aeroplane brooch.
- *5cm x 5cm*
- **Guide price £85/$161**

Lady and Dog Brooch ▼

- *circa 1922*
American Art Deco lady and dog brooch
made of white metal.
- *height 6cm*
- **Guide price £78/$150**

Jade Pendant ▶

- *1930*

Carved green flower jade pendant with gold leaf ring fittings and an amethyst drop.

- *width 3cm*
- **Guide price £1,250/$2,363**

Plane Pin ▲

- *1940s*

Unusual metal pin in the shape of a plane with a map of south-west United States.

- *5cm*
- **Guide price £85/$161**

Czechoslovakian Necklace ▲

- *1930*

Czechoslovakian glass necklace made up of 18 triangular emerald glass segments.

- *length 33cm*
- **Guide price £95/$180**

Coral Zuni Earrings ▲

- *1950*

Coral diamond fashioned Zuni earrings, with a smaller diamond inside.

- *length 8cm*
- **Guide price £169/$320**

Rhinestone Bracelet ▼

- *1938*

Metal and rhinestone banded bracelet by DRGM, Germany.

- *length 20cm*
- **Guide price £120/$227**

French Earrings ▼

- *1930s*

Early French Egyptian revival glass earrings.

- *7cm x 2cm*
- **Guide price £95/$180**

Lapis and Crystal Brooch ◀

- *1912*

Lapis and moulded panel brooch with bands of diamonds set in platinum, made in San Francisco, USA.

- *width 4.5cm*
- **Guide price £3,300/$6,237**

Navajo Bull Bracelet ▼

- *1960*

Navajo silver sand-cast bracelet with two large silver bull's heads on a scrolling border, flanked by turquoise stones.

- *height 6cm*
- **Guide price £499/$943**

Navajo Bracelet ▼

- *1950*

Navajo coral and turquoise set on a circular engraved base, signed 'P.M.'

- *diameter 6cm*
- **Guide price £499/$943**

Night and Day Pin ▼

- *1950*

Gold metal flower 'night and day' brooch made by Warner, USA.

- *6cm x 4cm*
- **Guide price £85/$161**

Navajo Shadow Box Bracelet ▲

- *1960*
Navajo silver shadow box bracelet set with five large coral pieces stamped by the artist P. Benally.
- *length 17cm*
- **Guide price £699/$1,321**

Bow Brooch ▲

- *1930*
Rhinestone and black enamel brooch fashioned as a bow tie.
- *4cm x 12cm*
- **Guide price £85/$161**

American Watch Bracelet ▲

- *1940*
Gold-plated American watch bracelet, similar to one worn by Gloria Swanson.
- **Guide price £250/$473**

Brooch by Andrew Grima ▼

- *1967*
Andrew Grima asymmetric crystal brooch with three gold leaves set with diamonds.
- *diameter 5cm*
- **Guide price £1,850/$3,497**

Navajo Coral Bracelet ▲

- *1920*
Navajo cast silver scrolled bracelet with a natural coral set in the centre.
- *length 16cm*
- **Guide price £599/$1,132**

Brooch and Earrings ▲

- *circa 1950*
American brooch and earrings by Miriam Haskell.
- **Guide price £850/$1,607**

Snail Brooch ▶

- *1930*
A snail brooch in paste and silver.
- **Guide price £65/$123**

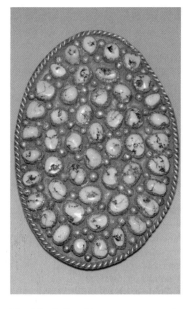

Zuni Belt Buckle ▲

- *1930*
Zuni oval belt buckle with turquoise nuggets on a silver setting.
- *length 8cm*
- **Guide price £699/$1,321**

Mic-Mak Indian Belt ▼

- *1920*
Glass Mic-mak 'Morning Star' Indian belt made from glass beads with butterflies and geometric blue and black design with a cream background, lined with antique pink material with floral design.
- *length 87cm*
- **Guide price £399/$754**

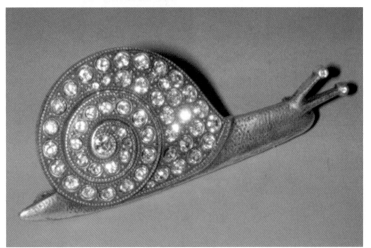

Flapper and Dog Brooch ▲

- *early 1920s*

American white metal Art Deco brooch of a flapper lady with a dog tugging at the leash.

- *6cm x 5cm*
- **Guide price £68/$129**

Green Lozenge-shaped Brooch ▲

- *1950*

Czechoslovakian brooch set with a dark green lozenge stone surrounded by bright green, faceted stones.

- *diameter 5cm*
- **Guide price £55/$104**

Amethyst Necklace ▶

- *1950*

Amethyst necklace consisting of 25 lozenge amethysts of varying sizes set in gold with a nine-stone amethyst flower design pendant.

- *size of pendant 6cm*
- **Guide price £2,750/$5,198**

Spider Brooch ▼

- *1940s*

Gilt metal spider brooch with two cut glass amethysts.

- *5cm x 5cm*
- **Guide price £45/$85**

Kokopelli Brooch ◀

- *circa 1970s*

An American Indian silver brooch showing the fertility god Kokopelli blowing a flute, inset with a circular turquoise stone.

- *length 5cm*
- **Guide price £129/$244**

Padlock Brooch ▲

- *1940*

An American heart-shaped brooch in the shape of a padlock connected to a key, with paste diamonds. Designed by Castlecliff and set in sterling silver.

- *diameter 2cm*
- **Guide price £120/$227**

Art Nouveau Brooch ▲

- *1900*

Art Nouveau 9ct. gold brooch set with a turquoise and baroque pearl drop. Marked 'Liberty & Co'.

- *length 3cm*
- **Guide price £480/$908**

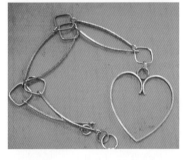

Silver Necklace ▲

- *1960s*

Silver heart necklace with a bridle link chain.

- *length 30cm*
- **Guide price £65/$123**

Czechoslovakian Brooch ▲

- *1930s*

Czechoslovakian shield brooch with numerous cut glass stones within gilt metal settings.

- *7.5cm x 5cm*
- **Guide price £85/$161**

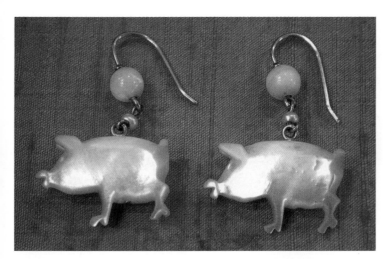

Pig Earrings ▲
- *1930s*

English mother-of-pearl earrings styled as little pigs.
- *2.5cm x 2cm*
- **Guide price £95/$180**

Christian Dior Brooch ▲
- *1966*

Christian Dior brooch with pearls.
- *height 8.5cm*
- **Guide price £275/$520**

Zuni Pendant ▲
- *circa 1940*

Zuni pin pendant showing an eagle dancer with turquoise, spiney oyster shell, jet, and mother of pearl on a silver base with beading.
- *diameter 7cm*
- **Guide price £950/$1,796**

Turquoise Pendant ▲
- *circa 1970*

Zuni silver and beaded pendant set with four lozenge-shaped turquoise stones surmounted by a sun symbol with red coral insert.
- *length 6cm*
- **Guide price £399/$754**

Navajo Concha Belt ▲
- *circa 1960*

Navajo silver concha engraved belt set with turquoise stones.
- *length 98cm*
- **Guide price £699/$1,321**

Zuni Concha Belt ▶
- *circa 1930s*

Zuni belt with alternating conchas of bow and lozenge form, set with turquoise, signed 'VMB'.
- *length 107cm*
- **Guide price £1,999/$3,778**

Navajo Ring ▼
- *circa 1970s*

Silver Navajo ring with two oval turquoise stones set within a feather design.
- *length 4cm*
- **Guide price £169/$320**

Czechoslovakian Brooch ▼
- *circa 1930*

A Czechoslovakian brooch of blue glass on a plenal base. Of diamond shape with a large, central diamond-shaped stone with a clasp mount.
- *length 7.5cm*
- **Guide price £40/$76**

Chanel Linked Brooch ▲
- *circa 1960*

Dramatic Chanel brooch encrusted with paste diamonds and blue, red and black stones.
- *length 12cm*
- **Guide price £650/$1,229**

Miriam Haskell Brooch ▲
- *circa 1950*

American Miriam Haskell brooch with glass stones, set within a stylised floral arrangement.
- *length 4cm*
- **Guide price £450/$851**

Green Fashion Ring ▼

- *1960*

A fun fashion green plastic and metal fun ring.

- *width 1cm*
- **Guide price £45/$85**

French Brooch ▼

- *1950*

A French brooch styled as a pair of lady's legs with paste garters and red high-heeled shoes.

- *height 7cm*
- **Guide price £85/$161**

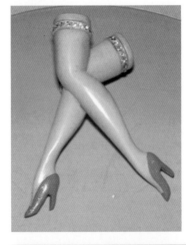

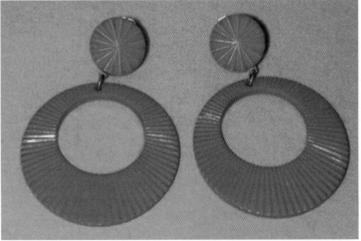

Burmese Ruby Ring ▲

- *1930*

Burmese Art Deco gold ring with four large rubies surrounded by diamonds.

- **Guide price £2,000/$3,780**

Egyptian-Style Pendant ▲

- *1920*

An Egyptian-style hexagonal shaped pendant with silver sphinx and teardrop amber stone.

- *length 2cm*
- **Guide price £120/$227**

French Art Deco Necklace ▼

- *1930*

A French green bakelite and silver link necklace.

- *diameter 2cm*
- **Guide price £120/$227**

Arts and Crafts Brooch ▼

- *circa 1910*

Silver and gold Arts and Crafts brooch set with crystal and turquoise flowers.

- *diameter 3cm*
- **Guide price £650/$1,229**

Fun Hooped Earrings ◄

- *1960*

English green plastic hooped earrings made in London.

- *diameter 4cm*
- **Guide price £25/$48**

Schiaparelli Bracelet ▼

- *circa 1950*

Bracelet with emerald green and sea green stones, designed by Schiaparelli.

- *length 12cm*
- **Guide price £550/$1,040**

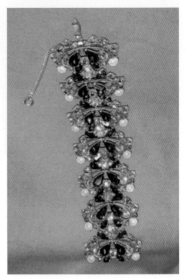

Linked Pearl Bracelet ▼

- *circa 1950*

Miriam Haskell bracelet linked with flowers and set with pearls.

- *length 14cm*
- **Guide price £750/$1,418**

Ball Pendant ▼

- *circa 1925*

Lapis ball-drop pendant with diamonds within a star-shaped platinum setting.

- *diameter 5cm*
- **Guide price £850/$1,607**

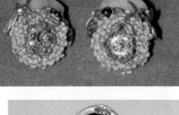

Silver Choker ▼

- *circa 1950*

American Indian silver-beaded necklace with an almond-shaped turquoise pendant set in silver.

- *length 3.5cm*
- **Guide price £289/$547**

Brooch and Earrings ▲

- *circa 1950s*

American jewellery set consisting of a brooch and a pair of earrings styled as flowers by Miriam Haskell.

- *length 5cm/brooch*
- **Guide price £550/$1,040**

Navajo Ring ◄

- *circa 1930s*

A Navajo silver ring with a lozenge-shaped and elongated Kingman turquoise stone.

- *length 5.6cm*
- **Guide price £299/$565**

Swedish Metal Ring ▲

- *1960*

Swedish ring with large central stone surrounded by metal band.

- **Guide price £95/$180**

French Ceramic Brooch ▲

- *1950*

A green French ceramic brooch in the shape of a poodle with bronze decoration and metal clasp.

- *length 5cm*
- **Guide price £45/$85**

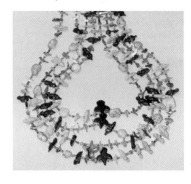

Zuni Fetish Necklace ▲

- *circa 2000*

Four-stranded Zuni fetish necklace with a menagerie of animals including eagles, ravens, turtles, coyotes and crows set in jet, turquoise, coral and other semi-precious stones.

- *length 89cm*
- **Guide price £699/$1,321**

American Indian Bracelet ▲

- *circa 1980s*

Gentleman's channel-work silver bracelet inset with chrysocolla and azurite stones.

- *diameter 23.2cm*
- **Guide price £299/$565**

Masonic Gold Locket ►

- *1900*

Masonic gold locket formed as a ten-page book with various engravings.

- *height 2cm*
- **Guide price £500/$945**

Diamond Bracelet ▲

- *circa 1920*

Art Deco diamond bracelet set with a rare marquis-shaped natural fancy blue diamond, mounted in platinum.

- **Guide price £155,000/$292,950**

Zuni Brooch ▲

- *circa 1999*

Circular silver Zuni brooch with graduated teardrop and lozenge-shaped turquoise stones set in a radiating sunburst pattern.

- *diameter 11cm*
- **Guide price £899/$1,699**

Crystal Beads ▼

- *circa 1940*

A necklace of crystal glass, amber, faceted beads with the principal pendant an extremely large, cushion-cut stone in a pierced, filigree mounting.
- **Guide price £35/$66**

Tab Necklace ▼

- *circa 1936*

Santa Domingo Pueblo tab necklace of red coral, spiny oyster shell and natural matrix turquoise, strung on double-strand original cord.
- *length 46cm*
- **Guide price £499/$943**

Bow Brooch ▼

- *circa 1940s*

Bow brooch with baguettes of faux sapphire and paste. Signed by Marcel Boucher.
- *height 6cm*
- **Guide price £95/$180**

KJL Brooch ▲

- *circa 1965*

A 'KJL' brooch, by Kenneth J. Lane. The brooch is of a flamboyant, baroque design, formed as a four-pointed star with rounded ends, set with a central, square cut faux cabochon ruby, and French lapis lazuli.
- *height 8cm*
- **Guide price £150/$284**

Mourning Pendant ▲

- *circa 1910*

An Edwardian mourning pendant, with 18 carat gold backing and silver front surrounding glass containing a strand of hair in the form of a feather.
- *length 4cm*
- **Guide price £1,250/$2,363**

Zuni Bracelet ▲

- *circa 1998*

A Zuni bracelet with three panels of geometric design, showing the four-direction medicine wheel for the protection of the wearer. Made of jet, coral, lapus lazuli and turquoise. By H. Kalfestewa.
- **Guide price £1,499/$2,833**

Wedding Necklace ▼

- *circa 1930*

Navajo squash-blossom wedding necklace with naga centrepiece, representing union, and silver, handcast beads with turquoise stones.
- **Guide price £1,499/$2,833**

Blue-beaded Brooch ▼

- *circa 1940*

Brooch of glass-encrusted flowers with blue beads.
- *length 7cm*
- **Guide price £45/$85**

Fertility Necklace ▼

- *circa 1970*

Turkmen silver choker fertility necklace with pendants. Made in Afghanistan.
- **Guide price £65/$123**

Bakelite Necklace ▲

- *circa 1940*

A continental necklace of the Art Deco period, fashioned with interlinked chrome rings hung with green bakelite discs.
- **Guide price £75/$142**

Silver Tiara ▲

- *circa 1910*

Silver and paste belle epoque tiara in original box. French provenance, with Greek key pattern and wreath design.
- *length 15cm*
- **Guide price £1,250/$2,363**

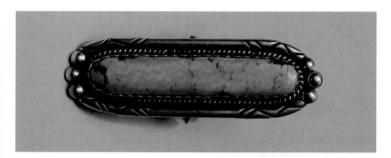

Coral Necklace ▼
- *circa 1938*
Red coral necklace of the Zuni tribe, of natural red coral, hand-drilled and strung. Red is a sacred colour to the Zuni, bringing good luck and longevity.
- *length 44cm*
- **Guide price £399/$754**

Art Deco Brooch ▼
- *circa 1925*
An unusual brooch of the Art Deco period, made in the form of an undulating diamond and onyx scroll, with carved emerald terminals, mounted in platinum. By Boucheron of Paris.
- *length 5.5cm*
- **Guide price £75,000/$141,750**

Bead Necklace ▼
- *circa 1940s*
A necklace of turquoise blue beads with glass encrusted flowers interwoven. The pendant is a flower cluster in pink, white blue and yellow.
- *length 45cm*
- **Guide price £35/$66**

Navajo Ring ▼
- *circa 1940*
Turquoise and silver ring with stones set on circular plate. Turquoise has four globules of silver to each side.
- **Guide price £199/$376**

Art Deco Bracelet ▶
- *circa 1925*
An Art Deco bracelet by Paulcho of Vienna, with enamel plaques, representing water, with floating flowers of craved jade and agate mounted on platinum and gold.
- *length 17cm*
- **Guide price £100,000/$189,000**

Amazonite Ring ◀
- *circa 1930*
A Navajo amazonite ring with traditional setting in silver, the whole of an elongated lozenge shape, with beading around the stone and moulded bezel.
- *height 5cm*
- **Guide price £329/$622**

Acrylic Rings ▲
- *circa 1965*
Moulded, clear acrylic rings with panels of colour running vertically throughout. Designed by Mary Quant.
- **Guide price £20/$38**

Silver Necklace ▲
- *circa 1950s*
American Indian silver-beaded necklace with a silver Naga inset with coral, with fleur-de-lis terminals.
- *diameter 5.5cm*
- **Guide price £699/$1,321**

Enamel Cat Brooch ▲
- *circa 1950*
Silver-gilt cat with turquoise enamelled eyes and an enamelled butterfly to the tail.
- *length 6cm*
- **Guide price £85/$161**

Zuni Ring ▲
- *circa 1950*
A Zuni flower design ring consisting of a central lozenge of turquoise, surrounded by twelve smaller stones interspersed with silver globules.
- *diameter 4cm*
- **Guide price £299/$565**

Basket Brooch ▲
- *circa 1925*
An Art Deco basket brooch by Cartier of Paris, of carved onyx with ruby flowers and cabochon emeralds and sapphires, mounted on platinum.
- **Guide price £9,000/$17,010**

KITCHENALIA

Kenwood Mixer ▼
- *1952*
Classic design steel Kenwood "Chef" food mixer with red dial and red lid, together with a steel bowl.
- *36cm x 37cm*
- **Guide price £60/$114**

Worcester Ware Cake Tin ▼
- *1950*
Worcester Ware tin with a red lid and 'Cakes in red letters on the front and 'Worcester Ware made in England' on the base.
- *diameter 22cm*
- **Guide price £28/$54**

Copper Dish ▼
- *1920*
Medium size copper dish with cover and brass handles.
- *9cm x 22cm*
- **Guide price £58/$110**

Bread Board ▲
- *circa 1940*
Circular wood bread board with the inscription 'Bread' and a foliate design surrounding a central flower.
- *diameter 28cm*
- **Guide price £28/$54**

Sputnik Egg Cups ▲
- *circa 1950*
Set of red, yellow, grey, black, blue, and green Sputnik egg cups with matching spoons.
- *height 3cm*
- **Guide price £20/$38**

Sucre and Café Pots ▶
- *1920*
French enamel blue and white marbled pots printed in black with the words 'sucre' and 'café'.
- *height 23cm*
- **Guide price £45/$85**

Bakelite Cruet ▲
- *1960*
Salt and pepper pots made from Bakelite styled as a red pepper and green chilli.
- *height 9cm*
- **Guide price £10/$19**

Kosy Kraft Teapot, Sugar Bowl, and Water Jug ▲
- *1958*
Pale pink china and stainless steel teapot, sugar bowl, and water jug. Unused in their original with 'Kosy Kraft Ever-Hot: The Greatest Name in Thermal Tableware' box and wrapper.
- *35cm x 35cm*
- **Guide price £75/$142**

Weighing Scales ▼
- *1950*
Beige Salter 10lb kitchen scales.
- *height 24cm*
- **Guide price £12/$23**

Bovril Cup ▼
- *1960*
Red plastic cup with 'Bovril warms and cheers' in white writing.
- *height 9cm*
- **Guide price £20/$38**

Milk Shake Mixer ▲
- *circa 1940*
Classic stainless steel café milk shake mixer, with wood handle and metal stand.
- *height 47cm*
- **Guide price £75/$142**

Small Iron ▲
- *circa 1920*
Small iron with a moulded base made by W. Cross and Son.
- *length 12cm*
- **Guide price £18/$34**

Enamel Casserole Dish ▲
- *1910*
French enamel casserole dish with painted cornflowers and variegated blue, white and turquoise, with white handles.
- *height 18cm*
- **Guide price £68/$129**

Storage Jar ▼
- *1930*
Hanging enamelled storage jar with a wooden lid and flue and white check design.
- *height 24cm*
- **Guide price £38/$72**

Hoover Janitor ▼
- *circa 1950*
Classic metal and cloth Hoover Janitor.
- *height 106cm*
- **Guide price £35/$66**

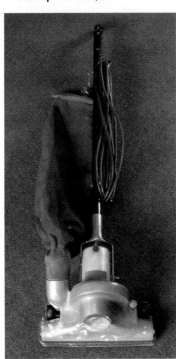

Porcelain Jars ▶
- *1910*
Five French cream pottery storage jars in three different sizes for café, sucre, thé, farine and poivre, each one decorated in blue with wild flowers.
- *height 22cm*
- **Guide price £95/$180**

Metal Weighing Scales ▲
- *1950*
Metal Hanson 5lb weighing scales.
- *height 25cm*
- **Guide price £55/$104**

Fruitwood Flour Scoop ▲
- *1940*
Fruitwood flour scoop carved from one piece of wood with a turned handle.
- *length 28cm*
- **Guide price £20/$38**

Large Brass Kettle ▼
- *1920*
Oversized brass English kettle.
- *height 20cm*
- **Guide price £68/$129**

Green Thermos ▼
- *1950*
Green Vacwonder metal thermos painted with a selection of sportsmen including runners, cyclists, shotputters and swimmers, made to commemorate the Olympic Games.
- *height 27cm*
- **Guide price £65/$123**

Plastic Container Set ▲

• *circa 1959*

A set of flour, sugar, rice, tea and coffee containers in variegated sizes, each one having a figurative design, and also a set of five smaller containers on a plastic shelf.

• *height 26cm*
• **Guide price £85/$161**

Cornish Ware Jug ▲

• *1959*

Blue and white-striped Cornish Ware milk jug

• *height 18cm*
• **Guide price £85/$161**

Set of Egg Cups ▲

• *circa 1930*

A set of four green bakelite egg cups on a circular tray.

• *height 8cm*
• **Guide price £12/$23**

Kitchen Material ▲

• *circa 1950*

Unused kitchen curtain fabric with red coffee grinders and assorted containers and floral arrangements in baskets on a white background.

• *width 94cm*
• **Guide price £75/$142**

Sugar Shaker ▲

• *circa 1950*

Glass sugar shaker with metal lid and spout.

• *height 18cm*
• **Guide price £10/$19**

Tea Towel Rail ▼

• *circa 1960*

Metal tea towel rail coated with yellow plastic.

• *length 16cm*
• **Guide price £8/$16**

Peugeot Frères Coffee Grinder ▲

• *1950*

Wooden coffee grinder with the maker's mark in brass, Peugeot Frères Valentigney (Doubs) with a large metal handle and wood knob.

• *height 19cm*
• **Guide price £50/$95**

Spice Containers ▲

• *circa 1950*

A set of five cream Australian bakelite spice containers with red lids on a shelf.

• *height 8cm*
• **Guide price £90/$171**

Bakelite Egg Cups ▼

• *circa 1950*

A set of four bakelite egg cups: two yellow, one blue and one red.

• *6cm x 10cm*
• **Guide price £7/$14**

Sputnik Butter Dish ▲

- *circa 1950*

Red plastic Sputnik-style butter dish with white spots, standing on three legs.
- *height 12cm*
- **Guide price £9/$17**

Art Deco Allumettes ▲

- *1920*

Art Deco allumettes storage box decorated with a purple floral and geometric design with red spots.
- *height 13cm*
- **Guide price £45/$85**

Cheese Dish ▲

- *circa 1950*

Clear plastic cheese dish with plastic stand and geometric plastic handle.
- *10cm x 18cm*
- **Guide price £18/$34**

English Sugar Jar ▲

- *1950*

English white porcelain sugar jar with a circular wood lid with a royal blue geometric design with the words 'Sugar' in black.
- *height 17cm*
- **Guide price £28/$54**

Metal Salad Sieve ▲

- *1920*

Metal salad sieve with handles and two feet.
- *height 24cm*
- **Guide price £15/$28**

Ham Stand ▼

- *1910*

English white pottery ham stand.
- *height 20cm*
- **Guide price £45/$85**

Wood Butter Pat ▼

- *1910*

Wood butter pat moulded one side with a handle.
- *length 19.5cm*
- **Guide price £10/$19**

Flour Shaker ▼

- *circa 1940*

Green enamelled flour shaker with the words 'Fine Flour' in cream writing, decorated with yellow banding.
- *height 12cm*
- **Guide price £10/$19**

Rocket Ice Crusher ▼

- *1950*

American rocket ice crusher made from aluminium with red plastic handle and container. Made by Fortuna.
- *height 32.5cm*
- **Guide price £150/$284**

Toast Rack ▶

- *circa 1950*

Yellow plastic toast rack with black spots.

- *length 12cm*
- **Guide price £8/$16**

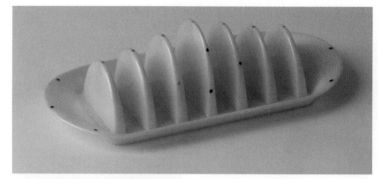

Metal Saucepan ▲

- *circa 1940*

Blue and grey metal saucepan with lid.

- *height 30cm*
- **Guide price £15/$28**

Pink Pyrex Dish ◀

- *circa 1950*

Pink Pyrex casserole dish with snowflake design, set on a metal stand with two burners.

- *15cm x 36cm*
- **Guide price £12/$23**

Porcelain Wall Box ▼

- *1950*

Porcelain wall box with wooden lid and decorated with fruit and blue banding with 'Allumettes' in gold writing.

- *height 15.5cm*
- **Guide price £45/$85**

Royal Blue Pot ▼

- *1920*

French enamel variegated blue coffee pot with noughts and crosses design.

- *height 27cm*
- **Guide price £60/$114**

Dessert Knives ▲

- *circa 1960*

A set of six pink, green, blue, purple, white and yellow Sheffield stainless steel dessert knives.

- *length 22cm*
- **Guide price £12/$23**

Caldor Ware ▼

- *circa 1950*

Green ceramic casserole dish with white lid decorated with a yellow cooker, blue sink, whisk, spatula, blue kettle and a frying pan.

- *height 13cm*
- **Guide price £55/$104**

Ceramic Cruet Set ▲

- *circa 1960*

White ceramic cruet decorated with pink fish.

- *height 16cm*
- **Guide price £15/$28**

Sugar Shaker ▲

- *circa 1950*

Pale blue plastic sugar shaker with star-pierced design on the lid and handle.

- *height 10cm*
- **Guide price £7/$14**

Brass Jelly Mould ▼

- *circa 1950*

Circular brass jelly mould with a stepped pattern.

- *diameter 22cm*
- **Guide price £15/$28**

Cast Iron Scales ▲

- *1920*

European cast iron weighing scales with copper pans and iron weights.
- *height 32cm*
- **Guide price £45/$85**

Café and Chicorée Pots ▲

- *1920*

Café and chicorée brown enamelled pots with white writing and banding.
- *height 20cm*
- **Guide price £45/$85**

Copper Kettle ▼

- *1950*

Copper kettle of bulbous shape with four feet and a tortoiseshell coloured glass handle.
- *height 21cm*
- **Guide price £78/$150**

French Storage Jar ▼

- *1920*

French hanging storage jar with a wood lid with red and white panels and the word 'Sel' in black.
- *height 27cm*
- **Guide price £65/$123**

Harlequin Cups ▼

- *1950*

Harlequin melamine set of six plastic cups and saucers. Argosy Ware made by Melmex.
- *height 3cm*
- **Guide price £45/$85**

Wagon Train Teapot, Sugar Pot, and Milk Jug ▲

- *circa 1958*

Teapot, sugar pot and milk jug stylised to represent vehicles from the *Wagon Train* TV programme
- *height 14cm*
- **Guide price £130/$246**

Enamelled Teapot ▲

- *1950s*

Blue-enamelled tin teapot.
- *height 23cm*
- **Guide price £25/$48**

French Red Pot ▲

- *1920*

French red coffee pot with variegated panels of red and white and red handle and spout.
- *height 27cm*
- **Guide price £78/$150**

Copper Ice Bucket ▼

- *1940*

Copper ice bucket with foliate design.
- *height 13.5cm*
- **Guide price £15/$28**

French Enamel Jar ▼

- *1930*

Royal blue wall storage jar with the word 'Sel' in gold with two rows of gold banding.
- *height 23cm*
- **Guide price £28/$54**

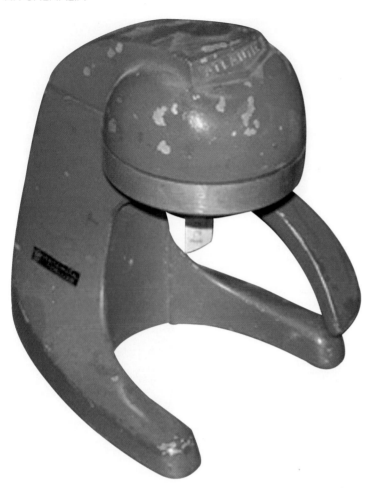

Bread Bin ▼

- *1930*
Enamelled bread bin with lettering.
- *height 40cm*
- **Guide price £44/$83**

Enamelled Bread Bin ▲

- *1940s*
English enamelled bread bin with the letters in stylised font.
- *height 50cm*
- **Guide price £25/$48**

Cheese Cutter ▼

- *circa 1910*
An Edwardian oak, brass and marble cheese cutter.
- *length 33cm*
- **Guide price £295/$558**

Cream Maker ▲

- *1950s*
Bakelite and glass cream maker with alloy handle
- *height 21cm*
- **Guide price £15/$28**

Squeezer ▲

- *1950s*
Solid aluminium vegetable or fruit squeezer made by Atlantic.
- *height 20cm*
- **Guide price £15/$28**

Cornish Ware Mug ▼

- *1940*
Cornish ware mug decorated with blue and white hoops.
- *height 8cm*
- **Guide price £11/$21**

Glass Creamer ▲

- *1940*
Jubilee model glass hand-creamer with primrose yellow plastic cup and handle designed by Bel.
- *height 22cm*
- **Guide price £16/$30**

Bakelite Thermos ▲

- *1930*
English green bakelite thermos with metal handle.
- *height 34cm*
- **Guide price £11/$21**

Flour Jar

- *1940s*

Enamelled tin flour container in flaked white and grey paint.

- *height 32cm*
- **Guide price £25/$48**

Potato Masher

- *20th century*

Wooden potato masher with turned shaft in fruitwood on a circular wooden base.

- *height 15cm*
- **Guide price £15/$28**

Tea Tins

- *1920s*

Numbered and pre-painted tea tins, with oriental designs.

- **Guide price £950/$1,796**

Brass Weights ▼

- *1910*

Selection of English brass weights with imperial measurements.

- **Guide price £38/$72**

Tin Opener ▼

- *1920*

A cast-iron late Victorian tin-opener shaped like a bull's head. With steel blade and in good condition.

- *length 16cm*
- **Guide price £15/$28**

Kitchen Scales ▶

- *1940s*

Set of British-made "Popular" kitchen scales in green enamel paint, with an accompanying set of brass weights.

- *height 45cm*
- **Guide price £45/$85**

Herb Chopper ▲

- *1910*

Victorian double-handled herb chopping knife, with wood-turned handles.

- *length 21cm*
- **Guide price £22/$44**

Rolling Pin ▲

- *1950s*

Good quality wooden rolling pin with turned painted handles.

- *length 40cm*
- **Guide price £10/$19**

Pestle and Mortar ▲

- *1940*

Pestle and mortar in white stone.

- *height 11.5cm*
- **Guide price £28/$54**

Coffee Pot ▼

- *1950*
Coffee pot by Kleen Kitchenware, with green concentric banding.
- *height 24cm*
- **Guide price £28/$54**

Hen-shaped Dish ▼

- *1970*
Ceramic hen dish produced by Susan Wilkans Ellis, Portmeirion.
- *height 13cm*
- **Guide price £25/$48**

Herb Storage Jar ▼

- *1950*
Herb jar and cover with red banding and the word 'Marjoram' on the body. Produced by Kleen Kitchenware.
- *height 10cm*
- **Guide price £6/$12**

Flour Jar ▲

- *20th century*
Glossed pottery flour jar by Hunts of Liverpool.
- *height 28cm*
- **Guide price £48/$91**

Pie Crust Funnel ▼

- *1940*
Ceramic pie crust funnel formed as a blackbird.
- *height 13cm*
- **Guide price £10/$19**

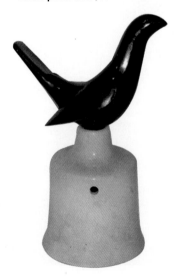

Pestle and Mortar ▶

- *1960*
Fruitwood pestle and mortar with turned decoration.
- *height 10cm*
- **Guide price £12/$23**

Brass Saucepot ▲

- *1910*
Sauce pot made of brass with iron handles and copper rivets
- *height 6cm*
- **Guide price £45/$85**

Devon Coffee Pot ◀

- *1950s*
Sandygate Devon coffee pot, with white polka dots on blue.
- *height 18cm*
- **Guide price £38/$72**

Ceramic Coffee Jar ▼

- *1950*
Ceramic container for coffee, by Red Lamp Kitchenware.
- *height 16cm*
- **Guide price £18/$34**

Metal Funnel ▼

• 1940
Blue enamelled metal funnel with handle.
• height 17cm
• **Guide price £9/$17**

Storage Jar ▲

• circa 1940
Cornish Ware jar with characteristic blue and white banding.
• height 22cm
• **Guide price £11/$21**

Metal Candlestick ▲

• 1930
Metal candlestick with green and black enamelling.
• height 6cm
• **Guide price £12/$23**

Baker's Paddle ▼

• 1920
A baker's folding paddle with spatulate head.
• length 185cm
• **Guide price £45/$85**

Dartmouth Teapot ▲

• circa 1930
Dartmouth Pottery teapot, with small white dots on a blue ground.
• height 17cm
• **Guide price £38/$72**

Bean Slice ▼

• 1920
Iron bean slice with a brass handle, produced by Alexander Ware.
• **Guide price £12/£23**

Ceramic Rolling Pin ▲

• 1950
Ceramic white rolling pin with green handles, inscribed 'Nutbrowne'.
• length 41cm
• **Guide price £25/$48**

Food Storage Flask ▲

• 1930s
A vacuum flask for food storage. with eagle clasping the world.
• height 38cm
• **Guide price £40/$76**

Kitchen Dolly ▲

• 1920
A dolly made by Simplex with wooden shaft and turned handle.
• height 25cm
• **Guide price £25/$48**

LIGHTING

Wedgwood Lamp ▼
- *circa 1925*
Wedgwood desk lamp fitted with a trough-shaped shade and circular stepped base.
- *38cm x 23cm*
- **Guide price £1,300/$2,457**

Chrome Wall Lights ▼
- *circa 1925*
Set of six wall lights in chromed brass fitted with coolie-shaped shades.
- *20cm x 15cm*
- **Guide price £2,500/$4,725**

Skyscraper Lamp ▶
- *1930s*
Art Deco chrome lamp featuring a skyscraper frosted glass shade in a wonderful sepia colour.
- *height 45cm*
- **Guide price £255/$482**

Tiffany Lamp ▲
- *20th century*
Bronze lamp with caged green glass shade stamped 'Tiffany Studio'.
- *height 50cm*
- **Guide price £5,900/$11,151**

Tôle Lamps ▼
- *circa 1920*
One of a pair of French tôle lamps, cream with gilt decoration.
- *71cm x 35.5cm*
- **Guide price £1,850/$3,497**

Art Deco Lady Lamp ▼
- *1930s*
Art Deco figural lamp featuring a semi-naked female holding a white glass globe shade. The figure is white metal and has been gilded on top in copper and gold tones. She rests on an oval alabaster base.
- *40cm x 22cm x 12cm*
- **Guide price £525/$992**

Glass Wall Lights ▲
- *circa 1950*
Set of three Italian moulded glass wall lights fitted with vertical chrome bands.
- *20cm x 16cm*
- **Guide price £1,500/$2,835**

Chrome Table Lamp ▲
- *1930s*
Art Deco original chrome table lamp with square-sided marbled cream and brown glass shade which gives off a warm sepia toned glow. Fully rewired.
- *42cm x 12.5cm*
- **Guide price £165/$312**

Sepia Chrome Lamp ▲

- *1930s*

Art Deco chrome lamp with an all chrome base and a rare sepia coloured segmented shade with silvered detailing.

- *38cm x 12.5cm*
- **Guide price £285/$539**

"Vers l'Oasis" Lamp ▲

- *late 1920s*

"Vers l' Oasis", a signed spelter lamp by Fayral of a woman holding a yellow glass urn mounted on a Portorro base.

- *height 47cm*
- **Guide price £1,395/$2,637**

Art Deco Verdigris Lantern ▼

- *circa 1930*

Art Deco bronze lantern of tapered form, each side centred by a moulded oval motif below a stepped fan cresting, fitted with replaced glass, the sides at the base of the lantern centred by scrolls issuing palmettes, with S-scroll brackets leading to a lower suspended bracket.

- *94cm x 41.5cm sq*
- **Guide price £6,500/$12,285**

Large Classical Lady Lamp ▼

- *1920s–30s*

Large lamp made of green patinated spelter featuring a woman standing bare breasted and wearing a short brown skirt, on a black marble top-hat base.

- *height 69cm*
- **Guide price £1,195/$2,259**

Tubular Lamp ▲

- *1950*

Italian chrome graduated tubular lamp with coiled decoration.

- *height 44cm*
- **Guide price £250/$473**

Yellow Sunhat Lamp ▲

- *circa 1960*

Large yellow Italian sunhat lamp with a green ribbon and assorted floral design.

- *diameter 44cm*
- **Guide price £290/$548**

Italian Gold Mesh Lamp ▼

- *circa 1940*

Table lamp with mesh lampshade supported on a black and white marble base.

- *height 49cm*
- **Guide price £900/$1,701**

Alabaster and Spelter Lamp ▼

- *circa 1925*

Gold patinated lady-lamp with base of cream onyx, nude woman figure of spelter, and steps and urn shade – which glows when lit – of alabaster.

- *18cm x 25.4cm*
- **Guide price £495/$936**

Murano Glass Lamps ▼

- *circa 1960*

Murano Italian glass lamp with yellow and orange ribbed body. The metal covers are ashtrays.

- *height 32cm*
- **Guide price £450/$851**

Blue-stripe Freeform Lamp ▲

- *1954–7*
Poole pottery lamp with a cross-hatched abstract design.
- *height 24cm*
- **Guide price £275/$520**

Pan-pipes Lamp ▲

- *circa 1970*
Italian pan-pipes table lamp with chrome and perspex columns surmounted by lights.
- *height 85cm*
- **Guide price £1,000/$1,890**

Pink and Brown Marbled Lamp ▼

- *1930s*
Art Deco original chrome table lamp with glass shade marbled dusty pink and brown. Fully rewired and in excellent condition.
- *40cm x 12cm*
- **Guide price £235/$445**

Desk Lamp ▼

- *1950–60*
A steel blue metal desk lamp by 'Elekthermax' with chrome stem and finial.
- *42cm x 42cm*
- **Guide price £250/$473**

Arctic Scene Lamp ▶

- *mid-1930s*
An enormous spelter polar bear and a pair of penguins sitting either side of an iceberg lamp on a base of cream and pale green onyx.
- *33cm x 81cm x 22.9cm*
- **Guide price £1,695/$3,204**

Patterned Freeform Lamp ▲

- *1954–7*
Poole lamp with brown and black abstract design, a brown band to the upper and lower edges.
- *height 12cm*
- **Guide price £125/$237**

Poole Vine Lamp ▲

- *1954–7*
Poole pottery lamp base, the body of bulbous form decorated with a leaf ribboned pattern.
- *height 24cm*
- **Guide price £275/$520**

Solid Freeform Lamp ▼

- *1954–7*
Poole lamp with attractive ice green glaze.
- *height 24cm*
- **Guide price £95/$180**

Glass Table Lamp ▼

- *circa 1970*
Plum and black glass table lamp.
- *height 38cm*
- **Guide price £30/$57**

Poole Atlantis Lamp ▲

- *1972–7*
Poole pottery lamp with a brown and beige glaze.
- *height 36cm*
- **Guide price £195/$370**

Rye Sphere Lamp ▲

- *1950–60*
Spherical Poole pottery lamp with yellow glaze, very minimal in style.
- *height 15cm*
- **Guide price £60/$114**

Lady Pastille Burner Lamp ▶

- *1925*
A spelter lamp with two ladies on stepped tapering columns sitting on either side of a globe. Both women hold a container with removable lids which appear to be pastille burners.
- *25.4cm x 36.8cm*
- **Guide price £1,285/$2,429**

Slim Bottle Lamp ▼

- *1954–7*
Poole freeform lamp with negative leaf design on striped-coloured ground.
- *height 26.5cm*
- **Guide price £195/$370**

Lorenzl Spelter Lady Lamp ▼

- *mid-1920s*
Spelter lamp of a woman in her under-clothes with a silvered enamel patina and peach coloured hightlights. Mounted on a Portorro Extra marble base, unsigned by Lorenzl.
- *28cm x 15.3cm*
- **Guide price £650/$1,229**

Candy Stripe Lamp ▲

- *1950–60*
A red and white glaze striped Rye lamp.
- *height 16.5cm*
- **Guide price £60/$114**

Peanut Lamp ▲

- *1954–7*
Poole freeform lamp with negative leaf design on striped background of green, mauve and brown.
- *height 27cm*
- **Guide price £215/$406**

Aeroplane Lamp ▼

- *1930s*
French Art Deco figural lamp featuring a classic brass aeroplane sitting on a soft brown veined marble base.
- *16cm x 23cm x 10cm*
- **Guide price £135/$255**

Stylised Clown Lamp ▼

- *1930s*
French mood lamp of spelter with two stylised clowns who have fallen asleep on top of the original crackle-glaze shade, mounted on a pink marble base tall.
- *29cm x 30.5cm*
- **Guide price £950/$1,796**

French Desk Lamp ▼

- *1955–65*
French chromed steel desk lamp with light green painted shade and base.
- *height 35cm*
- **Guide price £60/$114**

Silvered Bronze Lamp ▲

• 1923
Art Deco silvered bronze lady lamp mounted on a verdigris marble base, made by the French artist Janle and signed on the bottom of the figure.
• 40cm x 30cm
• **Guide price £1,595/$3,015**

Seal Lamp ▲

• mid-1920s
French Art Deco spelter seal lamp by Carvin mounted on a marble base.
• 27cm x 31cm
• **Guide price £295/$558**

Small Carafe Lamp ▼

• 1957
Sky-blue glazed lamp by Poole in a carafe shape.
• height 27cm
• **Guide price £95/$180**

Celtic Lamp ▼

• circa 1960
Pottery lamp decorated with a yellow and black stylised dragon pattern, swirls and black banding to the upper and lower registers.
• height 35cm
• **Guide price £95/$180**

Italian Light ▲

• circa 1950
Italian light with a white conical shade supported on a black circular base.
• height 40cm
• **Guide price £280/$530**

Spelter Lady Lamp ▲

• early 1920s
A spelter Egyptian-themed French lady lamp, possibly by Voliente although very Chiparus in detail. This lamp is with a crackle-glass shade and is mounted on an ovular red marble base with pebbled detail.
• 35.5cm x 29.2cm
• **Guide price £740/$1,399**

Art Deco Gymnast Lamp ▲

• 1923
French Art Deco spelter lamp featuring a woman doing the splits supporting a globe, signed by Balleste.
• 28cm x 36cm
• **Guide price £760/$1,437**

Patterned Poole Helios Lamp ▼

• circa 1964
A bluish grey/white glaze decorated Poole lamp of grid-style design.
• height 12cm
• **Guide price £50/$95**

Bronze Art Deco Lamp ▼

• early 20th century
French Art Deco bronze lamp by Molins-Balleste. The lamp shade is made of hand-made glass fruit and flowers sitting in an alabaster basket.
• 45cm x 50cm
• **Guide price £2,945/$5,567**

Wall Lights by Vemini ▼

• circa 1950
One of a pair of abstract Italian glass wall lights with a design of assorted squares with amber, tobacco and clear glass, by Vemini.
• 31cm square
• **Guide price £1,280/$2,419**

Conical Lamp ▲
- *1930s*

Large French metal ceiling lamp in conical form with green patinated ring detailing and chrome outer ring.
- *45.7cm x 61cm*
- **Guide price £595/$1,125**

Poole Helios Lamp ▲
- *circa 1964*

Poole pottery square-shaped lamp of an abstract geometric design with moss green glaze.
- *12cm x 10cm*
- **Guide price £40/$76**

Art Deco Lamp ▲
- *1930*

French Art Deco chrome table lamp with a domed shade, curved stand and circular base.
- *height 32cm*
- **Guide price £250/$473**

Cube Floor Light ▲
- *1970*

Free-standing floor light made from three white and yellow glass cubes, connected by metal bands with a circular metal top and handle.
- *height 1.2m*
- **Guide price £1,100/$2,079**

Perspex Lamp ▼
- *1970*

Italian U-shaped perspex lamp on a metal base by Stilnovo.
- *38cm x 32cm*
- **Guide price £1,200/$2,268**

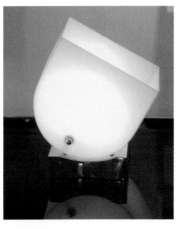

Brancusi Standing Light ▼
- *1990*

Brancusi standing light made from Japanese paper with a metal base, by Tom Dixon.
- *height 2.8m*
- **Guide price £1,600/$3,024**

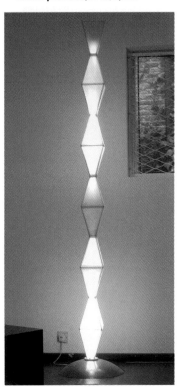

Crouching Woman Lamp ◄
- *late 1920s*

Art Deco lamp of a woman in a crouched position supporting the fixture. Made of spelter with a gold enamelled patina.
- *height 38cm*
- **Guide price £495/$936**

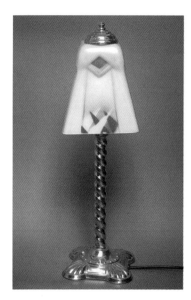

Art Deco Lamp ▲
- *circa 1930*

Art deco lamp with a twisted metal stand and a white glass lampshade with a grey geometric pattern.
- *height 47cm*
- **Guide price £75/$142**

Art Deco Lady Lamp ▲
- *early 1930s*

French Art Deco spelter lamp of a woman supporting a globe, mounted on a Portorro marble and onyx base.
- *height 46cm*
- **Guide price £495/$936**

Kodak Lampshade ▲

- *1970*

Plastic lampshade with the lettering 'Kodak' in red on a deep yellow background.

- *height 25cm*
- **Guide price £149/$282**

Baccarat-style Chandeliers ▲

- *20th century*

One of a pair of Baccarat-style cranberry glass chandeliers with scrolled moulded decoration and numerous crystal glass droplets, with 36 arms.

- *height 2.08m*
- **Guide price £20,000/$37,800**

Pagani Mesh Lamp ▲

- *circa 1970*

Italian black metal mesh lamp stylised as a flower by Luciano Pagani.

- *width 76cm*
- **Guide price £385/$728**

Italian Globe Lamps ▼

- *circa 1960*

One of a pair of clear and ripple-effect globe table lamps with a white band running through the body.

- *height 54cm*
- **Guide price £300/$567**

Table Lamp ▼

- *1968*

English table lamp designed for British Home Stores, with a green glass base, chrome neck and pale green perspex shade.

- *height 40cm*
- **Guide price £150/$284**

Spelter and Alabaster Lamp ▲

- *early 1930s*

English Art Deco lamp of a woman supporting a globe with one hand. Made of gold patinated spelter and mounted on an alabaster triangular base.

- *height 40cm*
- **Guide price £440/$832**

Gaku Light ▲

- *circa 1990*

Gaku light by Ingo Maurer made from Japanese paper on an aluminium stand.

- *height 95cm*
- **Guide price £560/$1,058**

Italian Wall Light ▼

- *circa 1970*

Italian wall light by Marlotta, with a perspex background with metal tubes projecting from it in a variety of sizes, the whole on a square metal frame.

- *60cm x 60cm*
- **Guide price £1,600/$3,024**

Italian Table Lamp ▼

- *1950*

Black Italian table lamp of baluster form with blue, yellow and red dots, within a white graffiti-patterned border.

- *height 15cm*
- **Guide price £50/$95**

Italian Desk Lamp ◄

- *circa 1970s*

Fully adjustable desk lamp with variable strength switch by Arteluce of Italy.

- *height 37.5cm*
- **Guide price £175/$331**

Mazzega Table Lamp ▲

- *circa 1960*

Italian Murano glass wave-effect table lamp by Mazzega.

- *54cm x 43cm*
- **Guide price £1,150/$2,174**

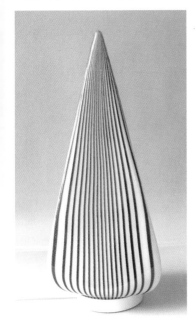

Italian Striped Lamps ▲

- *1950*

One of a pair of tear-shaped, brown and white striped Italian table lamps.

- *height 23cm*
- **Guide price £250/$473**

Vistosi Lamp ▼

- *1978*

Italian Murano white glass lamp of ovoid form by Vistosi.

- *height 57cm*
- **Guide price £1,200/$2,268**

Italian Hat Lamp ▼

- *circa 1960*

Large Italian table lamp in the form of a large striped sunhat with red flowers on one side and a large black ribbon.

- *diameter 44cm*
- **Guide price £290/$548**

Colomba Lamp ▼

- *1960*

Italian metal and glass, four globe, white Colomba lamp.

- *height 60cm*
- **Guide price £350/$662**

Ceiling Lamps ◄

- *circa 1950s*

Three perspex and metal ceiling lamps in aqua green, red and white.

- *diameter 45cm*
- **Guide price £800/$1,512**

Edwardian Ceiling Lights ▲

- *circa 1901*

One of a pair of Edwardian brass flash ceiling lights with frosted glass covers.

- *height 20cm*
- **Guide price £1,600/$3,024**

Raised Band Lamp ◄

- *circa 1950*

Pink Poole pottery lamp of pleasing proportions.

- *height 16cm*
- **Guide price £60/$114**

Cloth Lamp Covers ▲

- *1952*

Pair of English, moulded and stretched cloth wall lamp covers by George Nelson.

- *length 30cm*
- **Guide price £100/$189**

Italian Angled Lamp ▼

- *1970s*
Italian fully adjustable angled lamp.
- *height 37.5cm*
- **Guide price £175/$331**

Dome-shaped Lamp ▲

- *circa 1970s*
Italian dome-shaped glass lamp, with the light lit from within the glass base, by Mazzega.
- *height 52.5cm*
- **Guide price £650/$1,229**

Chrome Ceiling Lamp ▲

- *circa 1960s*
Chrome ceiling lamp with a series of interlocking metal tubes.
- *diameter 60cm*
- **Guide price £750/$1,418**

English Wall Lamps ▼

- *1950s*
Pair of English blue metal wall lamps with brass wall fittings.
- *height 25cm*
- **Guide price £90/$171**

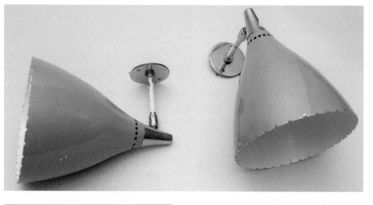

Italian Chrome Lamp ▲

- *1970*
Italian heavy chrome lamp of oval form with brass fittings.
- *diameter 35cm*
- **Guide price £350/$662**

Metal and Chrome Lamp ▲

- *1970*
Italian table lamp with painted black metal shade and chrome base.
- *height 56cm*
- **Guide price £350/$662**

Panthella Lamps ◄

- *1970*
Panthella lamps designed for Louis Poulson by Verner Panton, Denmark.
- **Guide price £550/$1,040**

English Ceiling Lamp ▲

- *1952*
Lantern-style ceiling lamp designed by George Nelson for Howard Miller.
- *width 46cm*
- **Guide price £350/$662**

Fruit-Shaped Lamp ▶

- *circa 1970s*
Italian plastic ceiling lamp in the shape of a peeled orange.
- *diameter 32.5cm*
- **Guide price £60/$114**

Wind Chime Lamp ▼

- *1970*

Wind chime ceiling lamp with crystal glass balls on chrome drops.

- *100cm x 40cm*
- **Guide price £1,700/$3,213**

White Chrome Lamp ▲

- *1950s*

Italian white chrome and plastic ceiling lamp by Harvey Guzzi.

- *diameter 58cm*
- **Guide price £450/$851**

Pistillo Wall Lamp ▲

- *1970*

Italian silverised wall lamp in a Pistillo design by Studio Tetrarch.

- *diameter 60cm*
- **Guide price £250/$473**

Italian Glass Lamp ▼

- *circa 1950s*

Italian white glass bowl shaped lamp on a chrome stand by Guzzi.

- *height 200cm*
- **Guide price £750/$1,418**

Fibre-optic Lamp ▲

- *1950*

Plastic fibre-optic lamp with plastic flowers within the base.

- *height 75cm*
- **Guide price £200/$378**

Amber Glass Lamp ▶

- *1960*

Amber glass ceiling lamp with a metal top to flex.

- *height 26cm*
- **Guide price £55/$104**

Etling Lamp ▲

- *1930*

French black lamp with red chinoisiere influence, designed by Etling.

- *47cm x 30cm*
- **Guide price £1,200/$2,268**

Plastic Ceiling Lamp ◀

- *1960*

Italian oval-shaped ceiling lamp in amber and yellow plastic.

- *diameter 42.5cm*
- **Guide price £350/$662**

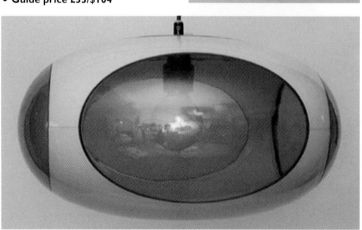

Table Lamp ▼

- *circa 1930*
Chrome and plastic table light with glass shade.
- *height 46cm*
- **Guide price £150/$284**

Hutschenreuther Candelabra ▼

- *20th century*
Candelabra with two branches of leaves supporting candleholders, with a central cherub standing on a gold circular ball, with a round white base, by Hutschenreuther.
- *height 22cm*
- **Guide price £1,400/$2,646**

Free-standing Lamp ▼

- *1960*
Large orange and brown free-standing lamp, with double handles.
- *height 60cm*
- **Guide price £80/$152**

Louis XVI-style Chandelier ◄

- *circa 1920*
Two-tiered Louis XVI-style, fine quality cut-crystal chandelier, with four light sconces at the top, and eight below.
- *height 120cm*
- **Guide price £6,000/$11,340**

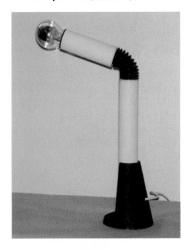

Italian Table Lamp ▲

- *1960*
Italian white table lamp with black base and rubber mobile arm.
- *height 40cm*
- **Guide price £45/$85**

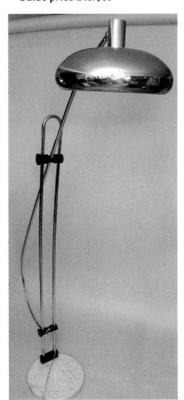

Adjustable Lamp ▲

- *circa 1970s*
Italian adjustable chrome lamp with marble base.
- *height 56cm*
- **Guide price £1,200/$2,268**

Metal Table Lamp ▲

- *circa 1960*
Metal table lamp with black lampshade and circular base.
- *height 41cm*
- **Guide price £85/$161**

Snowflake Chandelier ▲

- *1960–70*
Atomic metal chandelier of a snowflake design.
- *diameter 40cm*
- **Guide price £850/$1,607**

Desk Lamp ▲

- *circa 1960*
Table or desk lamp with white circular shade and metal base and stand.
- *height 37cm*
- **Guide price £35/$66**

American Plaster Lamp ▲

- *circa 1950*

American plaster lamp with lady dancer, with a yellow lampshade with black tassels.

- *height 92cm*
- **Guide price £175/$331**

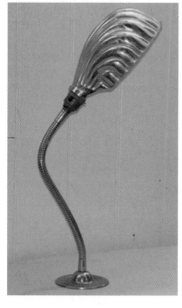

Reading Lamp ▲

- *1970*

Brass reading lamp on a flexible stand and circular base.

- *height 52cm*
- **Guide price £55/$104**

Italian Chandelier ▼

- *1900*

Italian brass chandelier with splayed leaves and blue drop crystals.

- *width 45cm*
- **Guide price £175/$331**

Hour-glass Candelabra ▼

- *1920*

Italian candelabra with a metal hour-glass base and wire and green glass flower decoration.

- *60cm x 40cm*
- **Guide price £475/$898**

Perspex Lamp ▶

- *1960*

Free-standing lamp with an amber perspex base and fine raffia shade.

- *height 36cm*
- **Guide price £40/$76**

White Lamp ◀

- *1960*

White ceiling lamp, with rubber flex and stainless steel collar.

- *height 35cm*
- **Guide price £50/$95**

Brass Desk Lamp ▲

- *circa 1930s*

Brass cylinder-shaped lamp on a stand with circular base.

- *height 32cm*
- **Guide price £250/$473**

Crystal Chandelier ▲

- *1920s*

Italian chandelier with a gilt metal foliate designed base, and crystal and red glass pendants.

- *65cm x 60cm*
- **Guide price £395/$747**

Ceiling Star Light ▼

- *1900*

Moroccan star ceiling light of mirrored glass.

- *diameter 62cm*
- **Guide price £240/$454**

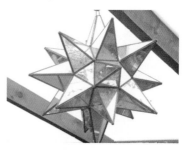

Adam-style Chandelier ▼

- *circa 1920*

Fine twelve sconce Adam-style chandelier with pink glass bowl.

- *height 85cm*
- **Guide price £1,450/$2,741**

British Spiral Lamp ▼

- *early 1990s*

Gold-coloured leaf spiral lamp on a circular base by Tom Dixon.

- *height 150cm*
- **Guide price £980/$1,852**

Oak Candelabras ▼

- *1920*
Pair of German, carved black, forest oak candelabra with a castellated influence.
- *height 48cm*
- **Guide price £1,950/$3,686**

Albini Chrome Lamp ▼

- *1969*
Italian chrome ceiling lamp by Franco Albini.
- *height 45cm*
- **Guide price £350/$662**

Painted Lamp Stand ▲

- *1920*
Naturalistically modelled and painted metal lamp stand showing a floral arrangement of daisies, poppies and wheatsheaves.
- *height 110cm*
- **Guide price £420/$794**

Alabaster Lamps ▲

- *20th century*
One of a pair of alabaster lamps with gilt wrought-iron appliqués.
- *width 45cm*
- **Guide price £1,200/$2,268**

French Empire Chandelier ▼

- *circa 1920*
Fine French Empire-style crystal and ormolu chandelier, with anthemion decoration to the rim and crystal tiers below.
- *30cm x 55cm*
- **Guide price £4,850/$9,167**

Cylindrical Steel Lamp ▼

- *2000*
Martin Herrick's BA cylinder-shaped steel lamp with an aluminum stand.
- *height 60cm*
- **Guide price £200/$378**

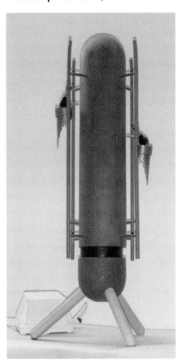

Brass Chandelier ▶

- *1930s*
Italian brass chandelier of foliate design, with turquoise teardrop glass pendants.
- *50cm x 40cm*
- **Guide price £375/$709**

Giltwood Chandeliers ◀

- *20th century*
One of a pair of giltwood, double-tier chandeliers.
- *70cm x 73cm*
- **Guide price £1,150/$2,174**

Star Light ▲

- *circa 1990s*
Star-shaped light made from paper and reinforced with metal, by Tom Dixon.
- *height 47.5cm*
- **Guide price £280/$530**

Brass and Crystal Chandelier ▲

- *1930s*
Italian brass chandelier with crystals swags and turquoise pendants.
- *height 80cm*
- **Guide price £795/$1,503**

American Silver Candlesticks ▲

- *1930s*

Unusual American horseshoe-shaped candelabra and two small circular candleholders on clear glass, designed by Chase.
- *height 25cm*
- **Guide price £270/$511**

Lamp on Cast-Iron Base ▲

- *1925*

Art Deco lamp with white glass lamp shade, on a tapered cast-iron base, signed Deguy.
- *height 39cm*
- **Guide price £500/$945**

Venetian Chandelier ▲

- *1940*

Art Deco Venetian glass chandelier with glass tendrils flowing from its base.
- *diameter 110cm*
- **Guide price £4,200/$7,938**

Beaded Chandelier ▼

- *1900*

Small chandelier with beaded frame and faceted pendant drops.
- *height 38cm*
- **Guide price £275/$520**

Art Nouveau Lamp ▼

- *1910*

American Art Nouveau lamp with green shade on a metal stand.
- *height 45cm*
- **Guide price £600/$1,134**

Daum Lamp and Shade ▶

- *1902*

French Art Nouveau lamp with glass lamp and shade, signed by Daum.
- *height 36cm*
- **Guide price £6,000/$11,340**

French Table Lamp ▲

- *1930*

French Art Deco table lamp with sandblasted glass shade and silvered bronze stand, signed by Sabino.
- *height 64cm*
- **Guide price £2,200/$4,158**

Decorative Chandelier ▼

- *1920*

Toile chandelier with scrolling ormolu pink flowers and green foliage.
- *length 35cm*
- **Guide price £435/$822**

Art Deco Lamp ▼

- *20th century*

Art Deco white ceramic vase-shaped lamp, with elongated slats for effective lighting.
- *height 32cm*
- **Guide price £350/$662**

Purzel Lamp ▼

- *circa 1925*

Very rare Art Deco lamp with an anodized bronze stand giving the appearance of copper, with sandblasted glass shade. Signed by Purzel.
- *height 64cm*
- **Guide price £2,400/$4,536**

American Batman Lamp ▼

- *circa 1940*

Polished steel adjustable lamp on a steel stand. Probably originally for medical use with heat-bulb. By Westinghouse.

- *height 106cm*
- **Guide price £275/$520**

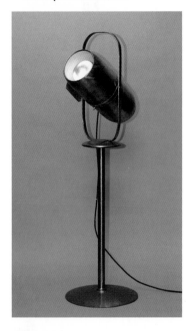

Table Lamp ▼

- *circa 1918*

A cast-brass table lamp fitted with a flakestone glass shade decorated with leaf motifs.

- *height 46cm*
- **Guide price £450/$851**

Oil Lamp Shade ▶

- *circa 1910*

Light blue opaque with waved, crimped edging. English, possibly Stourbridge.

- *height 21cm*
- **Guide price £150/$284**

Italian Table Lamp ▲

- *circa 1950*

Moulded plastic lamp, incorporating base and shade, designed by Flio Martinelli.

- *height 37cm*
- **Guide price £750/$1,418**

Cast-iron Lamp ▲

- *circa 1940*

An American industrial, adjustable lamp (ex-factory) with cast aluminium fittings, standing on a cast-steel base.

- *height 58cm*
- **Guide price £250/$473**

Italian Glass Lamp ▼

- *circa 1960*

By Mazzega in Murano glass with yellow and grey swirls.

- *height 57cm*
- **Guide price £850/$1,607**

Venetian Lamp Base ▼

- *circa 1950*

Cenedese Murano glass with three fish on dark green.

- *height 36cm*
- **Guide price £500/$945**

Italian Wall Lights ▼

- *circa 1920*

A pair of Italian wall lights with hanging crystals.

- *height 45cm*
- **Guide price £480/$907**

Hospital Lamp ▲

- *circa 1930*

With ball joint for lateral adjustment and telescopic shaft.

- *height 1.78m*
- **Guide price £350/$662**

Austrian Loetz Lamp ▲

- *1900*

Austrian Art Nouveau Loetz lamp with iridescent lampshade, the base by Gerchner.

- *height 46cm*
- **Guide price £7,500/14,175**

Table Lamp ▼

• *circa 1910*
A silver-plated brass table lamp decorated with a floral transfer printed glass shade.
• *height 37cm*
• **Guide price £600/$1,134**

Hand-painted Table Lamp ▼

• *circa 1920*
A copper-oxidised table lamp with handpainted shade showing an Egyptian landscape.
• *height 44cm*
• **Guide price £450/$851**

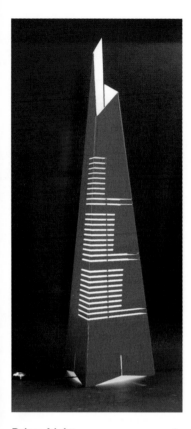

Prism Light ▲

• *circa 1960*
A red plastic triangular prism light with vertical cuts. Designed by Magistratti and produced by Francesconi.
• *height 1.37m*
• **Guide price £950/$1,796**

Laboratory Lamp ▼

• *circa 1930*
By Chas Hearson & Co Ltd, London. Brass stand on wooden base with maker's plaque.
• *height 45cm*
• **Guide price £145/$274**

Anglepoise Lamp ▲

• *circa 1930*
Polished aluminium and chrome, designed by Cawardine, based on the constant tensioning principles of the human arm, and made by Terry & Sons.
• *height 92cm*
• **Guide price £175/$331**

Table Lamp ▼

• *circa 1920*
Cast-brass lamp fitted with a flakestone glass shade, and decorated with Roman motifs.
• *height 51cm*
• **Guide price £575/$1,087**

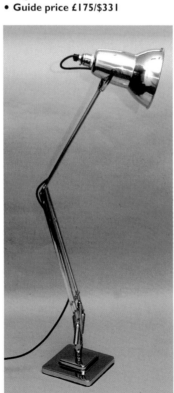

American Desk Lamp ▲

• *circa 1910*
An Edwardian American desk lamp in brass with a bell-shaped shade and circular plinth.
• *height 43cm*
• **Guide price £875/$1,654**

Chrome Desk Lamp ◀

• *circa 1930*
A chrome anglepoise desk reading lamp with heavy, stepped, square base.
• *height 90cm*
• **Guide price £125/$237**

LUGGAGE

Foxcroft Suitcase
- *circa 1950*
Cream plastic suitcase with leopard skin print on one side by Foxcroft.
- *45cm x 77cm*
- **Guide price £75/$142**

Antler Vanity Case
- *circa 1950*
Plastic leopard skin design vanity case by Antler with carrying handle.
- *height 30cm*
- **Guide price £68/$129**

Teenager's Case ▲
- *circa 1950*
Blue and white plastic teenager's case with figure of a young girl in jeans and a blue-check shirt using the telephone.
- *30cm x 35cm*
- **Guide price £75/$142**

Leather Suitcase ▼
- *circa 1940*
Leather suitcase with two straps and covered with labels of various destinations.
- *42cm x 74cm*
- **Guide price £50/$95**

Gents Hat Box ▼
- *1910*
Gents leather box for storing top hats with leather carrying handle, brass lock and leather strap.
- *height 23cm*
- **Guide price £160/$303**

Leather and Hide Vanity Case ▼
- *circa 1970*
Morocco leather and hide vanity case.
- *32cm x 23cm*
- **Guide price £90/$171**

Snakeskin Hat Box ▶
- *1912*
Ladies hardrock python snakeskin hat box with snakeskin handle, made in London for a family in Brunei.
- *23cm x 33cm*
- **Guide price £1,500/$2,835**

Crocodile Hat Box ▲
- *circa 1920*
Crocodile skin hat box with gilt over brass locks, with brown moiré silk lining.
- *26cm x 41cm*
- **Guide price £4,000/$7,560**

Army and Navy Hat Box ▲
- *1910*
Leather and canvas top hat box made by Army and Navy outfitters, comes with original top hat.
- *height 33cm*
- **£200**

Tartan Plastic Case ▼
- *circa 1950*
Tartan plastic case with black plastic trim and handle.
- *diameter 35cm*
- **Guide price £95/$180**

Gladstone Bag ▼
- *1930*
Ladies gladstone leather bag with brass fittings and leather handle.
- *width 37cm*
- **Guide price £75/$142**

Leather Briefcase ▼

- *circa 1920*

Leather briefcase with circular brass fitting and leather straps and handle.

- *length 40cm*
- **Guide price £500/$945**

Ladies Travelling Case ▼

- *circa 1930*

Ladies green leather travelling case in two separate sections, fitted with a silk interior incorporating a turquoise enamel brush set, boxes with silver gilt lids and a travelling clock.

- *width 32cm*
- **Guide price £600/$1,134**

Crocodile Skin Case ▼

- *1930*

Indian crocodile skin case with handles at each end and silver nickel locks.

- *32cm x 61cm*
- **Guide price £450/$851**

Picnic Set ◄

- *circa 1925*

A leather-cased picnic set with nickel-plated fittings and a setting for four people.

- *width 47cm*
- **Guide price £1,800/$3,402**

Black Crocodile Case ▲

- *circa 1920*

Black crocodile ladies vanity case relined with blue Moiré silk.

- *25cm x 32cm*
- **Guide price £350/$662**

Black Circular Case ▲

- *circa 1950*

Black circular vanity case with zip-action and black plastic carrying handle.

- *diameter 42cm*
- **Guide price £55 /$104**

Louis Vuitton Trunk ▼

- *1905*

Louis Vuitton patterned trunk with beechwood rails, leather binding, solid brass fittings and handles each side.

- *54cm x 110cm*
- **Guide price £7,200/$13,608**

Jewellery Case ▼

- *circa 1915*

Crocodile skin jewel case, with velvet and silk lining, with gilded brass fittings.

- *width 20cm*
- **Guide price £950/$1,796**

Brown Crocodile Case ▼

- *circa 1920*

Brown crocodile vanity case – relined with a new handle.

- *35cm x 40cm*
- **Guide price £850/$1,607**

Tapestry Case ▲

- *circa 1950*

Circular zip-action tapestry case, with labels of Rome, Casablanca and Brussels.

- *diameter 40cm*
- **Guide price £75/$142**

Fruitwood Case ▲

- *circa 1920*

Gents fruitwood carrying case.

- *30cm x 42cm*
- **Guide price £120/$227**

Goyard Hat Case ▲

- *1920*

Goyard canvas hat case with a painted chevron pattern and a tan leather trim with small brass nails, leather handle and brass fittings.

- *25cm x 49cm*
- **Guide price £1,500/$2,835**

MARINE ITEMS

Cunard Ashtray ▼
- *circa 1950*
Cunard *R.M.S. Queen Elizabeth* bone-china ashtray, showing starboard view of ship. With scalloped gilt edge.
- **Guide price £35/$66**

Cornish Skiff ▼
- *circa 1910*
Model of *The Vengeance*, a Cornish fishing skiff.
- *height 24cm*
- **Guide price £480/$908**

Model Yacht ▼
- *circa 1910*
Model yacht inscribed, 'Marine d'autrefois Gildas de Kerdrel, 80 Avenue des Ternes, Paris'.
- *height 27cm*
- **Guide price £750/$1,418**

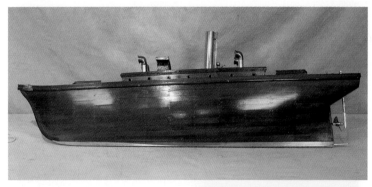

Steam Yacht ▲
- *circa 1910*
Model steam yacht complete with planked hull, working steam engine, brass funnel prop and lights and eight portholes.
- *length 1m*
- **Guide price £8,000/$15,120**

Ship's Bell ▲
- *early 20th century*
Ship's brass bell made for the *Grangeburn*.
- *height 31cm*
- **Guide price £780/$1,474**

Atlas Globe ◀
- *circa 1920*
Bronze figure of Atlas supporting a globe with brass supports.
- *height 53cm*
- **Guide price £1,250/$2,363**

"Faithful Freddie" Binnacle ▼
- *1930*
Brass binnacle from a submarine known as a "Faithful Freddie".
- *height 28cm*
- **Guide price £1,250/$2,363**

Nautical Match Holder ▼
- *circa 1920*
Porcelain match holder painted with a sailing yacht in a seascape.
- *diameter 8cm*
- **Guide price £365/$690**

Parallel Brass Rule ▼
- *circa 1920*
Brass parallel rule.
- *length 46cm*
- **Guide price £120/$227**

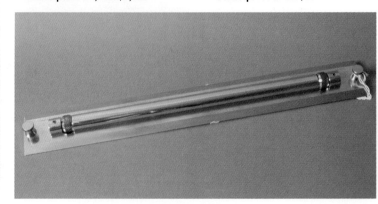

Model of "S.S. Rallus" ◀

- *circa 1900s*

A builder's scale model of the *S.S. Rallus*, which was built for the Cork Steam Ship Co Ltd, Cork, Ireland by Swan Hunter & Wigham Richardson Ltd. Masts, derricks and rigging with scale ivorine and nickel plated blocks, deck details including anchor winches, fairleads, bollards, ventilators, deck rails, hatches, and deck winches. The superstructure with lifeboats.

- *67cm x 2.34m*
- **Guide price £9,500/$17,955**

Pond Yacht ▲

- *circa 1910*

A pond yacht named *Bassett Lowke Britannia*'

- *length 60cm*
- **Guide price £1,600/$3,024**

First Aid Kit ▲

- *1920s*

A unique piece of shipping memorabilia, "First aid outfit for lifeboats", approved by the Ministry of Transport.

- *height 30cm*
- **Guide price £99/$187**

Globe ▼

- *20th century*

A reproduction of a 12-inch diameter, 19th-century globe on a mahogany stand. The original by Nerzbach & Falk, published in 1881.

- *height 43cm*
- **Guide price £680/$1,285**

Ship in a Bottle ▲

- *1900*

Three-masted ship in a bottle with coastal scene in the background.

- *length 30cm*
- **Guide price £480/$908**

Edinburgh & Leith Ship's Glass ◀

- *circa 1930*

Edinburgh & Leith ship's glass from the Aberdeen suite, consisting of a wine jug, decanters, water glasses, wine glasses, liqueur glasses, fruit cups, fruit saucer and seafood dishes.

- *height 33cm*
- **Guide price £4,600/$8,694**

Porthole ▲

- *1901–10*

Polished seven-inch diameter porthole made of brass with hinge and locking nut and six bevelled screw holes.

- *diameter 17cm*
- **Guide price £69/$131**

Celestial Globe ◀

- *circa 1950*

Celestial globe with brass fittings, and original oak box with carrying handle.

- *height 28cm*
- **Guide price £1,280/$2,419**

Model of the Queen Mary ▲

- *circa 1940*

Model of the *Queen Mary* by Bassett-Lowke, with display case.

- *width 32cm*
- **Guide price £400/$756**

Cylindrical Rule ▶

- *1929*

A very rare cranberry glass cylindrical rule with silver mounts.

- *length 30cm*
- **Guide price 399/$754**

Bone Model of a Boat ▲

- *circa 1940*

Bone prisoner-of-war model ship with three masts and the rigging made from hair, standing on a maple wood stand with satin wood inlay

- *height 36cm*
- **Guide price £8,600/$16,254**

Brass Lamp ▲

- *1912*

Polished and lacquered brass lamp, stamped on the base and lamp unit with manufacturer's details.

- *height 34cm*
- **Guide price £179/$339**

Oak Helm ▲

- *circa 1910*

A six-spar oak ship's wheel, bound in brass.

- **Guide price £299/$565**

Brass Telescope ▲

- *1910*

Brass telescope by Ladd of Chancery Lane London, in original mahogany box.

- *length 102cm*
- **Guide price £2,900/$5,481**

Prismatic Compass ▲

- *circa 1940*

An English brass, hand-held, military compass from World War II.

- **Guide price £99/$187**

Bulkhead Clock ▼

- *circa 1920*

An eight day ship's bulkhead clock marked 'Smiths Empire', with a painted enamelled dial and Arabic numerals.

- *diameter 18cm*
- **Guide price £240/$454**

Model of a Yacht ▼

- *circa 1910*

A shipbuilder's half-block model of a yacht, made of polished pine on a teak backboard.

- *length 95cm*
- **Guide price £1,850/$3,497**

Terrestrial Globe ▲

- *circa 1917*

Terrestrial globe by George Philip & Son Ltd, printed in colour.

- *25cm x 15cm*
- **Guide price £849/$1,605**

Signalling Telescope ▲

- *circa 1920*

A three-draw signalling telescope. Polished and lacquered brass on the outer barrel.

- **Guide price £339/$641**

Nelson's Last Signal ▼

- *circa 1910*

Nelson's last signal, "England expects that every man shall do his duty."

- *38cm x 57cm*
- **Guide price £430/$812**

Model of Yacht ▼
- *late 20th century*
Scale model of Americas Cup Yacht *Rainbow*.
- *81cm x 120cm*
- **Guide price £1,650/$3,119**

Luggage Labels ▼
- *circa 1930*
Cunard White Star luggage labels. Labels read 'Not Wanted on Voyage', indicating that trunks should be stored in the hold, and 'First Class', 'Cabin Class' and 'Tourist Class', in descending order of the social desirability of the owners.
- **Guide price £29/$56**

Four-volume Work ▲
- *circa 1997*
Jean Boudriot's four-volume opus, *The Seventy-Four Gun Ship*, published by Jean Boudriot Publications.
- *height 27.5cm*
- **Guide price £225/$426**

Viking Ship Brooch ▲
- *circa 1940*
Silver Scottish shawl brooch showing a Viking ship on a shielded base.
- **Guide price £39/$74**

Mary Tin ◄
- *1914*
A polished and embossed brass Mary Tin, presented by Princess Mary, aged 17, to all those wearing the King's uniform at Christmas, 1914.
- *width 13cm*
- **Guide price £79/$150**

Anchor Lamp ▲
- *circa 1940*
Copper and brass anchor lamp. With 'Seahorse' trade mark.
- *height 22cm*
- **Guide price £180/$341**

Ship's Linen ►
- *circa 1950*
Souvenir linen from the Cunard company's *RMS Mauretania*.
- **Guide price £19/$36**

Rolling Rule ▼
- *circa 1940*
Brass polished and lacquered parallel rolling rule in original box.
- *length 42cm*
- **Guide price £149/$282**

Small Pond Yacht ▲
- *circa 1930*
Mahogany model pond yacht with full rigging, on a mahogany stand.
- *length 82cm*
- **Guide price £510/$964**

Rock-Ola Princess ▲

- *1946*

American Rock-Ola Princess No.1422, manufactured in 1946, plays 20, 78 rpm records. In good original condition with pheonilic pilasters and a central panel with decorative metal scrolling.

- *149cm x 54cm*
- **Guide price £5,200/$9,828**

Seeburg HF100R ▲

- *1954*

Seeburg H.F. 100R. Holds 60 records with push button electric selection. Plays both sides. Considered by many to be the best design of a series of jukeboxes made by Seeburg in the 50s and 60. Made in the USA.

- *158cm x 87cm*
- **Guide price £7,000/$13,230**

Ami Continental ▼

- *1961*

American Ami Continental juke box, which has push-button electric selection and plays both sides. In good working condition and fully restored.

- *170cm x 70cm*
- **Guide price £6,500/$12,285**

Rock-Ola Juke Box ▼

- *1962*

Rock-Ola Princess stereophonic juke box, Model 1493. Takes 50 records. Stereo and auto mix, (plays with or without centres). In original condition. Made in the USA.

- *124cm x 76cm*
- **Guide price £4,000/$7,560**

Rock-Ola 1454 ▲

- *1956*

Rock-Ola 1454 juke box in original condition. The cabinet styling is based on a Seeburg M100 from 1954.

- *143cm x 77cm*
- **Guide price £4,000/$7,560**

Trashcan Juke Box ▲

- *1948*

Trashcan juke box made from bakelite and WWII scrap airplane aluminium, the whole in a wood grain finish. With 20 selections of 78 rpm, made by Seeburg.

- *144cm x 100cm*
- **Guide price £5,550/$10,490**

Ami H ▼

- *1957*

American Ami H, one of the first of the car-influenced style of juke box with a wraparound glass. It holds 100 records, with orange and blue push button electric selection, and plays both sides. Fully restored and in original condition.

- *159cm x 80cm*
- **Guide price £7,000/$13,230**

Continental 2 ▼

- *1962*

Continental 2 chrome juke box in red, with 200 selections. This was the first stereo juke box by AMI and has 100 records, with or without big centres (dinked/ undinked).

- *155cm x 72cm*
- **Guide price £7,500/$14,175**

Mystic 478 ▼

- *1978–9*
Rock Ola Mystic 478 juke box in wood and chrome, with a digital microcomputer music system and 200 selections.
- *136cm x 104cm*
- **Guide price £1,500/$2,835**

Rocket Juke Box ▲

- *1952*
Rocket juke box, type 1434, in chrome, wood and bakelite, with 50 selections. This was the last 78 rpm player and the first 45 rpm player, by Rock Ola Manufacturing Company.
- *150cm x 76cm*
- **Guide price £5,750/$10,868**

Singing Bird Musical Box ▼

- *circa 1900s*
Singing bird in polished brass cage with round embossed brass base, probably by Bontems.
- *height 28cm*
- **Guide price £1,750/$3,308**

Disc Table Polyphon ▶

- *1900*
Rare German 50cm disc table Polyphon with two combs, 118 notes. Carved mouldings to the case, shaped figured walnut panels and marquetry panel on the lid. Comes with original table with four turned legs at the corners supporting shelves for the discs.
- *113cm x 69cm*
- **Guide price £8,500/$16,065**

Ami J 200 ▲

- *1959*
Ami J.200. Holds 100 records. With pink plastic push-button electric selection, playing both sides. Made in USA. Fully restored.
- *152cm x 83cm*
- **Guide price £5,800/$10,962**

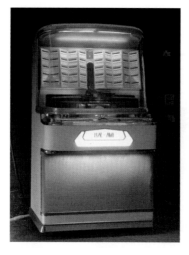

Bal-Ami S100 ▲

- *1960*
The Bal-Ami Jukebox, made in Britain by Balfoure. Engineering, using *High Tech* parts manufactured in the USA by Ami, to overcome import ban on luxury goods after World War 11.
- *147cm x 80cm*
- **Guide price £3,500/$6,615**

Portable Street Barrel Organ ▲

- *circa 1905*
Signed Thibouville Lamy but probably made by Marenghi of Paris. Seventeen-key action, playing six tunes – including Champagne Charlie – through three ranks of pipes. With rosewood veneered case and leather carrying strap.
- **Guide price £9,500/$17,955**

Musical Jewellery Box ▼

- *1960*
Red plastic musical jewellery box in the form of a radiogram with turn-table that rotates when music plays, Blue interior, red drawers and a gold *fleur de lis*.
- *height 11cm*
- **Guide price £55/$104**

Heart Musical Box ▼

- *1950*
Heart-shaped musical manicure box, lined with pink silk, with a circular mirror on the inside of the lid and a couple in evening dress dancing. Fitted with pink manicure set and two small circular metal boxes.
- *diameter 23cm*
- **Guide price £48/$91**

English Organette ▼

- *circa 1910*
By J.M. Draper, England. Fourteen notes, with three stops, flute, expression and principal which operate flaps over the reed box to control the tone.
- **Guide price £950/$1,796**

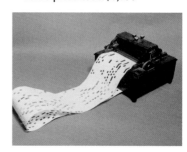

METALWARE

Italian Chrome Teapot ◄
- *circa 1950*
Round chrome teapot with cork stopper for the spout.
- *height 19cm*
- **Guide price £65/$123**

Robin Hood Figure ▲
- *1934*
French spelter and ivorine figure of a male archer modelled on Robin Hood.
- *height 68cm*
- **Guide price £995/$1,881**

Uriano Rock-man Figure ▲
- *late 1920s*
Large green and bronze patinated spelter male figure with base of black and Portorro Extra marbles. In excellent condition with original partina, by Uriano, unsigned.
- *38cm x 74cm*
- **Guide price £760/$1,437**

Chrome Coffee Pot ◄
- *circa 1950*
Italian circular chrome coffee pot.
- *height 24cm*
- **Guide price £50/$95**

Art Deco Lady ▲
- *circa 1930*
Bronze and ivory figure of a lady in theatrical costume. Excellent colour and detail, signed 'Josef Lorenzi'.
- *height 26cm*
- **Guide price £2,800/$5,292**

Dancing Maiden Figure ▲
- *circa 1930*
Bronze figure of a young lady dancing in striking pose, signed 'Georges Angerle', raised on an onyx base.
- *height 24cm*
- **Guide price £950/$1,796**

Young Girl in Bronze and Ivory ▲
- *circa 1925*
Highly detailed gilt bronze and ivory figure of a young girl, signed and inscribed 'Etling, Demetre Chiparus, Romania'.
- *height 19cm*
- **Guide price £3,300/$6,237**

Paul Philippe Bronze ▲
- *circa 1920*
Striking bronze figure of a young lady with arms outstretched with a golden patination standing on a circular marble plinth, signed by Paul Philippe.
- *height 46cm*
- **Guide price £3,950/$7,466**

Bronze Flute Player ▼

- *circa 1920*

Bronze figure of a young girl in a seductive dancing pose with golden patination, signed 'Claire Colinet'.

- *height 48cm*
- **Guide price £4,800/$9,072**

Bronze Lady ▲

- *1911*

Gilt bronze figure of a lady with a parasol by H. Varenne.

- *height 20cm*
- **Guide price £2,500/$4,725**

Italian Seal ▼

- *1950*

Italian silver torpedo-shaped seal stamp with base by Murini.

- *height 18cm*
- **Guide price £120/$227**

Etling Bronze ▼

- *circa 1925*

Detailed gilt bronze and ivory figure of a young girl, signed and inscribed 'Etling'.

- *height 19cm*
- **Guide price £3,300/$6,237**

Draped Bronze Dancer ▲

- *circa 1925*

Fine bronze and ivory figure of a beautiful young lady in dancing pose, stamped and signed 'Paul Philippe'.

- *height 24cm*
- **Guide price £4,950/$9,356**

Polychrome Figure ▲

- *circa 1930*

Etched steel model of a Greek Kouros princess. French.

- *height 190cm; width 60cm*
- **Guide price £3,500/$6,615**

Scarf Dancer Bronze ▲

- *circa 1930*

Cold-painted gilt and brown Austrian bronze figure of a young lady dancing with a scarf, signed 'Joseph Lorenzij'.

- *height 28cm*
- **Guide price £1,850/$3,497**

Letter Rack ▼

- *circa 1950*

Black wire cat letter rack, the body in the form of a spring with plastic eyes and rotating eye balls.

- *height 14cm*
- **Guide price £45/$85**

Josef Lorenzi Bronze ▼

- *circa 1930*

Austrian bronze figure of a dancer with carved ivory head, raised onyx base and signed 'Josef Lorenzi'.

- *height 24cm*
- **Guide price £1,950/$3,686**

Exotic Dancer Figure ◄

- *circa 1920*

A bronze figure of a young woman in exotic dress with rich green patina on cream marble base by Samuel Lypchytz.

- *height 33cm*
- **Guide price £1,795/$3,491**

Pantalon Dancer Bronze ▲

- *circa 1935*

Bronze cold-painted figure of a young lady dancing in a stylised pose by Josef Lorenzi.

- *height 24cm*
- **Guide price £1,450/$2,741**

Bird Brass Chargers ▲

- *20th century*

One of a pair of brass chargers of aesthetic movement design, this one depicting a bird on a branch.

- *diameter 31cm*
- **Guide price £600/$1,134**

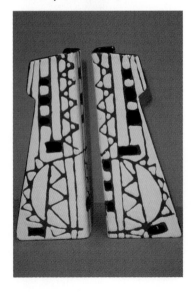

La Liseuse Figure ▼

- *circa 1920*

Figure of a lady in medieval dress seated on a chair with a book in one hand, signed on the skirt 'Dominique Alon'.

- *height 26cm*
- **Guide price £3,650/$6,899**

La Musicienne ▼

- *1912*

French gilt bronze of a lady with a Sistrum, by Muller.

- *height 18.5cm*
- **Guide price £2,500/$4,725**

Metal Door Handles ◄

- *1950*

Metal door handles with ceramic and enamel yellow and brown geometric design.

- *26cm x 10cm*
- **Guide price £155/$293**

Alphonse Saladin Bronze ▲

- *circa 1910*

Gilt bronze figure of a young naked woman holding a posy of flowers, signed and raised on a plinth.

- *height 31cm*
- **Guide price £2,250/$4,253**

"Puppet Dancer" Bronze ▲

- *1927*

A bronze by Ignacio Gallo of a nude dancer holding a jester puppet in her hand. She has a silvered finish with golden hair and a signed base made of Portorro Extra and Sienna marbles.

- *44.5cm x 12.7cm*
- **Guide price £1,995/$3,771**

WMF Fruit-knife Stand ▼

- *circa 1905*

WMF fruit-knife stand with an Art Nouveau maiden in profile, containing 12 knives.

- *height 30cm*
- **Guide price £295/$558**

Pop Art Metal Tray ▼

- *circa 1970*

A pop art metal tray decorated in typical 1970s colours and design. Made in Great Britain and marked 'Worcester Ware'.

- *diameter 38cm*
- **Guide price £45/$85**

Circular Electric Fan ▼

- *circa 1960*

Salmon-pink circular metal electric fan standing on metal legs.

- *diameter 65cm*
- **Guide price £120/$227**

Fish Brass Chargers ▲

- *20th century*
One of a pair of brass chargers of aesthetic movement design, this one depicting a leaping fish with water lilies.
- *diameter 31cm*
- **Guide price £600/$1,134**

World War I Frame ▲

- *circa 1914*
Iron sculpture of a winged angel of Mercury and a soldier with a lion, fashioned as a picture frame.
- *height 47cm*
- **Guide price £285/$539**

Lady on a Bridge Figure ▲

- *1928*
A signed figure of a lady and a deer on a metal slabbed bridge over a stream of green onyx with ribbed waterfall detail and a black marble river bank to either side.
- *36.8cm x 78.7cm*
- **Guide price £1,485/$3,807**

Lady and Deer Figures ▶

- *early 20th century*
"The Gift" by D.H. Chiparus, a spelter figure of a lady and deer group.
- *24cm x 49.5cm x 11.3cm*
- **Guide price £960/$1,815**

Chromed Dancer Figure ▲

- *late 1930s*
Tall Art Deco figure of a stylish lady, based on a 1920s dancer. Chromed on top.
- *height 40cm*
- **Guide price £155/$293**

Liberty Bombvase ▲

- *circa 1905*
A Liberty bombvase by Knox in polished pewter with a open-work tendril design.
- *height 17cm*
- **Guide price £700/$1,323**

Dianne Figure ▼

- *1928*
Large French "Dianne" figure in spelter by De Marco of the quality and weight of a bronze, and mounted on a Portorro Extra wedge-shaped marble base.
- *73.6cm x 32.5cm x 11.4cm*
- **Guide price £1,095/$2,070**

Nude Spelter Figure ▼

- *early 1930s*
Green patinated pointing figure of spelter, "Look'", by Joe De Roncourt, mounted on a Belgian black marble base and signed on the right-hand end.
- *48.3cm x 53.3cm*
- **Guide price £545/$1,031**

Silvered Bronze Dancer ▲

- *early 20th century*
A silvered bronze lady dancer by J.D. Guirande sitting on a wooden stepped base.
- *53cm x 57.2cm*
- **Guide price £3,640/$6,880**

Toga Dancer Figure ▲

- *1927*
A signed, green patinated spelter toga dancer figure by Carlier set on a pyramid marble base.
- *height 39.4cm*
- **Guide price £575/$1,087**

Spelter Mother and Child ▲

- *late 1920s–mid 1930s*

An unusual French spelter and ivoreen mother and child group by Menneville. The lady has an ivorine face and hands and is mounted on a signed ovular Portorro marble and onyx base.

- *28cm x 66cm*
- **Guide price £840/$1,588**

Italian Bronze Boy ▲

- *1904*

A fine Italian bronze of a naked young boy playing with kittens. He holds one up while cuddling the other. The bronze is signed Marcuse, Roma. On a chamfered marble base.

- *height 75cm*
- **Guide price £5,950/$11,246**

Figure by H. Varenne ▶

- *1912*

Figure of a lady with a large hat by H. Varenne, founder's mark Susse Frères.

- *height 19cm*
- **Guide price £2,500/$4,725**

Life-size Bronze Torso ▲

- *circa 1930*

Emotive life-size bronze torso by Hubert Yenge from the foundry of Alexis Rudier, Paris founder to Rodin.

- *71cm x 55cm*
- **Guide price £8,750/$16,538**

Chrome Egg Cups ▼

- *circa 1950*

Pair of Italian chrome egg cups with covers.

- *height 11cm*
- **Guide price £50/$95**

Japanese Bronze Peacock ▼

- *circa 1930*

A Japanese Showa period hakudo bronze peacock on original black lacquer stand decorated with inlaid abalone shell and the signature of the artist, Kano Seiun, on the reverse.

- *35.5cm x 53.3cm*
- **Guide price £1,900/$3,591**

Rivière Nude Bronze ▼

- *1920s*

"Balance", a silvered bronze nude athletic woman balancing on a brown marble ball by Guiraud Rivière. Her toes are spread for balance and she has a very stylised bobbed Deco hair detailing, all on a tapered base.

- *49.5cm x 10.2cm x 10.2cm*
- **Guide price £4,095/$7,738**

Turquoise Door Handles ▼

- *circa 1960*

Italian stylised pallette-shaped metal door handles with turquoise marbled enamel overlay and large brass mounts.

- *length 33cm*
- **Guide price £320/$605**

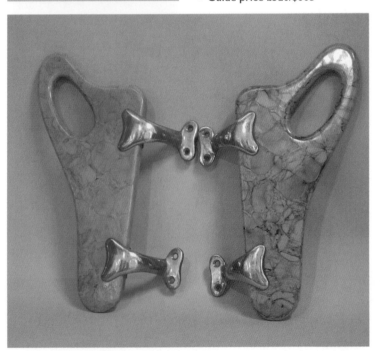

Spelter Woman and Peacock ▲

- *early 1930s*

Large French spelter figure of a woman feeding a peacock with berries, the base of green onyx and black and brown marble.

- *30.5cm x 78.7cm*
- **Guide price £765/$1,444**

Uriano Spelter Pair ▲

- *1930*

A spelter figure of a woman and a dog, unsigned but by Uriano. The woman has a natural skin patina and a blue and gold dress. The walled base is made of black marble, Portorro Extra and onyx sections.

- *43.2cm x 45.7cm*
- **Guide price £740/$1,399**

Gilt Bronze Lady ▲

- *1900*

Gilt patinated bronze figure of a lady by H. Varenne, signed and dated 1905, with bronze founder's mark of Susse Freres.

- *18.5cm*
- **Guide price £2,500/$4,725**

Bronze and Marble Figure ▶

- *mid-1920s*

French silvered bronze and chrome figure on a base of figured verdigris and black marbles with lovely verdigris columns.

- *30.5cm x 45.7cm x 25.4cm*
- **Guide price £4,380/$8,278**

Hunter and Leopard Figures ▲

- *early 1930s*

A French spelter man and leopard group mounted on a base of Portorro and brown marble and onyx, with a ziggurat back wall in brown marble and onyx. The man wearing enamel shirt and trousers, and holding a shield and chrome spear.

- *43cm x 63.5cm*
- **Guide price £1,145/$2,165**

Spelter Archer ▲

- *mid 1920s*

French green patinated male archer figure, signed by the artist Mellani, with original bow and mounted on a black and white marble base.

- *45.7cm x 61cm*
- **Guide price £695/$1,312**

Painted Silver Art Deco Bronze ◀

- *circa 1930*

Art Deco cold-painted silver bronze figure of a sensuous naked young lady.

- *height 35cm*
- **Guide price £950/$1,796**

Reclining Maiden Bronze ▼

- *circa 1920*

Bronze Art Deco figure of a naked young woman reclining, signed 'Amadeus Generalli'.

- *height 24cm*
- **Guide price £2,950/$5,576**

Circus Figure ▼

- *1926*

A large figure of a woman in circus costume juggling hoops. The base brown marble and cream onyx with circles and semi-circles of green onyx and brown marble.

- *55.8cm x 55.8cm*
- **Guide price £1,180/$2,230**

Diana the Huntress Figure ◀

- *1928*

French spelter figure of Diana the Huntress with brown skin tone and a bronzed scarf wrapped around her. Signed on the right-hand end of the marble base by Dauvergne.

- *length 83.8cm*
- **Guide price £875/$1,654**

Pair of Candelabra ▲

- *1900*

Highly decorative pair of bonze and gilded Regency-style candelabra with glass drops.

- *37cm x 35cm*
- **Guide price £750/$1,418**

"The Lesson" Spelter Figure ▼

- *1928*

"The Lesson" by Limousin, a huge French figural group of a black patinated spelter man giving his son a lesson in how to shoot an arrow. The base is of black marble with white striations, and is signed by the artist.

- *71cm x 76.2cm*
- **Guide price £995/$1,881**

"Group Atlante" Spelter Figure ▼

- *1920s–30s*

"Group Atlante", a spelter figure of Diane hunting a leaping gazelle on a granite stone base by De Marco.

- *762cm x 96.5cm*
- **Guide price £1,695/$3,202**

Mother and Child Spelter Group ▲

- *late 1920s–early 30s*

A signed figural group by Menneville, made in France of spelter and ivorine on a black Belgian marble and onyx base.

- *33cm x 58.4cm*
- **Guide price £1,140/$2,155**

Stacking Ashtrays ▲

- *1970*

Set of ten brass stacking ashtrays.

- *diameter 11cm*
- **Guide price £130/$246**

Spelter Male Hunter Figure ▲

- *late 1920s*

A male hunter figure made of spelter and signed by the artist Joe De Roncourt, sitting on a canted edged brown marble base.

- *38.1cm x 55.8cm x 17.8cm*
- **Guide price £795/$1,503**

Tribute to Flight ▲

- *1915*

A fine bronze which celebrated the flight of the Wright brothers. Entitled "Inspiration Humaine" by Kolakowski. It was reduced by the F. Barbedienne foundry.

- *height 19.5cm*
- **Guide price £1,250/$2,363**

Bronze and Ivory Figure ◄

- *circa 1920*

A lovely bronze and ivory figure of a young girl playing the accordion with original gilding and marble base.

- *height 25cm*
- **Guide price £4,900/$9,261**

Bronze Eagle ▼

• early 20th century
A German wall-mounted bronze eagle with three enamelled crowns, red tongue and talons.
• 51cm x 52cm
• **Guide price £750/$1,418**

Bronze Figure ▼

• 1921
Bronze figure entitled "Wind", signed and dated 1921. Exhibited by the Royal Academy.
• height 24cm
• **Guide price £1,100/$2,079**

Bronze Eagle ▲

• 1930
A bronze eagle with spread wings on a figured marble base.
• height 34cm
• **Guide price £1,200/$2,268**

Queen Victoria ▲

• 1901
Metal bust of Queen Victoria by Elkington & Co, England.
• height 22cm
• **Guide price £400/$756**

Harley Davidson Jacket ▼

• circa 1960
A unique, American, life-size bronze Harley Davidson motor cycle jacket hanging on a bronze rack, stamped 'H.G.M 1/1'.
• 90cm x 80cm
• **Guide price £5,000/$9,450**

Metal Lighter ▼

• 1970
Metal lighter with clear piezo perspex fluid container by Kogen-Kingsway.
• height 15cm
• **Guide price £70/$133**

Bronze Cow ◄

• circa 1925
Bronze reclining calf, signed by Richard Garve.
• 7cm x 14cm
• **Guide price £2,500/$4,725**

Silver Figurine ▲

• 1900
R. Bruchmann & Sonne silver sculpture on onyx base.
• height 50cm
• **Guide price £1,900/$3,591**

Spelter Figure ▲

• 20th century
Bronze spelter bust of the dancer Isadora Duncan, of a phantasmagorical theme.
• height 42cm
• **Guide price £4,500/$8,505**

Chrome Lighter ▲

• 1970
Chrome globe lighter raised on a circular base.
• height 10cm
• **Guide price £35/$66**

Art Deco Figure ▼

• *1930*
French Art Deco silvered bronze figure
of a dancer, by Henri Molins.
• *height 47cm*
• **Guide price £1,400/$2,646**

Bronze Vase ▼

• *1930s*
Dinanderie bronze vase designed by
Grange.
• *height 27cm*
• **Guide price £1,500/$2,835**

Dalou Bronze ▲

• *circa 1905*
Bronze figure of a man digging, by Aime
Joule Dalou. Pupil of Carpeaux and
Duret his debut was at the Salon in Paris
in 1867, signed with the Swiss French
Foundry mark.
• *height 9cm*
• **Guide price £1,650/$3,119**

Hussman Bronze Figure ▲

• *circa 1920*
Erotic bronze of a nude man on
horseback, Signed on the base
'Hussman'.
• *height 35.5cm*
• **Guide price £2,750/$5,198**

Bronze Dancer ▲

• *20th century*
Bronze figure of a female dancer by
Rena Rosenthal.
• *height 20cm*
• **Guide price £300/$567**

German Silver Tray ◄

• *1905*
German silver Art Nouveau tray
decorated with red poppies and head of
a girl with long red hair.
• *32cm x 40cm*
• **Guide price £7,000/$13,230**

Wall Sconces ▼

• *1940*
One of a pair of French metal wall
sconces with enamelled leaf and flower
design.
• *height 40cm*
• **Guide price £480/$907**

Tudric Jug ▼

• *1930*
Tudric jug of ovoid proportions made
for Liberty of London
• *height 25cm*
• **Guide price £85/$161**

Signed Bronze Plate ▼

• *20th century*
Bronze plate signed 'Tiffany Studios,
New York'.
• *diameter 23cm*
• **Guide price £350/$662**

Bronze Ibex ▲

- *1925*

Fine bronze of a leaping Ibex on a pink
marble plinth, by Fayral.
- *21cm x 28cm*
- **Guide price £750/$1,418**

Chrome Siphon ▲

- *1960*

British-made chrome siphon and ice
bucket.
- *height 40cm*
- **Guide price £240/$454**

Classical Figure ▼

- *20th century*

Bronze and ivory figure from a model
by Varnier, showing a classical maiden
holding a flower aloft. On an onyx and
marble base.
- *height 26.7cm*
- **Guide price £785/$1,484**

Bronze Figurine ▼

- *20th century*

Bronze figure of a female dancer by
Haggenauer for Wiener Werkstatte.
- *height 24cm*
- **Guide price £1,500/$2,835**

Lenoir Bronze ▲

- *20th century*

Patinated French bronze figurine of a
nude lady with an outstretched cloak,
standing on a pink marble plinth, by
Pierre Lenoir.
- *height 32cm*
- **Guide price £950/$1,796**

Warrior Figure in Bronze ▲

- *20th century*

Bronze figure of an African warrior
holding a gilt shield and throwing a
spear, by Rena Rosenthal.
- *height 20cm*
- **Guide price £300/$567**

Chrome Clocks ◄

- *1970*

Scottish-made chrome clocks with red,
purple and blue dials, by Westclox.
- *height 18.75cm*
- **Guide price £50/$95**

Bronze Prawn ▲

- *20th century*

A large, model of a prawn in mother-of-
pearl with verdigris bronze, in
naturalistic pose.
- *length 27.5cm*
- **Guide price £170/$322**

The Snake Charmer ▼

- *circa 1925*

Gilt bronze of a snake charmer, set on an onyx chamfered base. Signed by Rudolph Marcuse.

- *height 54cm*
- **Guide price £3,600/$6,804**

Copper Charger ▼

- *circa 1910*

Gilded, hand-crafted circular charger, exquisitely worked in a continuous band of flowerheads on a punched background.

- *height 30cm*
- **Guide price £475/$898**

Rosenthal Bronze ▲

- *20th century*

Bronze figure of a dancer in a straw skirt in a stylised form, by Rena Rosenthal.

- *height 20cm*
- **£300/$567**

Pair of Brass Candlesticks ▲

- *circa 1930*

A pair of candlesticks of barley-twist form on round bases.

- *height 31cm*
- **Guide price £88/$167**

Ivory Figure ▼

- *1925*

Very fine painted bronze and ivory and gold figure, by F. Preiss.

- *height 18cm*
- **Guide price £3,950/$7,466**

Art Deco Figure ▼

- *circa 1925*

Art Deco bronze of a young man holding a lariat, on a marble plinth.

- *height 30cm*
- **Guide price £1,275/$2,410**

Pair of Candlesticks ◀

- *circa 1930*

A pair of Art Deco chrome and decorative green plastic candlesticks with clear holders and conical sconces.

- *height 9cm*
- **Guide price £42/$80**

American Chrome Lighter ▲

- *1960*

Ball-shaped chrome lighter by Ronson of Newark, New Jersey, USA.

- *height 7.5cm*
- **Guide price £45/$85**

Mexican Horse ▲

- *20th century*

A naively modelled tin horse, with saddle and four straight legs, the whole on a square, tin base.

- *height 100cm; width 120cm*
- **Guide price £200/$378**

Chrome Ashtray ▲

- *circa 1970*

A chrome ashtray promoting Bridges' Tools, featuring a die-cast drill to centre.

- *height 8cm*
- **Guide price £25/$48**

Vegetable Dishes ▶

- *circa 1930*
A pair of silver-plated vegetable dishes with octagonal lids with wooden finials.
- *diameter 22cm*
- **£360/$680**

Metal Milk Churn ▶

- *circa 1920*
A large domestic milk churn.
- *height 51cm*
- **Guide price £45/$85**

Floor Standing Light ▲

- *20th century*
A decorative floor-standing light with wind-proof glass bowl.
- *height 116cm*
- **Guide price £425/$803**

Metal Bookends ▲

- *20th century*
A pair of bookends in the form of a bear's head in repose, set on a wooden stand.
- **£585/$1,106**

Silver-plate Vase ▲

- *circa 1930*
A conical, stepped, silver-plated vase on a stepped, circular base.
- *height 31cm*
- **Guide price £200/$378**

Standing Ashtray ◀

- *circa 1960*
Chrome floor ashtray with tiered trays, engraved pattern and rubber-coated stand.
- *height 65cm*
- **Guide price £60/$114**

'Ziglical' Column ▼

- *1966*
Stainless steel with stove enamelling. By Joe Tilson.
- *height 81cm*
- **Guide price £4,500/$8,505**

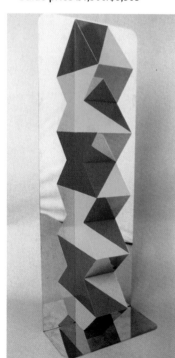

Tall Bronze Bottle ▲

- *circa 1950*
A Japanese Tsuro flower vessel of Kubi form. Vessel is signed by Roku IV.
- *height 40cm*
- **Guide price £1,600/$3,024**

Chrome Bath Rack ▶

- *circa 1930*
An early compartmentalised chromium bath rack with adjustable shaving mirror.
- *height 23cm*
- **Guide price £98/$185**

MUSICAL INSTRUMENTS

National Guitar ▼

- *1929*

National. Model Style 2. Irish rose tenor. Very rare. Original case. S/N 684.

- *height 89cm*
- **Guide price £2,250/$4,253**

Fender Stratocaster ▼

- *1964*

Fiesta red Stratocaster with rosewood neck, formerly owned by Richie Sanbora of *Bon Jovi*.

- **Guide price £9,500/$17,955**

Switchmaster Guitar ▲

- *1960*

Gibson Model: Switchmaster. Blonde finish, with original case. S/N A 33343

- *height 105cm*
- **Guide price £7,500/$14,175**

Gibson L-5 Guitar ▲

- *1935*

Gibson L-5 1935 guitar with F holes, scratch plate and mother-of-pearl inlaid fret board.

- *length 108cm*
- **Guide price £3,500/$6,615**

Gibson Guitar ▼

- *1964*

Gibson. Model: ES335TDC. Cherry finish. Original case. S/N 66236

- *height 104cm*
- **Guide price £5,500/$10,395**

Martin Guitar ▼

- *1960*

Brazilian rosewood Martin D-28 guitar.

- **Guide price £8,500/$16,065**

Gibson Guitar and Case ▲

- *1962*

Make: Gibson. Model: ES350TN. Blonde finish with original case. S/N 80935

- *height 105cm*
- **Guide price £4,250/$8,033**

Texan Epiphone Guitar ▲

- *1967*

Epiphone. Model: Texan. Natural finish. S/N 875125

- *height 108cm*
- **Guide price £1,895/$3,544**

Gretsch Guitar ▼
- *1957*

Gretsch guitar. Model 6120, with original white cowboy case. S/N:22080
- *height 1.05m*
- **Guide price £5,545/$10,481**

SJ200 Gibson Guitar ▼
- *1953*

Gibson Model SJ200. Sunburst finish. S/N A17263.
- *height 1.05m*
- **Guide price £5,850/$11,057**

Les Paul Guitar ▲
- *1960*

Gibson. Model Les Paul Special. Finish TV Yellow. S/N O 1432.
- *height 1m*
- **Guide price £3,850/$7,277**

Sunburst Gibson Guitar ▲
- *1960*

Gibson. Model: ES330. Sunburst finish. Dot neck. Factory order No. R29523.
- *height 99cm*
- **Guide price £2,850/$5,387**

Esquire Fender Guitar ▼
- *1959*

Fender. Model: Esquire. Blond finish. S/N 40511.
- *height 95cm*
- **Guide price £5,500/$10,395**

Jazzmaster Guitar ▼
- *1959*

Fender. Model: Jazzmaster. Sunburst finish. Original tweed case. S/N 31596.
- *height 1.04m*
- **Guide price £2,095/$3,960**

Martin Guitar ▲
- *1965*

Martin. Model: O18. S/N: 208 916.
- *height 99cm*
- **Guide price £1,895/$3,544**

Casino Guitar ▲
- *1967*

Epiphone. Model: casino. Long scale model. Near mint condition. Original card case.
- *height 108cm*
- **Guide price £2,500/$4,725**

Fender Guitar ▲

- *1952*

Fender. Model: Esquire with original thermometer case. S/N 4047.

- *height 98cm*
- **Guide price £7,500/$14,175**

SJ200 Gibson Guitar ▲

- *1949*

Gibson. Model: SJ200. Maple back and sides stained and a new scratch guard added by Gibson in the mid-1960s. S/N A3487.

- *height 105cm*
- **Guide price £4,950/$9,356**

Epiphone Guitar ▼

- *1958*

Epiphone. Model: Coronet. Refinished in black.

- *height 96cm*
- **Guide price £1,895/$3,544**

D28 Martin Guitar ▼

- *1965*

Martin. Model: D28. Brazilian rosewood. Replaced fingerboard. S/N 201923.

- *height 103cm*
- **Guide price £2,300/$4,347**

Stratocaster Guitar ▲

- *1963*

Fender. Model Stratocaster. Refinished in white. Some changes. S/N 95781

- *height 99cm*
- **Guide price £2,995/$5,661**

Rickenbacker Guitar ▲

- *1967*

Rickenbacker. Model: 365. Fireglow finish. S/N GC1415.

- *height 98cm*
- **Guide price £1,895/$3,544**

Jazzbase Fender Guitar ▼

- *1969*

Fender. Model: Jazzbase. Sunburst finish. Original case. S/N 283918.

- *height 115cm*
- **Guide price £2,250/$4,253**

Gretsch Guitar ▼

- *1962*

Gretsch. Model: 6120. Original case. S/N 67410.

- *height 109cm*
- **Guide price £2,500/$4,725**

Gretsch Country Club ▲
- *1959*

Chet Atkins 6119 Gretsch in western orange with single PAF filtertron pick-up.
- **Guide price £2,600/$4,914**

Epiphone Coronet ▼
- *1958*

Epiphone Coronet guitar with re-lacquered dark red body.
- *98cm x 33cm*
- **Guide price £1,850/$3,497**

Les Paul Guitar ▼
- *1954*

Gibson Les Paul guitar with gold top. Provenance: Richie Sanbora of American rock band *Bon Jovi*.
- **Guide price £7,000/$13,230**

Left-handed Gibson Guitar ▲
- *1963*

Custom-made Gibson guitar in sunburst with block markers and ebony fingerboard (left handed). Serial no. ES335.
- **Guide price £8,500/$16,065**

Gibson Firebird III ▼
- *circa 1968*

Firebird in gold finish, with non-reverse body, three pick-ups and a vibrato. All original fittings.
- **Guide price £2,650/$5,009**

Plexi Bass Guitar ▼
- *1969*

Dan Armstrong Plexi Bass. Model: Dan. In excellent condition, with instructions and OHSC.
- *110cm x 34cm*
- **Guide price £1,150/$2,174**

Casino Guitar ▲
- *1967*

Epiphone Casino guitar in sunburst.
- *110cm x 41cm*
- **Guide price £2,500/$4,725**

Fender Jaguar Guitar ▲
- *1968*

Fender Jaguar guitar with matching headstock in factory black custom colour.
- *103cm x 37cm*
- **Guide price £2,250/$4,253**

Framus Starbass

- *1960*

Cherry sunburst Framus Starbass guitar, as used by the *Rolling Stones*.
- **Guide price £1,960/$3,705**

White Falcon ▼

- *circa 1962*

Cutaway White Falcon, by Gretsch. Serial no. 50120, designed by Jimmy Webster, with 24-carat gold plating.
- **Guide price £4,950/$9,356**

Fender Jazzmaster ▲

- *1966*

Left-handed Fender Jazzmaster in fiesta red finish. It is very rare to find this type of left-handed custom coloured Fender.
- *109cm x 32cm*
- **Guide price £3,000/$5,670**

Ampeg Guitar ▲

- *1962*

AEB-1 scroll base Ampeg guitar in cherry with white pick-guard.
- **Guide price £1,580/$2,986**

Precision Bass ▼

- *1963*

Fender Precision bass in metallic turquoise with rosewood fingerboard, custom ordered.
- **Guide price £3,995/$7,551**

Epiphone Guitar ▼

- *1962*

Al Ciaola Cherry guitar made by Epiphone. Early 1960s' Epiphones are rare and this is in exceptional condition.
- *109cm x 41cm*
- **Guide price £1,895/$3,544**

Sunburst Gibson Guitar ▲

- *1959*

Gibson guitar in sunburst with dot neck. Serial No. ES 335.
- **Guide price £7,560/$14,289**

Gibson Trini Lopez ▲

- *1967*

Gibson Trini Lopez in cherry red finish with diamond inlay and sound holes.
- **Guide price £2,500/$4,725**

Silverjet Gretsch ▲
- *1955*

American Gretsch guitar in silverjet finish.
- **Guide price £5,500/$10,395**

Gibson ES-5 ▲
- *1952*

Natural body finish Gibson ES-5 with three P90s. Provenance: Gary Moore.
- **Guide price £8,500/$16,065**

Gretsch White Falcon ▼
- *1962*

Gretsch White Falcon double cut away guitar with black paint.
- **Guide price £4,950/$9,356**

Gibson Les Paul Junior ▼
- *1959*

Gibson Les Paul Junior in TV yellow with double cut away.
- **Guide price £4,250/$8,033**

Jazz Bass ▲
- *1972*

Fender jazz bass with maple neck, black binding and black markers with a natural body finish.
- **Guide price £1,500/$2,835**

Thunderbird Bass ▲
- *1976*

Rare black model with reverse body styling, bass, treble and volume knobs.
- **Guide price £1,750/$3,308**

Epiphone Frontier ▼
- *1960*

Epiphone Frontier guitar in sunburst finish.
- **Guide price £2,500/$4,725**

Fender Jazz Bass ▼
- *1961*

Sunburst Jazz Bass, Serial no. 44210. A fine example of the most sought-after vintage bass.
- **Guide price £7,250/$13,703**

Avocado Gretsch ▲

- *circa 1961*

Two-tone, smoked-green, semi-acoustic guitar with original scratch-plate and fittings.

- **Guide price £2,200/$4,158**

Gibson 12-String ▲

- *circa 1967*

Acoustic guitar in cherry sunburst, previously owned by Noel Gallagher, with authenticating letter.

- **Guide price £1,495/$2,826**

Silver Sparkle ▼

- *circa 1955*

A Gretsch Duo Jet with Bigsby tremelo and block inlays. Serial no. 17177.

- **Guide price £5,000/$9,450**

Les Paul Deluxe ▼

- *circa 1972*

Gold top finish with mini-humbuckers, the pick-up surrounds stamped 'Gibson'. A great investment.

- **Guide price £1,495/$2,826**

Gibson Les Paul ▲

- *1959*

With faded flame top, serial no. 91258. The '59, between the chubbier '58 and the flat '60, was regarded as the guitar player's favourite.

- **Guide price £35,000/$66,150**

Epiphone Riviera ▲

- *circa 1967*

Riviera, in sunburst, with a Frequentata tailpiece, mini-humbuckers and 'f' holes. Favoured by *The Beatles*.

- **Guide price £1,800/$3,402**

Fender Broadcaster ▼

- *1950*

Completely original Fender Broadcaster – serial no. 0729 – of which only 200 were made.

- **Guide price £15,000/$28,350**

Fender Stratocaster ▼

- *1964*

Pre-CBS Fender Stratocaster serial no. L70376. As-new finish with no playing wear – 'probably the cleanest in Europe'.

- **Guide price £6,000/$11,340**

Gretsch Guitar ▲

- *1953*

Model 35 made by Gretsch with DeArmond rhythm. Chief floating pick-up.
- *110cm x 41cm*
- **Guide price £1,295/$2,448**

Stratocaster Guitar ▲

- *1957*

Fender Stratocaster guitar, with tobacco sunburst finish. Completely original guitar with tweed case.
- *95cm x 32cm*
- **Guide price £1,085/$2,051**

Fender Broadcaster ▼

- *1950*

Fender Broadcaster with maple neck and black pick-guard and the first electric solid body guitar. Previously owned by John Entwhistle of the rock band, *The Who*.
- **Guide price £18,000/$34,020**

Gibson Les Paul Guitar ▼

- *1960*

Gibson Les Paul special model with original TV yellow finish.
- *98cm x 34cm*
- **Guide price £3,500/$6,615**

Gretsch Guitar ▲

- *1959*

Gretsch Anniversary model 6125 with 'f' holes and cream finish.
- *107cm x 41cm*
- **Guide price £1,895/$3,544**

Acoustic Guitar ▲

- *1929*

Model No. 00045 with Brazilian rosewood back and sides, and pearl inlay, by Martin.
- **Guide price £26,000/$49,140**

Gibson Flying Vee ▼

- *1958*

Korina wood Gibson Flying Vee, the Holy Grail of vintage solid body guitars. Only 100 were ever made.
- **Guide price £55,000/$103,950**

Fender Stratocaster ▼

- *1960*

Rare custom-ordered metallic blue sparkle Stratocaster with slab rosewood fingerboard. Believed to be one of only five ever made.
- **Guide price £18,500/$34,965**

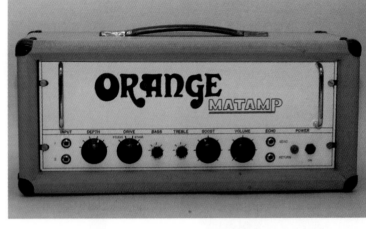

Lap Steel Guitar ▲
- *1933*

EH150 Lap Steel Gibson Guitar with a Charlie Christian pick-up, in sunburst finish, with original case.
- *68cm x 28cm*
- **Guide price £850/$1,607**

Orange Amplifier ▲
- *circa 1965*

A very early Orange Matamp with hand-painted Orange logo, finished in orange vinyl with single black handle.
- **Guide price £995/$1,881**

Amplifier ▼
- *circa 1958*

Tweed Fender amp with leather handle. Pre-CBS Fender.
- *height 42cm*
- **Guide price £795/$1,503**

Cherry Red Guitar ▲
- *1962*

Gibson guitar in cherry red with block markers. Serial no: ES 335.
- **Guide price £4,950/$9,356**

Valve Guitar Amp ▼
- *October 1956*

Gretsch 'Western Roundup' amp, with leather belt and brass studs.
- *height 40cm*
- **Guide price £2,000/$3,780**

Lead Amplifier ▲
- *circa 1970s*

A British Park 100-watt lead amplifier.
- **Guide price £950/$1,796**

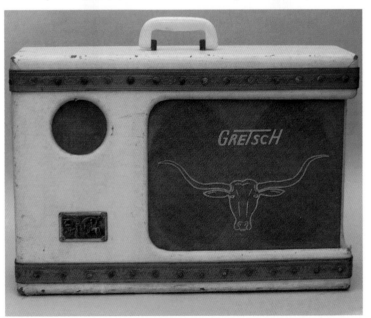

Lighting Ornament ▲
- *circa 1965*

Drum kit light – 110 volt – with green and red flashing alternately.
- *height 32cm*
- **Guide price £250/$473**

Sphere Speaker ▶
- *1970*

Metal sphere enclosing 12 speakers, with a chrome stand, by Grundig of Germany.
- *height 87.5cm*
- **Guide price £900/$1,701**

Concert Grand Piano ▼
- *1935*

Model D concert grand in a very unusual mahogany high gloss polish (most concert grands are black). Fully rebuilt by Steinway and Sons.
- *length 2.7m*
- **Guide price £58,500/$110,565**

Fender Stratocaster ▲
- *1960*

A Blue Sparkle Stratocaster, serial no. 50172. Unique, commissioned from Fender, with original brown Tolex case.
- **Guide price £18,500/$34,965**

Rosewood Satin Piano ▲
- *1906*

Model K. rosewood satin piano with inlay veneer. Fully rebuilt by Steinway & Sons. Made in Hamburg.
- *height 135cm*
- **Guide price £21,500/$40,635**

Wood and Skin Drum ▲
- *circa 1970*

Native American drum made of wood and skin and decorated with bone and feathers, with a green turtle on the skin.
- *height 65cm*
- **Guide price £400/$756**

Grand Piano ▲
- *circa 1939*

Steinway model M grand piano, fully rebuilt by Steinway, in high-polished mahogany.
- *length 1.7m*
- **Guide price £27,500/$51,975**

Art Deco Piano ▲
- *circa 1930*

An Art Deco, mahogany baby grand piano, by Monnington & Western, with German mechanism, resting on square, tapered legs.
- *length 1.26m*
- **Guide price £3,400/$6,426**

Ebonised Piano ▶
- *1958*

Model B. black ebonised piano in a high gloss finish, fully rebuilt by Steinway & Sons.
- *length 208cm*
- **Guide price £39,500/$74,655**

Steinway Grand Piano ▲
- *circa 1960*

Mahogany, model B grand piano, rebuilt by Steinway.
- *length 2.1m*
- **Guide price £40,000/$75,600**

PAPERWEIGHTS

Cat Paperweight ▼
- *1970*
Globular clear paperweight mounted with a metal cat.
- *height 10cm*
- **Guide price £45/$85**

Circular Italian Paperweight ▲
- *1960*
Circular Italian paperweight with a silver bubble effect with stylised pink and white flowers and a lime green border.
- *diameter 7cm*
- **Guide price £55/$104**

Baccarat Millefiori ▲
- *1960*
Millefiori closepack designed paperweight with various coloured and patterned canes.
- *diameter 7cm*
- **Guide price £65/$123**

Whitefriars Paperweight ▼
- *1976*
Whitefriars of London hemispherical shape paperweight, with six rings of composite cogwheels of indigo, white, blue, yellow and red, around a central cane.
- *diameter 8cm*
- **Guide price £195/$370**

Baccarat Sulphite ▶
- *1976*
Baccarat sulphite paperweight in facetop form, faceted with six lozenge cuts printed with a bust of Queen Elizabeth II.
- *diameter 7cm*
- **Guide price £1,670/$3,157**

Wedgwood Paperweight ▼
- *1981*
Wedgwood blue jasper and glass paperweight, to commemorate the marriage of the Prince of Wales and Lady Diana.
- *diameter 9cm*
- **Guide price £95/$180**

Baccarat Prince Charles Paperweight ▶
- *1976*
Baccarat sulphite paperweight in facet form, with six lozenge cuts and a bust of Prince Charles.
- *diameter 7.5cm*
- **Guide price £195/$370**

Whitefriars Paperweight ▲

- *1977*

Whitefriars paperweight from a limited edition to commemorate the Silver Jubilee of Her Majesty Queen Elizabeth 1952–1977 No. 418/1000.
- *diameter 8cm*
- **Guide price £135/$255**

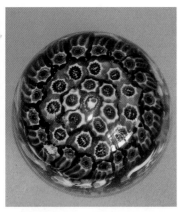

Hexagonal Paperweight ▼

- *1976*

English Whitefriars hexagonal faceted paperweight, with puce composite canes divided by six gauze tubes around a central turquoise cluster of canes.
- *diameter 7cm*
- **Guide price £195/$370**

Multicoloured Paperweight ◄

- *circa 1950*

Closepack designed paperweight with emerald green, red, cobalt blue and turquoise canes.
- *diameter 7cm*
- **Guide price £40/$76**

Queen Elizabeth II Plaque ▼

- *1977*

Glass paperweight with Wedgwood plaque of Queen Elizabeth II.
- *diameter 7cm*
- **Guide price £150/$284**

Jubilee Moonflower Paperweight ▲

- *1977*

Jubilee moonflower using abstract techniques. Echoes the glitter and ceremony of the Silver Jubilee. Engraved on the base with the Royal Cipher, designed by Colin Terris No. 2846.
- *diameter 7.5cm*
- **Guide price £85/$161**

Silver Jubilee Paperweight ▲

- *1977*

Crystal paperweight by Baccarat commissioned by Spinks. Limited edition of 500 to commemorate the Silver Jubilee of Queen Elizabeth II.
- *diameter 8.5cm*
- **Guide price £245/$463**

Purple Paperweight ►

- *circa 1970*

Purple faceted paperweight with a central flower.
- *diameter 8cm*
- **Guide price £55/$104**

Faceted Paperweight ▲

- *1970*

Faceted paperweight by Whitefriars of London, cut with five roundels and moulded turquoise purple and white canes.
- *diameter 7.5cm*
- **Guide price £195/$370**

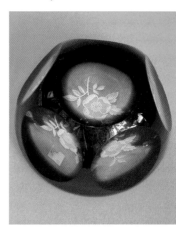

PHOTOGRAPHS

Film Makers ▲

- *1960*

Three Italian neo-realist filmmakers, from l to r: Vittorio de Sica (1901–74), Roberto Rossellini (1906–77) and Federico Fellini (1920–93) on the set of de Sica's film, "Generale delle Rovere". Black and white fibre, silver gelatin photograph. Limited edition: one of only four signed by the photographer Slim Aarons. Printed from original negative in Getty Images darkrooms.
- *length 25.4cm*
- **Guide price £1,500/$2,835**

Bacall and Bogart ▲

- *24th December 1951*

American actor Humphrey Bogart (1899–1957) with Lauren Bacall and their son Stephen at their home in Beverly Hills on Christmas Eve. Black and white fibre, silver gelatin photograph from a limited edition: one of only four signed by the photographer Slim Aarons. Printed from original negative in Getty Images darkrooms.
- *length 61cm*
- **Guide price £1,500/$2,835**

Take It ▼

- *September 1970*

Painter Salvador Dali (1904–1989) in a pose with his trademark walking stick, with some of his works at Port Ligat, Costa Brava, Spain. Colour Lambda photograph. Limited edition: one of only four signed by photographer Slim Aaron.
- *50.8cm x pro*
- **Guide price £2,400/$4,536**

Silver Gelatin Print ▼

- *1967*

'Manchester' by Shirley Baker.
- *length 30cm*
- **Guide price £200/$378**

Groucho Marx ▼

- *circa 1954*

American comic Julius "Groucho" Marx (1895–1977), member of the Marx brothers, in bed with a joke cigar in Beverly Hills. Black and white fibre, silver gelatin photograph, from a limited edition: one of only four signed by the photographer Slim Aarons. Printed from original negative in Getty Images darkrooms.
- *length 61cm*
- **Guide price £1,500/$2,835**

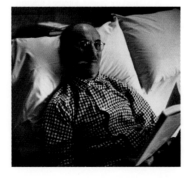

Capucine ▲

- *1957*

French actress Capucine, (Germaine Lefebvre) (1933–90) fanning herself at a New Year's Eve party held at Romanoffs in Beverly Hills. By Photographer Slim Aarons. Black and white fibre, silver gelatin photograph. Limited edition: one of only four signed by the photographer. Printed from original negative in Getty Images darkrooms.
- *length 50.8cm*
- **Guide price £1,500/$2,835**

Kings of Hollywood ▲

- *31st December 1957*

Film stars (from left to right) Clark Gable (1901–1960), Van Heflin (1910–71), Gary Cooper (1901–61) and James Stewart (1908–97) enjoy a joke at a New Year's party held at Romanoff's in Beverly Hills. A black and white fibre, silver gelatin photograph. Limited edition: one of only 250 signed by the photographer.
- *length 50.8cm*
- **Guide price £2,000/$3,780**

Sea Drive ▼

- *1967*

Film producer Kevin McClory takes his wife and family out in an "Amphicar" in the Bahamas. Colour Lambda photograph. Limited edition: one of only four signed by the photographer
- *length 1.52m*
- **Guide price £3,500/$6,615**

Jackie K ▼

- *circa 1959*

Jacqueline Kennedy (also known as Jackie Onassis 1929–94), wife of Senator Jack Kennedy at an "April in Paris" ball. Colour Lambda photograph. Limited edition: one of only four signed by the photographer.
- *50.8cm x pro*
- **Guide price £2,400/$4,536**

Signed Modern Print ▼

- *1931*

'Renée, Paris. January 1931' by Jacques-Henri Lartigue. Signed modern silver gelatin print.
- *length 50cm*
- **Guide price £3,000/$5,670**

Man's Work ▲

• 1960

Hugh Hefner working at his typewriter surrounded by 'bunny' girls. Publisher Hugh M Hefner at the Playboy Key Club in Chicago. He founded adult magazines, *Playboy*, *VIP* and *Oui*. Colour Lambda photograph. Limited edition: one of only four signed by the photographer.

• length 50.8cm

• **Guide price £2,400/$4,536**

The Rolling Stones ▲

• January 1967

British rock group The Rolling Stones; from left to right, Bill Wyman, Brian Jones (1942–69), Charlie Watts, Keith Richards and Mick Jagger. Photographer: Keystone Collection. Modern black and white fibre, silver gelatin archival photograph printed in Getty Images Darkrooms. Limited edition: 300.

• length 50.8cm

• **Guide price £225/$426**

Bolton Scene ▲

• 1937

Signed silver gelatin print by Humphrey Spender of two small children playing on a wasteland in Bolton, Lancashire. For mass observation.

• 30.5cm x 40cm

• **Guide price £300/$567**

Hitchcock Profile ▼

• July 1966

Film director Alfred Hitchcock (1889–1980) during the filming of "The Torn Curtain" by photographer Curt Gunther/BIPs Collection. Modern black and white fibre, silver gelatin archival photograph, printed in Getty Images Darkrooms. Limited edition: 300.

• length 50.8cm

• **Guide price £225/$426**

Night Time New York ▼

• 1936

Paramount Building in Times Square, New York, towers over Schenley's Chinese Restaurant. Photographer: Fox Photos Collection. Modern black and white fibre, silver gelatin archival photograph, printed in Getty Images darkrooms. Limited edition: 300.

• length 50.8cm

• **Guide price £225/$426**

Signed Silver Gelatin ▶

• circa 1994

'"Milton Keynes" by Leo Regan. Silver gelatin print, signed verso

• 30.5cm x 40cm

• **Guide price £300/$567**

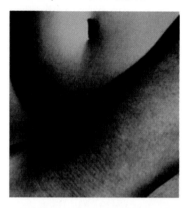

Limited C-Type Print ▲

• 1965

"Edie Sedgwick in Red Dress, 1965" by Nat Finkelstein. C-type print, from a limited edition of eight. Signed and numbered verso.

• 30.5cm x 40cm

• **Guide price £650/$1,229**

Signed Brandt Print ▼

• 1956

"Nude, London, 1956" by Bill Brandt. A silver gelatin print, signed recto.

• 30.5cm x 40cm

• **Guide price £1,800 /$3,402**

Bill Brandt Print ▼

• 1930

"Parlour Maid at Window, Kensington, 1930" by Bill Brandt. Silver gelatin print, signed recto.

• 30.5cm x 40cm

• **Guide price £1,300 /$2,457**

Silver Gelatin Print ◀

• 1991

'Kazaksthan', signed print by Sebastiao Salgado.

• length 35cm

• **Guide price £2,500/$4,725**

PHOTOGRAPHS

Fair Fun ▼

- *8th October 1938*

Two young women enjoying themselves on a roller coaster at Southend Fair, England by the photographer Kurt Hutton, Picture Post. Modern black and white fibre, silver gelatin archival photograph, printed in Getty Images Darkrooms. Limited edition: 300.

- *length 50.8cm*
- **Guide price £225/$426**

Solarized Portrait ▼

- *circa 1935*

One of an edition of 50 prints of 'Dorothy Hill, Solarized Portrait, New York 1935' by Lee Miller, estate stamped verso.

- **Guide price £300/$567**

Signed Modern Print ▶

- *1938*

'Good Reputation Sleeping' by Manuel Alvarez Bravo.

- *length 20cm*
- **Guide price £1,250/$2,363**

Snow in the Park ▲

- *1947*

A man trudging through Central Park West, New York City, in a blizzard by photographer: Nat Fein/Courtesy of Nat Fein's Estate. Exclusive. Black and white fibre, silver gelatin archival photograph, printed from original negative in Getty Images darkrooms.

- *length 50.8cm*
- **Guide price £485/$917**

Fonda in Town ▲

- *1951*

Film star Henry Fonda (1905–82) on a balcony overlooking a street in New York by photographer Slim Aarons. Black and white fibre, silver gelatin photograph, printed from original negative in Getty Images darkrooms. Limited edition: 300.

- *30.5cm x 30.5cm*
- **Guide price £185/$350**

Walking in the Rain ▼

- *circa 1955*

A man and his dog walking in the rain in Central Park, New York City by photographer: Nat Fein/Courtesy Of Nat Fein's Estate. Black and white fibre, silver gelatin archival photograph, printed from original negative in Getty Images darkrooms. Exclusive.

- *length 40.7cm*
- **Guide price £415/$784**

Guggenheim Window ▼

- *circa 1955*

The Guggenheim Museum of Modern and Contemporary Art in New York. Photographer: Sherman, Three Lions Collection. Black and white fibre, silver gelatin photograph, printed from original negative in Getty Images darkrooms. Limited edition: 300.

- *length 61cm*
- **Guide price £250/$473**

Jazz Scooter ▲

- *1949*

Lucille Brown takes control of the Vespa scooter as her husband Louis Armstrong (1898–1971) displays his musical appreciation of the ancient Coliseum in Rome. Black and white fibre, silver gelatin photograph, from a limited edition of 300 by photographer Slim Aarons. Printed from original negative in Getty Images darkrooms.

- *length 50.8cm*
- **Guide price £225/$426**

Bright Lights ▲

- *1970*

Aerial view of the Manhattan skyline at night, looking southeast down Fifth Avenue, from the RCA Building Rockefeller Center, New York City by photographer: Lawrence Thornton. Modern black and white fibre, silver gelatin archival photograph, printed in Getty Images Darkrooms. Limited edition: 300.

- *length 50.8cm*
- **Guide price £225/$426**

C-Type Colour Print ▲

- *20th century*

Adam Barfos, 'Conference Building Elevators', from his International Territory series.

- *length 50cm*
- **Guide price £1,000/$1,890**

Chrysler Building ▲

- *3rd May 1957*
The Chrysler Building in New York by photographer Phil Burcham, Fox Photos. Modern black and white fibre, silver gelatin archival photograph, printed in Getty Images darkrooms. Limited edition: 300.
- *length 50.8cm*
- **Guide price £225/$426**

Taylor Reclines ▲

- *1954*
American actress Elizabeth Taylor reclining in bed by the photographer Baron. Modern black and white fibre, silver gelatin archival photograph, printed in Getty Images darkrooms. Limited edition: 300.
- *length 50.8cm*
- **Guide price £225/$426**

John Lennon Profile ▼

- *26th June 1967*
John Lennon (1940–1980), singer, songwriter and guitarist with the Beatles by photographer Peter King, Fox Photos. Modern black and white fibre, silver gelatin archival photograph, printed in Getty Images darkrooms. Limited edition: 300.
- *length 50.8cm*
- **Guide price £225/$26**

Ali in Training ▼

- *August 1966*
American heavyweight boxer Muhammed Ali in training in London for his fight against Brian London. Photographer: R.McPhedran, Express Collection. Modern black and white fibre, silver gelatin archival photograph, printed in Getty Images darkrooms. Limited edition: 300.
- *length 50.8cm*
- **Guide price £225/$426**

Commissionaire's Dog ◄

- *22nd October 1938*
A hotel commissionaire talking to a small dog in London. Photographer: Kurt Hutton, Picture Post. Modern black and white fibre, silver gelatin archival photograph, printed in Getty Images darkrooms. Limited edition: 300.
- *length 40.7cm*
- **Guide price £185/$350**

The Beatles ▲

- *10th January 1964*
Paul McCartney, Ringo Starr, John Lennon (1940–80) and George Harrison (1943–2001) of The Beatles. Photographer: Terry Disney, Express Collection. Modern black and white, fibre silver gelatin archival photograph, printed in Getty Images darkrooms. Limited edition: 300.
- *length 50.8cm*
- **Guide price £225/$426**

Bert Hardy Print ▲

- *1957*
'US 6th Fleet in the Mediterranean' by Bert Hardy.
- *length 50cm*
- **Guide price £400/$756**

Royal Portraits ▼

- *1966*
A pair of portraits, this showing Queen Elizabeth II, the other of Prince Philip.
- **Guide price £950/$1,796**

Gorbals Boys ▼

- *31st January 1948*
Two boys in the Gorbals area of Glasgow. The Gorbals tenements were built quickly and cheaply in the 1840s. Conditions were appalling; overcrowding was standard and sewage and water facilities inadequate. The tenements housed about 40,000 people with up to eight family members sharing a single room, 30 residents sharing a toilet and 40 sharing a tap. By the time this photograph was taken 850 tenements had been demolished since 1920. Photographer: Bert Hardy, Picture Post. Modern black and white fibre, silver gelatin archival photograph, printed in Getty Images darkrooms. Limited edition: 300.
- *length 40.7cm*
- **Guide price £185/$350**

Silver Gelatin Print ◄

- *1934*
'Cafe Soho, London' by Wolfgang Suschitzky. Signed verso.
- *length 40cm*
- **Guide price £300/$567**

PHOTOGRAPHS

Cary in Rain ▼
- *1957*
British-born American actor Cary Grant (1904–86) sheltering in a hotel porch as he waits for the rain to stop. Photographer: Express Collection. Modern black and white fibre, silver gelatin archival photograph, printed in Hulton Getty darkrooms. Limited edition: 300.
- *length 40.7cm*
- **Guide price £185/$350**

SS Arctees ▶
- *26th January 1934*
The SS Arctees, designed by Sir Joseph Isherwood and christened by his wife. The ship was built to the 'Arcform' design of hull. This shot shows the unusual rudder design, before she was launched at Furness Shipbuilding Co's yard at Haverton-on-Tees, County Durham. Photographer: Douglas Miller, Topical Press Agency. Modern black and white fibre, silver gelatin archival photograph, printed in Hulton Getty Darkrooms. Limited edition of 300.
- *length 40.7cm*
- **Guide price £185/$350**

Racing Yacht ▲
- *6th August 1935*
Racing Yacht 'Candida' during a race at the Cowes Regatta. Photographer: E.Dean, Topical Press Agency. Modern black and white fibre, silver gelatin archival photograph, printed in Hulton Getty darkrooms. Limited edition: 300
- *length 61cm*
- **Guide price £250/$473**

Great Loss of Life ▲
- *16th April 1912*
Newspaper boy Ned Parfett selling copies of the *Evening News* telling of the Titanic maritime disaster. Photographer: Topical Press Agency. Modern black and white fibre, silver gelatin archival photograph, printed in Hulton Getty darkrooms. Limited edition: 300
- *length 40.7cm*
- **Guide price £185/$350**

Early Aircraft ▼
- *11th April 1907*
Mr Guillon attempts to fly his Guillon and Clouzy aeroplane on the Epsom Downs, Surrey. Photographer: Topical Press Agency. Modern black and white fibre, silver gelatin archival photograph, printed in Hulton Getty darkrooms. Limited edition: 300.
- *length 40.7cm*
- **Guide price £185/$350**

Lying on Deck ▼
- *1st July 1939*
The crew of a 12-metre racing yacht lying on the deck to lessen windage during a big race. Photographer: Kurt Hutton, Picture Post. Modern black and white fibre, silver gelatin archival photograph, printed in Hulton Getty darkrooms. Limited edition: 300.
- *length 50.8cm*
- **Guide price £225/$426**

Mike McKendrick ▼
- *1963*
Black and white fibre, silver gelatin photograph of American banjo player Mike McKendrick performing in Chicago by the photographer Slim Aarons. Printed from original negative in Hulton Getty darkrooms from a limited edition of 300.
- *length 40.7cm*
- **Guide price £185/$350**

Lady Day ▲
- *1954*
American jazz singer Billie Holiday (1915–59) in the spotlight during a performance by photographer Charles Hewitt, Picture Post. A modern black and white fibre, silver gelatin archival photograph, printed in Hulton Getty Darkrooms. Limited edition: 300.
- *length 40.7cm*
- **Guide price £185/$350**

Duke Ellington ▲
- *October 1958*
Modern black and white fibre, silver gelatin, archival photograph of American big band leader and legendary jazz pianist Duke Ellington (1899–1974) from the Evening Standard collection. Printed in Hulton Getty darkrooms. Limited edition: 300.
- *length 30.5cm*
- **Guide price £125/$237**

Jimi Hendrix ▲

- *August 1970*

Rock guitar virtuoso Jimi Hendrix (1942–70) caught mid-guitar break during his performance at the Isle of Wight Festival from the *Evening Standard* collection. Modern, black and white fibre, silver gelatin archival photograph, printed in Hulton Getty darkrooms. Limited edition: 300.

- *length 50.8cm*
- **Guide price £225/$426**

Delivery after Raid ▲

- *9th October 1940*

A milkman steadfastly delivering milk in a London street that has been devastated during a German bombing raid. Firemen are dampening down the ruins behind him. Photographer: Fred Morley, Fox Photos. Modern black and white fibre, silver gelatin archival photograph, printed in Hulton Getty darkrooms. Limited edition: 300.

- *length 40.7cm*
- **Guide price £185/$350**

Gelatin Print ▶

- *1999*

'Striped Wall and Cyclist' by Marcus Davies.

- *length 40cm*
- **Guide price £350/$662**

Grand Central Light ▲

- *circa 1930*

Beams of sunlight streaming through the windows at Grand Central Station, New York by the photographer Hal Morey, Fox Photos. Modern black and white fibre, silver gelatin archival photograph, printed in Hulton Getty darkrooms. Limited edition: 300.

- *length 50.8cm*
- **Guide price £225/$426**

Evening Dior ▶

- *4th September 1954*

An evening ensemble of tight-waisted jacket with long fur-trimmed sleeves worn over a full, ground-length skirt. Designed by Dior in Duchess satin. Photographer: John Chillingworth, Picture Post. Black and white toned fibre, silver gelatin photograph, printed from original negative in Hulton Getty darkrooms. Limited edition: 300.

- *length 30.5cm*
- **Guide price £187/$354**

Power Station ▶

- *circa 1935*

Smoke belches from the famous chimneys of London's Battersea Power Station. This photograph was taken before the chimneys increased to four in number. Photographer: Fox Photos Collection. Modern black and white fibre, silver gelatin archival photograph, printed in Hulton Getty darkrooms. Limited edition: 300.

- *length 40.7cm*
- **Guide price £185/$350**

Coronation Photograph ◀

- *12th May 1937*

George VI coronation photograph, by Dorothy Wilding. Autographed by the King and Queen Elizabeth.

- **Guide price £2,000/$3,780**

Jessie's Hands ▼

- *1930*

The hands of Jessie Matthews (1907–81), dancer and film star by the photographer Sasha. Black and white toned fibre, silver gelatin photograph, printed from original negative in Hulton Getty darkrooms. Limited edition: 300.

- *length 50.8cm*
- **Guide price £337/$637**

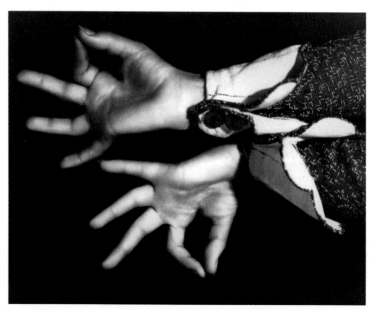

Silver Gelatin Print ▲

- *1929*

"Solange David, Paris, 1929", by Jacques-Henri Lartique. Silver gelatin print, signed recto.

- *30.5cm x 35.5cm*
- **Guide price £4,600/$8,694**

Untitled Print ▲

- *1999*

Untitled silver gelatin print taken in 1999 by Sheva Fruitman. Signed verso.

- *30.5cm x 35.5cm*
- **Guide price £600/1,134**

C-Type Print ▲

- *1999*

Untitled still life C-Type print taken in 1999 by Juliana Sohn. Signed verso.

- *30.5cm x 35.5cm*
- **Guide price £450/$851**

Colour Polaroid ▲

- *1999*

Untitled colour polaroid print taken by Sheva Fruitman in 1999. Signed verso.

- *12.7cm x 10.2cm*
- **Guide price £300/$567**

Trafalgar Square Print ▲

- *1965*

'March Climax, Trafalgar Square' London photograph by John 'Hoppy' Hopkins.

- *length 40cm*
- **Guide price £350/$662**

Signed Print ▼

- *1931*

"El Ensueno" (The Daydreamer) taken in 1931 in Mexico, by Manuel Alvarez Bravo. Silver gelatin print, signed verso.

- *25.5cm x 20cm*
- **Guide price £1,500/$2,835**

Platinum Print ▼

- *1949*

"Margarita de Bonampak, Mexico, 1949" by Manuel Alvarez Bravo. Platinum print, signed verso.

- *25.5cm x 20cm*
- **Guide price £2,000/$3,780**

Signed C-Type ▲

- *20th century*

Untitled photograph by Nigel Shafran, from 'Ruthbook', featuring blue hippo on radiator sill with green ground. Signed limited edition of 20.

- *length 40cm*
- **Guide price £450/$851**

Mishkov Sanatorium ▲

- *1999*

'Corridor of Hydrotherapy Treatment Rooms, Mishkov Sanatorium' by Jason Oddy.

- *length 50cm*
- **Guide price £775/$1,465**

Coronation Photograph ▼

- *1949*

Framed family group photograph of King George VI, Queen Elizabeth and Princess Margaret, with autographed letter by Princess Margaret.

- **Guide price £300/$567**

Finkelstein Print ▶

- *20th century*

Photograph 'Andy, Bob & Elvis' by Nat Finkelstein.

- *length 11.5cm*
- **Guide price £550/$1,040**

Stamford Bridge ◀

- *circa 1925*

Stamford Bridge, Chelsea Football Club's Stadium by the photographer A.H. Robinson. Black and white fibre, silver gelatin photograph, printed from original negative in Hulton Getty Darkrooms. Limited Edition: 300.

- *61cm x pro, panoramic format*
- **Guide price £250/$473**

Shirley Baker Print ▼

- *1964*

"Salford, 1964" by Shirley Baker. A silver gelatin print, signed verso.

- *30.5cm x 35.5cm*
- **Guide price £200/$378**

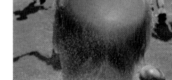

Marilyn Monroe Print ▼

- *1952*

Marilyn Monroe photographed in 1952 by Bob Willoughby. C-Type print, signed verso.

- *30.5cm x 40cm*
- **Guide price £600/$1,134**

Lartique Print ▼

- *1931*

"Cours automobile à Monthery, 1931" by Jacques-Henri Lartique. A silver gelatin print, signed verso.

- *30.5cm x 35.5cm*
- **Guide price £2,800/$5,292**

Bob Willoughby Print ▲

- *1962*

"Audrey Hepburn, 1962" by Bob Willoughby. A silver gelatin print, signed verso.

- *25.5cm x 30.5cm*
- **Guide price £600/$1,134**

Matthew Murray Print ▲

- *1999*

"Morris Dancers, 1999" by Matthew Murray. C-Type print, signed verso.

- *30.5cm x 35.5cm*
- **Guide price £200/$378**

Signed Willoughby Print ▼

- *1962*

"Billie Holliday, Tiffany Club, 1962" by Bob Willoughby. A silver gelatin print, signed verso.

- *30.5cm x 35.5cm*
- **Guide price £400/$756**

James Dean Print ▼

- *1955*

James Dean on the set of "Rebel Without a Cause" by photographer Bob Willoughby. Silver gelatin print, signed verso.

- *30.5cm x 40cm*
- **Guide price £400/$756**

Signed Print ▲

- *1955*

'Dreaming of Home' by Thurston Hopkins. Signed, modern silver-gelatin print.

- **Guide price £800/$1,512**

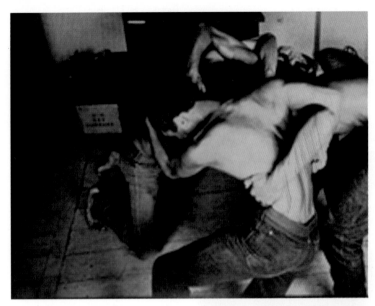

Berlin Bathers Print ▶

- *1959*

"Stoffe, Magda and Em Eating Popcorn, Berlin, 1959" by Will McBride. Silver gelatin print, signed verso.

- *30.5cm x 40cm*
- **Guide price £350/$662**

Signed C-Type Print ▼

- *1965*

"Hulme, 1965" by Shirley Baker. C-type print, signed recto.

- *30.5cm x 35.5cm*
- **Guide price £250/$473**

Fay Godwin Print ◀

- *1981*

"Flooded tree, Perwentnar, 1981" by Fay Godwin. Silver gelatin print, signed verso.

- *30.5cm x 35.5cm*
- **Guide price £500/$945**

Signed Gelatin Print ▲

- *1982*

"What she wanted and what she got, 1982" by Graham Smith. Silver gelatin print, signed verso.

- *30.5cm x 35.5cm*
- **Guide price £500/$945**

Signed McBride Print ◀

- *1957*

"Boys Romping at Jan's Place, 1957" by photographer Will McBride. Silver gelatin print, signed verso.

- *51cm x 35.5cm*
- **Guide price £500/$945**

C-Type Print ▼

- *1999*

Untitled C-type print by photographer Nigel Shafran. Signed verso.

- *25.5cm x 35.5cm*
- **Guide price £300/$567**

Palace of Nations Print ▼

- *1998*

Untitled C-type print taken in 1998 by Jason Oddy, from the "Palace of Nations" series. Signed verso.

- *30.5cm x 35.5cm*
- **Guide price £500/$945**

Nigel Shafran Print ▼

- *2000*

"Kitchen Sink" by Nigel Shafran. C-type print, signed verso.

- *51cm x 35.5cm*
- **Guide price £750/$1,418**

Silver Gelatin Print ▲

- *1987*

"North Islands in dry docks, Smith's Dock 1987" by Ian Macdonald. Silver gelatin print, signed verso.

- *51cm x 35.5cm*
- **Guide price £600/$1,134**

Ian Macdonald Print ▲

- *circa 1980*

Untitled silver gelatin print by photographer Ian Macdonald. Signed verso.

- *30.5cm x 40cm*
- **Guide price £500/$945**

Van der Elsken Print ▲

- *1957*

'Vali Reflected in the Mirror' by Ed Van
der Elsken.

- *length 42cm*
- **Guide price £650/$1,229**

Cibachrome Print ▲

- *20th century*

Untitled from 'The Wild West' series by
David Levinthal. Edition limited to 25.

- *length 25cm*
- **Guide price £500/$945**

'Footballers' Print ▼

- *1998*

Untitled silver gelatin print by Marcus
Davies from the "Footballers" series.
Taken in 1998 and signed verso.

- *12.8cm x 17.9cm*
- **Guide price £200/$378**

Signed Brandt Print ▼

- *1953*

'Nude, Eygalieres, France' by Bill Brandt.
Signed recto.

- *length 50cm*
- **Guide price £1,500/$2,835**

Audrey Hepburn ▼

- *1953*

Audrey Hepburn on Paramount Lot.
Signed modern silver-gelatin print by
Bob Willoughby.

- *length 30cm*
- **Guide price £400/$756**

Limited Edition Print ▼

- *1996*

'Making the Bed', c-type print, by Elinor
Carrucci. Limited edition of 15.

- *length 50cm*
- **Guide price £750/$1,418**

C-Type Print ◄

- *20th century*

Untitled, girl in hammock photograph by
Nat Finkelstein.

- *length 30cm*
- **Guide price £550/$1,040**

Bert Hardy Print ▲

- *circa 1950*

Untitled silver gelatin print from the
1950s, signed recto by photographer
Bert Hardy.

- *12cm x 16cm*
- **Guide price £1,300/$2,457**

Paris Print ▼

- *1951*

'Claudy and Vali in Claudy's Hotel Room'
by Ed Van der Elsken.

- **Guide price £2,050/$3,875**

Estate Print ▼

- *20th century*

'Asleep on the job' by Weegee. Silver
gelatin print.

- *length 27.5cm*
- **Guide price £500/$945**

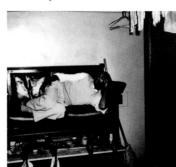

Blackpool Print ▲

- *1951*

"Maidens in waiting, Blackpool, 1951" by photographer Bert Hardy. Silver gelatin print, signed recto.

- *30.5cm x 35.5cm*
- **Guide price £500/$945**

Silver Gelatin Print ▲

- *1997*

"Le Grande Arche, Paris, 1997" by Marcus Davies. With photographer's signature verso.

- *16cm x 20cm*
- **Guide price £400/$756**

Signed Print ▶

- *1992*

"A detective amuses colleagues" taken in Oughtraud, C. Galway, in 1992 by Leo Regan. A silver gelatin print, signed verso

- *30.5cm x 40cm*
- **Guide price £300/$567**

Finkelstein Print ▲

- *1965*

"Andy and Cow Wallpaper, 1965" by Nat Finkelstein. Silver gelatin print from an edition limited to 10. Signed verso.

- *30.5cm x 40cm*
- **Guide price £600/$1,134**

Beatles Print ▶

- *1964*

The Beatles on the way to Teddington studios, 1964, by John 'Hoppy' Hopkins. Silver gelatin print, signed verso.

- *51cm x 61cm*
- **Guide price £500/$945**

John Hopkins Print ▲

- *circa 1964*

"The Rolling Stones, studio group" by John 'Hoppy' Hopkins. Silver gelatin print, signed verso.

- *35.5cm x 51cm*
- **Guide price £350/$662**

'Dunroamin' Print ▲

- *1998*

Untitled C-type print by Jason Oddy taken in 1998 as part of the "Dunroamin" series. Signed verso.

- *30.5cm x 35.5cm*
- **Guide price £500/$945**

Luther King Print ▲

- *1964*

"Martin Luther King at Oxford peace conference, 1964" by John 'Hoppy' Hopkins. Signed verso.

- *25.5 x 20cm*
- **Guide price £200/$378**

C-Type Print ▼

- *1994*

"Dog in back garden, 1994" by Matthew Murray. C-type print, signed verso.

- *30.5cm x 35.5cm*
- **Guide price £200/$378**

Bob Willoughby Print ▼

- *1967*

Silver gelatin print by Bob Willoughby of Katherine Hepburn walking in the Wicklow mountains in Ireland in 1967 during the filming of "The Lion in Winter". Signed recto.

- *30.5cm x 40cm*
- **Guide price £600/$1,134**

Louis Armstrong Print ◀

- *1950*

"Louis Armstrong with All Stars, 1950" by Bob Willoughby. A silver gelatin print, signed verso.

- *30.5cm x 35.5cm*
- **Guide price £600/$1,134**

Locomotive Print ▲

- *1955*

"Locomotive 605, about to be washed, 1955" by O. Winston Link. Silver gelatin print, signed verso.
- *30.5cm x 40cm*
- **Guide price £1,750/$3,308**

Chrystel Lebas Print ▲

- *2000*

"The Alps, 2000" from the "Moving Landscape" series by Chrystel Lebas. C-type print, signed and titled verso.
- *30.5cm x 40cm*
- **Guide price £400/$756**

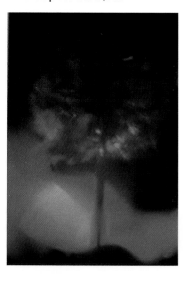

Humphrey Spender Print ▶

- *1937*

"Bolton, 1937" by Humphrey Spender. For mass observation. Silver gelatin print, signed and titled recto.
- *30.5cm x 40cm*
- **Guide price £300/$567**

'Moving Landscape' Print ▲

- *1999*

"Kent, 1999" from the "Moving Landscape" series by Chrystel Lebas. C-type print, signed and titled verso.
- *30.5cm x 40cm*
- **Guide price £400/$756**

Silver Gelatin Print ▲

- *1955*

"The Popes and the last passenger steam train, 1955" taken by O. Winston Link. Silver gelatin print, signed verso by the photographer.
- *30.5 x 40cm*
- **Guide price £1,750/$3,308**

C-Type Print ◀

- *2000*

"Hot Dandelion, 2000" by photographer Delilah Dyson. C-type print, signed verso.
- *30.5cm x 40cm*
- **Guide price £250/$473**

Cornel Lucas Print ▲

- *1948*

"Yvonne de Carlo as Salome" by Cornel Lucas. A silver gelatin print, signed recto and titled verso.
- *30.5cm x 40cm*
- **Guide price £400/$756**

South Pacific Print ▲

- *1948*

"Movie cameraman in the South Pacific, 1948" by Cornel Lucas. Silver gelatin print, signed recto.
- *30.5cm x 40cm*
- **Guide price £400/$756**

Dyson Print ▼

- *2000*

"Snow Drops, 2000" by Delilah Dyson. C-type print, signed verso.
- *30.5cm x 40cm*
- **Guide price £300/$567**

John Hopkins Print ▼

- *1964*

"Thelonius Monk" taken in 1964 by John 'Hoppy' Hopkins. Silver gelatin print, signed recto.
- *30.5cm x 40cm*
- **Guide price £350/$662**

POSTERS

Ovaltine Nightcap ▲

- *circa 1950*

An Ovaltine advertisement of a young smiling lady holding a cup and saucer with the words "Ovaltine – The World's Best Nightcap".

- *37cm x28cm*
- **Guide price £75/$142**

Marcella Cigars ▲

- *circa 1950*

Poster of a hand holding five Marcella cigars and the words "A Grand Shilling's Worth".

- *42cm x 36cm*
- **Guide price £120/$227**

Salamander Brandy ▼

- *circa 1950*

Advertising poster for Salamander Brandy with a view of a village and the sea in the background and a cartouche of the factory, a large bottle of cognac, and a bunch of grapes in the foreground.

- *41cm x 36cm*
- **Guide price £145/$274**

Metrovick Lamps ▼

- *circa 1950*

Advertising poster of a lady wearing a cream dress leaning over a red chair advertising Metrovick Lamps for Metropolitan.

- *48cm x 36cm*
- **Guide price £75/$142**

Grapefruit Breakfast ◄

- *circa 1950*

Gentleman in a suit and bowler hat seated on a grapefruit with the slogan "Start the day on a Grapefruit".

- *26cm x 46cm*
- **Guide price £55/$104**

Monarch Whisky ▲

- *circa 1950*

The Monarch Old Scotch Whisky advertising poster.

- *37cm x 23cm*
- **Guide price £65/$123**

Bullitt ▼

- *1969*

"Bullitt" with Steve McQueen. US One sheet.

- *27cm x 21cm*
- **Guide price £680/$1,285**

Way Out West
- *1937*
"Way Out West" with Laurel and Hardy.
- *28cm x36cm*
- **Guide price £650/$1,229**

Ice Cold in Alex
- *1958*
"Ice Cold in Alex" with John Mills and Sylvia Syms. Directed by Bruce Robinson.
- *height 102cm*
- **Guide price £350/$662**

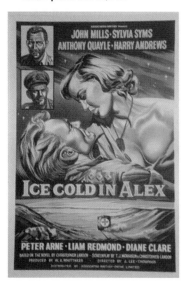

The Untouchables
- *1987*
"The Untouchables", with Kevin Costner, Sean Connery and Robert De Niro.
- *28cm x 36cm*
- **Guide price £75/$142**

Blade Runner
- *1982*
"Blade Runner" with Harrison Ford.
- *104cm x 58cm*
- **Guide price £400/$756**

Apocalypse Now
- *1979*
"Apocalypse Now" with Marlon Brando. German double panel.
- *85cm x 1.18m*
- **Guide price £1,300/$2,457**

The Birds
- *1963*
"The Birds" by Alfred Hitchcock, with Tippi Hedren and Rod Taylor.
- *1.02m x 79cm*
- **Guide price £500/$945**

The Apartment
- *1960*
"The Apartment" starring Jack Lemmon and Shirley McLaine.
- *28cm x 36cm*
- **Guide price £85/$161**

Sherlock Holmes Faces Death
- *1951*
"Sherlock Holmes Faces Death". Spanish one sheet.
- *1.04m x 29cm*
- **Guide price £450/$851**

315

Jaws II ▼

- *1961*

US linen-backed "Jaws II" poster with artwork by Mick McGinty.

- *104cm x 69cm*
- **Guide price £500/$945**

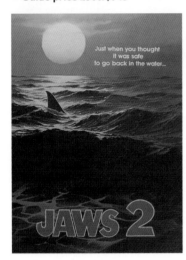

Bay of Naples ▶

- *1950*

Lady holding a guitar seated on a boat, with the words "A trip thro' the Bay of Naples".

- *48cm x 54cm*
- **Guide price £45/$85**

Cycles Favor Motos ◀

- *circa 1950*

Advertisement for Cycles Favor Motos featuring a mechanic wearing a cap and blue overalls, holding a bicycle in one hand and a motor bike in the other.

- *46cm x 50cm*
- **Guide price £75/$142**

Cruising the West Indies ▼

- *circa 1960*

"Southampton to the West Indies" travel poster showing a cruise liner, tropical fruit, and the words "French Line – A Service of Distinction".

- *80cm x 48cm*
- **Guide price £85/$161**

Psycho ▼

- *circa 1960*

Showing Alfred Hitchcock on a blank background. Printed in England by W.E. Berry and released by Paramount Pictures. In style B.

- *length 100cm, width 76cm*
- **Guide price £5,000/$9,450**

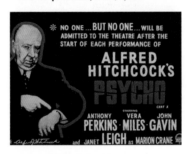

Night of the Demon ◀

- *circa 1960*

"The Night of the Demon"/"La notte del demonio" Italian linen-backed poster.

- *140cm x 99cm*
- **Guide price £1,500/$2,835**

The Italian Job ▼

- *1969*

"The Italian Job" with Michael Caine. UK Mini Quad.

- *31cm x 41cm*
- **Guide price £5/$9**

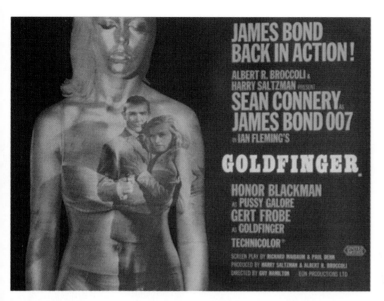

Goldfinger ◀

- *1964*

"Goldfinger" poster with Sean Connery as James Bond and Honor Blackman as Pussy Galore.

- *76cm x 101cm*
- **Guide price £2,800/$5,292**

The Godfather ▲

- *1972*

"The Godfather" and "Italian Photobusta".

- *45cm x 65cm*
- **Guide price £350/$662**

Othello ◀

- *1955*

Original Czech poster, linen backed, depicting Othello.

- *84cm x 58cm*
- **Guide price £500/$945**

Withnail and I ▼

- *1987*

"Withnail and I" starring Richard E. Grant and Paul McGann.

- *height 103cm*
- **Guide price £400/$756**

Alfie ▼

- *1966*

"Alfie", with Michael Caine.

- *28cm x 36cm*
- **Guide price £95/$180**

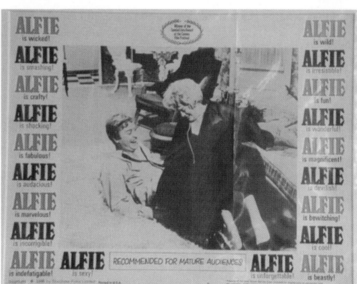

High Society ▼

- *1956*

"High Society" with Frank Sinatra, Grace Kelly and Bing Crosby.

- *28cm x 36cm*
- **Guide price £120/$227**

NA Vychod Od Raje/Giant ▲

- *1955*

Original Czech poster, linen backed, for the first Czech release of "Giant" starring James Dean.

- *84cm x 58cm*
- **Guide price £750/$1,418**

James Bond Poster ▶

- *1967*

"Goldfinger" with Sean Connery.

- *56cm x 102cm*
- **Guide price £1,200/$2,268**

Blow-Up ▲

- *circa 1967*

Framed behind glass, in style A. Designed by Acy R. Iehman.

- *length 100cm, width 76cm*
- **Guide price £500/$945**

Deserto Rosso ▶
- 1964

Italian linen backed poster for "Deserto Rosso".
- 2.01m x 1.4m
- **Guide price £2,500/$4,725**

Persona ◀
- 1966

Swedish linen-backed poster for Ingmar Berman's "Persona" with Bibi Andersson and Liv Ullmann.
- 99cm x 69cm
- **Guide price £1,800/$3,402**

Badlands ▼
- 1974

British linen-backed film poster for "Badlands".
- 76cm x 102cm
- **Guide price £375/$709**

Sporting Life ◀
- 1963

British linen-backed poster for "This Sporting Life" with art by Renatop Fratini.
- 104cm x 69cm
- **Guide price £300/$567**

Prazdniny V Rime/ Roman Holiday ▲
- 1953

Original Czech poster, linen backed, promoting the film "Roman Holiday" with Audrey Hepburn.
- 84cm x 58cm
- **Guide price £500/$945**

Stand-Up Card Sign ▲
- circa 1940

A Hartley's three-dimensional stand-up card sign.
- height 53cm
- **Guide price £160/$303**

French Cancan ▶

- *1955*

Linen-backed "French Cancan" poster with art by Rene Gruau.

- *1.6m x 1.19m*
- **Guide price £2,250/$4,253**

Battleship Potemkin ▲

- *1925*

Poster for first Japanese release of "The Battleship Potemkin".

- *76cm x 51cm*
- **Guide price £600/$1,134**

Apocalypse Now ▲

- *1979*

Australian linen-backed poster for "Apocalypse Now".

- *102cm x 69cm*
- **Guide price £350/$662**

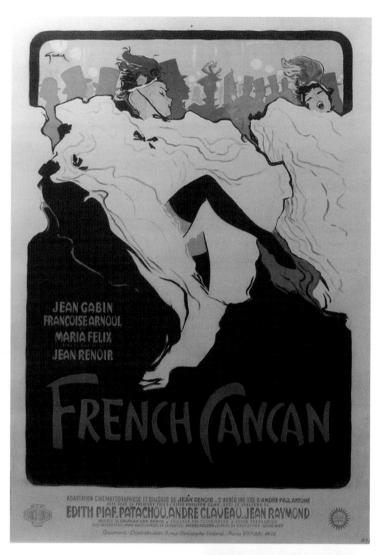

Italian Rififi ▶

- *1955*

Italian linen-backed poster for "Rififi" by Jules Dassin.

- *140cm x 99cm*
- **Guide price £1,250/$2,363**

Forbidden Planet ◀

- *1956*

American linen-backed poster for landmark science fiction film "Forbidden Planet" with Leslie Nielsen.

- *104cm x 69cm*
- **Guide price £7,500/$14,175**

Czerwona Pustynia ▼

- *1964*

Polish "Il Deserto Rosso"/"Czerwona Pustynia" poster with art by Witold Janowski.

- *84cm x 58cm*
- **Guide price £600/$1,134**

Embossed Tin Sign ▼

- *circa 1910*

An embossed tin sign showing an advertisement for alcohol.

- *height 31cm*
- **Guide price £175/$331**

Rear Window

- *1962*

"Rear Window" 1962 re-issue US sheet.

- *width 29cm*
- **Guide price £600/$1,134**

Gilda

- *1946*

"Gilda", American insert.

- *92cm x 35cm*
- **Guide price £1,600/$3,024**

Love Is My Profession ▼

- *1959*

"Love Is My Profession" (Freiheit dressiert), starring Brigitte Bardot.

- *83cm x 60.5cm*
- **Guide price £350/$662**

Breakfast at Tiffany's ▼

- *1961*

"Breakfast at Tiffany's", starring Audrey Hepburn.

- *28cm x 36cm*
- **Guide price £475/$898**

Manhattan ▼

- *1979*

"Manhattan" Lobby Carl.

- *28cm x 36cm*
- **Guide price £95/$180**

Revenge of the Creature ▲

- *1955*

"Revenge of the Creature" UK Quad John Agar Laurie Nelson.

- *102cm x 60.5cm*
- **Guide price £850/$1,607**

Sleeping Beauty ▼

- *circa 1959*

A paper-backed poster of Walt Disney's *Sleeping Beauty* showing various characters from the story and the title 'Awaken to a World of Wonders!'.

- *length 76cm, width 51cm*
- **Guide price £300/$567**

Ragtime ▼

- *1981*

Original east German poster, paper backed, featuring artwork by B. Krause.

- *81cm x 58cm*
- **Guide price £250/$473**

My Fair Lady ◄

- *1965*

"My Fair Lady" with Audrey Hepburn and Rex Harrison.

- *75cm x 1.37m*
- **Guide price £450/$851**

The Enforcer ▲

- *1977*

"The Enforcer" with Clint Eastwood as Dirty Harry.

- *28cm x 36cm*
- **Guide price £95/$180**

Turtle Diary ▲

- *1985*

Original British poster, paper backed, featuring artwork by Andy Warhol, for the film "Turtle Diary".

- *76cm x 102cm*
- **Guide price £225/$426**

Moulin Rouge ▲
- *1952*
Original Polish poster, paper backed and unfolded, by Lucjan Jagodzinski.
- *84cm x 58cm*
- **Guide price £1,800/$3,402**

Yellow Submarine ▼
- *1969*
"Yellow Submarine" with the Beatles. US One sheet.
- *height 104cm*
- **Guide price £12,500/$23,625**

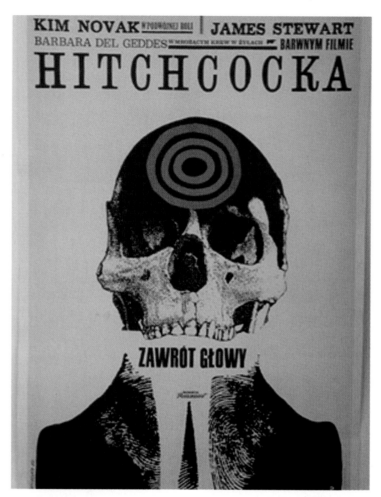

Planet of the Apes ◄
- *circa 1968*
A linen-backed, cartoon style Romanian poster with title 'Planeta Maimutelor'.
- *length 97cm, width 69cm*
- **Guide price £950/$1,796**

Zawrot Glowy/Vertigo ▲
- *1958*
Original polish poster, linen backed, with artwork by Roman Cieslewicz.
- *84cm x 58cm*
- **Guide price £1,200/$2,268**

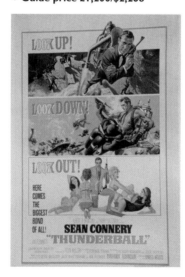

Casablanca ▲
- *circa 1961*
Original Italian 1961 re-release. Art by Campejgi Silvano. Showing stars' names and the Islamic skyline.
- *length 2m, width 1.4m*
- **Guide price £7,500/$14,175**

Thunderball ▲
- *1965*
"Thunderball" with Sean Connery.
- *41cm x 27cm*
- **Guide price £1,100/$2,079**

From Russia with Love ▲

- *1963*
"From Russia with Love", starring Sean Connery. Original UK quad.
- *76cm x 105cm*
- **Guide price £2,750/$5,198**

Breakfast at Tiffany's ▲

- *1961*
"Colazione da Tiffany" poster.
- *27.5cm x 51cm*
- **Guide price £1,000/$1,890**

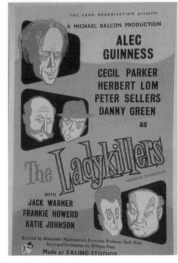

The Ladykillers ▲

- *1955*
"The Ladykillers" with Alec Guiness, Peter Sellers and Frankie Howard. Made at Ealing Studios. UK one sheet.
- *40cm x 69cm*
- **Guide price £2,000/$3,780**

Dial M For Murder ▼

- *1954*
"Dial M for Murder" by Alfred Hitchcock.
- *36cm x 41cm*
- **Guide price £1,000/$1,890**

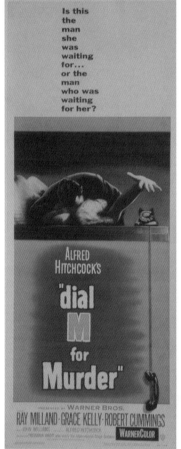

Midnight Cowboy ▼

- *1969*
"Midnight Cowboy" with Dustin Hoffman. UK quad.
- *76cm x 102cm*
- **Guide price £190/$360**

Anatomy of Murder ◄

- *circa 1959*
Graphic artist style by Saul Bass. Photographs by Sam Leavitt.
- *length 100cm, width 76cm*
- **Guide price £850/$1,607**

Le Mans ▲

- *circa 1971*
French poster showing Steve McQueen. Artist Rene Fenacci.
- *length 61cm, width 41cm*
- **Guide price £150/$284**

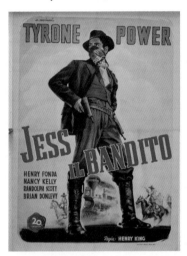

Jess Il Bandito ▲

- *circa 1939*
Showing actor Tyrone Power. Released by 20th Century Fox.
- *length 2m, width 1.4m*
- **Guide price £1,800/$3,402**

Goldfinger ▲

- *1964*
"Goldfinger" starring Sean Connery.
- *28cm x 36cm*
- **Guide price £325/$614**

Get Carter ▼

- *circa 1971*

With photographic captions from the film by M.G.M.

- *length 100cm, width 69cm*
- **Guide price £425/$803**

Il Diritto di Uccidere/ In a Lonely Place ▼

- *1950*

Original Italian poster, linen backed, featuring artwork by Anselmo Ballester.

- *140cm x 99cm*
- **Guide price £3,500/$6,615**

The Graduate ▼

- *1967*

"The Graduate", with Dustin Hoffman and Anne Bancroft (framed).

- *28cm x 36cm*
- **Guide price £350/$662**

Some Like it Hot ▲

- *1959*

"Some Like it Hot", with Marilyn Monroe, Tony Curtis and Jack Lemmon.

- *28cm x 36cm*
- **Guide price £450/$851**

La Mort Aux Trousses/ North by Northwest ▲

- *1959*

Original French poster, paper backed, for the Hitchcock film "North by Northwest".

- *79cm x 61cm*
- **Guide price £225/$426**

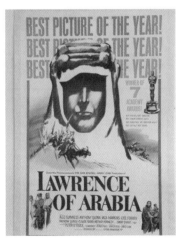

Lawrence of Arabia ▲

- *1963*

"Lawrence of Arabia" with Peter O'Toole. Re-issue 1963 of 1962 film.

- *102cm x 56cm*
- **Guide price £650/$1,229**

The Odd Couple ▼

- *1968*

"The Odd Couple", with Walter Matthau and Jack Lemmon.

- *28cm x 36cm*
- **Guide price £140/$265**

Vertigo ▼

- *1958*

"Vertigo", The International vision, by Alfred Hitchcock, with Kim Novak and James Steward.

- *83cm x 60.5cm*
- **Guide price £2,500/$4,725**

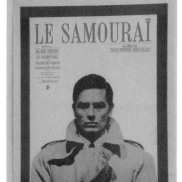

Le Samourai ▲

- *1967*

"Le Samourai", produced by Alain Delon, starring Nathalie Delon and François Perier.

- *height 76cm*
- **Guide price £450/$851**

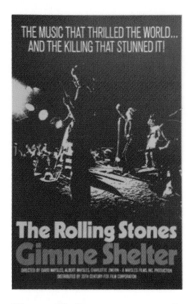

Gimme Shelter ▲

- *1970*

Original US poster, paper backed, for the Rolling Stones' film "Gimme Shelter".

- *104cm x 69cm*
- **Guide price £350/$662**

Jour de Fête ▼

- *1948*

Original French poster, linen backed, for the Jacques Tati film "Jour de Fête", featuring artwork by Eric.

- *160cm x 119cm*
- **Guide price £2,500/$4,725**

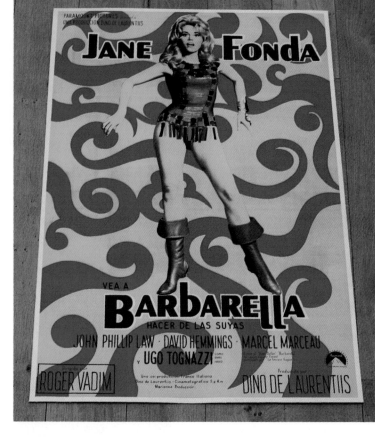

Que Viva Mexiko ◄

- *1932*

Original east German poster, paper backed, by Wenzer.

- *81cm x 58cm*
- **Guide price £180/$341**

Barbarella Poster ▲

- *circa 1968*

Argentinian poster showing Jane Fonda. Conservation backed.

- *height 107cm, width 71cm*
- **Guide price £500/$945**

Viaggio in Italia ▲

- *1953*

Original Italian poster, linen backed, by Mauro Innocenti for the film "Viaggio in Italia".

- *201cm x 140cm*
- **Guide price £1,800/$3,402**

2 Hommes Dans Manhattan ▲

- *1959*

Original French poster, linen backed, by Georges Kerfyser, for "2 Hommes dans Manhattan".

- *79cm x 61cm*
- **Guide price £250/$473**

Rosemary's Baby ▲

- *1968*
Original British poster designed by Steve Frankfurt.
- *104cm x 69cm*
- **Guide price £350/$662**

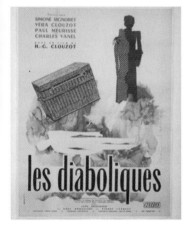

Les Diaboliques ▲

- *1955*
Original French poster, linen backed, style A, with artwork by Raymond Gid.
- *160cm x 119cm*
- **Guide price £1,500/$2,835**

Taxi Driver ▼

- *1976*
Original US poster, linen backed, featuring artwork by Guy Peelaert, Style A.
- *104cm x 69cm*
- **Guide price £500/$945**

Le Mépris ▼

- *circa 1963*
Starring Brigitte Bardot. Linen backed poster with artwork by George Allard.
- *length 79cm, width 61cm*
- **Guide price £600/$1,134**

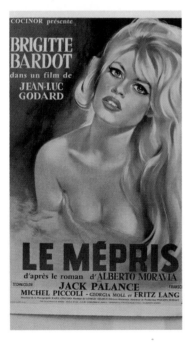

Goldfinger Poster ◄

- *circa 1964*
Original French poster by Jeism Mascii. Released by United Artists. Captions in French.
- *length 79cm, width 61cm*
- **Guide price £500/$945**

The Godfather Part II ▲

- *1974*
"The Godfather Part II", with Al Pacino.
- *28cm x 36cm*
- **Guide price £125/$237**

La Donna Che Visse due Volte/Vertigo ▲

- *1958*
Original Italian poster featuring art by Sandro Simeoni, for the Hitchcock film, "Vertigo".
- *140cm x 99cm*
- **Guide price £1,500/$2,835**

Sueurs Froides/Cold Sweat ◄

- *1958*
Original French poster, paper backed, art by Claude Venin.
- *79cm x 61cm*
- **Guide price £425/$803**

F for Fake ▼

- *1973*
Original US poster, linen backed, designed by Donn Trethewey.
- *104cm x 69cm*
- **Guide price £500/$945**

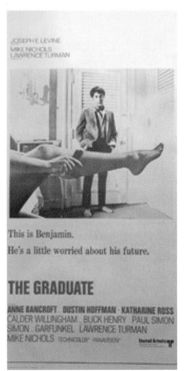

The Graduate ▼

- *1967*
Original US poster, linen backed, designed by United Artists Corporation.
- *2.06m x 1.04m*
- **Guide price £2,250/$4,253**

RADIOS, TV & SOUND EQUIPMENT

Wrist Radio ▼
- *1960*

Panasonic blue plastic radio worn around the wrist.
- *17cm x 18cm*
- **Guide price £50/$95**

Isis Plastic Radio ▲
- *circa 1960*

Isis white plastic radio in the form of the word "radio".
- *7cm x 25cm*
- **Guide price £55/$104**

Pye Record Player ▼
- *1955*

Pye record player in a bow-fronted teak case with cream turntable. Holds ten records on stack.
- *height 26cm*
- **Guide price £100/$189**

Panasonic Novelty Radio ▼
- *1960*

Yellow plastic wrist radio by Panasonic.
- *17cm x 18cm*
- **Guide price £50/$95**

Perdio Transistor ▼
- *1962*

Perdio Super Seven Transistor radio, inscribed with "Real Morocco leather made in England", on the back, with a dial for an aerial and phone or tape, and a large brass dial and gold writing.
- *height 12.5cm*
- **Guide price £38/$72**

Decca Gramophone ▲
- *1951*

Children's gramophone in original box with nursery rhyme pictures on each side and carrying handle.
- *18cm x 32cm*
- **Guide price £150/$284**

Radio and TV Diary 1957 ▲
- *1957*

Radio and TV Diary for 1957 with photographs on each page of actors and musicians. Showing a photograph of David Attenborough.
- *height 12cm*
- **Guide price £10/$19**

Dansette Portable Radio ◀
- *1961*

Grey plastic Dansette portable radio with beige plastic handle and large circular dial.
- *14cm x 21cm*
- **Guide price £45/$85**

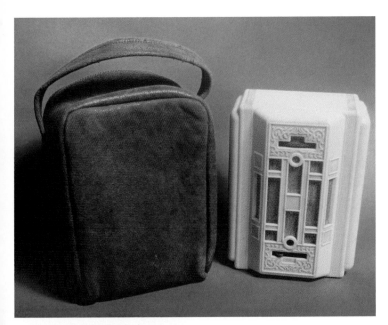

Portable Radio ◄

- *circa 1955*

A small portable radio with original leather protective case. Medium and long waves.
- *height 11cm*
- **Guide price £45/$85**

Crystal Set ▲

- *circa 1910*

An English Edwardian crystal set in mahogany case with brass fittings. In good condition.
- *height 30cm*
- **Guide price £585/$1,106**

Calypso Radio ▼

- *circa 1960*

Grey plastic Calypso radio with circular dial.
- *18cm x 23cm*
- **Guide price £28/$54**

Pye Record Player ▲

- *1955*

Pye record player in a grey with white polka dot case, with unusual curved sides, white plastic carrying handles and a black and gold sparkling grill.
- *height 25cm*
- **Guide price £75/$142**

Kidditune Record Player ▼

- *1962*

Red plastic battery-operated record player by Marx Toys in original box complete with original records.
- *13cm x 26cm*
- **Guide price £65/$123**

Ekco RS3 ▲

- *1931*

Art Deco bakelite radio standing on metal feet. This model was one of the first bakelite radios to be manufactured in the United Kingdom.
- *height 45cm*
- **Guide price £800/$1,512**

Roberts Metal and Teak Radio ▼

- *1968*

Roberts radio with metal and teak case and carrying handle.
- *23cm x 38cm*
- **Guide price £38/$72**

HMV Record Player ▲

- *1958*

His Master's Voice record player in a red and mottled grey case with red plastic carrying handles, with a Monarch deck.
- *height 25cm*
- **Guide price £75/$142**

Philips 930A ▲

- *1931*

Philips Art Deco radio with an unusual keel-shaped shaped body, and a stars and wavy line design, standing on a square base and legs.
- *height 48cm*
- **Guide price £800/$1,512**

Wondergram Record Player ▶

- *1959*

Very rare Wondergram record player for 45 rpm and 33/one-third rpm in anodised aluminium case, with folding legs. Made in England by Baird.
- *height 8.5cm*
- **Guide price £350/$662**

E.A.R. Triple Four ▲

- *1958*

E.A.R. Triple four record player in a blue and grey Rexine case with cream piping and handles.
- *height 27cm*
- **Guide price £80/$152**

Bakelite Radio ▲

- *1930*

Brown bakelite radio with lattice-effect front grille.
- **Guide price £95/$180**

Dansette Conquest ▼

- *1959*

Dansette Conquest green and cream record player, standing on four black tapered legs on circular base. Holds ten records on stack. Fully restored and re-conditioned. With cream handles each side for carrying.
- *height 67cm*
- **Guide price £80/$152**

HMV Record Player ▶

- *1957*

His Master's Voice record player in a chocolate brown case with cream interior and black handles.
- *height 27cm*
- **Guide price £75/$142**

Roberts Radio ◀

- *1970*

Roberts radio in red leather case.
- *15cm x 22cm x 8cm*
- **Guide price £60/$114**

Philips Radio ▲

- *circa 1931*

Hexagonal with oxidised bronze grill. Sought after for its unusual appearance.
- *height 43cm*
- **Guide price £500/$945**

Bush TV ▼

- *circa 1949*

Model 22 television produced by Bush. This was one of the most desired of all British bakelite models.

- *height 39cm*
- **Guide price £300/$567**

HMV TV/Radio Combination ▲

- *circa 1938*

Model No. 904 television and radio combined unit produced by HMV. This model uses the same chassis as Marconi model No. 706.

- *height 45cm*
- **Guide price £1,800/$3,402**

Fada Streamliner ▲

- *1940*

American onyx and amber streamlined Catalin radio, with large oval dial on the right.

- *height 19cm*
- **Guide price £1,000/$1,890**

Intercom Speaker ▲

- *1940s*

English Art Deco-style red intercom system speaker, tube operated.

- *height 28cm*
- **Guide price £100/$189**

GEC Radio ▼

- *circa 1950*

GEC radio with bakelite handles.

- *32cm x 44cm x 17cm*
- **Guide price £55/$104**

Sonorette ▲

- *1940s*

French brown radio in bakelite, with a bulbous form and grille-design speaker.

- *height 34cm*
- **Guide price £500/$945**

JVC Television ▲

- *circa 1968*

A JVC 'Space Helmet' television of spherical form on a square plinth. Monochrome reception.

- *height 60cm*
- **Guide price £200/$378**

CKCO Model AD75 ▲

- *circa 1940*

Wartime English bakelite radio designed by Wells Coates to meet marine needs.

- *height 35cm*
- **Guide price £700/$1,323**

Emersa Radio ▲

- *1932*

American Art Deco bakelite radio with a central fan design.

- *40cm x 50cm*
- **Guide price £300/$567**

German Radio ▼

• circa 1950
A rare post-war German bakelite mains radio.
• height 58cm
• **Guide price £175/$331**

Dansette Major De-luxe ▼

• 1960
Dansette Major de-luxe with a red and cream case, sloping front gold grill and light up Dansette badge, with cream plastic handles each side for carrying.
• height 27cm
• **Guide price £75/$142**

Red Radio ▲

• circa 1965
A typically 1960s round plastic portable radio, giving medium wave reception.
• **Guide price £80/$152**

Murphy Console ▲

• circa 1938
Model A56V. A good-quality middle of the range set costing £30, vision and TV sound only.
• height 86cm
• **Guide price £1,000/$1,890**

Silver Tone Bullet 6110 ◄

• circa 1938
Modern design push-button radio with enormous rotating turning scale. Designed by Clarence Karstacht.
• height 17cm
• **Guide price £1,100/$2,079**

TV/Radio and Gramophone ▲

• 1938
RGD (Radio Gramophone Developments) model RG. Top of the range radiogram. Image viewed through mirror in the lid.
• height 92.5cm
• **Guide price £3,250/$6,143**

Bendix Model 526C ▲

• 1946
Black bakelite American radio with the inscription "Strong Machine Age".
• 28cm x 35cm
• **Guide price £750/$1,418**

American Radio ▲

• circa 1930
Designed by Harold Van Doren. Skyscraper influence, produced by AirKing. Then the largest US bakelite moulding produced.
• height 30cm
• **Guide price £3,000/$5,670**

HMV TV/Radiocode ▲

• circa 1937
Model 900 with mirror lid. A very popular set despite its 80-guinea cost, with speakers extra at £5.
• height 96cm
• **Guide price £1,500/$2,835**

Wooden Radio ▼

• circa 1930
Valve radio housed in wooden display case.
• 30cm x 54cm
• **Guide price £85/$161**

Cossor Table Model ▼

• *1938*

Costing 23 guineas when new, the cheapest pre-war set with sound. A rare set.

• *height 44cm*
• **Guide price £1,000/$1,890**

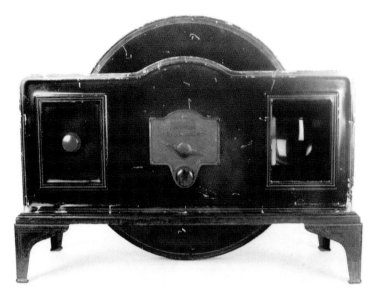

Hacker ▲

• *1964*

Hacker record player in a black and grey case with metal fittings.

• *height 27cm*
• **Guide price £50/$95**

Baird Televisol ▲

• *circa 1930*

'The world's first television', actually a mechanical system as opposed to the later electronic tubes. Viewed through small lens.

• *height 54cm*
• **Guide price £5,000/$9,450**

Grille Radio ▲

• *circa 1945*

Chunky automobile fender grille radio. Made by Sentinel. Very desirable.

• *height 19cm*
• **Guide price £1,000/$1,890**

Mains Radio ▼

• *circa 1950*

A very small, red-cased mains radio by Packard Bell of the USA, with large central dial and minimal controls.

• *height 14cm*
• **Guide price £140/$265**

English Radio ▲

• *circa 1950*

Kiather Brandes BM 20, rare green bakelite radio, made of two exact halves. Made in many colours, some quite unique.

• *height 22cm*
• **Guide price £500/$945**

Invicta Table Model ▲

• *1939*

Model TL5, made by Pye of Cambridge. This is the only known model of Invicta.

• *height 47.5cm*
• **Guide price £800/$1,512**

'KB' Wooden Radio ▲

• *circa 1940*

Fully working radio. One of many produced in Great Britain during World War II.

• *height 46cm, width 53cm*
• **Guide price £125/$237**

Transistor Radio ▲

• *1970*

Roberts transistor radio, in wood and grey plastic.

• *14cm x 22cm*
• **Guide price £60/$114**

ROCK & POP

Record Bag ▶
- *circa 1950*
Plastic multi-coloured bag for carrying
45 rpm records with various musical
instruments.
- *diameter 24cm*
- **Guide price £26/$50**

ABBA Mirror ▲
- *circa 1970*
Mirror with photograph of the band
ABBA.
- *24cm x 20cm*
- **Guide price £16/$30**

Record Case ▶
- *circa 1950*
White plastic carrying case for 45rpm
records with jazz and dancing design.
- *diameter 26cm*
- **Guide price £28/$54**

"Rubber Soul" Test Press ▼
- *circa 1965*
A Parlophone test press features side
two of "Rubber Soul" with white label
and track listing.
- **Guide price £2,250/$4,253**

Top Pop Stars ◀
- *circa 1950*
"Book of Top Pop Stars" with Cliff
Richard on the cover.
- *28cm x 24cm*
- **Guide price £14/$26**

The Move Demo ▼
- *1965*
The only surviving demo by *The Move*,
with one vocal per member and featuring
'Winter Song'.
- **Guide price £7,000/$13,230**

No New York ▼
- *circa 1978*
Produced by Brian Eno and recorded at
Big Apple Studio, NY Cover by Steve
Keisler.
- **Guide price £65/$123**

Sex Pistols ▼
- *circa 1980*
Sex Pistols t-shirt with a picture of the
Queen and the words "God Save the
Queen".
- *50cm x 42cm*
- **Guide price £25/$48**

Pat As I See Him ▲

• *1966*

"Pat As I See Him", a pen and ink portrait on an envelope by Joe Meek of his lover. Annotated in verso "Pat was Meek's boyfriend and was present at the landlady's shooting and Meek's subsequent suicide".

• **Guide price £5,250/$9,923**

Michael Jackson Doll ▲

• *1995*

A singing Michael Jackson doll wearing a white shirt and black trousers in original box.

• **Guide price £47/$89**

Stone Age ▲

• *1971*

"Stone Age" by *The Rolling Stones*.

• **Guide price £580/$1,097**

The Beatles Live at BBC ▲

• *circa 1995*

The only existing maquette for the proposed HMV box set, 'Live at the BBC', permission for which was withdrawn by Apple.

• **Guide price £5,025/$9,497**

Beatles Album ▼

• *circa 1966*

'The Beatles Yesterday and Today'. Original USA stereo with 'Butcher' cover.

• **Guide price £825/$1,559**

Andy Warhol Magazine ▶

• *December 1966*

Set of postcards and flip-book magazine incorporating Velvet Underground flexidisc.

• **Guide price £950/$1,796**

Andy Warhol ▼

• *1967*

"Andy Warhol's Index Box". First hardback edition-Random House USA complete and in working order including flexi-disc recorded by the *Velvet Underground*. Lou Reed's eye has not even popped!

• **Guide price $1,500/$2,835**

Instant Karma ▲

• *1971*

John Ono Lennon "Instant Karma" produced by Phil Spector.

• **Guide price £117/$221**

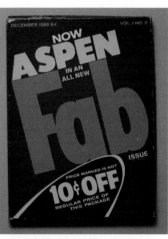

Time Will Pass ▼
• 1977
"Time Will Pass" by the Spriguns. Distributed by The Decca Record Company Limited, London.
• **Guide price £175/$331**

Status Quo ▼
• 1970
"In my Chair/Gerdundula" Status Quo.
• **Guide price £72/$137**

Equinoxe 4 ▲
• 1979
"Equinoxe 4", an album by Jean Michel Jarre, with a signed autograph in black biro on front cover.
• **Guide price £60/$114**

Yellow Submarine ▲
• 1960s
The Beatles "Yellow Submarine and Eleanor Rigby".
• **Guide price £72/$137**

Bob Dylan ◄
• 1961
Bob Dylan's first recording produced by John Hammond.
• **Guide price £735/$1,369**

Beatles' Lady Madonna ▼
• 1968
"The Inner Light, Lady Madonna" by The Beatles.
• **Guide price £72/$137**

Agogo ►
• 1963
"Agogo", with Ray Charles, The Supremes, Petula Clark, and The Everly brothers.
• **Guide price £35/$66**

The Monkees ▼
• 1968
The Monkees. Original motion picture sound track "Head".
• **Guide price £95/$180**

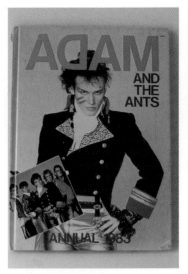

Adam and the Ants ▲
• circa 1970
Annual of Adam and the Ants.
• 24cm x 20cm
• **Guide price £14/$26**

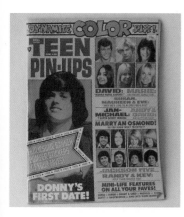

Donny Osmond ▲
- *circa 1970*
Teen Pin-Ups dynamite colour comic featuring Donny Osmond.
- *23cm x 28cm*
- **Guide price £10/$19**

The Who Album ▲
- *1965*
The Who's 'My Generation' album, by Brunswick, with original band line up on cover. Poor condition.
- **Guide price £40/$76**

The Beatles ▶
- *circa 1960*
"The Beatles: An Illustrated Record" by R. Carr and T. Tyler.
- *23cm x 30cm*
- **Guide price £20/$38**

Latin ala Lee ▲
- *circa 1950*
Peggy Lee album and cover.
- *width 42cm*
- **Guide price £7/$13**

Beatles First No. 1 ◀
- *circa 1963*
A copy of the 'Red A' label demo 45 rpm recording of 'From Me to You' and 'Thank You Girl' – The Beatles first No. 1.
- **Guide price £695/$1,314**

'The Beautiful Freaks' ▲
- *circa 1969*
Oz magazine issue no. 24, with cover by Robert Crumb.
- **Guide price £30/$57**

Slade in Flame ◀
- *circa 1970*
Rare album and cover of *Slade* in Flame.
- *42cm x 42cm*
- **Guide price £20/$38**

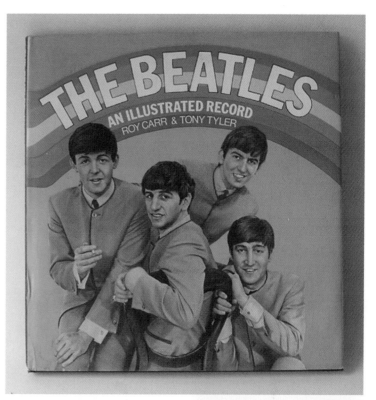

Powder Compact ▲
- *circa 1963*
A circular powder compact featuring a Dezo Hoffman black and white shot of *The Beatles*.
- **Guide price £475/$898**

Collage Postcard ▲
- *9th November 1978*
'Que serait la vie sans les soirs?', signed by Genesis P. Orridge and dedicated to Mark Penny.
- **Guide price £950/$1,796**

The Police Box ▼

• *1997–87*

"The Police Box" (Sting, Stewart Copeland and Andy Summers) from 1977 to 1987.

• **Guide price £150/$284**

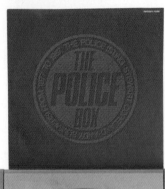

Elvis ▼

• *1971*

"You'll Never Walk Alone" by Elvis. Manufactured and distributed by RCA Limited.

• **Guide price £1,800/$3,402**

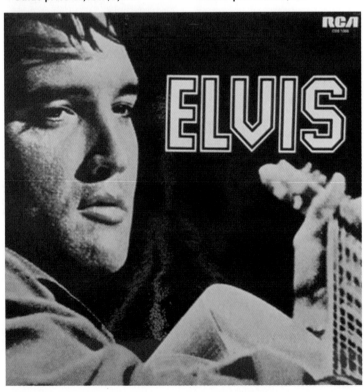

HMS Donovan ▲

• *1971*

"HMS Donovan" record produced by Donovan Engineered by Mike Bobak at Morgan Studios London. All paintings by Patrick.

• **Guide price £130/$246**

Sticky Fingers: Rolling Stones ▲

• *1972*

"Sticky Fingers", an album by *The Rolling Stones*.

• **Guide price £220/$416**

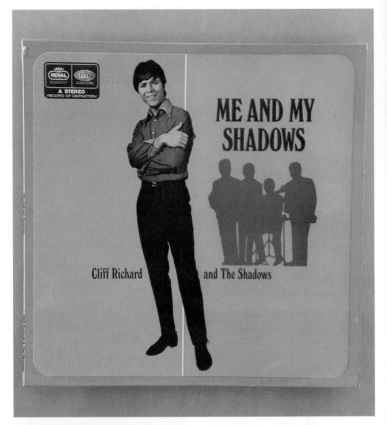

Roy Harper Sophisticated ▼

• *1966*

Roy Harper "Sophisticated Beggar" Strike JHL 105. Test pressing. W/Proff Sleeve in excellent condition.

• **Guide price £550/$1,040**

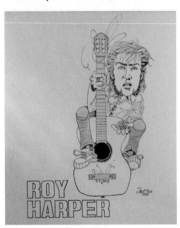

Me and My Shadows ▲

• *1960*

"Me and My Shadows" Cliff Richard export copy in excellent condition.

• **Guide price £70/$133**

The Velvet Underground ◄

• *circa 1967*

Andy Warhol presents the "The Velvet Underground and Nico", original German Issue with Erice Emmerson Sleeve (No Banana).

• **Guide price £248/$469**

Hollywood Blues ▲

• *1970*

"Johnny Almond Music Machine/ Hollywood Blues" by Deram Records.

• **Guide price £60/$114**

The Beatles ▲
• 1994
The Beatles "Live at the BBC". The only existing Marquette for the proposed HMV box set edition-permission for which was refused by Apple as the delayed production was considered potentially detrimental to the 'Anthology' launch.
• **Guide price £4,995/$9,441**

Cliff Richard and the Shadows ▲
• 1964
"A Forever Kind of Love" by Cliff Richard and the Shadows.
• **Guide price £33/$62**

Captain Beefheart ▲
• 1965
Captain Beefheart and his Magic Band/ "Mirror Man" with a broken mirror on the cover.
• **Guide price £95/$180**

John Lennon Signature Watch ◄
• 1991
John Lennon signature watch produced for Toshiba and given to visiting signees.
• **Guide price £200/$378**

Michael Jackson Doll ▼
• 1997
Michael Jackson doll wearing a red leather jacket with zippers and black trousers holding a microphone in original box and sings 'Beat It'.
• **Guide price £37/$70**

Brenda Lee ▼
• 1950
Brenda Lee "Speak to Me Pretty".
• **Guide price £27/$52**

U.F. Orb ▲
• 1992
"U.F. Orb" presented to Kris Weston to recognise sales in the United Kingdom of more than 60,000 copies of the "Big Life/ Wau!" Mr Modo Album. U.F. Orb.
• **Guide price £265/$501**

Travelling Wilburys ▲
• 1990
"Travelling Wilburys", manufactured and distributed by Warner Bros. Records.
• **Guide price £25/$48**

David Bowie CD ▼
• circa 1996
Sampler of 'David Bowie's BBC Sessions 1969–1972', released by Worldwide Music.
• **Guide price £400/$756**

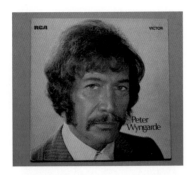

Peter Wyngarde ▲
- *circa 1970*
Cult 1960s–70s TV actor Peter Wyngarde's departure into music. Recorded at Olympic Sound Studios, Surrey.
- **Guide price £120/$227**

Beatles Fan Badge ▲
- *circa 1964*
Official Beatles' Fan Club badge, featuring faces of the Fab Four with their names beside them for identification (for true fans).
- **Guide price £45/$85**

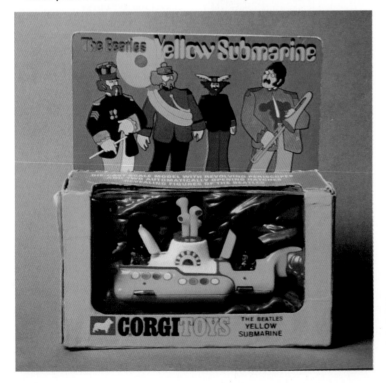

Captain Beefheart ▶
- *1975*
Trout mask replica by *Captain Beefheart and his Magic Band*.
- **Guide price £44/$83**

Mail Art ▲
- *circa 1977*
A double-sided postcard collage by Genesis P. Orridge, featuring an industrial seaside scene and the Queen of England.
- **Guide price £300/$567**

Authentic Corgi Toy ▼
- *1968*
Die-cast metal yellow submarine with revolving periscope and one yellow and one white hatch. From the movie.
- **Guide price £375/$709**

The Dixie Cups ▼
- *1962*
The Dixie Cups "Riding High".
- **Guide price £47/$89**

The Gordon Beck Trio ▼
- *1968*
The Gordon Beck Trio Twin Stereo MJ1 Jazz series, "Gyroscope".
- **Guide price £495/$936**

Beatles' Scarf ▲
- *1960*
Souvenir scarf decorated with pictures of each of *The Beatles*.
- *50cm x 50cm*
- **Guide price £55/$104**

Brum Beat ▲
- *1964*
"Brum Beat" including The Strangers, The Mountain Kings, The Blue Stars, The Cavern Four, and Dave Lacey and The Corvettes.
- **Guide price £120/$227**

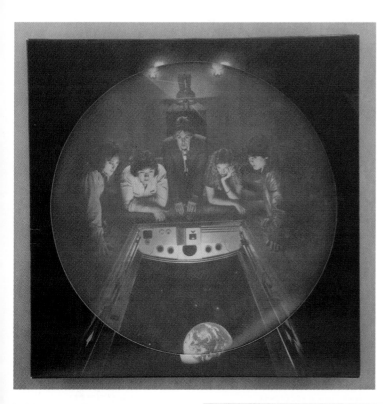

Wings "Back To The Egg" ◀

- *1979*

Wings "Back to the Egg" Promo only picture disc manufactured for the MPL christmas party 1979 but delivered too late for use.

- **Guide price £1,250/$2,363**

Happily Ever After ▲

- *1980*

The Cure, "Happily Ever After".

- **Guide price £45/$85**

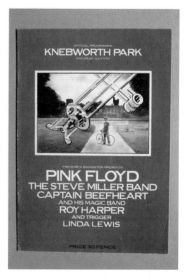

Pink Floyd Programme ▲

- *5th July 1974*

Official programme for Pink Floyd's open-air concert at Knebworth Park, in performance with other bands.

- **Guide price £65/$123**

Whitehouse Present Total Sex ▼

- *circa 1980*

Whitehouse present "Total Sex".

- **Guide price £125/$237**

Psychic TV ◀

- *circa 1982*

A trophy cast in solid brass with an incription around the head and the base and recipient companies on shaft.

- **Guide price £500/$945**

'The Beatles' ▼

- *circa 1964*

The JD 33 rpm of *The Beatles* 'Deutscher Schallplattenclub' edition with red club label. Limited run.

- **Guide price £575/$1,087**

Rolling Stones Hologram ▼

- *1967*

Rolling Stones hologram "Their Satanic Majesties Request" fully signed on front cover.

- **Guide price £249/$471**

Oz Magazine ▲

- *1970*

A copy of issue no. 28, the famous School Kids' Issue.

- **Guide price £80/$152**

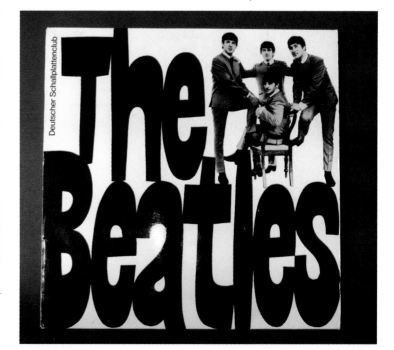

Beatles Poster with John Lennon Signature ▲

- *1977*

Pull-out poster from American magazine "People". Signed by band member John Lennon in 1977.

- *70cm x 45cm*
- **Guide price £700/$1,323**

Rolling Stones Album ◄

- *1971*

Export edition of the *Rolling Stones* "Stone Age" album.

- *30cm x 30cm*
- **Guide price £700/$1,323**

Kylie Promotional Handbag ▼

- *2000*

Promotional "Puma" handbag produced for Kylie Minogue's "Light Years" album. Contains full album and interview CDs.

- *20cm x 20cm*
- **Guide price £100/$189**

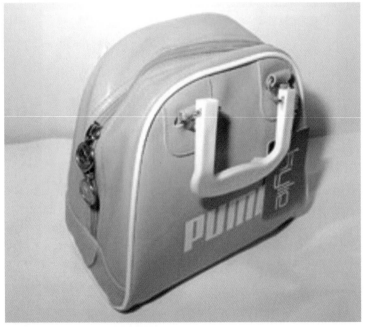

The Verve ▼

- *circa 1992*

Mint condition copy of "Voyager 1" recorded live in New York by The Verve.

- **Guide price £65/$123**

Lennon Lithographs ◄

- *1970*

Packet of explicit lithographs from John Lennon's "Bag One" exhibition. Numbered edition of 1,000.

- *30cm x 50cm*
- **Guide price £500/$945**

Tote Bag with Five 12-inch Singles ▲

- *1985*

Duran Duran tote bag containing five maxi 12-inch singles.

- *30cm x 35cm*
- **Guide price £75/$142**

Brute Force Album ▲

- *circa 1971*

'Extemporaneous', recorded at Olmstead studios, with design and photography by Hal Wilson. Published by Jingle House Music.

- **Guide price £499/$943**

Manic Street Preachers Single ▼

- *1990*

"UK Channel Boredom" flexi-disc supplied with both fanzines.

- *18cm x 18cm*
- **Guide price £120/$227**

Heavy Metal ▼

- *circa 1977*

Issue no. 1 of Heavy Metal magazine, pursuivant on the cult film of the same name.

- **Guide price £20/$38**

Straight No Chaser ▼

• *December 1988*

Issue no.1 of the jazz magazine entitled 'Straight No Chaser'. Issue no. 1 dated December 1998.

• **Guide price £10/$19**

Mojo ▼

• *circa 1995*

Mojo issue no. 24 – They're Back! – published with three different covers – this one in black and white.

• **Guide price £20/$38**

Coil Album ▼

• *circa 1988*

Album entitled 'Gold is the Metal with the Broadest Shoulders', by Coil. Deluxe limited edition, no. 29 of 55.

• **Guide price £500/$945**

U2 Single ▲

• *1979*

U2's first single "Three", individually numbered.

• *20cm x 30cm*

• **Guide price £350/$662**

Madonna Lucky Star Single ▲

• *1983*

Full-length version of the single "Lucky Star" by Madonna.

• *30cm x 30cm*

• **Guide price £80/$152**

Pair of Beatles Stockings ◄

• *1960*

Pair of unused Beatles souvenir stockings in original packet.

• *23cm x 17cm*

• **Guide price £55/$104**

Beatles Film Book ▼

• *Circa 1960*

Book based on the story and making of *The Beatles'* film "Help!", illustrated with black and white photographs.

• *25cm x 14cm*

• **Guide price £15/$28**

John and Yoko "Wedding Album" ◄

• *1969*

USA release of "Wedding Album" eight-track tape including box, slice of wedding cake, poster, photographs, postcard, bag, book, and copy of wedding certificate.

• *30cm x 30cm*

• **Guide price £175/$331**

Siouxsie and The Banshees Memorabilia ▶

- *1981*

Half-page artwork for promotion of the Arabian Knights tour by *Siouxsie and the Banshees*.

- *40cm x 35cm*
- **Guide price £175/$331**

Bruce Springsteen Single ▲

- *1981*

"Cadillac Ranch" single by Bruce Springsteen.

- *18cm x 18cm*
- **Guide price £25/$48**

Beach Boys Album ▲

- *circa 1966*

Special disc jockey/producer copy of "The Best of the Beach Boys" album, released by EMI Records, London.

- **Guide price £184/$348**

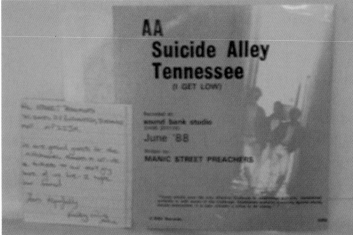

The Police Singles Box ▲

- *1990*

Embossed wooden box containing 10 gold vinyl singles together with a picture disc by *The Police*.

- *18cm x 18cm*
- **Guide price £195/$370**

Manic Street Preachers Single ◀

- *1988*

Double A-side single "Suicide Alley Tennessee" containing a letter from the band.

- *18cm x 18cm*
- **Guide price £995/$1,881**

Black Sabbath Album ▼

- *1971*

Vertigo records album 'Masters of Reality', produced by Roger Bain for Tony Hall Enterprises.

- **Guide price £85/$161**

Sex Pistols Press Pack ▼

- *circa 1976*

'Glitterbest' press pack for 'Anarchy in the UK' album. Twenty pages on white, pink and yellow stock, hand stamped.

- **Guide price £482/$912**

John and Yoko ▼

- *circa 1968*

Album cover for 'Two Virgins' in limited mono version, available by mail order only.

- **Guide price £3,250/$6,143**

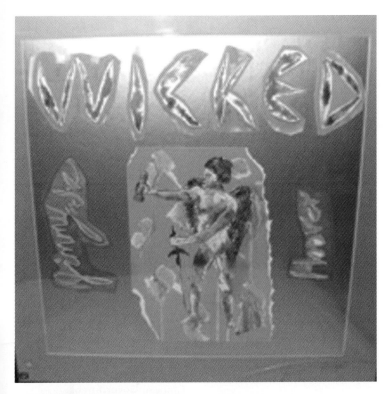

Album Artwork ◀

- *1984*

Unused album artwork for Jimmy the Hoover by Jamie Reid, with glass broken and damaged intentionally for the "Leaving the 21st Century" series held at the Mayfair gallery.
- *50cm x 50cm*
- **Guide price £200/$378**

U2 Helmet ▲

- *1998*

U2 helmet issued to promote the "Best of 1980–1990" album. Limited edition of 50 units.
- *30cm x 25cm x 23cm*
- **Guide price £250/$473**

4AD Calendar ▲

- *1993*

Collector's item calendar issued by record company, 4AD, and designed by 23 Envelope.
- *35cm x 55cm*
- **Guide price £25/$48**

Mojo Magazine ▲

- *circa 1995*

Issue no. 24 showing *The Beatles*. Published in three colours – this one with a red background.
- **Guide price £20/$38**

Withdrawn Single ▼

- *1981*

"Ha ha I'm drowning" single by *The Teardrop Explodes*. Withdrawn issue.
- *18cm x 18cm*
- **Guide price £60/$114**

Brute Force Album featuring John Lennon ▲

- *1970*

"Extemporaneous" album by Brute Force featuring John Lennon.
- **Guide price £395/$748**

Rolling Stones Album ▲

- *1971*

Copy of the *Rolling Stones* album "Sticky Fingers".
- *30cm x 30cm*
- **Guide price £240/$454**

Beatles Dolls ▼

- *1966*

Set of four NEMS/King Features syndicate inflatable cartoon dolls of *The Beatles*.
- *35cm x 15cm*
- **Guide price £120/$227**

Beatles Dress ▲

- *circa 1964*

Official Dutch Beatles' cotton dress in mustard with polka dots. With the makers' card tag.
- **Guide price £395/$748**

Official Carded Jewellery Box ▶

- *1964*

Oval leather and brass accessories, with The Beatles' faces featured on the lid of the box.
- **Guide price £225/$426**

SCRIPOPHILY & PAPER MONEY

Thailand Note ▲

- *1987*

Thailand 60 Baht, Government.

- **Guide price £9/$17**

Israel Shekel ▲

- *1975*

Israeli 100 Shekel with a picture of a building with the 'Bank of Israel' beneath.

- **Guide price £5/$9**

Uzbekistan Note ▼

- *1993*

Uzbekistan '5 sum' note with a decorative wreath and an eagle spreading its wings.

- **Guide price £1/$2**

Rhodesian Pound Note ▶

- *1952*

Southern Rhodesia pound note, showing Queen Elizabeth II.

- **Guide price £125/$237**

Indo China Note ▲

- *1938*

Bank de l'Indochine 1,000 Francs 'Mille Francs' painted with ladies and camels on one side and on the reverse a lady carrying a basket with the sea in the background.

- **Guide price £65/$123**

Mozambique Note ▲

- *1919*

Mozambique 5 Libras note Banco da Beira.

- **Guide price £20/$38**

Romanian Bank Note ▲

- *1938*

Romanian bank note 500 Lei showing two seated Romanian women, one with a baby.

- **Guide price £15/£$28**

Portuguese Note ▲

- *1960*

Banco de Portugal 50 Escudos.

- **Guide price £7/$14**

Chinese Government Treasury Notes ▼

- *1925/29*

Chinese Government 8 per cent 10 year. Treasury note for L100. Sterling.

- **Guide price £50/$95**

Chinese Bond ▼

- *1913*

'Banque Industrielle de Chine' bond decorated with a picture of China and two dogs of Fo.

- **Guide price £42/$80**

Zaire Note ◀

- *1992*

Banque du Zaire cinque millions Zaires.

- **Guide price £4/$8**

Chinese Bond ▼

- *1920*

'Gouvernement de la Republique Chinoise bon du tresors 8 per cent de 1921. Chemin de fer lung Tsing U Hai'.

- **Guide price £15/$28**

Polish Bond ▼

- *1928*

Polish Bond Banku Gospodarstwa Krajowego.

- **Guide price £20/$38**

Chinese Bond ▼

- *1920*

Chinoise bon du tresors 8 per cent. Francs 50,000,000.

- **Guide price £15/$28**

Titanic Stock Certificate ▲

- *1919*

Titanic stock certificate, with the words 'International Mercantile Marine Company' which owned the White Star Line, and showing the *Titanic*.

- **Guide price £50/$95**

Chinese Gold Loan ▲

- *1912*

Chinese Government gold loan of 1912 for L10,000,000 sterling.

- **Guide price £30/$57**

Mexican Bond ▲

- *1921*

Mexican Bond Minas Pedrazzini. Gold and Silver Mining Co.

- **Guide price £20/$38**

Quebec Railway Company Bonds ▼

- *1907*

The Atlantic Quebec and Western Railway Company. Five per cent. First mortgage debenture bonds for 9,050,000 dollars.

- **Guide price £45/$85**

Mining & Railway Co. Ltd. ▼

- *1936*

The El Oro Mining & Railway Company, Limited.

- **Guide price £52/$99**

Russian Bond ▲

- *1914*

Russian South Eastern bond to the value of 945 roubles.

- **Guide price £7/$14**

Gold Mining Share Certificate ▼

- *1900*

The Road Block Gold Mining Company of India Limited share certificate.

- **Guide price £28/$54**

White English Note ▼

- *1944*

Bank of England white five pound note.

- **Guide price £70/$133**

National Currency $20 Dollar Note ▼

- *1900*

$20 dollar note issued by the Citizen's Bank of Eureka, Kansas, during the Battle of Lexington.

- **Guide price £595/$1,125**

American Note ▼

- *1995*

American note in the amount of $2.

- **Guide price £3/$6**

Bank of England Note ▼

- *1950*

White £5 note issued by the Bank of England.

- **Guide price £90/$171**

£50 Banknote ▶

- *1987*

English £50 note signed by David Somerset.

- **Guide price £95/$180**

Military Payment Note ▲

- *1970*

Military payment certificate to the value of 10 cents.

- **Guide price £6/$12**

Seychelles Note ▲

- *1972*

Government of Seychelles Rs. 50 note, carrying a portrait of Queen Elizabeth II.

- **Guide price £385/$728**

Columbia Pictures Note ▲

- *circa 1960*

Shares note issued by Columbia Pictures Corporation.

- **Guide price £9/$17**

Chinese Bond ▶

- *1913*

Gold bond note issued by the Chinese Government.

- **Guide price £25/$48**

Scottish Pound Note ▼

- *1969*

£1 note issued by the Bank of Scotland.

- **Guide price £25/$48**

Lebanese Bond ▼

- *1949*

L5,000 bond issued by the Lebanese government.

- **Guide price £8/$16**

Shares Note ▲

- *1913*

Shares note issued by the Marconi Wireless Company.

- **Guide price £35/$66**

Bolivian Note ▲

- *1928*

$b1 note issued by the Central Bank of Bolivia.

- **Guide price £4/$8**

Queen Victoria Letter ▼

• *19th August 1954*
To M. le Comte de Mensdorff Pouilly.
Written in German and sent from
Windsor Castle.

• **Guide price £600/$1,134**

Mexican Bond ▼

• *1921*
Mina Pedrazzini Gold and Silver Mining
Co.

• **Guide price £20/$38**

Caribbean Note ▼

• *1975*
EC$100 dollar note issued by the East
Caribbean Currency Authority, bearing a
portrait of Queen Elizabeth II.

• **Guide price £175/$331**

German Bond ▶

• *1909*
DM 10,000 bond from Germany

• **Guide price £15/$28**

Scottish Pound Note ▲

• *1921*
£1 note issued by The Bank of Scotland.

• **Guide price £95/$180**

Irish Banknote ▲

• *1977*
£50 note issued by The Central Bank of
Ireland.

• **Guide price £175/$331**

Swiss Note ▼

• *1952*
SFr 5 note issued by the national bank of
Switzerland.

• **Guide price £38/$72**

Iraqi Note ▼

• *1931*
ID banknote, numbered A 157545, from
Iraq.

• **Guide price £450/$851**

Chinese Bond ▲

• *1911*
£20 bond issued by the Imperial Chinese
Government.

• **Guide price £65/$123**

Scottish Banknote ▲

• *1915*
£1 note issued by The National Bank of
Scotland

• **Guide price £85/$161**

Portugese Bond ▲

• *1922*
Bond issued by the Companhia Colonial
Navegaedo.

• **Guide price £7/$14**

SILVER & PEWTER

Silver Wall Sconce ▲

- *1912*

This silver wall sconce was made by L A Crichton in London in a style that would have been popular during the reign of Charles II. The decoration shows two cherubim amid flowers and birds with the two candleholders having gadroon borders.

- *30cm x 20cm*
- **Guide price £1,800/$3,402**

Silver Milk Jug ▼

- *circa 1940*

Silver milk jug with a lobed body, engraved and embossed decoration and a reeded handle.

- *height 11cm*
- **Guide price £300/$567**

Basket Centrepiece ▼

- *1918*

A silver three-basket centrepiece made by Sharman Dermott Neill in Chester. The centre bowl would have been used for fruit or flowers while the side baskets, which are detachable, would contain nuts, fruit or sweets.

- *30cm x 22cm*
- **Guide price £3,000/$5,670**

Sovereign Case with Sovereign ◀

- *1900*

A fine sovereign case cum Vesta/match safe; initialled 'CE' and well decorated. The case was made in Birmingham by Constantine & Floyd and holds a 1914 gold sovereign.

- *length 7.6cm*
- **Guide price £245/$464**

Salts with Shell Feet ▶

- *1913*

Pair of silver circular salts with a serpentine scalloped rim, standing on three scalloped feet.

- *diameter 7.5cm*
- **Guide price £395/$747**

Pair of Silver Candlesticks ▲

- *1911*

Pretty pair of silver candlesticks of George II design, made in Sheffield.

- *height 16cm*
- **Guide price £875/$1,654**

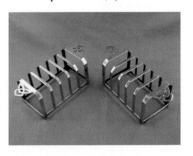

Pair of Scottish Toast Racks ▲

- *1937*

A pair of Scottish five-piece toast racks of rectangular form with celtic knot lug handles. Made in Edinburgh by Hamilton & Inches.

- *length 10cm*
- **Guide price £275/$520**

Silver Perfume Spray ◀

- *circa 1910*

Silver perfume spray on a faceted glass circular bottle.

- *height 17cm*
- **Guide price £175/$331**

Edwardian Photo Frame ▼

- *1903*

A beautiful Edwardian pierced and embossed photo frame, decorated with lion mask, cherubs, birds, foliage and wild beasts. The frame was made by WJ Myatt & Co. in Birmingham and has a dark blue velvet backing.

- *13cm x 9cm*
- **Guide price £585/$1,106**

Asprey Square Waiter ▼

- *1927*

A small square salver/waiter with serpentine corners to the raised border, on four hoof feet. Made in London by Asprey & Co.

- *17.5cm x 17.5cm*
- **Guide price £295/4558**

Chick Pepperette ▼

- *1908*

A finely modelled chick pepperette, sitting on a flat base with pierced removable head. Import marks for Chester; imported by Berthold Muller.

- *4cm x 4cm*
- **Guide price £195/$370**

Aeroplane Cruet Stand ▼

- *circa 1930*

A rare and fine early 20th century silver-plated cruet stand in the form of an aeroplane, with four bottles, salt container and toothpick holder.

- *25.5cm x 38cm x 35.5cm*
- **Guide price £5,600/$10,584**

Horse's Hoof Cigar Lighter ▼

- *circa 1908*

A rare and unusual cigar lighter in the shape of a horse's hoof, in tortoiseshell and silver. The hunting horn unscrews to reveal a reservoir. A small wick would go up through the horn to light cigars.

- *height 10cm*
- **Guide price £1,450/$2,741**

Edwardian Porringer Christening Cup ▲

- *1906*

An Edward VII porringer christening cup, circular with everted rim, embossed with gadroons and flutes, with reeded strap handles. Inscribed 'Pamela Ann Sutherland, 1906'. Made by C J Vander Ltd.

- *7.5cm x 14.5cm*
- **Guide price £365/$690**

Aeroplane Desk Set ▲

- *circa 1930*

Exceptionally fine early twentieth century silver-plated desk set in the form of an aeroplane.

- *16.5cm x 36cm x 37cm*
- **Guide price £4,800/$9,072**

Art Nouveau Mirror ▲

- *circa 1930*

Art Nouveau silver mirror with elaborate scrolling and a young lady holding a light in the shape of a lily.

- *height 59cm*
- **Guide price £4,500/$8,510**

Cigarette Case ▼

- *circa 1920*

Silver cigarette case with meshed effect and lines of gold inlay.

- *length 12cm*
- **Guide price £65/$123**

Pewter Continental Bowl ▼

- *circa 1900s*

Continental pewter bowl with a wide border and moulded rim.

- *diameter 30cm*
- **Guide price £120/$227**

Silver Bowl ▼

- *1930*

Silver "Crumpled Paper" bowl with fruit decoration.

- *height 16cm*
- **Guide price £1,100/$2,079**

Silver Salt and Pepper Pots ▲

- *circa 1923*

Matching silver salt and pepper pots, of octagonal baluster form with finial lids, from E. Johnson & Son Ltd., Derby.

- *height 9cm*
- **Guide price £240/$454**

Silver Pheasant ▲

- *1966*

Hand chased sterling silver pheasant, hallmarked 'London'.

- *length 19cm*
- **Guide price £975/$1,843**

Silver Goblets ▲

- 1970

Set of four silver goblets with silver gilt interiors with rusticated stems on circular bases, by Christopher Lawrence.

- height 15cm
- **Guide price £1,000/$1,890**

Glass Sugar Shaker ▲

- circa 1906

Glass sugar castor of baluster form, with a pierced silver cover, engraved floral designs and ball finial.

- height 16.5cm
- **Guide price £225/$426**

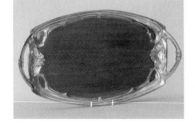

Twenties Toastrack ▼

- circa 1929

Silver Art Deco toastrack with six bays, canted corners and a pierced apron.

- height 6cm
- **Guide price £190/$360**

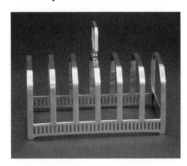

Pair of Decanters ▼

- 1910

Pair of glass decanters with silver mounts and handle, made by Walker and Hall.

- height 23cm
- **Guide price £3,900/$7,371**

Art Nouveau Pewter Tray ◀

- 1900

Art Nouveau pewter and mahogany tray designed by Orivit.

- length 45cm
- **Guide price £650/$1,229**

Leaf Dish ▶

- 1900

Silver leaf-shaped dish with curled rim and vein pattern. Made in Birmingham by Joseph Gloster.

- length 17.5cm
- **Guide price £125/$237**

Silver Tea Strainer ▼

- circa 1920

Silver tea strainer, made in Sheffield, England, with pierced and engraved decoration and lattice handle.

- length 13cm
- **Guide price £160/$303**

Silver and Glass Jar ▶

- 1945

Glass cosmetic container with a silver cover and a bone moon-shaped thumb piece, made in London.

- height 9cm
- **Guide price £150/$284**

Silver Bon-Bon Dish ▼

- 1901

Liberty & Co. cymric silver bon-bon dish designed by Oliver Baker. Hallmarked 'Birmingham 1901'.

- 9cm x 10.5cm
- **Guide price £1,500/$2,835**

Hancock Silver Bowl ▲

- *1911*

Sterling silver bowl with cut card decoration, hallmarked in London by George Hancock.

- *diameter 12cm*
- **Guide price £365/$690**

Stamp and Cigarette Case ▲

- *circa 1910*

Silver stamp and cigarette case with blue enamel lid.

- *width 9cm*
- **Guide price £275/$520**

Teak Cigarette Box ▲

- *1903*

Teak cigarette box within a silver frame with 'Cigarettes' in silver on the lid.

- *width 13cm*
- **Guide price £260/$492**

Art Nouveau Creamer ▼

- *circa 1936*

Art Nouveau silver cream jug, with moulded lip, strap handle and raised on a square moulded base.

- *height 8.5cm*
- **Guide price £160/$303**

Sheffield Pierced Dish ▼

- *1919*

Sterling silver pierced dish, hallmarked in Sheffield by William Hutton.

- *width 26cm*
- **Guide price £995/$1,881**

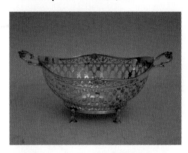

Silver Ashtray ▲

- *1900*

Silver ashtray made in London with five recesses within the border.

- *width 8cm*
- **Guide price £1,900/$3,591**

Silver Cruet Set ▼

- *circa 1930*

Silver Art Deco cruet set consisting of mustard, salt and pepper in the style of tankards.

- *height 5cm*
- **Guide price £360/$681**

Cigar Case ▼

- *circa 1920*

Silver cigar case with three compartments allowing for half coronas.

- *length 12cm*
- **Guide price £160/$303**

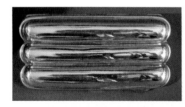

Four-section Cigar Case ◄

- *circa 1930*

Four-section silver plate cigar case.

- *length 13cm*
- **Guide price £49/$93**

Edwardian Candlesticks ▲

- *1905*

Pair of Edwardian sterling silver square based candlesticks, hallmarked.

- *height 22cm*
- **Guide price £1,425/$2,693**

Condiment Set ▲

- *1911*

Condiment set comprising two glass bottles with faceted stoppers, on a silver stand with extended ring handle, supported on silver ball feet.

- *height 21cm*
- **Guide price £240/$454**

Silver Photograph Frame ▲

- *1935*

Silver photograph frame with a concave design.
- *height 26cm*
- **Guide price £350/$662**

Liberty & Co. Tea Set ▶

- *1903*

Pewter tudric tea set with turquoise enamel mount, and tray designed by Archibald Knox for Liberty & Co.
- *length 42cm*
- **Guide price £4,500/$8,505**

Archibald Knox Barrel ▼

- *1902*

Tudric pewter biscuit barrel designed by Archibald Knox, with blue and green enamelling.
- *15cm x 13cm*
- **Guide price £1,500/$2,835**

Vignelli Carafe ▶

- *1970*

Christofle and Venini silver carafe and six shots, designed by Vignelli. Stamped 'Christofle, Italy'.
- *height of carafe 22.5cm*
- **Guide price £2,000/$3,780**

Sheffield Silver Dish ▲

- *1937*

Octagonal silver dish with double handles of ivory, made in Sheffield, England.
- *diameter 30cm*
- **Guide price £180/$341**

Silver Gilt Heron Cigarette Box ▼

- *circa 1909*

Silver gilt heron standing on a silver box, the mechanism opens the cover for the heron to bend and pick out a cigarette. Made by W. H. Sparrow of Birmingham.
- *height 30cm*
- **Guide price £4,250/$8,033**

Napkin Rings ▼

- *1937*

Boxed set of six, solid silver Art Deco napkin rings with engraved, engine-turned scallop-shell design. Birmingham.
- **Guide price £650/$1,229**

Tudric Pewter Tankard ▲

- *1903*

Tudric pewter tankard with two large scrolled handles. Designed by David Veazey for Liberty & Co.
- *height 32cm*
- **Guide price £995/$1,881**

Silver Pierced Dish ▲

- *1950*

Silver dish with pierced border, supported on a pedestal base with banded decoration.

- *height 15cm*
- **Guide price £175/$331**

Silver Condiment Set ▲

- *1964*

Silver condiment set consisting of a salt, mustard and pepper pot. Made in Sheffield, England.

- *height 8cm*
- **Guide price £400/$756**

Silver Postal Weighing Scale ▼

- *1909*

Rare silver postal weighing scale with blue enamel, made in Birmingham.

- *height 7cm*
- **Guide price £750/$1,418**

Conical Silver Vases ◄

- *circa 1930*

Two tall conical vases with chased scrolling and cartouches of cherubs, musicians, dancers and revellers, surrounded by foliage birds and flowers, standing on a circular base, made in Germany.

- *height 61cm*
- **Guide price £5,500/$10,395**

Silver and Glass Bowl ►

- *1920*

Ladies' melon-shaped glass bowl with a silver banded collar and tortoiseshell insert.

- *diameter 15cm*
- **Guide price £280/$530**

Small Silver Teapot ▼

- *circa 1904*

Edwardian silver teapot of small proportions with bone handle and finial lid.

- *height 15cm*
- **Guide price £240/$454**

Silver Sugar Caster ▼

- *1906*

Silver sugar caster of baluster form made in Chester, with banded decoration a finial lid.

- *height 23*
- **Guide price £395/$748**

Irish Dish Ring ▲

- *1916*

Irish silver dish ring decorated with foliage, flowers, birds and animals by Weir of Dublin.

- *8cm x 19cm*
- **Guide price £2,700/$5,103**

Liberty Pitcher ▲

- *circa 1910*

Liberty green glass pitcher with a pewter lid, handle and base.

- *height 21cm*
- **Guide price £1,200/$2,268**

Letter Rack ▼

- *1937*

Silver letter rack, with a double circle design, mounted on a mahogany base.

- *height 17cm*
- **Guide price £350/$662**

Silver Tea Infuser ▲

- *circa 1919*

Rare silver tea infuser in the form of an egg, of two sections with silver chain.

- *length 9.5cm*
- **Guide price £485/$917**

Silver Horse Figurine ▲

- *1903*

Silver figure of a horse in motion with mouth open and flowing mane and tail, by Nereisheimer in Chester.

- *17cm x 23cm*
- **Guide price £2,500/$4,725**

Silver Ink Stand ▶

- *1997*

A silver ink tray with reservoir of simple design, made in Birmingham.

- *width 24cm*
- **Guide price £490/$927**

Silver Blotter ▲

- *1921*

Silver blotter of plain design with chalice-shaped thumb piece.

- *length 17cm*
- **Guide price £280/$530**

Pewter Ice Bucket ▼

- *circa 1920*

Pewter ice bucket with tulip pattern, designed by Orivit.

- *20cm x 21cm*
- **Guide price £700/$1,323**

Cigarette Case ▲

- *circa 1920*

Silver cigarette case with canted corners and diamond pattern design within plain borders.

- *length 14cm*
- **Guide price £68/$129**

Circular Mustard Pot ▲

- *circa 1929*

Mustard pot of drum design with blue glass liner, hinged lid, scrolled handle and scalloped thumb piece.

- *height 5.5cm*
- **Guide price £248/$469**

Silver Cigar Box ▲

- *circa 1912*

Fine silver cigar case with four sections engraved with a floral design centered with a vacant panel.

- *length 13cm*
- **Guide price £425/$803**

Silver Snuff Box ▲

- *circa 1939*

Small silver snuff box made in Sheffield, England.

- *6cm square*
- **Guide price £110/$208**

Double-handled Chalice ▲

- *1937*

A simply designed silver bowl with double scrolled handles and moulded rim on a splayed shaped foot, made in Birmingham.

- *8cm x 21cm*
- **Guide price £1,100/$2,079**

French Pewter Plate ▼

- *1900*

A French pewter plate from Orleans with embossed designs to the rim and centre.

- *diameter 24cm*
- **Guide price £65/$123**

Art Nouveau Pewter Vase ▲

- *1903*

Art Nouveau pewter vase with green glass liner designed by Archibald Knox for Liberty & Co.

- *height 18cm*
- **Guide price £950/$1,796**

Tudric Rose Bowl ▲

- *circa 1903*

Liberty & Co tudric rose bowl with stylised foliate designs signed by Archibald Knox. Previously attributed to Rex Silver.

- *23cm x 19cm*
- **Guide price £2,250/$4,253**

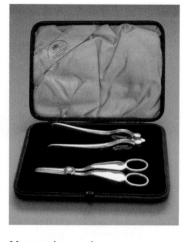

Nutcracker and Grape Peeler ▲

- *circa 1904*

Silver nutcracker and grape peeler, made in Sheffield, in original silk-lined and blue velvet box.

- *length 14cm*
- **Guide price £675/$1,276**

English Sauce Boats ▲

- *1928*

A pair of George III-style sauce boats made by Thomas Bradbury of London.

- *height 6cm*
- **Guide price £6,775/$12,805**

Silver Tea Strainer ▼

- *1942*

Silver double-handled tea strainer made in London with pierced and chased decoration.

- *length 16cm*
- **Guide price £250/$473**

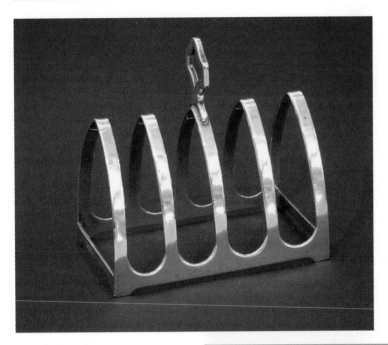

Silver Oval Basket ▼

- *1918*

An oval silver basket with a pierced diamond lattice design and plain splayed rim, made in London.

- *length 33cm*
- **Guide price £600/$1,134**

Silver Toast Rack ◀

- *circa 1930*

Elegant silver toast rack with an ecclesiastical theme and a cross-shaped thumb piece.

- *width 8cm*
- **Guide price £95/$180**

Sheffield Caster ▲

- *1911*

A fine caster of conical form with fluted designs, finial top and serpentine moulded base. Made in Sheffield.

- *height 13cm*
- **Guide price £600/$1,134**

Dublin Dish Ring ▼

- *1913*

Irish dish ring, made in Dublin, decorated with gadrooned borders, and pierced floral designs with oval cartouches.

- *10cm x 19cm*
- **Guide price £3,500/$6,615**

Silver Cream Jug ▼

- *circa 1920*

Silver cream jug with scallop shell design and scrolled handle, supported on a raised circular foot.

- *height 11.5cm*
- **Guide price £317/$599**

Victorian Montieth ▲

- *1900*

Victorian montieth by Goldsmith & Silversmith, based on a seventeenth century design with shaped collar and ring handles from mask decoration.

- *26cm x 41cm*
- **Guide price £9,000/$17,010**

Peppermill ▲

- *1910*

Ivory peppermill banded with silver.

- *height 7.5cm*
- **Guide price £525/$992**

Sweet Box ◀

- *1918*

Unusual sweet box shaped as paint tin, by H. Woodward & Co, Birmingham.

- *height 7.5cm*
- **Guide price £1,270/$2,401**

Silver Champagne Cup ▽

- *1902*

A silver champagne cup with saucer-shaped bowl, made by William Adams Ltd, Birmingham.

- *height 14cm*
- **Guide price £1,160/$2,193**

Edwardian Centrepiece ▽

- *1902*

A silver centrepiece with pierced and moulded floral designs on a raised foot, made by C.S. Morris of London.

- *14cm x 23cm*
- **Guide price £990/$1,871**

Wine Coolers ▲

- *1905*

A pair of silver urn-shaped wine coolers raised on pedestal feet on a plain square base, by Walker and Hall Sheffield of London.

- *27cm x 25cm*
- **Guide price £12,750/$24,098**

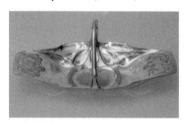

Osiris Fruit Basket ▲

- *1905*

Art Nouveau pewter fruit basket, with a handle engraved with cherries, by Osiris.

- *34cm x 18cm*
- **Guide price £250/$473**

Silver Candlesticks ▲

- *1910*

A set of four silver candlesticks made by E. J. Greenberg of London.

- *height 29cm*
- **Guide price £6,750/$12,758**

Covered Serving Dish ▶

- *1900*

A silver covered serving dish with gadrooned borders and asymmetric scrolled designs made by Hatkins of Sheffield.

- *diameter 22cm*
- **Guide price £1,200/$2,268**

Edwardian Silver Card Box ▽

- *1900*

A silver card box profusely engraved with floral meanderings, including two original sets of cards from Vienna. Made in Birmingham.

- *height 6cm*
- **Guide price £475/$898**

Frosted Sugar Basket ▽

- *1913*

A fine silver sugar basket made by Charles Stuart Harris of London, with a frosted glass liner.

- *height 14cm*
- **Guide price £675/$1,276**

Pair of Candelabras ▲

- *1911*

A finely detailed pair of silver, five branch candelabras, with four removable branches, transforming to a single candlestick on square gadrooned bases.

- *45cm x 38cm*
- **Guide price £15,000/$28,350**

Goldsmiths Vases ▲

- *1912*

A set of three vases made by Goldsmiths of London with tapered conical necks on a splayed foot.

- **Guide price £1,450/$2,741**

Chinese Teapot ▲

- *1930*

A pewter Chinese teapot with Hadite spout, handle and finial.

- *height 15cm*
- **Guide price £85/$161**

Pewter Fruit Bowl ▲

- *1905*

Art Nouveau pewter fruit bowl with green glass liner and pewter mounts incorporating organic designs, by Orivit.

- *11cm x 16.5cm*
- **Guide price £380/$719**

Art Nouveau Pewter Tureen ▲

- *1900*

Art Nouveau pewter tureen finial top with twin handles on a splayed foot.

- *9.5cm x 24cm*
- **Guide price £280/$530**

Raised Silver Dish ▲

- *1932*

A silver shallow dish on a raised splayed foot with scrolled border, made by Walker & Hall of Sheffield.

- *10cm x 23cm*
- **Guide price £525/$992**

Knox Pewter Dish ◄

- *1903*

Art Nouveau pewter fruit bowl with green glass liner raised on three legs reserved on a circular base, designed by Archibald Knox for Liberty & Co.

- *13cm x 13cm*
- **Guide price £650/$1,229**

Three-handled Cup ▼

- *1914*

A silver cup on a raised splayed foot with three ribbon handles, made in Birmingham.

- *height 15cm*
- **Guide price £700/$1,323**

Water Jug ▼

- *1930*

A pewter water jug of bulbous proportions with unusual splayed lip and curved handle.

- *height 24cm*
- **Guide price £60/$114**

Goldsmiths Scent Bottle ▼

- *1902*

A silver and glass scent bottle with profuse foliate designs to the body and stopper, made by Goldsmiths of London.

- *height 14cm*
- **Guide price £1,275/$2,410**

Pewter Dish ▼

- *1905*

Art Nouveau pewter dish with three lobed sections decorated with an organic design of stylised leaves by Gallia.

- *20cm x 31cm*
- **Guide price £250/$473**

Set of Pewter Goblets ▼

- *20th century*

A set of five, half-pint capacity, pewter goblets of typical form, in fine condition on a circular base. Handcrafted by Aquineas Locke of London.

- *height 15cm*
- **Guide price £100/$189**

Edwardian Ink Stand ▼

- *1904*

A fine ink stand with two silver-mounted cut glass ink bottles on a tray with ball feet, made in London.

- *20cm x 15cm*
- **Guide price £1,950/$3,686**

Double-handled Dish ▶

- *1905*

A silver double-handled chalice-shaped dish, raised on a pedestal foot, made in London.

- *23cm x 38cm*
- **Guide price £2,750/$5,198**

Banded Tankard ▼

- *1908*

Silver tankard with scrolled handle, domed lid and moulded banding. By H. Atkin, Sheffield.

- *height 17cm*
- **Guide price £790/$1,494**

Cigarette Case ▲

- *circa 1910*

With enamelled plaque of a robust Cleopatra with asp at her breast. European 900 mark.

- *length 9.5cm*
- **Guide price £1,400/$2,646**

Silver Pierced Basket ▼

- *1907*

A pierced silver basket with floral designs, gadrooned borders and cartouche on four ball feet. Made by C.S. Hennell of London.

- *14cm x 27cm*
- **Guide price £2,450/$4,631**

Stirrup Cups ▲

- *1920*

Set of four large German stirrup cups with 835 standard mark. The cups rest on fox-head bases.

- *height 13cm*
- **Guide price £1,500/$2,835**

Fruit Dish ▼

- *1910*

A silver pierced Edwardian fruit dish with floral swag decoration on three scrolled feet. London.

- *diameter 23cm*
- **Guide price £900/$1,701**

Gilded Fruit Bowl ◀

- *1910*

Silver-plated fruit bowl with gilded interior and a glass liner on a pedestal foot with geometric designs and gadrooned border, engraved 'W.M.F'.

- *12cm x 24cm*
- **Guide price £650/$1,229**

Claret Jugs ▲

- *1901*

Pair of highly ornate Edwardian silver-gilt claret jugs in hand-etched crystal. Made by Walter Keith of London.

- *height 41cm*
- **Guide price £16,750/$31,658**

Sheffield Silver Basket ◀

- *1916*

A silver basket with shaped borders hand crafted by J. Dickson of Sheffield.

- *14cm x 39cm x 29cm*
- **Guide price £6,000/$11,340**

Sovereign Case ▲

- *1912*

Heart-shaped silver sovereign case, engraved with floral designs. By E.J. Houlston, Birmingham.

- *length 5cm*
- **Guide price £250/$473**

Mustard Pot ▼

- *1910*

Elegant George V drum mustard pot with pierced pattern and blue glass liner.

- *height 9cm*
- **Guide price £375/$709**

Note Clip ▼

- *1900*

Unusual silver and tortoiseshell note clip, in the form of a seesaw. By H.A. Batson, London.

- *length 14cm*
- **Guide price £2,300/$4,347**

Cigarette Case ▲

- *1928*

Silver, turquoise and black enamel cigarette case with silver gilt interior. European with London import mark.

- *length 8cm*
- **Guide price £950/$1,796**

Punch Bowl ▲

- *1911*

Punch bowl with fluted body with inverted beading, pedestal foot and serpentine rim with moulded edge. Made in London.

- *diameter 29cm; height 22cm*
- **Guide price £2,475/$4,678**

Photograph Frame ▼

- *1903*

Silver and green/grey and red agate photograph frame in the style of two basket-hilt swords and shields. Birmingham.

- *height 8cm*
- **Guide price £890/$1,681**

Stamp Dispenser ▼

- *1904*

Rare English piece made in Birmingham by Gray & Co.

- *length 8cm*
- **Guide price £1,250/$2,363**

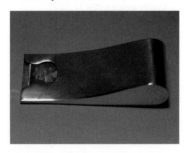

Edwardian Monteith ▶

- *1906*

A fine silver bowl in the style of an eighteenth century monteith with scalloped collar and floral designs on a raised foot. Made in Birmingham.

- *20cm x 37cm*
- **Guide price £2,450/$4,631**

Condiment Set ▶

- *1935*

Six-piece condiment set comprising two salt, two pepper and two mustard pots of rectangular form with champfered corners. Art Deco by Mappin & Webb of London.

- **Guide price £600/$1,134**

Liberty Cup ▲

- *1900*

Liberty cup of beaten pewter with traditional tree pattern typical of Art Nouveau period.

- *height 20cm*
- **Guide price £600/$1,134**

Fabergé Bowl and Ladle ▲

- *circa 1917*

Imperial Russian silver bowl and ladle, made by Fabergé in St Petersburg immediately prior to the revolution.

- **Guide price £24,750/$46,967**

Silver Filigree Frame ▼

- *20th century*

Pierced silver photograph frame with original leather back and velvet backing to filigree. By L. Emmanuel, Birmingham.

- *height 19cm*
- **Guide price £790/$1,494**

Leaf Design Candelabra ▲

- *1901*

An unusual pair of silver candelabra of woven stem and branches with leaf motif. On gadrooned square bases. By Charles Stuart Harris, London.

- *height 42cm*
- **Guide price £6,750/$12,758**

Fluted Goblet ▲

- *1909*

With beaded base and knop stem; the bowl has fluting. By Walker & Hall, Sheffield.

- *height 20cm*
- **Guide price £400/$756**

Monkey Pepperpot ◀

- *1908*

Rare monkey pepperpot, seated with one arm tucked under the other. By H. Heywood.

- *height 7cm*
- **Guide price £2,300/$4,347**

Dressing Table Set ▶

- *1966*

Three-piece enamel and silver set consisting of hairbrush, clothes brush and mirror in white enamel with red rose design. By Barker, Ellis Silver Co, Birmingham.

- **Guide price £360/$681**

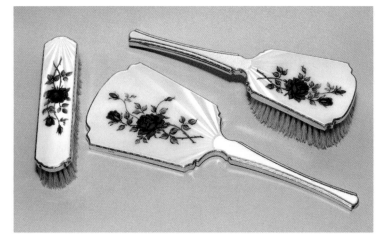

Silver Neff ▲

- *1902*

A four-wheeled neff in the shape of a schooner, with several figures, cannon, pennants, anchors and all exaggerated detail. By B. Müller.

- *height 41cm*
- **Guide price £6,000/$11,340**

SPORTING ITEMS

Child's Football Boots ▶

- *1930*

Child's leather football boots in original condition.

- *length 18cm*
- **Guide price £125/$237**

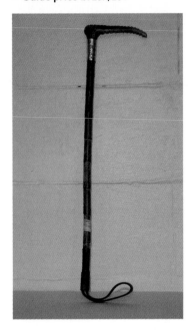

Riding Crop ▲

- *circa 1930*

Bamboo riding crop with 13 crosses on the bone handle, above a silver collar, engraved with the letters 'H. S.'

- *length 61cm*
- **Guide price £65/$123**

Goggles ▲

- *1940*

Goggles with brass and metal rim on a leather backing with adjustable rubber straps.

- *width 18cm*
- **Guide price £28/$54**

Miniature Football ▼

- *circa 1940*

Novelty miniature leather football.

- *miniature*
- **Guide price £20/$38**

Leather Gaiters ▲

- *circa 1920*

Pair of leather gaiters with leather straps and metal buckles.

- *length 29cm*
- **Guide price £28/$54**

Football Trophy ▶

- *1956*

Football trophy presented to Mr. and Mrs. Clarke of Berkhampstead Football Club 1956.

- *height 17cm*
- **Guide price £45/$85**

Trophy Cap ▼

- *1923–4*

Black velvet cap with gold braiding and tassel with the letters 'S. S. O. B.' in gold.

- *medium*
- **Guide price £45/$85**

Leather Riding Boots ▼

- *1930*

Pair of gentleman's brown leather polo boots with laces, three straps with brass buckles and wood shoe trees.

- *height 61cm*
- **Guide price £170/$322**

Hotspur Football Boots ▼

- *1920*

Pair of brown leather football boots with leather studs and cream laces, from a Hotspur footballer.

- *length 30cm*
- **Guide price £225/$426**

Child's Skis ▼

- *1920s*

Child's wooden skis with matching poles and bindings.

- *1.05m x 8cm*
- **Guide price £120/$227**

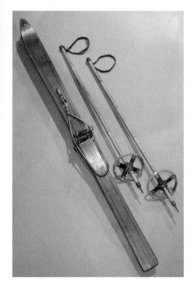

Leather Football ▼

- *1950s*

Brown leather football in original condition.

- *25cm*
- **Guide price £70/$133**

Rugby Ball ▼

- *1950s*

Brown leather rugby ball with original stitching.

- *33cm x 18cm*
- **Guide price £85/$161**

Leather Football Boots ◄

- *1930*

Leather football boots in excellent condition appointed by Stanley Matthews.

- *length 30cm*
- **Guide price £125/$237**

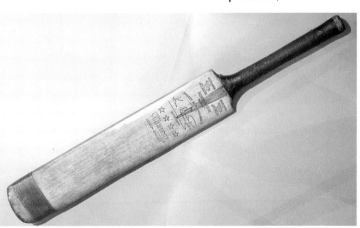

York Rowing Cap ▲

- *1940s*

Rowing cap with the braid and cap badge of York City Rowing Club.

- *29cm x 18cm*
- **Guide price £50/$95**

Leather Flying Helmet ▼

- *circa 1940*

Leather flying helmet with leather chin strap and headphone connectors.

- *medium*
- **Guide price £110/$208**

Stuart Surridge Bat ▲

- *1940s*

Stuart Surridge autographed Ken Barrington cricket bat.

- *78cm*
- **Guide price £72/$137**

B C F C Cap ▲

- *1933*

B C F C velvet blue and maroon football cap with silver braiding and tassle. On the inside 'English manufactured Christys, London, Horton Stephens, Ltd., The Shops Brighton College and Ward 1933–45'.

- *diameter 20cm*
- **Guide price £45/$85**

Saddle Bags ▲

- *circa 1930*

Brown leather saddle bags in fine condition with leather straps and brass buckles.

- *length 18cm*
- **Guide price £155/$293**

Billiard Scorer ▼

- *circa 1910*

Wall-mounted mahogany billiard scorer, with brass numerals and sliding markers.

- *92cm x 35cm*
- **Guide price £280/$530**

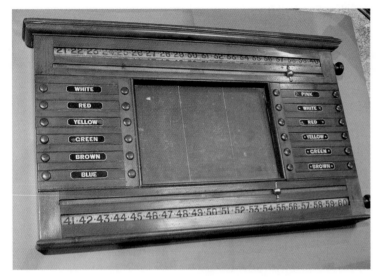

Wall Billiard Scorer ▲

- circa 1910

Mahogany and brass billiard scorer, with a slate panel in the centre.

- 60cm x 105cm
- **Guide price £700/$1,323**

Silver Football Trophy ▲

- 1928

Silver footballer trophy presented to the Alexanders Welfare Football League for the Annual Competition London.

- 45cm x 22cm
- **Guide price £680/$1,285**

Swiss Army Ice Pick ▶

- 1940s

Wooden ice pick with steel head and spike made for the Swiss Army.

- 90cm
- **Guide price £70/$133**

Polo Player on Pony ▲

- 1970

Bronze figure of a polo player on a galloping pony, one of a limited edition of ten, signed the artist.

- height 40cm
- **Guide price £4,950/$9,356**

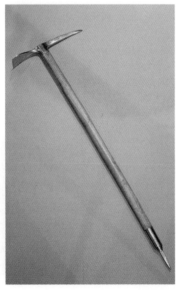

Richie Benaud Bat ▼

- 1940

Richie Benaud autographed cricket bat.

- 78cm
- **Guide price £68/$129**

Croquet Set ▼

- 1930

Portable croquet set on mahogany stand with brass handle and feet, containing four mallets, hoops and red, black, yellow and blue balls.

- **Guide price £495/$936**

Leather Sandwich Case ▲

- 1910

Leather sandwich case with brass clasp and a leather shoulder strap, inscribed: 'J.S.W'.

- 19cm square
- **Guide price £295/$558**

Sporting Magazines ▲

- 1930

Two tennis magazines signed by Fred Perry and a selection of lawn tennis books.

- 30cm x 25cm
- **Guide price £125–£145/ $237–$274**

Bottle Opener ▼

- circa 1940

Metal bottle opener in the form of a jockey's riding cap, decorated with red and white enamel.

- diameter 7cm
- **Guide price £45/$85**

Tennis Press

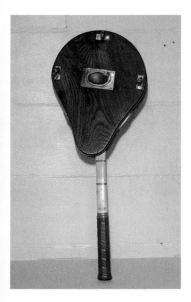

- *circa 1920*

Mahogany tennis press in excellent condition with brass fittings.

- *diameter 27cm*
- **Guide price £155/$293**

Hunting Crop

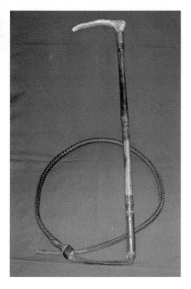

- *1940*

Hunting whip with braided leather strap, ivory handle and brass collar.

- *length 120cm*
- **Guide price £145/$274**

Black Rugby Boots ▶

- *1930*

Pair of black leather rugby boots with white laces and leather studs.

- *length 29cm*
- **Guide price £165/$312**

Steel Pick Axe ▼

- *circa 1920*

A steel pick axe with a mahogany handle and leather strap.

- *length 58cm*
- **Guide price £68/$129**

Ice Axes ▶

- *1930*

Continental ice axes with wood handles and metal axe head, of various sizes. Hickory shafted.

- *length 84cm*
- **Guide price £60/$114**

Football Player ◀

- *circa 1930*

Spelter figure of a football player poised and about to kick a ball.

- *height 25cm*
- **Guide price £425/$803**

Pond Yacht ◀

- *circa 1960*

Model Gaff rigged pond yacht on a brass stand.

- *height 98cm*
- **Guide price £325/$614**

Leather Binocular Case ▲

- *1910*

Leather binocular case with leather carrying handle and shoulder strap.

- *5.5cm x 4cm*
- **Guide price £95/$180**

Riding Boots ▲

- *circa 1915*

Gentleman's leather riding boots, with wooden trees with brass handles.

- *height 58 cm*
- **Guide price £200/$378**

Riding Crop ▲

- *1930*

A leather riding crop with notched ivory handle and silver collar.

- *length 55cm*
- **Guide price £85/$161**

Ivory Binoculars ▲

- *1920*

Elliott Bros ivory binoculars with brass trim.

- *4cm x 3.5cm*
- **Guide price £145/$274**

Football Trophy ▼

- *1900*

Continental red football trophy with silver metal finial and circular base.

- *height 44cm*
- **Guide price £645/$1,219**

Badminton Rackets ▶

- *circa 1920*

Wooden with presses. Gut strings. Feather shuttlecocks.

- **Guide price £65/$123 racket;
£7/$14 shuttlecock**

Polo Helmet and Knee Pads ▼

- *circa 1930*

White Polo helmet with red ribbon trim, and leather knee pads.

- *diameter 28cm*
- **Guide price £65/$123 helmet;
£35/$66 knee pads**

Brass Dinner Gong ▶

- *circa 1930*

Brass dinner gong flanked by two brass tennis racquets, supported on an oval mahogany stand.

- *30cm x 24cm*
- **Guide price £695/$1,314**

Willow Cricket Bat ▼

- *1900*

Leather cricket bag with leather handle and straps, and willow cricket bat.

- *length 75cm*
- **Guide price £120/$227**

Nickel-plated Binoculars ▲

- *circa 1930*

Nickel-plated binoculars with leather grips.

- *length 6cm*
- **Guide price £125/$237**

Bowling Balls ▲

- *circa 1910*

Lignum Vitie bowling balls with bone monogram panels.

- *diameter 16cm*
- **Guide price £60/$114**

Football Trophy ▼

- *1900*

Silver-plated football trophy in the form of early football with a silver foliate tripod stand on a circular base.

- *height 45cm*
- **Guide price £775/$1,465**

Alpine Equipment ▼

- *circa 1930*

Wooden skis, continental ice axe and pair of early wooden skates with leather bindings.

- *210cm, 85cm, 28cm*
- **Guide price £55–£120/$104–$227**

Aeroplane Propellor ▲

- *circa 1925*

Aeroplane propellor in laminated mahogany with brass edges. From Cirrus III. Boss stamped.

- **Guide price £1,400/$2,646**

Golf Ball Vesta ▲

- *circa 1907*

Golf ball vesta in the form of a golf ball. Shows incised patterns. Made by Henry Williamson Ltd, Birmingham.

- *length 5cm*
- **Guide price £745/$1,409**

Cricket Bats ▼

- *circa 1920*

'Autographed' cricket bats – incised with names of famous players. Quality willow, English.

- **Guide price £85/$161**

Boxing Gloves ▼

- *1920*

Leather boxing gloves stuffed with horsehair.

- *30cm*
- **Guide price £95–£145/$180–$274**

Mounted Car Mascot ▼

- *circa 1950*

A horse-racing figure with an enamelled rider. On marble.

- *height 16cm*
- **Guide price £225/$426**

Leather Punchball ◄

- *1920*

Leather punchball with leather strap used to suspend from the ceiling.

- *diameter 30cm*
- **Guide price £185/$350**

Photograph and Tennis Racquet ▲

- *1932*

Photograph of Bunny Dusten and Hazell Streamline, together with a Hazell Streamline Blue Star lawn tennis racquet.

- **Guide price £795/$1,503**

Hickory Golf Clubs ▲

- *circa 1910*

Hickory shafts. Leather grips and makers' names. Persimmon headed wood, hand-forged.

- **Guide price £45–£75/$85–$142**

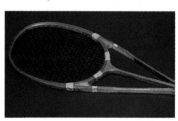

Hazell Tennis Racket ▲

- *1934*

Hazell streamline tennis racket of first aerodynamic design. Blue star, gut strings.

- *length 68cm*
- **Guide price £425/$803**

Wicker and Leather Pelota Cradles ▲

- *circa 1910*

Early 20th-century pelota cradles. Made from wicker with leather gloves. Used for high-speed ball game of Spanish origins.

- *length 50cm*
- **Guide price £110/$208 each**

Football Medals ▲

- *circa 1920*

A collection of football medals. Silver enamelled.

- **Guide price £80–£120/$152–$227**

Golf Putters ▼

- *circa 1905*

Hickory-shafted patent aluminium putters. Made by, from left; Schenectady, Fred Saunders and Mallet putter.

- **Guide price £460–£840/ $870–$1,588**

Lizard-skin Flask ▼

- *circa 1930*

Early 20th-century large silver lizard-skin flask. Flask is hallmarked with inscription 'Death to Filias'. Shows a silver hinged screw to the stopper. Has a glass reservoir inside. Flask is in very good condition.

- **Guide price £435/$822**

Polished Pewter Figure ◄

- *circa 1920*

Naturalistically styled polished pewter golfing figure. The figure is mounted on a pewter rectangular base. Signed by Zwick.

- *height 34cm*
- **Guide price £1,075/$2,032**

Croquet Mallets ▲

- *circa 1920*

From top, brass-bound croquet mallet by Jacques of London, and square mallet by Slazenger of London. Made from box wood.

- *height 95cm*
- **Guide price £65–£110/$123–$208**

Signed Leather Football ▲

- *1950*

Mid 20th-century leather football recently signed by Vialli. The ball is constructed using twelve panels of handstitched leather.

- **Guide price £120/$227**

Cigar Polo Mallets ▼

- *circa 1925*

Pair of cigar polo mallets with bamboo shafts, sycamore or ash heads. Made by Salters.

- *length 130cm*
- **Guide price £48/$91**

Signed World Cup Football ▼

- *1990*

Football signed by the English team from the Italian World Cup of 1990. The signatures include those of Gazza, Lineker and Platt.

- **Guide price £850/$1,607**

Bronze Football Figure ▼

- *circa 1910*

Naturalistically styled bronze on oval base showing a footballer in period costume. Art deco period.

- *height 48cm*
- **Guide price £2,480/$4,687**

Sporting Books ▼

- *circa 1910*

Sporting books on golf, tennis, fishing, and cricket, including a Morocco-bound limited edition book on British Sports and Sportsmen.

- **Guide price £65–£280/$123–$530**

Pigskin Flask ▲

- *circa 1930*

Early 20th-century tan flask. Made from pigskin leather. Shows a silver hinged screw stopper and also has a glass reservoir.

- **Guide price £225/$426**

Squash Rackets ▲

- *circa 1910*

Pair of early 19th-century squash rackets. Shown with heavy gut stringing. Rackets bound with leather grips. In good condition.

- *length 68cm*
- **Guide price £125/$237 each**

Croquet Set ▲

- *circa 1950*

Boxed croquet set by John Jacques, London. Pine box.

- *110cm x 25cm x 30cm*
- **Guide price £225/$426**

Silver Sandwich Box and Leather Pouch ▶

- *circa 1930*

From left; a leather carrying pouch with a strap and two belt loops and a sandwich box made from silver.

- **Guide price £500/$945**

Group of Handstitched Footballs ▲

- *circa 1920*

Group of 20th-century handstitched leather footballs. Made with 12 and 18 leather panels. Best English cowhide. With laces and bladders.

- **Guide price £95/$180 each**

Football Tobacco Box ▼

- *1905*

Silver tobacco box styled as a rugby ball. Hinged flap. Made in Birmingham.

- *length 8cm*
- **Guide price £525/$992**

Bronze Figure of a Skier ▶

- *1930*

A stylized bronze of a downhill skier. Art deco. Signed.

- *height 25cm*
- **Guide price £3,250/$6,143**

Set of Initialled Lawn Bowls ◀

- *circa 1910*

Set of four lignum vitae lawn bowls. Ivorine inserts with owner's initials and numbers. Pictured with white porcelain jack.

- **Guide price £26–£38/$50–$72**

Signed Liverpool Football ▲

- *1999–2000*

Liverpool team ball from the 1999-2000 season. Signatures from the team include players such as Owen, Redknapp, Fowler and Berger.

- **Guide price £150/$284**

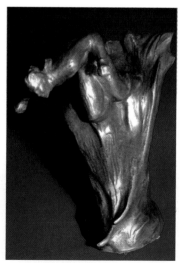

Cricket Bats ▲

- *circa 1940*

Two standard cricket bats. Leather or whipped handles.

- **Guide price £35/$66 each**

Football Rattle ▲

- *circa 1920*

Early 20th-century football rattle. Made from wood and used by football supporters. In good condition.

- **Guide price £75/$142**

Football Collectables ▲

- *circa 1940*

Leather-covered trinket box in shape of a football. Marble ashtray. Football tankard.

- **Guide price £95–£135/$180–$255**

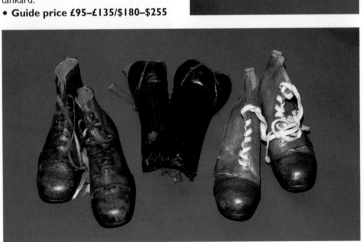

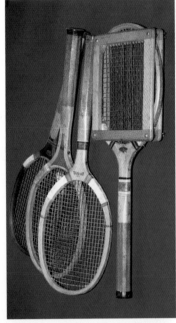

1920s Tennis Rackets ▼

- *circa 1920*

Tennis rackets with wooden handles and presses.

- **Guide price £38/$72 each**

Cricket Bat Bookmark ▲

- *1907*

Early 20th-century bookmark in the form of a cricket bat. The top of the bat shows an ivory ball. Made by A. & J. Zimmerman of Birmingham.

- *length 9.5cm*
- **Guide price £425/$803**

Leather Footballs ▲

- *circa 1930*

Handstitched leather footballs. Show various team names with names in gilt lettering. Top is a leather medicine ball.

- *diameter 19cm and 33cm*
- **Guide price £65–£95/$123–$180**

Football Items ◄

- *circa 1920*

Selection of football items from early 20th century. From left of picture: football boots, shin pads and hotspur boots. All items are handmade from leather. Made in England.

- **Guide price £65–£225/$123–426**

Dayton Badminton Racket ▲

- *circa 1920*

Badminton racket made by Dayton, U.S.A. Shuttlecock with natural feathers.

- **Guide price £190/$360 racket; £7/$14 shuttlecock**

Golfing Figure ▲

- *circa 1930*

Donald Duck plaster figure.

- *height 23cm*
- **Guide price £850/$1,607**

Selection of Boxing Items including Boots, Gloves and Bag ▲

- *circa 1920*

Group of sporting items comprising, from left to right, leather boxing boots, leather boxing gloves and a leather punch bag. Made by various English sporting manufacturers.

- **Guide price £60–£165/$114–$312**

Framed Photograph of Michael Owen ▼

- *1998–99*

Recently photographed single mounted photograph of footballer Michael Owen, one of Britain's rising stars. Matted with Owen's signature. Photograph shows the Liverpool team's yellow strip.

- **Guide price £50/$95**

Gianfranco Zola Photograph ▼

- *1998*

Signature with photographs of Gianfranco Zola scoring the winning goal in the Cup Winners Cup Final, Stockholm, 1998.

- **Guide price £200/$378**

European Cup Photograph ▲

- *1998–99*

Manchester United squad photo taken in the 1998–99 season at a European Cup match. Photo and signatures include Beckham, Cole and Schmeichel.

- **Guide price £350/$662**

Team Barcelona Photograph ▲

- *1999–2000*

Photograph of the 1999–2000 Barcelona squad. Signed at Wembley stadium, in the match against Arsenal. Includes Rivaldo, Kluivert and Figo.

- **Guide price £350/$662**

Manchester United Football Shirt ▲

- *1998–99*

Signed Manchester United football shirt of treble winners. Showing 21 signatures from the 1998–99 season squad. Signatures include Beckham, Sheringham, Schmeichel and Keane.

- **Guide price £1,750/$3,308**

Signed Chelsea Team Photograph ▶

- *1999–2000*

Chelsea team photograph including signatures of the players. Taken prior to playing AC Milan in Champions League.

- **Guide price £350/$662**

Signed Liverpool Team Shirt ▲

- *circa 1999–2000*

Football jersey from the Liverpool team, 2000 season. With all the team signatures including football greats such as Owen, Fowler, Hyppia and Camara.

- **Guide price £350/$662**

Signed Manchester United Shirt ▲

- *1999–2000*

Manchester United football shirt from the 2000 season. The shirt is signed by the team including key players such as Beckham, Giggs and Keane.

- **Guide price £350/$662**

Signed Chelsea Football Shirt ▼

- *2000*

Chelsea football shirt from the 2000 season. Shirt is signed by the team, including Zola, Vialli and De Goey.

- **Guide price £350/$662**

Signed Arsenal Shirt ▼

- *2000*

Signed Arsenal shirt from the 2000 season. Signatures include popular football players such as Bergkamp, Overmars and Kanu.

- **Guide price £350/$662**

Trout Priest ▲

- *1910*

An unusual trout priest in staghorn, carved in the form of an eagle with a dragonfly motif.

- *length 30cm*
- **Guide price £200–£300/ $378–$567**

Perfect Fly Reel ▲

- *1920–1*

Rare Hardy "Perfect" duplicated MK-2 salmon fly reel with smooth alloy foot held with two screws, ivorine handle, nickel silver line guide and duplicated check.

- *diameter 10.8cm*
- **Guide price £120–£180/ $227–$341**

Cased Flies ▲

- *1920*

A case of 70 fishing flies.

- *15cm x 10cm*
- **Guide price £100–£200/ $189–$378**

Allcocks Reel ▲

- *circa 1920–40*

Wood fishing reel by Allcocks with brass fittings and ebonised handles.

- *diameter 9cm*
- **Guide price £50/$95**

Fly Box ▼

- *circa 1915*

Leather-lined box with 12 glass and alloy containers for flies, with original tweezers and pocket.

- *13cm x 10cm*
- **Guide price £90/$171**

Leather Fly Wallet ◄

- *circa 1920–40*

Leather fly wallet with eight compartments.

- *width 16cm*
- **Guide price £28/$54**

Brass Telescopic Gaff ▼

- *circa 1920*

Brass telescopic gaff with turned wooden handle.

- *length 61cm*
- **Guide price £120/$227**

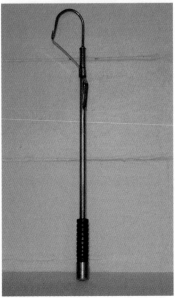

Fishing Flies ▼

- *1920*

A case of 45 fishing flies.

- *15cm x 10cm*
- **Guide price £100–£200/ $189–$378**

Small Fishing Reel ▲

- *circa 1920–40*

Small wood fishing reel with a brass plate and turned decoration.

- *diameter 7cm*
- **Guide price £25/$48**

Bamboo Rod Holder ▼

- *circa 1920*

Hardy Brothers bamboo rod holder. String-bound with leather carrying handle and cover.

- **Guide price £145/$274**

Uniqua Fly Reel ▼

- *circa 1923*

Hardy "Uniqua" duplicated MK-2 trout fly reel with horseshoe latch, ivorine handle, smooth brass foot and retaining most of the black lead finish.

- *diameter 7.3cm*
- **Guide price £130–£150/ $246–$265**

Fishing Reel ▲

• circa 1920–40
Wood fishing reel with brass handles and plate with turned decoration.
• diameter 10cm
• **Guide price £45/$85**

Hercules Fly Reel ▲

• early 20th century
Hardy "Hercules" raised-face brass fly reel with ivoreen handle, wasted and ventilated foot, and oval logo.
• diameter 10.2cm
• **Guide price £150/$284**

Nottingham Walnut Reel ▼

• 1912
Rare Hardy Nottingham reel made of seasoned walnut, with patent lever "Silex" action, fitted with twin cow horn handles on elliptical brass seats and Bickerdyke line guide.
• diameter 10.2cm
• **Guide price £150/$284**

Wood Fishing Reel ▼

• circa 1920–40
Wood fishing reel with banded decoration, brass fittings and ebonised double handles.
• diameter 8cm
• **Guide price £35/$66**

Sea Fishing Reel ▼

• Early 20th century
A Nottingham sea fishing reel made of walnut with twin bulbous handles on elliptical brass seats, brass cross on the back with sliding on/off check button and fitted with a brass Bickerdyke line guide.
• diameter 14cm
• **Guide price £25–£80/$48–$152**

Bernard & Sons Reel ▲

• circa 1928
J. Bernard & Sons salmon fly and trolling or harling reel with a fixed calliper check, strap over rim mounted tension adjuster and unventilated drum with ivorine handle.
• diameter 12.7cm
• **Guide price £80–£100/$152–$189**

St George Fly Reel ▲

• 1935
Hardy "St George" fly reel with ridged brass foot, three screw drum release, grey agate line and ebonite handle.
• diameter 8.6cm
• **Guide price £100–£140/ $189–265**

Hardy Fly Box ▲

• circa 1920
Hardy alloy fly box, includes collection of trout flies.
• 13cm x 10cm
• **Guide price £110/$208**

Wide Drum Perfect Reel ▲

• circa 1955
Hardy wide drum salmon "Perfect" fly reel fitted with revolving nickel silver line guide, and duplicated check and ridged brass foot reel.
• diameter 9.5cm
• **Guide price £120–£160/ $227–$303**

Dry Fly Tin ▲

• 1900
A Hardy black japanned dry fly tin with lift lid and ivorine pencil inside lid.
• 15cm x 10cm
• **Guide price £100–£200/ $189–$378**

SPORTING ITEMS

Hardy Fishing Reel ▼

- *circa 1930*
Hardy platewind fishing reel. Silex no 2.
- *diameter 10cm*
- **Guide price £280/$530**

Brass Reels ▼

- *circa 1910*
Three brass fly fishing reels.
- *7cm/left; 5.5cm/centre; 5cm/right*
- **Guide price £35–£50/$66–$95**

Japanned Fly Box ▼

- *circa 1910*
Tortoiseshell bakelite fly box with ten ranks of fly hooks, containing assorted flies.
- *21cm x 12cm*
- **Guide price £95/$180**

Wood Reels ▶

- *circa 1920*
Two wooden fly fishing reels with brass cross backs.
- *9cm/left; 9cm/right*
- **Guide price £45–£90/$85–$171**

Wicker Creel ▲

- *circa 1940*
Wicker fishing creel with adjustable leather carrying strap with fasteners.
- *width 26cm*
- **Guide price £55/$104**

Fishing Basket ▲

- *circa 1940*
Fine split reed fishing basket with leather carrying strap and buckle fasteners, on circular legs with a canvas strap.
- *35cm x 42cm*
- **Guide price £65/$123**

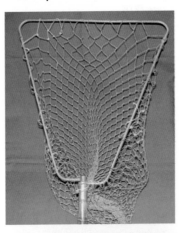

Landing Net ◀

- *1930*
Landing net with cane handle.
- *length 150cm*
- **Guide price £175/$331**

Starback Fishing Reel ▼

- *circa 1920–40*
Starback wood fishing reel with turned decoration and brass fittings.
- *diameter 12cm*
- **Guide price £55/$104**

John Macpherson Reel ▼

- *1930*
John Macpherson bakelite reel with original box, by Allcock & Co.
- *diameter 9cm*
- **Guide price £95/$180**

Brown Salatopia ▲

- *circa 1920*
Brown linen Salatopia hunting hat with a leather lining and the maker's inscription in gold lettering 'by S. H. Batcha & Sons, Moore Market, Madras'.
- *width 34cm*
- **Guide price £60/$114**

Starback Reel ▲

- *circa 1920–40*
Starback wooden fishing reel with brass fittings and double handles.
- *diameter 9cm*
- **Guide price £58/$110**

Fishing Nets ▲

- *1900*
Fishing net with bamboo shafts. The net on the right is patent collapsible.
- *length 78cm/left; 130cm/right*
- **Guide price £90/$171**

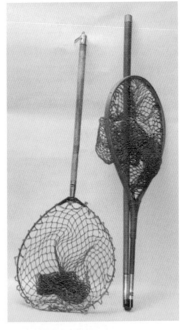

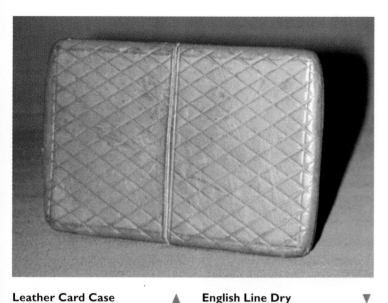

Leather Card Case ▲
- 1910

Leather card case with a diamond-shaped design on the cover.
- *length 8cm*
- **Guide price £25/$48**

Pot-bellied Creel ▲
- 1900

Wicker-weave pot-bellied creel with sloping lid and fish slot, and webbing handle.
- *22cm x 22cm*
- **Guide price £125/$237**

Brass Salmon Reel ▲
- circa 1910

Solid brass salmon fly fishing reel with bone handle and original leather case, by C. Farlow.
- *diameter 11cm*
- **Guide price £450/$851**

English Line Dry ▼
- 1990

An English mahogany Line Dry with bone handle.
- *height 32cm*
- **Guide price £288/$545**

Three Fishing Reels ▼
- circa 1900-1930

Selection of fishing reels. The reels are made, from left to right, of walnut and brass, and a combination of brass and steel.
- **Guide price £45–£65/$85–$123**

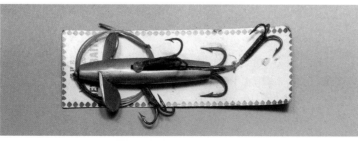

Starback Reel ▼
- 1910

Starback wooden sea fishing reel, with star-shaped brass mounts.
- *diameter 10cm*
- **Guide price £115/$217**

Trout Rod ▼
- circa 1975

A split cane trout rod with a Hardy's cork end, by the Harris and Sheldon Group.
- *length 150cm*
- **Guide price £700/$1,323**

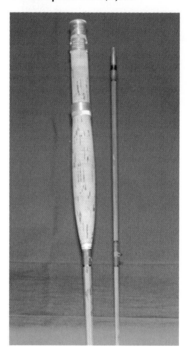

Devon Bait Lure ▼
- circa 1930

Artificial bait lure, with four triple hooks, manufactured by Devon. With original case.
- **Guide price £40/$76**

Fly Wallet ▲
- 1930

Pigskin fly wallet with leather strap, in excellent original condition.
- *length 18cm*
- **Guide price £280/$530**

Fishing Flies ▲
- 1920

Alloy cases containing trout and salmon flies.
- *5cm x 9 cm/small; 15cm x 9 cm/large*
- **Guide price £90/$171**

Murdoch Rod ▲
- circa 1920

The Murdoch split cane fishing rod made by Hardy.
- *length 395cm*
- **Guide price £295/$558**

Small Creel ▼

- *circa 1940*

Mid 20th-century small child's creel. Made from wicker.

- **Guide price £95/$180**

Hardy 3-inch Reel ▲

- *circa 1903*

A Hardy Perfect 3-inch metal body with ivory handle.

- **Guide price £475/$898**

Fly Rod ▲

- *1975*

A Hardy 'Palakona' fly fishing rod. Split-cane, 7 feet 2 inches with canvas sleeve.

- **Guide price £500/$945**

Hardy Telescopic Gaff ▶

- *early 20th century*

Deep-sea telescopic gaff, for big game fishing. With belt clip. Brass with rosewood handle and spring safety clip.

- **Guide price £250/$473**

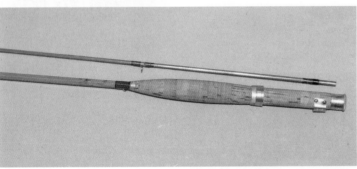

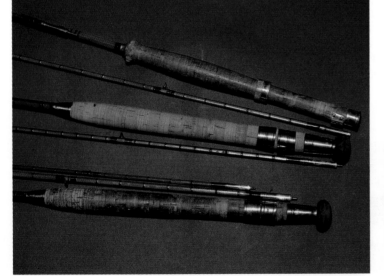

Hardy Reel Case ▼

- *circa 1930*

Well-preserved Hardy reel case. For 4 inch reel. Made from leather and lined in red velvet.

- **Guide price £125/$237**

Hardy Neroda Dry Fly Box ▶

- *circa 1920*

Hardy Neroda case with nickle plated fittings, in tortoiseshell and bakelite. Compartmentalised into six sections with trout flies.

- **Guide price £245/$463**

Split-cane Rods ◀

- *circa 1900–30*

Assortment of split-cane trout and salmon rods. Various makers; cork handles, brass or alloy fittings. All in excellent condition.

- **Guide price £65–£220/ $123–$416**

Hardy 'St George' ▲

- *circa 1932*

Hardy 'St George' 3⅜ inch. Brass and metal components. Agate line guard.

- **Guide price £295/$558**

Leather Reel Case – 3⅛ Inch ▼

- *circa 1920s*

Early 20th-century reel case. The case is made from leather and has red velvet lining.

- **Guide price £145/$274**

Boat Rod ◀

- *circa 1910*

Split-cane boat rod. 7 feet. Two sections.

- **Guide price £125/$237**

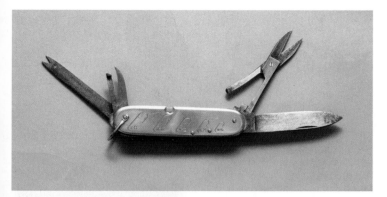

Angler's Knife ◄

- *mid 20th century*

Unnamed angler's knife with six attachments including scissors in steel and brass. Sideplates marked with imperial scale 1–3 inches.

- **Guide price £245/$463**

Farlows Spring Balance ▼

- *circa 1920*

Farlows spring balance. Metric and imperial weights up to 100lbs and measuring 9 inches. Made in London.

- **Guide price £95/$180**

French-weave Creel ▲

- *circa 1910*

Fine French weave wicker split reed pot-bellied creel with sloping lid and fish slot.

- **Guide price £145/$274**

Reel and Case ▼

- *circa 1920*

Early 20th-century unmarked reel with velvet-lined leather case.

- **Guide price £345/$652**

Brass Fly Case ▲

- *1910*

Circular brass fly case with hinge. Three cloths.

- *diameter 10cm*
- **Guide price £75/$142**

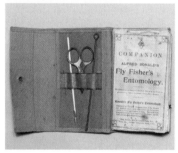

Canvas/Leather Fly Wallet ▲

- *1930*

Canvas and leather fly wallet with fly-making equipment and Alfred Randle's 'Fly Fisher's Entymology'. With various compartments.

- **Guide price £175/$331**

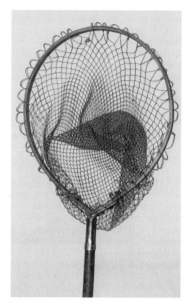

Landing Net ▲

- *early 20th century*

Poker pattern, bamboo landing net. Bowed wood hoop and brass fittings.

- **Guide price £275/$520**

The Dry Fly Dresser ▲

- *circa 1930*

Used as a line dryer. Made by Hardy Brothers Ltd.

- **Guide price £75/$142**

Fishing Priest ▼

- *circa 1940*

A fishing priest of antler horn, with leather strap.

- **Guide price £85/$161**

Hardy Allinono

- *1925*

An early 20th-century fisherman's companion from Hardy Neroda, containing a brass weighing measure. The item incorporates various pouches.

- **Guide price £495/$936**

Ammunition Case ◄

- *circa 1920*

Ammunition case with brass fittings and leather straps by Penry Williams, Middlesbrough.

- *41cm x 16cm*
- **Guide price £950/$1,796**

Magazine Case ►

- *circa 1930*

Leather magazine case with brass fittings. Cogswell and Harrison. Six compartments with leather pull straps.

- **Guide price £750/$1,418**

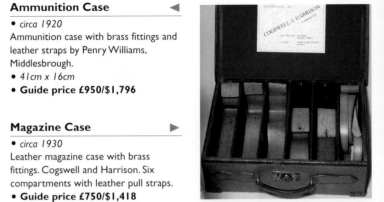

Holland & Holland Rifle ▼

- *2001*

Holland & Holland 375 H&H. New bolt-action magazine rifle.

- *length 1.19m*
- **Guide price £15,615/$29,512**

Royal Rifle ►

- *1945*

Holland & Holland Royal model 300 back-action double rifle, with sights.

- *length 1.14m*
- **Guide price £32,000/$60,480**

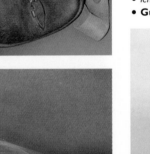

Cartridge Bag ◄

- *1930*

Leather cartridge bag with webbing shoulder strap and the monogram "M.G.F." on the buckle.

- *length 38cm*
- **Guide price £145/$274**

Shooting Stick ▼

- *1940s*

Leather-bound shooting stick, with metal spike.

- *length 90cm*
- **Guide price £144/$272**

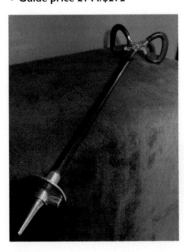

Four-Bore Shotgun ▲

- *1928*

Holland and Holland four-bore shotgun with black powder only.

- *length 1.5m*
- **Guide price £5,500/$10,395**

Gun Case ►

- *circa 1930*

Leg of mutton gun case. Brass fittings. Cogswell and Harrison. Six compartments with leather pull straps.

- **Guide price £375–£425/ $709–$803**

Shotgun Belt ▲

- *circa 1930*
Leather shotgun belt. Twenty-five cartridge compartments and a brass buckle.
- **Guide price £55/$104**

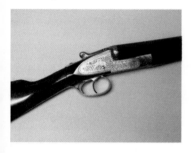

Twelve-bore Self Opener ▲

- *1960*
12-bore Royal self opener with 26.5-inch barrel with double trigger. Royal scroll engraved with coin finish to action. Stock and fore. Superb walnut finish.
- **Guide price £18,000/$34,020**

Shooting Bag ▼

- *circa 1950*
Canocs leather and net shooting bag with leather strap.
- **Guide price £175/$331**

Leather Gun Case ▼

- *circa 1930*
Single oak and leather gun case, with red base interior and leather straps. Brass mounts with carrying handle. Various compartments.
- **Guide price £1,250/$2,363**

Hunter's Display Case ▼

- *circa 1923*
Display case showing tusks and moths of India.
- *32x30cm*
- **Guide price £420/$794**

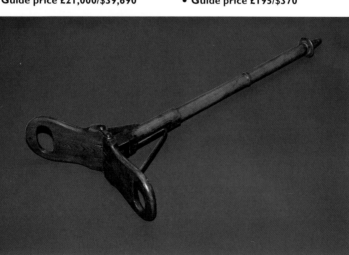

.375 (2½ inch) Calibre Rifle ▲

- *1901*
.375 calibre Royal rifle. Folding leaf sights, double trigger; 26-inch barrels.
- **Guide price £21,000/$39,690**

Shooting Stick ▼

- *circa 1910*
Malacca shooting stick with a walnut seat. Excellent condition.
- *height 68cm*
- **Guide price £195/$370**

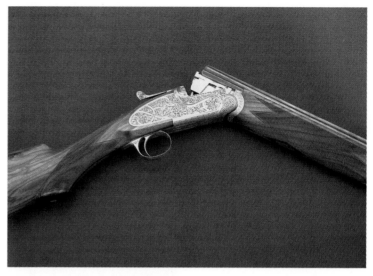

Twenty-Bore Shotgun ▲

- *2001*
Holland & Holland sporting over and under 20-bore single-trigger shotgun.
- *length 1.15m*
- **Guide price £25,000/$47,250**

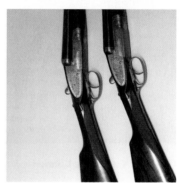

16-bore Guns ▲

- *1911*
A composed pair of Royal non-self openers; 28-inch barrels, scroll engraved. Coin finish to action. All French walnut wood. New barrels fitted. Gold inlay.
- **Guide price £25,000/ $47,250 for pair**

Magazine Rifle ▼

- *1975*
Excellent quality Holland & Holland 7mm calibre magazine rifle, with telescopic sight.
- *length 64cm*
- **Guide price £7,000/$13,230**

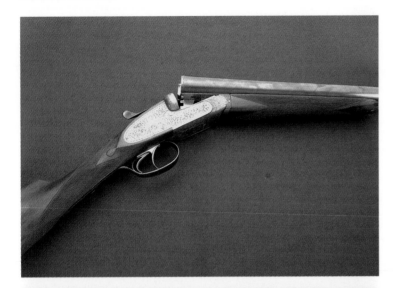

12-Bore Shotgun ◄

- *1939*

Holland & Holland Royal self opener. 12-bore shotgun, with double trigger.
- *length 115cm*
- **Guide price £18,000/$34,020**

Double Barrel Rifle ►

- *1945*

A 300 calibre Holland & Holland Royal, double barrelled rifle, belted and rimless.
- *length 61cm*
- **Guide price £32,000/$60,480**

Crocodile Rifle Case ▲

- *circa 1925*

Rifle case made from a fine crocodile skin, with leather straps and carrying handle, made by Manton and Co, Delhi & Calcutta, India.
- *76cm x 18cm*
- **Guide price £1,200/$2,268**

Royal Deluxe Shotgun ▼

- *1956*

Holland & Holland Royal Deluxe, 12-bore side by side shotgun, with figured walnut furniture.
- *length 71cm*
- **Guide price £24,000/$45,360**

Canochy Cartridge Loader ▼

- *1930*

Canochy cartridge loader encased in leather with a leather strap.
- *diameter 15cm*
- **Guide price £1,500/$2,835**

Hunting Tankards ▲

- *circa 1940*

A set of three pottery tankards with hunting motifs. Made by Arthur Wood. Shows a treacle glaze.
- *height 12cm*
- **Guide price £130/$246 set**

Holland & Holland Gun ►

- *1929*

Holland and Holland leather gun and rifle case, with original inscription, brass fitting and well-fitted red felt interior.
- *74cm x 24cm*
- **Guide price £1,500/$2,835**

Decoy Duck ▲

- *1940s-50s*

Mid-20th-century vintage duck decoy. Made from apple wood. With painted highlights and realistic colouring.
- **Guide price £225/$426**

Badminton Shotgun ▲

- *1937*

Holland & Holland Badminton model
12-bore side by side shotgun.
- *length 71cm*
- **Guide price £14,000/$26,460**

Holland & Holland Royal ▼

- *1908*

Holland & Holland 12-bore, Royal, side
by side shotgun.
- *height 76cm*
- **Guide price £10,500/$19,845**

Canochy Loader ▼

- *circa 1930*

Leather canochy loader, with carrying
strap.
- *diameter 15cm*
- **Guide price £2,250/$4,253**

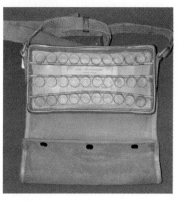

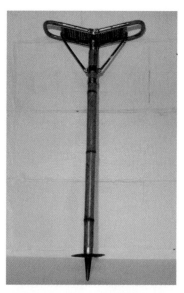

Holland & Holland Shotgun ▼

- *2000*

Holland & Holland deluxe 28-bore
sporting model, over and under shotgun,
with figured walnut furniture.
- *length 71cm*
- **Guide price £30,300/$57,267**

Bamboo Shooting Stick ▲

- *circa 1920*

Bamboo shooting stick with a folding
rattan seat, with metal spike and brass
fittings.
- *length 75cm*
- **Guide price £195/$370**

Leg of Mutton Gun Case ▼

- *circa 1930*

Leg of mutton leather gun case with
carrying handle and shoulder strap.
- *length 89cm*
- **Guide price £550/$1,040**

Tartan Shooting Stick ▲

- *1950s*

Chrome shooting stick with hinged seat
and tartan liner.
- *83cm*
- **Guide price £48/$91**

Oak Shooting Stick ▼

- *circa 1920*

Light oak shooting stick, with plain
wooden seat and metal spike.
- *82cm*
- **Guide price £140/$265**

Ammunition Pouch ▼

- *circa 1920*

Leather ammunition ten-pouch belt with
well-preserved and polished leather
pouches and straps and brass mounts. In
good condition.
- **Guide price £75/$142**

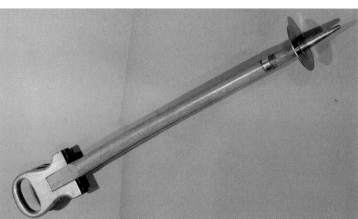

Double Barrel Hunting Rifle ▲

- *1949*

A 300 calibre Flanged Dominion double
barrel hunting rifle, made by Holland and
Holland
- *length 71cm*
- **Guide price £19,750/$37,328**

TAXIDERMY

Albino Cobra ▼

- *20th century*
Albino cobra shown in an aggressive pose.
- *60cm x 28cm*
- **Guide price £195/$370**

Tawny Owl ▼

- *20th century*
Tawny owl naturalistically posed and mounted on a circular base, with original glass dome.
- *55cm x 27cm*
- **Guide price £395/$748**

Eagle Owl ▶

- *20th century*
Eagle owl in fine condition with a good expression mounted on a circular base.
- *65cm x 35cm*
- **Guide price £550/$1,040**

Mallards ▲

- *20th century*
Two male mallards, one shown standing and the other recumbent.
- *40cm x 64cm*
- **Guide price £295/$558**

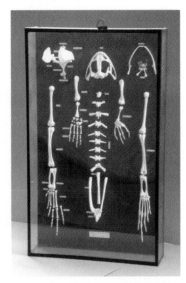

Roach ▶

- *20th century*
Roach surrounded by marine vegetation and displayed within a bow-fronted case.
- *length 48cm*
- **Guide price £475/$898**

Hooded Crow ▼

- *20th century*
Hooded crow shown perched on a branch and mounted on a plinth base.
- *57cm x 28cm*
- **Guide price £125/$237**

Bullfrog Skeletons ◀

- *20th century*
Bullfrog skeleton in sections with documentation.
- *30cm x 40cm*
- **Guide price £140/$265**

Sparrowhawk ▲

- *20th century*
Sparrowhawk with wings pinned back.
- *27cm x 35cm*
- **Guide price £190/$360**

Chameleon ▲

- *20th century*
Chameleon with a curious expression shown with branch.
- *23cm x 38cm*
- **Guide price £175/$331**

Red Fox ▼

- *20th century*
Red fox vixen shown recumbent with head slightly raised.
- *35cm x 57cm*
- **Guide price £200/$378**

Yorkshire Terrier ▲

- *20th century*

Yorkshire terrier seated with a curious expression and a red ribbon.

- *30cm x 20cm*
- **Guide price £245/$463**

Barn Owl ▲

- *20th century*

Barn owl with wings outstretched at the point of take off, mounted on a branch.

- *70cm x 70cm*
- **Guide price £275/$520**

Welsh Raven ▲

- *20th century*

Welsh raven perched on a stump on a square wood base.

- *height 67cm*
- **Guide price £275/$520**

Magpie ▼

- *20th century*

Magpie perched on a wooden branch and mounted on a mahogany base.

- *52cm x 32cm*
- **Guide price £95/$180**

Cock Pheasant ▼

- *20th century*

Cock pheasant in flight supported by a branch and mounted on an oval wooden base.

- *64cm x 70cm*
- **Guide price £175/$331**

Bush Baby ▲

- *20th century*

Bush baby in good condition, naturalistically posed within the branches of a tree.

- *60cm x 54cm*
- **Guide price £195/$370**

Teal ▲

- *20th century*

Teal with striking markings mounted on a branch.

- *27cm x 25cm*
- **Guide price £95/$180**

Hedgehog ▼

- *20th century*

Adult hedgehog on all fours, mounted on oval wooden base.

- *23cm x 15cm*
- **Guide price £175/$331**

Amazon Parrots ▼

- *20th century*

Two Amazon parrots, theatrically mounted on a branch.

- *55cm x 32cm*
- **Guide price £195/$370**

Capucin Monkey ▼

- *20th century*

Capucin monkey mounted on a branch on a large circular base.

- *60cm x 38cm*
- **Guide price £180/$341**

Snipe ▼

- *20th century*

Snipe in good condition and poised on a branch.

- *22cm x 25cm*
- **Guide price £75/$142**

Red Fox Cub ▲

- *20th century*
British Red fox cub shown reclining, mounted on wooden base.
- *height 24cm*
- **Guide price £225/$426**

Sparrow Hawk ▼

- *20th century*
Sparrow hawk with wings spread, mounted on a branch set on a polished wood base.
- *height 61cm*
- **Guide price £195/$370**

Baboon ▶

- *20th century*
Baboon shown on all fours baring his teeth in an aggressive stance.
- *71cm x 81cm*
- **Guide price £450/$851**

Asian Insects ▼

- *20th century*
Display cabinet showing three Asian insects: a scorpion, horned beetle and ghost beetle.
- *length 40cm*
- **Guide price £60/$114**

Snowy Owl ▼

- *20th century*
Snowy owl shown on a snow covered wooden stump on a circular wood base.
- *height 57cm*
- **Guide price £590/$1,116**

Mongrel Dog ▼

- *20th century*
Naturalistically seated mongrel dog shown in an alert pose.
- *height 62cm*
- **Guide price £295/$558**

Egyptian Bat ▼

- *20th century*
Egyptian bat with extended wings on a circular wood base.
- *width 80cm*
- **Guide price £145/$274**

Pelican ▼

- *20th century*
Pelican shown standing with open beak.
- *95cm x 63cm*
- **Guide price £75/$142**

Prevost's Squirrel ◄

- *20th century*
Prevost's squirrel posed on a branch on an oval wood base.
- **Guide price £195/$370**

Armadillo ▼

- *20th century*
Adult armadillo on all fours.
- *length 65cm*
- **Guide price £240/$454**

Blackbird ▼

- *20th century*
Blackbird traditionally perched upon a branch, with oval wood base.
- *height 27cm*
- **Guide price £95/$180**

Polar Bear Skin Rug ▲

- *circa 1920*
A Canadian polar bear skin rug, well preserved, with a fearsome expression.
- *285cm*
- **Guide price £2,500/$4,725**

Jungle Cat ►

- *20th century*
Asiatic jungle cat shown on a branch set upon a polished wooden base.
- *height 105cm*
- **Guide price £650/$1,229**

White Rabbit ▲

- *20th century*
White rabbit modelled on the theme of *Alice in Wonderland*.
- *height 48cm*
- **Guide price £190/$360**

Crow and Skull ▲

- *20th century*
Crow picking at an eyeball of a human skull decorated with fake blood, on a metal base.
- *height 59cm*
- **Guide price £395/$748**

Rooster ▼

- *20th century*
Magnificent rooster naturalistically posed in crowing position, without a base.
- *height 57cm*
- **Guide price £245/$463**

Rudd ▼

- *20th century*
A rudd displayed in a bow-fronted case decorated with marine vegetation.
- *length 48cm*
- **Guide price £475/$898**

Guinea Pig ▼

- *20th century*
Tan and white guinea pig on all fours.
- *length 15cm*
- **Guide price £95/$180**

TAXIDERMY

Beaver ▼

- *20th century*

Adult North American or Canadian beaver. Shown on hindlegs with forearms raised.

- *height 55cm*
- **Guide price £395/$748**

Finch ▲

- *20th century*

Goldfinch mounted on twig upon an oval polished wood base.

- *height 17cm*
- **Guide price £95/$180**

Lesser Anteater ▶

- *20th century*

An African lesser anteater posed on a branch.

- *height 56cm*
- **Guide price £375/$709**

Lemur ▲

- *20th century*

Madagascan black and white ruffed lemur on natural perch.

- *height 100cm*
- **Guide price £750/$1,418**

Crowned Crane ▼

- *20th century*

African crowned crane shown on an oval base.

- *height 103cm*
- **Guide price £295/$558**

Lizard ▼

- *20th century*

Egyptian monitor lizard modelled in an alert posture.

- *length 1.0m*
- **Guide price £375/$709**

Squirrel ▼

- *20th century*

An adult grey squirrel perched upon a tree-stump set within a wooden base.

- *height 28cm*
- **Guide price £95/$180**

Wolf ▲

- *20th century*

Adult North American timber wolf, on all fours baring teeth.

- *height 88cm*
- **Guide price £1,800/$3,402**

Tortoise ▲

- *20th century*

An adult leopard tortoise with finely preserved shell.

- *height 16cm*
- **Guide price £185/$350**

Grey Rabbit ▼

- *20th century*

Adult grey rabbit with white tail, shown in an alert pose.

- *height 25cm*
- **Guide price £125/$237**

Peacock ▼

• *20th century*
A peacock, shown with tail closed, set on a square base.
• *height 1.8m*
• **Guide price £395/$748**

Red Fox ▶

• *20th century*
Adult European Red Fox standing naturalistically on all fours, without a base.
• *height 51cm*
• **Guide price £200/$378**

Butterfly Collection ▲

• *20th century*
A collection of nine South American butterflies, mounted in a display case.
• *height 31cm*
• **Guide price £65/$123**

Falcon and Partridge ▶

• *20th century*
A well-preserved Saker falcon, mounted on a branch with an English partridge clasped in its talons, the whole on an oval base.
• *height 69cm*
• **Guide price £650/$1,229**

Mallard Drake ▶

• *20th century*
Mallard drake shown with wings outstretched, mounted on a base.
• *height 45cm*
• **Guide price £195/$370**

Spider and Insect ▼

• *20th century*
A South American spider and insect, mounted in display case.
• *length 40cm*
• **Guide price £75/$142**

Pheasant ▶

• *20th century*
A cock pheasant in mating pose, with erect tail feathers, mounted on a branch, on a wooden base.
• *height 95cm*
• **Guide price £175/$331**

Tibetan Dog ▼

• *20th century*
Lhasa Apso Tibetan dog on all fours, with attentive expression.
• *height 36cm*
• **Guide price £425/$803**

TELEPHONES

English Telephone ▼

- *circa 1950*
Cream Bakelite telephone with nickel rotary dial and black numerals, inscribed "Portobello 4559", rare in any colour but black.
- *height 15cm*
- **Guide price £290/$549**

Black Bakelite Telephone ▲

- *circa 1930*
Black Bakelite telephone with large dial and drawer.
- *18cm x 25cm*
- **Guide price £165/$312**

Call Exchange Telephone ▲

- *circa 1950*
Black telephone cast in Bakelite with large central rotary dial and small drawer.
- *20cm x 26cm*
- **Guide price £135/$255**

Genie Telephone ▼

- *circa 1970*
Red Genie designer telephone by A. P. Besson manufactured by British Telecom, with push button dial.
- *11.5cm x 22cm*
- **Guide price £65/$123**

Gecophone Telephone ▶

- *circa 1930*
Gecophone black bakelite telephone with bell ringing.
- *18cm x 24cm*
- **Guide price £185/$350**

Ivory Telephone ▼

- *circa 1950*
Ivory bakelite telephone with drawer and ringing bell.
- *14cm x 25cm*
- **Guide price £225/$426**

Red GPO Telephone ▲

- *circa 1960*
Unusual GPO telephone cast in red.
- *14cm x 18cm*
- **Guide price £53/$101**

Candlestick Telephone ◀

- *circa 1920*
Candlestick telephone with Steal handle with black bakelite top and brass and separate wood and brass ring box.
- *44cm x 15cm*
- **Guide price £395/$748**

Trimphone ▶

- *circa 1970*
Two-tone beige trimphone with push-button dialing.
- *10cm x 19cm*
- **Guide price £55/$104**

Two-tone Telephone ▲

• circa 1970
Two-tone, adjustable volume stone coloured British GPO telephone in plastic.
• 12cm x 10cm
• **Guide price £48/$91**

Desk Telephone ▼

• 1908
A desk phone with magneto handle, raised on a wooden base by Thomson-Houston, France.
• 33cm x 18cm
• **Guide price £385/$728**

Belgian Desk Telephone ▼

• circa 1950
European ivory desk telephone with large numerals and clear plastic rotary dial.
• height 12.5cm
• **Guide price £75/$142**

Lyssell and Bloomberg Telephone ▲

• circa 1957
The first ever one piece telephone designed by Ralph Lysell and Hugo Bloomberg in cream with rotary dial underneath.
• height 23.5cm
• **Guide price £100/$189**

Pyramid Telephone ▲

• circa 1930
Black bakelite pyramid telephone with drawer and bell ringing.
• 16cm x 23cm
• **Guide price £185/$350**

Belgian Wall Phone ▲

• circa 1960
A Belgian wall phone repainted in red. Made in Antwerp by Bell Telephones, a subsidiary of the American Bell Telephones.
• **Guide price £180/$341**

R2D2 Telephone ◄

• circa 1980
A telephone in the form of the character R2D2, from the 'Star Wars' films. His head moves and lifts up when the phone rings.
• **Guide price £99/$187**

Ericsson Telephone ►

• circa 1950
Cream bakelite Ericsson telephone with original handset and cord and large rotary dial with black numerals.
• height 14cm
• **Guide price £185/$350**

Candlestick Telephone ▼

- *1916*

French candlestick telephone with metal and chrome handset and wooden candlestick base by Grammont.

- *height 34cm*
- **Guide price £415/$784**

Red Telephone ▲

- *circa 1960*

Red plastic British GPO telephone.

- *13cm x 24cm*
- **Guide price £45/$85**

Bakelite Telephone ▲

- *circa 1950*

Black bakelite British GPO telephone with ringing bell.

- *16cm x 24cm*
- **Guide price £105/$198**

GPO Pyramid Telephone ▼

- *circa 1930*

British Ivory bakelite GPO Pyramid telephone with ringing bell.

- *15cm x 24cm*
- **Guide price £295/$558**

French Wooden Telephone ▲

- *1924*

French wooden candlestick telephone with metal dial and handset, and original wiring, by P. Jacquesson.

- *height 22.5cm*
- **Guide price £475/$898**

British Telephone ▼

- *circa 1970*

British GPO plastic telephone with Warble ringing and adjustable volume.

- *12cm x 10cm*
- **Guide price £48/$91**

Burgunder Telephone ▲

- *1912*

A candlestick telephone by A. Burgunder, made in Paris, France.

- *height 32cm*
- **Guide price £285/$539**

Betacom 'Golphone' ▼

- *mid 1980*

Model GFl. Made in Hong Kong with golf-bag handset and push buttons, mute tone and redial.

- **Guide price £18/$34**

Ericsson Telephone ▼

- circa 1905
A Swedish-made, Ericsson, wooden 936wall-mounted phone with bell-ring display to top.
- 69cm x 26cm
- **Guide price £495/$936**

Series 300 Telephone ▼

- 1940s–50s
An English acrylic golden yellow telephone with drawer for addresses and integral bell.
- 19cm x 18cm
- **Guide price £300/$567**

Plastic Telephone ▲

- circa 1950
Blue plastic telephone with cream dial and handle and silver banding.
- 14cm x 14cm x 24cm
- **Guide price £55/$104**

Pink Plastic Metallic Telephone ▲

- circa 1965
Pink plastic metallic telephone with black flex.
- 14cm x 14cm x 24cm
- **Guide price £55/$104**

Orange Plastic Telephone ▲

- 1970
Orange plastic telephone with cream numerals and orange flex.
- 12cm x 10cm x 21cm
- **Guide price £20/$38**

Green Plastic Telephone ▲

- circa 1960
Green plastic British GPO telephone. Slightly older than telephone # 9965.
- 13cm x 24cm
- **Guide price £45/$85**

Chrome Handset ▲

- 1900
A French candlestick telephone with a metal base and chrome handset by Thomson-Houston.
- height 32cm
- **Guide price £385/$728**

Black Bakelite Telephone ▶

- circa 1950
Black bakelite British GPO telephone with drawer and ringing bell.
- 16cm x 24cm
- **Guide price £135/$255**

English Telephone ▲

- *circa 1900s*

An English telephone with a wooden base, chrome bell and metal handset by Electric and Ordnance Accessories Ltd.

- *22.5cm x 20cm*
- **Guide price £295/$558**

Elvis Presley Telephone ▲

- *circa 1980*

'Jailhouse Rock' shown with guitar and period clothes. Touchtone handset.

- **Guide price £99/$187**

Western Electric Telephone ▼

- *1930*

An American candlestick telephone with original ringer box by Western Electric.

- *height 29cm*
- **Guide price £345/$652**

Black Telephone ▼

- *circa 1940*

Black bakelite telephone with rotary dial issued by GPO.

- **Guide price £180/$341**

Pink Plastic Wall Telephone ◄

- *1950*

Pink plastic wall telephone with cream and silver banding to the ear and mouthpiece.

- *7cm x 13cm x 21cm*
- **Guide price £75/$142**

GPO Telephone ►

- *circa 1946*

Black bakelite British GPO telephone with function on/off switch for ringing.

- *16cm x 24cm*
- **Guide price £175/$331**

Series 200 Telephone ▼

- *1930s–40s*

An English acrylic cream coloured telephone. This type of telephone did not have a bell; the bell was installed on the wall.

- *17cm x 18cm*
- **Guide price £420/$794**

Cream Telephone ▼

- *circa 1970*

An English cream plastic telephone.

- *width 20.5cm*
- **Guide price £75/$142**

Black Plastic Telephone ▼

- *1960*

Black plastic telephone with white letters and numbers, and black flex.

- *13cm x 13cm x 21cm*
- **Guide price £55/$104**

German Telephone ◄
- *1900*
A German-made magneto telephone with metal base and handset, and chrome earpiece and microphone.
- *30cm x 20cm*
- **Guide price £285/$539**

Swiss Telephone ▲
- *circa 1950*
A Swiss wall-mounted telephone with bell-ring displayed to top and hook connection.
- **Guide price £100/$189**

Danish Telephone ▲
- *circa 1935*
A Danish magneto telephone based on an L.M. Ericsson design. Cannot be used on today's system.
- **Guide price £270/$511**

Belgian Telephone ▶
- *circa 1940*
Copper-bodied telephone by the Bell Company, with pleasant ring and carrying handle.
- **Guide price £89/$169**

Audioline 310 Telephone ▲
- *circa 1980*
Red Audioline 310, with oversized keypad with numbers also in red, push-button controls and black flexicord extension.
- **Guide price £30/$57**

Viscount Telephone ▲
- *circa 1986*
A British Telecom-supplied telephone in burnt orange with cream flexcord extension.
- **Guide price £20/$38**

300 Series Telephone ▶
- *circa 1955*
A 300 series black bakelite office telephone with original handset, cord and draw.
- **Guide price £230/$435**

Blue Plastic Telephone ▶
- *1960*
Blue plastic telephone with red dial, on a cream base with red flex.
- *14cm x 14cm x 24cm*
- **Guide price £55/$105**

Post Office Telephone ▼

• *circa 1935*
GPO series 300. Made by Ericsson with bakelite body, rotary dial and address drawer.

• **Guide price £295/$558**

Candlestick Telephone ▼

• *circa 1923*
Candlestick telephone 150 with original No.1 solid back transmitter.

• **Guide price £600/$1,134 (set 25)**
• **Guide price £780/$1,475 (set 1)**

Bakelite Telephone ▼

• *circa 1955*
A British-made green, bakelite telephone, made for the GPO, model number 332. Shows original label on all-metal rotary dial, cheese-dish address drawer and gold-coloured, fabric-covered, interwoven flex. Green is a particularly rare colour.

• **Guide price £500/$945**

Genie Telephone ▼

• *circa 1978*
BT special range, a much sought-after designer telephone in white with metal dial.

• **Guide price £39/$74**

200 Series Telephone ◀

• *circa 1940*
English cream telephone with original undermounted bell box. Rare in any colour but black.

• **Guide price £550/$1,040**

Mickey Mouse Telephone ▲

• *circa 1980*
British-made showing Mickey Mouse standing on faux-wooden base with push-button dial.

• **Guide price £189/$358**

Belgian Desk Telephone ▲

• *circa 1960*
A Belgian ivory desk telephone. Most of these were made in black, making this very collectable.

• **Guide price £190/$360**

Rare Green 200 Series ▲

• *circa 1938*
Almost the rarest colour in the 200 series. Made by Siemens Brothers of Woolwich.

• **Guide price £1,100/$2,079**

Ericofon Telephone ▲

• *circa 1955*
Designed in 1953 by Ralph Lysell and Hugo Blomberg. In white and red with dial underneath.

• **Guide price £70/$133**

300 Series Telephone ▲

• *circa 1957*
A rare 328 telephone made by Plessey, Ilford, Essex. With bell-on and bell-off push buttons.

• **Guide price £650/$1,229**

Danish Telephone ▲
- *circa 1920*
Made in Copenhagen to a Swedish design and also known as the corporation telephone.
- **Guide price £330/$624**

Star Trek Telephone ▲
- *circa 1994*
Modelled on Star Trek's 'Enterprise' with sound effects and push-button dial to base.
- **Guide price £89/$169**

Ivory Telephone ▶
- *circa 1930*
A GPO telephone in ivory, rare for the period. Shows all-metal rotary dial with original central label and number/letter display.
- **Guide price £395/$748**

Danish Telephone ▲
- *circa 1935*
A variation on the D30, with two exchange lines coming in. Supplied with a separate bell set.
- **Guide price £420/$794**

300 Series Telephone ▲
- *circa 1954*
By Siemens Brothers, Woolwich. Rarest colour in this series. Used for shared or party lines.
- **Guide price £600/$1,134**

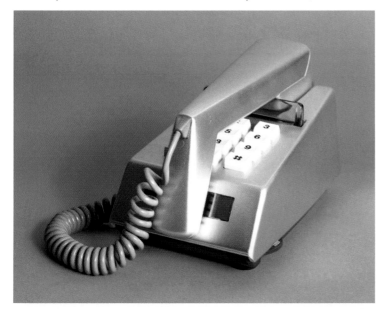

Desk Telephone ▲
- *circa 1960*
A Belgian desk telephone in black plastic, with black rotary dial and white base on rubber feet.
- **Guide price £150/$284**

Darth Vader Telephone ▲
- *circa 1980*
Telephone in the form of Darth Vader, from 'Star Wars', with moving head.
- **Guide price £99/$187**

Trimphone ◀
- *circa 1970*
Silver-painted British 'Trimphone' made for the GPO, with push-button dialling. With distinctive ringing tone.
- **Guide price £85/$161**

Magneto Telephone ▼
- *circa 1925*
A classic design by L. M. Ericsson, Stockholm, made from around 1896. Also known as Eiffel Tower.
- **Guide price £850/$1,607**

Candlestick Telephone ▼
- *circa 1927*
Type 150, in bakelite, featuring a replacement microphone. Made by Ibex Telephones.
- **Guide price £460/$870**

TEXTILES

Art Deco Evening Dress ▼
- *1920*

Black Art Deco silk chiffon evening dress with silver beading.
- *full length*
- **Guide price £900/$1,701**

Pink Cocktail Dress ▲
- *circa 1950*

Short pink satin cocktail dress.
- *length 1.06m*
- **Guide price £225/$426**

Short Velvet Jacket ▼
- *circa 1920*

Pale pink velvet short evening jacket.
- *length 44cm*
- **Guide price £125/£237**

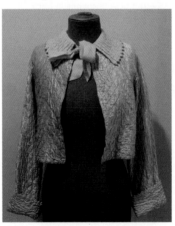

Ivory Fan ▼
- *circa 1904*

Cream silk fan with a trailing design of pink and yellow apple blossom mounted on carved ivory spines.
- *length 35cm*
- **Guide price £125/$237**

Silk Day Dress ▲
- *circa 1940*

Silk day dress with lace design background and stripes of pink, yellow and green with matching bow.
- *full length*
- **Guide price £135/$255**

Chinese Evening Coat ▲
- *1918*

Chinese black ladies' coat embroidered with pink yellow and blue floral design and lined with white rabbit.
- *full length*
- **Guide price £2,000/$3,780**

Strapless Cocktail Dress ▲
- *circa 1950*

Yellow and white cotton strapless cocktail dress by Frank Usher with swathed bodice detail and gathered skirt.
- *mid-length*
- **Guide price £100/$189**

Silk Floral Hat ▼
- *circa 1950*

A summer hat lavishly decorated with silk faux flowers and leaves intertwined with fine veiling.
- *length 22cm*
- **Guide price £49/$93**

Cloche Hat ▼
- *1920*

Brown silk cloche hat with velvet brim and a large gold silk flower and leaf.
- *height 23cm*
- **Guide price £195/$370**

Rafia Cocktail Dress ▼
- *circa 1960*

Pink hand-crocheted raffia sleeveless shift dress.
- *short*
- **Guide price £130/$246**

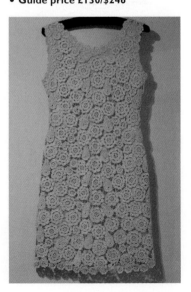

Blue Evening Dress ▼
- *circa 1930*
Royal blue net evening dress.
- *full length*
- **Guide price £175/$331**

Silk Cape ▼
- *circa 1910*
Silk cape decorated with red chrysanthemums within a trailing foliate design.
- *length 96cm*
- **Guide price £165/$312**

Gold Cocktail Dress ▲
- *circa 1960*
Hand-beaded gold cocktail dress with gold beading and topaz stones.
- *mini*
- **Guide price £130/$246**

Silver Lurex Dress ▲
- *circa 1965*
Silver lurex hand-crocheted dress.
- *mid-length*
- **Guide price £125/$237**

Chiffon Dress ▼
- *circa 1960*
Layered chiffon evening dress with large pink satin ribbon.
- *full length*
- **Guide price £175/$331**

Patchwork Quilt ▼
- *circa 1950*
Patchwork quilt with a bold, multi-coloured and patterned geometric design.
- *1.6m x 1.56m*
- **Guide price £195/$370**

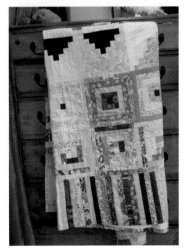

Navy Blue Cocktail Dress ▶
- *circa 1960*
Navy blue strapless cocktail dress with white frill.
- *mid-length*
- **Guide price £100/$189**

Lady's Parasol ◀
- *circa 1920*
Lady's parasol with a black floral design and a handle with a black and beige geometric pattern.
- *length 53cm*
- **Guide price £95/$180**

Nylon Flower Dress ▲
- *circa 1960*
Nylon flower power print dress with smock detail on the hips and interesting orange belt.
- *long dress*
- **Guide price £75/$142**

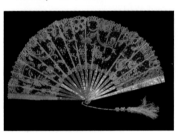

Mother-of-Pearl Fan ▲
- *circa 1910*
Cream silk lace fan covered with cream floral lace and a mother-of-pearl handle.
- *length 29cm*
- **Guide price £275/$520**

Lilac Petal Hat ▶

- *circa 1950*
Faux lilac petals and lilac wire and mesh 'leaves' arranged to form a decorative summer headpiece.
- *diameter 22cm*
- **Guide price £22/$42**

Military Breeches ▲

- *circa 1910*
Gentleman's war-issue military tweed breeches.
- *medium*
- **Guide price £95/$180**

Shibori Kimono Designs ▼

- *circa 1920*
A bold set of nine Japanese blue and white designs for kimono decorated in Shibori, stylised from traditional designs. Framed and glazed.
- *48cm x 79cm*
- **Guide price £2,800/$5,292**

Lace Fan ▼

- *circa 1905*
Cream lace fan with silk backing and cream ivory handle with a cartouche of a raised lily.
- *length 32cm*
- **Guide price £375/$709**

Paisley Silk Dressing Gown ▲

- *circa 1930*
Gentleman's black and gold paisley design silk dressing gown.
- *full length*
- **Guide price £125/$237**

Ladies Red Hat ▲

- *circa 1920*
Ladies red soft silk mesh hat by Pauline Louy's, decorated with red felt flowers.
- *medium*
- **Guide price £145/$274**

Russian-style Cape and Hat ▼

- *circa 1950*
Dramatic red Russian-style cape with black embroidery and white fur lining, with matching hat.
- *medium*
- **Guide price £695/$1,314**

Gleneagles Coat ▼

- *circa 1980*
Gents single-breasted three-quarter length cream light wool coat.
- *three-quarter length*
- **Guide price £120/$227**

Orange Silk Dressing Gown ◀

- *circa 1980*
Orange silk dressing gown with design, by Georgina Von Ernodof.
- *full length*
- **Guide price £195/$370**

Chinese Silk Jacket ▲

- *circa 1960*

Cream cotton Chinese design jacket with wide burgundy silk lapels and belt.
- *full length*
- **Guide price £60/$114**

Pink Mini Dress ▲

- *circa 1960*

Pink floral silk mini dress with chiffon sleeves and a matching hat.
- *mid-length*
- **Guide price £150/$284**

Velvet Waistcoat ▼

- *circa 1970*

Velvet waistcoat with broad paisley pattern and wide lapels.
- *length 60cm*
- **Guide price £95/$180**

Silk Evening Scarf ▼

- *circa 1920*

Cream silk evening scarf with black and white wool tassels.
- *length 1.3m*
- **Guide price £30/$57**

Silk Top Hat ▶

- *1910*

Black silk top hat by Battersby, Northumbland Av, Trafalgar Square, London.
- *circumference 17cm*
- **Guide price £75/$142**

Panama Hat ◀

- *1940*

Gents Panama hat with black band around the crown base.
- *circumference 21cm*
- **Guide price £32/$61**

Burgundy Scarf ▲

- *circa 1940*

Burgundy paisley silk gents scarf with gold and burgundy tassels.
- *length 1.1m*
- **Guide price £28/$54**

Corduroy Breeches ▲

- *circa 1920*

Olive green corduroy breeches with side lacing below the knee and cotton with buttoning. Two large angled pockets and one smaller.
- *length 1m*
- **Guide price £100/$189**

Animal Print Scarf ▼

- *circa 1950*

Burgundy wool gentleman's scarf with ethnic print of figures, animals and flowers.
- *length 70cm*
- **Guide price £30/$57**

Tartan Umbrella ▼

- *circa 1930*

Tartan umbrella with a handle in the shape of a swan with glass eyes.
- *length 67cm*
- **Guide price £65/$123**

Straw Hat ▼

- *circa 1935*

Black straw hat by Wooland Brothers, trimmed with two large beige flowers. Crown decorated with top-stitching.
- **Guide price £48/$91**

TOOLS

Mathieson Plane ▲

- *circa 1920s*

A Mathieson dovetailed parallel-sided smoothing plane with rosewood infill made as a special order for a man with large hands.

- *length 26.3cm*
- **Guide price £575/$1,087**

Webb Lawnmower ▲

- *circa 1955*

A Webb's push mower with cross-over handles and rubber grips. With grass box, adjustable cutter bar and cutter base-plate and adjustable height nuts on the front roller.

- **Guide price £40/$76**

Lawn Edger ▼

- *circa 1950*

Steel and cast-iron lawn edger with aluminium handle and rubber grips. The edger cuts by means of a rotating serrated blade and wheel.

- **Guide price £55/$104**

Pair of Garden Tools ▼

- *early 20th century*

Tools for aid in the growing of asparagus. A hoe for the amassing of soil over and round the 'head', and a cutter for harvesting the plant by cutting it off under the soil.

- *height 139cm*
- **Guide price £48/$92 each**

A1 Panel Plane ◀

- *1930*

A Norris A1 panel plane with dovetailed and rosewood infill.

- *length 44cm*
- **Guide price £2,050/$3,875**

Garden Sprayer ▲

- *circa 1930*

Pressurised sprayer with copper and brass components, with copper cylinder and brass pump with turned wooden handle. Webbing carrying straps. All original materials.

- *height 77cm*
- **Guide price £140/$265**

Garden Shears ▲

- *circa 1930*

A pair of tempered steel-bladed garden shears with turned ash handles. In working order.

- **Guide price £25/$48**

Lawn Edger ▼

- *circa 1940*

A well-worn half-moon lawn edger with rustic shaft of hornbeam construction and rusted steel blade. For sale as decorative artefact.

- *height 94cm*
- **Guide price £15/$28**

Pruner ▼

- *1920*

Trademarked 'Mighty Cutter' pruner, with patented action for use with lever arms or worked by wire on pole. Made in England for fruit tree pruning.

- **Guide price £48/$92**

Norris A1 Jointer ▼

- *1925*

A Norris A1 jointer with rosewood infill and dovetailed body in excellent condition.

- *length 56cm*
- **Guide price £4,100/$7,749**

Watering Can ▼

- *circa 1940*

Galvanised steel watering can with a large, detachable nozzle rose and handle of a tubular construction. Possibly a converted milk-churn.

- *height 42cm*
- **Guide price £38/$72**

French Watering Can ▲

- *circa 1930*

Enamelled French watering can of drum construction and screw-on lid, for indoor use.

- *height 38cm*
- **Guide price £110/$208**

Lawn Aerator ▲

- *circa 1950*

A lawn aerator with a turned, polished wood shaft and handle. The mechanism is a rotating cylinder with flat spikes driven by the forward motion of the front rollers. English made in full working order.

- **Guide price £65/$123**

Stanley 45E ▲

- *1923*

An immaculate Stanley 45E, a presentation piece in 1923. Type 15 Sweetheart, in a tin box, complete with instructions and original screwdriver.

- *length 25cm*
- **Guide price £130/$246**

Beech Ogee ▼

- *1910*

A little used handled beech ogee by T. Hall, Newcastle.

- *length 7.6cm*
- **Guide price £60–£90/$114–$171**

Garden Fork ▲

- *circa 1940*

An English classic four-tine garden fork. Steel with turned wooden shaft and half-turned, all wooden handle.

- *height 94cm*
- **Guide price £15/$28**

Shovel ▼

- *circa 1940*

Classic English shovel of steel and wood construction with turned shaft and partly turned, all-wooden handle.

- *height 94cm*
- **Guide price £15/$28**

Stanley Plane ▲

- *1925*

A Stanley 85 plane with original decal.

- *length 20cm*
- **Guide price £600/$1,134**

Norris Smoothing Plane ▼

- *1920*

A Norris 20R gunmetal smoothing plane in its original box.

- *length 22cm*
- **Guide price £700/$1,323**

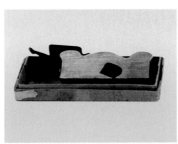

Drawing Instrument Set ▲

- *1910*

A quality with two ivory rulers, an ivory parallel rule, and brass protractor.

- *15cm x 20cm*
- **Guide price £100–£150/$189–$284**

TOYS, GAMES & DOLLS

Gold Cadillac ▲
- *circa 1950*

American gold cadillac with red interior and chromed fittings, made by Bandai, Japan.
- *length 29cm*
- **Guide price £150/$284**

Smiley of the Seven Dwarfs ▲
- *circa 1930*

Padded soft toy of "Smiley", one of the dwarfs from the children's story, "Snow White and the Seven Dwarfs".
- *height 27cm*
- **Guide price £160/$303**

Steiff Owl ▶
- *circa 1950*

Steiff owl with large glass eyes and a menacing expression.
- *height 14cm*
- **Guide price £49/$93**

Noddy ▼
- *1980*

Noddy wearing a red shirt, yellow spotted scarf and blue hat with a yellow pom-pom, in his yellow rubber car with red fenders.
- *19cm x 27cm*
- **Guide price £30/$57**

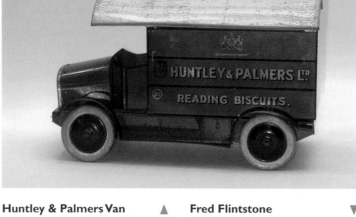

Huntley & Palmers Van ▲
- *circa 1920*

Brown toy van with a hinged lid to store biscuits and the gilt inscription, "Huntley & Palmers Ltd, Reading Biscuits" and a Royal Crest above.
- *19cm x 25cm*
- **Guide price £875/$1,654**

Fred Flintstone ▼
- *1960*

Tin plate "Fred Flintstone" sitting astride his dinosaur "Dino", made by Louis Marks in Japan.
- *length 20cm*
- **Guide price £265/$501**

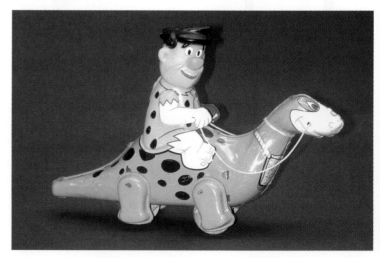

Mickey Mouse ▲
- *circa 1930*

Velvet padded Mickey Mouse with a large smiling expression.
- *height 33cm*
- **Guide price £110/$208**

Japanese Motor Launch ▲
- *circa 1950*

Japanese red, yellow, orange and blue motor launch with driver in a helmet, and hand crank.
- *length 21cm*
- **Guide price £73/$139**

Tin Plate Racing Car ▲
- *circa 1930*

English tin plate cream racing car, with a red radiator grille and red line decoration, bonnet straps, and the number five on the side and on the tail back.
- *length 38cm*
- **Guide price £265/$501**

Dream Baby ▼
- *circa 1920*

Porcelain jointed black "Dream Baby", in perfect condition.
- *height 28cm*
- **Guide price £398/$752**

Red Double Decker Bus ▲
- *1960*

Red bus with "Mobilgas" and "Double Decker Bus" decals on the side, in fine condition.
- *height 22cm*
- **Guide price £145/$274**

Ovaltine Van ▲
- *circa 1950*

Blue Dinky Bedford 10cwt Ovaltine van, inscribed "Ovaltine" and "Ovaltine Biscuits" on the side, with original box.
- *length 8cm*
- **Guide price £65/$123**

Mummy Bear ▲
- *circa 1930*

Padded jointed bear with glass eyes and cloth paws.
- *height 39cm*
- **Guide price £85/$161**

Drummer Boy ◄
- *1930*

Drummer boy with a tin plate body, legs and arms, and a celluloid head, with the makers name "Fecuda", Japan.
- *24cm*
- **Guide price £275/$520**

Spanish Racing Car ▲
- *circa 1920*

Blue and yellow racing car with driver and passenger, and the number seven on the side. Manufactured by Paya in Spain.
- *length 27cm*
- **Guide price £225/$426**

Mickey Mouse ▲
- *1950*

Mickey Mouse puppet carved from wood with yellow composition feet, by Pelham.
- *height 29cm*
- **Guide price £75/$142**

Austin Seven ▼

- *circa 1940*
Cornflower-blue Austin Seven, 35 series
with pneumatic tyres.
- *height 3cm*
- **Guide price £38/\$72**

Dutch Silk Plush Bear ▲

- *1950s*
Dutch brown art silk plush bear in
superb original condition with bulging
cheeks, black and white plastic eyes,
brown plastic nose, black stitched
mouth, white plush pad, and excelsior
filling.
- *height 43.2cm*
- **Guide price £65/\$123**

Ferrari Pedal Car ▲

- *1970*
Red Ferrari pedal car with the number
three on the side.
- *length 1.17m*
- **Guide price £250/\$473**

Oriental Baby Doll ◄

- *circa 1930*
Small oriental porcelain jointed baby doll
with brown glass eyes and a painted
face.
- *height 18cm*
- **Guide price £300/\$567**

German Fire Engine ▲

- *1950*
Red German fire engine with fireman,
manufactured by Gamma.
- *length 43cm*
- **Guide price £110/\$208**

Telstar Kaleidoscope ►

- *1960*
Telstar kaleidoscope with a rocket, stars
and satellite and a blue background,
made by Green Monk of England.
- *height 17cm*
- **Guide price £20/\$38**

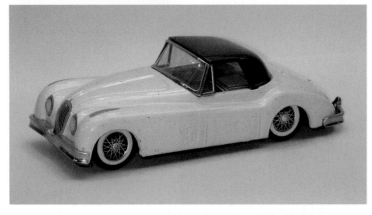

XK Jaguar ▲

- *circa 1950*
XK Jaguar with bottle green top, and
chromed bumper, made by Hoku.
- *length 25cm*
- **Guide price £225/\$426**

Tri-ang Red Racing Car ►

- *1950*
Red Tri-ang Mimic racing car with driver,
the car bearing the number three.
- *length 15cm*
- **Guide price £45/\$85**

American Racing Car ◄

- *1930*

Red and silver racing car and driver, made from an interesting combination of metals, die cast and cast iron, probably by Hubbly American. No. 22 on the side.
- *length 25cm*
- **Guide price £67/$127**

Terrafish ▼

- *1960*

Green Terrafish with yellow spots and large white eyes, from the Gerry Anderson TV show, by Lakeside Toys, Japan.
- *length 23cm*
- **Guide price £275/$520**

Golden Blonde Mohair Bear ▲

- *circa 1910*

Early American golden blonde mohair bear, probably by Harman. Brown glass eyes, black fabric nose, black stitched mouth and claws, peach felt pads, excelsior filling, humped back and front final seam.
- *height 49.5cm*
- **Guide price £685/$1,295**

Yellow Milk Float ▼

- *circa 1960*

Rare yellow Dinky promotional milk float, with "Jobs Dairy" inscribed on the front and rear, with red interior and hubs.
- *length 7cm*
- **Guide price £145/$274**

Blonde Mohair Bear ▼

- *circa 1920*

English blonde mohair bear with glass eyes, black stitched nose and mouth, original linen pads (extensively darned), inoperative tilt growler, excelsior filling and pronounced humped back.
- *height 50.8cm*
- **Guide price £325/$614**

Horse and Milk Float ▲

- *1950*

Matchbox horse-drawn red milk float with driver.
- *height 3cm*
- **Guide price £18/$34**

Orober Fire Engine ▲

- *1920*

Fire engine set of two vehicles with a driver on a pumper, and three figures on the fire engine carrier, complete with red garage, made by Orober in Germany.
- *19cm x 33cm*
- **Guide price £650/$1,229**

Tri-ang Blue Van ▶

- *1950*

Tri-ang Mimic navy-blue London and North Eastern Railway van.
- *length 18cm*
- **Guide price £225/$426**

Nestlé's Austin Van ▲

- *circa 1950*

Red Austin van inscribed with "Nestlé's" in gold letters on the side, made by Dinky, no. 471.

- *length 9cm*
- **Guide price £125/$237**

Daimler Ambulance ▲

- *circa 1950*

Dinky Daimler ambulance, no. 253, with a red cross on the side, red hub plates and original box.

- *height 4cm*
- **Guide price £45/$85**

Chad Valley Teddy ▲

- *1950*

Chad Valley padded teddy with glass eyes and a pleasant expression.

- *height 44cm*
- **Guide price £250/$473**

Gold Mohair Bear ▲

- *circa 1918*

A dark gold German short bristle mohair bear with black boot button eyes, black stitched nose and mouth, replaced tan felt pad, and excelsior filling.

- *height 36cm*
- **Guide price £285/$539**

Vespa and Driver ▲

- *1960*

Green Vespa with a driver wearing red, made in England by Benbros.

- *height 5cm*
- **Guide price £22/$41**

Matchbox Fire Engine ▲

- *1950*

Red Matchbox fire engine with driver.

- *height 3cm*
- **Guide price £22/$41**

Petrol Tanker ▲

- *1930*

Red lead petrol tanker by Taylor and Barrett.

- *length 10cm*
- **Guide price £85/$161**

Round the World Space Toy ▶

- *circa 1950*

Round the World space toy made by Technofix, Germany.

- *length 60cm*
- **Guide price £265/$501**

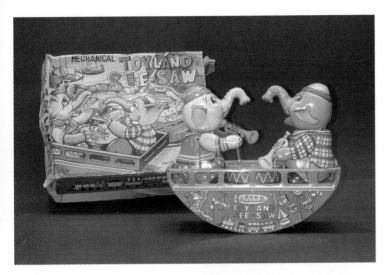

Elephant See-Saw ▲

- *1950*
Two elephants on a toyland see-saw, with key winder playing drums, made by M. S. Toys, Japan.
- *18cm*
- **Guide price £335/$633**

Snow White ▲

- *circa 1930*
French padded doll of Snow White with composition face and hands.
- *height 44cm*
- **Guide price £368/$696**

Black Seal ▼

- *circa 1950*
Black seal balancing a striped ball, manufactured in Japan.
- *height 16cm*
- **Guide price £90/$171**

Scalextric Green BRM ▼

- *1960*
Scalextric tin plate green BRM with racing driver. No. Three on the side.
- *length 15cm*
- **Guide price £95/$180**

Cottage Doll ▼

- *circa 1950*
Small padded "Cottage Doll" made by Glenda O'Connor, with blonde plaits, blue eyes and a pleasant expression, wearing a pink gingham dress, green hat, top and shoes.
- *height 21cm*
- **Guide price £58/$110**

Motorbike with Rider ▶

- *1930*
Grey motorbike with rider made by Arnold Germany, Reg A643.
- *length 25cm*
- **Guide price £230/$435**

Alfa Romeo ▲

- *circa 1960*
Red Alfa Romeo 1900 "Super Sprint", by Dinky, no. 185, with original box.
- *length 10cm*
- **Guide price £62/$118**

Steiff Pekinese ▶

- *circa 1940*
Velvet padded pekinese by Steiff, with glass eyes.
- *height 10cm*
- **Guide price £48/$91**

Tin Metal Boxers ▲

- *1920*
Tin metal boxers on wheeled base made by Einfeilt, Germany.
- *13cm x 19cm*
- **Guide price £275/$520**

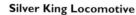

Silver King Locomotive ▶

- *1953–54*
Hornby Dublo EDL11 Silver King
locomotive.
- *length 28cm*
- **Guide price £68/$129**

Bobby Bear ▲

- *1950*
Padded "Bobby Bear" made by Pedigree,
in good overall condition.
- *height 44cm*
- **Guide price £89/$169**

Shoe-Shine Panda ▼

- *circa 1960*
Shoe-shine soft panda, battery-operated,
sitting with a pipe in its mouth and a
brush in each paw, wearing red
dungarees.
- *height 25cm*
- **Guide price £80/$152**

Shell Chemical Tanker ◀

- *circa 1950*
Dinky no. 591 red Shell chemical tanker,
with yellow roof and hubs, and original
box.
- *7cm x 16cm*
- **Guide price £250/$473**

Hornby Dublo Signal Home ▲

- *1950s*
Rare Hornby Dublo 5065 Single Arm
Signal Home, an electrically operated
signal.
- *length 8cm*
- **Guide price £45/$85**

Tri-ang Tank Locomotive ▲

- *1961–67*
Tri-ang TT Railways T99 2-6-2 Class 4MT
Tank Loco in excellent boxed condition
with internal packing and oil bottle.
- *length 14cm*
- **Guide price £75/$142**

Velam Bubble Car ▲

- *1960*
French cream Velam bubble car with
grey roof, made by Quiralu, with original
box.
- *height 4cm*
- **Guide price £78/$148**

Topsy-Turvy Doll ▲

- *1930s*
A British Topsy-Turvy doll which changes
from black to white when turned upside
down. The heads are composition with
painted features.
- *height 30cm*
- **Guide price £150/$284**

Tri-ang Hornby Tank Loco ▼

- *1967–70*
Triang Hornby R754 0-4-4 Class M7
Tank Locomotive. Complete with
instructions, service sheet and crew.
- *length 15cm*
- **Guide price £70/$133**

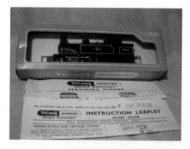

Wrenn Locomotive ◀

- *1976–89*
Wrenn W2221 Cardiff Castle
locomotive in excellent condition
with box.
- *length 25cm*
- **Guide price £100/$189**

Tinplate Crane ▲

- *circa 1950*
Tinplate tower three function crane
N.B.L., made in Western Germany.
- *height 42cm*
- **Guide price £85/$161**

Tri-ang Hornby Train Station ▼
- *1965–71*

Tri-ang Hornby R459 train station set, part of their range of accessories and rolling stock with "Picture Boxes".
- *32cm x 19cm*
- **Guide price £95/$180**

Hornby Duplo Train ▼
- *1962–64*

Hornby Dublo 2234 Deltic Diesel Electric 2 Rail train in excellent condition with box.
- *length 25cm*
- **Guide price £150/$284**

Red Fiat ▼
- *1960*

Red Fiat 600 made in Japan, in excellent condition, with working spring-back sunshine roof.
- *length 22cm*
- **Guide price £180/$341**

MG Midget TD ▶
- *1950*

Matchbox yellow MG Midget TD with red interior, driver, grey wheels and a wheel on the boot.
- *height 2cm*
- **Guide price £24/$47**

Minic Red Steam Lorry ▼
- *1966–68*

Minic Motorway M1564 Red Steam Lorry to complement and run with Tri-ang OO scale railways.
- *length 7cm*
- **Guide price £175/$331**

German-Made Giraffe ◀
- *1950*

German elastoline Giraffe.
- *height 28cm*
- **Guide price £75/$142**

Coal Truck ▼
- *1931–36*

Hornby "O" gauge Meccano coal truck.
- *length 17cm*
- **Guide price £88/$167**

Shirley Temple Doll ▼
- *1934*

Shirley Temple porcelain doll with blonde hair, wearing suede dungarees with silver studs and a red check shirt.
- *height 325cm*
- **Guide price £325/$614**

Brown Steiff Bear ▲
- *1993*

Brown Steiff bear. Limited edition of 3,000.
- *height 61cm*
- **Guide price £375/$709**

Roman Chariot ▼

- *1960*

Plastic roman chariot by Timber Toys, in the original box.

- *width 42cm*
- **Guide price £350/$662**

Tri-ang Accessories ▲

- *1960s*

Tri-ang TTRailways T27 signal box.

- *length 9cm*
- **Guide price £40/$76**

Hornby Metal Train ▲

- *1958*

Metal train by Hornby in original box.

- *length 28cm*
- **Guide price £125/$237**

Twin Rotor Helicopter ▲

- *circa 1960*

ALPS Japanese tinplate battery-driven twin rotor helicopter with plastic rotors.

- *length 35cm*
- **Guide price £180/$341**

Steiff Bear Watches ▶

- *1992*

Steiff bear watch collection.

- *height 51cm*
- **Guide price £350/$662**

Merrythought Cheeky ▲

- *circa 1994*

One of the largest 'Cheekies', in cream mohair with cream pads, a cream bow and yellow nose.

- *height 60cm*
- **Guide price £230/$435**

Annabette Himstedt Doll ▲

- *1993–4*

Limited edition of an Annabette Himstedt doll. Hand painted with long blonde hair and original white dress.

- *height 68cm*
- **Guide price £650/$1,229**

CN Budd Dummy Railcar ▼

- *1965–71*

Rare r352cn CN Budd Dummy unpowered locomotive.

- *length 25cm*
- **Guide price £40/$76**

LNER 504 Locomotive ▲

- *circa 1930*

Bing for Bassett Lowke 4-4-0 George V LNER Locomotive 504, with clockwork, "O" gauge.

- *length 42cm*
- **Guide price £375/$709**

Tinplate Fire Engine ▶

- *circa 1960*

Tinplate clockwork fire engine with three-piece extending ladder. Made in Japan and marked with "K" trademark.

- *length 33cm*
- **Guide price £145/$274**

Frazer Nash Sports Car ▲

• 1940
Frazer Nash sports car made by Dinky, with a blue body and wheels, and a grey interior.
• length 8cm
• **Guide price £48/$91**

American Ford ▶

• 1920
Tan American Ford with black wheels and brass radiator, made by Tootsie.
• length 10cm
• **Guide price £27/$52**

Rolls Royce ▲

• 1960
Cream and silver Rolls Royce Phantom V made by Dinky.
• length 8cm
• **Guide price £75/$142**

Austin Healey ▲

• 1960
Cream Austin Healey sports car with red wheels and interior, with driver and the number "23" on the side.
• length 8cm
• **Guide price £113/$214**

American Tootsie Car ▲

• 1930
American brown Tootsie car, by La Salle.
• length 12cm
• **Guide price £120/$227**

Limited Edition Doll ▼

• 1994
Annabette Himstedt doll, one of a limited edition.
• height 75cm
• **Guide price £750/$1,418**

Blue Mini ▼

• 1966
Unusual blue Mini in original box, made by Dinky.
• length 8cm
• **Guide price £125/$237**

Robot Money Bank ▼

• 1960
Silver robot with large round eyes, designed with a silver scoop for the money, sitting on a circular brown container.
• height 14cm
• **Guide price £25/$48**

Circus Elephant ▼

• 1950
Clockwork grey circus elephant with blue eyes and red decorative trimmings.
• height 14cm
• **Guide price £88/$167**

Steiff Bear and Golly ▲

- *1996*

Jolly Golly and Steiff Bear set, part of a limited edition of 1,500.

- *height 45cm*
- **Guide price £295/$558**

German Doll ▲

- *1930*

Original porcelain and hand-painted German doll, wearing original black coat with lace collar, red dress and hat with lace trim, and black laced boots.

- *height 37cm*
- **Guide price £175/$331**

Porcelain Doll ▶

- *circa 1940*

A Burggrub-Princess Elizabeth Pozellanlabrik porcelain doll with blonde hair and a white organza dress.

- *height 38cm*
- **Guide price £1,200/$2,268**

Merrythought Golly ▼

- *1960*

Merrythought golly, limited edition of 100.

- *height 32cm*
- **Guide price £40/$76**

American School Bus ▲

- *1950*

Yellow American school bus.

- *length 30cm*
- **Guide price £190/$359**

American Fastback ▲

- *1920*

American fastback orange car with black running boards and red enamel wheels, by Mano IL.

- *length 8cm*
- **Guide price £75/$142**

American Footballer ▼

- *1950*

American footballer with red and white helmet.

- *height 9cm*
- **Guide price £85/$161**

Morris Car ▲

- *1960*

Bull-nosed Morris commemorative toy with a band called The Beat.

- *length 7cm*
- **Guide price £45/$85**

Phantom Brown Bear ▲

- *circa 1910*

Brown Bear made by Phantom, limited edition of 4,000.

- *height 61cm*
- **Guide price £380/$719**

Red Mercedes Racing Car ▲
- *1930*
Red German Mercedes racing car, by Marklin.
- *length 26cm*
- **Guide price £750/$1,418**

Batmobile Car ▼
- *1960*
American black Batmobile, with red interior.
- *length 10cm*
- **Guide price £48/$91**

Blue and Silver Metal Dalek ▼
- *1950s*
Unusual blue and silver metal dalek from the 1950s.
- *height 12cm*
- **Guide price £225/$426**

Wellington Bear ▲
- *1992*
Limited edition of Merrythought Wellington Bear.
- *height 54cm*
- **Guide price £125/$237**

Clockwork Clown ▼
- *1950*
Clockwork clown with red jacket and yellow and black hat, riding a bike, with original key.
- *height 7cm*
- **Guide price £155/$293**

Curatt Car ▼
- *20th century*
Red motor car with black roof and a brass radiator and side lamp, red running boards, and a man driving, made by Curatt.
- *length 44cm*
- **Guide price £2,350/$4,442**

Black Clockwork Robot ▲
- *1960*
American black clockwork robot with red boots, with original cardboard box.
- *height 125cm*
- **Guide price £168/$320**

Green Racing Car ▲
- *1980*
Green Connaught Dinky racing car with driver, with its original box.
- *length 16cm*
- **Guide price £80/$152**

Police Van ▼
- *1930s*
Black police van, made by Wells.
- *length 11cm*
- **Guide price £75/$142**

Merrythought Mohair Bear ▲

- *1930s*

Merrythought mohair bear. A limited edition of 50 was produced in white brown and black.
- *height 38cm*
- **Guide price £55/$104**

Barbie Doll ▼

- *1960*

Plastic flexible Barbie doll with long blonde hair, a pink hairband and pink pumps, by Mattel.
- *height 30cm*
- **Guide price £75/$142**

Messerschmitt Car ▼

- *1960*

Messerschmitt with red body and a clear cover and three wheels.
- *length 21cm*
- **Guide price £360/$681**

Red London Bus ▲

- *1950s*

Red London double-decker bus, by Triang toys.
- *length 17cm*
- **Guide price £170/$322**

Clown on Stilts ▼

- *circa 1950s*

Clown on stilts with red and white striped trousers, red top and green hat, playing a violin, with original box and key.
- *height 20cm*
- **Guide price £100/$189**

Milk Van ▼

- *1950*

English blue and white milk van by Chad Valley toys.
- *length 15cm*
- **Guide price £115/$217**

Red Fire Engine ▲

- *1960s*

Red fire engine operated by battery with a box snorkel.
- *34cm x 20cm*
- **Guide price £85/$161**

Clockwork Circus Clown ▲

- *1930*

Clockwork Shiuko circus clown with a drum.
- *height 6cm*
- **Guide price £145/$274**

French Racing Car ▲

• 1930
French blue racing car with red decoration, the number "54" on the side and white wheels.
• length 24cm
• **Guide price £85/$161**

Tudor Doll's House ▲

• 1930s
Mock Tudor doll's house with white walls and black beams, circa 1930.
• height 87cm
• **Guide price £125/$237**

Delivery Van ▲

• 1950
Green delivery van made by Dinky with its original cardboard yellow box.
• length 8cm
• **Guide price £67/$127**

VW Beetle Model ▼

• 1998
A gold beetle of 1:⅛ scale modelled after 1955 car, 1,000,000 off the production line. In dye-cast aluminium, with opening doors, boot and bonnet.
• **Guide price £20/$38**

Steiff Bear ◄

• circa 1991
A Steiff bear, one of a limited edition of 300 which were made only for the UK market in 1991. This is a replica of a Steiff bear salvaged from the Titanic and sold for £94,400.
• height 48cm
• **Guide price £450/$851**

Green Flying Scotsman ▼

• 1950
Green Flying Scotsman by Bassett, coke O-gauge.
• length 28cm
• **Guide price £1,950/$3,686**

Woodbine Dominoes ▲

• circa 1930
A box of dominoes in original green box with cream lettering with the words, "Wills Woodbine Dominoes" inscribed on the front of the tin.
• length 27cm
• **Guide price £36/$70**

Clockwork Steamboat ◄

• circa 1925
Clockwork white steamboat boat with yellow funnels and red wheels and trim.
• length 12cm
• **Guide price £238/$450**

Welsh Doll ▲

• circa 1930
A Welsh Moa 200 porcelain hand-painted doll, wearing an emerald green velvet dress with a large ribboned belt with diamante clasp, bonnet and black shoes.
• height 61cm
• **Guide price £395/$748**

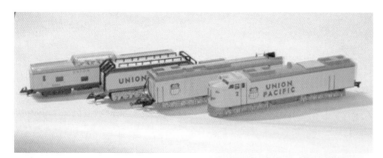

Yellow Union Pacific Train ◄

- *1960*

Yellow Union Pacific train by Wese. TT-gauge.

- *length 64cm*
- **Guide price £225/$426**

Racing Car ▼

- *1930*

Clockwork metal French racing car with driver, by Charles Rossignol, Paris.

- *length 40cm*
- **Guide price £485/$917**

Clockwork Windmill ▼

- *1900*

English clockwork metal windmill with orange sails.

- *height 4cm*
- **Guide price £90/$171**

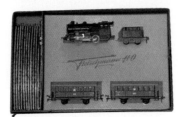

Fleischmann Train ▲

- *1955*

Fleischmann train with rails, in original box. HO-gauge.

- *width 38cm/box*
- **Guide price £85/$161**

Figure with Drum ▼

- *1940*

German clockwork figure with drum and cymbal.

- *height 10cm*
- **Guide price £130/$246**

Royal Mail Van ▼

- *1950*

Red Royal Mail van made by Dinky, with the original yellow box and picture.

- *height 9cm*
- **Guide price £120/$227**

Hornby Train ▼

- *circa 1930*

Brown Hornby train with yellow trim around the windows and black wheels. O-gauge.

- *length 32cm*
- **Guide price £120/$227**

Tin-Head Doll ▲

- *1930*

Tin-head hand-painted china doll, with long blonde hair, wearing a white silk dress.

- *height 34cm*
- **Guide price £195/$369**

Dumper Truck ▼

- *1950s*

Yellow and red dumper truck, made in Japan by Haji for the American market.

- *length 23cm*
- **Guide price £60/$114**

Oriental Doll Family ▲

- *20th century*

Japanese family of dolls wearing traditional costumes, the girls having black wigs and hand painted faces.
- *height 36cm/girl*
- **Guide price £250/$473**

Chad Valley Train ▼

- *1950*

An English brown bakelite toy train with two carriages with black wheels on the train, and ivory on the carriages. Maker's name: Chad Valley.
- *length 58cm*
- **Guide price £700/$1,323**

Toy Pheasant ▼

- *1920*

German clockwork toy pheasant.
- *4cm x 6cm*
- **Guide price £125/$237**

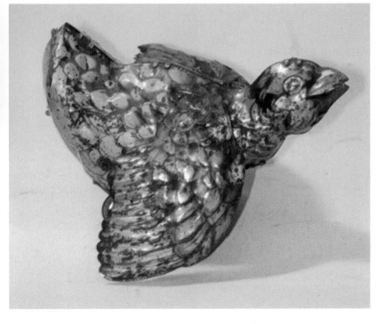

Alfa Romeo ▼

- *1978*

Red Alfa Romeo Dinky racing car with red wheels and a figure of a racing driver at the wheel in white, with original box.
- *length 14cm*
- **Guide price £78/$148**

Bluebird Car ▼

- *1930*

Blue Bluebird racing car, by Kosuge & Co.
- *length 21cm*
- **Guide price £425/$803**

Yellow Ferrari ▼

- *1960*

Yellow Ferrari with original box, made by Dinky.
- *length 10cm*
- **Guide price £40/$76**

Horse Van ▼

- *1950*

Yellow and orange horse van, with original packaging.
- *length 21cm*
- **Guide price £69/$131**

Magic Roundabout ▲

- *1970*

Magic roundabout characters, on a red bicycle with a trailer, made by Corgi Toys.
- *length 8cm*
- **Guide price £45/$85**

Silver XK120 ▲

- *1950s*

Silver clockwork metal Jaguar XK 120 with original box and key.
- *length 10cm*
- **Guide price £200/$378**

Mickey Mouse Driving a Car ▲

- *1961*

Mickey Mouse driving a blue open car, with yellow spoked wheels.
- *length 12cm*
- **Guide price £60/$114**

German Doll ▲

- *1930*

German doll with hand painted porcelain face, blue eyes and blonde hair, wearing a red hat jacket and dress, with white lace trim and black leather boots.
- *height 57cm*
- **Guide price £325/$614**

Peugeot Fire Engine ▲

- *circa 1930*

Peugeot 601 fire engine in painted bright red tinplate. Made by Charles Rossignol, Paris. Three firemen inside and a swivelling ladder on the top.
- *height 37cm*
- **Guide price £485/$917**

Mussolini Figure ▼

- *circa 1940*

Hand-painted, lead figure of Il Duce in typically aggressive arms akimbo pose.
- *height 25cm*
- **Guide price £150/$284**

Robot ▼

- *circa 1970*

A tin robot spaceman, made in Japan, with walking mechanism. Silver painted with yellow and blue design.
- *height 14cm*
- **Guide price £75/$142**

Rope Swinging Cowboy ▼

- *circa 1950*

Rodeo cowboy made of tinplate and celluloid. Dressed in cotton trousers and printed shirt. Also equipped with felt hat, tin feet, tin arms and tin gloves. Contains clockwork mechanism which swings the lasso and moves his hips. Original box. Japan.
- *height 22cm*
- **Guide price £165/$312**

German Crocodile Train ▲

- *circa 1960*

Green German crocodile train by Marklin. HO-gauge.
- *length 23cm*
- **Guide price £445/$841**

Rocking Horse ▲

- *circa 1960*

Pressed steel arm with seat and painted head. With leather ears. Simulated rocking action caused by spring and lever movement.
- *length 52cm*
- **Guide price £54/$102**

Metal Soldiers ◄

- *1950*

Set of lead, hand-painted, model British soldiers and horses.
- *height 4cm/soldier*
- **Guide price £1,500/$2,835**

Union Pacific Train ▲

- *1957*

Plastic orange Union Pacific train with black wheels by Lionel & Co.
- *length 28cm*
- **Guide price £85/$161**

11th Hussars Models ▲

- *1949*

Britains lead soldiers set 182, with hussars dismounted with officer and horses. Original Fred Whisstock hand-painted box. Immaculate condition.

- *length 60 cm*
- **Guide price £200/$378**

Ford Sedan ▼

- *1950s*

Marusan Ford Sedan toy car. A lovely bright yellow with lithographed seat and crosshatched floor. Chrome bumper, lights and trim.

- *length 25.5cm*
- **Guide price £250/$473**

Horse Roller ▲

- *1940*

Farm roller with farm hand and horse, from Britains Home Farm series, set of nine. Patriotic wartime toy in original strong cardboard box.

- **Guide price £80/$152**

Thunderbirds Doll ◄

- *circa 1966*

A 'Brains' doll from the Gerry and Sylvia Anderson TV programme, 'Thunderbirds', complete with original clothing, plastic spectacles, spanner and pliers.

- *height 30cm*
- **Guide price £200/$378**

Dumper Truck ▼

- *circa 1950*

English, all wood dumper truck. The moving wheels activate the tipping action. In original painted livery of red and green.

- *length 67cm*
- **Guide price £75/$142**

Ford Zodiac Model ▼

- *circa 1960*

Model of a Ford Zodiac convertable. Matchbox toy number 39. Pink bodywork with a white and green interior and green towbar. Original box.

- *length 9cm*
- **Guide price £45/$85**

Hornby 4-4-4 Train ▼

- *circa 1920s*

Clockwork Hornby model of L.M.S. 4-4-4 locomotive, with original burgundy and black paint and brass fittings.

- *length 26.5cm*
- **Guide price £195/$369**

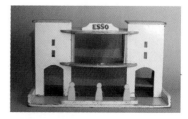

Skedoodle ▲

- *1979*

A Skedoodle etching game with stencils made in Brevete, France, by Estanger. Complete with all original attributes.

- **Guide price £16/$30**

Wooden Garage ▲

- *circa 1950*

Wooden Esso garage with forecourt and petrol pumps. Original white paint with blue details. Includes hand-operated lift.

- *height 26cm*
- **Guide price £85/$161**

Miss Piggy ▼

- *1979*

The Muppet Show's Miss Piggy shown in pink sports car in famous waving pose.

- *length 11cm*
- **Guide price £10/$19**

Snap ▲

- *1920*

Pack of Snap cards, complete and in good condition with original box, depicting characters from the pantomime and nursery rhymes. British.
- **Guide price £55/$104**

Bébé Jumeau Doll ▲

- *1907*

Jumeau doll, with small firing mark to right ear, otherwise perfect china head, with original white lace costume, white shoes and mob cap.
- *height 47cm*
- **Guide price £1,250/$2,363**

Black Fleischmann Train ▶

- *1955*

Black Fleischmann train with red trim and wheels. O-gauge.
- *length 23cm*
- **Guide price £135/$256**

Green Centurion Tank ▲

- *1954–60*

English green centurion tank.
- *length 12cm*
- **Guide price £50/$95**

Trix Twin Train ▼

- *circa 1937*

Train of four coaches, loco and tender. L.M.S '00' gauge. Maroon with dark green roofs. Each coach has four wheels.
- *length 50cm per coach*
- **Guide price £110/$208**

Britains' Zoo Series ▼

- *1950*

Set 908 Indian rhinoceros, grey with cream-coloured horn. With original box and paint.
- *height 5cm*
- **Guide price £50/$95**

Green MG ◀

- *1950*

Green MG TF sports car made by Band Japan for the USA market.
- *length 22cm*
- **Guide price £60/$114**

Light Goods Van ▲

- *1948*

Van from Britains' Motor and Road Series set 2024, with driver. All original paintwork with 'Britains Ltd' signwritten on side panels. Original box.
- **Guide price £350/$662**

Teddy Bear ▲

- *circa 1993*

A replica of a 1907 Steiff bear, one of the largest made. The materials used are all as the original. The bear is in the sitting position, wearing a red bow.
- *height 70cm*
- **Guide price £750/$1,418**

Kiddy Computer ▲

- *late 1970s*

Kiddy computer, with original box, which features addition, subtraction, multiplication and division, but looks as if it does rather more.
- *height 19cm*
- **Guide price £18/$34**

Royal Scot Train ▲
- *1935*

Red English Royal Scot metal train with black trim and wheels.
- *length 26cm*
- **Guide price £425/$803**

Mickey Mouse Toy ▶
- *1930s*

Cardboard Mickey Mouse 'rolly' toy with bakelite round base. Made from cardboard. Chad Valley, USA.
- *height 23cm*
- **Guide price £180/$341**

GI Soldier ▲
- *1987*

US soldier in combat uniform with helmet and rifle. Battery-operated sequence where soldier crawls and fires weapon.
- *length 34cm*
- **Guide price £40/$76**

Black Train ▼
- *1930*

Black metal train with red and gold trim. The maker's name is Maerklin.
- *length 42cm*
- **Guide price £2,500/$4,725**

Tin Motorcyclist ▲
- *1950*

German tin model of a clockwork motorcyclist with an expression of speed.
- *length 16cm*
- **Guide price £225/$426**

Celluloid Doll ▲
- *circa 1930*

A French celluloid doll in a green velvet suit and white blouse – both original. A 'bent limb boy'.
- *height 45cm*
- **Guide price £145/$274**

Clockwork Cat ▼
- *1950*

German clockwork tabby cat, playing with yellow and green striped ball.
- *length 5cm*
- **Guide price £45/$85**

Cloth Doll ▲
- *1920*

All original and in good condition, with red hair, a red hair ribbon and flirting eyes.
- *height 59cm*
- **Guide price £298/$563**

Rubik's Cube ▲
- *1980*

Rubik's cube in box shown in complete form with sticker 'Toy of the Year 1980'. From the Ideal Toy Corporation. Made in Hungary.
- *8cm square*
- **Guide price £20/$38**

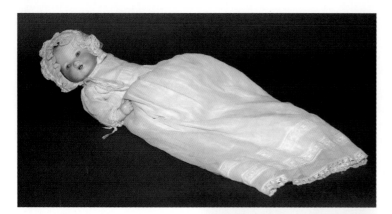

Dream Baby ▲

- *1920*

Dream Baby doll in excellent condition with open and close eyes, original white apparel and painted features.

- *length 34cm*
- **Guide price £325/$614**

Shirley Temple Doll ▲

- *circa 1930s*

Very collectable Shirley Temple composition doll, with all original clothes and club badge.

- *height 65cm*
- **Guide price £450/$851**

Model T Ford Model ▲

- *1960s*

Dinky toy 109 cabriolet model of a Model T Ford car. Based on Gerry Anderson's TV series "The Secret Service". Black and yellow in colour. England.

- *length 8.5cm*
- **Guide price £78/$148**

ET Doll ▲

- *1982*

Plastic stuffed doll from the feature film 'ET' by Stephen Spielberg.

- *height 24cm*
- **Guide price £18/$34**

Bucking Bronco ▲

- *1910*

Bucking bronco horse with rider. Made in Germany by Lehmann, serial no. 625. Tinplate clockwork and base. Man is in red shirt and brown trousers.

- *height 19cm*
- **Guide price £585/$1,106**

Master Blaster Station ▼

- *1981*

UFO Master Blaster Station battery operated by Bambino, made in Japan.

- *length 21cm*
- **Guide price £15/$28**

Model Pandas ▲

- *1949*

Set 9011 in Britains Zoo series. Giant panda standing on all fours and two baby pandas (one on two legs and the other on all fours). With original box.

- **Guide price £35/$67**

Wild West Models ▲

- *1960*

A set of Britains' Swoppets Wild West plastic models, hand-painted and all complete with the original box shaped to accommodate the ten scale models.

- **Guide price £150/$284**

Jousting Knights ▼

- *circa 2000*

Hand-made and painted pewter 15th-century Jousting Knight (right) and Crusader Knight. 90mm scale.

- *height 17cm*
- **Guide price £1,000/$1,890 (Jousting); £850/$1,607 (Crusader)**

Military Band ▲
- *circa 1948*

Imperial Napoleonic Band with escort. Twenty-one piece figure set. Made in Belgium by M.I.M.
- **Guide price £1,000/$1,890**

Simon and Halbig Doll ▲
- *1910*

Simon and Halbig 1078 doll with perfect bisque head. Contains glass flirty eyes and moveable joints.
- *height 69cm*
- **Guide price £795/$1,503**

Somersault Bear ▲
- *circa 1990*

A replica of a 1909 Som709ersault bear with clockwork mechanism which makes him lift his arma and do his trick. In old gold mohair. Edition limited to 5,000.
- *height 29cm*
- **Guide price £375/$709**

Clockwork Whoopee Car ▲
- *circa 1930*

American clockwork tin plate orange Whoopee car. Grafitti on bonnet, for example 'squeak easy'. Makes crazy erratic movements. Illustrated on Maxime Pinksy volume 2. Made by Louis Marx toys. Clown shown driving.
- *length 19cm*
- **Guide price £245/$464**

UFO Jigsaw ◄
- *1970*

A complete UFO jigsaw puzzle comprising 320 pieces by Arrow Games ltd., after a TV series. Shows a scene with 'Shadows' space engineers – one of a series of three designs.
- *18 x 18cm*
- **Guide price £10/$19**

Fischer Car ▼
- *circa 1910*

Stylish version of Fischer car cabriolet with driver. Predominantly white with brown canopy. Was featured in 'American Motor Toys' by Lillian Gottschalk.
- *length 19cm*
- **Guide price £1,780/$3,364**

Robot ▼
- *1985*

Battery-operated robot named 'Crackpot'. By Tomy, made in Singapore, with animated preset moves, moving arms, head and flashing lights.
- *height 17cm*
- **Guide price £55/$104**

Hornby 'O' Garage ▼
- *1950s*

French Hornby 'O' gauge model representing the main station at Bordeaux. White and orange handpainted wood, decorated with small posters of Normandy and a painted clock.
- *length 53cm*
- **Guide price £125/$237**

View Master ▲
- *1980*

A GAF View Master and one ornothological slide. In working order. Circular slides contain several transparencies which are selected by lever on side of viewer.
- *width 15cm*
- **Guide price £8/$16**

Pedigree Doll ▲
- *1950*

Pedigree doll in original dress. Walking doll with flirting eyes, naturalistic hair and red hair ribbon.
- *height 56cm*
- **Guide price £110/$208**

Model Train ◄

• *circa 1947*

Lionel GG1 model train. Rare USA train '0' gauge. Black cast metal. 'Pennsylvania' written on the side. This is one of the first models produced by the company.

• *length 36cm*
• **Guide price £450/$851**

Battery-Operated Robot ◄

• *late 1970s*

Robot with preset animated programme with moving head and illuminating eyes.

• *height 11cm*
• **Guide price £18/$34**

Snow White ▼

• *1938*

Snow White and the Seven Dwarfs, in painted lead. Part of Britains' Civilian Series.

• *height 4-6.5cm*
• **Guide price £225/$426**

Sailorboy and Girl Doll ▲

• *circa 1930*

A Schuco sailor and girl doll, made in Germany, both made of tinplate and celluloid, with clothes in felt. Clockwork mechanism in full working order.

• *height 7cm*
• **Guide price £250/$473**

Rock and Roll Flower ▲

• *1988*

Sound-activated, dancing 'rock and roll' flower shown with painted face upside-down glasses and yellow trumpet, in white flower pot.

• *height 35cm*
• **Guide price £18/$34**

Formula 1 Car ▼

• *circa 1950*

Lancia Formula 1 by Mercury of Italy. Unusual with petrol tanks on the side. With original box.

• *length 9cm*
• **Guide price £78/$148**

Timpo Models ▼

• *1970*

Clay County Jail Wagon and horse with seven cowboys in different poses. Still boxed.

• **Guide price £80/$152**

Doll ►

• *circa 1920s*

A German character doll from the 1920s, in original woollen romper suit with open and shut eyes and a china head.

• *height 25cm*
• **Guide price £265/$501**

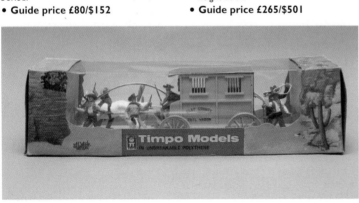

Troll ▲

• *circa 1990*

One of the celebrated Troll family, made in Denmark. This particular model has long white hair and is wearing a yellow dress with white trim.

• *height 26cm*
• **Guide price £18/$34**

Model Soldier ▲

- *1940*

First Empire Imperial Guard mounted standard bearer. Made in Belgium by M.I.M.

- *height 6cm*
- **Guide price £80/$152**

Heinrich Doll ▲

- *1905*

Pretty doll made by Heinrich. Hand-worked head with perfect open and shut eyes. Body in good condition.

- *height 57cm*
- **Guide price £450/$851**

Sailor Doll ▼

- *1910*

A doll representing a boy in original sailor costume. Small firing crack in forehead, otherwise perfect.

- *height 39cm*
- **Guide price £450/$851**

Animated Santa Bank ▼

- *circa 1960s*

Deluxe animated Santa piggy bank with original box. Battery-and coin-operated. Eyes flash, head moves, and bell rings. Santa has a vinyl face and sits on a tinplate house, holding presents and a bell. Japan.

- *height 30cm*
- **Guide price £285/$539**

Tailless Donkey Game ◄

- *circa 1905*

"Pin the tail on the Donkey" game, complete with donkey poster and tails and a curious snake.

- *49 x 27cm*
- **Guide price £55/$104**

Yeomen Guard Models ▲

- *1950*

Britains set 1257 Yeomen of the Guard from their "Original Historical Series", complete with box displaying the nine figures.

- **Guide price £140/$265**

Merrythought Bear ▲

- *circa 1980*

A Merrythought Sloth Bear – one of a limited edition of 250 – in black and white, with very long hair and growler. Fully jointed and with hand-embroidery.

- *height 60cm*
- **Guide price £225/$426**

Railway Signal Box ▲

- *circa 1950s*

Tinplate signal box made by Hornby. Green roof and orange brick work. In good condition and with original box.

- *length 6.5cm*
- **Guide price £45/$85**

Clockwork Sparrow ▼

- *1976*

Chinese clockwork sparrow in full working order and complete with original box. Sparrow is vividly painted and pecks the ground when activated.

- *height 8.5cm*
- **Guide price £13/$25**

Mounted Drummer ▼

- *circa 2000*

Hand-made and painted pewter mounted French drummer, with plumes to rider and mount, on a modelled painted base and a wooden plinth.

- *height 17cm*
- **Guide price £850/$1,607**

Le Loto Comique ▼

- *circa 1905*

Lotto/Bingo style game. Contains games pieces with numbers, pictures and boards with pictorial montages.

- *43 x 35cm*
- **Guide price £118/$223**

TRIBAL ART

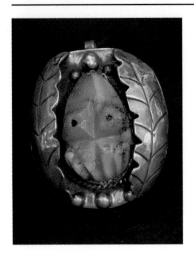

Zuni Fetish Frog ▲
- *1930*
Large Zuni fetish circular silver pendant with a central turquoise styled frog flanked by silver leaves.
- *length 4.5cm*
- **Guide price £59/$112**

Zuni Pot ▲
- *circa 2000*
Zuni ceramic seed pot with two painted frogs, by A. Peynetsa.
- *height 6cm*
- **Guide price £90/$171**

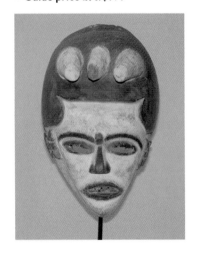

Nigerian Delta Region Mask ▼
- *circa 1910*
Spirit mask from the Nigerian Delta region, the head crowned by four men and a boat, with classical red pigmentation. The figures, originally white, have been overpainted black.
- *height 53cm*
- **Guide price £1,100/$2,079**

Igbo Tribe Figures ▼
- *circa 1910*
One of a pair of figures from the Igbo tribe. A terracotta seated ancestorial couple, with typical central crested headdress and multiple anklets, bracelets and necklaces symbolising wealth.
- *height 54cm*
- **Guide price £6,500/$12,285**

African Ogni Mask ◄
- *early 20th century*
African Ogni mask.
- *26cm x 14cm*
- **Guide price £350/$662**

Tshokwe-Mbuna Mask ▲
- *circa 1910*
Striking Tshokwe-Mbuna mask with natural patination and fibre additions.
- *height 37cm*
- **Guide price £400/$756**

Apache Smoking Pouch ▼
- *1950*
Apache Indian smoking pouch with a red, white and black butterfly, and an orange background made from glass beads sewn on leather.
- *12cm x 7cm*
- **Guide price £160/$303**

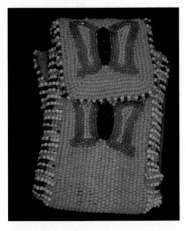

Native American Pot ◄
- *circa 2000*
Native American ceramic pot with a painted black and red geometric pattern, signed "P Beneto".
- *height 24cm*
- **Guide price £129/$245**

Indian Gloves ▼
- *1950*
Pair of Indian gloves with a glass beadwork woodland design and fringing. Lined with pink silk and worn in Wild West Shows.
- *length 28cm*
- **Guide price £299/$565**

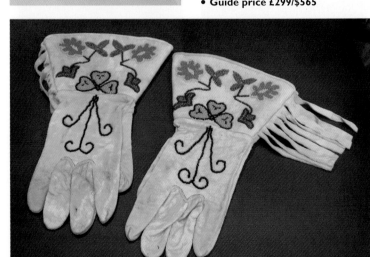

Hopi Indian Pot ▶

- *circa 1999*

Hopi Indian ceramic pot with black painted geometric design signed "ACC".

- *height 5cm*
- **Guide price £40/$76**

African Wall Hanging ▼

- *early 20th century*

An unusual ceremonial dance skirt with black abstract patterns on a light brown background, from the Neongo tribe, Zaire.

- *76cm x 40cm*
- **Guide price £2,800/$5,292**

Kple Kple Mask ▲

- *circa 1920*

Kple Kple junior mask of the Golidance, one of the most abstracted masks of Africa, from a collection in France.

- *height 43cm*
- **Guide price £5,500/$10,395**

Yoruba Crown ▲

- *20th century*

Yoruban crown decorated with coconut hair and a face created from cowrie shells.

- *height 35cm*
- **Guide price £650/$1,229**

Calabar Mask ▲

- *circa 1910*

Calabar mask from Benue River, Nigeria, with a strong Cameroon influence.

- *height 29cm*
- **Guide price £720/$1,360**

Ivory Coast Mask ▶

- *circa 1910*

Heavily encrusted Dan mask from the Ivory Coast, Africa.

- *height 24cm*
- **Guide price £680/$1,286**

Pair of Naga Figures ◀

- *circa 1910*

Carved wood Naga figures depicting a standing male with hands clasped and a standing female with hands held across her stomach and head looking down.

- *height 64cm*
- **Guide price £950/$1,796 the pair**

Himachal Pradesh Mask ▼

- *early 1900s*
A most unusual form with the upper features on a dome-like area, with exaggerated slit eyes and a stylised mouth, with signs of applied silver and other applications.
- *26cm x 40cm*
- **Guide price £1,300/$2,457**

Zuni Fetish Pot ▼

- *circa 2000*
Zuni fetish pot shaped as an owl with its owlet.
- *height 8cm*
- **Guide price £90/$171**

Buffalo Helmet Mask ▲

- *circa 1920*
Kanos buffalo carved wood mask from the Ivory coast of Africa.
- *height 38cm*
- **Guide price £1,400/$2,646**

Native American Ceramic Pot ▲

- *circa 1998*
Native American pot with black incised design painted with porcupine quills, inscribed, "ACOCMA NM KSC".
- *height 7cm*
- **Guide price £150/$284**

Heavily Patinated Mask ▲

- *circa 1910*
Heavily patinated tribal mask.
- *height 26cm*
- **Guide price £740/$1,399**

Yoruban Iron Staff ▼

- *early 1900s*
Ancient ceremonial wrought-iron staff, from Yoruba, Nigeria.
- *64cm x 24cm*
- **Guide price £720/$1,361**

Mask with Cowrie Shells ▼

- *circa 1910*
Mask with applied cowrie shells on the nose and cheeks, iron rings through the nose and ears, and erect hair.
- *height 36cm*
- **Guide price £3,200/$6,048**

Javanese Mask ▶

- *early 1900s*
Javanese mask of a Mahabarata/ Ramayana character.
- *19cm x 14cm*
- **Guide price £550/$1,040**

Dan Mask ▲

- *early 20th century*
Dan mask from Liberia.
- *25cm x 16cm*
- **Guide price £400/$756**

Gable Mask ▲

- *early 20th century*
A Gable mask from Papua New Guinea decorated with cowrie shells and pig tusks.
- *height 90cm*
- **Guide price £550/$1,040**

Baule Tribe ▼

• *circa 1910*
Well formulated naturalistic human face with a delicate pouting mouth, finely shaped nose, almond eyes painted white, crossbanded hair and surmounted by a white crescent moon, in excellent condition, from the west coast of Africa.
• *height 48cm*
• **Guide price £3,200/$6,048**

Naga Mask ▶

• *20th century*
Naga wooden mask.
• *30cm x 18cm*
• **Guide price £550/$1,040**

Apache Bag ▲

• *1950*
Apache suede pipe bag with a long strap and fringing and a central glass bead work of a red and black frog.
• *length 50cm*
• **Guide price £169/$320**

Yonba Maternity Figure ▲

• *circa 1910*
Yonba carved wood maternity figure of a seated woman with a child at her breast.
• *height 59cm*
• **Guide price £1,700/$3,213**

African Mask ▲

• *early 1900s*
A finely drawn mask with a good patination from the Incangala Tshokwe.
• **Guide price £800/$1,512**

Kuba Dance Skirt ▼

• *mid 20th century*
Zairean Neongo tribe Kuba dance skirt. Dyed raffia appliquéd.
• *76cm x 400cm*
• **Guide price £1,900/$3,591**

African Wooden Sculptures ◀

• *early 1900s*
Three African tribal carved wood sculptures.
• *11cm x 70cm*
• **Guide price £360/$681**

Ebony Pot ▲

• *circa 2000*
An ebony pot and stand, carved from one piece of wood, with zoomorphic and figurative designs. From Zimbabwe.
• *height 22cm*
• **Guide price £20/$38**

Native American Pot ◀

• *circa 1999*
Native American pot and lid with a rust, white and black geometric design painted with porcupine quills, inscribed "ACOMA".
• *height 6cm*
• **Guide price £50/$95**

Fang Wooden Pulley ▼

- *20th century*

An African Fang wooden pulley with carved and turned decoration.

- *height 39cm*
- **Guide price £390/$737**

Kota Figure ▼

- *early 20th century*

Kota wooden figure decorated with brass and copper plaques.

- *71cm x 33cm*
- **Guide price £850/$1,607**

Bookends ▶

- *circa 2000*

A pair of large, water-buffalo bookends made from kiaat wood. From Zimbabwe.

- *height 41cm*
- **Guide price £150/$284**

Iron Lamp ▲

- *early 1900s*

Ancient wrought-iron lamp decorated with birds.

- **Guide price £820/$1,550**

Embroidered Panel ▲

- *circa 1935*

A Shoowa tribe velvet knotted and embroidered panel, with geometric, repeated diamond patterns. From Zaire, formerly the Belgian Congo.

- *1.3cm square*
- **Guide price £330/$624**

Mahogany Stool ▼

- *circa 1970*

A red mahogany stool, carved from one piece of wood, showing an elephant. From the Shona or Matabele tribe of Zimbabwe.

- *height 51cm*
- **Guide price £230/$435**

Ebony Table ▼

- *circa 1990*

An ebony table, with interlocking carved support and top carved with rhino pattern and elephant pattern on reverse.

- *height 42cm*
- **Guide price £30/$57**

Double-Edged Weapon ▲

- *circa 1910*

Ngombe Doko-Mbudja double-edged cutting weapon from Zaire, formerly the Belgian Congo.

- *height 40cm*
- **Guide price £220/$416**

Bapende Mask ▲

- *20th century*

Bapende tribal mask decorated with shells and coconut hair.

- *40cm x 17cm*
- **Guide price £490/$926**

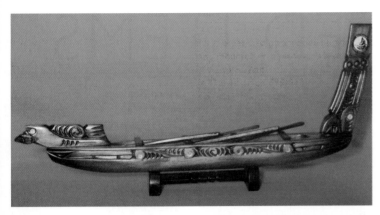

Tree of Life Carving ▼

- *circa 1990*

A carved ebony statue showing a small tree of life with ancestral characters about a central figure.
- *height 31cm*
- **Guide price £48/$91**

Painted Drum ▼

- *circa 1980*

A wooden painted drum with calfskin drumskin, pegged for tension, the body decorated with masks and geometric patterns.
- *height 58cm*
- **Guide price £48/$91**

Kongo Figure ▲

- *early 20th century*

Kongo wooden fetish with snake skin strands and monkey hair, with traces of gesso decoration.
- *height 35cm*
- **Guide price £650/$1,229**

Hat and Pipe Man ▲

- *circa 2000*

A traditional Southern African hat and pipe man, carved into a piece of verdit granite.
- *height 37cm*
- **Guide price £38/$72**

Maori Canoe ◄

- *circa 1992*

A model of a Maori war canoe, with space for four oarsmen, with traditional Maori carvings to sides and heavily carved prow.
- *length 50cm*
- **Guide price £80/$152**

Wrought-Iron Sculpture ▲

- *early 1900s*

Three wrought-iron currency forms.
- *18cm x 48cm*
- **Guide price £380/$719**

Gable Mask ▼

- *early 20th century*

A gable mask from Papua New Guinea with cowrie shells.
- *height 90cm*
- **Guide price £550/$1,040**

Ceremonial Sword ▼

- *circa 1915*

An Ngombe Doko Poto sword from Central Africa.
- *length 61cm*
- **Guide price £285/$539**

Story Board ◄

- *circa 1992*

Traditional story board from Papua New Guinea, showing half-man, half-crocodile central figure. From the Sepik river.
- *width 1.03m*
- **Guide price £200/$378**

Tribal Mask ▲

- *early 1900s*

Heavily patinated tribal mask (code 9427).
- *22cm x 15cm*
- **Guide price £740/$1,499**

WINE-RELATED ITEMS

Brass Cocktail Shaker ▲

- *circa 1930*
Brass cocktail shaker with screw lid.
- *height 20cm*
- **Guide price £48/$91**

Italian Lever Corkscrew ▲

- *20th century*
All brass Italian lever corkscrew making use of the cog and ratchet principle. Rosati's patent. Archimedian worm, crown cork opener in handle and marked "ITALY" below.
- *17.5cm x 7cm*
- **Guide price £130/$246**

Silver Hip Flask ▼

- *1904*
Edwardian silver hip flask in excellent condition with silver hinged lid made in London.
- *height 16cm*
- **Guide price £550/$1,040**

Silver Champagne Flute ▼

- *1910*
Silver champagne flute made by Aspreys of London, dated 1910.
- *height 15cm*
- **Guide price £300/$567**

Spirit Labels ▶

- *1910*
Spirit labels on chains. Port, Shrub, and Madeira.
- *length 5cm*
- **Guide price £45/$85**

Silver Wine Taster ▲

- *1939*
Silver wine taster engraved "Souvenir of Schroder and Schyler & Co. Bordeaux 1739–1939".
- *diameter 8cm*
- **Guide price £145/$274**

Horn Corkscrew ▲

- *circa 1910*
Corkscrew with a horn handle and metal screw.
- *length 12cm*
- **Guide price £44/$83**

Horn Beakers ▼

- *circa 1906*
Pair of English horn beakers with a silver rim and shield cartouche.
- *12cm x 8cm x 7cm*
- **Guide price £150/$284**

Ice Bucket ▼

- *circa 1930*
Silver-plate ice bucket with plain moulded handles to the sides.
- *height 21cm*
- **Guide price £185/$350**

Crocodile Hip Flask ▲

• *1920*

Glass hip flask with crocodile skin cover, silver mounts and silver cup, made by J. Dixon of Sheffield.

• *height 18cm*

• **Guide price £595/$1,125**

Ice Bucket ▲

• *circa 1930*

Silver-plate ice bucket with bun handles each side and two sets of ring patterns.

• *height 21cm*

• **Guide price £130/$246**

Expanding Corkscrew ▲

• *circa 1902*

English expanding corkscrew by Armstrong.

• *27cm x 16cm*

• **Guide price £120/$227**

Pair of Silver Coasters ▼

• *circa 1920*

Pair of silver coasters with scrolled rim and teak base with a circular silver disc.

• *diameter 16cm*

• **Guide price £180/$341**

Spirit Decanter ▼

• *1930*

Spirit decanter with moulded body and lozenge-shaped stopper with foliate and bird engraving.

• *height 27cm*

• **Guide price £320/$605**

Dachshund Corkscrew ▼

• *1930*

Dachshund novelty corkscrew, with brass corkscrew tail.

• *length 8cm*

• **Guide price £45/$85**

Cocktail Shaker ▼

• *1920*

Silver-plated cocktail shaker.

• *height 20cm*

• **Guide price £68/$129**

Silver Beer Mugs ▲

• *circa 1940*

Silver beer mugs with glass bottoms and bamboo decoration.

• *height 13cm*

• **Guide price £130/$246 the pair**

Metal Corkscrew ▲

• *circa 1910*

Expanding polished metal corkscrew.

• *length 14cm*

• **Guide price £50/$95**

Silver Coasters ▼

• *circa 1920*

Silver-plated circular coaster, one of a pair, with scrolled rim and a teak base.

• *diameter 17cm*

• **Guide price £160/$303**

WORKS OF ART & SCULPTURE

Italian Bronze Boy ▲

- *1904*

A fine Italian bronze of a naked young boy playing with kittens. He holds one up while cuddling the other. The bronze is signed "Marcuse, Roma 1904". On a chamfered marble base.

- *height 73cm*
- **Guide price £5,950/$11,246**

Boy Archer ▲

- *circa 1925*

Carved ivory figure of a naked young boy holding a bow raised on onyx base, signed "Ferdinand Preiss".

- *height 15cm*
- **Guide price £3,800/$7,182**

Bronze Sculpture ▼

- *20th century*

Amorphous French polished bronze sculpture after Jean Arp.

- *width 23cm*
- **Guide price £4,450/$8,411**

Bronze Spaniel Bookends ▼

- *circa 1930*

Cold-painted Austrian bronze spaniels, one black and the other liver and white.

- *13cm x 8cm*
- **Guide price £780/$1,474**

Limestone Head ▼

- *circa 1970*

English head of a girl carved from limestone, on a square wooden base, by Mike Grevatte.

- *height 70cm*
- **Guide price £2,850/$5,387**

Nue Debout ▲

- *circa 1920*

Exquisite hand-carved ivory figure of a standing nude lady raised on a rouge marble base, signed "Joe Descomps".

- *height 27cm*
- **Guide price £3,800/$7,182**

Bronze Study of Rhinoceros ▼

- *circa 1920*

Detailed study of a rhinoceros on a rectangular base. Madlestickse of Germany.

- *6cm x 8cm*
- **Guide price £840/$1,588**

Terracotta Bust ▼

- *20th century*

An Italian terracotta bust of David after Michelangelo.

- *56cm x 14cm*
- **Guide price £850/$1,607**

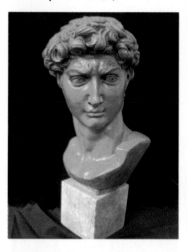

Wolfhound Bronze ▼

- *circa 1920*

French cast of Gayrad's peaceful wolfhound, from the Susse Frères foundry.

- *8cm x 16cm*
- **Guide price £1,070/$2,028**

Gilt Bronze Cat ▲

- circa 1920

Delightful gilt bronze model of a seated cat signed by Thomas Carter.

- 15cm x 13cm
- **Guide price £1,400/$2,646**

Bust of Bacchus ▲

- 20th century

A plaster bust of Bacchus, with head inclined to dexter.

- height 67cm
- **Guide price £950/$1,796**

Bronze Gymnast ▲

- 1979

English bronze of a female gymnast on the bar, with a rectangular marble plinth, signed "K.Carter 1979 2/4".

- height 42cm
- **Guide price £1,850/$3,497**

Danish Sculpture ▼

- 1960

An abstract wooden sculpture designed by Simon of Denmark.

- height 37.5cm
- **Guide price £800/$1,512**

Bust of Child ▼

- circa 1910

A good patinated bronze bust of a child with a rose in her hair by H. Jacobs, standing on an integral plinth inscribed 'H. Luppens & Cir Editeurs'.

- height 56cm
- **Guide price £2,953/$5,582**

Bronze Plaque ▶

- circa 1930

Bronze Art-Deco plaque depicting Hermes, the Greek messenger of the gods shown in his winged sandals carrying a twin snaked staff.

- 26cm x 28cm
- **Guide price £750/$1,418**

Sculpted Head ▲

- 1970

English carved limestone head of a female with her hair in a chignon, on a square wooden base, by Mike Grevatte.

- height 70cm
- **Guide price £2,850/$5,387**

Bronze Gymnast ▲

- 1976

English bronze of a female gymnast on the vault, with a marble plinth, signed by Kelsey.

- height 35cm
- **Guide price £1,850/$3,497**

Bronze Group ▼

- circa 1930s

Bronze group of a mother clutching her child astride a horse, executed in a richly patinated bronze. Signed by E. de Valeriola.

- 56cm x 23cm
- **Guide price £4,250/$8,033**

Limestone Maquette ▼

- circa 1930

Limestone maquette of two seated and embracing figures, after Henry Moore.

- 23cm x 24cm
- **Guide price £12,500/$23,625**

Syrian Table ▲

- *circa 1920*

Hexagonal mother-of-pearl and bone inlay table with pierced masharabi panels on turned legs.

- *49cm x 35cm*
- **Guide price £200/$378**

Vase Bowl and Saucer ▲

- *circa 1910*

Matching blue and turquoise floral pattern vase bowl and saucer.

- *height 37cm*
- **Guide price £300/$567**

Mother-of-Pearl Table ▼

- *circa 1920*

Mother-of-pearl and bone inlay in geometric patterns with architecturally carved legs.

- *64cm x 44cm*
- **Guide price £400/$756**

Cleopatra Stands ▼

- *circa 1920*

A pair of cast-iron stands showing Cleopatra as a caryatid supporting a table above her head.

- *height 119cm*
- **Guide price £1,800/$3,402**

Syrian Tea Table ◄

- *circa 1910*

A tea table from Damascus with a brass circular top.

- *47cm x 59cm*
- **Guide price £150/$284**

Mother-of-Pearl Chair ▲

- *circa 1930*

Mother-of-pearl and bone inlay chair, with carved top rail and scrolled arms.

- *93cm x 64cm*
- **Guide price £500/$945**

Damascus Table ▲

- *circa 1920*

Side table from Damascus with mother-of-pearl and bone inlay, single small drawer with brass handle, standing on cabriole legs.

- *43cm x 36cm*
- **Guide price £150/$284**

Algerian Brass Teapot ▲

- *circa 1930*

Brass inlay teapot on a tall brass stand with circular base.

- *length 1.72m*
- **Guide price £650/$1,229**

Persian Vases ▲
- *circa 1930*
A pair of fluted Persian blue and turquoise floral pattern vases with two handles on circular bases.
- *height 56cm*
- **Guide price £200/$378**

Persian Charger ▲
- *circa 1940*
Persian oval brass charger or tray.
- *diameter 75cm*
- **Guide price £200/$378**

Inlaid Wooden Box ▲
- *circa 1915*
Turkish wooden box with mother-of-pearl inlay to the front panel and rim of the lid.
- *height 50cm*
- **Guide price £400/$756**

Persian Brass Dish ▼
- *circa 1910*
A Persian oval dish with engraved floral designs to centre.
- *width 40cm*
- **Guide price £130/$246**

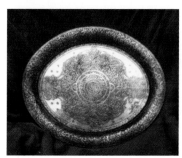

Moroccan Chair ▼
- *1910*
A Moroccan cedar chair inlaid with a floral and star pattern, in bone and boxwood. With a moulded seat and shaped legs.
- *height 103cm*
- **Guide price £350/$662**

Islamic Tray ▼
- *circa 1920*
Persian circular brass tray with engraved Islamic lettering and geometric patterns to centre.
- *diameter 58.75cm*
- **Guide price £110/$208**

Architectural Table ▲
- *circa 1910*
Mother-of-pearl hexagonal table with geometric patterns and architectural legs.
- *55cm x 43cm*
- **Guide price £200/$378**

Persian Beaker ▲
- *circa 1910*
Persian silver beaker with embossed foliate designs within shaped borders.
- *height 11.25cm*
- **Guide price £50/$95**

Syrian Box ▲
- *1910*
Wooden box with mother-of-pearl inlay and red satin interior from Damascus.
- *25cm x 16.25cm*
- **Guide price £120/$227**

Turkish Vase ▼
- *circa 1930*
Twentieth-century Turkish, bottle-shaped vase with turquoise enamelling to body and neck and orange banding.
- *height 26cm*
- **Guide price £90/$171**

Persian Copper Vase ▼
- *circa 1950*
A Persian copper and brass vase.
- *height 75cm*
- **Guide price £250/$473**

Fabergé Hand Mirror ▲

• *1910*
Silver hand mirror by Fabergé, with raised engraved crest.
• *length 21cm*
• **Guide price £1,400/$2,646**

Soviet Pen Tray ▲

• *circa 1930*
Soviet pottery pen tray with a reclining Uzbek reading *Pravda* after Natalia Danko.
• *width 19cm*
• **Guide price £650/$1,229**

Soviet Tea Holder ▲

• *1967*
Soviet silver propaganda tea glass holder with a scene showing a man in the foreground with a harvest and a rocket flying into space and the sun in the background.
• *height 10cm*
• **Guide price £80/$152**

Russian Revolutionary Plate ▼

• *circa 1920*
Soviet Russian large porcelain revolutionary plate decorated with a fantasy architectural scene of Rome by Vladimir Mosyagin, painted by Vasilii Timorev (1870–1942).
• *diameter 31cm*
• **Guide price £2,750/$5,198**

Fabergé Kovsh ▼

• *1910*
Fabergé ceramic and silver kovsh with set cut amethysts. Provenance: Princess of Baden, from the Baden collection.
• *height 15cm*
• **Guide price £5,000/$9,450**

Small Fabergé Mirror ▼

• *1910*
Small Fabergé silver mirror with raised engraved crest.
• *length 17.5cm*
• **Guide price £1,400/$2,646**

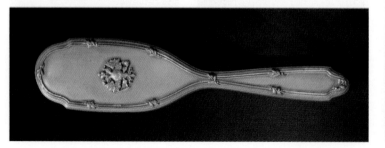

Brass Cigarette Box ▲

• *circa 1970*
Musical cigarette box in brass, depicting the first Russian space flight.
• *10cm x 8cm*
• **Guide price £250/$473**

Bronze Ballerina ▲

• *circa 1950s*
Russian bronze Ballerina shown standing on a stone base.
• *height 61cm*
• **Guide price £5,250/$9,923**

Baboushka ▼

• *circa 1930*
Soviet white glazed porcelain figure of a baboushka with impressed hammer and sickle mark and initials of Boris Kustodiev (1878–1927) from the Lomonosov factory.
• *height 27cm*
• **Guide price £1,250/$2,363**

Football Trophy ▼

• *1960*
Russian football trophy painted under glass, decorated with a cartouche showing footballers.
• *height 38cm*
• **Guide price £250/$473**

Russian Frame ▲

- *circa 1920*

Russian rosewood picture frame with brass borders and bearing the crest of two eagles with a portrait of Tsar Nicholas II of Russia.

- *28cm x 21cm*
- **Guide price £1,300/$2,457**

Opaline Glass Sweet Jars ▲

- *circa 1905*

Opaline glass sweet jars modelled as busts of the Tsar and Tsarina Nicholas and Alexandra, made for the Imperial visit to France.

- *height 35cm*
- **Guide price £500/$945 the pair**

Puss in Boots ▼

- *circa 1930*

A brightly coloured Soviet figure of Puss in Boots, unmarked, probably by Boris Kustodiev.

- *height 23cm*
- **Guide price £450/$851**

Soviet Inkwell ▼

- *circa 1929*

Soviet pottery inkwell, surmounted by a young lady with a red headscarf reading a book, the lid modelled as books and pamphlets. After Danko.

- *height 16cm*
- **Guide price £1,250/$2,363**

Fedoskino Box ▲

- *1951*

Black lacquer box with a painting of playful couples shown on a bridge over a stream, by the Fedoskino factory.

- *14cm x 7cm*
- **Guide price £590/$1,115**

Lenin Figure ▲

- *circa 1925*

Porcelain figure of Lenin shown standing on a circular base.

- *height 66cm*
- **Guide price £1,250/$2,363**

Musicians by Yakovlevich ◄

- *circa 1910*

Pair of terracotta musicians by Golovin Alexander Yakovlevich.

- *height 28cm*
- **Guide price £5,500/$10,395 (pair)**

Stalin ▼

- *circa 1920*

Soviet white glazed porcelain figure of Stalin shown in his youthful revolutionary "Hero" style. Signed.

- *height 36cm*
- **Guide price £2,450/$4,631**

Lenin ▼

- *circa 1920*

Rare plaster figure of Lenin by Mauetta.

- *height 34cm*
- **Guide price £2,450/$4,631**

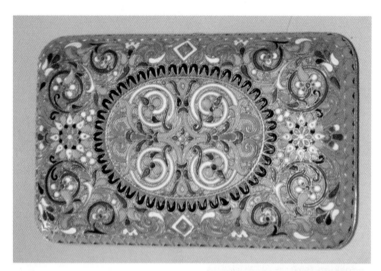

Soviet Porcelain Plate ▼

- *circa 1920*

Russian, Soviet porcelain plate with floral design and stylised "CCCP" by Natalya Girshfeld.

- *diameter 23cm*
- **Guide price £1,650/$3,119**

Icon of St. Samon, Gury and Aviv ▲

- *1900*

Russian icon showing the Saints Samon, Gury and Aviv, covered with a silver and turquoise blue enamel riza, by Michelson, Moscow, 1900.

- *7cm x 6cm*
- **Guide price £1,250/$2,363**

Enamelled Case ▲

- *circa 1900s*

Russian cigarette case with an enamelled geometric and foliate design.

- *10cm x 8cm*
- **Guide price £1,250/$2,363**

Constructivist Plate ▼

- *1928*

Constructivist plate painted with female skiers in linear form with strong colours. Signed and dated 1928.

- *diameter 24cm*
- **Guide price £1,650/$3,119**

Soviet Bowl ▲

- *circa 1921*

Soviet bowl painted with strong brush-strokes in vibrant colours by Rudolf Vilde (1868–1942).

- *diameter 26cm*
- **Guide price £2,200/$4,158**

Grey Horses with Riders ▲

- *circa 1930*

Pair of grey horses with riders, one pointing, on a foliate square base.

- *26cm x 18cm*
- **Guide price £2,650/$5,009**

Accordion Player ▲

- *circa 1930*

Soviet white glazed figure of an accordion player by Boris Kustodiev.

- *height 23cm*
- **Guide price £490/$926**

Arctic Rescue Tea Set ▼

- *circa 1925*

Tea set commemorating an Arctic rescue of the Swedish Arctic Expedition, led by Nobel, by the Soviet icebreaker "Krasin".

- *diameter of plate 24cm*
- **Guide price £2,500/$4,725**

Imperial Cigarette Case ▲

- *circa 1900s*

Silver Russian cigarette case repoussé with Adam and Eve, with a dedication to Tsar Nicholas II on the reverse, and a gold coin, Imperial flags, crown and coat of arms.

- *10cm x 8cm*
- **Guide price £1,950/$3,686**

Stalin in Uniform ▲

- *1945*

Black painted lacquer box showing Stalin in uniform standing by a railtrack. Made by the Fedoskino factory.

- *height 8cm*
- **Guide price £890/$1,682**

Reclining Man Reading Newspaper ▲

- *circa 1930*

Reclining figure of a man reading a newspaper dressed in white with a black and white hat.

- *length 21cm*
- **Guide price £580/$1,097**

Commemorative Tea Holder ▲

- *1970*

Soviet silver tea holder with a central cartouche showing Lenin's head, an industrial scene and the dates "1920–1970", surrounded by a foliate design.

- *height 10cm*
- **Guide price £80/$152**

Russian Radio ▲

- *circa 1950s*

A Soviet radio in bakelite, made in the style of an American 1950s car dashboard.

- *35cm x 54cm*
- **Guide price £750/$1,418**

Iron Statue ▲

- *circa 1950*

Iron statue of Ivan the Terrible in armour on horseback.

- *height 15cm*
- **Guide price £50/$95**

Lenin Inkwell ▲

- *circa 1924*

The Lenin inkwell, with facsimile signatures and inscription "Proletariat of the World unite" and anniversary inscription on the cover. By Natalia Danko (1892–1942) from the Lomonosov factory.

- *height 17cm*
- **Guide price £1,250/$2,363**

Bronze Seated Ballerina ▼

- *circa 1950s*

Bronze showing a ballerina seated on a stool, on a square base.

- *height 29cm*
- **Guide price £3,950/$7,466**

Weightlifter ▶

- *circa 1950*

Alloy model of a weightlifter in black enamel. In the act of final lift. On an oval base.

- *height 52cm*
- **Guide price £890/$1,682**

Cloisonné Cigarette Case ▼

- *circa 1900s*

Russian cloisonné cigarette case with blue, red, white and turquoise floral decoration.

- *height 9cm*
- **Guide price £1,350/$2,552**

Portrait of Pushkin ▲

- *1951*

Russian painted lacquer box with a portrait of Pushkin on the front by the Fedoskino factory.

- *height 8cm*
- **Guide price £750/$1,418**

Bronze Figures ▲

• *circa 1950s*
Bronze of a man teaching his young son archery, on a triangular base.
• *height 48cm*
• **Guide price £1,450/$2,741**

Revolutionary Plaque ▲

• *1917–20*
Russian revolutionary monumental cast bronze plaque, with a rusticated finish, showing a gun, helmet and cartridges and the date "1917–1920".
• *190cm x 105cm*
• **Guide price £7,500/$14,175**

Paperweight ▲

• *circa 1940*
Obsidian and onyx paperweight with intaglio of Lenin in profile, looking to sinister.
• *height 15cm*
• **Guide price £490/$926**

Commemorative Vase ▼

• *circa 1950s*
Russian commemorative vase showing Stalin in military costume on a red glazed ground.
• *height 49cm*
• **Guide price £1,250/$2,363**

Russian Soldier ▼

• *circa 1950*
Ceramic figure of a Russian soldier shown seated playing the accordion.
• *height 42cm*
• **Guide price £850/$1,607**

Bronze Sculpture ▼

• *circa 1920*
Bronze sculpture depicting Lenin in discussion.
• *height 16cm*
• **Guide price £2,650/$5,009**

Ceramic Urn ▲

• *circa 1950*
Russian ceramic urn with a sepia portrait of Lenin surrounded by floral decoration, with two scrolled and gilded handles, and gilded banding to the neck and base.
• *49cm x 32cm*
• **Guide price £750/$1,418**

Painted Lacquer Box ▲

• *1947*
Rare wartime allegorical lacquered painted box showing the invasion of Russia by Germany, and the eventual defeat of the German army. The box is painted in icon form with the moon on the left hidden by the burning buildings, by F. Kolosov.
• *21cm x 17cm*
• **Guide price £1,650/$3,119**

Bronze Partisan ▲

• *circa 1940*
Revolutionary bronze Russian partisan shown holding a gun above his head, on a rectangular plinth.
• *height 100cm*
• **Guide price £3,750/$7,088**

Mould of Lenin ◄

• *circa 1950*
A plaster mould of Lenin made for the production of bronze casts.
• *height 71cm*
• **Guide price £400/$756**

Commemorative Plaque ▼

- *circa 1971*

Gilt bronze with red glass inserts, and central enamelled plaque showing a nuclear power station within a wreath.
- *diameter 30cm*
- **Guide price £750/$1,418**

Ceramic Platter ▼

- *circa 1920*

Commemorative ceramic platter, only one other recorded. Showing Lenin in centre with various faces of revolutionary Russia in red and grey charcoal glaze.
- *diameter 42cm*
- **Guide price £5,500/$10,395**

Commemorative Vase ◄

- *circa 1940*

Baluster-shaped vase, showing Lenin, in red glaze with gilded lettering and floral decoration.
- *height 37cm*
- **Guide price £750/$1,418**

Presentation Vase ▲

- *circa 1950*

Made for the anniversary of the birth of Lenin. Cut and applied decoration of social realism.
- *height 59cm*
- **Guide price £6,500/$12,285**

Wooden Toboggan ▲

- *1901*

Russian painted red wooden toboggan from the Volodga region.
- *length 65cm*
- **Guide price £120/$227**

Bronze High-Jumper ▼

- *circa 1960*

Cast bronze high-jumper naturalistically styled in the act of landing on a stone landing mat.
- *height 94cm*
- **Guide price £4,500/$8,505**

'The Partisan' ▲

- *circa 1979*

Painting entitled 'The Partisan' by M. S. Prokopyuk, in charcoal and watercolour.
- *86 x 61cm*
- **Guide price £850/$1,607**

Marshall Voroshilov on Skis ►

- *1929*

Russian lacquer box depicting the Marshall Voroshilov skiing.
- *18cm x 7cm*
- **Guide price £1,300/$2,457**

Plate by Freze ◄

- *circa 1921*

Soviet plate decorated with a vase and flowers by Varvara Freze (1883–1970).
- *diameter 22.5cm*
- **Guide price £1,200/$2,268**

WRITING EQUIPMENT

Limoges Inkwell ▲
- *1930*

Limoges enamel inkwell with red flowers on a white ground and brass banding.
- *height 5.5cm*
- **Guide price £115/$217**

Gold Waterman Pen ▲
- *1920*

Gold Waterman fountain pen with basketweave pattern, No.5552½, with original glass ink dropper.
- *length 14cm*
- **Guide price £600/$1,134**

Pen Wipe and Pen ▼
- *1911*

Silver pen wipe with plain oval dip pen, made in London by S. Mordan.
- *height 7cm*
- **Guide price £165/$312**

Parker Pencil ▼
- *1934–5*

Mottled green Parker pencil.
- *length 11cm*
- **Guide price £175/$331**

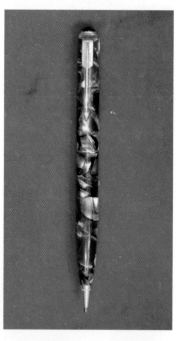

Silver Inkwell ◄
- *1930*

Small silver circular inkwell with a hinged lid.
- *diameter 9cm*
- **Guide price £60/$114**

Circular Inkwell ▲
- *circa 1930*

Large silver circular inkwell with a hinged lid.
- *diameter 11.5cm*
- **Guide price £190/$360**

Telescopic Pencil ▲
- *1902*

Silver telescopic pencil in sheaf with stirrup loop by Alfred Deeley, Birmingham, 1902.
- *length 3.75cm*
- **Guide price £220/$416**

Stone Inkwell ▲
- *circa 1950*

Inkwell in the shape of a curling stone with a brass lid and handle.
- *diameter 6cm*
- **Guide price £45/$85**

American Eversharp Pen ▼
- *1930*

American Eversharp black and red desk pen with gold banding, with a penholder on a square base.
- *length 22cm*
- **Guide price £320/$605**

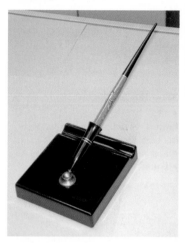

'Lucky Cup' Pen ▼
- *circa 1928*

Canadian duofold junior, mandarin yellow Parker pen.
- *length 14cm*
- **Guide price £640/$1,210**

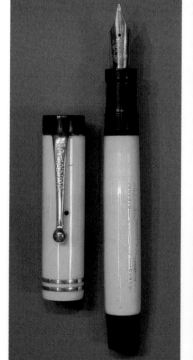

Salter Letter Balance ▲

• 1930

Small metal letter balance with a brass dial, with the manufacturer's mark "Salter-and-made in England" on the dial.

• height 22cm

• **Guide price £48/$91**

Fountain Pen ▲

• 1951

English fountain pen with green herringbone design and wide gilt band, by Conway Stewart Duro, No.60, 1951.

• length 12.5cm

• **Guide price £380/$719**

Pencil Sharpener ▼

• 1930

White plastic pencil sharpener showing a cricketer, made for the Australian Cricket team.

• height 4cm

• **Guide price £55/$104**

Waterman Fountain Pen ▼

• circa 1920

Waterman 0552 gold plated basket weave fountain pen with half G. P.

• length 14cm

• **Guide price £900/$1,701**

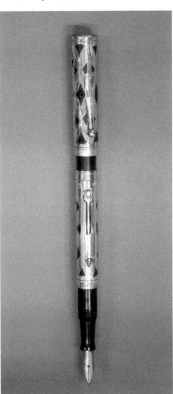

Double Glass Inkwell ◄

• circa 1910

Double glass inkwell with silver rims around the lids, in a square oblong container.

• width 11cm

• **Guide price £96/$181**

Propelling Pencil ▲

• 1900s

Ivory propelling pencil, decorated with painted enamel flowers, and silver mounts.

• length 9cm

• **Guide price £79/$150**

Silver Tray with Inkwell ▲

• circa 1901

Silver moulded tray on raised feet, with a pen holder and faceted glass ink pot with scrolled silver lid.

• height 11cm

• **Guide price £375/$709**

Glass Ink Stand ▼

• circa 1925

Art Nouveau green glass ink bottle resting on a brass stand.

• height 8cm

• **Guide price £180/$341**

Beehive Ink Pot ▼

• circa 1905

Silver ink pot with hinged lid. Made in London by Mappin & Webb.

• height 6.5cm

• **Guide price £350/$662**

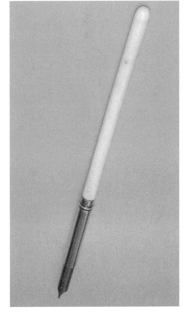

Ivory-Handled Pen ▼

• 1912

English pen with ivory handle and silver nib, made in London, 1912.

• length 26cm

• **Guide price £145/$274**

Edwardian Ink Stand ▲

- *1904*

Highly decorative ink stand with pierced gallery, two crystal glass reservoirs, and moulded apron raised on shaped feet. Made in London.

- *26cm x 15cm*
- **Guide price £2,350/$4,442**

Parker Propelling Pencil ▲

- *circa 1930–5*

Mottled green Parker propelling pencil.

- *length 13cm*
- **Guide price £220/$416**

Glass Inkwell ▲

- *circa 1901*

Glass inkwell with faceted base and silver hinged lid.

- *height 9cm*
- **Guide price £290/$549**

Silver Paper Knife ▲

- *1923*

English rat-tail silver paper knife with cedar pencil, by Sampson Mordan.

- *length 18cm*
- **Guide price £220/$416**

Silver Ink Pot ▲

- *circa 1937*

Silver ink pot with hinged lid within a glass moulded base, and pen holder. Made in Birmingham.

- *length 14.5cm*
- **Guide price £295/$558**

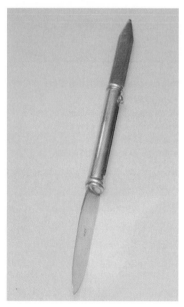

Pencil and Paper Knife ▲

- *1903*

Edwardian combination pencil and silver paper knife, made in Birmingham by Perry & Company.

- *length 15cm*
- **Guide price £185/$350**

Waterman Pen ▼

- *1931–8*

Black and grey marbled Waterman Ideal fountain pen, No 32.

- *length 10cm*
- **Guide price £270/$511**

Gold-Plated Fountain Pen ▼

- *1920*

Maybie Todd & Co gold-plated fountain pen with a rosette design.

- *length 13cm*
- **Guide price £800/$1,512**

Art Deco Ink Pot ◄

- *circa 1920*

Moulded brass art deco inkwell with cover and porcelain bowl.

- *width 13cm*
- **Guide price £68/$129**

Ball Inkwell ▼

- *1914*

Brass inkwell consisting of four brass balls resting on each other, one of which contains the ink, with a metal and wood base.
- *diameter 17cm*
- **Guide price £78/$148**

Parker Pen ▼

- *1942*

Parker Victory fountain pen in black and green laminated plastic.
- *length 12.5cm*
- **Guide price £380/$719**

Conway Stewart Dinkie Pen ▼

- *circa 1935*

Conway Stewart dinkie pen with a blue and amber marbling effect.
- *length 12cm*
- **Guide price £220/$416**

American Fountain Pen ▲

- *1920*

Gold-plated American fountain pen with a gothic design by Maybie Todd & Co.
- *length 13cm*
- **Guide price £800/$1,512**

Quill Box ▲

- *1920*

Quill box made from ebonised wood and quills.
- *5cm x 16cm*
- **Guide price £45/$85**

Ormolu Inkstand ▲

- *circa 1901*

Elkington ormolu inkstand decorated with blue and turquoise enamel, with two cherubs holding a monogrammed plaque, standing on bracket feet, with two clear cut glass bottles with brass and enamelled lids.
- *length 32cm*
- **Guide price £850/$1,607**

Silver Capstan Ink Pot ▼

- *1913*

Capstan silver inkwell with hinged lid and large splayed base. Made in Birmingham by H. Greaves Ltd.
- *diameter 14cm*
- **Guide price £640/$1,210**

Brass Blotter ▲

- *circa 1912*

Arts and crafts brass boat blotter period. Marked GESCi 9121.
- *length 15cm*
- **Guide price £260/$492**

Waterman Pen ▲

- *1920*

American Waterman fountain pen with gold basketweave pattern, No.5552.1½.
- *length 10cm*
- **Guide price £600/$1,134**

Inlaid Stationery Box ▲

- *1900*

Edwardian mahogany inlaid stationery box with satinwood fan-shaped inlay.
- *height 28cm*
- **Guide price £375/$709**

Silver Inkwell ▼

- *circa 1931*
Capstan silver inkwell with glass reservoir and large spayed base. Made in Birmingham.
- *diameter 20cm*
- **Guide price £500/$945**

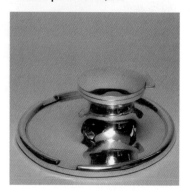

Parker Duofold Set ▲

- *circa 1928*
A pristine Parker Duofold set with button-filler pen with 18-carat gold nib and propelling pencil.
- **Guide price £225/$426**

Waterman Gothic ▼

- *1924*
A Waterman 452 gothic design in sterling silver with American lever fill and 12-carat gold nib.
- *length 15cm*
- **Guide price £1,000/$1,890**

Parker 51 ▲

- *circa 1950*
A Parker 51 Special classic, commemorating 51 years in the business, with burgundy body, rolled gold cap and pearlescent hooded nib.
- *length 15cm*
- **Guide price £250/$473**

Ladies' Parker Pen ▼

- *1928*
Canadian Duofold Ladies' pen with lapis permanite body. Pump filled with three gold-plated bands on cap.
- *length 14cm*
- **Guide price £300/$567**

Inkwell ▲

- *circa 1920*
Decorative inkwell with metal eagle figure on marble base.
- *length 30cm*
- **Guide price £85/$161**

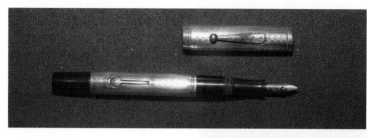

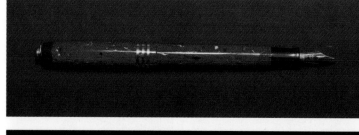

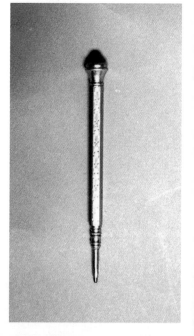

Glass Ink Pot ▼

- *circa 1930*
Multi-sided glass amethyst colour American ink pot with sliding glass lid.
- *height 5.5cm*
- **Guide price £260/$492**

Parker 51 ▶

- *1950*
Aeromatic filling system with teal-blue body and solid gold cap and medium nib.
- *length 16cm*
- **Guide price £180/$341**

Bridge Pencil ▲

- *circa 1930*
Silver-plated bridge pencil, originally one of a set of four, with propelling action.
- *length 15cm*
- **Guide price £22/$41**

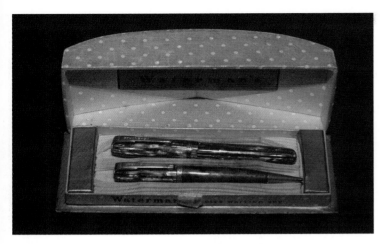

Waterman 512V Set ▲

- *circa 1930*
Pen and propelling pencil in laminated plastic jet and mother-of-pearl.
- *length 14cm*
- **Guide price £275/$520**

Silver Pencil ▼

- *circa 1930*
Silver-plated propelling pencil of the Art Deco period.
- *length 15cm*
- **Guide price £15/$28**

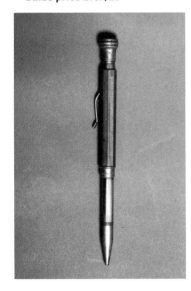

English Writing Desk Set ▶

- *circa 1940*
20th-century English Phendic desk set with blotter sponge holder, double inkwell, and paper holder.
- **Guide price £250/$473**

Waterman Ideal 452½ ▼

- *circa 1925*
Ladies' pen with basketweave design in sterling silver and American lever fill.
- *length 14cm*
- **Guide price £750/$1,418**

Silver Capstan Inkwell ▲

- *1912*
Inkwell made in Birmingham with porcelain bowl.
- *height 7cm*
- **Guide price £285/$539**

Waterman Ideal 0552½ ▼

- *1924*
Ladies' pen with gold-plated gothic pattern and lever fill.
- *length 14cm*
- **Guide price £450/$851**

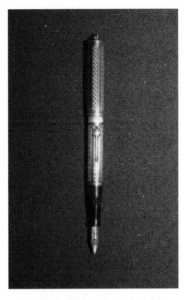

Bone-Handle Pen ▼

- *circa 1910*
A souvenir, bone handle with steel nib inscribed 'A Present from Skegness'.
- *length 18cm*
- **Guide price £28/$55**

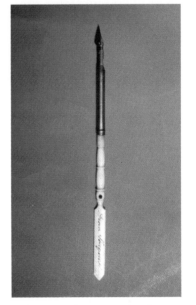

Parker Duofold ▼

- *circa 1940*
A Parker Duofold pen, made in the U.S.A., with button filler, gold band and clip.
- *length 15cm*
- **£100/$189**

Waterman Ideal 0552½ ▼

- *1920*
Ladies' pen with lever-fill action and gold-plated nib.
- *length 14cm*
- **Guide price £750/$1,418**

Dinkie 540J ▼

- *circa 1920*
Conway Stuart Dinkie 540J. Rare ladies' pen with 14-carat gold nib and multicoloured body.
- *length 15cm*
- **Guide price £220/$416**

GLOSSARY

acacia Dull yellow hardwood with darker markings used for inlay and bandings.

acanthus A leaf motif used in carved and inlaid decoration.

air-beaded Glass with air bubbles resembling beads.

air-twist Spiral pattern enclosed in a glass stem with air bubbles.

albarello Waisted ceramic drug jar.

alder Wood used for country-style furniture in the eighteenth century.

amboyna Light brown with speckled grain wood from West Indies.

annulated Ringed (of glass).

applied Attached or added, rather than modelled or carved as part of the body.

apron Decorative panel of wood between the front legs of a chair or cabinet.

arbor The axle on which the wheel of a clock's mechanism is mounted.

arch (clockmaking) The arch above the dial of a post-1700 longcase clock.

argyle Double-skinned metal pouring jugs and tea and coffee pots.

armoire French wardrobe, linen press or large cupboard.

ash Hardwood used for making country furniture and for its white veneer.

astragal Small semi-circular moulding, used as glazing bar in furniture.

automaton clock A clock where the strike is performed by mechanically operated figures.

backboard The unseen back of wall furniture.

backplate The rear plate supporting the movement of a clock, often the repository of engraved information relating to its manufacture.

balance Device counteracting the force of the mainspring in a clock's movement.

balloon-back chair Popular, rounded-backed Victorian dining or salon chair.

baluster (adj.) Having a dominant convex swell at the base, culminating in a smaller, concave one at the neck. (noun) One of a set of upright posts supporting a balustrade.

barley-sugar twist Spiral-turned legs and rails popular in the seventeenth century.

bat printed Transfer printed (ceramics).

beech Hardwood used in the manufacture of country furniture and, when stained, as a substitute for mahogany.

bergère Chair with caned back and sides.

bevel Decorative, shaved edge of glass, particularly mirror.

bezel Metal rim of a glass cover or jewel.

bird-cage Support mechanism at the top of the pedestal of some eighteenth-century tilt-top tables.

birch Hardwood used principally for carcassing or low-quality veneer.

bird's eye maple Wood of the sugar maple with distinctive figure caused by aborted buds. Used in veneering.

biscuit/bisque Ceramics fired but unglazed.

blind fretwork Fretwork carving on a solid background.

block front Front shaped from thick boards allowing for a recessed centre section.

bob The weight at the bottom of a pendulum.

bobbin Turned furniture element, resembling a row of connected spheres.

bocage Foliage, bushes and shrubs supporting, surrounding or standing behind porcelain or pottery figures.

bombé Having an outswelling front.

bone china Clay with bone ash in the formula, almost entirely porcellanous.

bonheur du jour Small, ladies writing desk with a cabinet and drawers above.

boxwood Pale yellow, close-grained hardwood.

bow front Convex curve on the front of chests of drawers.

bracket foot Plain foot carved into the rail or stretcher to form an ornamental bracket.

breakfront Piece of furniture with a central section which projects forward.

breech Rear end of the barrel of a gun.

broken pediment Pediment with a symmetrical break in the centre.

bun foot Flattened spherical foot.

bureau Desk with a fall front enclosing a fitted interior, with drawers below.

bureau bookcase Bureau with glazed bookcase above.

burr Veneer used in furniture making, with a decorative pattern caused by some abnormality of growth or knotting in the tree. Usually from the base of the tree.

cabriole leg Furniture leg that curves out at the foot and in at the top.

calendar/date aperture Window in the dial of a clock displaying day, month or date.

canted corner Decoratively angled corner.

canterbury Container for sheet music.

carcase/carcass The inner frame of a piece of furniture, usually made of inferior wood for veneering.

card case Case for visiting cards.

carriage clock Portable timepiece, with handle above.

case furniture Furniture intended as a receptical, e.g. chest of drawers.

caster/castor 1. Sprinkling vessel for e.g. sugar. 2. Pivoted wheel attached to foot.

Castleford ware Shiny white stoneware made in Castleford and elsewhere.

cellaret A wine cooler or container.

centrepiece Ornament designed to sit in the centre of a dining table.

chain fusée The fusée of a clock from which a chain unwinds on to the barrel of the mainspring.

chamfer A flattened angle; a corner that has been bevelled or planed.

chapter ring The ring on a clock dial on which the numbers of the hours are inscribed.

Chesterfield Deep-buttoned, upholstered settee from the nineteenth century.

chest on chest Tallboy having two chests fitting together, the lower with bracket feet, the upper with pediment.

chest on stand Known as a tallboy or highboy, a chest of drawers on a stand.

cheval mirror Tall mirror supported by two uprights on swivels.

chiffonnier Side cupboard, with solid, latticed or glazed doors.

chinoiserie Oriental-style decoration on lacquered furniture or artefacts.

chronometer Precision timepiece, often for navigation.

circular movement Clock movement of circular plates.

cistern Chamber containing mercury at the base of the tube of a barometer.

claw-and-ball foot Foot modelled as a ball clutched in a claw, frequently used to terminate a cabriole leg.

coaster Small, circular tray, often in silver, for holding a bottle.

cockbeading Bead moulding applied to the edges of drawers.

cock bracket Bracket supporting a watch mainspring.

coin glass English drinking glass with a coin moulded into the knop of the stem.

commode Decorated chest of drawers or cabinet, with applied mounts.

composition Putty-like substance for moulding and applying to e.g. mirror frames, for gilding.

corner chair Chair with back splats on two sides and a bowed top rail, designed to fit into a corner.

cornice Horizontal top part of a piece of furniture; a decorative band of metal or wood used to conceal curtain fixtures.

coromandel Wood from India's Coromandel coast.

country furniture Functional furniture made outside the principal cities. Also provincial furniture.

countwheel strike Clock mechanism determining the number of strikes per hour.

cow creamer Silver or china cream jug.

crazing Fine cracks in glaze.

creamware Earthenware glazed in a cream colour giving a porcelain effect.

credenza Long Victorian side cabinet with glazed or solid doors.

crenellated Crinkly, wavy.

crested china Ware decorated with heraldic crests.

crinoline stretcher Crescent-shaped stretcher supporting the legs of some Windsor chairs.

cross-banding Decorative edging with cross-grained veneer.

cruet Frame for holding condiment containers.

crutch The arm connecting a clock's pendulum to the pallet arbor.

damascene Inlay of precious metal onto a body of other metal for decorative purposes.

deadbeat escapement Version of the anchor escapement that eliminates recoil and improves accuracy.

deal Sawn pine wood.

dentil Small, block-shaped moulding found under a furniture cornice.

dialplate Frontplate of a clock.

diamond cut (of glass) Cut in diamond shape.

dinanderie Brass artefact from the factories of Dinant, Belgium.

dished table top Hollowed-out, solid top, particularly of a pie-crust, tripod table.

distressed Artificially aged.

dovetails Interlocking joints used in drawers.

dowel Peg holding together wooden joint.

dram glass Small, short-stemmed glass with rounded bowl.

drop-in seat Framed, upholstered seat which sits in the framework of a chair.

drop handle Pear-shaped brass furniture handle.

drop-leaf table Table with a fixed central section and hinged flaps.

drum table Circular writing table on a central pedestal with frieze drawers.

dry-edge With unglazed edges.

Dutch strike Clock chime which strikes the next hour on the half hour.

ebonise To stain a wood to the dark colour of ebony.

ebony Exotic black hardwood, used as veneer in Europe.

electroplate The technique of covering one metal with the thin layer of another.

elm Hardwood used in the manufacture of chair seats, country furniture and coffins.

embossing Relief decoration.

enamel Second, coloured glaze fired over first glaze.

endstone In a clock mechanism, jewel on which an arbor pivots.

épergne Centrepiece of one central bowl surrounded by smaller ones.

escritoire Cabinet with a fall-front for a writing surface. With a fitted interior.

escutcheon Brass plate surrounding the edges of a keyhole.

étuis Small, metal oddments box.

everted Outward turned, flaring.

facet-cut (of glass) Cut criss-cross into straight-edged planes.

faience Tin-glazed earthenware.

fairings Porcelain figures, usually comical and carrying descriptive captions.

fall front Flap of a bureau or secretaire that pulls out to provide writing surface.

fauteuil Open-sided, upholstered armchair with padded elbows.

feather banding Two bands of veneer laid at opposite diagonals.

field Area of a carpet within its decorated borders.

fielded panel Raised panel with chamfered edge fitting into a framework.

figure Natural pattern created by the grain through the wood.

finial Decorative, turned knob.

flamed veneer Veneer cut at an angle to enhance the figuring.

flute glass Glass with tall, slender bowl.

fluting Decorative parallel grooving.

foliate Flower and leaf motifs.

fretwork Fine pierced decoration.

frieze Long ornamental strip.

frit The flux from which glass is made. An ingredient of soft-paste porcelain.

fruitwood Generally the wood of apple, cherry and pear trees, used for ebonising and gildings.

fusee The conical, grooved spool from which a line or chain unwinds as it is pulled by the mainspring of a clock movement.

gadroon Carved edge or moulded decoration consisting of a series of grooves, ending in a curved lip, with ridges between them.

Gainsborough chair Deep, upholstered armchair with padded, open arms and carved decoration.

galleried Having a wood or metal border around the top edge.

garniture Set of ornamental pieces of porcelain.

gateleg Leg that pivots to support a drop leaf.

gesso Plaster-like substance applied to carved furniture before gilding or moulded and applied as a substitute for carving.

gilt-tooled decoration Gold leaf impressed into the edges of leather on desktops.

girandole Wall-mounted candle holder with a mirrored back.

Greek key Ancient key-shaped decoration often repeated in fretwork on furniture.

gridiron pendulum Clock pendulum consisting of rods of a mix of metals positioned in such a way that the dynamics of their behaviour when subjected to heat or cold keep the pendulum swing uniform.

half hunter Watch with an opening front cover with glass to the centre and a chapter ring, giving protection to the glass over the dial.

hallmark The mark by which silver can be identified by standard, place of assay and date.

hard-paste porcelain Porcelain made with kaolin and petuntse in the Chinese fashion.

hunter Watch with a hinged, opening front cover in solid metal.

husk Formalised leaf motif.

ice glass Glass with uneven, rippling surface.

Imari Japanese porcelain made in and around Arita and shipped to Europe from the port of Imari. Blue, red and gold coloured.

improved A pejorative term implying that a piece has been altered in order dishonestly to enhance its value.

inlay The decorative setting of one material into a contrasting one.

intaglio Incised design.

ironstone Patented stoneware, in which slag from iron furnaces was mixed with the clay to toughen the ware.

japanned Painted and varnished in imitation of Oriental style lacquer work.

jardinière An ornamental pot or vase for plants.

jasper ware Coloured stoneware developed by the Wedgwood factory.

joined Manufactured with the use of mortice and tenon joints and dowels, but without glue.

kingwood Exotic, purplish hardwood used in veneer.

kneehole desk Desk with a recessed cupboard beneath the frieze drawer.

knop Rounded projection or bulge in the stem of a glass.

lacquer Resinous substance which, when coloured, provides a ground for chinoiserie and gilding.

ladder-back Chair with a series of horizontal back rails.

lantern clock Clocks driven entirely by weights and marking only the hours. Similar in appearance to a lantern.

lappit Carved flap at the top of a leg with a pad foot.

lead crystal Particularly clear, brilliant glass including lead in the process.

lead-glazed the earliest glaze for Western pottery, derived from glass making.

lever escapement Modification of the anchor escapement for carriage clocks and, particularly, watches.

lion's paw foot Foot carved as a lion's paw.

longcase clock The 'grandfather' clock, housed in a tall wooden case containing the weights and pendulum.

loper Pull-out arm that supports the hinged fall of a bureau.

lustre ware Ceramic ware decorated with a metallic coating which changes colour when fired.

mahogany Hardwood used as solid wood until its rarity led to its use for veneer.

majolica Originally tin-glazed earthenware produced in Renaissance Italy.

mantel clock Clock with feet designed to stand on a mantelpiece.

maple North American hardwood used for its variety of veneers.

marine chronometer Precision clock for use in navigation at sea.

marquetry The use of wooden and other inlays to form decorative patterns.

married Pejorative term applied to a piece of furniture made up of more than one piece of the same period.

mercury twist Air-twist in glass of a silver colour.

millefiori Multi-coloured or mosaic glass.

moonwork Clock mechanism which computes and displays moonphases.

mortice Slot element of a mortice and tenon joint.

moulding decorative, shaped band around an object or a panel.

mount Invariably metal mounting fitted to a piece of furniture.

mule chest Coffer with a single row of drawers to the base.

musical clock Clock with a cylinder which strikes bells to play a tune.

oak Hardwood which darkens with age.

obverse The front side of a coin or medal.

ogee An S-shaped curve.

ogee arch Two S-shaped curves coming together to form an arch.

ormolu From French *dorure d'or moulu*: 'gilding with gold paste'.

orrery Astronomical clock which shows the position of heavenly bodies.

overmantel mirror Mirror designed to hang over a mantelpiece.

ovolo A rounded, convex moulding, making an outward curve across a right angle.

oyster veneer Veneer resembling an open oyster shell, achieved by slanting the cut across the grain of a branch.

pallet Lever that engages in a clock's escapement wheel in orderb to arrest it.

papier mâché Moulded and lacquered pulped paper used to make small items of furniture and other artefacts.

parian Uncoloured, biscuit-style porcelain named after Parian white marble.

parquetry Veneered pattern using small pieces of veneer, often from different woods, in a geometrical design.

patera Circular ornament made of wood, metal or composition.

patina The layers of polish, dirt, grease and general handling marks that build up on a wooden piece of furniture over the years and give it its individual signs of age, varying from wood to wood.

pediment Architectural, triangular gable crowning a piece of furniture or a classical building.

pembroke table Small, two-flapped table standing on four legs or a pedestal.

pepperette Pepper sprinkler.

pewter Alloy of tin, lead and often various other metals.

pie-crust Decorative edge of a dished-top tripod table.

pier glass Tall mirror for hanging on a pier between windows.

pillar (watchmaking) A rod connecting the dial-plate and backplate of a movement.

pine Softwood used for carcassing furniture.

platform base Flat base supporting a central pedestal and table-top above and standing on scrolled or paw feet.

plinth base Solid base not raised on feet.

pole screen Adjustable fire screen.

pontil mark Mark made by the blowpipe, (pontil) on the base of hand-blown glass.

print decoration Mass-produced decoration. Not hand painting.

punch bowl Large bowl for the retention and dispensation of punch.

quartered top Flat surface covered with four pieces of matching veneer.

rail A horizontal member running between the outer uprights on furniture.

rating nut Nut under the bob of a clock's pendulum to adjust rate of swing.

reeding Parallel strips of convex fluting.

re-entrant corner Shaped indentation at each corner of a table.

relief Proud of the surface.

repeating work Mechanism that operates the striking mechanism of a clock or watch to the last hour.

repoussé An embossed design which has been refined by chasing.

rosewood Named after its smell when newly cut, a dark-brown hardwood with an attractive stripe or ripple.

rule joint Hinge on furniture which fits so well that, when open, no join can be detected between two hinged parts.

runners Strips of wood, fitted to furniture, on which drawers slide.

saltglaze Stoneware in which salt is added to create a porcellanous, glassy surface.

salver A large metal dish or tray for transporting smaller dishes.

satinwood A light golden-coloured, close-grained hardwood.

sconce 1. Cup-shaped candle holder. 2. Metal plate fixed to the wall, supporting candle holder or light.

scroll, scrolling Carving or moulding of a curled design.

seat rail Horizontal framework below the chair seat uniting the legs.

secretaire Writing desk with false drawer front which lets down to reveal a writing surface and fitted interior.

settee Upholstered settle.

tripod table Small, round-topped table on three-legged base.

tulipwood Pinkish, naturally patterned hardwood used in veneer.

tureen Large bowl in porcelain or metal, usually with a lid and two handles.

underglaze Colour or design painted below the glaze of a ceramic artefact.

uniface Medal or coin with modelling on one side only.

veneer A thin sheet of wood laid across a cheaper carcase or used as inlay decoration.

verge escapement Mechanism for regulating a clock movement before the anchor escapement.

Vesta case Match box for Vesta matches.

wainscot chair Joined chair with open arms and a panelled back.

walnut Hardwood used in England for the manufacture of furniture.

well Interior of a plate or bowl.

wheel-back chair Chair with circular back with radiating spokes.

windsor chair Wooden chair with spindle back.

yew Tough, close-grained hardwood.

INDEX